SUSTAINABLE DEVELOPMENT LAW
PRINCIPLES, PRACTICES AND PROSPECTS

Sustainable Development Law

Principles, Practices and Prospects

MARIE-CLAIRE CORDONIER SEGGER
and
ASHFAQ KHALFAN

OXFORD

UNIVERSITY PRESS

*This book has been printed digitally and produced in a standard specification
in order to ensure its continuing availability*

OXFORD
UNIVERSITY PRESS

Great Clarendon Street, Oxford OX2 6DP

Oxford University Press is a department of the University of Oxford.
It furthers the University's objective of excellence in research, scholarship,
and education by publishing worldwide in

Oxford New York

Auckland Cape Town Dar es Salaam Hong Kong Karachi
Kuala Lumpur Madrid Melbourne Mexico City Nairobi
New Delhi Shanghai Taipei Toronto
With offices in
Argentina Austria Brazil Chile Czech Republic France Greece
Guatemala Hungary Italy Japan South Korea Poland Portugal
Singapore Switzerland Thailand Turkey Ukraine Vietnam

Oxford is a registered trade mark of Oxford University Press
in the UK and in certain other countries

Published in the United States
by Oxford University Press Inc., New York

ISBN 0-19-927671-4

The Centre for International Sustainable Development Law thanks the World
Bank Legal Vice-Presidency, the United Nations Environment Programme
and the International Law Association, co-hosts of
Sustainable Justice 2002: Implementing International Sustainable Development Law
Montreal, Canada, 13–15 June 2002.

UNEP

CISDL

THE WORLD BANK
Legal Vice-Presidency

This anthology is published under the auspices of the Partnership on
International Law for Sustainable Development that was launched at the 2002
World Summit on Sustainable Development by the CISDL, the International
Development Law Organization and the International Law Association.

INTERNATIONAL DEVELOPMENT LAW ORGANIZATION
ORGANISATION INTERNATIONALE DE DROIT DU DÉVELOPPEMENT

The partners gratefully acknowledge the financial support of the Government
of Canada, the Policy Research Initiative, the International Development
Research Centre (IDRC) of Canada, the Government of Québec and
McCarthy Tétrault LLP.

 **Government
of Canada** **Gouvernement
du Canada**

IDRC  **CRDI** Policy Research
Initiative Projet de recherche
sur les politiques

McCarthy
Tétrault Québec

Dedicated to my spouse and family, with gratitude for their constant love and support, to our CISDL colleagues and advisers, and to McGill University, especially the Faculty of Law, as well as Yale and Oxford Universities, for making us welcome.

– Marie-Claire Cordonier Segger

Dedicated to my family, for always understanding, to McGill University's Faculty of Law for its support, and to the diverse members of CISDL for their constant inspiration and subversive humour over the last four years.

– Ashfaq Khalfan

Foreword

BY H.E. JUDGE CHRISTOPHER G. WEERAMANTRY
Former Vice-President of the International Court of Justice

Sustainable development is one of the most vibrant current topics in the development of domestic and international law. It is also one of the least developed topics in international law, legal jurisprudence and scholarship. This book provides an important new understanding based on a solid academic study of integrated principles, practical instruments and prospects for future legal research. It presents a long-awaited and coherent vision of an emerging international sustainable development law.

There is a belief on the part of many that the concept of sustainable development is simply "soft" law. Some may even say that this concept is only aspirational. However, I believe that sustainable development is a substantive area of the law in a very real sense. Courts and countries must endeavour to administer and implement sustainable development law, just as is done with other "hard" and established rules.

In the first place, what is sustainable development? The notion of sustainable development has gathered much strength from a variety of international declarations, conventions, and academic writings. The Brundtland Commission describes it as development which meets the needs of the present without compromising the ability of future generations to meet their own needs. As such, it represents a delicate balancing of competing interests. In this book, a new generation of scholars, taking note of my judgments at the International Court of Justice and the work of other jurists, will argue that sustainable development law is necessary in the areas where three highly important areas of law today – the social, the economic and the environmental – overlap, balance and integrate. Development is a human right – there is no longer any reason to deny it. As we saw in the 2002 Johannesburg Summit, extreme poverty violates human dignity, upon which all human rights are founded, and a new kind of equitable economic growth is needed to redress and eradicate such poverty. Environmental protection is also a very important foundation of various human rights such as the right to life, the right to an adequate standard of living, and the right to health and a clean environment.

These rights are part of international law. International law arises initially from the realm of aspirations. All of its principles are formulations of aspirations, gradually hardened into concrete law. For instance, the Universal Declaration of Human Rights began with the formulation of a series of aspirations. But as time advanced, these aspirations became firmer, crystallized, and became part of accepted international law. These were infused into domestic law, becoming hard law subject to judicial settlement and enforcement. I believe that the same process is taking place for sustainable development law. It may begin in the realm of the aspirational, but as time progresses and its importance becomes clearer, it is accepted into the established legal order and is infused into established domestic legal orders.

I believe that the concept of sustainable development is a new truly global concept which is fast gathering momentum, and has become part of accepted international law. The recognition of the concept of sustainable development is not merely a concern for the developing world, but is also accepted as a criterion of State conduct by the developed world.

How do we achieve global sustainable development through law? In modern legal systems, a number of impediments to widespread acceptance remain.

Primary among these difficulties is a short-sighted concept that is very strongly entrenched in modern law. This concept holds that only the living generation have rights under the law. Most of our current legal systems, common law or civil law, concentrate exclusively on the rights of those who are living here and now. They are the only bearers of rights in our modern legal systems. This is, indeed, a very limited view. It does not accord with the philosophies that traditional wisdom has bequeathed to us. Those philosophies teach us that there is a duty on the present generation to look beyond itself to those who are to come after us as well as to look back at the past and respect those who went before us. This is very beautifully expressed in the traditional African concept to which Archbishop Desmond Tutu, Nobel Peace Prize Laureate, has referred in his sermons – that the human community consists of three elements; those who went before us, those who are with us here and now, and those who are yet to come. All three together constitute the human community.

Other challenges also exist. Modern law seems to suggest, quite narrowly, that only human beings have any recognizable rights. However, in many traditional legal systems, there was a very deep understanding of the rights of other living creatures to this planet which we all share. In addition, modern law seems to characterize all in terms of rights rather than duties. The entire emphasis seems to be on rights, whereas traditional legal systems heavily accentuated duties. Every individual had duties towards his or her group, every villager had duties towards the village. The ancient irrigation systems of many countries could not have been maintained in all their complexity if the members of each village did not have duties of maintenance and repair in regard to the village tank and the local irrigation channels.

Much guidance can be gained from traditional wisdom. In these respects, such wisdom surpasses the rather limited vision of modern legal systems. Modern law, rich though it may be, neglects an important and fertile source of nourishment by neglecting the traditional wisdom of humanity. In environmental matters, the traditional wisdom of humanity can teach us how we can live in harmony with our environment without destroying it in the manner resulting from the pursuit of legal concepts to the limit of their logic, without applying also the restraining influence of the traditional wisdom of the human family.

The old international law (the international law that prevailed until the end of World War II) was based upon individualism. It was founded in the individual sovereignty of different States that are members of the world community. But today's international law is moving toward a more socially oriented international law. Various pressures have forced this recognition. One is the pressure of environmental needs. Ozone depletion, global climate change, loss of bio-diversity and advancing deserts bring possible damage not merely to individual States, but to the world at large. Such damage does not respect national boundaries. Pollution does not recognize the doctrine of State sovereignty and end at the boundaries of a nation state. If we are to fight pollution, this must be done as a global community.

I believe that we have passed out of the era of co-existence, into the era of cooperation. This is not merely passive cooperation, but rather, active cooperation. If we are to save our global inheritance, we must do so actively. We need, for this purpose, to be willing to surrender some part of sovereignty to the rest of the world, accepting common guidance by the global community.

Similarly, our vision must not only extend in space, to States beyond national frontiers, but also in time, beyond generational frontiers. We have to cast our vision beyond the present generation and look forward into the future. In sustainable development law, we are in the realm of future generations. We become responsible for the rights not only of ourselves but of generations to come.

We must marshal all our resources to this task. International law must draw upon the principles of different civilizations. Many regions of the world are rich in a particular resource – the resource of traditional wisdom – and we as lawyers must see how we can best tap into that reservoir of wisdom. If we fail to look to the past for its traditional wisdom, we may be depriving ourselves of one of our richest resources. When we think in terms of formal law and modern formalistic legal systems, we rather superciliously deny ourselves the benefit of this very important source of wisdom. Let me illustrate this from the traditional people of Australia. They, the historians tell us, have to their credit one of the greatest achievements that any human race can claim. They were able to maintain a stable life style, for 60,000 years, on the world's most inhospitable continent. Reflect on what this means. The great civilizations, those we see as being very ancient, such as Ancient Egypt, or the Indus Valley civilization, were not much more than 6,000 years old. Aboriginal people have maintained a stable life style in such a challenging environment with great success for such a period of time. Is there not some wisdom we can gather from them?

For example, such peoples believe that land has a vitality of its own, living and growing with the people. If the land withers and dies, so also will the people, because the health of a community is dependent on the health of the land. And the health of the land is lost unless you pay due regard and reverence to that land, caring for it as you would any other living thing. Another piece of aboriginal wisdom was built on using every species to the maximum advantage one could. Fauna and flora were comparatively meagre on the continent, but every species of plant and animal was used carefully. Nothing was discarded.

Such are the sustainable development traditions of numerous countries. We can and must weave these aspirations back into the fabric of modern international law by developing the concept of sustainable development law, for the benefit of present and future generations. This book is an important contribution to this far-reaching and momentous task. It is a first step in the direction of making international law broader in its conceptions, less formalistic in its procedures and more harmonious with the global inheritance of traditional human wisdom than it has been thus far. Sustainable development law is in a sense leading the way. This book seeks to gather together the principles that should guide it on its journey.

Biographies of the Authors & Contributors

Marie-Claire Cordonier Segger, MEM (Yale), B.C.L. & LL.B. (McGill), B.A. Hons (Carl) is Director of the Centre for International Sustainable Development Law (CISDL). She lectures in law for the International Development Law Organization (IDLO), the United Nations Environment Programme (UNEP), the United Nations Economic Commission for Latin America and the Caribbean and at several universities. With former Vice-President of the International Court of Justice, Judge C.G. Weeramantry, she edited *Sustainable Justice* (Leiden: Martinus Nijhoff, 2004), and with Dr. Markus Gehring, she edited *Sustainable Developments in World Trade Law* (The Hague: Kluwer Law International, 2005). She is also director of a joint UNEP, International Institute for Sustainable Development and CISDL Americas project, where she chairs a hemispheric research consortium and was lead author of four books on regional trade and sustainable development issues. A member of the International Law Association's (ILA) Committee on International Law on Sustainable Development, she chairs a joint CISDL–ILA–IDLO Partnership on International Law for Sustainable Development. Ms. Cordonier Segger has served as an editor on the *Revue québécoise de droit international*, on the Board of Directors of the Canadian Environment Network, and on several Canadian delegations to the United Nations. She has been twice appointed an AVINA Fellow, a Visiting Scholar at the Lauterpacht Research Centre for International Law at Cambridge University, and Associate Fellow at the Royal Institute of International Affairs (Sustainable Development Programme). A British Chevening Scholar, she holds an SSHRC Doctoral Fellowship for a Ph.D. in International Law at Oxford University. She is fluent in English, French and Spanish with a notion of Portuguese and German.

Ashfaq Khalfan, B.C.L & LL.B (McGill), B.A. Hons. (McGill), is Director of the CISDL, and initiated the Human Rights and Poverty Eradication programme. He has published on a range of topics including human rights and sustainable development, minority rights and constitutional reform and poverty eradication. He led CISDL's research project on debt legitimacy, co-authored the CISDL working paper, *Advancing the Odious Debt Doctrine*, and regularly advises civil society advocates of Southern debt cancellation of their legal and strategic options. He also serves as Coordinator of the Right to Water Programme at the Centre on Housing Rights and Evictions, where he co-authored two books on the right to water. In this capacity, he has monitored violations of the rights to housing and water in a range of countries and provided legal advice to other civil society organizations. He has served as an editor on the *Revue québécoise de droit international*, a Montreal-based law journal. He has previously worked with the Kituo Cha Sheria (Legal Advice Centre) in Kenya carrying on research on insecurity in informal settlements and with the Law & Society Trust, a Sri Lankan human rights NGO, where he coordinated the work of a civil society coalition on constitutional reform. He has also worked with the Investigations Branch of the Canadian Human Rights Commission, and with the Federal Department of Justice in Canada. He speaks English, Swahili and French.

Salim A. Nakhjavani, LL.M (Cantab), B.C.L. & LL.B (McGill) is Lead Counsel for Crosscutting Issues at the Centre for International Sustainable Development Law (CISDL). He currently serves as Assistant Legal Adviser in the Office of the Prosecutor of the International Criminal Court. He was elected to the Whewell Scholarship in International Law in the University of Cambridge in 2003. He has lectured on international human rights law in several universities in Australia, and on specialist topics in international criminal law in Germany, Italy and Norway. He is past Research Director of the McGill Legal Information Clinic, and was commended by the Government of Quebec for his work with youth. Mr. Nakhjavani is fluent in French, English and Persian, with notions of German and Dutch.

Sumudu Atapattu, Ph.D Law & LL.M (Cantab) is Lead Counsel for Human Rights and Poverty Eradication with the CISDL, and an Attorney-at-Law of the Supreme Court of Sri Lanka (first in order of merit at the final examination). She held a Senior Fulbright scholarship for "Environmental Rights and Human Rights" at the New York University Law School and the George Washington University Law School. She was a Senior Lecturer at the Faculty of Law, University of Colombo, Sri Lanka. She also serves as Consultant to the Law & Society Trust, and was editor of the *LST Review*. She has worked on the draft fundamental rights chapter of the proposed Constitution of Sri Lanka, and the draft legislation on equal opportunity, edited several publications and coordinated research for the annual *State of Human Rights Report* of the Trust, which she edited in 2002. In 2001 she served on a panel of experts on liability and compensation issues for the WHO's proposed Framework Convention on Tobacco Control. She is presently a visiting scholar at the Institute for Legal Studies of the University of Wisconsin-Madison Law School.

Jorge Cabrera Medaglia, B.C.L & LL.M (University of Costa Rica) is Lead Counsel for International Sustainable Biodiversity Law with the CISDL. A professor at the University of Costa Rica's Faculty of Law, and the UNED University in Costa Rica, he also serves as a tutor for WIPO's distance learning courses on intellectual property. Prof. Cabrera acts as a legal adviser to Costa Rica's National Biodiversity Institute (INBio). He has acted as a Consultant for UNCTAD, ECLAC, IICA, SICA, CCAD, IPGRI, CYMMIT, REMERFI, CATIE, University of California, Environmental Law Center of IUCN in Bonn,

COSUDE, EU projects, IISD, TNC, IDB, and the Institute of Economic Development of the World Bank, amongst others. Prof. Cabrera is also a member of the International Advisory Committee of the Public Interest Intellectual Property Association (PIIPA), the International Advisory Group of the UNEP initiative on capacity building on access to genetic resources, and the National Biodiversity Commission of Costa Rica. He has acted as a negotiator at the Convention on Biological Diversity (CBD) on behalf of the Government of Costa Rica, served as co-chair of the CBD's Expert Panel on Access and Benefit Sharing and chaired the CBD Sub-working Group on IPR and Capacity-Building. He is also a member of the delegation to the WIPO Committee on Genetic Resources and Traditional Knowledge and the Group of Like-minded Megadiverse Countries. He has published in the areas of intellectual property rights, access to benefits sharing, biosafety, trade and environment, and has served as a legal adviser and instructor on these issues in Africa, Asia and Latin America.

Carolyn Deere, M.A. (Johns Hopkins SAIS), B.Econ. (Hons) (Sydney) is Lead Research Fellow for Natural Resources Law with the CISDL. She also leads the trade and development work of the Global Economic Governance Programme at Oxford University. She was previously Assistant Director in the Global Inclusion theme of the Rockefeller Foundation, a Founder of the Funders' Network on Trade and Globalization and served on its Steering Committee, and a member of the Steering Committee of Grantmakers Without Borders. She is Founder and Chair of the Board of Directors of Intellectual Property Watch (IP Watch). Ms. Deere has also worked with the World Conservation Union (IUCN); the International Center for Trade and Sustainable Development (ICTSD); and the Congressional Staff Forum for International Development at the Overseas Development Council in Washington, DC. She has published on natural resources, development, intellectual property and trade issues, and has consulted for UNCTAD, UNDP and the Soros Foundation, among others.

Kathryn Garforth, LL.B. (Osgoode Hall), M.E.S (York) is a Research Fellow with the CISDL. She conducts research on access to genetic resources and benefit-sharing as well as biosafety, has served as a consultant to the UNEP-GEF project on the Development of National Biosafety Frameworks, and led the CISDL delegation to the 7th Conference of the Parties to the Convention on Biological Diversity as well as the second meeting of the Ad Hoc Open-Ended Working Group on Access to Genetic Resources and Benefit-Sharing. She is currently developing manuals for publication in the areas of access and benefit-sharing and biosafety.

Markus W. Gehring, LL.M (Yale), Ph.D. Law (Hamburg) is Lead Counsel for Sustainable International Trade, Investment and Competition Law with the CISDL. He has led the CISDL delegation in various WTO Ministerial Meetings. He is also a legal researcher with Prof. Vaughan Lowe at All Souls College, Oxford University, a tutor in public international law at University College,

Oxford University, and a member of the Concerted Action on Trade and Environment (CATE), funded by the European Commission. He served as Legal Fellow for the International Centre for Trade and Sustainable Development in Geneva, Switzerland, and editor of their legal column in the *BRIDGES Journal*. He also taught German Constitutional and Administrative Law at the Faculty of Law, University of Hamburg, Germany. He was Walter Oberreith Fellow, and is candidate for his second Ph.D, a J.S.D. in European and Comparative Constitutional Law, at Yale Law School. He also studied at the Universidad de Deusto in Bilbao, Spain, where he specialized in International and European Law, and at the University of Hamburg. His recent book is *Sustainable Developments in World Trade Law* (The Hague: Kluwer Law International, 2005). He has also served as an Alderman on his town council in Germany, and is fluent in German, English and Spanish with a notion of French.

María Leichner Reynal, B.C.L (Buenos Aires), Ph.D. Law (Litoral) is Lead Counsel for Crosscutting Issues with the CISDL. She is also Founder and Executive Director of the Fundación Ecos, and former President of Patagonia Land Trust (PLT) Argentina. Dr. Leichner Reynal served as Professor at Buenos Aires University, School of Social Sciences and Economics, and co-ordinated "Informa MERCOSUR", and has served as a consultant to the World Wildlife Fund (WWF). She was named by the World Economic Forum as a "Global Leader for Tomorrow 2002" and is part of its Environmental Sustainability Index Task Force. Dr. Leichner Reynal is a partner of the International Investment Rules Project, and President of Fundación Ecos Corrientes, which was established as an ECOS subsidiary organization in Argentina, to develop the "Management and Conservation of Biodiversity in the Wetlands of the Esteros del Iberá", a nature conservation programme with a strong social component. She serves as a consultant to the Organization of American States (OAS), the UNEP, and the World Wildlife Fund, and is the MERCOSUR Partner of the Americas project of the UNEP, the IISD and the CISDL.

Alhagi Marong, D.C.L., LL.M. (McGill), LL.B & B.L. (Sierra Leone) is a Senior Research Fellow at the Centre for International Sustainable Development Law (CISDL). Dr. Marong is currently Co-Director for Africa Programs at the Environmental Law Institute in Washington, DC. He taught at the Department of Law, American University of Armenia and has served as Senior State Counsel at the Ministry of Justice in Gambia and Legal Adviser for the National Environment Agency of The Gambia. He has published on norm creation in international law and the confluence of international business regimes, social and environmental concerns in Africa. Dr. Marong also worked with the Law Reform Commission of The Gambia, the United Nations Food and Agriculture Organization, and the Legal Affairs Division of the World Trade Organization in Geneva, and studied at the International Development Law Organization, in Rome. He has held the McGill Greenshields Fellowship, the McGill Major Fellowship, and a Commonwealth Scholarship.

Maya Prabhu, LL.B. (McGill), M.D. (Dalhousie Medical School), M.Sc. (Political Economy, LSE), A.B. (Social Studies, Harvard) is Lead Counsel for Sustainable International Health Law at the CISDL. A medical doctor and a lawyer, her legal interests include international humanitarian law, medical ethics and various issues at the nexus of health and human rights. Dr. Prabhu's past experience includes health policy analysis at the United Nations Policy Development Branch, the International Affairs Division of Health Canada, the Canadian International Development Agency and the Manitoba Center for Health Policy and Evaluation. Her field work has taken her to Thailand and India for research on HIV/AIDS. While in medical school she did extensive work in psychiatry and post-traumatic stress disorder, especially among civilians and combatants in post-conflict situations. She is currently practising law in New York.

Witold Tymowski, B.C.L & LL.B (McGill), B.A. (McGill) is a Research Fellow at the CISDL. He is also presently a Legal Counsel at the Supreme Court of Canada, and collaborates with IUCN and the United Nations Food and Agriculture Organization (FAO) on a legal guide to the International Treaty on Plant Genetic Resources for Food and Agriculture. Mr. Tymowski has practised in the field of international trade and intellectual property law with the law firm Stikeman Elliott LLP. He has worked for the Environmental Law and Policy Center (ELPC) in Chicago, Illinois and the Trade Law Programme of the Center for International Environmental Law (CIEL) in Geneva, Switzerland. He has also worked for the World Conservation Union (IUCN) Environmental Law Centre in Bonn, Germany. He is fluent in English, French, Polish, and has basic German.

Xueman Wang, LL.M. (Wu Han, China), M.A. (Fletcher School, Tufts) is Lead Counsel for Climate Change and Vulnerability Law at the CISDL. She works with the Secretariat of the Convention on Biodiversity (CBD), and is responsible for legal and policy issues related to the Biosafety Protocol, specifically on liability, compliance and trade. Before she joined the CBD, she worked for four years with the Climate Change Secretariat, mainly responsible for developing compliance regimes for the Climate Change Convention and its Kyoto Protocol, as well as trade and environment. Ms. Wang worked for seven years with the Treaty and Law Department of the Ministry of Foreign Affairs of China, and is fluent in Chinese, English and German.

Acknowledgements

This book was developed through three years of work by the Centre for International Sustainable Development Law (CISDL). The authors, Marie-Claire Cordonier Segger and Ashfaq Khalfan, Directors of CISDL, owe particular thanks and acknowledgement to various contributors. First, we would like to thank Salim Nakhjavani, Lead Counsel for Crosscutting Issues of CISDL, who was an editor of the first edition of this book under the title *Weaving the Rules for Our Common Future*, for his contribution. We also wish to thank Witold Tymowski, CISDL Research Fellow, Alhagi Marong and Cairo Robb, CISDL Senior Research Fellows, as well as the Lead Counsel of the CISDL for their contribution to this book: Sumudu Atapattu, Sri Lanka, Human Rights and Poverty Eradication, Jorge Cabrera Medaglia, Costa Rica, Sustainable International Biodiversity Law, Carolyn Deere, Australia, Sustainable Natural Resources Law, Markus Gehring, Germany, Sustainable International Trade, Investment and Competition Law, Maya Prabhu, Canada, Sustainable International Health Law, Xueman Wang, China, Sustainable Climate Change and Vulnerability Law, and María Leichner Reynal, Uruguay, Crosscutting Issues.

The CISDL owes a sincere debt of gratitude to the members of the CISDL International Council, and roster of distinguished advisers, who provided intellectual guidance, review and support throughout the development of the book and related consultation events. These include Kamal Hossain, International Law Association, Stephen Toope, Pierre Elliot Trudeau Foundation, Université de Québec à Montréal, Armand de Mestra, Peter Leuprecht, McGill University Faculty of Law, Justice Charles Gonthier, former Judge of the Supreme Court of Canada, Daniel Esty and Harold Koh, Yale University, Gérald Tremblay, McCarthy Tétrault LLP, Simon Potter, Canadian Bar Association, Bakary Kante and Brennan van Dyke, United Nations Environment Programme, David Runnalls and Konrad von Moltke, International Institute for Sustainable Development, David Freestone, World Bank, Pia Rodriguez and Yohannes Kassahuhn, International Development Law Organization, Vaughan Lowe, All Souls College at Oxford University, and Christopher Gregory Weeramantry, former Vice-President of the International Court of Justice. Special thanks are also owed to Nicholas Kasirer, Richard Janda, Adelle Blackett, Robert Godin, Myron Frankman, Rene Provost, and Jaye Ellis at McGill University, among many others there.

The authors and contributors would also like to acknowledge and thank Sidney Thompson, Karin Baqi, Michelle Toering, Audrey Demarsico, and Rachel Bendayan, CISDL, for their substantial editing work and review, Debbie Locker and Alicen Chow, CISDL, for research assistance, Rene Steiner at SteinerGraphics for his work on layout, as well as John Louth, Gwen Booth, Louise Kavanagh, and Dominic Shryane at Oxford University Press for their work on this book.

About the CISDL

It is the mission of the Centre for International Sustainable Development Law (CISDL) to promote sustainable societies and the protection of ecosystems by advancing the understanding, development and implementation of international sustainable development law (SDL). The CISDL is an independent legal academic research centre which has a close partnership with the McGill University Faculty of Law. It works in cooperation with other Faculties of McGill University, the Université de Montréal, the Université de Québec à Montréal and a network of developed and developing country law faculties. It is guided in its work by a roster of distinguished experts in international environmental, economic and social law, representing developing and developed countries, from intergovernmental and non-governmental organizations, academic institutions and private practice.

The CISDL, after hosting "Sustainable Justice 2002: Implementing International Sustainable Development Law" in Montreal, June 2002, presented its results at the 2002 UNEP Global Judges Symposium on Sustainable Development and the Role of Law, and to the 2002 *World Summit for Sustainable Development* in Johannesburg, South Africa. CISDL has now taken on a United Nations-sanctioned partnership to implement the WSSD outcomes with regard to International Law for Sustainable Development, with the International Development Law Organization in Rome, the International Law Association in London, the United Nations Environment Programme and the World Bank. The partnership reports annually to the United Nations Commission on Sustainable Development. For further information, see www.cisdl.org.

CISDL thanks all the sponsors, speakers and participants of "Sustainable Justice 2002", held in Montreal 13–16 June 2002 for their contributions which influenced the final draft of this book. For their help in organizing and chairing "Sustainable Justice 2002: A Conference on Implementation of International Sustainable Development Law", and their intellectual contributions, the CISDL would like to acknowledge other senior research fellows, research fellows and associate fellows, and faculty members, including Bradnee Chambers, Beatrice Chaytor, François Crepeau, François Joubert, Phillipe LePrestre, Desiree McGraw, and Catherine-Zoi Varfis. CISDL should also thank honorary fellows Richard Ballhorn, Eric Dannenmaier, Ahmed Ihab Gamaledin, Ricardo Melendez-Ortiz, Catherine Redgewell, Nicolas Robinson, Naresh Singh, Matthew Stillwell, and advisers Phillip Alston, New York University, Louise Arbour, former Judge of the Supreme Court of Canada, James Cameron, of Baker & McKenzie, James Crawford and Nick Sinclair-Brown of the Cambridge Lauterpacht Research Centre for International Law, Elizabeth Dowdeswell, Omar El-Arini of the Montreal Protocol Multilateral Fund, Janine Ferretti of the Inter-American Development Bank, Maurice Kamto of the International Law Commission, Albie Sachs of the Supreme Court of South Africa, Nicolas Schrijver of the University of Amsterdam, Maurice Strong of the Earth Council, Hamdullah Zedan and Dan Ogolla of the United Nations Convention on Biological Diversity. Finally, the CISDL would like to thank the dedicated members of its secretariat, François Massé, Karin Kessaris, Sidney Thompson, Alejandro Gomez, Ana Luisa Georgescu and Joana Ali.

Intellectual guidance was provided by those mentioned above, and by Phillipe LaRoche, Beat Nobs and Franz Perrez of Switzerland, Knut Opsal of Norway, Lars Goran and Viveka Bohn of Sweden, Micheal Katz and Dhesigen Naidoo of South Africa, Inab Gamaledin of Egypt, Hossein Moeini of Iran, at the United Nations Commission on Sustainable Development and the 2002 *World Summit on Sustainable Development* in Johannesburg, South Africa.

Contents

Introduction

There is an observable increase in conflicts throughout the world between the demands of economic development, the environment and human rights. The frequency of these disputes is linked to current global patterns of natural resource degradation, over-consumption, inequitable distribution of resources and poverty. These are placing unprecedented demands on the regenerative capacity of ecosystems and jeopardize the livelihoods of vulnerable groups.

A fundamental disconnection lies at the core of the conflicts. Environmental conservation initiatives can be indifferent or hostile to economic development, and have at times ignored human rights considerations, such as the needs of local communities directly dependent on natural resources. Economic development projects often appear to subordinate environmental and human rights concerns to financial results. This approach has not slowed increasing inequalities within and among nations. Similarly, international human rights obligations are generally not applied in a manner which addresses environmental issues. International instruments with a primarily human rights focus do not explicitly refer to environmental protection; efforts to link these domains are embryonic. Attempts to deal with these three fields of development separately run counter to the fundamentally interconnected nature of the international systems themselves, and are proving to have serious consequences.

The problem lies not so much in the social, economic and environmental goals or rules themselves, but in their governance. In essence, a global tapestry of laws is being crafted – without weaving together the strands.

Respect for human rights, environmental protection, and economic development are complementary rather than unrelated or opposing objectives. Measures to address them require balanced, integrated approaches. "Sustainable development" can provide new insights and solutions,[1] guiding relationships at the interstices of the three systems.

The *World Summit for Sustainable Development* (WSSD) and its myriad parallel events took place in 2002 in Johannesburg, South Africa, drawing an estimated 45,000 participants, including over 100 heads of state. In the Johannesburg Declaration on Sustainable Development, and the Johannesburg Plan of Implementation, countries assume a collective responsibility to advance and strengthen the interdependent and mutually reinforcing pillars of sustainable

---

[1] The need for such integrated approaches is ancient in its origins. See the Separate Opinion of International Court of Justice Vice-President Weeramantry in *Case Concerning the Gabčíkovo-Nagymaros Project (Hungary/Slovakia)* (1997), ICJ Rep. 7, where the concept of sustainable development is traced to the practices of ancient tribes in Sri Lanka, Eastern Africa, America and Europe, and in Islamic legal traditions.

development – economic development, social development and environmental protection – at the local, national, regional and global levels.[2]

SUSTAINABLE GLOBALIZATION?

Central to the global consensus in Johannesburg was the understanding that sustainable development needs to be implemented on many levels, in changing situations. In particular, the 2002 Johannesburg Declaration recognizes that globalization has added a new dimension to development challenges. For globalization to be sustainable, it must become equitable. The rapid integration of markets, mobility of capital and significant increases in investment flows around the world open new challenges and opportunities for the pursuit of sustainable development. But the benefits and costs of globalization are unevenly distributed, with developing countries facing special difficulties. External factors have become critical in determining the success or failure of developing countries in their national development efforts. And globalization must also become environmentally sound. As such, according to the 2002 *World Summit for Sustainable Development* (WSSD), there are three interdependent and mutually reinforcing pillars of sustainable development – economic development, social development and environmental protection. Challenges in all three areas must be addressed if the new "global community" is to last. International cooperation founded on mutually agreed commitments is more necessary than ever, for global progress towards sustainable development.

> Sustainable development is "development that meets the needs of the present without compromising the ability of future generations to meet their own needs".
>
> *Brundtland Report, 1987*

The international language of sustainable development has dominated legal debates in the fields of social and economic development and environmental protection since the seminal report of the World Commission on Environment and Development (WCED) in 1987, *Our Common Future*, popularly known as the *Brundtland Report*.[3] The definition agreed therein, adopted in this book, sees sustainable development as "development that meets the needs of the present without compromising the ability of future generations to meet their own needs." The *Brundtland Report* highlights two elements of the concept. First, there is a substantive recognition that development must be geared toward

---

[2] See *Johannesburg Declaration on Sustainable Development*, in Report of the *World Summit on Sustainable Development*, Johannesburg, South Africa, 26 Aug.–4 Sept. 2002, A/CONF.199/20 (New York: United Nations, 2002). See also *Johannesburg Plan of Implementation*, Report of the *World Summit on Sustainable Development*, Johannesburg, South Africa, 4 Sept. 2002, UN Doc. A/CONF.199/20: <http://www.un.org/esa/sustdev/documents/WSSD_POI_PD/English/POIToc.htm>.

[3] World Commission on Environment and Development, *Our Common Future* (Oxford: Oxford University Press, 1987) at 8. See also Report of the World Commission on Environment and Development: "Our Common Future" 4 Aug. 1987, U.N GA Res., A/42/427 (1987).

meeting basic human needs. It must seek to end poverty, starting with the most vulnerable first. Secondly, it is also recognized that there are limits. Development must meet human needs, but it is bounded by the evolving constraints of human abilities (technology, governance), and also by diverse environmental limitations. The tension between environmental limits and economic and social development pressures is bridged through the concept of "sustainable development". The bridge is achieved by recognizing a common obligation toward future generations. These generations are "our common future" – a global future, one that is interconnected at all subsidiary levels. Sustainable development seeks to create the conditions for long-term sustainability for present and future generations; it requires an accommodation between economic development, social justice and environmental protection. This is important. Sustainable development, as a concept, is constructed to frame cooperative, integrated solutions to some of the most significant challenges of our era. These challenges evolve. For example, in 1987, global priorities related to population and human resources, food security, species and ecosystems, energy, industry and urbanization, while in 2004, global climate change and health might also be high priorties.[4] Furthermore, sustainable development has significant procedural elements. It is done through empowerment, through consultation, through impact and risk assessment, through the expansion of opportunities and capacities, and through public participation. It is a process, not just a goal.

The concept of sustainable development received the approval of over 140 governments in the 1992 *United Nations Conference on Environment and Development* (UNCED), the "Earth Summit", whose key consensus statements, the 1992 *Rio Declaration and Programme of Action* and *Agenda 21* addressed mostly environmental, but also social and economic concerns. Despite that general agreement, however, there are hundreds of formulations of sustainable development, each reflecting particular values and priorities.[5] For example, the International Institute for Sustainable Development (IISD) provides a rather sophisticated definition, describing sustainable development as:

an open and participatory process of environmental, social, economic, cultural and political change that can be achieved through protecting and enhancing ecosystems, transforming the direction of investments and the orientation of technology, and re-designing institutions to ensure current and future potential to meet the needs and aspirations of communities.[6]

In contrast, in 1991 the International Union for the Conservation of Nature (IUCN) published a sequel to the *World Conservation Strategy* entitled *Caring for the Earth*, which emphasizes ecological limits. Herein, sustainable

---

[4] *Our Common Future, supra* note 3.

[5] T.C. Trzyna, ed., *A Sustainable World: Defining and Measuring Sustainable Development* (Sacramento: California Institute of Public Affairs, 1995) 23. See also N. Schrijver and F. Weiss, eds., *International Law and Sustainable Development* (Leiden: Martinus Nijhoff, 2004).

[6] International Institute for Sustainable Development (IISD), *Impoverishment and Sustainable Development* (Winnipeg: IISD, 1996).

development was defined as "improving the quality of human life while living within the carrying capacity of supporting ecosystems".[7] The UNDP, in 1998, proposed a "sustainable human development" which "seeks to expand choices for all people – women, men and children, current and future generations – while protecting the natural systems on which all life depends..." and "aims to eliminate poverty, promote human dignity and rights, and provide equitable opportunities for all through good governance, thereby promoting the realization of all human 'rights' – economic, social, cultural, civil and political".[8]

The vagueness in the concept of sustainable development may have been appropriate in 1992, for it allowed the idea to be adopted almost universally. This inclusiveness was essential for sustainable development to begin to provide guidance for diverse communities, on many levels (local, sub-national, national, sub-regional, regional and global). In the *Brundtland Report* formulation, sustainable development was clearly a political and social construct, not a scientific blueprint.[9] But international law and policy have moved on. Even in 1997, in the Earth Summit + 5 Programme for Further Implementation of *Agenda 21*, the United Nations General Assembly observed that "it is necessary to continue the progressive development and, as and when appropriate, codification of international law related to sustainable development."[10]

The multiplicity of meanings, and consequent lack of clarity, now causes difficulties at the national and international level. Indeed, as one scholar notes:

the advance of 'international law in the field of sustainable development' raises basic questions about the connection between norms arising in different areas of international law, in particular the environmental, economic and social/human rights fields.[11]

Laws and policies have been designed to implement policy objectives in the three separate spheres of sustainable development – the economic, environmental and social – without coherence or even co-ordination between them. As international legal regimes become more complex, and institutions are established to implement obligations, countries are faced with overlapping and sometimes even conflicting legal rules. The situation has become particularly unmanageable for developing countries. Valuable resources, political will and capacity are squandered in an attempt to harmonize programmes which were never meant to

---

[7] D.A. Munro and M.W. Holdgate, eds., *Caring for the Earth: A Strategy for Sustainable Living* (Gland: IUCN, 1991).

[8] J.G. Speth, *Integrating Human Rights with Sustainable Human Development: A UNDP Policy Document* (New York: United Nations Development Programme, 1998).

[9] See in particular, World Commission on Environment and Development, *Our Common Future* (Oxford: Oxford University Press, 1987) at 51, where it states: "No single blueprint for sustainability will be found, as economic and social systems and ecological conditions differ widely among countries." See also S. Baker, M. Kousis, D. Richardson & S. Young, eds., *The Politics of Sustainable Development* (London: Routledge, 1997).

[10] UNGA Res. A/RES/S-19/2 (19 Sept. 1997) at 109.

[11] P. Sands, "Sustainable Development: Treaty, Custom and the Cross-fertilization of International Law" in D. Freestone and A. Boyle, *International Law and Sustainable Development: Past Achievements and Future Challenges* (Oxford: Oxford University Press, 1999) at 39.

conflict. Furthermore, international treaties and institutions charged with sustainable development mandates begin to suffer from a lack of respect and credibility. The instruments for cooperation are accused of organizational inefficiencies, or found to have ineffective compliance and enforcement mechanisms.

In 1992 at the Rio de Janeiro Earth Summit, in *Agenda 21*, governments called for "[t]he further development of international law on sustainable development, giving special attention to the delicate balance between environmental and developmental concerns"; and identified a "need to clarify and strengthen the relationship between existing international instruments or agreements in the field of environment and relevant social and economic agreements or instruments, taking into account the special needs of developing countries".[12]

The 2002 *World Summit on Sustainable Development* reaffirmed these priorities, and assumed "a collective responsibility to advance and strengthen the interdependent and mutually reinforcing pillars of sustainable development – economic development, social development and environmental protection – at the local, national, regional and global levels". Countries reaffirmed their "commitment to the principles and purposes of the Charter of the United Nations and international law, as well as to the strengthening of multilateralism". They mandated the United Nations Commission on Sustainable Development to "[t]ake into account significant legal developments in the field of sustainable development, with due regard to the role of relevant intergovernmental bodies in promoting the implementation of Agenda 21 relating to international legal instruments and mechanisms". Moving forward from the *World Summit on Sustainable Development*, there is a need to coordinate and integrate social, economic and environmental regimes. Important tasks are ahead. A new generation of dedicated jurists, from both developed and developing countries, is needed to design, strengthen, implement and monitor policies, laws and integrated instruments that can achieve sustainable development on all levels. Increasing globalization presents both opportunities and serious challenges.[13] International rules must become more coherent, especially in the critical areas of human rights, environmental protection and economic development. This not a matter of joining three areas of law into one. However, if globalization is to be harnessed and channelled toward sustainability, collective, binding international principles and instruments become essential. International law is needed to govern the intersections between conflicting global priorities and norms in this area, to ensure a balanced outcome. The emerging international law of sustainable development, or, in short, "sustainable development law", a body of treaties, legal instruments and emerging substantive principles, supported by distinctive procedural elements, provides ways to address these critical challenges.

---

[12] *Agenda 21*, Report of the UNCED, I (1992) UN Doc. A/CONF.151/26/Rev.1, (1992) 31 ILM 874 at para. 39.1 See also P. Sands, "International Law in the Field of Sustainable Development" (1994) 65 *BYBIL* 303.

[13] For a better understanding of the meaning of globalization as it is intended here, see J. Stiglitz, *Globalization and its Discontents* (London: Penguin Books, 2002).

SUSTAINABLE DEVELOPMENT LAW: THE BOOK

This book, *Sustainable Development Law: Principles, Practices and Prospects* seeks to advance the understanding, development and implementation of international sustainable development law. It has two principal aims. First, it seeks to advance the understanding of sustainable development by providing a discussion of international law in this area. As such, it explores current concepts of sustainable development law, surveys innovative aspects of key treaties in international social, economic and environmental law, analyses the proposed principles of sustainable development law, provides preliminary practical case studies of relevant legal instruments, and identifies prospects for further legal research. Secondly, it aims to strengthen the implementation of sustainable development law. In this first volume, there is not scope to provide a comprehensive exploration of this rich and complex area of law, nor a full resource on either international judgments or treaty law in this area. However, the book does provide an up-to-date guide to this emerging area, for use in capacity-building programmes and courses for lawmakers, jurists, scholars and educators in developed and developing countries, from environmental protection, economic progress and social development communities.

The text of *Sustainable Development Law: Principles, Practices and Prospects* is presented in five parts. After this brief introduction, Part I (The Foundations) surveys the origins of the concept of sustainable development in depth. It identifies the legal aspects of the concept, and describes the formation of a body of "international law on sustainable development". In particular, after providing brief descriptions of the evolving fields of international social, economic and environmental law, it explains how sustainable development law is emerging at the area of intersection between the three.

Part II (The Principles) examines principles of international law related to sustainable development that were proposed by the International Law Association Committee on the Legal Aspects of Sustainable Development,[14] in light of debates in the *World Summit for Sustainable Development*. It takes a balanced approach, drawing on examples from international social, economic and environmental law, and focuses on recent developments and reflection of these principles in international treaty instruments. Then, legal instruments in this field are

---

[14] See ILA Resolution 3/2002: *New Delhi Declaration Of Principles Of International Law Relating to Sustainable Development*, in ILA, Report of the Seventieth Conference, New Delhi (London: ILA, 2002). Available online: http://www.ila-hq.org and excerpted and discussed extensively herein. See also "ILA New Delhi Declaration of Principles of International Law Relating to Sustainable Development" in Kluwer Academic Publishers, *International Environmental Agreements: Politics, Law and Economics* 2, 2 2002, 209–16, available online: http://www.Kluweronline.com/issu/1567–9764/current. See also N. Schrijver and F. Weiss, eds., *International Law and Sustainable Development* (Leiden: Martinus Nijhoff, 2004) at 699. And see M.-C. Cordonier Segger and C.G. Weeramantry, eds., *Sustainable Justice: Reconciling Economic, Social and Environmental Law* (Leiden: Martinus Nijhoff, 2004).

analysed according to a typology describing the degree of integration between international social, economic and environmental law. This "continuum" ranges from instruments displaying little or no integration to fully-integrated international sustainable development law.

Part III (The Practices) provides practical case studies of law and policy instruments at these various degrees of integration, illustrating challenges and innovative methodologies that have been implemented over recent years. Three case studies are presented. First, the development and application of "sustainability impact assessment" is analysed, as an instrument for the integration of social and environmental concerns into economic development projects, programmes and policies. Secondly, "regional integration agreements" are examined from five sub-regions of the Americas, and new social, economic and environmental developments are briefly surveyed. Thirdly, the role of economic, social and cultural rights in international sustainable development law is discussed, demonstrating the movement towards applying human rights law in economic and environmental governance, and assessing its implications. A second section in this Part focuses on challenges to implementation of international sustainable development law, including an analysis of the current international architecture for sustainable development governance and, in a section with Salim Nakhjavani, the issue of compliance-building.

Part IV (The Prospects) identifies cutting-edge research agendas in six priority areas of intersection between international social, economic and environmental law, and identifies several themes which cross-cut these substantive agendas. These priority areas of intersection are drawn, in a balanced manner, from all three fields. The first section, with Markus W. Gehring, identifies emerging social and environmental issues in international trade, investment and competition law. The second section, with Carolyn Deere, examines economic and social issues in international natural resources law. The third section, with Maya Prabhu, examines emerging sustainable development issues in international health law. The fourth section, with Sumudu Atapattu, discusses economic and environmental applications of international human rights and poverty law. The fifth section, with Xueman Wang, considers economic and social aspects of international climate change law. The sixth section, with Jorge Cabrera Medaglia and Kathryn Garforth, analyses emerging social and economic aspects of international biodiversity law. A seventh section, with María Leichner Reynal and Salim Nakhjavani, briefly examines cross-cutting issues. Finally, this Part provides a brief general conclusion to this book, drawing the analysis and proposals together.

The Conclusion presents recommendations for further investigation into the rich and developing fields of international environmental law, international economic law and international social law, and provides a bibliography for the book.

Sustainable Development Law: Principles, Practices and Prospects, is designed as a beginning guide, resource, exploration and reference source for multiple stakeholders: academics, policy-makers, negotiators, students and practitioners of international sustainable development law. It serves both the legal community, and a broader group of development, environment and human rights scholars and professionals affected by intersections of laws in these fields. It lays out some of the key concepts and illustrative instruments for sustainable development law, and proposes future legal research agendas. It is intended to be used in conjunction with specific manuals on particular instruments and fields of international sustainable development law, and curriculum or workshop outlines designed for teaching and discovering international sustainable development law.

As such, *Sustainable Development Law: Principles, Practices and Prospects* is meant for lawyers and non-lawyers alike. The following paragraphs provide a quick overview of the nature of international law, for readers from non-legal disciplines. It describes the principal sources of international law, explains "soft law", and provides short explanations of the key legal concepts used throughout this book, citing sources for a reader's further explorations.

KEY CONCEPTS IN PUBLIC INTERNATIONAL LAW

Where does international law come from? The basic rules of international law are drawn from several sources of law. The three major sources, as defined at Article 38 of the Statute of the International Court of Justice, are treaty, custom and general principles of law recognized by civilized nations.[15]

Treaty law

Treaty law is the most common source of international law and includes rules of international law expressed in writing. Like a contract, a treaty only binds those States that become "party" to the treaty; that is, States that signal their intention to be bound by the rights and duties imposed by a treaty. Treaties may include specific rules or may be "framework" treaties, spelling out general objectives and principles. Some treaties require regular meetings of a "conference of parties" in order to make decisions about treaty implementation. Certain treaties also designate supervisory bodies to monitor compliance with the treaty. The

---

[15] There are also two subsidiary means; international courts can draw upon judicial decisions, and the teachings of the most highly qualified publicists of the various nations. International Court of Justice Statute 26 June 1945, T.S. No. 933, 59 Stat. 1055, 3 Bevans 1179. This is not an exhaustive statement of the foundations of all international law, that might be used by all international dispute settlement bodies, or obeyed by nations. Unilateral acts of international law, the decisions and resolutions of international organs, and other sources may contribute to the development of international law. In this section, only a brief overview of concepts is provided. For an introduction to this field see D.J. Harris, *Cases and Materials on International Law*, 5th edn. (London: Sweet & Maxwell, 1998) at 21–68 and generally, see also J. Collier and V. Lowe, *The Settlement of Disputes in International Law: Institutions and Procedures* (Oxford: Oxford University Press, 2000). And see International Court of Justice, online: http://www.icj-icj.org>.

decisions of these supervisory bodies are not usually formally binding on the parties, but are of significant weight and can influence the conduct of States.

Custom

Customary law is derived from the behaviour of States, according to norms generally accepted as binding. In order to constitute customary law, such State behaviour must be consistent and widespread (state practice), and there must also be evidence that States act as they do because they actually believe they are bound by these norms (*opinio jures*). These international customary norms, whether recognized or in the process of being recognized (*lex ferenda*) are normally called "principles". Principles of customary law that are consistently obeyed and reinforced across context and time can emerge as a form of "super-custom" and become "peremptory" norms of international law (sometimes referred to as *jus cogens*). Some obligations under customary law, typically those involving matters of global concern, are owed to the international community as a whole, not just to a particular, identifiable State (*erga omnes* rules). All members of the international community have an interest in seeing these obligations respected.

General principles

International law can also be drawn from general principles common to the major legal systems, as a secondary source of law. Much of international law, whether customary or constituted by agreement, reflects principles analogous to those found in the major legal systems of the world, and historically may derive from them or from a more remote common origin. When there has not been practice by states sufficient to give the particular principle status as customary law, and the principle has not been legislated by general international agreement, the ICJ or other tribunals may resort to these general principles as a source to develop international law interstitially in special circumstances. Rules that have been drawn from general principles include rules relating to the administration of justice (such as the rule that no one may be judge in his own cause) and rules of fair procedure generally. General principles may also provide "rules of reason" of a general character, such as acquiescence, *estoppel*, the principle that rights must not be abused, or the obligation to repair a wrong. International practice may sometimes convert such a principle into a rule of customary law.[16]

Soft law

"Soft law" refers to a vast body of legally non-binding or incompletely binding norms, the most important of which are guidelines, resolutions, declarations and

[16] C. Ford, "Judicial Discretion in International Jurisprudence: Article 38(1)(C) and 'General Principles of Law'" (1994) 5 *Duke J. of Comp. & Int'l Law* 35–86.

recommendations that are made by parties to an international agreement in the course of its implementation. Soft law is not a source of international law. However, certain "soft law" documents can constitute evidence of emerging customary international law, act as tools to interpret treaties and custom, and serve as templates for generating the precise text of treaty law. Compliance with "soft law" can shape legitimate expectations, and demonstrate good faith. The *Rio Declaration* and *Agenda 21* from the 1992 United Nations Conference on Environmental and Development, UN General Assembly resolutions, and the 2002 *World Summit for Sustainable Development Johannesburg Plan of Implementation* are all examples of "soft law" statements. Indeed, Edith Brown Weiss argues that international agreements need to be viewed as *living agreements*, into which parties continuously breathe life and to which they give new directions by acting as informal legislatures. In many cases, States will follow "soft law" although they may not be required to do so.[17]

The international legal system

How does the international system function? It is important to identify which actors play a role in the international system and how the international system is evolving.

Traditionally, international law was seen as "the body of rules and principles of action which are binding upon civilized States in their relations with one another".[18] The Peace of Westphalia sought to establish an international order based on sovereign, independent, territorially-defined States, each having an interest in maintaining political independence and territorial integrity.

As such, according to the classical definition, international law governs relations between independent States, and the rules of law binding upon States emanate from their free will expressed in treaties, or in customs generally accepted as based on binding principles of law. From this viewpoint, international law exists to regulate relations between co-existing independent communities, and to provide mechanisms for the achievement of common aims.[19] While still relevant, this perspective of the international system cannot paint the full picture. First, it assumes that States' primary interests (political independence and territorial integrity) have not evolved over time. In addition, by char-

---

[17] "Soft law", consisting of non-binding international declarations, consensus statements and other agreements, is not binding in the traditional sense in international law. For the International Court of Justice, the sources of "hard" international law include treaties, custom, general principles and subsidiary methods. As described above, for the International Law Commission, further sources might include the binding decisions of international organizations and the judgments of international courts and tribunals. However, "soft law" is not only persuasive in the way that it influences the conduct of States in the international system, but can also be a basis for legitimate expectations of other States, and for "good faith" in international relations. See K. Abbott and D. Snidal, "Hard and Soft Law in International Governance" 45:3 *International Governance* 421–456. See also D. Shelton, "Law, Non-Law and the Problem of Soft Law", in D. Shelton, ed., *Commitment and Compliance: The Role of Non-Binding Norms in the International System* (Oxford: Oxford University Press, 2000) at 4–10.

[18] J.L. Brierly, *Law of Nations*, 6th edn. (Oxford: Clarendon Press, 1963).

[19] See *S.S. Lotus (France v. Turkey)*, (1924) PCIJ (Series A) No. 10.

acterizing States as monolithic bodies, this view limits the recognition of other relevant entities within States, not to mention transnational organizations. It would, perhaps, be more helpful to conceive of public international law as the rules, or framework, for a broad transnational legal process, one that increasingly seeks to achieve global public interest goals.[20]

While the global system still encompasses 191 sovereign, decision-making government entities, "effective power is increasingly being organized in a non-hierarchical manner".[21] Thousands of non-governmental as well as inter-governmental organisations have emerged to play a relevant role in the making, implementation and monitoring of international law.[22] Today, international law provides normative frameworks and procedures for co-ordinating behaviour, controlling conflict, facilitating cooperation and establishing common values.

Implementation: compliance, enforcement and monitoring

How is respect for the rule of law ensured in such a system? Unlike domestic legal systems, the international system does not include a centralized core – such as an integrated police force and justice system – to *enforce* international law generally.[23] Rather, States come to *comply* with international law for a number of reasons; including the incremental effect of a process of continuous interaction, the development of shared values, and the use of incentives between parties to a treaty,[24] although political and economic considerations also play a role.

This gradual evolution in the nature of the international system has many consequences. The once sharp lines between the public international law, regulating the international conduct of States, and private international law, regulating the activities of individuals, corporations and private entities engaged in trans-border transactions, are fading. The harmonization of national laws, the human rights movement and globalizing trends are gradually meshing international law and domestic law. The formally "binding" or "non-binding" nature of international instruments is less likely to result in any practical difference in

---

[20] The classical framework of international law centres exclusively on States, relies on binding legal instruments to provide solutions to clearly defined problems, and assumes that States comply with the obligations they have assumed. See H. Koh, "The Globalization of Freedom" (2001) 26 *Yale J Intl L* 305. See also P. Allot, "The Concept of International Law", in M. Byers, ed., *The Role of Law in International Politics: Essays in International Relations and International law* (Oxford: Oxford University Press, 2000).

[21] H.K. Jacobson, *Networks of Interdependence: International Organizations and the Global Political System*, 2nd edn. (New York: Knopf, 1984) 386.

[22] *Ibid.* See also S. Toope, "Emerging Patterns of Governance and International Law", in M. Byers, ed., *The Role of Law in International Politics: Essays in International Relations and International Law* (Oxford: Oxford University Press, 2000); and H. Koh, "Transnational Legal Process" (1996) 75 *Nebraska LR* 181.

[23] A key exception is the role of the Security Council to respond to threats to international peace and security, under chapter VII of the *Charter of the United Nations*.

[24] See J. Brunnée and S.J. Toope "International Law and Constructivism: Elements of an Interactional Theory of International Law" (2000) 39(1) *Col. J. Trans'l Law* 19.

State behaviour. Indeed, a significant part of international law now consists of so-called "soft law".[25] Further, primary binding legal norms are not the only way that international customary law is developed. Recent scholarship has also identified the existence of "interstitial norms", norms that modify the effect of other primary norms of international law.[26] The likelihood that these interstitial norms will take root is determined primarily by their effectiveness in reconciling conflicts between other norms of international law and filling gaps in the law, rather than by their formal status as "treaty law", "customary law" or "soft law".[27]

The changing nature of the international system is also affecting the role of organizations of civil society – non-governmental organizations, labour unions, chambers of commerce, professional associations, and other groups. The actions of civil society now seem to influence the development of international law, albeit in a limited way. The international system is not blind to powerful statements coming from a large number of people. When the International Court of Justice considered the legality of nuclear weapons in international law, Judge Christopher Gregory Weeramantry noted in a dissenting opinion that the two million signatures received by the Court on that issue were "evidence of a groundswell of global public opinion which is not without legal relevance".[28] While we should not exaggerate the relevance of civil society statements in relation to a particular case, the views of civil society expressed over time can filter into the general understanding of the law.

On a fundamental level, then, international law seems increasingly subject to concurrent forces of integration and fragmentation, each serving to oppose and yet reinforce the other. This beautiful paradox is fundamentally re-shaping the structures and processes of the international system, and is important to efforts to understand significant developments in the field of sustainable development.

Forty-five thousand people participated in the *World Summit for Sustainable Development* in 2002. International law in the field of sustainable development is rapidly evolving, and its governance is relevant to scholars and practitioners all over the world. The lack of detailed content and specific guidelines for the achievement of sustainable development is certainly central to the challenges of developing and implementing appropriate international law. It is important, then, to start by examining how the concept of sustainable development emerged, to identify the legal regimes that aim to achieve its essential goals, and to ask how these regimes can begin to balance economic, environmental and social priorities.

---

[25] For discussion of the meaning of "soft law", see P. Dupuy, "Soft Law and the International Law of the Environment" (1991) 12 *Mich. J. Int'l L.* 420; and F.V. Kratochwil, *Rules, Norms and Decisions: On the Conditions of Practical and Legal Reasoning in International Relations and Domestic Affairs* (Cambridge: Cambridge University Press, 1989) 201.

[26] V. Lowe, "The Politics of Law-Making: Are the Method and Character of Norm Creation Changing?" in M. Byers, ed., *The Role of Law in International Politics: Essays in International Relations and International Law* (Oxford: Oxford University Press, 2000) at 214–215.

[27] *Ibid.* at 215 and 219–221.

[28] *Advisory Opinion on the Legality of the Use by a State of Nuclear Weapons in Armed Conflict,* Advisory Opinion, [1996] ICJ Rep. 226 at 438.

PART I

THE FOUNDATIONS

1

*Origins of the Sustainable Development Concept**

The need for sustainability has been recognized since ancient times across diverse civilizations.[1] The last twenty-five years have nevertheless witnessed the emergence of sustainable development as an important concept in global efforts to balance economic, social and environmental policies and laws. The idea may have first emerged from the environmental field; part of international efforts to find a "compromise" term for more environmentally sound natural resource exploitation, or to describe conservation policies in developing countries.[2] But it was not until the report of the World Commission on Environment and Development, "Our Common Future" or *"the Brundtland Report"*[3] and the 1992 *United Nations Conference on Environment and Development* (UNCED, or the "Earth Summit") that the term "sustainable development" gained truly global currency. Over 7,000 delegates from 178 countries, including 115 heads of state, gathered at this Conference alongside over 1,400 non-governmental organizations (NGOs). They recognised a global need for environmental protection with

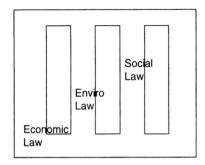

* The authors acknowledge and thank Alhagi Marong for his contribution to this section.

[1] See *Case Concerning the Gabčíkovo-Nagymaros Project (Hungary/Slovakia)* (1997), ICJ Rep. 7 (Separate Opinion of Vice-President Weeramantry), where the concept of sustainable development is traced to the practices of ancient tribes in Sri Lanka, Eastern Africa, America and Europe, and in Islamic legal traditions.

[2] It was proposed on a global level in 1980 as part of the *World Conservation Strategy* of the International Union for the Conservation of Nature (IUCN). See UNGA Res. 7, UN GAOR 36th Sess., Supp. No. 51, UN Doc. A/51 (1982) [hereinafter *World Conservation Strategy*]. Several of the central ideas of sustainable development may have crystallized in earlier global processes, such as in the 1972 United Nations Conference on the Human Environment (UNCHE) and the *Stockholm Declaration on the Human Environment*, UN Doc. A/C. 48/14 (1972), 11 ILM 1461 (1972) [hereinafter *Stockholm Declaration*]. For discussion, see G.D. Meyers & S.C. Muller, "The Ethical Implications, Political Ramifications and Practical Limitations of Adopting Sustainable Development as National and International Policy" (1996) 4 *Buff. Envt'l. L.J.* 1.

[3] World Commission on Environment and Development, *Our Common Future* (Oxford: Oxford University Press, 1987) [hereinafter *Our Common Future*].

economic and social development, and called for sustainable development. In 1997, governments met in the United Nations General Assembly Special Session on Sustainable Development (the "Earth Summit+5") to review progress; they urged further development of the concept, and greater efforts for its implementation on all levels. In 2002, at the *World Summit for Sustainable Development* in Johannesburg, South Africa, more than 22,000 official delegates, with 10,000 representatives of 193 countries, including over 100 heads of state, and 8,096 individuals from 925 accredited civil society organisations, gathered to call for coherence between, and integration of, the three pillars of sustainable development – social justice, economic growth and environmental protection. This section will briefly examine the evolution of the concept of sustainable development and its prospects beyond the "Johannesburg Summit".

"SUSTAINABLE DEVELOPMENT" PRIOR TO STOCKHOLM

Although the 1987 *Brundtland Report* popularized the concept of sustainable development in international discourse, its underlying environmental principles are not as recent. It has long been recognized that humanity must live within the carrying capacity of the earth, and manage natural resources so as to meet both current demand and the needs of future generations. In the eighteenth century, scholarly debates recognized the existence of essential links between environment and development, and proposed consequent environmental constraints on economic development.[4] Throughout the nineteenth century, it remained unclear to what extent these issues were of international concern, and how international legal rules might govern the balance between environmental protection and economic development. Equity issues, human rights and other social concerns were only barely touched upon at first, in the environmental debates.

In the mid-twentieth century, the UN began to support greater recognition for an international sustainable development agenda. As a forum for the development and negotiation of cooperative strategies and binding rules, the UN has had a critical role in promoting sustainable development. For example, in 1962, the UN General Assembly passed a resolution for governments to take natural resource preservation measures at the earliest stages of economic development, and called for assistance to be provided to developing countries in that respect.[5]

---

[4] Thomas Malthus and David Ricardo were 18th-century economic thinkers who were both pessimistic about the prospects for long-term economic growth. T. Malthus posited that populations would increase until diminishing returns from agricultural production, due to the fixed quantity of land, forced standards of living to subsistence levels. D. Ricardo similarly believed that economic growth would be limited by the scarcity of natural resources. These premises gained currency and influenced world opinion, though they have since been considerably revised and updated. D.W. Pearce and R.K. Turner, *Economics of Natural Resources and the Environment* (Baltimore: Johns Hopkins University Press, 1990) at 6–7.

[5] UNGA Res. 1831, UN GAOR, 17th Sess. (1962).

The 1972 Stockholm UN Conference on the Human Environment, and the Stockholm Declaration

In 1968, a second resolution by the UN General Assembly pledged to find solutions to problems related to the environment.[6] Subsequently, in 1972, the UN hosted the *Conference on the Human Environment* (UNCHE) in Stockholm. The conference provided a forum to discuss international co-operation in the area of environmental protection. As the 26 principles embodied in the *Stockholm Declaration* make clear, the numerous ecological crises threatening the planet at the time demanded worldwide attention and effort. Principle 4, for instance, recognizes a special responsibility to safeguard and wisely manage the imperilled heritage of wildlife and its habitat. The *Stockholm Declaration* also led to UNGA Resolution 2997 (XXVII), which established the United Nations Environment Programme (UNEP). UNEP began operations in 1973, and focused on strengthening and coordinating environmental policy, particularly in developing countries.[7] The subsequent adoption by the UN General Assembly of the *World Charter for Nature* in 1982 provided further support for the general principles and attitudes of environmental conservation expressed in the *Stockholm Declaration*. Like the *Stockholm Declaration*, the *World Charter for Nature* was not binding international law. However, it represented a degree of international convergence on the core elements of international environmental law and policy.

Sustainable development as a socio-political concept began to be incorporated into the international debate in the early 1980s.[8] As mentioned above, sustainable development first appeared in the IUCN's *World Conservation Strategy*, followed shortly thereafter by the book, *Building a Sustainable Society*,[9] and many other studies. On the whole, this conceptual framework promoted a set of seemingly conflicting priorities. It recognized the need to ensure that economic and social development, a pressing concern of developing countries, became more equitable and sustainable. Many of the most urgent problems were seen to impact on the global environment, but were understood to be intricately

---

[6] See (1968) *UNYB* 84, 430 for the text of a UN pledge to find solutions to environmental problems.

[7] For further information on the development of international environmental law, see, e.g. P. Sands, *Principles of International Environmental Law: Frameworks, Standards and Implementation*, vol. 1 (Cambridge: Cambridge University Press 2003). See also A. Timoshenko, "From Stockholm to Rio: The Institutionalization of Sustainable Development", in W. Lang, ed., *Sustainable Development and International Law* (London: Graham and Trotman/Martinus Nijhoff, 1995). And see D. Hunter, J. Salzman & D. Zaelke, *International Environmental Law and Policy* (New York: Foundation Press, 2002).

[8] See A. Timoshenko, "From Stockholm to Rio: The Institutionalization of Sustainable Development", in W. Lang, ed., *Sustainable Development and International Law* (London: Graham and Trotman/Martinus Nijhoff, 1995). See also L. Sohn, "The Stockholm Declaration on the Human Environment" (1973) 14 *Harv. Int'l L. J.* 423.

[9] L.R. Brown, *Building a Sustainable Society* (New York: W.W. Norton & Company, 1981) [hereinafter *Brown*].

related to development strategies. At the same time, it was also noted that economic growth alone would not solve many of the most urgent problems, especially for the most poor. The need for environmental protection and conservation was internationally acknowledged, and public pressure (mainly in developed countries) increased for new policies (and laws) to this end. In 1983, the General Assembly established the World Commission on the Environment and Development (WCED) to investigate these issues, and seek ways forward.[10]

THE 1987 "BRUNDTLAND REPORT"

The WCED, chaired by Gro Harlem Brundtland, popularized the term sustainable development in *Our Common Future*, also known as the 1987 *Brundtland Report*.[11] *Our Common Future* called for a world political transformation based on the concept of sustainable development, that the parallel problems of environmental degradation and lack of social and economic development be addressed together.[12] As stated earlier, sustainable development was defined as development that "meets the needs of the present without compromising the ability of future generations to meet their own needs".[13]

> "Ecology and economy are becoming ever more interwoven – locally, regionally, nationally, and globally – into a seamless net of causes and effects."
>
> *Brundtland Report, 1987*

The WCED formally recognized the interrelationships among crises facing citizens throughout the world: "An environmental crisis, a development crisis, an energy crisis. They are all one. Ecology and economy are becoming ever more interwoven – locally, regionally, nationally, and globally – into a seamless net of causes and effects."[14] The WCED further articulated the pursuit of sustainable development as an important goal for the nations of the world, explaining that "the key element of sustainable development is the recognition that economic and environmental goals are inextricably linked."[15]

The WCED also discussed social development priorities, mainly by addressing the concept of "needs", in particular the essential needs of the world's poor, to which overriding priority should be given, recognizing the need for "equitable opportunities for all" and noting: "it is futile to attempt to deal with environmental problems without a broader perspective that encompasses the factors

---

[10] *Our Common Future, supra* note 3 at ix.   [11] *Ibid.*   [12] *Ibid.*

[13] *Ibid.* ("The members of the World Commission on Environment and Development came from 21 very different nations. [. . .] We are unanimous in our conviction that the security, well-being, and very survival of the planet depend on such changes, now"). See also T. Panayotou, *Economic Instruments for Environmental Management and Sustainable Development* (Nairobi: UNEP, 1994). And see R. Goodland and H. Daly, "Environmental Sustainability: Universal and Non-Negotiable" (1996) 6:4 *Ecological Applications* 1003–1013. And see S. Hart, "Strategies for a Sustainable World" (1997) Jan.–Feb. *Harvard Business Rev.* 67–76.

[14] *Our Common Future, supra* note 3.   [15] *Ibid.*

underlying world poverty and international inequality."[16] Social issues and human rights were not fully considered, though it was recognized that the "inability to promote the common interest in sustainable development is often a product of the relative neglect of economic and social justice within and amongst nations." As such, the *Brundtland Report* decried the disconnection between existing environmental and development law, and emphasized the increasing interdependence of ecosystems and resource availability with the economic components of development. Noting that international law often lagged behind advancements in economy and industry, the Commission called for gap-filling measures, to catch up with the "accelerating pace and expanding scale of impacts on the ecological basis of development".[17] It went on to explain how some "forms of development erode the environmental resources upon which they must be based", and how environmental degradation can undermine economic development and prevent the enjoyment of its benefits.[18] In calling for a realignment of humanity's relationship with the environment, countries were urged to reorient their development strategies towards more sustainable paths by taking environmental considerations into account. The adoption of the *Brundtland Report* is widely viewed as the moment at which sustainable development became a broad global policy objective.[19]

Some argued that the WCED did not go far enough. They sought to question economic development as an objective, critiquing the "neo-liberal" focus on progress, growth and material wealth in order for there to be an effective response. While these voices were heard, others noted that international processes are not often meant to directly impose a particular development path. They observed that sustainable development can seldom provide a universal solution: it mainly serves to curb worse excesses. In addition, given that developing countries have different developmental challenges and needs, it could be impossible to make a catch-all prescription. It was also pointed out that while developed countries may invest in environmental or development aid programmes, many do not adjust their own unsustainable consumption patterns. Accordingly, it seemed hypocritical for developed countries to insist on conservation in developing countries. These conceptual debates, often heated, sought ways of acknowledging the divergent priorities of the "haves" and "have-nots", while recognizing the full importance of their common interest. The search for compromises led the international community to the 1992 UNCED, the 2002 WSSD and the body of emerging rules referred to as "international law in the field of sustainable development".[20]

---

[16] *Ibid.* at 3 and 43   [17] *Our Common Future, supra* note 3 at 3.   [18] *Ibid.*

[19] See e.g. FAO, *Law and Sustainable Development Since Rio: Legal Trends in Agriculture and Natural Resource Management* (Rome: FAO, 2002). See also A. Lowenfeld, *International Economic Law* (Oxford: Oxford University Press, 2002) 304. And see W. Lang, *Sustainable Development and International Law* (London: Graham and Trotman/Martinus Nijhoff, 1995).

[20] *Rio Declaration on Environment and Development*, Report of the *United Nations Conference on Environment and Development*, UN Doc. A/CONF.151/6/Rev.1, (1992), 31 ILM 874 (1992),

THE 1992 RIO "EARTH SUMMIT", THE RIO DECLARATION AND *AGENDA 21*

The *Brundtland Report* led the UN to convene a second global conference, held in 1992 in Rio de Janeiro – the *United Nations Conference on Environment and Development* (UNCED). The very name of the conference reflected a change in approach since the *Conference on the Human Environment* in Stockholm.[21] While the focus had once been on the human impact on the environment and assessing the relevance of the environment in terms of human need, the UNCED's approach was in marked contrast. In Rio de Janeiro, the emphasis was on the protection of the environment and the advancement of development, giving priority to both, and calling for social and economic development processes to take the environment into account. The *Rio Declaration*, a short document of twenty-seven principles, reaffirms the *Stockholm Declaration* of 1972 on which it seeks to build, but with a new approach and philosophy. Its central concept is sustainable development, as defined by the *Brundtland Report*, which urges integration of environment and development so that both may be sustained, over the long term. Principle 4 is important in this regard as it affirms that in order to achieve sustainable development, environmental protection must constitute an integral part of the development process. These views are also reflected in Principle 1, which advances the admittedly anthropocentric position that "[h]uman beings are at the centre of concerns for sustainable development. They are entitled to a healthy and productive life in harmony with nature."[22] The *Declaration* also reflects the *Brundtland Report*'s emphasis on poverty and equity by noting in Principle 3 the right of "peoples" to development and in Principle 5 the indispensable role of poverty alleviation in achieving sustainable development. The social aspect of sustainable development was embryonically recognized in this way.

---

especially at Principle 27 on international law [hereinafter *Rio Declaration*] and *Agenda 21*, Report of the UNCED, I (1992) UN Doc. A/CONF.151/26/Rev.1, (1992) 31 ILM 874, especially at ch. 39, on international law [hereinafter *Agenda 21*].

[21] A. Kiss and D. Shelton, *International Environmental Law*, 2nd edn. (New York: Transnational Publishers, 1994) at 67 [hereinafter *Kiss & Shelton*]. The *Rio Declaration* covers both substantive aspects of sustainable development, in certain Principles, and its procedural elements, in Principles 10, and 15–22. Thus, according to the *Rio Declaration*, sustainable development involves: intergenerational equity (3); the integration of environmental protection into the development process (4); intragenerational equity and poverty alleviation (5); particular attention for countries with special development and environment needs (6); the reduction of unsustainable consumption and production and population reductions (8); and effective environmental legislation (11). Its procedures include broad public participation and access to information and judicial review (10); use of precaution where there are threats of serious or irreversible damage (15); internalization of costs (16); environmental impact assessment (17); notification and consultation with affected States (18 and 19); and the involvement of major groups (20–22). See e.g. D. Hunter, J. Salzman & D. Zaelke, *International Environmental Law and Policy* (New York: Foundation Press, 2002).

[22] *Ibid.* at 70–71.

Agenda 21, an 800-page blueprint for international action in the twenty-first century, was another major outcome of the UNCED.[23] *Agenda 21* provides a comprehensive plan complete with strategies and programmes to halt and reverse the effects of environmental degradation and to promote sustainable development in all countries.[24]

The text of *Agenda 21* comprises four sections and a preamble. Its four sections are entitled "Social and Economic Dimensions",[25] "Conservation and Management of Resources for Development",[26] "Strengthening the Role of Major Groups"[27] and "Means of Implementation".[28] Unlike the "Rio Treaties" (the 1992 *United Nations Framework Convention on Climate Change*, the 1992 *United Nations Convention on Biological Diversity*, and the 1994 *United Nations Convention to Combat Desertification*, which will be examined below), the Rio Declaration and *Agenda 21* are not legally binding; however, they are considered "soft law".[29] When they left the Earth Summit, the signatories to *Agenda 21* had agreed on much in principle. Yet, most of the details on environmental goals and standards and commitments of the developed world to the developing world remained to be worked out through more specific treaties, conventions, laws, and institutional changes in the years ahead.[30]

Chapter 38 of *Agenda 21* on institutional matters called for the creation of a new United Nations institution. This body was to ensure the effective follow-up of decisions made at the Earth Summit, enhance international co-operation toward integration of environment and development, and examine progress in the implementation of *Agenda 21*.[31] The UN responded by creating the United Nations Commission for Sustainable Development (CSD) on November 25,

---

[23] *Agenda 21, supra* note 20. See also N. Robinson, ed., *Agenda 21 and the UNCED Proceedings* (New York: IUCN/Oceana Publications, 1993).

[24] N.A. Robinson, ed., "Agenda 21: Earth's Action Plan" IUCN Environmental Policy & Law Paper No. 27 (1993) [hereinafter *Robinson*].

[25] Containing chapters on international co-operation to accelerate sustainable development in developing countries, poverty, consumption patterns, demographic dynamics, human health, human settlements, and integrating environment and development in decision-making.

[26] This section deals with the more traditional environmental problems and contains chapters concerning atmosphere, land resources, deforestation, desertification and drought, mountain ecosystems, sustainable agriculture and rural development, biological diversity, biotechnology, oceans and seas, fresh waters, toxic chemicals, hazardous wastes, solid and sewage wastes, and radioactive wastes.

[27] Section 3 contains chapters pertaining to the roles in achieving sustainable development to be played by women, children and youth, indigenous people, non-governmental organizations, local authorities, workers and trade unions, business and industry, science and technology, and farmers.

[28] This section addresses financing mechanisms, technology transfers, science, education, capacity building in developing countries, international institutional arrangements, international legal instruments, and information for decision-making.

[29] *Agenda 21, supra* note 20, chs. 11, 12, 18, 20, 21 & 22. See also I. Porras, "The Rio Declaration: A New Basis for International Cooperation" (1992) 1 *RECIEL* 245. And see D. Hunter, J. Salzman & D. Zaelke, *International Environmental Law and Policy* (New York: Foundation Press, 2002) at 202–214.

[30] See FAO, *Law and Sustainable Development since Rio: Legal Trends in Agriculture and Natural Resource Management* (Rome: FAO, 2002).

[31] *Agenda 21, supra* note 20 at 38.11.

1992.[32] The CSD is comprised of 53 UN member States elected for three-year terms.[33] Meeting on a yearly basis, the UN CSD was to review State implementation at national, regional and international levels of the various chapters of *Agenda 21*, addressing all chapters every three years.[34]

Since 1992, many countries have embraced the goal of sustainable development.[35] Indeed, many governments have developed national *Agenda 21s*, authorized special bodies to implement *Agenda 21*,[36] or even negotiated regional blueprints for sustainable development. International organizations have also adopted the principles and goals of sustainable development, including the European Union and the United Nations Economic Commissions in each region. Indeed, over the course of the last decade, organizations such as the UNEP, the World Bank, the Organization for Economic Cooperation and Development, and the IUCN have been actively working to identify specific empirical "indicators" for measuring progress towards sustainable development.[37]

THE 1997 NEW YORK UN GENERAL ASSEMBLY SPECIAL SESSION ON SUSTAINABLE DEVELOPMENT

In 1997, a special session of the United Nations General Assembly, widely referred to as "Earth Summit+5", was held in New York. The session saw the attendance of heads of State and Government from across the world. Although a relatively modest event, it reviewed and appraised implementation of *Agenda*

---

[32] Timoshenko, *supra* note 8. *Robinson, supra* note 24 at 655.

[33] See UNGA Res. A/1993/207. The UN CSD mandate includes: to monitor progress on the implementation of *Agenda 21* and activities related to the integration of environmental and developmental goals by governments, NGOs, and other UN bodies; to monitor progress towards the target of 0.7% GNP from developed countries for Overseas Development Aid; to review the adequacy of financing and the transfer of technologies as outlined in *Agenda 21*; to enhance dialogue with NGOs, the independent sector, and other entities outside the UN system, within the UN framework; and to provide recommendations to the General Assembly through the Economic and Social Council (ECOSOC). The allocation of seats is 13 from Africa, 11 from Asia, 6 from Eastern Europe, 10 from Latin America and the Caribbean and 13 from Western Europe and North America. The Secretariat is the Division of Sustainable Development, in the UN Department of Economic and Social Affairs (DESA). See United Nations Commission on Sustainable Development (www.un.org).

[34] M.-C. Cordonier Segger, "Significant Developments in Sustainable Development Law and Governance: A Proposal" (2004) *United Nations Natural Resources Forum* 28:1.

[35] United Nations Commission on Sustainable Development, *National Information Report of the Secretary-General* (New York: UN CSD, 1995). This document consists of a table summarizing national level co-ordination of actions pursuant to *Agenda 21*, and a matrix summarizing national priorities assigned to the various issues and current status. According to CSD, nations having taken these steps towards implementation included Australia, Benin, Belgium, Cameroon, Cuba, Canada, China, Egypt, Germany, Italy, Korea, Malaysia, Mongolia, New Zealand, Netherlands, Norway, Niger, Philippines, Portugal, Peru, Senegal, Switzerland, Sweden, United Kingdom, and Zaire. In addition, over 55 nations were submitting reports to the CSD on *Agenda 21* implementation.

[36] *Ibid.*

[37] T.C. Trzyna, ed., *A Sustainable World: Defining and Measuring Sustainable Development* (Sacramento: California Institute of Public Affairs, 1995) 23.

21, and other commitments adopted by the 1992 Earth Summit. It sought to assess global progress made in sustainable development since Rio; to demonstrate the effectiveness of sustainable development by highlighting "success stories" from around the world; to identify reasons why goals set in Rio have not always been met and suggest corrective action; to highlight special issues – such as finance and technology transfer, patterns of production and consumption, use of energy and transportation, scarcity of freshwater – and to identify priorities for future action; and finally, to call on governments, international organizations and major groups to renew their commitment to sustainable development. The whole resulted in a Declaration, the *Programme of Further Action to Implement Agenda 21*, which laid out priorities for action to promote sustainable development worldwide, including specific commitments to further strengthen and codify international law related to sustainable development.[38]

[38] Programme of Further Action to Implement *Agenda 21*, UN Doc. A/Res/s-19/2 Annex (1997).

2

Results of the 2002 World Summit for Sustainable Development

The *World Summit on Sustainable Development*, held from 26 August to 4 September 2002, brought together an estimated 45,000 participants in Johannesburg, South Africa. Over 100 heads of state and more than 22,000 government delegates, international experts and non-governmental organizations and media representatives attended the Summit itself, from 193 countries, and another 23,000 were represented at parallel events for business, scientists, civil society and other major groups.[1]

The United Nations objectives for the Summit were to review the 1992 UN Conference on Environment and Development (UNCED) and reinvigorate global commitment to sustainable development.[2] The WSSD was the last meeting in a cycle of global conferences held over the decade of 1992–2002, which were considered important precursors to the event. These had specifically focused on building global consensus on the new meaning of, and challenges to, development for all. The United Nations Adoption of the Millennium Development Goals (2000), which included commitments to human rights, economic development and environmental sustainability, provided an important milestone and a series of concrete targets as reference points.[3] The World Trade Organization (WTO) Doha, Qatar meeting of World Trade Ministers (2001) had launched a new round of trade and economic liberalization negotiations, the so-called "Development Agenda", and many countries were still seeking to

---

[1] See *Johannesburg Declaration on Sustainable Development*, in Report of the *World Summit on Sustainable Development*, Johannesburg, South Africa, 26 Aug.–4 Sept. 2002, A/CONF.199/20 (New York: United Nations, 2002). See also *Johannesburg Plan of Implementation*, Report of the *World Summit on Sustainable Development*, Johannesburg, South Africa, 4 Sept. 2002, UN Doc. A/CONF.199/20: <http://www.un.org/esa/sustdev/documents/WSSD_POI_PD/English/POIToc.htm>.

[2] In Dec. 2000, the UN General Assembly (UNGA) decided to convene a ten-year review of progress since UNCED (A/RES/55/199). Despite ongoing efforts since the Stockholm Conference in 1972 to protect the environment and natural resources, the UNGA expressed concern about continuing deterioration. Therefore, the UNGA called for the *World Summit on Sustainable Development* to focus on the status of *Agenda 21*'s implementation and the other Earth Summit outcomes. The WSSD's mandate was to identify further measures to implement the Rio agreements, accomplishments and areas where more effort and action-oriented decisions were needed, as well as new challenges and opportunities. The WSSD was to ensure balance among economic, social and environmental concerns and reinvigorate the global commitment to sustainable development.

[3] UNGA Res. 53/239 (5 Sept. 2000). See also Millennium Development Goals, online: http://www.developmentgoals.org/.

understand the potential impacts and opportunities of these plans for greater economic interdependence.[4] Finally, the International Conference on Financing for Development in Monterrey (2002) had led to concrete commitments for new and additional developed country resources, earmarked for development spending.[5] As noted informally by one leading international expert and WSSD Bureau member, in the lead-up to the WSSD, "Monterrey committed new resources, but WSSD still needs to decide how to spend them."[6]

The WSSD sought to address social, environmental and economic problems in an integrated way. It negotiated and adopted two main documents: the *Johannesburg Declaration on Sustainable Development* and the *Johannesburg Plan of Implementation* (JPOI).

The *Johannesburg Declaration* outlines the path taken from UNCED to the WSSD, highlights present challenges, expresses a commitment to sustainable development, underscores the importance of multilateralism and emphasizes the need for implementation. (See Table 2.1.)

The *Johannesburg Plan of Implementation* is designed as a framework for action to implement the commitments originally agreed at UNCED and includes eleven chapters. After an Introduction (1), substantive chapters cover: Poverty Eradication (2); Changing Unsustainable Patterns of Consumption and Production (3); Protecting and Managing the Natural Resource Base of Economic and Social Development (4); Sustainable Development in a Globalizing World (5); Health and Sustainable Development (6); Sustainable Development of Small Island Developing States (7): Sustainable Development in Africa (8); and Other Regional Initiatives (9). Further chapters cover Means of Implementation (10) and the Institutional Framework for Sustainable Development (11). Table 2.1 summarizes the JPOI.[7] The JPOI shifts the focus of sustainable development from primarily "environmental protection" to an integrated environmental,

---

[4] The results of the WTO Ministerial Meeting in Doha, Qatar, Nov. 2002, included the Ministerial Declaration WT/MIN(01)/DEC/1 (20 Nov. 2001); a Declaration on the TRIPS Agreement and Public Health, a Decision on implementation-related issues and concerns, a Decision on Subsidies related to procedures for extensions under Article 27.4 (of the Subsidies and Countervailing Measures Agreement) for certain developing country members, a Decision on a waiver for EU–ACP Partnership Agreement, and a Decision on the EU transitional regime for banana imports. See WTO, http://www.wto.org/english/thewto_e/minist_e/min01_e/min01_e.htm#declarations. See also M. Gehring and M.-C. Cordonier Segger, eds., *Sustainable Developments in World Trade Law* (The Hague: Kluwer Law International, 2005).

[5] Report of the International Conference on Financing for Development, A/Conf.198/11 (18–22 Mar. 2002). See also Financing for Development, online: http://www.un.org/esa/ffd/.

[6] Notes from conversation with Mr. Richard Ballhorn, Director General, Environment and Sustainable Development Affairs Bureau, Canadian Department of Foreign Affairs and International Trade, on file with authors.

[7] The other significant commitments from the meeting include: using and producing chemicals in ways that do not harm human health and the environment; reducing biodiversity loss by 2010; restoring fisheries to their maximum sustainable yields by 2015; establishing a representative network of marine protected areas by 2012; improving developing countries' access to environmentally-sound alternatives to ozone depleting chemicals by 2010; and undertaking initiatives by 2004 to implement the Global Programme of Action for the protection of the Marine Environment from Land Based Sources.

Table 2.1: Structure of the Johannesburg Plan of Implementation (JPOI)

Chapter	Summary
I. Introduction	– poverty-reduction programmes (health, education, food security)
II. Poverty eradication	– clean drinking water and sanitation
	– access to energy services and industrial development
	– urban poor and slum dwellers, and child labour
III. Changing unsustainable patterns of consumption and production	– consumption policies and economic instruments
	– corporate social and environmental responsibility
	– renewable energy and energy efficiency
	– transportation and urban planning
	– waste management and recycling
	– chemicals and hazardous waste management
IV. Protecting and managing the natural resource base of economic and social development	– fresh water resources, fisheries, oceans and coastal resources
	– vulnerability, risk assessment and disaster management
	– climate change and trans-boundary air pollution
	– agriculture and food security, desertification and land degradation,
	– mountain ecosystems, sustainable tourism
	– biodiversity, forestry and mining
V. Sustainable development in a globalizing world	– international financial system
	– International Labour Organization conventions
	– international trade negotiations (and the Doha Development Agenda)
	– corporate responsibility and public/ private partnerships
	– regional trade and cooperation agreements
	– the digital divide
VI. Health and sustainable development	– basic health-care systems, access to public health services
	– infant and maternal mortality rates, reproductive and sexual health
	– HIV/AIDS, respiratory diseases and lead poisoning
VII. Sustainable development of small island developing states	– fisheries, waste management vulnerability to disaster
	– access to energy, access to health care, and other priorities

(Continued)

Table 2.1: (Continued)

Chapter	Summary
VIII. Sustainable development for Africa	– NEPAD, poverty-reduction strategies, conflict, mining, energy – public participation, climate change, health, agriculture and others
IX. Other regional initiatives	A. Sustainable development in Latin America and the Caribbean B. Sustainable development in Asia and the Pacific C. Sustainable development in the West Asia region D. Sustainable development in the Economic Commission for Europe region
X. Means of implementation	– international cooperation, investment and financing institutions – global and regional trade – rights of peoples to self-determination – environmentally sound technologies, tech transfer and assistance – risk assessment and risk management, global information systems – education, capacity building and research
XI. Institutional framework for sustainable development	A. Objectives B. Strengthening the institutional framework for sustainable development at the international level C. Role of the General Assembly D. Role of the Economic and Social Council E. Role and function of the Commission on Sustainable Development F. Role of international institutions G. Strengthening institutional arrangements for sustainable development at the regional level H. Strengthening institutional frameworks for sustainable development at the national level I. Participation of major groups

social and development agenda, with attention for poverty eradication, sanitation and health. New resources were committed to the Global Environment Facility and desertification was included as a new focal area. Specific attention was focused on certain important priorities identified by the UN Secretary-General, in the areas of water and sanitation, energy, health, agriculture and biodiversity (the so-called "WEHAB" issues). By the end of the Summit, a number of the WEHAB commitments set out in the JPOI had been linked to new partnerships and financial commitments.[8]

The JPOI is noteworthy for treatment of issues in a way that reflects new developments since 1992. First, there is a separate section on globalization – a phenomenon which had barely registered on political agendas in 1992. Another development is in the treatment of cross-cutting issues. In particular, poverty and unsustainable production and consumption patterns were identified as "cross-cutting", and addressed throughout the text as well as in specific chapters. Unlike *Agenda 21*, the JPOI recognizes poverty as a running theme, linked to its multiple dimensions, from access to energy, water and sanitation, to the equitable sharing of the benefits of biodiversity. This reflects a shift from a uni-dimensional income focus on poverty to a multidimensional approach that embraces a vision of "sustainable livelihoods".

Although critical evaluation of the negotiated texts is important, other outcomes of the Summit should not be neglected in assessing progress since the Rio de Janeiro "Earth Summit". Indeed, certain conceptual and procedural advances were apparent in Johannesburg. Primary among them was the renewed emphasis given to the need for greater coherence and integration among "the three pillars of sustainable development". In the 1992 "Earth Summit", social justice and poverty eradication were mainly seen as simply part of (or a goal of) economic development. Just as in the *Brundtland Report*, where social issues were addressed, it was mainly through hortatory references to the need for greater equity and more focus on the poor, and occasional notes about the special roles of women or other groups. Human rights, including social, economic and cultural rights, were not clearly part of the programme, or given equal weight. In Johannesburg, perhaps to the consternation of many "pure environment" advocates, social issues, human rights and poverty were highlighted as integral to sustainable development. The more integrated, balanced treatment of the three social, economic and environmental pillars in the 2002 WSSD provides an indication of how the sustainable development agenda has evolved over the past ten years. The conceptual shift may also be a reflection of recent international recognition that, as explained by both Jeffrey Sachs and Amartya Sen, economic development is not synonymous with social development, and one does not automatically lead to the other, either.[9] This improved integration was apparent in nearly every discussion, including the calls

---

[8] For example, a number of initiatives publicized at the Summit will support the JPOI commitment to halve the proportion of people without access to sanitation by 2015 together with the Millennium Declaration Goal to halve the proportion without access to safe drinking water by 2015. The US has announced US$970 million in investments on water and sanitation projects; the EU announced its "Water for Life" initiative; and the UN has received an additional 21 water- and sanitation-related initiatives worth at least US$20 million. Similarly, the JPOI commitment on energy access will be accompanied by financial commitments from the EU (US$700 million), the US (US$43 million), and 32 separate partnership initiatives worth up to US$26 million.

[9] A. Sen, *Development as Freedom* (Oxford: Oxford University Press, 1999). See also J. Sachs and A. Warner, "Globalization and International Competitiveness: some Broad Lessons of the Past Decade", in World Economic Forum, *The Global Competitiveness Report* (New York: Oxford University Press, 2000) at 18– 27.

for increased synergy among the Rio Conventions and the attention to concurrent UN processes on financing and social development issues. A greater proportion of officials from development, commerce, and foreign ministries participated in the WSSD, and it was hoped that future meetings will see even greater representation from sectors other than the environment.

The JPOI and associated outcomes, however, do not amount to the complete picture of the WSSD. The official business of the Summit ran alongside a host of activities, networking and presentations – all of which trace their original inspirations back to the Rio Summit.[10] The WSSD held Partnership Plenaries on the five WEHAB issues: water and sanitation, energy, health, agriculture, and biodiversity, as well as on cross-cutting issues and regional implementation took place during the first week of the WSSD.[11] Four Round Tables also took place from 2 to 4 September under the theme "Making It Happen", focusing on how to fulfil *Agenda 21*, the Rio Conventions, the UN Millennium Summit and the WSSD commitments.[12] Over 300 new partnerships were announced, representing a significant commitment of United Nations-sanctioned initiatives to implement the WSSD outcomes.[13] With regard to international law, several important announcements and agreements were also reached.[14]

The fact that the Summit was held in Africa was also significant. It afforded the opportunity to highlight the particularly severe social, economic and environmental problems on the continent, including the impact of HIV/AIDS, desertification, food security and other critical problems. While the divergent interests of the countries necessarily limit the formal outcomes of these UN "expos", this should not diminish the unique role that the UN plays in forging global agreements, or the catalytic role that these Summits can play in changing what takes place in workplaces, communities and institutions around the world.[15] Many treaties relate directly to sustainable development, and even

---

[10] From the non-State perspective, the participation of women, youth, NGOs, parliamentarians, unions, local authorities, scientists and other stakeholders was greater in the meeting halls than it was in Rio, where many key groups were almost exclusively involved outside the negotiation sessions. Combined with the activities of these groups outside the convention halls, the various alternative venues around Johannesburg showed a range of innovative and non-negotiated visions of sustainable development. Another group whose participation had significantly increased was business. The private sector's understanding of the need for sustainable development, the conference organizers recognition of business and industry's key role in it, and the business community's involvement in and funding of numerous partnerships were new and largely welcome developments.

[11] Summaries of the Partnership Plenaries were adopted with the meeting's report (A/CONF.199/ L.2/Add.1–3).

[12] A report on the Round Tables (A/CONF.199/L.2/Add.4) was adopted in the closing Plenary on 4 Sept.

[13] Summaries of the Partnership Events (A/CONF.199/16 and 16/Add.1–3).

[14] Canada and the Russian Federation announced their intent to ratify the Kyoto Protocol. This meant that multilateral support for the UN-sponsored climate change regime was intact and there is a possibility that the Protocol may enter into force by 2005. Modest commitments on measures to contribute to the recovery of fish stocks, action on chemicals and a potential new international benefit-sharing regime under the Convention on Biological Diversity (CBD) also meet the UNGA challenge to identify areas where more international effort is needed.

[15] UNTS, *Focus 2002: Sustainable Development, Multilateral Treaties* (New York: UNTS, 2002).

more declarations, action plans and other non-binding instruments are also relevant. Tables 2.2 and 2.3 below summarize the binding international treaties and "soft law" instruments highlighted in the JPOI from the *World Summit for Sustainable Development*. These may be considered part of the body of international sustainable development law. Several challenges and opportunities for international law emerged during the WSSD and were highlighted for future attention. Examples of these include the Doha round of WTO negotiations; the need for a regime on corporate responsibility and accountability; the need for negotiation of a new regime on access to genetic resources and benefit-sharing; and an emerging sense that the multilateral system of governance may have to find new structures to advance the cause of sustainable development in a globalizing world.[16]

Beyond the confines of the negotiating halls where practical sustainable development activities were constantly showcased, it became evident that "sustainable development" is more than a vague concept and, as an area of law and policy, can help to address the need to balance and coordinate widely divergent priorities related to economic growth, social development and environmental protection. Like Stockholm and Rio, however, the effects of this Summit cannot be fully measured in the immediate aftermath. Their impact on the international process and on national, local and individual levels will only become more visible with time.

A SUMMARY OF THE *JOHANNESBURG DECLARATION ON SUSTAINABLE DEVELOPMENT*[17]

"*The Johannesburg Declaration on Sustainable Development*" is a three-page, six-section document.[18] It reaffirms, "from this continent, the cradle of humanity," a commitment to sustainable development and building a humane, equitable and caring global society

---

[16] The WSSD issues unfolded within the larger context of a post-Cold War world of globalization, WTO ascendancy, and the recent efforts of the international community to globalize a social and development agenda through the Millennium Declaration Goals and the Monterrey commitments. In the absence of a World Environment Organization, the WSSD provided a rare opportunity for the world's political leaders to support and press for further progress in the sustainable development agendas within and beyond the core UN system, notably in the WTO, the World Bank and the GEF. Some viewed the hotly disputed paragraph on corporate accountability in the JPOI as a possible stepping stone for civil society to press its case for the negotiation of an international regulatory framework for corporations. However, an interpretive statement from the contact group on globalization, suggesting that the issue would be addressed within existing agreements, was clearly an attempt to diminish the prospect of the negotiation of a new international instrument.

[17] See *Johannesburg Declaration on Sustainable Development*, *supra* note 1.

[18] The completed text was issued in the final hours of the Summit as A/CONF.199/L.6/Rev.2 with a corrigendum (Corr.1). It can now be found at *Johannesburg Declaration on Sustainable Development*, in Report of the *World Summit on Sustainable Development*, Johannesburg, South Africa, 26 Aug.–4 Sept. 2002, A/CONF.199/20 (New York: United Nations, 2002). See also *Johannesburg Plan of Implementation*, Report of the *World Summit on Sustainable Development*, Johannesburg, South Africa, 4 Sept. 2002, UN Doc. A/CONF.199/20: <http://www.un.org/esa/sustdev/documents/WSSD_POI_PD/English/POIToc.htm>.

Table 2.2: The binding international treaties highlighted in the JPOI from the World Summit for Sustainable Development

WSSD Priority Area	Binding Treaty Instruments
Johannesburg Declaration	1945 Charter of the United Nations
Poverty eradication	1994 United Nations Convention to Combat Desertification in Those Countries Experiencing Serious Drought and/or Desertification, particularly in Africa 1999 International Labour Organization Convention No. 182 to Eliminate the Worst Forms of Child Labour
Changing unsustainable patterns of consumption and production	1989 Basel Convention on the Control of Transboundary Movements of Hazardous Wastes and Their Disposal 1998 Rotterdam Convention on Prior Informed Consent Procedures for Certain Hazardous Chemicals and Pesticides in International Trade 2001 Stockholm Convention on Persistent Organic Pollutants
Protecting and managing the natural resource base of economic and social development	1971 Convention on Wetlands of International Importance Especially as Waterfowl Habitat 1982 United Nations Convention on the Law of the Sea (UNCLOS) 1982 Agreement for the Implementation of the Provisions of the UNCLOS Relating to the Conservation and Management of Straddling Fish Stocks and Highly Migratory Fish Stocks 1992 United Nations Convention on Biological Diversity 1993 Agreement to Promote Compliance with International Conservation and Management Measures by Fishing Vessels on the High Seas Protocols and Treaties of the International Maritime Organization (IMO) IMO Draft International Convention on the Control and Management of Ships' Ballast Water and Sediments 1966 International Covenant on Economic, Social and Cultural Rights 1985 Vienna Convention for the Protection of the Ozone Layer

(*Continued*)

Table 2.2: (Continued)

WSSD Priority Area	Binding Treaty Instruments
	1987 Montreal Protocol on Substances that Deplete the Ozone Layer
	1992 United Nations Framework Convention on Climate Change (UNFCCC)
	1997 Kyoto Protocol to the UNFCCC
	2001 International Treaty on Plant Genetic Resources for Food and Agriculture
	2001 Cartagena Protocol on Biosafety to the UNCBD
Sustainable development in a globalizing world	1994 Agreements Establishing the World Trade Organization
	Conventions of the International Labour Organization Agreements establishing multilateral and regional financing institutions
Health	International programmes on tobacco (may include WHO Tobacco Convention)
Regional Initiatives	Caribbean Regional Fisheries Mechanism
	Convention on the Conservation and Management of Highly Migratory Fish Stocks in the Western and Central Pacific Ocean
	Convention on International Trade in Endangered Species of Wild Fauna and Flora
	Convention on Access to Information, Public Participation in Decision-Making and Access to Justice in Environmental Matters (Aarhus Convention)
	Alpine Convention
	North American Commission for Environmental Cooperation
	International Boundary Waters Treaty Act
Means of Implementation and Institutional Matters	WTO Agreement on Agriculture
	WTO Agreement on Trade-Related Aspects of Intellectual Property Rights (TRIPs)

cognizant of the need for human dignity for all. It emphasizes the three pillars of sustainable development at all levels and a common resolve to eradicate poverty, change consumption and production patterns, and protect and manage the natural resource base. After tracing the road from Stockholm to Rio to Johannesburg, it addresses present challenges, such as the deepening fault line between rich and poor, biodiversity depletion, desertification, pollution, the benefits and costs of globalization, and the loss of confidence in democratic systems.

The Declaration also stresses the importance of human solidarity and urges the promotion of dialogue and cooperation among the world's civilizations. It welcomes decisions on targets, timetables and partnerships to improve access to clean water, sanitation, energy, health care, food and to protect biodiversity. It highlights the need for access to financial

Table 2.3: The non-binding "soft law" instruments highlighted in the JPOI from the World Summit for Sustainable Development

WSSD Priority Area	Non-Binding "Soft Law" Instruments
Johannesburg Declaration	1972 Stockholm Declaration,
	1992 Rio Declaration and Agenda 21
	1997 Programme for the Further Implementation of Agenda 21
	1998 ILO Declaration on Fundamental Principles and Rights at Work
	2000 UN Millennium Development Goals
	2001 Doha Ministerial Declaration (the Doha Development Agenda)
	2002 Monterrey Consensus on Financing for Development
Poverty eradication	1998 ILO Declaration on Fundamental Principles and Rights at Work
	2000 UN Millennium Development Goals
Consumption and production	Bahia Declaration and Priorities for Action Beyond 2000 of the Intergovernmental Forum on Chemical Safety
Protecting and managing the natural resource base of economic and social development	Reykjavik Declaration on Responsible Fisheries in the Marine Ecosystem
	United Nations General Assembly Resolution 54/33
	1995 Code of Conduct for Responsible Fisheries
	FAO International Plan of Action to Prevent, Deter and Eliminate Illegal, Unreported and Unregulated Fishing
	1999 FAO International Plan of Action for the Management of Fishing Capacity
	1999 FAO International Plan of Action for Reducing Incidental Catch of Seabirds in Longline Fisheries
	1999 FAO International Plan of Action for the Conservation and Management of Sharks
	Jakarta Mandate on the Conservation and Sustainable Use of Marine and Coastal Biological Diversity of the UN CBD
	International Coral Reef Initiative Programme of Action of the UNCBD
	2001 Montreal Declaration on the Protection of the Marine Environment from Land-based Sources of Marine Pollution
	2001 Global Programme of Action for the Protection of the Marine Environment from Land-based Activities
	Resolution GC (44)/RES/17 of the General Conference of the International Atomic Energy Agency

(Continued)

Table 2.3: (*Continued*)

WSSD Priority Area	Non-Binding "Soft Law" Instruments
	International Strategy for Disaster Reduction 2001 Marrakesh Accords of the UNFCCC 2001 UNCBD Bonn Guidelines on Access to Genetic Resources and Fair and Equitable Sharing of Benefits 2002 Quebec Declaration of World Eco-tourism World Tourism Organization Global Code of Ethics for Tourism Collaborative Partnership on Forests of the United Nations Forum on Forests
Sustainable development in a globalizing world	2001 Monterrey Consensus on Financing for Development 2001 Doha Ministerial Declaration (the Doha Development Agenda)
Health and sustainable development	World Health Organization Health for All Strategy Declaration of the World Summit for Children Declaration of the International Conference on Population and Development Declaration of the World Summit for Social Development Declaration of the Fourth World Conference on Women UN General Assembly Declaration of Commitment on HIV/AIDS ILO Code of Practice on HIV/AIDS and the World of Work
Regional Initiatives	Barbados Programme of Action for the Sustainable Development of Small Island Developing States New Partnership for Africa's Development (NEPAD) 2002 Rio Platform for Action on the Road to Johannesburg 2002 Phnom Penh Regional Platform on Sustainable Development for Asia Pacific Regional Action Programme for Environmentally Sound and Sustainable Development Kitakyushu Initiative for a Clean Environment Economic Commission for Europe Ministerial Statement to the WSSD

(*Continued*)

Table 2.3: (Continued)

WSSD Priority Area	Non-Binding "Soft Law" Instruments
	Iqaluit Declaration of the Arctic Council
	Baltic Agenda 21
	Mediterranean Agenda 21
Means of Implementation and Institutional Matters	Brussels Programme of Action for the Least Developed Countries for the Decade 2001–2010
	2000 UN Millennium Development Goals
	2001 Monterrey Consensus on Financing for Development
	2001 Doha Ministerial Declaration (the Doha Development Agenda)
	WTO New Strategy for Technical Cooperation for Capacity-Building, Growth and Integration
	WTO Integrated Framework for Trade-Related Technical Assistance to Least Developed Countries
	Doha Declaration on the Agreement on Trade-Related Aspects of Intellectual Property Rights (TRIPs Agreement) and Public Health
	Declaration on Principles of International Law concerning Friendly Relations and Cooperation among States in accordance with the Charter of the United Nations
	Dakar Framework for Action on Education for All
	Declaration of the World Summit for Social Development,
	Decision on International Environmental Governance of the Governing Council of the United Nations Environment Programme
	UN General Assembly Resolutions 48/162 and 50/227 on the ECOSOC
	UN General Assembly Resolution 47/191 on the UN CSD

resources, opening of markets and technology transfer. It reaffirms pledges to address threats posed by foreign occupation and armed conflict, corruption, terrorism and intolerance in all forms, and to combat communicable and chronic diseases, such as HIV/AIDS, malaria and tuberculosis.

The document stresses women's empowerment and emancipation, and the vital role of indigenous peoples. It recommits support to achieving Millennium Development Goals, increase official development assistance (ODA), regional initiatives such as NEPAD, and the requirements of small island developing states (SIDS) and least developed countries (LDCs). It emphasizes the need for better employment opportunities, and for the private sector to enforce corporate accountability.

The Declaration reaffirms all countries' commitment to the UN Charter and international law, calls for strengthening multilateralism and pledges to an inclusive process involving all major groups.

A SUMMARY OF THE *JOHANNESBURG PLAN OF IMPLEMENTATION*[19]

I. Introduction

The introduction reaffirms the outputs of UNCED and states that the intent of the implementation plan is to build thereon. It acknowledges that implementation of the plan should benefit all, and that good governance, peace, security and stability are essential to attain sustainable development.

II. Poverty eradication

This chapter states that poverty eradication is the greatest global challenge, and presents targets and timetables for poverty eradication at all levels. In relation to poverty eradication, the JPOI reaffirms the Millennium Declaration commitments to halve by 2015 the proportion of the world's people living on less than US$1 a day and who suffer from hunger; and establish a world solidarity fund to eradicate poverty; and to halve by 2015 the proportion of people unable to reach or afford safe drinking water. It adds the new target to halve by 2015 the proportion of people who do not have access to basic sanitation.

In relation to energy access, the JPOI contains the following key commitments: take joint efforts to improve access to reliable and affordable energy services; promote sustainable use of biomass; and support a transition to cleaner use of fossil fuels.

In relation to industrial development, the JPOI contains the following key commitments: to provide assistance to increase income-generating employment opportunities, taking into account the International Labour Organization (ILO) Declaration on Fundamental Principles and Rights at Work; to promote micro, small and medium-sized enterprises; and to enable rural communities to benefit from small-scale mining ventures.

In relation to slum dwellers, the JPOI contains the following key commitments: to improve access to land and property for the urban and rural poor; to use low-cost and sustainable materials and appropriate technologies to construct housing for the poor; and to support local authorities in slum upgrading programmes.

In relation to child labour, the JPOI contains the following key commitments: to take immediate measures to eliminate the worst forms of child labour; and promote international cooperation to assist developing countries requesting help in addressing child labour and its root causes.

---

[19] See JPOI, *supra* note 1.

III. Changing unsustainable patterns of consumption and production

This chapter proposes action to be taken by governments, relevant international organizations, the private sector and all major groups, to fundamentally change the way societies produce and consume resources with the goal of achieving global sustainable development.

In relation to sustainable consumption and production, the JPOI contains the following key commitments: increase eco-efficiency, with financial support for capacity building, technology transfer and exchange of technology with developing countries and countries with economies in transition; increase investment in cleaner production and eco-efficiency in all countries through incentives and support schemes and policies directed at establishing appropriate regulatory, financial and legal frameworks; provide incentives for investment in cleaner production and eco-efficiency in all countries, such as state-financed loans, venture capital and technical assistance; integrate the issue of production and consumption patterns into sustainable development policies, programmes and strategies, including into poverty reduction strategies; enhance corporate environmental and social responsibility and accountability; and encourage financial institutions to incorporate sustainable development considerations into their decision-making processes.

In relation to energy for sustainable development, the JPOI contains the following key commitments: promote the internalization of environmental costs and the use of economic instruments; establish domestic programmes for energy efficiency; accelerate the development, dissemination and deployment of affordable and cleaner energy efficiency and energy conservation technologies; recommend that international financial institutions and other agencies' policies support countries to establish policy and regulatory frameworks that create a level playing field; support efforts to improve the functioning, transparency and information about energy markets with respect to both supply and demand; strengthen and facilitate, as appropriate, regional cooperation arrangements for promoting cross-border energy trade; implement transport strategies for sustainable development; and promote investment and partnerships for the development of sustainable, energy efficient multi-modal transportation systems.

In relation to waste and chemicals management, the JPOI contains the following key commitments: encourage countries to implement the new globally harmonized system for the classification and labelling of chemicals, with a view to having the system operational by 2008; prevent and minimize waste and maximize reuse, recycling and use of environmentally friendly alternative materials; develop waste management systems, with highest priorities placed on waste prevention and minimization, reuse and recycling, and environmentally sound disposal facilities; promote the ratification and implementation of relevant international instruments on chemicals and hazardous waste; and promote efforts to prevent international illegal trafficking of hazardous chemicals and hazardous wastes and to prevent damage resulting from the transboundary movement and disposal of hazardous wastes.

IV. Protecting and managing the natural resource base of economic and social development

Acting at all levels, governments agreed to reverse the current trend in natural resource degradation where possible. In relation to water resources, the JPOI contains the following key commitments: launch a programme of actions to achieve safe drinking water and sanitation goals; mobilize international and domestic financial resources, transfer technology, promote best practices and support capacity building; promote and provide new and additional financial resources and innovative technologies to implement Chapter 18 of *Agenda 21*; and develop integrated water resource management and water efficiency plans by 2005.

In relation to oceans, the JPOI contains the following key commitments: where possible, maintain or restore depleted fish stocks to maximum sustainable yield levels not later than 2015; eliminate subsidies contributing to illegal, unreported and unregulated fishing and to over-capacity; implement the Ramsar Convention; implement the Global Programme of Action for the Protection of the Marine Environment from Land-based Activities; and establish a regular process under the UN for global reporting and assessment for the state of the marine environment by 2004. On air pollution, the JPOI agrees to improve access by developing countries to alternatives to ozone-depleting substances by 2010. On desertification, the JPOI calls on the Global Environment Fund (GEF) to designate land degradation as a focal area of GEF and to consider making GEF a financial mechanism for the Convention to Combat Desertification. In relation to biodiversity, the JPOI contains the following key commitments: achieve by 2010 a significant reduction in the current rate of biodiversity loss; and negotiate an international regime to promote and safeguard the fair and equitable sharing of benefits arising from the utilization of genetic resources. On forests, the JPOI commits to take immediate action on domestic forest law enforcement and illegal international trade in forest production. In relation to mining, the JPOI supports efforts to address the environmental, economic, health and social impacts of mining, minerals and metals and calls for fostering sustainable mining practices.

V. Sustainable development in a globalizing world

The chapter addresses globalization, acknowledging that serious challenges include financial crises, insecurity, poverty, exclusion and inequality, and calling for national- and international-level policies. The first paragraph also offers support for the successful completion of the work programme in the World Trade Organization's *Doha Ministerial Declaration*, implementation of the 2002 Monterrey Consensus on Financing for Development, encourages efforts to ensure that decision-making is open and transparent, supports enhanced capacity for developing countries to benefit from liberalized trade opportunities, supports the ILO's ongoing work on the social dimension of globalization, and calls for enhanced delivery of trade-related technical assistance and capacity building. Other paragraphs call for: active promotion of corporate responsibility and accountability, based on the Rio Principles; strengthening developing country capacity to encourage public/private initiatives that enhance the ease of access, accuracy, timeliness and coverage of information on countries and financial markets; strengthening regional trade and cooperation agreements; and assisting developing countries and economies in transition in narrowing the digital divide.

VI. Health and sustainable development

The JPOI commits to strengthen the capacity of health-care services' providers to deliver basic health-care services to all. Agreed commitments include actions at all levels to:

provide technical and financial assistance to developing countries and countries with economies in transition to implement the Health for All Strategy; develop partnerships to improve global health literacy by 2010; develop programmes to reduce infant/child mortality rates by two-thirds by 2015, and maternal mortality rates by three-fourths of the prevailing rate in 2000; promote the preservation, development and use of effective traditional medicine knowledge and practices. Delegates agreed to reduce the incidence of HIV prevalence among the young (15–24) by 25 per cent in the most-affected countries by 2005 and globally by 2010. Agreed commitments in this regard include: to provide resources to support the Global Fund to Fight AIDS, Tuberculosis and Malaria; and to mobilize public and encourage private financial resources for research and development on diseases of the poor, such as HIV/AIDS, malaria and tuberculosis. Delegates also agreed to target health impacts resulting from air pollution, with particular attention to women and children, and lead exposure.

VII. Sustainable development of Small Island Developing States (SIDS)

The chapter recognizes the special needs of SIDS and calls for action in the following areas: to strengthen national and regional implementation with adequate financial resources, including through GEF focal areas; to undertake technology transfer and assistance for capacity building; to enhance sustainable fisheries management and strengthen regional fisheries management organizations; to support development and implementation of, *inter alia*, work programmes on marine and coastal biological diversity; freshwater programmes; development of community-based initiatives on sustainable tourism by 2004; comprehensive hazard and risk management, disaster prevention, mitigation and preparedness, and relief from the consequences of disasters, extreme weather events and other emergencies; operationalization of economic, social and environmental vulnerability indices and related indicators; mobilization of adequate resources and partnerships to address adaptation to the adverse effects of climate change, sea-level rise and climate variability; capacity building and institutional arrangements to implement intellectual property regimes; to support the availability of adequate, affordable and environmentally-sound energy services and new efforts on energy supply and services by 2004; to undertake a comprehensive review of the implementation of the Barbados Programme of Action for the Sustainable Development of SIDS in 2004; and request the General Assembly to consider convening an international meeting for the sustainable development of SIDS.

VIII. Sustainable development for Africa

The chapter affirms the international community's commitment to support sustainable development in Africa, through concrete action to implement *Agenda 21* in Africa, within the framework of the New Partnership for Africa's Development (NEPAD). The chapter highlights, *inter alia*, the need to support programmes and partnerships to ensure universal energy access to at least 35 per cent of the African population within 20 years; mobilize resources to address Africa's adaptation to the adverse impacts of climate change, including sea-level rise, climate variability and the development of national climate change strategies; support the sustainable use, and fair and equitable sharing of benefits arising out of the use of Africa's genetic resources; promote technology development and diffusion; support land tenure reform; increase capacity to achieve internationally-agreed development goals related to education, hunger and food security; bridge the digital divide and create opportunities including access to infrastructure and technology transfer and application; support sustainable tourism; strengthen health care systems; mobilize financial support to make available necessary drugs and technology in a sustainable and affordable manner to control communicable diseases such as HIV/AIDS, malaria, tuberculosis and diseases caused by poverty.

IX. Other regional initiatives

This chapter recognizes initiatives at the regional, subregional and trans-regional level to promote sustainable development. In the section on Sustainable Development in Latin America and the Caribbean; governments target actions to address biodiversity, water resources, vulnerabilities and sustainable cities, social aspects (including health and poverty), economic aspects (including energy) and institutional arrangements (including capacity building, indicators and participation of civil society). They encourage actions that foster South–South cooperation.

In the section on sustainable development in Asia and the Pacific, the text calls for action in the following areas: capacity building for sustainable development; poverty reduction; cleaner production and sustainable energy; land management and biodiversity conservation; protection and management of and access to freshwater resources; oceans, coastal and marine resources and sustainable development of SIDS; and atmosphere and climate change.

In the section on sustainable development in the West Asia Region, the text endorses the following areas for further action: poverty alleviation; debt relief; and sustainable management of natural resources, including, *inter alia*, integrated water resources management, implementation of programmes to combat desertification, integrated coastal zone management, and land and water pollution control.

Finally, in the section on sustainable development in the Economic Commission for Europe (ECE) Region, the JPOI recognized the need to address the three pillars of sustainable development in a mutually-reinforcing way, and endorsed the regions' priority actions identified in the 2001 ECE ministerial statement for the WSSD.

X. Means of implementation

This chapter contains sections on finance, trade, technology transfer, capacity building and education. The section on Finance states that internationally-agreed development goals, including those in the Millennium Declaration and *Agenda 21*, require significant increases in financial resources as elaborated in the Monterrey Consensus, cites the common but differentiated responsibilities principle and calls for implementing the outcomes of major UN conferences. The section also describes financial mobilization as a first step to ensuring that the twenty-first century becomes the century of sustainable development for all; identifies the challenge of ensuring the internal conditions for savings and investment; calls for the facilitation of greater flows of foreign direct investment to support developing countries; recognizes that a substantial increase in official development assistance (ODA) and other resources is required and calls for the delivery of the relevant ICFD commitments; encourages more efficient and effective use of ODA; addresses efforts to reform the international financial architecture to foster transparency and equity; welcomes the third replenishment of the GEF; calls for the exploration of ways to generate new public and private sources of finance; and calls for a reduction of the unsustainable debt burden and for the speedy implementation of the enhanced Highly Indebted Poor Countries (HIPC) initiative.

The section on trade recognizes the major role that trade can play in achieving sustainable development and eradicating poverty, and encourages WTO members to pursue the work programme agreed at the Fourth WTO Ministerial Conference. They are also encouraged to: facilitate the accession of all developing countries; implement substantial trade-related technical assistance and capacity-building measures and support the Doha Development Agenda Global Trust Fund; implement the New Strategy for WTO Technical Cooperation; and support the implementation of the Integrated Framework for Trade-Related Technical Assistance to Least Developed Countries.

It also calls for: a determination to address developing country issues regarding the implementation of some WTO agreements and decisions; the fulfilment of WTO members' commitments, notably on market access; fulfilment of a commitment to comprehensive WTO negotiations initiated under the Agreement on Agriculture, aiming, *inter alia*, to phase out all forms of export subsidies; developed countries to work towards duty-free and quota-free access for all least developed country (LDC) exports; commitments to address trade-related issues and concerns affecting the integration of small, vulnerable economies; capacity building for commodity-dependent countries to help them diversify; and enhanced benefits for developing countries and countries with economies in transition from trade liberalization, including through public–private partnerships.

The section also calls to enhance the mutual supportiveness of trade, environment and development, with a view to achieving sustainable development through actions at the WTO Committee on Trade and Environment and the WTO Committee on Trade and Development, the completion of the Doha work programme, and technical assistance through cooperation between the Secretariats of the WTO and UN bodies. The trade section also encourages the use of environmental impact assessments and promotes mutual supportiveness between the multilateral trading system and environmental agreements, consistent with sustainable development goals, in support of the WTO work programme. The section also addresses: the *Doha Declaration* on the TRIPS Agreement and Public Health; environmental measures as disguised restrictions on trade; unilateral measures; self-determination of peoples; and the Declaration on Principles of International Law Concerning Friendly Relations and Cooperation among States.

Other sections call for enhanced technology transfer, capacity building, education as a critical contribution to sustainable development, and access to environmental information and judicial and administrative proceedings.

XI. Institutional framework for sustainable development

The chapter's introduction states that an effective institutional framework for sustainable development at all levels is based on the "full implementation" of *Agenda 21*, WSSD outcomes, and other internationally-agreed development goals. It outlines objectives, including to strengthen coherence, coordination and monitoring, and to increase effectiveness and efficiency within and outside the UN system, enhance participation, and strengthen capacities, especially in developing countries.

In the section on the international level, the chapter agrees to integrate sustainable development goals in the policies, work programmes and operational guidelines of UN agencies and international trade and finance institutions, "within their mandates"; strengthen collaboration within the UN system; implement decisions on international environmental governance adopted by the UNEP Governing Council and invite the UN General Assembly to address the issue of universal membership of the Governing Council; promote good governance at the international level; commits to the ideals of the UN and to strengthen the UN and other multilateral institutions.

The chapter also calls for the UN General Assembly to adopt sustainable development as the key element of the overarching framework for UN activities.

The section on the United Nations Economic and Social Council (ECOSOC) reaffirms its role in overseeing system-wide coordination and integration of the three pillars of sustainable development in the UN, and, *inter alia*, ensuring that there is a "close link" between its role in the follow-up of the Summit and to the Monterrey Consensus, "in a sustained and coordinated manner".

The chapter agrees to enhance the role of the UN Commission on Sustainable Development (UNCSD), to review progress in the implementation of *Agenda 21*, address new challenges, and limit the number of themes addressed in each session. The UNCSD, it concludes, will serve as a focal point for discussion of partnerships, consider more effective use of national reports and regional experiences, and exchange and promote best practices.

The section on international institutions notes that it is an evolutionary process to strengthen them. It stresses the need to enhance coordination among them in implementing *Agenda 21*, WSSD outcomes, the sustainable development aspects of the Millennium Declaration, the Monterrey Consensus on Financing for Development and the WTO *Doha Ministerial Declaration*. It requests the UN Secretary-General to promote system-wide coordination by utilizing the UN System Chief Executives Board. It also emphasizes the need to support the UN Development Programme's Capacity 21 programme and to strengthen cooperation among UNEP and other UN bodies, the specialized agencies, Bretton Woods Institutions and the WTO. It agrees to streamline the sustainable development meetings calendar, reduce the number of meetings in favour of implementation, and make greater use of information technologies.

The section on institutional arrangements at the regional level calls for the regional commissions to enhance their capacity; it encourages multi-stakeholder participation, partnerships, and support for regional programmes.

The section on institutional frameworks at the national level notes that States should strengthen existing mechanisms, formulate strategies for sustainable development immediately and "begin their implementation by 2005", promote public participation and access to information, policy formulation and decision-making, promote the establishment of sustainable development councils, enhance national institutional arrangements for sustainable development and the role and capacity of local authorities.

The last section agrees to enhance partnerships, including all major groups, acknowledges the "consideration being given to the possible relationship between environment and human rights, including the right to development", and urges youth participation.

3

Sustainable Development in Policy and in Law

Sustainable development has been accepted as global policy. The concept appears, often as an objective or preambular reference, in most international statements and declarations related to environmental, social and economic issues since the 1992 Rio de Janeiro Earth Summit. However, for the purposes of this book, it is important to consider the legal status of sustainable development in international law. What is "international law on sustainable development"? Is sustainable development a binding principle of international customary law? Is it simply a broad policy goal, found in certain international treaties but without specific meaning? Or is it something else?

It is not clear that "sustainable development", as such, can be accurately described as a single emerging principle of international environmental law, or as a customary norm that will eventually be accepted as binding on all States. First, as is further discussed below with regard to differences between international law on sustainable development, and international environmental law, sustainable development is not only about protection of the environment. Sustainable development is not simply a "softer" way to describe environmental law when it is done in developing countries, or to describe the environmental laws applied to natural resource development. Secondly, as noted by David Freestone, Vaughan Lowe and others, it is perhaps unlikely that sustainable development has become a customary norm of international law, in itself. International legal obligations may have been assumed with regard to certain economic development sectors, regional cooperation initiatives, or resource management challenges, in treaties and in international practice. However, sober assessment of significant developments to date, including the debates and outcomes of the WSSD, reveals little clear *opinio juris*, and less state practice, to support the proposal that states feel bound by some kind of general legal obligation to "develop sustainably". As noted by Gunther Handl, cited by David Freestone and Alan Boyle:

[n]ormative uncertainty, coupled with the absence of justiciable standards for review, strongly suggest that there is as yet no international legal obligation that development

must be sustainable,[1] and that decisions on what constitutes sustainability rest primarily with individual governments.[2]

As such, it is difficult, at present, to describe "sustainable development" as a binding international legal principle in the traditional sense. As stated by Vaughan Lowe, "the argument that sustainable development is a norm of customary international law, binding on and directing the conduct of states, and which can be applied by tribunals, is not sustainable."[3]

But neither is it accurate to describe sustainable development as simply a vague international policy goal, void of normative value. As observed by Judge Weeramantry in his extraordinary Separate Opinion in the *Case Concerning the Gabčíkovo-Nagymaros Dam (Hungary/Slovakia)*,[4] there is "wide and general acceptance by the global community" of sustainable development. There is also emerging global consensus on the need to strengthen "international law on sustainable development", and the need for further implementation of this law. The sheer weight of legal instruments and treaties which have been set in place to implement the sustainable development obligations, and its significant procedural elements, argue against such a facile dismissal.

Neither of these two options (a principle of customary international environmental law, or a meaningless notion) serves to accurately characterize "international law on sustainable development", after the 2002 WSSD. Rather, sustainable development, in international law, can be understood through a combination of two complementary approaches. First, it can be seen as an emerging area of international law in its own right.[5] As such, "international law on sustainable development", or, for short, "sustainable development law" describes a "group of congruent norms",[6] a corpus of international legal principles and treaties which address the areas of intersection between international economic law, international environmental law and international social

---

[1] See G. Handl, "Environmental Security and Global Change: The Challenge to International Law" (1990) 1 *YbIEL* 25. For the same reasons Handl also rejects the possibility that sustainable development is a peremptory norm of international law. See also G. Handl, "The Legal Mandate of Multilateral Development Banks as Agents for Change towards Sustainable Development" (1998) 92 *AJIL* 641.

[2] A. Boyle and D. Freestone, *International Law and Sustainable Development: Past Achievements and Future Challenges* (Oxford: Oxford University Press, 1999) at 16.

[3] V. Lowe, "Sustainable Development and Unsustainable Arguments" in A. Boyle and D. Freestone, eds., *International Law and Sustainable Development: Past Achievements and Future Challenges* (Oxford: Oxford University Press, 1999) at 30.

[4] (1997) ICJ Reports, 7.

[5] M.-C. Cordonier Segger, "Significant Developments in Sustainable Development Law and Governance: A Proposal" (2004) *United Nations Natural Resources Forum* 28:1. See FAO, *International Law and Sustainable Development Since Rio* (Rome: FAO, 2002). See also M.-C. Cordonier Segger, A. Khalfan, M. Gehring & M. Toering, "Prospects for Principles of International Sustainable Development Law after Johannesburg: Common but Differentiated Responsibilities, Precaution and Participation" (2003) 12:3 *RECIEL*. For examinations of international legal instruments on sustainable development, see N. Schrijver and F. Weiss eds., *International Law and Sustainable Development* (Leiden: Martinus Nijhoff, 2004)

[6] V. Lowe, "Sustainable Development and Unsustainable Arguments" in Boyle and Freestone, eds., *supra* note 3, at 26.

law aiming toward development that can last. Procedural and substantive norms and instruments, which help to balance or reconcile these fields, form part of this body of international law and play a role in its implementation. And secondly, sustainable development may also serve as a different type of norm in its own right,[7] one that facilitates and requires a balance and reconciliation between conflicting legal norms relating to environmental protection, social justice and economic growth. As proposed by Vaughan Lowe, it can be analysed as a "meta-principle, acting upon other legal rules and principles – a legal concept exercising a kind of interstitial normativity, pushing and pulling the boundaries of true primary norms when they threaten to overlap or conflict with each other".[8] The substantive aspect of this "interstitial norm" is the requirement of reconciliation, in the interest of present and future generations: development that can last. All three sets of priorities should be reflected in the substantive outcomes of a given dispute or conflict – while there are few bright lines, and no hard and fast rule, it is not "sustainable" to allow one or the other priority to completely "fall off the table" in situations where common international concerns are at stake. Viewed in this way, sustainable development helps to curb the worst social and environmental impacts of economic development activities,[9] it coordinates the internalization of otherwise externalized common concerns. There is "an immense gravitational pull exerted by concepts such as sustainable development, regardless of their standing as rules or principles of lex lata. That is plain when they are used by judges as modifiers; but it is also true when they are used in the same way by states as they negotiate (either with other states, or within their own governmental apparatus) on ways of reconciling conflicting principles."[10]

This characterization fits with recent guidance from international tribunals in relation to international law in the evolving fields of economic cooperation, human rights and environmental protection. In the *Gabčíkovo-Nagymaros* case, the ICJ invoked the concept of sustainable development in order to reconcile environmental protection, and the need for economic development. It stated:

Throughout the ages, mankind has, for economic and other reasons, constantly interfered with nature. In the past this was often done without consideration of the effects upon the environment. Owing to new scientific insights and to a growing awareness of the risks for mankind – for present and future generations – of pursuit of such interventions at an unconsidered and unabated pace, new norms and standards have been developed, [and] set forth in a great number of instruments during the last two decades. Such new norms have to be taken into consideration, and such new standards given proper weight, not only

---

[7] V. Lowe, "The Politics of Law-Making: Are the Method and Character of Norm Creation Changing?" in M. Byers, ed. *The Role of Law in International Politics: Essays in International Relations and International Law* (Oxford: Oxford University Press, 2000) at 214–215.

[8] V. Lowe, "Sustainable Development and Unsustainable Arguments" in Boyle and Freestone, eds., *supra* note 3, at 31.

[9] M. Decleris, *The Law of Sustainable Development: General Principles, A Report for the European Commission* (Brussels: European Commission, 2000) 40.

[10] V. Lowe, "Sustainable Development and Unsustainable Arguments" in Boyle and Freestone, eds., *supra* note 3, at 35.

when States contemplate new activities, but also when continuing with activities begun in the past. This need to reconcile economic development with protection of the environment is aptly expressed in the concept of sustainable development. For the purposes of the present case, this means that the Parties together should look afresh at the effects on the environment of the operation of the Gačíkovo power plant. In particular they must find a satisfactory solution for the volume of water to be released into the old bed of the Danube and into the side-arms on both sides of the river.[11]

The World Trade Organization Appellate Body has also provided clarification on this point, noting, in the *Shrimp/Turtle* case, that the Preamble to the WTO Agreement specifically refers to "the objective of sustainable development" and characterizing it as a concept that has "been generally accepted as integrating economic and social development and environmental protection".[12]

The concept of sustainable development, in international law, may be binding in a treaty or as an interstitial norm used by judges or governments. It may also be non-binding, but still persuasive. International law is increasingly including legal instruments that may not be formally binding.[13] Both the 1972 Stockholm UNCHE and the 1992 Rio UNCED conferences contributed significantly toward the development of this new model of international policy discourse.[14] In international law related to sustainable development, so-called "soft law" instruments abound. The *Stockholm Declaration* and the *Rio Declaration* are both non-binding instruments, as are the *Forest Principles* adopted at UNCED. The many guidelines, principles, and recommended practices adopted by the Organization for Economic Co-operation and Development (OECD), the UNEP, or the UN Food and Agriculture Organization (FAO), while non-binding, are often influential legal instruments. For example, the 1989 UNEP *London Guidelines for the Exchange of Information on Chemicals in International Trade* or the 1985 FAO *International Code of Conduct on the Distribution and Use of Pesticides*,

---

[11] *Gabčíkovo-Nagymaros Case* [1997] ICJ Rep. 78 at para. 140.

[12] *United States – Import Prohibition of Certain Shrimp and Shrimp Products* (20 Sept. 1999) WT/DS58/AB/R (Appellate Body Report), WT/DS58/R (Panel Report) at para. 129 and note 107. See also Case C-371/98, *R. v. Secretary of State for the Environment, Transport and the Regions, ex parte First Corporate Shipping Ltd.* [2000] ECR I-9235 which observes that the concept of sustainable development "emphasizes the necessary balance between various interests which sometimes clash, but which must be reconciled".

[13] Edith Brown Weiss, "The Emerging Structure of International Environmental Law" in N.J. Vig and R.S. Axelrod, eds., *The Global Environment: Institutions, Law, and Policy* (Washington: Congressional Quarterly, 1999) 98, argues that "[i]nternational law now consists of other important legal instruments in addition to binding agreements and rules of customary international law, namely, legally non-binding or incompletely binding norms, or what has been called 'soft law'. These instruments exist in all areas of international law, although they appear to be more abundant in human rights, environment, and financial dealings." She points out that "one of the most important sources of international 'soft law' is the myriad of guidelines, resolutions, and recommendations that are made by parties to an international agreement in the course of implementing it" and argues that the "old vision of an international agreement as an unchanging normative document binding upon the parties is obsolete. International agreements need to be viewed as living agreements, into which parties continuously breathe life and to which they give new directions by acting as informal legislatures."

[14] M.A. Hajer, *The Politics of Environmental Discourse: Ecological Modernization and the Policy Process* (Oxford: Clarendon Press, 1995) 97–98.

and the 1990 FAO *Guidelines on the Operation of Prior Informed Consent* have been widely respected, although they are non-binding.[15] There are various reasons that States sometimes prefer non-binding documents. The negotiation of legally non-binding instruments is more likely than the negotiation of formal international conventions in at least certain areas of international law. Agreement appears easier to achieve, the transaction costs are lower, the opportunity to detail strategies is greater, and often, such norms seem to respond better to rapid economic changes in scientific understanding or economic or social conditions.[16]

Emerging international regimes consist of networks, partnerships between States and non-state actors such as intergovernmental organizations, civil society and private sector associations. In this regard, an important factor has been the emergence of international and regional organizations within which government officials and experts, as well as non-governmental individual and group actors, interact and consider alternative policy options for the emerging problem.[17] The debate that led to the emergence of sustainable development was partially the result of emerging institutional processes within international organizations that allowed non-governmental actors to direct their claims to the plenary of States as a whole, in addition to seeking to influence States in their individual capacity. Thus, the new institutions served as focal points for a discursive process involving both States *inter se*, and between States and non-state actors.

As many have recently observed, international law itself is being re-designed. It is being broadened to include actors other than States among those who make international norms. Non-state actors implement and comply with norms. From this perspective, international law can be seen as a manifestly dynamic system with numerous interconnected instruments organized around a common statement of values and principles. These gain clarity and specificity at the intermediate levels of the system, as directives are developed to implement the general international rules in that area.

As argued by Edith Brown Weiss, traditional international law is healthy in the sense that there are more international agreements than ever, and States continue to serve important roles in the international system. It is no longer, however, the sole focus of international legal efforts. While the sovereign State remains the principal actor, its freedom to make decisions unilaterally appears increasingly restricted. Today, numerous non-State entities influence international decisions, and perform complex tasks for the implementation of international norms and treaties. By allowing a large group of non-governmental actors to attend the conferences as observers, the UN established a new standard of decision-making

---

[15] P. Sands, "Environmental Protection in the Twenty-First Century: Sustainable Development and International Law" in N.J. Vig and R.S. Axelrod, eds., *The Global Environment: Institutions, Law, and Policy* (Washington: Congressional Quarterly, 1999) 120.

[16] Brown Weiss, *supra* note 13 at 98.

[17] On the role of international organizations as sites of interaction and arenas for coalition building at the international level, see H. Breitmeier, "International Organizations and the Creation of Environmental Regimes" in O. Young, ed., *Global Governance: Drawing Insights From the Environmental Experience* (Cambridge: MIT Press, 1997) at 87–114.

at the international level.[18] At Stockholm, non-governmental organizations (NGOs) presented their own statement of principles to the conference, in Rio the NGO Forum developed "alternative" accords among civil society groups,[19] and in Johannesburg, roundtable dialogues were held between heads of states and other experts, and non-State actors committed to "Type II Partnerships" to implement the intergovernmentally agreed outcomes of the Summit.

In sustainable development treaties, this procedural phenomenon is particularly evident, and binding outcomes are produced. In economic, environmental and social law, there are clearly several levels of interactive process between States *inter se*, between States and NGOs, and between NGOs themselves, and these processes affect substantive outcome. Viewed in this way,[20] sustainable development law derives a significant amount of its normative power from its negotiated, incremental acceptance among States, as well as a wide variety of other actors and interest groups. The process of debate around the concept of sustainable development requires participation from the international community as a whole, regulating the conduct of both its legislators and civil society. It represents a global consensus as to future direction of environmental, economic and social decision-making.

As such, while there is doubt that a legally binding "principle of sustainable development" exists as such, a growing body of "international law in the field of sustainable development" or "sustainable development law" can be identified, analysed and implemented. This is not just a change in semantics. It is a conceptual shift, one that facilitates and may even require, through new procedural and substantive obligations in different contexts, a balance between three intersecting systems of international law.[21]

---

[18] An estimated 2,000 NGOs were said to be in attendance at the UNCED Conference. L.K. Caldwell, *International Environmental Policy* (Durham: Duke University Press 1996) 106; also A. Kiss and D. Shelton, *International Environmental Law*, 2nd edn. (New York: Transnational Publishers, 1994) at 23.

[19] *Caldwell, supra* note 18 at 66.

[20] See J. Brunnée and S.J. Toope "International Law and Constructivism: Elements of an Interactional Theory of International Law" (2000) 39(1) *Col. J. Trans'l. Law* 19 at 48. The writers refer to lawmaking as a mutually generative activity, and the dual function of States as both makers and observers of international law.

[21] For guidance on how international law can resolve overlaps between customary norms and treaty law related to the environment and sustainable development, through application of the terms of the 1969 *Vienna Convention on the Law of Treaties,* especially Articles 30 and 31, see P. Sands, "Sustainable Development: Treaty, Custom and the Cross-fertilization of International Law" in A. Boyle and D. Freestone, *International Law and Sustainable Development: Past Achievements and Future Challenges* (Oxford: Oxford University Press, 1999). See also a similar chapter by P. Sands, "International Law and Sustainable Development" in R. Revesz, P. Sands & R. Stewart, *The Environment, the Economy and Sustainable Development* (Cambridge: Cambridge University Press, 2000). The *Vienna Convention on the Law of Treaties* addresses relationships between treaties relating to the same subject matter, between treaties and *jus cogens* rules of international law, and between treaties and other relevant rules of international law (including customary principles that are not *jus cogens* norms). It does not address relationships between regimes, decisions of international organizations, fields of law, or between intersecting customary principles of law.

4

The Intersections of International Economic, Social and Environmental Law

International sustainable development law is found at the intersection of three principal fields of international law, each of which contribute to sustainable development. Since the call for a clarified and strengthened relationship between international agreements in the field of environment and relevant social and economic agreements in Chapter 39 of *Agenda 21*, the areas of intersection between international economic law, international law related to social development, especially human rights, and international environmental law have been growing. The scope of potential conflicts between international norms represented in treaties is limited to certain circumstances. A true conflict occurs where there is overlap *ratione materiae, personae* and *temporis* between norms, and one constitutes, has led to, or may lead to, the breach of the other.[1] For example, in instances where the implementation of one treaty requires or permits the use of measures that would explicitly violate obligations or rights set out in another treaty. Such conflicts, between treaties, are governed by formal rules of treaty interpretation laid out in the 1969 *Vienna Convention on the Law of Treaties*: in the absence of other directions, the *lex posteriori* normally prevails,[2] though not necessarily when one norm is customary and the other treaty-based.[3] In the absence of an overarching international body that can balance such priorities, different treaties related to sustainable development attempt to ensure that they can be "mutually supportive" with other potentially conflicting accords. For example, the Preamble of the 1994 *Marrakesh Agreement Establishing the World Trade Organization* (WTO) recognizes sustainable development as an

---

[1] J. Pauwelyn, *Conflict of Norms in Public International Law: How WTO Law Relates to Other Rules of International Law* (Cambridge: Cambridge University Press, 2003) at 170–180.

[2] *Vienna Convention on the Law of Treaties* (adopted 23 May 1969, entered into force 27 Jan. 1980) 1155 UNTS 331.

[3] See *Case Concerning the Gabčíkovo-Nagymaros Project (Hungary/Slovakia) (Separate Opinion of Judge C.G. Weeramantry)* [1997] ICJ Rep 92 at 114: "Unfortunately, the Vienna Convention offers very little guidance regarding this matter which is of such importance in the environmental field." And see P. Sands, "International Law and Sustainable Development", in R. Revesz, P. Sands and R. Stewart, *Environmental Law, the Economy and Sustainable Development* (Cambridge: Cambridge University Press, 2000).

objective of the world trading system,[4] and WTO members have agreed to seek a mutually supportive relationship between international trade, environmental and development policies.[5] Recent decisions from the Appellate Body of the WTO have also shown a growing sensitivity to the environmental and social (especially health) objectives of challenged trade measures.[6] However, the problem of "reconciliation" between international treaties in these different areas is far from being solved at the global level.[7] The Doha Development Agenda calls for negotiations on the relationship between the WTO and multilateral environmental accords (MEAs), and directs both the Committee on Trade and Environment and the Committee on Trade and Development to help to ensure that the objective of sustainable development is appropriately reflected in negotiations.[8] These debates are also evident in multilateral environmental agreements (MEAs) and in the International Labour Organization (ILO), where hortatory commitments to "mutual supportiveness" with trade law obligations have recently appeared.[9] As will be further discussed in Part III on Practices, several regional and sub-regional trade agreements have sought to liberalize trade while simultaneously improving enforcement of environmental laws and norms.[10] Recent trade agreements in the Americas have included explicit provisions or instruments

---

[4] *Marrakesh Agreement Establishing the World Trade Organization* (adopted 15 Apr. 1994, entered into force 1 Jan. 1995), 1867 UNTS 154 (WTO Agreement) Preamble.

[5] Ministerial Declaration of Doha (20 November 2001) WT/MIN(01)/DEC/1, reprinted at (2002) 41 *ILM* 746, 2, 3 and 6. Johannesburg **Plan of Implementation**, Report of the *World Summit on Sustainable Development*, Johannesburg (South Africa) (4 Sept. 2002) UN Document A/CONF.199/20 <http://www.johannesburgsummit.org/html/documents/summit_docs/ 2309_planfinal.htm> (18 May 2004) 92. *Rio Declaration on Environment and Development* (adopted 14 June 1992) (1992) 31 *ILM* 874, 12.

[6] *United States – Import Prohibition of Certain Shrimp and Shrimp Products: Recourse to Article 21.5 of the DSU by Malaysia* (21 November 2001) WT/DS58/AB/RW (Appellate Body Report), WT/DS58/RW (Panel Report). See also *European Communities – Measures Affecting Asbestos and Asbestos-Containing Products* (5 Apr. 2001) WT/DS135/AB/R (Appellate Body Report), WT/DS135/R (Panel Report). For discussion, see M.-C. Cordonier Segger and M. Gehring, "Precaution, Health and the World Trade Organization: Moving Toward Sustainable Development" (2003) *Queen's Law Journal* 29:1 at 133–140. And see H. Mann and S. Porter, *The State of Trade and Environment Law 2003: Implications for Doha and Beyond* (Winnipeg: IISD/CIEL, 2003).

[7] Pauwelyn, *supra* note 1, at 10–22.

[8] Ministerial Declaration of Doha (20 November 2001) WT/MIN(01)/DEC/1 (reprinted at (2002) 41 *ILM* 746, 2, 3, and 6) at 31(i) and 51.

[9] *Cartagena Protocol on Biosafety to the Convention on Biological Diversity* (*Cartagena Protocol*) (adopted 29 Jan. 2000, entered into force 11 Sept. 2003) (2000) 39 *ILM* 127, Preamble. See also *Stockholm Convention on Implementing International Action on Certain Persistent Organic Pollutants* (adopted 22 May 2001, entered into force 17 May 2004) UNEP/POPS/CONF/4 (POPs Convention), Preamble.

[10] *North American Agreement on Environmental Cooperation* (Canada-USA-Mexico) (adopted 13 Sept. 1993, entered into force 1 Jan. 1994) (1993) 32 *ILM* 1480, Preamble. See also *North American Agreement on Labour Cooperation* (Canada-USA-Mexico) (adopted 17 Dec. 1992, entered into force 1 Jan. 1994) (1993) 32 *ILM* 1502; *North American Free Trade Agreement*, (Canada-USA-Mexico) (adopted 17 Dec. 1992, entered into force 1 Jan. 1994) (1993) 32 *ILM* 289 and 32 *ILM* 605; *Free Trade Agreement between Canada and Costa Rica*, (Canada-Costa Rica) (adopted 23 Apr. 2001, entered into force 1 Nov. 2002) published in La Gaceta of Costa Rica, No. 127 (3 July 2002); and *Environmental Cooperation Agreement between the Government of Canada and the Government of the Republic of Costa Rica* (Canada-Costa Rica) (*Canada-Costa Rica Agreement on Environmental*

aimed to ensure that integration can support social development, and does not encourage the violation of core labour rights.[11] It remains to be seen how such treaty provisions will be interpreted. There is still uncertainty as to how, exactly, to reconcile economic, environmental and social treaties and regimes in cases of conflicts between norms. Sustainable development may play a role in resolving such situations. However, the present book has a broader focus. First, it addresses intersections, rather than simply conflicts. There are increasing incidences of overlaps and intersections between social, economic and environmental *fields of international law*. Only a few of these situations lead to formal conflicts of legal norms. Secondly, it addresses international policy as well as law. As will be seen below, both formally binding treaty provisions and non-binding commitments often form part of a legal regime in a particular field of international law. In order to analyse the body of principles and practices which have developed to mediate and provide coherence between these fields, it is important to begin with a survey of recent developments in each of these three areas. In this section, each area is very briefly summarized in turn, by laying out several of the recognized principles, and describing some of the major legal instruments, dispute-resolution bodies, and domestic implementation mechanisms that form part of the respective legal regimes. Each area is, of course, a body of law in itself, and as such, legal resources are recommended with relation to each field to provide a more in-depth survey for those seeking greater detail.

INTERNATIONAL ECONOMIC LAW

A broad view of international economic law encompasses both the law governing the conduct of States in international economic relations, and the rules of conduct of private parties involved in cross-border economic and business transactions. As economic interrelationships among countries continue to grow, new challenges appear, and international economic law develops. This law is not derived from a single or even several sources of law; but finds its genesis in a wide variety of sources and continues to evolve through the decisions of international tribunals and relevant international organizations. National, regional, and international law (public and private) and policy form part of international economic law. International economic law encompasses a wide range of subjects including trade in goods and services and resolution of related disputes, international investment law, international competition law, certain aspects of development law such as the rules of the international financial system, international economic integration regimes, and laws governing use of economic sanctions.

Cooperation) (adopted 23 Apr. 2001, entered into force 1 Nov. 2002) published in La Gaceta of Costa Rica, No. 127 (3 July 2002).

[11] *Canada–Chile Agreement on Labor Cooperation* (Canada-Chile) (entered into force 2 June 1997) (1997) 36 *ILM* 1216.

International business transactions continue to grow in number and size. Various international organizations play a role in the coordination of this growing area of international law. Chief among them are the World Trade Organization (WTO), the World Customs Organization (WCO), the Organization for Economic Cooperation and Development (OECD), the United Nations Conference on Trade and Development (UNCTAD), as well as the International Labour Organization (ILO), the Bretton Woods Institutions (such as the International Monetary Fund, the World Bank and its affiliates), and many regional or bilateral trade, investment and economic integration treaties.

This short overview will simply survey existing international institutions and treaties of international economic law, focusing on the areas of (1) international trade law, (2) international investment law, (3) international competition law, (4) the treaties governing international and regional economic integration, (5) the rules of the international financial system, and (6) other international economic groupings and actors. It will highlight relevant principles and recent trends, to lay a foundation for later discussions of intersections between international economic, social and environmental law. For those interested in further analysis or information, several key resources are recommended at the end of this section.

International trade law

International trade law focuses on how countries conduct trade in goods and services across national borders. It enshrines the principles of "most-favoured nation" (MFN) treatment, no increased trade barriers, "national treatment", tariffs only, regular negotiations, and "transparency".[12] The MFN principle holds that trade should be conducted on the basis of non-discrimination, it requires a country to apply duties and similar changes on the import of goods equally, so that products or services from one country are treated the same as products and services from another. The commitment not to increase trade barriers means that governmental restraints on the movement of goods should be kept to a minimum, and if changed, should be reduced not increased. The principle of "National treatment" requires that a country's internal taxes, charges and other regulations should not discriminate between domestically produced and imported products or services. The commitment to "tariffs only" holds that the accepted form of trade restraint is the customs tariff rather than, subject to exceptions, quotas or licensing schemes. The "regular negotiations", or "agreement to meet regularly" principle means that parties will continue to seek to lower trade barriers on the basis of reciprocity within a multilateral

---

[12] See A. Lowenfeld, *International Economic Law* (Oxford: Oxford University Press, 2002) at 28–30. See also J. Jackson, *The World Trading System: Law and Policy of International Economic Relations* 2nd edn. (Boston: MIT Press, 1997). And see M. Matsushita, T.J. Schoenbaum & P.C. Mavroidis, *The World Trade Organization – Law, Practice, and Policy* (Oxford: Oxford University Press, 2004).

framework. The principle of "transparency" requires a country's trade and economic rules to be made available to other countries, it is the reason for notification and publication requirements.

Several organizations have mandates concerning the export and import issues that arise in the international trade of goods and services. Chief among them is the World Trade Organization (WTO), established through a coordinated body of treaties linked to a quasi-judicial, binding dispute settlement mechanism.[13] The *General Agreement on Tariffs and Trade* (GATT) came into being in 1948 as a multilateral instrument to promote trade and gradual liberalization. In 1994, the Uruguay Round of the GATT established the WTO as an international organization. The GATT/WTO system has four principal elements. First, it encompasses the traditional GATT on trade in goods, augmented by twelve multilateral agreements binding on all WTO members, and two plurilateral agreements, binding on those that have accepted them. Secondly, WTO members are parties to the General Agreement on Trade in Services (GATS), which applies basic principles of the GATT to trade in services, subject to many exemptions and using a "positive-list" approach (members are only bound to liberalize sectors that they have agreed). Thirdly, the Agreement on Trade Related Intellectual Property Rights (TRIPs) applies basic trade law principles to intellectual property (including patents, copyright, trade marks and counterfeit goods). Fourthly, an Understanding on Dispute Settlement builds on early mechanisms from the GATT, but becomes applicable (with exceptions) to all agreements of the GATT/WTO system, and provides for binding decisions in state-to-state disputes, with compensation or retaliation for non-compliance.[14] With regard to its relationship to social and environmental concerns, the GATT contains an important exception, GATT Article XX, which permits the use of otherwise incompatible trade measures in certain circumstances; these issues have been raised in several important disputes.[15] The WTO also addresses electronic commerce, trade and investment, environment, development, trade policy reviews, government procurement,[16] regionalism, competition policy and dispute settlement.[17] Over 100,000 official

---

[13] M. Moore, *Doha and Beyond: The Future of the Multilateral Trading System* (Cambridge: Cambridge University Press, 2004). And see P. Gallagher, *Guide to the WTO and Developing Countries* (The Hague: Kluwer Law International, 2000).

[14] See Lowenfeld, *supra* note 12, at 70–71. See also P. Gallagher, *Guide to the WTO and Developing Countries* (The Hague: Kluwer Law International, 2000).

[15] See M. Gehring and M.-C. Cordonier Segger, eds., *Sustainable Developments in World Trade Law* (The Hague: Kluwer Law International, 2005, forthcoming). See also D. Esty, *Greening the GATT: Trade, Environment and the Future* (Washington: Institute for International Economics, 1994). And see WTO Secretariat, *Trade, Development and the Environment* (The Hague: Kluwer Law International, 2000).

[16] This area is expanding, especially in regional economic law. See P. Trepte, *Regulating Procurement – Understanding the Ends and Means of Public Procurement Regulation* (Oxford: Oxford University Press, 2004). And see S. Arrowsmith, *Government Procurement in the WTO* (The Hague: Kluwer Law International, 2002).

[17] Some have argued that it should extend further. See P.S. Watson, J.E. Flynn & C. Conwell, *Completing the World Trading System, Proposals for a Millennium Round* (The Hague: Kluwer Law International, 1999).

documents are produced by or for the WTO's councils, committees, and working groups.[18]

The WTO Dispute Settlement mechanism is building a separate body of law through the adoption of dispute settlement panel reports, appellate body reports, and adopted panel reports within its framework.[19] These build on the adopted Panel Reports from the 1947 GATT framework, which were produced from 1948 to 1994. A significant difference between the GATT and WTO dispute settlement procedures is that now Panel and Appellate Body reports enjoy near-immediate application. Specifically, these reports become binding at the panel level unless one of the parties decides to appeal, or the Dispute Settlement Body (DSB) decides by consensus not to adopt the report.[20] Similarly, Appellate Body reports are adopted by the DSB and accepted by the parties unless the DSB decides, again by consensus, within thirty days of the issuance of the report, not to adopt it.[21] The fact that these new procedures have taken away the power of veto which, under the previous GATT regime, enabled an aggrieved party to block the adoption of panel reports, promises to contribute to the advancement of jurisprudence in this area. A significant body of disputes, in the WTO, in which many required Appellate Body rulings on specific legal and interpretative matters, have begun to build up a substantive body of persuasive, if not nearly authoritative, international trade law.[22]

Other institutions also provide assistance and support to international trade through market and country reports and economic analyses, and these are also governed by international laws and play important roles in the regime.[23] The World Customs Organization (WCO) is an independent intergovernmental body with worldwide membership (currently 159 members) which deals specifically with customs issues. The WCO addresses the harmonization of customs systems, valuation, origins of goods, cross-border crime, and information technology. Further relevant international actors include the International Labour Organization (ILO), a specialized UN agency, which develops international labour standards called conventions and recommendations. These are critical in setting minimum standards of basic labour rights. Select "International Labour Standards" have been developed, through particular labour conventions and international labour guidelines processes. Similarly, the International Organization for Standardization (ISO) is a non-governmental organization established in

[18] See WTO, which has an excellent online document retrieval system <http://docsonline.wto.org>.

[19] D. Palmeter & P.C. Mavroidis, *Dispute Settlement in the World Trade Organization: Practice and Procedure* 2nd edn. (Cambridge: Cambridge University Press, 2004).

[20] See paragraph 16.3 of the *Dispute Settlement Understanding*, being Annex 2 to the *Marrakech Agreement Establishing The World Trade Organization*, 15 April 1994 (in force: 1 January 1995), 33 ILM 1125.

[21] *Ibid.*, para. 17.14.

[22] P. Gallagher, *Guide to the WTO and Developing Countries* (The Hague: Kluwer Law International, 2000).

[23] I. Seidl-Hohenveldern, *International Economic Law*, 3rd edn. (The Hague: Kluwer Law International, 1999).

1947, consisting of a worldwide federation of national standards bodies representing over 140 countries. The ISO develops international agreements of technical specifications to be used consistently as rules or guidelines to ensure that materials and products are suitable for their purposes in a global marketplace. These agreements are published as non-binding international standards to break down barriers to trade and facilitate the international exchange of goods and services.

International investment law

The corpus of international law concerning international investment, and in particular the relation between host countries and foreign investors, has greatly expanded in the last two decades. In early international investment law, there were divergent sources of customary law of state responsibility for foreign investors,[24] which was applied in international arbitrations and adjudication.[25] Several recent tribunal awards, and many international investment treaties now govern much of current investment flows. Key issues, on the international level, include the debates about regulation and expropriation, the acceptance of limits on performance requirements, and investor-state dispute mechanisms.[26]

Major treaties sponsored by the World Bank have sought to improve the investment climate and to encourage transborder investment as a vehicle for economic growth. The *Convention on the Settlement of Investment Disputes between States and Nationals of Other States*[27] established the International Centre for the Settlement of Investment Disputes. If both the home country of the investor and the host country of the investment are parties to the Convention,

---

[24] An excellent survey is provided in Lowenfeld, *supra* note 12, at 391–415, which has served as a guide for this section. See also C.H. Schreuer, *The ICSID Convention: A Commentary* (Cambridge: Cambridge University Press, 2001). And see F.V. Garcia-Amador, "The Proposed New International Economic Order: A New Approach to the Law Governing Nationalization and Compensation" (1980) 12 *Lawyer of the Americas* 1, commenting on the *Charter of Economic Rights and Duties of States* GA Res. 3281, 29 UN G.A.O.R. Supp. (No. 31) 50, UN Doc. A/9631; 14 ILM 251 (1975).

[25] See *Anglo-Iranian Oil Co. Case (United Kingdom v. Iran)* [1952] ICJ Rep. 93; *Case concerning the Barcelona Traction, Light and Power Company Limited* (New Application: 1962) (*Belgium v. Spain*) Second Phase [1970] ICJ Rep. 3; and *Case concerning Elettronica Sicula S.p.A. (ELSI) (United States v. Italy)* [1989] ICJ Rep. 15. And see S. Murphy, "The ELSI Case: An Investment Dispute at the International Court of Justice" (1991) 16 *Yale J. Int'l L.* 391. Arbitrations arising out of the termination of Libyan petroleum concessions granted to western oil companies led to three influential cases. See *TOPCO/Calasiatic Award* 19 Jan. 1977 53 Int'l Law Reports 389; *BP Award* 1 Aug. 1974 53 Int'l Law Reports 297; and *LIAMCO Award* 12 Apr. 1977 20 ILM 1 (1981). For commentary see R.B. von Mehren and P. Nicholas Kourides, "International Arbitrations between States and Foreign Private Parties: The Libyan Nationalization Cases" (1981) 75 *Am. J. Int'l L.* 476. See also *Kuwait v. American Independent Oil Company* 21 ILM 976 (1982). For discussion, see P. Kahn, "Contrats d'Etat et Nationalisation – Les Apports de la Sentence Arbitrale du 24 Mars, 1982" (1982) 109 *J. Droit Int'l* 844.

[26] See M. Sornarajah, *The International Law on Foreign Investment*, 2nd edn. (Cambridge: Cambridge University Press, 2004). See also A.A. Asouzu, *International Commercial Arbitration and African States: Practice, Participation and Institutional Development* (Cambridge: Cambridge University Press, 2001).

[27] 575 UNTS 159, entered into force 16 Oct. 1966.

and a dispute is subject of a consent to arbitrate under the auspices of the ICSID (either through an agreement at the time the project in question was undertaken, or an ad hoc agreement after the dispute arises), the ICSID Convention provides rules for the establishment of an independent arbitral tribunal, granting of an award, and its enforcement.[28] The ICSID Convention provides that the tribunal will apply international law in specific situations, such as where the subject matter or issue is regulated by international law, for instance, a treaty between the host state and the home state of the investor. This links directly to the hundreds of bilateral investment treaties (BITs) that have been signed in recent years.[29] Over 149 countries have signed that ICSID Convention, and of these, more than 134 have completed the process of ratification. In 2001, more than 80 disputes had been submitted to the ICSID for arbitration or conciliation and 51 had been concluded. ICSID awards are published in the *ICSID Review*, and made available on their website.[30] Parties to a dispute may also use the rules of the UNCITRAL or the ICC.[31]

Hundreds of decisions were rendered, over the course of more than a decade, by the Iran-US Claims Tribunal.[32] Though the law applied in these tribunals could be considered *lex specialis*, specific to the particular circumstances, it has been convincingly argued that the Iran-US Claims Tribunals decisions make a significant contribution to the development of international investment law.[33]

Other treaties are also relevant to international investment law. The World Bank has established the Multilateral Investment Guarantee Agency (MIGA) to encourage the flow of investment for productive purposes among member countries (in particular to developing country members), by guaranteeing investments (based on certain conditions in the country), encouraging the

---

[28] See IBRD, *The Convention on the Settlement of Investment Disputes: Documents Concerning the Origin and Formulation of the Convention* (Washington: IBRD, 1970). See also M. Sornarajah, *The International Law on Foreign Investment*, 2nd edn. (Cambridge: Cambridge University Press, 2004). And see E.C. Nieuwenhuys & M.M.T.A. Brus, *Multi-lateral Regulation of Investment* (New York: Kluwer Law International, 2001).

[29] A.A. Asouzu, *International Commercial Arbitration and African States: Practice, Participation and Institutional Development* (Cambridge: Cambridge University Press, 2001).

[30] See ICSID <http://www.worldbank.org/icsid>.

[31] See UNCITRAL <http://www.uncitral.org> and ICC <http://www.iccwbo.org>. See, for general information on UNCITRAL, G. Herrmann, "The role of UNCITRAL" in I. Fletcher, L. Mistellis & M. Cremona, eds., *Foundations and Perspectives of International Trade Law* (London: Sweet & Maxwell, 2001) 28–36. And see M. Sornarajah, *The International Law on Foreign Investment*, 2nd edn. (Cambridge: Cambridge University Press, 2004).

[32] The Iran-US Claims Tribunals, which judged hundreds of claims from US national and companies against Iran (and vice versa) related to the "interventions", expropriations or abandonments and withheld payments surrounding the Islamic Revolution. For further details, see C. Brower and J. Brueschke, *The Iran-United States Claims Tribunal* (The Hague: Martinus Nijhoff, 1998). Also see the 29 volumes of the *Iran-United States Claims Tribunal Reports* (Cambridge: Grotius, 1981–1993). These tribunals addressed issues such as whether a claimant was eligible, whether the deprivation suffered by the foreign investor or the gain to the state is most relevant in terms of state liability, whether a claimant must first exhaust local remedies, the nature of an expropriation, the standard and quantum of compensation owed (including whether interest should be paid, and from whence it should run). These issues are key to international investment law.

[33] Lowenfeld, *supra* note 12, at 464.

amicable settlement of disputes, and providing certain technical and other assistance to developing countries. In 2001, the MIGA had 22 developed and 132 developing country members. In addition, there is a WTO Agreement on Trade-Related Investment Measures (TRIMs): this is quite narrow in scope but covers investment measures that directly affect trade.[34] Negotiations for a Multilateral Investment Agreement (MIA) in the OECD were not, after a debate, successful, and while the 2001 WTO Doha Development Agenda specifically discusses the relationship between trade and investment, negotiations within the WTO system seem unlikely at present.[35] The *North American Free Trade Agreement*'s Chapter 11 is more extensive, and several recent arbitral awards under its controversial investor-state dispute settlement provisions may be of interest to those interested in intersections between international investment law and health or environmental regulatory regimes.[36]

One of the more significant new developments involves the conclusion of bilateral investment treaties (BITs). Over 1,100 were in effect in 2001; more than 800 of these had been concluded since 1987. These treaties provide specific protections and guarantees for foreign investors. They usually address admission of an investment (giving a broad definition for investments that will be covered), obligations of fair and equitable treatment for investors, commitments, by a host state, to full protection and security, and provisions on expropriation (laying out the conditions upon which it is permitted, including a commitment for compensation), and dispute settlement (usually referring the parties to special investor-state tribunals governed by ICSID or UNCITRAL rules). These accords, and their effects on developing countries, have been subject to recent scholarly debate.[37]

Based on these treaties, statutes and arbitral awards, the international investment law that emerges is not wholly uniform.[38] However, it is being interpreted. The pace and content of international arbitration of investment disputes has

---

[34] WTO TRIMs Agreement, which recognizes that certain investment measures can cause trade-restrictive and distorting effects, agrees to certain principles (such as national treatment), and provides that such TRIMs should be notified to the WTO Council on Trade in Goods and eliminated on a schedule tied to the stage of the WTO member state's development.

[35] For an overview of the OECD-MAI negotiations, see E. Neumayer, "Multilateral Agreement on Investment: Lessons for the WTO from the Failed OECD Negotiations" (1999) 46 *Wirtschaftspolitische Blätter* 618–628. See WTO Ministerial Declaration, "Doha Development Agenda", adopted 14 Nov. 2001 WT/MIN(01)1. And see R. Pritchard, *Economic Development, Foreign Investment and the Law* (The Hague: Kluwer Law International, 1996).

[36] See J.C. Thomas, "Investor-State Arbitration under NAFTA Chapter 11" (1999) 37 *The Canadian Yearbook of International Law* 99–137. See also J. Kirton and V. Maclaren, eds., *Linking Trade, Environment, and Social Cohesion: NAFTA Experiences, Global Challenges* (Aldershot: Ashgate, 2002). And see M.K. Omalu, *NAFTA and the Energy Charter: Treaty Compliance with, Implementation and Effectiveness of International Investment Agreements* (The Hague: Kluwer Law International, 1999).

[37] See, e.g., A. Guzman, "Why LDCs Sign Treaties that Hurt Them: Explaining the Popularity of Bilateral Investment Treaties" (1998) 38 *Va. J. Int'l Law* 639 and J. Kurtz, "A General Investment Agreement in the WTO?: Lessons from Chapter 11 NAFTA and the OECD Multilateral Agreement on Investment" (2002) 23 *Journal of International Economic Law* 713–789.

[38] Lowenfeld, *supra* note 12, at 493.

vastly increased. The resolution of disputes under international law directly between foreign investors and host states is becoming more established, though not without debate.

International competition law

Competition law[39] regulates business practices and transactions that create or abuse market power, and interfere with the free play of market forces.[40] In modern economies, competition law constitutes a core aspect of economic regulation, and new rules have proliferated.[41] More than 80 countries, including South Korea, South Africa, Indonesia, Brazil, Mexico, Bulgaria and Croatia, have competition laws: most of these were adopted since 1990.[42] Most competition laws contain rules that prohibit cartels,[43] and prohibit or control certain conduct of dominant firms,[44] refusals to deal, horizontal and vertical contractual restraints[45] and mergers.[46]

Competition has a significant international dimension. Multinational enterprises act in domestic markets and often, only these companies have the economic power to engage in uncompetitive activities or create dominant market positions. However, there is, as yet, little truly global competition law.[47] The OECD has produced a number of non-binding instruments dealing with hard-core cartels, cooperation between competition authorities, pre-merger

[39] The term anti-trust law is more widely used in North America, while other jurisdictions more frequently refer to the same legal field and key issues as "competition law". International bodies, such as the OECD, the WTO and the UNCTAD refer to competition law as does the new cooperative International Competition Network of national competition authorities, online <http://www.internationalcompetitionnetwork.org>.

[40] See E. Fox, "Competition Law" in Lowenfeld, *supra* note 12, at 340–383. See also M. Gehring and M.-C. Cordonier Segger, eds., *Sustainable Developments in World Trade Law* (The Hague: Kluwer Law International, 2005, forthcoming).

[41] A.I. Gavil *et al.*, *Antitrust Law in Perspective: Cases, Concepts and Problems in Competition Policy* (St. Paul: Thomson West, 2002) 38. See also F. Jenny, "Globalization, Competition and Trade Policy: Convergence, Divergence and Cooperation" in Yang-Ching Chao, Gee San, Changfa Lo & Jiming Ho, eds., *International and Comparative Competition Law and Policies* (The Hague: Kluwer Law International, 2001).

[42] Fox, *supra* note 4.

[43] As defined by Fox, *ibid* at 353, cartels, or "hard-core cartels" are agreements among competitors to lessen the competition among them. This is typically done by price-fixing, bid-rigging, allocating customers or territories, assigning quotas or a combination of these devices. The word "cartel", in Europe, can also be used to describe all private firm collaborations. If they work, cartels clearly harm competition, raise prices, and lower output – they are seen as harmful to the economy. They can also been seen as harmful to other, often smaller, market actors (firms, etc).

[44] Acts of monopolization and attempts to monopolize, agreements among competitors or potential competitors that are not cartels but create or facilitate use of market power, can also harm competition and other actors.

[45] Mergers, acquisitions, alliances and other joint ventures can create or facilitate the use of market power.

[46] Agreements or ownership between a buyer and supplier, or between buyers or suppliers to lessen or harm competition.

[47] D. Gerber, *Law and Competition in Twentieth-Century Europe – Protecting Prometheus* (Oxford: Oxford University Press, 2001).

notification and reporting of mergers.[48] In the European Union, cartels come within Article 81 of the Treaty of Rome, which declares that anti-competitive agreements are incompatible with the common market and void unless exempted.[49] Legislation entered into force May 01, 2004, which amends competition law enforcement in Europe and merger reviews,[50] and determines that no price-fixing is allowed. Article 82 of the Treaty of Rome prohibits abuse of a dominant market position. The European Union "exports" EC competition law through free trade agreements, which require their trading partners to apply European Community competition law to restraints in the free trade area, and revisions of national laws among countries that apply for EU membership.[51] Some bilateral accords exist, which formalize cooperation between competition authorities,[52] but there are very few transnational or international competition rules.

It has been proposed that the World Trade Organization (WTO) become an umbrella for international competition disciplines.[53] In the WTO, though the Agreement on Trade-Related Aspects of Intellectual Property Rights (TRIPS) contains some disciplines that could be considered anti-trust law, the General Agreement on Trade in Services (GATS) does not contain competition rules, and glancing references in other Agreements have little substance.[54] However, negotiations in September 2003 at the Cancun 5th WTO Ministerial Conference failed to produce an agreement to launch negotiations.[55] The objectives and goals of competition law are actually very different from traditional trade law disciplines. The competition dossier is demanding. It requires extraordinarily

---

[48] A 30 March 1998 Recommendation states that Members should make every effort to enforce their own anti-cartel laws, and increase co-operation. The primary purpose of competition law is to improve economic efficiency so that consumers enjoy lower prices, increased choice, and improved product quality. See *A Framework for the Design and Implementation of Competition Law and Policy* (Paris: World Bank and Organization for Economic Co-operation and Development, 1999).

[49] See R. Wesseling, *The Modernisation of EC Antitrust Law* (Oxford: Hart, Studies in European Law and Integration, 2000).

[50] See Council Regulation (EC) No 1/2003 of 16 December 2002 on the implementation of the rules on competition laid down in Articles 81 and 82 of the Treaty, <*http://europa.eu.int/cgi-bin/eur-lex/udl.pl?REQUEST=Seek-Deliver&COLLECTION=oj&SERVICE=eurlex&LANGUAGE=en& DOCID=2003l001p00010025&ext=.pdf*> and Council Regulation (EC) No 139/2004 of 20 January 2004 on the control of concentrations between undertakings (the EC Merger Regulation), <*http:// europa.eu.int/cgi-bin/eur-lex/udl.pl?REQUEST=Seek-Deliver&COLLECTION=oj&SERVICE=eur-lex&LANGUAGE=en&DOCID=2004l024p00010022&ext=.pdf*> and D.G. Goyder, *EC Competition Law*, 4th edn. (Oxford: Oxford University Press, 2003).

[51] See E. Fox, "Anti-trust and Regulatory Federalism: Races Up, Down and Sideways" (2000) 75 *NYUL Rev.* 1781. See also T. Jakob, "EEA and Eastern European Agreements with the European Community" (1993) 18 *Fordham Corp. L. Inst.* 403.

[52] Such as the 1991 *Agreement between the Government of the United States of America and the European Communities Regarding the Application of Their Competition Laws*, 23 Sept. 1991 4 *Trade Ref. Rep* (CCH) 13,504.

[53] *Doha Ministerial Declaration, supra* note 5.

[54] See M. Matsushita, T.J. Schoenbaum & P.C. Mavroidis, *The World Trade Organization – Law, Practice, and Policy* (Oxford: Oxford University Press, 2004).

[55] *Doha Ministerial Declaration, supra* note 5.

sophisticated domestic institutions (Competition Authorities), backed by legislation, jurisdiction and quasi-judicial independence.[56] Many of these Competition Authorities are highly independent, and have the power to directly review, investigate or sue large private corporations. While many countries (or regions, in the case of the EU) have such domestic authorities, many others do not, especially in least developed countries. Any new mechanisms for international cooperation will need to reflect these and other specific conditions.[57]

Straightforward competition rules do not always apply – certain exceptions have been designed to ensure that governments retain freedom to regulate for social or environmental priorities.[58] For example, a specific segment of a market can be guaranteed in order to promote the development of a desirable new technology. The European Court of Justice (ECJ) recently upheld a German law that reserved a certain percentage of the German energy market for alternative, renewable energy sources.[59] The ECJ ruled that as renewable energy was a legitimate social goal, the measure would be exempted from European Union competition laws, which otherwise might have prevented the use of such policies.[60] Social and environmental competition measures also exist in developing countries.[61] India's competition law puts a strong emphasis on consumer protection, Jamaica's courts have recognized valid exceptions where full application of anti-trust measures would jeopardize legitimate sustainable development goals, and South African's competition laws and policies include ownership measures aimed at "historically disadvantaged individuals" to complement economic empowerment programmes.[62] Regional bodies of the Caribbean Community (CARICOM) have also developed community legislation which boosts member state codes.[63]

---

[56] D. Gerber, *Law and Competition in Twentieth-Century Europe – Protecting Prometheus* (Oxford: Oxford University Press, 2001).

[57] F. Jenny, "Globalization, Competition and Trade Policy: Convergence, Divergence and Cooperation" in Yang-Ching Chao, Gee San, Changfa Lo & Jiming Ho, eds., *International and Comparative Competition Law and Policies* (New York: Kluwer Law International, 2001). See also M. Matsushita, "International Cooperation in the Enforcement of Competition Policy" (2002) 1 *Washington University Global Studies Law Review* 463.

[58] See, e.g., G. Marceau, *Anti-Dumping and Anti-Trust Issues in Free-Trade Areas* (Oxford: Clarendon Press, 1994).

[59] Case C-379/98 *Preussen Elektra AG v. Schleswag AG* [2002] E.C.R I-2099, Celex No. 698J0379, 13 Mar 2001.

[60] *Ibid.*

[61] M.-C. Cordonier Segger, *Sustainable Development Implications of Competition Law and Policy*, IISD WTO Policy Briefing Paper Series (Winnipeg: IISD, 2003).

[62] WTO Working Group on the Interaction between Trade and Competition Policy, *Overview of Members' National Competition Legislation – Note by The Secretariat*, WT/WGTCP/W/128/Rev.2, 4 July 2001(counting the EU and its members separate since all EU member states have competition laws), Appendix 3. See also F. Jenny, "Globalization, Competition and Trade Policy: Convergence, Divergence and Cooperation" in Yang-Ching Chao, Gee San, Changfa Lo & Jiming Ho, eds., *International and Comparative Competition Law and Policies* (The Hague: Kluwer Law International, 2001).

[63] *Ibid*, WTO Working Group on the Interaction between Trade and Competition Policy Report.

The International Competition Network (ICN) has been recently launched as a network of government competition authorities, to assist developing and developed countries with practical competition enforcement and policy issues.[64] It aims to become a forum to improve worldwide cooperation and enhance convergence on international competition law and policy, through dialogue. It has working groups on Mergers, Capacity Building & Competition Policy Implementation, Antitrust Enforcement in Regulated Sectors, Funding and Memberships. The ICN might offer a consensus-oriented alternative venue to accomplish much of the "international cooperation on competition" agenda, in a more "cooperative" manner. Much depends on its capacity to use all available tools and participatory mechanisms to ensure that deliberations remain open and accessible, avoiding perceptions of "regulatory capture" by special interests, and to ensure that a delicate balance of independence and legislative oversight is preserved in a governmental network structure.[65] In the short term, neither WTO negotiations nor the ICN, alone, provide a "perfect" institutional framework to negotiate international competition law. Rather, progress may be needed in both forums. The ICN can provide a short-term option to build links between competition authorities, starting an exchange of highly technical information, bridging gaps between different levels of competition authority development, and building consensus on important issues. When characterized by inclusivity and expertise, the network structure may serve to facilitate the development of a global epistemic community on key international issues.

Current discussions in the WTO have been understandably tentative.[66] Countries may eventually proceed with negotiations on a tentative multilateral framework of principles, but the only issues of substance mentioned to date are measures to address so-called "hard-core" cartels (those that engage in price-fixing, bid-rigging and market sharing) at the international level.

---

[64] The founding conference of the International Competition Network (ICN) was held in Naples, Italy, 28–29 September, 2002, and its second annual conference was in Merida, Mexico, 23–25 June, 2003. It provides antitrust agencies from developed and developing countries with a focused network for addressing practical antitrust enforcement and policy issues of common concern. It facilitates procedural and substantive convergence in antitrust enforcement through a results-oriented agenda and informal, project-driven organization. It seeks to "bring international antitrust enforcement into the 21st century". According to the ICN, "[b]y enhancing convergence and cooperation, [it] promotes more efficient, effective antitrust enforcement worldwide". The network states that "[c]onsistency in enforcement policy and elimination of unnecessary or duplicative procedural burdens stands to benefit consumers and businesses around the globe." The organization has already announced a series of best practice proposals aimed at improving merger review and competition advocacy. For further information, visit <http://www.internationalcompetitionnetwork.org/index.html>.

[65] M. Gehring, "Sustainable Competition Law" in M.-C. Cordonier Segger and C.G. Weeramantry, eds., *Sustainable Justice: Reconciling Economic, Social and Environmental Law* (Leiden: Martinus Nijhoff, 2004). A new legal research agenda in this area is further discussed in Part V. of this book.

[66] L.H. Summers, "Reflections on Managing Global Integration" [1999] *J. Econ. Perspectives* 3.

Law of international economic integration

Regional economic cooperation regimes

Regional affiliations range from loosely defined free trade areas to customs unions to highly structured and regulated economic and monetary unions. They are almost always framed or governed by a regional economic treaty, which provides the backbone of the economic relations between the parties in the region.[67] These regional organizations generally provide public access to documents and legislation as well as information from member countries. An illustrative survey of several major regional economic cooperation instruments includes:

- AFRICA: The Common Market for Eastern & Southern Africa (COMESA) is a regional grouping of 21 countries of Eastern and Southern Africa and was established in 1994 to replace the Preferential Trade Area for Eastern and Southern Africa (PTA), which had been in existence since 1981. The Economic Community of West African States (ECOWAS) is a sub-regional grouping of fifteen West African Countries established in 1975 to foster the economic and monetary integration of its Member States. The constitutive treaty of 1975, adopted in Lagos, was revised in 1993. Significantly, this revised treaty provides, as one of the objectives, " ... to protect, preserve and enhance the natural environment of the region".[68] Similarly, the *Constitutive Act* of the African Union adopted in Lomé, Togo in 2000, aims to accelerate the political and socio-economic integration of Africa, and to promote sustainable development at the economic, social and cultural levels.[69] The New Economic Partnership for Africa's Development (NEPAD) is also relevant in this context.
- ASIA AND THE PACIFIC: The Asia-Pacific Economic Cooperation (APEC) was established in 1989. APEC currently has 21 member countries that border the Pacific Ocean, working together to promote open trade and economic cooperation in the region. In addition, the Association of Southeast Asian Nations (ASEAN) was established in 1967 with the signing of the Bangkok Declaration by Indonesia, Malaysia, Philippines, Singapore and Thailand. Brunei Darussalam, Vietnam, Laos, Myanmar, and Cambodia later became members. The ASEAN *Bangkok Declaration* aimed to join Member States in an effort to promote regional economic cooperation and welfare. Objectives from ASEAN summits include the creation of an ASEAN Free Trade Area and a preferential tariff scheme.
- EUROPE: The Council of Europe is an international organization whose objectives include the strengthening of democracy, the promotion of social and economic programmes, human rights and the rule of law among its 43

---

[67] J.H.H. Weiler, *The EU, the WTO and the NAFTA – Towards a Common Law of International Trade* (Oxford: Oxford University Press, 2000).

[68] See *Revised Treaty of the Economic Community of West African States* (ECOWAS) 1993, Art. 29, reprinted at (1996) 8 *Afr.J.I.C.L* 189. The 1975 *Lagos Treaty* can be found at 14 ILM 1200 (1975).

[69] See *Constitutive Act of the African Union*, adopted in Lomé, 12 June, 2000, Arts. 3(d) and 3(j).

Member States. The 1958 *Treaty establishing the European Economic Community (Rome Treaty)*, established a European Common Market, whose objective was to gradually develop integrated economic policies, a common customs tariff scale and the elimination of customs duties among members. The 1993 *Treaty on European Union (Maastricht Treaty)* established the European Union with the aim to achieve an economic and monetary union. Much law has also developed through the European Court of Justice and Court of First Instance, which has jurisdiction to hear disputes between Member States, Community institutions, undertakings and individuals. Decisions from the Court of Justice and Court of First Instance have led to a particular quasi-constitutional order specific to the region. The European Free Trade Association (EFTA) also deserves brief mention. Originally founded in 1960 by six European nations, EFTA now includes Iceland, Liechtenstein, Norway and Switzerland. The legal instrument of the Association is the *Stockholm Convention*. EFTA's objective is to remove trade barriers among members. Finally, the European Economic Area (EEA) came into being on January 1, 1994 extending the internal market of the EU to three EFTA countries, Iceland, Liechtenstein, and Norway. The Secretariat administers the *Stockholm Convention*, the EEA Agreement, and other conventions and agreements. The 1995 *Treaty of Amsterdam* clearly introduced the objective of sustainable development in EU law.[70]

- WESTERN HEMISPHERE: The Free Trade Area of the Americas (FTAA) aims to integrate the economies of 34 nations in the Western Hemisphere into a single free trade area with a launch date in 2005. This process was initiated in 1994 at the Summit of the Americas, and is built upon five sub-regional blocks.[71] The Andean Community, a customs union, is comprised of Bolivia, Colombia, Ecuador, Peru, and Venezuela. Andean integration focuses on economic and social cooperation to promote the growth of member economies. The Central American common market, which includes Nicaragua, El Salvador, Guatemala, Honduras, and often Costa Rica and Panama, aims for trade liberalization, a common external tariff, the progressive harmonization of socio-economic policies and the coordination of national legislation. The Caribbean Community (CARICOM) is an organization focusing on Caribbean regional integration. The MERCOSUR – Southern Common Market Agreement, also known as the *Treaty of Asunción*, established a common

---

[70] The *Treaty of Amsterdam* was adopted at the Amsterdam European Council on 16 and 17 June 1997 and signed on 2 October 1997 by the Foreign Ministers of the fifteen Member States. It entered into force on 1 May 1999. It established sustainable development as a goal of the European Union. A European Union strategy for sustainable development was adopted in May 2001, and was given an external dimension by the global partnership for sustainable development which the Commission adopted in 2002. See Europa, *The Amsterdam Treaty: A Comprehensive Guide*, available online: http://europa.eu.int/scadplus/leg/en/lvb/a15000.htm.

[71] M. Salazar Xirinchas, *Towards Free Trade in the Americas* (Washington: OAS/Brookings Institute, 2002). See also M.-C. Cordonier Segger *et al.*, *Trade Rules and Sustainability in the Americas* (Winnipeg: IISD, 1999). See also online: www.oas.org.

market among Argentina, Brazil, Paraguay and Uruguay. MERCOSUR aims for a programme of trade liberalization, reductions of customs tariffs, the elimination of non-tariff barriers and other restrictions to trade. Finally, the *North American Free Trade Agreement* (NAFTA) entered into force on 1 January 1994, which aims to eliminate tariffs on qualifying goods between Canada, Mexico and the United States. Other objectives include fair competition, greater investment opportunities, and the protection and enforcement of intellectual property rights.

Other economic cooperation treaties

While not a "regional" but rather a "regionalizing" treaty, the European–African Caribbean Pacific economic cooperation treaty, called the 2000 "Cotonou Agreement", deserves special mention in the area of international economic development law. Signed in June 2000, the Cotonou Agreement is an extension to the Lomé Convention (established in 1975). The Agreement provides the 77 ACP countries (South Africa excepted) with an extension of existing non-reciprocal preferential access for certain ACP agricultural and other goods to the EU market at least through 2002, when a preparatory period will begin during which ACP countries will build their capacities to withstand freer trade.[72] The Agreement is built on three interrelated components: political dialogue, trade and investment, and development co-operation. The new accord emphasizes a joint approach to combat poverty, promote sustainable development and work towards gradual integration of ACP countries into the world economy and the WTO system.[73] It emphasizes five "pillars": a comprehensive political dimension, participatory approaches, a strengthened focus on poverty reduction, a new framework for economic and trade cooperation, and a reform of financial cooperation.

Commencing 2002–2008, the EU and ACP are negotiating WTO-compatible and reciprocal trade agreements to be implemented from 2008 to 2020. Cotonou Economic Partnership Agreements (EPA) are performance-based and subject to peer review – they aim to establish an entirely new framework for trade and investment flows between the EU and the ACP based on reciprocity, regions and special treatment for LDCs.[74] EPA negotiations between the EU and each region were launched in September 2002. As part of the accord, the EU has pledged to provide ACP countries with about US$12.5 billion (EUR $13.5 billion) in official development assistance (ODA). ACP-EU cooperation is formally steered by

---

[72] See online: www.acpsec.org/gb/lome/lome1.htm. See also online: europa.eu.int/comm/development/cotonou/index_en.htm.

[73] K. von Moltke, *Sustainable Development Governance* (Winnipeg: IISD, 2003) available online: www.iisd.org. See also ICTSD, online: www.ictsd.org/html/weekly/story1.27–06–00.htm.

[74] ECDPM, *Cotonou Infokit: Regional Economic Partnership Agreements* (14). (Maastricht: ECDPM, 2001). Online: *http://www.ecdpm.org/Web_ECDPM/Web/Content/Navigation.nsf/index? readform&http://www.ecdpm.org/Web_ECDPM/Web/Content/Content.nsf/0/ED09769D167CB32 7C1256C520059BBD4?OpenDocument&Cotonou_Agreement.*

three "official" bodies : the ACP-EU Council of Ministers, (charged with political guidance, and made up of members of the Council of the EU, representatives of the European Commission, and a member of the government of each ACP country, with an alternating presidency and annual meetings), the ACP-EU Committee of Ambassadors (assists the Council of Ministers, and monitors implementation, made up of member representatives) and the Joint Parliamentary Assembly (a forum for dialogue and consultation, to discuss issues pertaining to development and raise public awareness, and to adopt resolutions and make recommendations, made up of equal numbers of EU and ACP parliamentary representatives). It is supported by an ACP Secretariat in Brussels and the European Commission Directorate General (represented by the Development Director General, with support from Humanitarian Aid Office (ECHO)), the External Relations DG and the Common Service for External Relations (SCR), and a National Authorizing Officer (NAO) and specialized agencies in the field.[75]

The participatory approach established under the Cotonou Agreement offers new hope for better integrating social and economic concerns and for more democracy. Those provisions have already led to a number of initiatives. Non-State actors were consulted on nearly all the Country Strategy Papers elaborated until now and specific funding has been earmarked for civil society in two-thirds of them for a total amount of €170 million over the next five years. The Commission is convinced that trade and regional integration can make an important contribution to poverty reduction, sustainable growth and beneficial integration into the world economy.[76]

The international financial system

International financial law was substantially influenced by the 1944 Bretton Woods regime. Significant changes, brought about by the establishment and development of the International Monetary Fund (IMF), the World Bank and other Bretton Woods institutions, shape this area of international economic law. In the international financial system, rules, practices and institutions are based on a mix of "soft law" and "hard law", though constitutive documents of the Bretton Woods institutions remain highly relevant. A detailed discussion of this emerging global regime is beyond the scope of this book.[77] Here, it will simply be noted that relevant treaties and institutions can be divided into four categories.

[75] ECDPM, *Cotonou Infokit: The Institutions* (6). (Maastricht: ECDPM, 2001). Online: http:// www.ecdpm.org /Web_ECDPM/Web/Content/Navigation.nsf/index?readform&*http://www.ecdpm. org/Web_ECDPM/Web/Content/Content.nsf/0/ED09769D167CB327C1256C520059BBD4?Open Document&Cotonou_Agreement.*

[76] European Commission, The Cotonou Agreement Enters Into Force Today (Brussels 1 April 2003), EC online: http://europa-eu-un.org/article.asp?id=2201&lg=5.

[77] For accessible overviews of relevance to sustainable development law, see, e.g., B.J. Richardson, *Environmental Regulation through Financial Organisations, Comparative Perspectives on the Industrialised Nations* (The Hague: Kluwer Law International, 2002). And see G. Handl, *Multilateral Development Banking: Environmental Principles and Concepts Reflecting General International Law and Public Policy* (The Hague: Kluwer Law International, 2001).

First, the IMF,[78] a revolving Fund which draws all its resources from governments, continues to be a major source of assistance and impetus for adjustment for developing countries, as well as a source of funds for economies in transition from centrally planned to market economies. Its discipline of fixed exchange rates, requirement of balance of payments equilibrium for States whose currency is willingly held or used by other States, and programme of surveillance of economic policies of all member States under Article IV of the Amended Articles of Agreement, have not been maintained. Its programme of conditionally for member States seeking to draw on the resources of the Fund remains controversial. However, the IMF remains the major forum for discussion of international financial issues, and its Articles of Agreement remain a major source of international economic law, and it continues to play a major role in addressing regional balance of payments and other economic crises.

Secondly, the International Bank for Reconstruction and Development (the World Bank),[79] and its affiliates, including the International Development Association and the International Finance Corporation play an important role. The most important of these, the World Bank, is financed primarily through the sale of its bonds in the capital markets of the principal industrial shareholders (member States), and under its Articles of Agreement, is required either to lend directly to member States or, if the borrower is a private enterprise or a subsidiary of a member, to lend subject to a guarantee by the member State. The World Bank usually grants loans on terms designed to cover its own cost of funds, and on condition that the project financed will be permitted to service the loan and meet development needs of the beneficiary state.

Thirdly, the United Nations Economic and Social Council increasingly addresses international monetary issues, including through engaging with the IMF and World Bank in yearly meetings. Under the auspices of the United Nations, and with the participation of the IMF and World Bank, a series of conferences led to the agreement by States on the *Monterrey Consensus on Financing for Development*.[80] The *Monterrey Consensus* is a non-legally binding document, yet it provides important guidance for States and recommendations to the relevant international organization on foreign direct investment, international financial architecture, international trade as an engine for development, international financial and technical cooperation, external debt and coherence and

---

[78] The IMF functions under a three-tiered system of governance. It has a Board of Governors, formed from member State ministers of finance or central bank officials, a Board of Executive Directors, and an independent staff headed by a Managing Director. Voting power depends on a quota and most decisions are taken by consensus, reflecting only paid-in capital, and the Managing Director has always been European.

[79] Like the IMF, the World Bank functions under a three-tiered system of governance. It has a Board of Governors, formed from member State ministers of finance or central bank officials, a Board of Executive Directors, and an independent staff headed by a President chosen for 5 year terms. Voting power depends on a quota and most decisions are taken by consensus, like the IMF, but for the World Bank, the quota reflects both paid-in capital and subscribed capital, and the President has always been American.

[80] *Monterrey Consensus on Financing for Development* UN Doc. A/Conf. 198/11, 22 March 2002.

consistency of international monetary, financial and trading systems. The *Monterrey Consensus* also addressed the issue of mobilising domestic financial resources for development.

Fourthly, regional financial systems have become increasingly important. The most significant of these regional regimes is the European Monetary System, now transformed by use of the common single currency of the euro. However, other regional monetary systems (such as the monetary union of the Eastern Caribbean States, or the Community of East African States (COMESA)), are also relevant to a study of international economic law, and provide useful experiences for developing countries seeking economic integration.

Other international economic actors

Other informal groupings of interest include the so-called Group of 8 (G8) and the Group of 20 (G20). The G8 meetings deal with macroeconomic issues, including international trade, and relations between developed and developing countries. G8 members include France, the United States, Britain, Germany, Japan, Italy, Canada, European Union, and Russia. Decisions of interest from G8 Summit Meetings, G8 Ministerial Meetings, and scholarly publications form part of the background to this decision-making process. The G20 is a relatively new forum of finance ministers and central bank governors from twenty large developed and developing economies. The G20 aims to bring together systemically significant economies and to promote cooperation between them to achieve stable and sustainable world economic growth.

In terms of non-governmental actors in this area, the International Chamber of Commerce (ICC) deserves mention. The ICC has consultative status with the United Nations Economic and Social Council (ECOSOC), representing the views of business in the area of international trade and investment. It promulgates voluntary practices in the conduct of transnational business in such areas as banking, arbitration, commercial crime, e-commerce, energy, financial services, taxation, and trade and investment. These practices have found widespread acceptance and are widely adhered to in international transactions.[81] The ICC International Court of Arbitration is a leading international arbitral institution, governed by 1998 *Rules for ICC Arbitration.*

This section does not seek to summarize international law on economic issues, rather, it simply presents a brief survey of the field of law to help describe the context and lay a foundation for an exploration of intersections where sustainable development law is relevant.[82]

---

[81] T. Padoa-Schioppa, *Regulating Finance – Balancing Freedom and Risk* (Oxford: Oxford University Press, 2004).

[82] For further exploration of this important area, the authors recommend A.F. Lowenfeld, *International Economic Law* (Oxford: Oxford University Press, 2002), I. Seidl-Hohenveldern, *International Economic Law* (The Hague: Kluwer Law International, 2003), and J.H. Jackson, *The Jurisprudence of the GATT and the WTO: Insights on Treaty Law and Economic Relations* (Cambridge: Cambridge University Press, 2000).

INTERNATIONAL SOCIAL LAW[83]

This section surveys international social law relevant to sustainable development. Chapter 39 of *Agenda 21* refers to "relevant" social and economic agreements without explicitly defining them. However, *Agenda 21* and the JPOI address a broad range of social issues and the international instruments governing them, ranging from poverty eradication, access to water and sanitation, health, labour standards and human rights.

International law in the social domain comprises four broad categories. The first three are specialized bodies of law – international human rights law, international labour law and international humanitarian law (the law of armed conflict). These are based on a body of treaties and declarations, elements of which also have expression in customary international law. International human rights and labour law are linked to multilateral international monitoring bodies. The fourth category is a growing corpus of international instruments relating to social development issues, such as food, health and population. International law in this area is composed primarily of multilateral "soft law" declarations and decisions of international organizations, which often reflect human rights norms. Each of these categories is surveyed below.

International human rights law

International human rights law is probably the most relevant body of social treaty law in the context of sustainable development as it comprises a wide range of legally binding obligations relating to civil, political, social, economic and cultural rights. As will be illustrated in Part III, Chapter 6, human rights bodies are increasingly addressing environment and economic development concerns. The programmes of action in *Agenda 21* and the JPOI explicitly recognize the need to realize key human rights, such as the right to an adequate standard of living, the right to adequate housing and the right to water.[84]

Human rights law is based on a number of theories influenced by religion, the philosophies of the law of nature, positivist utilitarianism and social movements.[85] Human rights treaties have distinct characteristics. The first is that its treaties are arranged in a series of affirmations, each affirmation introducing a right that all individuals have by virtue of the fact that they are human. Therefore, the law concentrates on the value of the persons themselves, who have the right to expect the benefit of particular freedoms and forms of protection. Secondly, human rights treaties are relatively short and simple. As a result of these two characteristics, human rights law is not limited to any particular

---

[83] The research assistance of Debbie Locker for parts of this section is gratefully acknowledged.

[84] See JPOI, *supra* note 5, paras. 40(a), 109, 169, *Agenda 21*, Report of the UNCED, 1992, UN Doc. A/CONF. 151/26/Rev. 1 (1992) 31 ILM 874, Chapters 7.6 and 18.47.

[85] For a good presentation of human rights theories and background, see H. Steiner and P. Alston, *International Human Rights in Context: Law, Politics, Morals*, 2nd edn. (Oxford: Oxford University Press, 2000).

sphere of activity. In theory, human rights law should apply as much to environmental and economic issues as to political and social issues.

The pre-eminent human rights international declaration is the *Universal Declaration of Human Rights* (UDHR), which contains both civil and political rights as well as economic, social and cultural rights.[86] Aspects of the UDHR are considered customary law, and two legally binding treaties were developed to implement it; the *International Covenant on Economic, Social and Cultural Rights* (ICESCR)[87] and the *International Covenant on Civil and Political Rights* (ICCPR).[88] Together, the UDHR, the ICCPR and the ICESCR enshrine global human rights standards and principles, which are indivisible and interdependent.[89] The ICCPR requires each State party to "respect and to ensure to all individuals ... the rights recognized in this Covenant ...".[90] Civil and political rights are usually perceived as not requiring any particular level of economic development.[91] On the other hand, the ICESCR requires each State party to "take steps, individually and through international assistance and cooperation, especially economic and technical, to the maximum of its available resources, with the view to achieving progressively the full realization of the rights recognized in this Covenant ...".[92] There are immediate obligations within this formulation, as well as the possibility of identifying State actions inconsistent with the Covenant.[93]

There are a broad range of treaties and declarations relating to specific classes of persons including the *Convention on the Rights of the Child*,[94] the *Convention on the Elimination of All Forms of Discrimination Against Women*[95] and the UN *Declaration on the Rights of Ethnic, National and Linguistic Minorities* (1992).[96] In addition, a category of "solidarity rights" has emerged, comprising rights to development and to a healthy

---

[86] *Universal Declaration of Human Rights*, 10 Dec. 1948, GA Res. 217A, UN GAOR, 3rd Sess., UN Doc. A/810 (1948).

[87] 19 Dec. 1966, 993 UNTS 3, (entered into force 3 Jan. 1976).

[88] 19 Dec. 1966, 999 UNTS 171 (entered into force 23 Mar. 1976).

[89] One of the central reaffirmations of the equal nature of these two sets of rights is: "(a) All human beings and fundamental freedoms are indivisible and interdependent: equal attention and urgent consideration should be given to the implementation, promotion and protection of both civil and political, and economic, social and cultural; (b) The full realisation of civil and political rights without the enjoyment of economic, social and cultural rights is impossible, the achievement of a lasting progress in the implementation of human rights is dependent upon sound and effective national and international policies of economic and social development, as recognised by the Proclamation of Tehran of 1968 ... "; World Conference on Human Rights 1993, GA Res.32/130 16 Dec. 1977, para. 1.

[90] ICCPR, *Supra* note 88, Art. 2

[91] In spite of the fact that the right to trial in the ICCPR, for example, calls for certain infrastructures and professional training.

[92] ICESCR, *Supra* note 87, Art. 2.

[93] Committee on Economic, Social and Cultural Rights, General Comment No. 3, UN ESCOR, 1990, UN Doc. E/1991/23.

[94] GA Res. 44/25, UN GAOR, 44th Sess., Annex, Supp. No. 49, UN Doc. A/44/49 (1989) 167 (entered into force 2 Sept. 1990).

[95] 4 Jan. 1969, Can. T.S. 1982 No. 31.

[96] GA Res. 47/135 of 18 Dec. 1992, available online at www.unhchr.ch/html/menu3/b/d_minori. htm.

environment.[97] The right to development is recognized in the 1986 *Declaration on the Right to Development* and is the subject of a UN Working Group established by the Commission on Human Rights.[98] While the right to a healthy environment has not achieved comparable formal recognition at the international level, it is gaining recognition at the regional and national level.[99]

Human rights related intergovernmental discussion and review procedures occur in the United Nations Commission on Human Rights (CHR), established in 1948. The CHR comprises fifty-three elected member States. The CHR procedures and mechanisms are mandated to examine, monitor and publicly report either on human rights situations in specific countries or territories (known as country mechanisms or mandates) or on major phenomena of human rights violations worldwide (known as thematic mechanisms or mandates). These procedures and mechanisms are collectively referred to as the Special Procedures of the Commission on Human Rights. The CHR's plenary gives its observations and recommendations. There is also a Sub-Commission on the Protection and Promotion of Human Rights composed of twenty-six experts elected by the Commission. This body carries out studies and develops resolutions on various themes related to human rights that are then passed on to the Commission on Human Rights for further consideration.

International human rights treaties each include a treaty body composed of independent experts that assess reports by State parties on a regular basis, and which release concluding observations on the State's performance of its treaty obligations. The treaty bodies also release General Comments and Recommendations that provide authoritative interpretations of the relevant treaty. In addition, four of the six major human rights treaties (the ICCPR, CEDAW, the Convention Against Torture, the Convention on the Elimination of All Forms of Racial Discrimination) include an Optional Protocol whereby States consent to permit individual complaints from persons within their jurisdiction to the Committee supervising the treaty.[100] The "views" of the treaty bodies on individual complaints are not legally binding, although often accepted by States. Unlike environmental treaties, human rights treaties generally do not have conferences of parties that monitor progress on treaties.

---

[97] See P. Alston, "Peoples' Rights: Their Rise and Fall", in P. Alston, ed., *Peoples' Rights* (Oxford: Oxford University, 2001) at 282–3.

[98] For a good overview of the right to development, see K. de Feyter, *World Development Law: Sharing Resources for Development* (Antwerp: Intersentia, 2001) at 20 ff.

[99] It is recognized in Article 11 of the *Additional Protocol to the American Convention on Human Rights in the Area of Economic, Social and Cultural Rights* (Protocol of San Salvador), 1988. In addition, the right to a healthy environment, or a similar right, has been formally included in most constitutions adopted since 1992, as recognized in UN High Commissioner for Human Rights and the United Nations Environmental Programme, *Meeting of Experts on Human Rights and the Environment, 14–15 January, 2002: Conclusions*; see www.unhchr.ch/environment/conclusions.

[100] There is currently a working group established by the CHR to consider options related to an Optional Protocol to the ICESCR.

There are three regional human rights systems covering Europe, the Americas and Africa.[101] The primary regional instruments are the *European Convention on Human Rights*,[102] the *European Social Charter*,[103] the *Inter-American Convention on Human Rights*[104] and the *African Charter on Human and People's Rights*.[105] Each system includes a commission or committee that addresses individual complaints (in the European case, this applies only to social rights issues). In addition, the European Court of Human Rights adjudges upon the European Convention on Human Rights[106] while the Inter-American Court on Human Rights addresses complaints referred to it from the Inter-American Commission on Human Rights.

Human rights law is increasingly being implemented at the national level as binding and justiciable obligations in constitutions, and in legislation in certain cases. For the most part, States draw heavily upon the ICCPR and UDHR. Social and economic rights provisions, primarily drawn from the ICESCR, are increasingly being included in constitutions. The overwhelming majority of new constitutions adopted in developing countries from 1990 onwards have included social and economic rights provisions.

Human rights law provides legal content and institutional mechanisms that include key rights such as the right to political participation, the right to free expression, the right to an adequate standard of living and the right to equality of social welfare and poverty and equality rights for women and minorities, the right to self-determination and the right to development. The role of human rights law in sustainable development is elaborated upon in Part III, Chapter 6.

International labour law

International labour standards, developed and monitored under the auspices of the International Labour Organization (ILO), regulate a range of sustainable development concerns such as child labour and health and safety in the workplace. The JPOI recognized the urgent need to support the ILO and its work on the social dimensions of globalization.[107] The ILO was developed as a result of

[101] See Steiner and Alston, *supra* note 85. For the Americas, see D. Harris and S. Livingstone, eds., *The Inter-American System of Human Rights* (Oxford: Clarendon Press, 1998) as well as the website of the Inter-American Commission on Human Rights, www.cidh.oas.org. For Europe, see M. Janis, R. Kay and A. Bradley, *European Human Rights Law: Texts and Materials* (Oxford: Oxford University Press, 2000). To supplement the latter text on the rapidly developing social rights issues, see the website of the European Committee on Social Rights, www.coe.int/T/E/Human_Rights/Esc/. For Africa, see the website of the African Human Rights Resource Centre, www1.umn.edu/humanrts/africa/comision.html.

[102] *European Convention for the Protection of Human Rights and Fundamental Freedoms*, 4 Nov. 1950, 213 UNTS 222 (entered into force 3 Sept. 1953).

[103] 18 Oct. 1961, Eur. TS No. 35, 529 UNTS 89.

[104] 22 Nov. 1969, 1144 UNTS 123.

[105] *Banjul Charter on Human and Peoples' Rights*, 27 June 1981, OAU Doc. CAB/LEG./67/3/ Rev.5. reprinted 21 ILM 59 (1982).

[106] *Supra* note 102.

[107] JPOI, *supra* note 5, para. 47(d). See also paras. 10(b) and 12–13.

discussions at the Treaty of Versailles to end World War I. The organization was established in 1919 and is based on the tripartite representation of governments, employer organizations and labour unions. The objectives of the ILO include, *inter alia*, the achievement of full employment and the raising of the standards of living, the effective recognition of the right to collective bargaining and the cooperation of management and labour in the continuous improvement of productive efficiency.

The ILO's *Philadelphia Declaration* established that the UN does not deal with explicitly labour matters. It recognizes the ILO as the specialized agency responsible for taking appropriate action for the accomplishment of the purposes set out in its constitution. However, UN human rights instruments in a more general scope have also covered labour matters. The ICESCR and the ICCPR, because of their comprehensive nature, are drafted in general terms; therefore, various rights in relation to labour, which they recognize, are dealt with in a less precise way. In addition, the *Convention on the Elimination of All Forms of Racial Discrimination*, *Convention on the Elimination of All Forms of Discrimination against Women* and the *Convention on the Rights of the Child* also address labour matters.

The ILO comprises an extensive series of instruments, including the constitution of the ILO, numerous conventions and recommendations. There is a supervisory machinery in the ILO that applies to State parties to each convention. In exceptional cases, sanctions may be declared.

While ILO conventions are not ranked in terms of importance, there is an underlying hierarchy. The conventions of primary importance are: *Freedom of Association and Protection of the Right to Organize Convention* (Convention No. 87, 1948), *Right to Organize and Collective Bargaining Convention* (1949, Convention No. 98), *Forced Labour Convention* (1930, Convention No. 29) and the *Abolition of Forced Labour Convention* (1957, Convention No. 105), *Equal Remuneration Convention* (1951, Convention No. 100), *Discrimination (Employment and Occupation) Convention* (1958, Convention No. 111) and the *Minimum Age Convention* (1973, Convention No. 138). These core conventions were identified and given prominence in the Conclusion of the *World Summit for Social Development* in 1995 (see *Copenhagen Declaration on Social Development*), where the heads of States and government attending the conference adopted specific commitments and a Programme for Action relating to "basic workers' rights" which are the seven core conventions previously mentioned. Other treaties that are also of central relevance to sustainable development include the *Indigenous and Tribal Peoples Convention*, 1989 (ILO Convention No. 169) and the *Maintenance of Social Security Rights Convention*, 1982 (ILO Convention No. 157).

The ILO enacted the *Declaration on the Fundamental Principles and Rights at Work* on 18 June 1998. The Declaration requests States parties to the core ILO conventions, listed above, fully to implement them and other States to take into account the principles embodied in them. The Declaration recognizes that the members of the ILO, even if they have not ratified the core conventions, have the obligation to respect in "good faith" and in accordance with the Constitution, the principles concerning the fundamental rights which are the subject of those conventions. Each year States that have not ratified the core conventions will be asked to submit a report on the progress made in implementing the principles enshrined in them.

International humanitarian law (IHL)

International humanitarian law (or laws of armed conflict) contains the rules which in times of armed conflict seek to protect persons who are not or are no longer taking part in the hostilities, and to restrict the methods and means of warfare employed. International humanitarian law does not strictly relate to the process of development and whether such development is sustainable. Lack of armed conflict is often seen as a precondition of sustainable development. However, several humanitarian law instruments aim to reduce the impact of armed conflict upon civilians and the environment, which is relevant for sustainable development. Specific components of humanitarian law may, therefore, contribute to sustainable development law.

International humanitarian law concentrates on the reality of a conflict without considering the reasons for or legality of resorting to force. It is intended to protect war victims and their fundamental rights, no matter to which party they belong. IHL legal instruments are universal. There are no regional systems. IHL are applicable to the following situations: (1) international armed conflicts; (2) non-international armed conflicts; and (3) international disruptions and other situations of internal violence only if the violence is of the same intensity as an armed conflict. The main legal instruments of international humanitarian law are the four *Geneva Conventions* of 1949 and the two *Additional Protocols* of 1977.[108] These conventions cover military personnel who are not or are no longer taking part in the fighting and persons not actively involved in hostilities, particularly civilians. They also cover the rights and obligations of the belligerents in the conduct of military operations, and limit the means of harming the enemy.

There are a number of means by which IHL is implemented. The instruments place the emphasis on cooperation between the parties to the conflict and a neutral intermediary with a view to preventing violations. The first measure is preventative, requiring States to spread knowledge of humanitarian law,[109] train

---

[108] The Four Geneva Conventions are: (I) Amelioration of the condition of the wounded and sick in armed forces in the field; (II) Amelioration of the condition of wounded, sick and shipwrecked members of armed forces at sea; (III) Treatment of prisoners of war; and (IV) Protection of civilian persons in time of war. The two Protocols additional to the four 1949 Geneva Conventions strengthen the protection of victims of international (Protocol I) and non-international (Protocol II) armed conflicts.

[109] Additional Protocol I, Art. 82.

qualified personnel to facilitate the implementation of humanitarian law, appoint legal advisers in the armed forces,[110] and adopt legislative and statutory provisions to ensure compliance with humanitarian law.[111] The measures for monitoring compliance of IHL for the duration of the conflict include action by the Protecting Powers[112] and action by the ICRC.[113] Repressive measures are based on the duty of the parties to the conflict to prevent and put a halt to all violations, including the obligation by the national courts to repress grave breaches considered as war crimes, the criminal and disciplinary responsibility of superiors and the duty of military commanders to repress and denounce offences and mutual assistance between States on criminal matters.[114] Other lesser-utilized measures include: the enquiry procedure; the International Fact-Finding Commission;[115] examination procedures concerning the application and the interpretation of legal provisions;[116] and cooperation with the United Nations.[117]

International social development agreements

A fourth area of law comprises international social development agreements that set out programmes of action to realize social development with regard to issues such as food, water, population and development, housing, women and development and health. Multilateral soft law declarations may not comprise a formally recognized source of international law, as such, but as is explained later in this book, they are part of the broader international legal system. They can indicate emerging consensus on customary norms, influence the decisions of intergovernmental organizations, affect legitimate expectations as to a State's behaviour, and provide evidence of good faith on the part of a State.

Most agreements and declarations are developed in world conferences, organized under the auspices of the United Nations and its specialized agencies. Key declarations in the last ten years have included, for example, the United Nations Fourth World Conference on Women which developed the *Beijing Declaration and Platform for Action* (1995),[118] the *Report of the International Conference on Population and Development* (1994),[119] the *Programme of Action of the World Summit for Social Development* (1995),[120] the 1996 *Habitat Agenda* of the UN Conference on Human Settlements (1996), the *Rome Declaration on*

---

[110] Additional Protocol I, Art. 6.
[111] Geneva Convention (II), Art. 45.
[112] Common article 1 to the Geneva Conventions.
[113] Geneva Convention (I), Art. 9; Geneva Conventions (I), (II) and (III), Art. 10; Geneva Conventions (IV), Art. 11.
[114] Art. 49/50/129/146 common to all four Geneva Conventions.
[115] Additional Protocol I, Art. 90.
[116] *Ibid.*, Art. 7.
[117] *Ibid.*, Art. 89.
[118] UN Doc. A/CONF.177/20 (1995).
[119] UN Doc. A/CONF.171.13 (1994).
[120] UN World Summit for Social Development, UN Doc. A/CONF.166/9 (1995).

World Food Security and the *World Food Summit Plan of Action* (1996) as well as the *Declaration of the World Food Summit* (2002).[121]

Social development agreements often refer explicitly to human rights and labour treaties that address similar issues (see the section on "International Labour Law" above, for an example). One innovative approach to weave together social development and human rights norms occurred at the 2002 *World Food Summit* where it was agreed to establish an Inter-Governmental Working Group (IGWG) within the Food and Agricultural Organization (FAO) to elaborate a set of Voluntary Guidelines to support the progressive realization of the right to adequate food. It can be argued that human rights laws, particularly those in the Universal Declaration of Human Rights, can serve a similar role in the social domain to the role played by principles of environmental law in the environmental domain.[122]

A significant number of resolutions and declarations are developed in United Nations institutions such as the General Assembly, for example, the *Declaration on Social Progress and Development* (1969)[123] and the *Millennium Declaration* (2000).[124] The *Millennium Development Goals* set out in the *Millennium Declaration*, have an important normative force as a result of the political profile given to these Goals in other agreements, the UN system and by member States.[125]

The social development agreements considered in this subsection are conspicuous by the general absence of formally binding treaties or governance institutions at the multilateral level. Social development issues have been viewed by governments as properly falling within the domain of national sovereignty, with the exception of issues of human rights, humanitarian and labour issues that have considerable moral force. Unlike international economic cooperation or international environmental regimes, States have therefore preferred to set out only policy commitments and targets in social development agreements.[126] There are, however, a few exceptions. For instance, the 2003 *Framework Convention on Tobacco Control* (FCTC) was recently developed through the World Health Organization.[127] The FCTC is a "framework convention" that establishes an ongoing diplomatic process to reduce the global public health threat posed by tobacco consumption. States parties to the FCTC intend to negotiate

---

[121] WFS Doc. FYL 2002/3.

[122] One important difference is that while the UDHR is a declaration, portions of which form customary law, many of its provisions are reflected in binding legal treaties, chief of which are the *International Covenant on Civil and Political Rights* and the *International Covenant on Economic, Social and Cultural Rights*. The latter treaties have, respectively, 149 and 152 ratified States parties as of May 2004.

[123] GA Res. 2542, UN GAOR 1969.

[124] GA Res. 55/9, UN GAOR, 2000, ch. III.

[125] See JPOI, *supra* note 5, Chapter 2.

[126] See Part IV, Chapter 12, "International Health and Sustainable Development Law" which considers why the World Health Organization has rarely exercised its power to develop legally binding health law instruments.

[127] For more information on the Framework Convention see the World Health Organization's website at www.who.int.

protocols on specific issues connected to global tobacco control, such as tobacco advertising, promotion, and sponsorship; tobacco-product regulation; illicit trade in tobacco; and liability.[128] As with the "framework-protocol" approach taken in certain international environmental treaties, the strategy in the FCTC contemplates progressive development of the international law on tobacco control. It is discussed further later in this book.

This section does not seek to summarize international law on human rights and social issues, rather, it simply presents a brief survey of the field of law to help describe the context and lay a foundation for an exploration of intersections where sustainable development law is relevant.[129]

INTERNATIONAL ENVIRONMENTAL LAW

International environmental law is distinct from, but related to sustainable development law. The goal of international environmental law, broadly stated, is protection of the environment. Many multilateral environmental agreements (MEAs) have two objectives. They focus both on conservation and protection of the environment, and also on a second (less studied) objective related to "sustainable use" or "sustained economic growth".[130] This section will focus on the first "environmental preservation, conservation and protection" objectives of these treaties, as well as the principles and regimes that surround them. Together,

---

[128] Intergovernmental Negotiating Body on the WHO Framework Convention on Tobacco Control, 6th Session, *Future Protocols: Note by the Secretariat*, Doc. No. A/FCTC/INB6/INF.DOC./2, 18 Jan. 2003, available online at www.who.int. For commentary on the need for international legal strategies, see A.L. Taylor, "An International Regulatory Strategy for Global Tobacco Control" (1996) 21 *Yale J. Int'l Law* 257.

[129] For further exploration of this important area, the authors recommend H. Steiner and P. Alston, *International Human Rights in Context: Law, Politics, Morals*, 2nd edn. (Oxford: Oxford University Press, 2000); an international labour law, see B. Hepple, ed., *Social and Labour Rights in a Global Context: International and Comparative Perspectives* (Cambridge: Cambridge University Press, 2002) and on international humanitarian law, D. Fleck, ed., *Handbook of Humanitarian Law in Armed Conflicts* (Oxford: Oxford University Press, 2000). For an enlightening comparison of the human rights and humanitarian law systems, see R. Provost, *International Human Rights and Humanitarian Law* (Cambridge: Cambridge University Press, 2002).

[130] As discussed above, sustainable development law focuses on integration of environmental, social and economic norms for development that can last. According to both the 1992 *Rio Declaration*, and the 1987 *Brundtland Report*, sustainable development centres on human beings and their communities, seeking to satisfy the needs of present generations, without compromising the ability of future generations to meet their own needs. Sustainable development law involves poverty eradication, social cohesion, sustained use of natural and other resources, and equitable sharing of benefits. It is about empowering human beings and their communities to improve their quality of life, though in order to be sustainable, this must be done in a way that respects environmental limits. Environmental law, in contrast, focuses on preservation, conservation and protection of the environment. It involves the needs of all species and natural systems, which it values for their intrinsic worth. Both are valuable and essential areas of international law with significant overlaps and intersections, but they should not be artificially conflated. See M.-C. Cordonier Segger, "Significant Developments in Sustainable Development Law and Governance: A Proposal" (2004) United Nations *Natural Resources Forum* 28:1. See also M.-C. Cordonier Segger and C.G. Weeramantry, eds., *Sustainable Justice* (Leiden: Martinus Nijhoff, 2004).

these form the existing body of international law for the protection of the environment.[131]

The framework of international environmental law is based on several key principles, implemented through MEAs and national regulatory instruments, and coordinated through a system of international environmental governance (IEG). This section briefly mentions certain key judgments and principles, identifies certain "clusters" of significant international treaties in this field, surveys relevant national environmental management techniques, and summarizes recent efforts to strengthen and enhance international environmental institutions.

Environmental law is a relatively new field. However, certain precepts date from over a century ago. One of the first recorded international legal processes relating to the conservation of the environment was the *Pacific Fur Seal Arbitration* of 1893, when a dispute arose between the United States and the United Kingdom regarding the right of the United Kingdom to hunt migratory fur seals on the high seas, just outside the three-mile limit of US territorial waters.[132] The USA argued that it held rights of property and protection in the seals, and consequently the right to take conservation measures extraterritorially as trustees "for the benefit of mankind". The US position was overwhelmingly rejected by the arbitral tribunal in favour of UK arguments on freedom of fishing on the high seas.[133] However, the tribunal also "adopted regulations for the protection and preservation of fur seals", effectively establishing a 60-mile radius safe haven for the seals.[134] In another leading case, the 1938 *Trail Smelter Arbitration* between the United States and Canada, sulphur dioxide fumes from a smelter in British Columbia were found to be damaging agricultural and timberland in the State of Washington. The tribunal resolved the dispute by setting a strict limit on the permissible output of sulphur dioxide from the smelter, and held that under the principles of international law, as well as the law of the United States, no State has the right to use or permit the use of its territory in such a manner as to cause injury in or to the territory of another or the properties of persons therein, when the case is of serious consequence and the injury is established by clear and convincing evidence.[135] Such cases illustrate the

---

[131] For further resources, see D. Hunter, J. Sommer and S. Vaughan, *Concepts and Principles of International Law* (Nairobi: UNEP, 1998). See also N. de Sadeleer, *Environmental Principles – From Political Slogans to Legal Rules* (Oxford: Oxford University Press, 2002).

[132] 1 Moore's Int'l Arb. Awards 755.

[133] See A. Cassese, *International Law* (Oxford: Oxford University Press, 2001) 376.

[134] *Ibid.*

[135] *Trail Smelter Arbitration (United States v. Canada)*, 3 R. Int'l Arb. Awards 1911 (1938), reprinted in 33 *AJIL* 182 (1939), 3 R. Int'l Arb. Awards 1938 (1941), reprinted in 35 *AJIL* 684 (1941). The Trail Smelter dispute lasted for a number of years. Damage within the United States was reported as early as 1925. In 1928 the two countries established a joint commission to examine the dispute. A report was issued, and damages were awarded to the US in 1931. *Convention for Settlement of Difficulties Arising from Operation of Smelter at Trail, B.C.*, 15 April 1935, U.S.T.S. No. 893, reprinted in 30 *AJIL* (Supp.) 163. Continued pollution and disagreements led to the creation of a mixed arbitral tribunal that issued opinions in 1938 and 1941. *See* generally, A.K. Kuhn, "The Trail Smelter Arbitration – United States and Canada" Comment (1938) 32 *AJIL* 785.

central tenets of international environmental law: trans-boundary preservation and protection of the environment.[136]

Principles of International Environmental Law

The principles of international environmental law have gained increasing recognition over the past decades; while some are still considered influential "soft law", others are increasingly emerging as "norms of customary international environmental law". Principles of environmental law have also been "codified" in key MEAs, which as treaties, are binding upon their state Parties in international law.

A widely accepted principle of international environmental law is that States are required to ensure that activities within their jurisdiction or control do not damage the environment of other States or areas beyond national jurisdiction.[137] The duty not to allow damage is often written to require States to take all "practicable" steps to avoid or prevent harm.[138] The reliance on a standard of "practicable" steps suggests that the duty to prevent harm may not be absolute, but requires at least that States diligently and in good faith make all reasonable efforts to avoid such environmental damage. This principle has been accepted in many treaties, and as an international customary norm by the International Court of Justice and other tribunals.[139] It is related to respect for the jurisdiction of other states that is embodied in the concept of sovereignty.[140]

A second, related principle involves the duty to prevent pollution, which can be considered a specific articulation of the general duty to avoid environmental damage. Avoiding or reducing pollution is almost always less expensive than attempting to restore a contaminated area, especially since it can be impossible

---

[136] See further X. Hanqin, *Transboundary Damage in International Law* (Cambridge: Cambridge University Press, 2003).

[137] As provided in Principle 21 of the *Stockholm Declaration on the Human Environment*, UN Doc. A/C. 48/14 (1972), 11 ILM 1461 (1972) (and, more recently, Principle 2 of the *Rio Declaration*, *supra* note 5), "States have, in accordance with the Charter of the United Nations and the principles of international law, . . . the responsibility to ensure that activities within their jurisdiction or control do not cause damage to the environment of other States or of areas beyond the limits of national jurisdiction." For further analysis and critical commentary, see M. Bowman and A. Boyle, *Environmental Damage in International and Comparative Law – Problems of Definition and Valuation* (Oxford: Oxford University Press, 2002).

[138] See, e.g., the 1991 *Convention on Environmental Impact Assessment in a Transboundary Content* (25 Feb. 1991) 30 ILM 800, 803 at Art. 21(1), or the 1989 *Basel Convention on the Control of Transboundary Movements of Hazardous Wastes and Their Disposal* (Basel Convention) (opened for signature 22 March 1989, entered into force 5 May 1992) (1989) 28 ILM 649 at Art. 2(8).

[139] *Advisory Opinion on the Legality of the Use by a State of Nuclear Weapons in Armed Conflict*, Advisory Opinion, [1996] ICJ Rep. 226. See also the *United Nations Convention on the Law of the Sea*, 10 December 1982, UN Doc. A/CONF.62/122; 21 ILM 1245 (entered into force 16 November 1994) at Part XII and the IUCN, *Draft International Covenant on Environment and Development* (Gland, Switzerland: IUCN, 1995) at Article 11. See also the 1985 *ASEAN Agreement on the Conservation of Nature and Natural Resources* (9 July 1985, Kuala Lumpur) at Art. 20.

[140] See F. Perrez, "The Relationship Between Permanent Sovereignty and the Obligation Not to Cause Transboundary Environmental Damage" (1996) 26 *Environmental Law* 1187. See also F. Perrez, *Cooperative Sovereignty: From Independence to Interdependence in International Environmental Law* (London: Kluwer Law International, 2000).

to remedy certain types of environmental damage.[141] The International Court of Justice has recognized this principle, specifically as it relates to environmental protection.[142] Pollution prevention has been adopted, in general terms, by numerous conventions and resolutions restricting the introduction of pollutants into the environment.[143] MEAs can also prescribe concrete quantitative standards for pollution abatement, including in some cases specific timetables for reducing or eliminating certain emissions. In some contexts, pollution prevention refers to minimizing waste through design changes, input substitutions and other cleaner production methods. Beginning with the initial design of a product and of its production process and continuing all the way through the life-cycle of a product to disposal, the minimization of waste is often more cost-effective than relying on "end-of-pipe" technologies or disposal options.

A third principle is that of "common heritage" of humankind. Areas beyond the limits of national jurisdiction – the high seas, the sea-bed, Antarctica, outer space, and possibly the outer atmosphere (such as the ozone layer) are part of the environment and frequently referred to as the "global commons". Several important preservation-focused treaties have been negotiated in order to recognize, preserve and manage an area beyond sovereign control of any State, as "common heritage"[144] of humanity. The principle implies that States will avoid appropriating such heritage, that it will be internationally managed and its benefits will be shared by humanity, and that it will be used only for peaceful purposes.[145]

A fourth principle of international environmental law is a general obligation on States to cooperate in identifying, investigating and avoiding trans-boundary environmental harms. The duty to cooperate is a general principle of international law as recognized in Article 1.3 of the Charter of the United Nations,

---

[141] N. de Sadeleer, *Environmental Principles – From Political Slogans to Legal Rules* (Oxford: Oxford University Press, 2002).

[142] *Gabčíkovo-Nagymaros Case*, *supra* note 3, para 140, where the ICJ noted it was "mindful that, in the field of environmental protection, vigilance and prevention are required on account of the often irreversible character of damage to the environment and of the limitations inherent in the very mechanism of reparation of this type of damage."

[143] Principle 6 of the *Stockholm Declaration, supra* note 137, sets out the principle in sweeping terms: "The discharge of toxic substances or of other substances and the release of heat, in such quantities or concentrations as to exceed the capacity of the environment to render them harmless, must be halted in order to ensure that serious or irreversible damage is not inflicted upon ecosystems." For a list of key treaties, see P. Sands, *Principles of International Environmental Law* 2nd edn. (Cambridge: Cambridge University Press, 2003) at 248.

[144] This principle is recognized in the UNESCO 1972 *Convention Concerning the Protection of World Cultural and Natural Heritage* 11 ILM 1358 at the Preamble, and also in the *Treaty on Principles Governing the Activities of States in the Exploration and Use of Outer Space, Including the Moon and Other Celestial Bodies* (27 Jan. 1967) 610 UNTS 205 (1967); and in the *Agreement Governing the Activities of States on the Moon and Other Celestial Bodies* (5 Dec. 1979), at Art. 11. It was also recognized in the 1982 *United Nations Convention on the Law of the Sea*, 10 December 1982, UN Doc. A/CONF.62/122; 21 ILM 1245 (entered into force 16 November 1994) at Articles 136, 137 and 140, on the deep-sea bed, though it was later removed to convince the USA to join the Convention. It was also recognised in the 1959 *Antarctic Treaty* (1 December 1959) 402 UNTS 71; and its 1991 *Protocol on Environmental Protection* XI ATSCM/2 (21 June 1991).

[145] D. Hunter, J. Salzman & D. Zaelke, *International Environmental Law and Policy* (New York: Foundation Press, 2003).

and the 1970 United Nations Declaration of Principles on International Law.[146] When used in environmental law, this general obligation can lead to specific duties relating, for example, to the exchange of information, the need to notify and consult with potentially affected States, and the requirement to coordinate international scientific research. It may also, in certain circumstances, incur an obligation to conduct an environmental impact assessment if a project seems likely to result in transboundary effects.[147] It is at the core of many international treaties on environmental matters, and it has been recognized by the International Court of Justice in leading cases.[148]

A fifth principle, precaution, can apply both in general environmental law, and also in the law relating to specific sustainable development law issues such as health, sustainable use of biodiversity and natural resources. This is a key principle of international environmental law, as it is central to the prevention of environmental damage.[149] The precautionary principle underlies a number of international legal instruments. It also applies in a variety of contexts from protecting endangered species to preventing pollution. The precautionary principle evolved from the growing recognition that scientific certainty often comes too late to design effective legal and policy responses to potential environmental threats. In essence, it switches the burden of proof necessary for triggering policy responses. The far-reaching implications of the precautionary principle for sustainable development are considered more fully in Part III, The Principles, which also discusses its status in international law.

The "polluter pays principle" is also widely recognized. This principle implies that the polluter should bear the expenses of carrying out pollution prevention measures or paying for damage caused by pollution.[150] Instituting the polluter

---

[146] *United Nations Declaration of Principles on International Law Concerning Friendly Relations and Cooperation Among States in Accordance with the Charter of the United Nations* (24 Oct. 1970) 9 ILM 1292.

[147] See UNEP, *Goals and Principles of Environmental Impact Assessment* (Nairobi: UNEP, 1987). See also IBRD, *International Bank for Reconstruction and Development Operational Policy* 4.01 (Washington: IBRD, 1999) at 15–16, which requires public consultations and disclosure of any adverse effects, as a pre-condition to the granting of international loans for development projects.

[148] This principle is found with related concepts, in Principle 27 and Principle 19 of the 1992 *Rio Declaration*. It is embodied in the *Convention on the Protection of the Environment Between Demark, Finland, Norway and Sweden* (19 Feb 1974) 13 ILM 591, and recognized by the International Court of Justice in both the *Lac Lanoux Arbitration (France v. Spain)* [1957] 24 ILR 101 & the *Gabčíkovo-Nagymaros Case, supra* note 3.

[149] As set forth in the *Rio Declaration, supra* note 5 at Principle 15, the precautionary principle states that: "Where there are threats of serious or irreversible damage, lack of full scientific certainty shall not be used as a reason for postponing cost-effective measures to prevent environmental degradation." See A. Trouwborst, *Evolution and Status of the Precautionary Principle in International Law* (The Hague: Kluwer Law International, 2002). And see T. O'Riordan, A. Jordan & J. Cameron, eds., *Reinterpreting the Precautionary Principle* (London: Cameron May, 2001).

[150] Originally recommended by the OECD Council in May 1972, the polluter pays principle has been increasingly accepted as an international environmental principle. It has been explicitly adopted in several bilateral and multilateral resolutions and declarations, including Principle 16 of the *Rio Declaration, supra* note 5, which provides: "National authorities should endeavour to promote the internalisation of environmental costs and the use of economic instruments, taking into account the approach that the polluter should, in principle, bear the cost of pollution, with due regard to the public interest and without distorting international trade and investment."

pays principle ensures that the prices of goods reflect the costs of producing that good, including costs associated with pollution, resource degradation, and environmental harm. Environmental costs are reflected (or "internalized") in the price of every good. The result is that goods that pollute less will cost less, and consumers may switch to less polluting substitutes. This will result in a more efficient use of resources and less pollution.

It is doubtful that these principles have all been accepted as international customary law, and neither is this brief survey intended to be viewed as an exhaustive list. For example, the principle of common but differentiated responsibility, which will be discussed below, has been proposed as a principle of international environmental law,[151] as have principles related to subsidiarity, access to environmental information, public participation in environmental decision-making, and a duty to assess environmental impacts.[152] Some authors perceive sustainable development itself as a principle of international environmental law,[153] though this is not the approach adopted in this book. The issue of whether there is a broad principle of State responsibility and liability for environmental harm remains contested. A distinction continues to emerge in international environmental law between international "responsibility" and international "liability": the former arises from unlawful acts, the latter can arise from the consequences of otherwise lawful acts (although it is still used at times with reference to unlawful acts).[154] There is a concern that imposing liability for acts not prohibited by international law irrespective of fault or the lawfulness of the activity will emphasize the harm, rather than the conduct. Traditional principles of State responsibility can merge with the concept of State liability, particularly in instances such as ultra-hazardous activities where States must meet such a strict standard of care that for all practical purposes they will be "responsible" for any activity leading to harm.[155] In any case,

---

[151] See, e.g., Sands, *supra* note 143, at 285.

[152] Hunter, Salzman and Zaelke, *supra* note 145, at 379–438.

[153] See, e.g., Sands, *supra* note 143, at 252. But see V. Lowe, "Sustainable Development and Unsustainable Arguments" in *International Law and Sustainable Development: Past Achievements and Future Challenges*, A. Boyle and D. Freestone, eds. (Oxford: Oxford University Press, 1999) at 19–37. And see Hunter, Salzman and Zaelke, *supra* note 145, at 213–214.

[154] Under the rubric of State responsibility, the recent *Articles on State Responsibility*, adopted by the International Law Commission, establish that the obligation to make reparations is premised on "injury" or "damage", but there is no requirement that an international dispute be premised on the fact of harm. This is particularly evident in the analysis of damage in J. Crawford, *The International Law Commission's Articles on State Responsibility – Introduction, Texts & Commentaries* (Cambridge: Cambridge University Press, 2002) 29–31 [hereinafter *Crawford*].

[155] The new Articles are highly relevant to cases of environmental harm attributable to a State, in particular where the obligations breached are peremptory norms of international law (such as the prohibition on "massive pollution" of the atmosphere and seas) or obligations owed to the international community as a whole (such as an obligation aimed at protection of the marine environment, the obligation to refrain from massive pollution of the sea and atmosphere, or even a general obligation of States to ensure that activities within their jurisdiction and control respect the environment of other States (and of areas beyond national control), recognized by the ICJ in the *Nuclear Weapons* case and reiterated in the *Gabčíkovo/Nagymaros* case). See I. Brownlie, *Principles of Public International Law* (New York: Oxford University Press, 1998) 288 [hereinafter *Brownlie*]; *Gabčíkovo/Nagymaros*, *supra* note 3, para. 53; *Advisory Opinion on the Legality of the Use by a State of Nuclear Weapons in Armed Conflict*, *supra* note 139.

liability for pollution-related injuries is also addressed, albeit generally, in many treaties.

Multilateral Environmental Accords (MEAs)

International environmental law is enshrined in a body of international treaties and legal instruments, many of which contain integrated provisions related to sustainable development, as well. For example, Philippe Sands lists 346 treaties that relate to environmental protection dating from as far back as 1867.[156] In terms of international environmental governance, these treaties are not at present organized into any hierarchical relationship or otherwise coherent system. Rather, each environmental accord was negotiated, the majority in the last four decades, to provide a framework for international collaboration addressing a specific environmental challenge. Often, the first step was simply to collate, in a cooperative way, enough scientific information to clearly define a problem and identify the steps needed to address it. This approach often led to the negotiation of a "framework convention" laying out common objectives and a schedule of meetings (of the "conference of the parties"), and this was later followed by specific protocols, as well as a series of non-binding decisions, guidelines and technical programmes aimed at achieving the common objectives. Most leading scholars "cluster" these instruments according to the substantive environmental challenge or concern that they address, and this approach has also been proposed in the United Nations Environment Programme.[157] A comprehensive examination is beyond the scope of this book, but a few well-known treaties with environmental protection objectives will be mentioned briefly below.[158] Several treaties appear in more than one cluster, as environmental problems are interrelated and many conventions address more than one issue.

   One cluster of international agreements relates to the protection of the international atmospheric environment, in particular addressing urban and transboundary air pollution, depletion of the ozone layer, climate change and international management of outer space. These include, for example, the *1979 ECE Convention on Long Range Transboundary Air Pollution* and its Protocols, such as the 1984 Protocol on *Long Term Financing of the Co-operative Programme for Monitoring and Evaluation of the Long-Range Transmission of Air Pollutants in Europe,* its 1985 Protocol on *Reduction of Sulphur Emissions or*

---

[156] See Sands, *supra* note 143.

[157] See K. von Moltke, *The Organisation of the Impossible* (Winnipeg: IISD, 2001), available online: <http://www.iisd.org/publications/publication_list.aspx?themeid=12>. See also D. Hunter, J. Salzman and D. Zaelke, *International Environmental Law and Policy* (New York: Foundation Press, 2003). And see Sands, *supra* note 143. And see A. Kiss and D. Shelton, *Judicial Handbook on Environmental Law (Draft)* (Nairobi: UNEP, 2004).

[158] International environmental law benefits from a strong coordinating and promotional role played by the United Nations Environment Programme. Excellent resources on international environmental law, as well as links to many of the MEAs listed here, are available online: <http://www.unep.org>. For brevity, only the year that the treaties were concluded will be mentioned in this survey. Full citations are available in the Table of Treaties in this book.

Their Transboundary Fluxes by at Least 30 Per Cent and its 1991 *Protocol on Control of Emissions of Volatile Organic Compounds and Their Transboundary Fluxes*.[159] They also include the 1991 *Agreement Between the United States of America and Canada on Air Quality*. In terms of protection of the ozone layer, the most significant treaty is the 1985 *Vienna Convention for the Protection of the Ozone Layer* and its 1987 *Montreal Protocol on Substances that Deplete the Ozone Layer*. In terms of climate change, which is both about protection of the environment, and creation of a carbon market and financing system to encourage development of sustainable energy sources, the 1992 *United Nations Framework Convention on Climate Change* (UNFCCC) and its 1987 *Kyoto Protocol* are particularly significant.[160] The 1994 *United Nations Convention to Combat Desertification* (UNCCD) is also important, and will be discussed elsewhere in this book. Treaties on management of outer space and the moon are also relevant.

A second cluster of treaties relates to the protection of biological diversity. Environmental concerns have been raised as rates of species extinction continue to grow, often a result of the destruction of habitat or lack of common parameters for the protection and sustainable use of the earth's biological diversity. A growing body of MEAs exists to coordinate state efforts for the preservation and protection of biological diversity, many of which are administered by UNEP. One of the most significant in the group relating to biological diversity is the 1992 *United Nations Convention on Biological Diversity* which seeks the protection of biodiversity, sustainable use of biological diversity, and sharing of its benefits.[161] Another example is the 1973 *Convention on International Trade in Endangered Species of Flora and Fauna* (CITES), which lists endangered species through a system of Annexes. If a particular species is listed as particularly vulnerable or endangered in one of the Annexes, Parties to the MEA will limit its exploitation, and establish trade restrictions for countries not in compliance with the protection regimes.[162] Further conservation treaties include the *Agreement on the Conservation of African-Eurasian Migratory Waterbirds* (AEWA); the *Agreement on the Conservation of Small Cetaceans of the Baltic & North Seas* (ASCOBANS); the *Agreement on the Conservation of the Black Seas, Mediterranean and Contiguous Atlantic Area* (ACCOBAMS); and the 1979 *Bonn Convention on Migratory Species*, as well as many species-specific accords, such as the 1973 *Oslo Agreement on the Conservation of Polar Bears*. Such

---

[159] For further information, see P. Okawa, *State Responsibility for Transboundary Air Pollution in International Law* (Oxford: Oxford University Press, 2000).

[160] For further exploration, see F. Yamin and J. Depledge, *The International Climate Change Regime: A Guide to Rules, Institutions and Procedures* (Cambridge: Cambridge University Press, 2004). See also P.D. Cameron and D. Zillman, *Kyoto: From Principles to Practice* (The Hague: Kluwer Law International, 2001).

[161] For further resources, see M. Bowman & C. Redgwell, *International Law and the Conservation of Biological Diversity* (The Hague: Kluwer Law International, 1995).

[162] See, e.g., S. Lyster, *International Wildlife Law: An Analysis of International Treaties concerned with the Conservation of Wildlife* (Cambridge: Cambridge University Press, 1985).

treaties often establish joint management regimes for protected areas or ecosystems, and threatened or otherwise significant species.[163]

A third cluster of international treaties have also been agreed to govern hazardous substances and activities, as well as waste. Treaties governing hazardous substances and activities often provide for accident prevention, preparedness and response in transportation and trade of hazardous substances, as well as specific regimes to govern the production, trade and use of chemicals, pesticides and other dangerous substances. These conventions set regimes in place to regulate, and in some cases even ban or control, international trade and use of hazardous and dangerous substances, including chemicals and pesticides.[164] They can help to ensure safe use of hazardous substances, or prevent them from entering a country where such safe use cannot be assured.[165] Environmental law can even apply in situations of war.[166] Chemical- and pesticides-related conventions include the 1987 *Montreal Protocol on Substances that Deplete the Ozone Layer* and its *Multilateral Fund for the Implementation of the Montreal Protocol*; the 1998 *Rotterdam Convention on the Prior Informed Consent Procedure for Certain Hazardous Chemicals and Pesticides in International Trade*, which shares a joint interim secretariat with the UN Food and Agriculture Organization (FAO); and the 2001 *Stockholm Convention on Persistent Organic Pollutants*. Other treaties have been negotiated to address radioactive substances and biotechnology, such as the 2001 *Cartagena Protocol on Biosafety*. Finally, several treaties seek to address the international aspects of prevention and treatment, as well as disposal, recycling and re-use of wastes, especially as they are traded internationally.[167] These include the 1989 *Basel Convention on the Control of Transboundary Movements of Hazardous Wastes and Their Disposal*, and its 1999 *Protocol on Liability and Compensation*.

A fourth cluster of international treaties address regimes to govern the shared management of the oceans and seas.[168] Though much broader than international

---

[163] *Ibid.* And see M. Austen and T. Richards, *Basic Legal Documents on International Animal Welfare and Wildlife Conservation* (The Hague: Kluwer Law International, 2000).

[164] For further exploration, see, e.g., G. Handl and R.E. Lutz, *Transferring Hazardous Technologies and Substances* (The Hague: Kluwer Law International, 1990).

[165] *Ibid.*, and see X. Hanqin, *Transboundary Damage in International Law* (Cambridge: Cambridge University Press, 2003).

[166] J.E. Austin and C.E. Bruch, *The Environmental Consequences of War: Legal, Economic, and Scientific Perspectives* (Cambridge: Cambridge University Press, 2001).

[167] See e.g. K. Kummer, *International Management of Hazardous Wastes – The Basel Convention and Related Legal Rules* (Oxford: Oxford University Press, 1995). And see M. Bowman and A. Boyle, *Environmental Damage in International and Comparative Law – Problems of Definition and Valuation* (Oxford: Oxford University Press, 2002).

[168] R. Churchill and V. Lowe, *The Law of the Sea* (Oxford: Oxford University Press, 1999). See also M. Nordquist and J. Norton Moore, *Current Marine Environmental Issues and the International Tribunal for the Law of the Sea* (Leiden: Martinus Nijhoff, 2001), as well as T. Treves, "The Settlement of Disputes According to the Straddling Stocks Agreement of 1995" and M. Goransson, "Liability for Damage to the Marine Environment" in *International Law and Sustainable Development: Past Achievements and Future Challenges*, A. Boyle and D. Freestone, eds. (Oxford: Oxford University Press, 1999).

environmental law, certain aspects of these fisheries and oceans conventions focus specifically on environmental conservation and protection purposes. An extensive collection of protocols, regional treaties and non-binding but influential guidelines and declarations regulate pollution by dumping, marine pollution from land-based sources, vessels, and sea-bed activities, as well as environmental emergencies and liability and compensation.[169] In this area, the 1983 *United Nations Convention on the Law of the Sea* (UNCLOS) is undoubtedly the most significant, but other accords include an early trajectory of treaties relating to oil pollution, such as the 1954 *International Convention for the Prevention of Pollution of the Sea by Oil*, the 1958 *High Seas Fishing and Conservation Convention*, the 1973 *International Convention for the Prevention of Pollution from Ships* (MARPOL), and over thirty UNEP Regional Seas Conventions, including the 1992 *Convention for the Protection of the Marine Environment of the North-East Atlantic* and the 1992 *Convention on the Protection of the Baltic*.

A fifth cluster governs freshwater resources, it includes principally one recent global treaty, backed by customary law, regional and bilateral rules and other agreements. The 1997 *Convention on the Law of Non-Navigational Uses of International Watercourses* applies to uses of international watercourses and their waters for purposes other than navigation, establishes a framework of principles, and encourages watercourse States to enter into watercourse agreements.[170] Regional treaties include, for example, the 1992 *Convention on the Protection and Use of Transboundary Watercourses and International Laws*, which was negotiated under the auspices of the UN Economic Commission for Europe, and the 1987 *Agreement on the Action Plan for the Environmentally Sound Management of the Common Zambezi River System* among eight African countries, a precedent to the 2000 *Maseru Protocol on Shared Watercourses in the SADC Region*, under the auspices of the South African Development Community (SADC). Many bilateral agreements also exist to manage shared watercourses or watersheds. One classic example is the original 1909 *Washington Treaty Relating to Boundary Waters and Questions Arising Along the Boundary Between the US and Canada* and its later 1978 *Great Lakes Water Quality Agreement*, which established an International Joint Commission, with a Great Lakes Water Quality Board and a Science Advisory Board to assist it.[171]

Other treaties relate to international heritage protection. These include the UNESCO *Man and the Biosphere Programme* (MAB), the *World Heritage Convention* (WHC), the Arctic Council and the 1959 *Antarctic Treaty*. The

---

[169] N. Klein, *Dispute Settlement in the UN Convention on the Law of the Sea* (Cambridge: Cambridge University Press, 2004). And see A. Kirchner, *International Marine Environmental Law: Institutions, Implementation and Innovations* (The Hague: Kluwer Law International, 2003).

[170] For further exploration, see S. McCaffrey, *The Law of International Watercourses – Non-Navigational Uses* (Oxford: Oxford University Press, 2003).

[171] J. Brunnée and S.J. Toope, "Freshwater Regimes: The Mandate of the International Joint Commission" (1998) 15 *Ariz. J. Int'l & Comp. L.* 273.

Antarctic regime is a good example of environmental law in many respects,[172] and includes, the 1972 *Antarctic Seals Convention,* the 1980 *Convention on the Conservation of Antarctic Marine Living Resources,* the 1988 *Convention on the Regulation of Antarctic Mineral Resource Activities,* as well as the 1991 *Protocol on Environmental Protection to the Antarctic Treaty,* as well as the *Arctic Environmental Protection Strategy* and the 1996 *Declaration on the Establishment of the Arctic Council,* which sets up a council on which both the eight circum-Arctic countries, and the Arctic indigenous peoples, are represented. These regimes are being used to conserve important natural areas.

Other environmental treaties have also been developed on the regional level with regard to certain particular techniques of environmental protection,[173] such as the 1991 *Espoo Convention on Environmental Impact Assessment in a Transboundary Context,* or the 1998 *Aarhus Convention on Public Participation, Access to Environmental Information and Access to Justice.* Finally, beyond the scope of this section, a comprehensive new regime of international or "supranational" environmental law has been developed in the European Community,[174] and similar regional environmental cooperation schemes are being attempted elsewhere, as part of political and economic integration projects.

MEAs provide for a variety of specific techniques to implement the agreed international obligations. As Phillipe Sands observes, several of these techniques appear common to most MEAs.[175] Parties will often agree to conduct environmental impact assessments. They will also agree on provisions related to environmental information, requiring data collection and information exchange, reporting and provision of information, consultations, notification of emergency situations, monitoring, access to environmental information, public education and awareness-building, eco-labelling of products, or even eco-auditing and accounting.[176] In addition to increasing understanding of environmental issues, the exchange of information through specific, periodic reporting requirements is one of the most important tools for monitoring the domestic implementation of international environmental obligations. MEAs have institutionalized the col-

---

[172] For further exploration, see K. Bastmeijer, *The Antarctic Environmental Protocol and its Domestic Legal Implementation* (The Hague: Kluwer Law International, 2003).

[173] See, e.g., J. Holder, *Environmental Assessment – Legal Regulation of Decision Making* (Oxford: Oxford University Press, 2003).

[174] For further information on European Community environmental law, see, e.g., T.F.M. Etty and H. Somsen, *Yearbook of European Environmental Law* 4 (Oxford: Oxford University Press, 2004) and earlier editions. See also A. Weale, G. Pridham, M. Cini, D. Konstadakopulos, M. Porter & B. Flynn, *Environmental Governance in Europe – An Ever Closer Ecological Union?* (Oxford: Oxford University Press, 2000).

[175] For an excellent review, see P. Sands, *Principles of International Environmental Law,* 2nd edn. (Cambridge: Cambridge University Press, 2003) at 799–1073. See also A. Timoshenko, *Environmental Negotiator Handbook* (The Hague: Kluwer Law International, 2003).

[176] Some of these strategies are more appropriate in industrialized societies than in the majority of the world. See, e.g., W.M. Lafferty and J. Meadowcroft, *Implementing Sustainable Development – Strategies and Initiatives in High Consumption Societies* (Oxford: Oxford University Press, 2000). But see J. Razzaque, *Public Interest Environmental Litigation in India, Pakistan and Bangladesh* (The Hague: Kluwer Law International, 2004) for a description of other techniques.

lection and distribution of information by creating international bodies (such as clearing houses or secretariats) with explicit information generating and distribution functions. They can also agree on provisions for explicit State or civil liability for environmental damage. Parties will sometimes choose to include trade measures in MEAs, such as restrictions on trade with non-parties.[177] They can also include measures encouraging or permitting the use of subsidies, or restrictions on competition, in order to promote, for example, the development and marketing of environmentally sound technologies. In addition, they may include specific provisions related to investment, public–private partnerships or even insurance. MEAs may agree on certain jointly developed performance-based or product standards; they may also establish mutual recognition systems for existing or future standards. Most MEAs will commit to provide the necessary financial resources for their implementation, or will otherwise establish financing mechanisms that are expected to generate funding for new and additional burdens related to compliance.[178] They often also provide for technology transfer, and technical assistance. Several MEAs have also included provisions on intellectual property. Finally, global MEAs will often provide for regional collaboration to promote capacity-building, enforcement and monitoring, and some provide procedures for use in the event of non-compliance, including party-to-party consultations, peer review processes, or even access to international dispute settlement mechanisms.

National Environmental Management Techniques

To clarify the nature of the international environmental legal regime, it is also necessary to briefly review the nature of national environmental management. This is conducted through a variety of means, including species and habitat conservation measures, environmental taxes and charges, negotiated voluntary agreements, deposit and refund (or take-back) schemes, and also restrictions on certain goods and practices. Environmental standards can play a strong role.

Five specific national environmental management techniques can be highlighted.[179] First, environmental quality standards, which seek to set a certain state of the environment. These are done with the designation of permissible

---

[177] See, e.g., D. Brack, "Multilateral Environmental Agreements: An Overview" in *Trade, Investment and the Environment*, H Ward and D Brack, eds. (London: Royal Institute of International Affairs and Earthscan, 2000).

[178] See, e.g., R.A. Westin, *Environmental Tax Initiative & International Trade Treaties* (New York: Kluwer Law International, 1997). See also A. Kiss, D. Shelton & K. Ishibashi, *Economic Globalization and Compliance with International Environmental Agreements* (The Hague: Kluwer Law International, 2003). And see B.J. Richardson, *Environmental Regulation through Financial Organisations: Comparative Perspectives on the Industrialised Nations* (New York: Kluwer Law International, 2002). In addition, see G. Handl, *Multilateral Development Banking: Environmental Principles and Concepts Reflecting General International Law and Public Policy* (The Hague: Kluwer Law International, 2001).

[179] United Nations Environment Programme (UNEP) and International Institute for Sustainable Development (IISD) *Environment and Trade: A Handbook* (Winnipeg: IISD/UNEP, 2000).

concentrations of substances (pollution) in the air, water or soil, or population standards which require the protection of certain species that have become threatened or endangered. The second are emission standards, which identify the amount of certain substances a facility may emit. The third are product standards, which specify certain characteristics that are deemed necessary to avoid environmental harm from the use or disposal of products. This includes bans on certain chemicals in products, and these standards are often used to protect human health. The fourth are process and production standards, which specify how products are to be produced and what kinds of impact they may have on the environment. Finally, performance standards can require certain actions, such as environmental impact assessment to improve environmental management, but focus mainly on the relative environmental performance of a product itself. The overall effect of all these techniques is to require producers, traders and consumers to consider the environmental impact of the economic decisions they take, internalizing external environmental costs. Market mechanisms such as taxes, charges, tradable permits or subsidies can achieve the same goal, and are often also part of national environmental management systems.[180]

International Environmental Governance

International environmental governance has recently been detailed, clarified and strengthened, through a comprehensive intergovernmental process, which, through an open-ended intergovernmental group of ministers or their representatives, with the United Nations Environment Programme (UNEP) Executive Director as an ex-officio member, was mandated to undertake a comprehensive policy-oriented assessment of existing institutional weaknesses, future needs and options for strengthened international environmental governance, including the financing of the United Nations Environment Programme. The final decision to establish an international environmental governance (IEG) regime,[181] was the result of a ministerial-level intergovernmental process, established by the UNEP governing council, addressing issues and options for strengthening international environmental governance.[182] This group held several consultative meetings, discussing, for example, ways to improve collaboration and coordination between MEAs. It considered the potential to cluster MEAs on sectoral (as for example, among biodiversity-related conventions in the management of ecosystems and species); functional (for example, on trade-related issues); and

---

[180] United Nations Environment Programme (UNEP) and International Institute for Sustainable Development (IISD) *Environment and Trade: A Handbook* (Winnipeg: IISD/UNEP, 2000).

[181] International environmental governance will be mainly carried out through the implementation of the outcomes of UNEP's Governing Council Seventh Special Session, Decision I: International Environment Governance (IEG); ss. VII/1 (15 February 2002), UNGA Res. 57/251.

[182] More information on international environmental governance negotiations can be found at the UNEP website, online: http://www.unep.org/IEG. See also M.-C. Cordonier Segger, A. Khalfan & M. Gehring, *International Environmental Governance for Sustainable Development* (Montreal: CISDL, 2001), available online: <http://www.cisdl.org>.

regional (capacity-building, compliance and enforcement, pooling of resources, and complementary legislation) grounds. To implement such coordination, there would be consultations with the MEAs and specific proposals from them. The group presented a report containing analysis and options to the Governing Council/Global Ministerial Environment Forum. The outcomes of this process were mentioned with approval in the 2002 *Johannesburg Plan of Implementation* (JPOI), although the issue of universal membership was left outstanding for debate in the United Nations General Assembly.[183]

This process defined five essential building blocks for a greatly strengthened global environmental regime. First, UNEP is to be greatly strengthened and secondly, given adequate, more secured financing. As UNEP has been both a deliberative and operational, or at least catalytic agency, this is appropriate. There is also a special role for the Global Environmental Facility (GEF) in terms of financing environmental projects. Thirdly, coordination will be enhanced, including through the further development of an Environmental Management Group (EMG) composed of relevant international organizations and treaty secretariats. Fourthly, there will be "clustering" or collaborative grouping of Multilateral Environmental Agreements (MEAs) along functional and programmatic lines, and streamlining of their meeting schedules. Fifthly, and this call was reinforced by its reference in the JPOI, the General Assembly was invited to consider establishing universal membership for the Governing Council/Global Ministers of Environment Forum (GMEF).[184]

This section does not seek to summarize international environmental law, rather, it simply presents a brief survey of the field to help describe the context and lay a foundation for an exploration of its intersections with international social and economic law.[185]

---

[183] Universal membership in the UNEP Governing Council would essentially mean ratification of the Global Ministers of the Environment Forum and provide the foundations for a potential global environmental organization.

[184] JPOI, *supra* note 5 at Chapter XI, IEG, *supra* note 181.

[185] For further exploration of this important field of international law, the authors recommend D. Hunter, D. Zaelke, & J. Salzman, *International Environmental Law and Policy* (New York: Foundation Press, 2001), A. Kiss and D. Shelton, *International Environmental Law* (New York: Transnational Publishers, 2000) and also P. Sands, *Principles of International Environmental Law*, 2nd edn. (Cambridge: Cambridge University Press, 2003). For a civil law perspective, see C. Dommen and P. Cullet, *Droit International de L'Environment, Textes de base et reference* (The Hague: Kluwer Law International, 2001).

PART II

THE PRINCIPLES

5

Principles of International Law Relating to Sustainable Development *

In recent years discussions of the role of international law in sustainable development have expanded considerably.[1] Increasing numbers of international treaties, particularly in the fields of international economic and environmental law, have set sustainable development as an objective or part of their purposes.[2] International human rights law is increasingly being applied to sustainable development concerns such as poverty eradication and environmental protection,

---

* The authors acknowledge and thank Witold Tymowski for his contributions to this section.

[1] These include, *inter alia*, a report by the *World Commission on Environment and Development Experts Group on Environmental Law* (1987), the 1992 *Rio Declaration on Environment and Development*, Report of the *United Nations Conference on Environment and Development*, UN Doc. A/CONF.151/6/Rev.1, (1992), 31 ILM 874 (1992), final documents of various large UN Conferences, including the 18th *UNGA Special Session on International Economic Co-operation* (1990), the Vienna *World Conference on Human Rights* (1993), the Cairo *UN Conference on Population and Development* (1994), the Beijing *UN Womens Conference* (1995) and the Copenhagen *Social Summit* (1995), the *Agenda for Development* by the UN Secretary General (1995); the *Report of the Expert Group Meeting on Identification of Principles of International Law for Sustainable Development*, UN Secretariat, September 1995, International Law Association committee research seminar publications, including "*The Right to Development in International Law*" (1992), "*Sustainable Development and Good Governance*" (1995), and "*International Economic Law with a Human Face*" (1997); the UNEP *Position Papers on International Environmental Law Aimed at Sustainable Development*, UNEP (1997) and *Montevideo Programmes II and III* (2000), and the *Earth Charter* (2000).

[2] See *United Nations Framework Convention on Climate Change*, 9 May 1992, 31 ILM 849 [hereinafter *Climate Change Convention*], *United Nations Convention on Biological Diversity*, 5 June 1992, 31 ILM 822, Arts. 8 & 10 [hereinafter *Biodiversity Convention*], *Convention to Combat Desertification in Those Countries Experiencing Serious Drought and/or Desertification, particularly in Africa*, 17 June 1994, 33 ILM 1328, Arts. 4 & 5 [hereinafter *Desertification Convention*]. See also the *United Nations Convention on the Non-Navigational Uses of International Watercourses*, UN Doc. A/51/869 (1997) [hereinafter *Watercourses Convention*]. See also several trade treaties that recognize the promotion of sustainable development as a preambular objective, including the *North American Free Trade Agreement*, (Canada-USA-Mexico) (adopted 17 Dec. 1992, entered into force 1 Jan. 1994) (1993) 32 ILM 289 and 32 ILM 605; the *Free Trade Agreement between Canada and Costa Rica* (Canada-Costa Rica) (adopted 23 Apr. 2001, entered into force 1 Nov. 2002) *La Gaceta of Costa Rica*, No. 127 (3 July 2002); and the *United States–Chile Free Trade Agreement* (USA-Chile) (adopted 6 June 2003, entered into force 1 Jan. 2004) (www.ustr.gov/new/fta/chile.htm (18 May 2004)). And see several regional sustainable development treaties, such as the 2002 *Antigua Convention for Co-operation in the Protection and Sustainable Development of the Marine and Coastal Environment of the North East Pacific* (18 Feb. 2002) (not yet in force), which includes a legally binding definition of sustainable development, and the 1995 *Chiang Rai Agreement on Co-operation for the Sustainable Development of the Mekong River Basin* (5 Apr. 1995) 34 ILM 864.

in particular through growing recognition of social, economic, and cultural rights. The decisions of international courts and tribunals are beginning to explicitly recognize sustainable development goals and instruments,[3] and its concepts are increasingly being invoked before national courts and tribunals around the world.[4]

The question remains as to whether, in this changing context, the international principles related to sustainable development are sufficiently substantive at this time to be capable of establishing the basis of an international cause for action.[5] There is an emerging body of legal principles, and treaties based on these principles, which can facilitate reconciliation between social, environmental and economic norms and regimes. Their integrated social, economic and environmental purposes are often focused on development of a resource or resolution of a development challenge, in a more sustainable way. Can such principles give rise to an international customary legal obligation, the violation of which would give rise to a legal remedy? To answer this question, it is important to identify substantive principles of international law related to sustainable development, consider whether they have a "fundamentally norm-creating character such as could be regarded as forming the basis of a general rule of law", and to analyse the practice and *opinio juris* of States.[6] Not all principles of international law on

---

[3] See *Case Concerning the Gabčíkovo-Nagymaros Project (Hungary/Slovakia)* (1997), ICJ Rep. 7), [hereinafter *Gabčíkovo-Nagymaros*], *Advisory Opinion on the Legality of the Use by a State of Nuclear Weapons in Armed Conflict*, [1996] ICJ Rep. 226 at 438 [hereinafter *Nuclear Weapons*] and *Certain Phosphate Lands in Nauru (Nauru/Australia)* (1993), ICJ Rep. 322. See also *United States – Import Prohibition of Certain Shrimp and Shrimp Products*, 20 Sept. 1999, WTO Doc. WT/DS58/AB/R (Appellate Body Report) [hereinafter *Shrimp Turtle*], for example, and *LCB v. United Kingdom* (1999) 27 EHRR 212.

[4] See, for example, the cases of *Bulankulama v. The Secretary, Ministry of Industrial Development* (2000) Vol 7, No. 2 South Asian Environmental Law Reporter 1 (Sri Lankan Supreme Court) and *Shehla Zia and others v. WAPDA*, Case No 15-K of 1992 (Pakistan Supreme Court).

[5] See W. Lang, ed., *Sustainable Development and International Law* (London: Martinus Nijhoff/ Graham & Trotman, 1995) [hereinafter *Lang*], P. Sands, "International Law in the Field of Sustainable Development" (1994) 65 *Byb. I. L.* 303, and H. McGoldrick, "Sustainable Development: The Challenge to International Law" (1994) *Review of European Community and International Environmental Law* 3. See also A. Boyle and D. Freestone, *International Law and Sustainable Development: Past Achievements and Future Challenges* (Oxford: Oxford University Press, 1999), which questions whether "sustainable development", in itself, can be considered a principle of international law, but suggests that certain substantive or procedural elements of sustainable development may become principles. For more recent anthologies of judges, scholars and other experts, see M.-C. Cordonier Segger and C.G. Weeramantry, *Sustainable Justice: Reconciling Economic, Social and Environmental Law* (Leiden: Martinus Nijhoff, 2004), and see N. Schrijver and F. Weiss, *International Law and Sustainable Development* (Leiden: Martinus Nijhoff, 2004).

[6] *North Sea Continental Shelf Cases (Federal Republic of Germany/Denmark; Federal Republic of Germany/Netherlands)* (1969) ICJ Rep. 3 at 4. See also *Military and Paramilitary Activities Case (Nicaragua v. United States)* [1986] ICJ Rep. 14 at 99–101. See International Law Association, *London Statement of Principles Relating to the Formation of General Customary International Law* (London: ILA, 2000). And see M. Mendelson, "The Formation of Customary International Law" (1998) 272 *R.d.C.* 155. But see M. Byers, *Custom, Power and the Power of Rules* (Cambridge: Cambridge University Press, 1999); and see P. Allot, "The Concept of International Law", in M. Byers, ed., *The Role of Law in International Politics: Essays in International Relations and International Law* (Oxford: Oxford University Press, 2000) at 76.

sustainable development, or reflected in recent treaties related to sustainable development have also been recognized as international customary law.

The following section suggests that a body of substantive principles of sustainable development law is emerging, supported by distinctive procedural elements. These principles have a normative character in international law, they generate obligations (requirements to act or not act) or rights (permissions to act or not act) for the states that are bound by them. They can play a role in interpretation or application of international law. The principles help to resolve disputes related to sustainable development, and to guide law and policy at the intersections of international environmental, social and economic norms towards development that can last.[7]

The international processes described earlier are culminating in a general, though not universal, acceptance of a type of normative power for sustainable development. In the aftermath of the *World Summit on Sustainable Development*, there can be legitimate expectations that States and other actors will make good faith efforts to live up to their global commitments to sustainable development. However, much could be gained from further elaboration of a more coherent legal concept of sustainable development, especially as bundles of rights and norms that are beginning to be reflected in international negotiations, treaties and the decisions of tribunals. As explained above, the changing structure of international law has allowed a multiplicity of actors, both State and non-State, to generate knowledge and participate in the development of sustainable development discourse through domestic and international legal systems. Greater international recognition of norms and principles holds the potential to further strengthen

> A substantive body of legal norms has developed, supported by distinctive procedural elements, that can reconcile perceived conflict and guide further integration at the intersection of environmental, social and economic law.

---

[7] For guidance on how international law can resolve overlaps between customary norms and treaty law related to sustainable development, with a focus on the environmental aspects, through application of the terms of the 1969 *Vienna Convention on the Law of Treaties*, especially Arts. 30 and 31, see P. Sands, "Sustainable Development: Treaty, Custom and the Cross-fertilization of International Law" in A. Boyle and D. Freestone, *International Law and Sustainable Development: Past Achievements and Future Challenges* (Oxford: Oxford University Press, 1999). See also a similar chapter by P. Sands, "International Law and Sustainable Development" in R. Revesz, P. Sands & R. Stewart, *Environmental Law, the Economy and Sustainable Development* (Cambridge: Cambridge University Press, 2000). The traditional rules are hard pressed to reconcile conflicts between broader legal regimes, overlapping mandates or acts of international organizations, or intersecting customary norms. While certain specific conflicts of norms may be satisfactorily resolved through careful drafting of international instruments, or through the traditional rules of public international law enshrined in the *Vienna Convention on the Law of Treaties*, and international law of state responsibility, broader intersections between regimes, particularly regimes related to sustainable development, might better be reconciled with a principled approach. Traditional conflict rules, in public international law, address conflicts of treaties, *jus cogens* norms and customary norms dealing with the same subject matter. For an excellent discussion of conflicts of norms emerging from the field of international economic law, see J. Pauwelyn, *Conflict of Norms in Public International Law: How the WTO Relates to Other Rules of International Law* (Cambridge: Cambridge University Press, 2003).

sustainable development law.[8] Emerging mainly from "soft-law instruments", such as declarations and international statements, such principles are starting to assert certain persuasive force.[9] But much more work is needed to properly analyse and understand the implications and level of acceptance of each, in international law, even as increasing use of and compliance with these norms contributes to the unfolding process of sustainable development.[10] The 2002 *Principles of International Law Related to Sustainable Development*, recently identified by the Committee on the Legal Aspects of Sustainable Development of the International Law Association, provide a useful starting point. These will be examined in this section.

Over the course of a decade of legal scholarship and debate, efforts have been made by the International Law Association (ILA), and elsewhere, to identify general substantive and procedural principles of international law for sustainable development.[11] In the 2002 *New Delhi Declaration on the Principles of International Law Related to Sustainable Development*,[12] the ILA Committee on the Legal Aspects of Sustainable Development identified seven principles in particular. The text of the New Delhi Declaration is excerpted below.

---

[8] M. Decleris, *The Law of Sustainable Development: General Principles, A Report for the European Commission* (Brussels: European Commission, 2000) at 14.

[9] But see V. Lowe, "Sustainable Development and Unsustainable Arguments" in A. Boyle and D. Freestone, *International Law and Sustainable Development: Past Achievements and Future Challenges* (Oxford: Oxford University Press, 1999), where it is argued that there are still real questions about how several proposed principles related to sustainable development, such as inter-generational equity, or sustainable use, can be applied in practice. Lowe suggests that "the careful elaboration of a coherent concept of sustainable development could make a crucial contribution to the ability of the international legal system to . . . rise to the challenges that face it."

[10] This is not to say that all proposed principles must be present in conjunction in order to facilitate sustainable development, nor that application of a principle, alone, can somehow ensure that a regime is sustainable. Indeed, depending on the particular context and circumstances, it may not be necessary to invoke certain principles. For example, the principle of "common but differentiated responsibility" may not be applicable where members of a sustainable development regime are all developing countries at similar levels of development, or where members have a common historical trajectory in relation to a particular challenge.

[11] In particular, see United Nations, *Report of the Expert Group Meeting on Identification of Principles of International Law for Sustainable Development* (UN Secretariat, Sept. 1995); UNEP, *Position Papers on International Environmental Law Aimed at Sustainable Development* (1997) and *Montevideo Programmes II and III* (2000); and Earth Council, *The Earth Charter* (2000). These also include, *inter alia*, a report by the *World Commission on Environment and Development Experts Group on Environmental Law* (1987), the *Rio Declaration* (1992), final documents of various large UN Conferences, including the 18th UNGA Special Session on International Economic Co-operation (1990), the Vienna World Conference on Human Rights (1993), the Cairo UN Conference on Population and Development (1994), the Beijing UN Womens Conference (1995), the Copenhagen Social Summit (1995), and UN Secretary General, *The Agenda for Development* (1995). See also efforts by environmental law experts to clarify principles, such as IUCN – The World Conservation Union Commission on Environmental Law/ICEL – International Council of Environmental Law, No. 31 *Draft International Covenant on Environment and Development* (Bonn: IUCN, 1995) and 2nd edn.: *Updated Text, IUCN Environmental Law and Policy Series* (Bonn: IUCN, 2000).

[12] Most notably, see International Law Association 2002 *New Delhi Declaration on Principles of International Law Relating to Sustainable Development* (London: ILA, 2002). See ILA Resolution 3/2002: *New Delhi Declaration Of Principles Of International Law Relating to Sustainable Devel-*

NEW DELHI DECLARATION OF PRINCIPLES OF INTERNATIONAL LAW
RELATING TO SUSTAINABLE DEVELOPMENT

The duty of States to ensure sustainable use of natural resources

It is a well-established principle that, in accordance with international law, all States have the sovereign right to manage their own natural resources pursuant to their own environmental and developmental policies, and the responsibility to ensure that activities within their jurisdiction or control do not cause significant damage to the environment of other States or of areas beyond the limits of national jurisdiction.

States are under a duty to manage natural resources, including natural resources solely within their own territory or jurisdiction, in a rational, sustainable and safe way so as to contribute to the development of their peoples, with particular regard for the rights of indigenous peoples, and to the conservation and sustainable use of natural resources and the protection of the environment, including ecosystems. States must take into account the needs of future generations in determining the rate of use of natural resources. All relevant actors (including States, industrial concerns and other components of civil society) are under a duty to avoid wasteful use of natural resources and promote waste minimization policies.

The protection, preservation and enhancement of the natural environment, particularly the proper management of climate system, biological diversity and fauna and flora of the Earth, are the common concern of humankind. The resources of outer space and celestial bodies and of the sea-bed, ocean floor and subsoil thereof beyond the limits of national jurisdiction are the common heritage of humankind.

The principle of equity and the eradication of poverty

The principle of equity is central to the attainment of sustainable development. It refers to both *inter-generational equity* (the rights of future generations to enjoy a fair level of the common patrimony) and *intra-generational equity* (the rights of all peoples within the current generation of fair access to the current generation's entitlement to the Earth's natural resources).

The present generation has a right to use and enjoy the resources of the Earth but is under an obligation to take into account the long-term impact of its activities and to sustain the resource base and the global environment for the benefit of future generations of humankind. "Benefit" in this context is to be understood in its broadest meaning as including, *inter alia*, economic, environmental, social and intrinsic benefit.

opment, in ILA, *Report of the Seventieth Conference, New Delhi* (London: ILA, 2002). Available online: http://www.ila-hq.org and excerpted here. See also "ILA New Delhi Declaration of Principles of International Law Relating to Sustainable Development" in Kluwer Academic Publishers, *International Environmental Agreements: Politics, Law and Economics* 2, 2 2002, 209–216, available online: http://www.kluweronline.com/issn/1567–9764/current. And see N. Schrijver, and F. Weiss, "Editorial" in (2002) 2:2 *International Environmental Agreement: Politics, Law and Economics* 105–8; online: http://www.kluweronline.com/issn/1567-9764/current. See also N. Schrijver and F. Weiss, *International Law and Sustainable Development* (Leiden: Martinus Nijhoff, 2004), 699.

The right to development must be implemented so as to meet developmental and environmental needs of present and future generations in a sustainable and equitable manner. This includes the duty to cooperate for the eradication of poverty in accordance with Chapter IX on International Economic and Social Co-operation of the Charter of the *United Nations and the Rio Declaration on Environment and Development* as well as the duty to cooperate for global sustainable development and the attainment of equity in the development opportunities of developed and developing countries.

Whilst it is the primary responsibility of the State to aim for conditions of equity within its own population and to ensure, as a minimum, the eradication of poverty, all States which are in a position to do so have a further responsibility, as recognised by the Charter of the United Nations and the Millennium Declaration of the United Nations, to assist States in achieving this objective.

The principle of common but differentiated responsibilities

States and other relevant actors have common but differentiated responsibilities. All States are under a duty to cooperate in the achievement of global sustainable development and the protection of the environment. International organizations, corporations (including in particular transnational corporations), non-governmental organizations and civil society should cooperate in and contribute to this global partnership. Industrial concerns have also responsibilities pursuant to the polluter pays principle.

Differentiation of responsibilities, whilst principally based on the contribution that a State has made to the emergence of environmental problems, must also take into account the economic and developmental situation of the State, in accordance with paragraph 3.3.

The special needs and interests of developing countries and of countries with economies in transition, with particular regard to least developed countries and those affected adversely by environmental, social and developmental considerations, should be recognized.

Developed countries bear a special burden of responsibility in reducing and eliminating unsustainable patterns of production and consumption and in contributing to capacity-building in developing countries, *inter alia* by providing financial assistance and access to environmentally sound technology. In particular, developed countries should play a leading role and assume primary responsibility in matters of relevance to sustainable development.

The principle of the precautionary approach to human health, natural resources and ecosystems

A precautionary approach is central to sustainable development in that it commits States, international organizations and the civil society, particularly the scientific and business communities, to avoid human activity which may cause significant harm to human health, natural resources or ecosystems, including in the face of scientific uncertainty.

Sustainable development requires that a precautionary approach with regard to human health, environmental protection and sustainable utilization of natural resources should include accountability for harm caused (including, where appropriate, State responsibility), planning based on clear criteria and well-defined goals, consideration of all possible means in an environmental impact assessment to achieve an objective (including, in certain instances, not proceeding with an envisaged activity) and, in respect of activities which may cause serious long-term or irreversible harm, establishing an appropriate burden of proof on the person or persons carrying out (or intending to carry out) the activity.

Decision-making processes should endorse a precautionary approach to risk management and in particular should proceed to the adoption of appropriate precautionary measures even when the absence of risk seems scientifically assured.

Precautionary measures should be based on up-to-date and independent scientific judgment and be transparent. They should not result in economic protectionism. Transparent structures should be established which involve all interested parties, including non-state actors, in the consultation process. Appropriate review by a judicial body or administrative action should be available.

The principle of public participation and access to information and justice

Public participation is essential to sustainable development and good governance in that it is a condition of responsive, transparent and accountable governments as well a condition for the active engagement of equally responsive, transparent and accountable civil society organizations, including industrial concerns and trade unions. The vital role of women in sustainable development should be recognized.

Public participation in the context of sustainable development requires effective protection of the human right to hold and express opinions and to seek, receive and impart ideas. It also requires a right of access to appropriate, comprehensible and timely information held by governments and commerce on economic and social policies regarding the sustainable use of natural resources and the protection of the environment, without imposing undue financial burdens upon the applicants and with due consideration for privacy and adequate protection of business confidentiality.

The empowerment of peoples in the context of sustainable development requires access to effective judicial or administrative procedures in the State where the measure has been taken to challenge such measure and to claim compensation. States should ensure that where transboundary harm has been, or is likely to be, caused, individuals and peoples affected have non-discriminatory access to the same judicial and administrative procedures as would individuals and peoples of the State from which the harm is caused if such harm occurred in that State.

The principle of good governance

The principle of good governance is essential to the progressive development and codification of international law relating to sustainable development. It commits States and international organizations:

(a) to adopt democratic and transparent decision-making procedures and financial accountability;
(b) to take effective measures to combat official or other corruption;
(c) to respect due process in their procedures and to observe the rule of law and human rights; and
(d) to implement a public procurement approach according to the WTO Code on Public Procurement.

Civil society and non-governmental organizations have a right to good governance by States and international organizations. Non-state actors should be subject to internal democratic governance and to effective accountability.

Good governance requires full respect for the principles of the 1992 *Rio Declaration on Environment and Development* as well as the full participation of women in all levels of decision-making. Good governance also calls for corporate social responsibility and socially responsible investments as conditions for the existence of a global market aimed at a fair distribution of wealth among and within communities.

The principle of integration and interrelationship, in particular in relation to human rights and social, economic and environmental objectives

The principle of integration reflects the interdependence of social, economic, financial, environmental and human rights aspects of principles and rules of international law relating to sustainable development as well as of the needs of current and future generations of humankind.

All levels of governance – global, regional, national, sub-national and local – and all sectors of society should implement the integration principle, which is essential to the achievement of sustainable development.

States should strive to resolve apparent conflicts between competing economic, financial, social and environmental considerations, whether through existing institutions or through the establishment of appropriate new ones.

In their interpretation and application, the above principles are interrelated and each of them should be construed in the context of the other principles of this Declaration. Nothing in this Declaration shall be construed as prejudicing in any manner the provisions of the Charter of the United Nations and the rights of peoples under that Charter.

After the *World Summit for Sustainable Development*, greater attention is being paid to these international principles as they can offer substantive guidance when it seems difficult to integrate environmental, economic and social development objectives and regimes. This section will examine these principles in greater detail, from the perspective that they form part of an emerging body of law that can deliver on the objective of sustainable development, with sources in environmental, human rights, and economic law.

The principle of integration and interrelationship will be considered first, as it provides a conceptual framework for "integrated thinking" in international law relating to sustainable development, which can guide consideration of the other principles. The integration of environmental, economic and social law in international regimes is part of an incremental, nuanced process. It is not a matter of joining three areas of law into one. There is no one chronological linear progression toward integration, nor is there necessarily a single "pull" toward greater integration as such, except in certain specific situations. Rather, there are particular patterns to this weaving of social, environmental and economic bodies of law, patterns that are also greatly influenced by different conditions, requirements and policy choices of each specific context.

THE PRINCIPLE OF INTEGRATION AND INTERRELATIONSHIP IN
RELATION TO SOCIAL, ECONOMIC AND ENVIRONMENTAL
OBJECTIVES

The concept of sustainable development integrates economic, environmental and social (including human rights) priorities. As a point of departure, international sustainable development law addresses the area of intersection between three fields of international economic, environmental and social law. As such not all aspects of international environmental law are international sustainable development law. For example, as noted by Alan Boyle and David Freestone, animal rights, the conservation of "charismatic megafauna", and trans-boundary environmental disputes do not necessarily deal with issues of sustainable development.[13] The same may be true for various aspects of international trade, tax, financial or investment law in the economic field, or certain specific laws for the international protection of human rights, social development or humanitarian assistance in the social field. As not all international law in these three areas is (or even needs to be) integrated, the term "sustainable development law" refers to a specific, narrower set of legal instruments and provisions where environment, social and economic considerations are integrated to varying degrees in different circumstances. And by extension, the principle of integration is fundamental to sustainable development law.

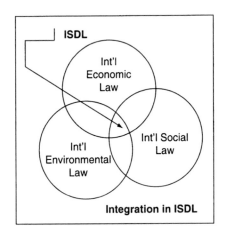

The need for integration was strongly reinforced and highlighted in the 2002 *World Summit on Sustainable Development* (WSSD). Indeed, in the 2002 *Johannesburg Declaration on Sustainable Development*, states assumed "a collective responsibility to advance and strengthen the interdependent and mutually reinforcing pillars of sustainable development – economic development, social development and environmental protection...". In the *Johannesburg Plan of Implementation* (JPOI), this recognition also appears in numerous instances, for example at paragraph 2, stating the objectives of the JPOI, governments accord that it "will promote the integration of the three components of sustainable development – economic development, social development and environmental protection – as interdependent and mutually reinforcing pillars".[14] Is a "collective

---

[13] A. Boyle and D. Freestone, "Past Achievements and Future Challenges" in *Lang, supra* note 5 at 6.

[14] See *Johannesburg Declaration on Sustainable Development*, in Report of the *World Summit on Sustainable Development*, Johannesburg, South Africa, 26 Aug.–4 Sept. 2002, A/CONF.199/20 (New

responsibility" to "promote the integration of the three components of sustainable development" also a legal norm, though? What would be the formulation of such a rule? Is there a formulation of "fundamentally norm-creating character", and if so, is there enough practice, and *opinio juris*, to allow it to be described as an emerging customary norm?

There may be a useful normative formulation of this principle. In the negative, it would be based on a three-fold obligation relating specifically to the need to take all three aspects into account in development decision-making. As such, the norm would hold that States must "ensure that social and economic development decisions do not disregard environmental considerations, and not undertake environmental protection without taking into account relevant social and economic implications". While the exact formulation and application of this norm would vary according to the circumstances of its use, its general purpose would be to ensure the necessary integration between social, economic and environmental policies and laws, responding to the "collective responsibility" assumed by States in the *Johannesburg Declaration*.

From this obligation would flow several increasingly accepted procedures, practices and instruments of sustainable development law. For example, the use of sustainability or "integrated" impact assessments, described in more detail in Part III, can ensure that economic development decisions (including decisions about policies, plans, programmes or projects) consider, and do not ignore, their potential social and environmental impacts. From this principle, too, would stem the reverse sustainable development obligations for environmental protection not to be carried out without consideration of relevant social and economic aspects. For example, decision-making bodies for conservation projects, such as large parks, should ensure that their plans provide for, or even have the prior informed consent of, local peoples and other socially vulnerable groups who could be affected by the new park boundaries and restrictions. A project that did not do so would be violating the second part of this principle, the obligation not to consider environmental protection in isolation from its social and economic implications. The creation of "inter-locking mechanisms", such as environmental or social units in international development organizations, or the World Bank Inspection Panel, to monitor and investigate the social and environmental implications of their economic development projects, would be likewise encouraged, supported and even potentially required by this norm.

Emergence of the principle

The need for the integration of social and economic development and environmental policy permeates soft law, including the 1972 *Stockholm Declaration*,

York: United Nations, 2002). See also *Johannesburg Plan of Implementation*, Report of the *World Summit on Sustainable Development*, Johannesburg, South Africa, 4 Sept. 2002, UN Doc. A/CONF.199/20: <http://www.un.org/esa/sustdev/documents/WSSD_POI_PD/English/POIToc.htm>.

the 1992 *Rio Declaration* and *Agenda 21*, and, as mentioned above, the 2002 *Johannesburg Declaration* and *Plan of Implementation*.

Principle 4 of the 1992 *Rio Declaration* States that "in order to achieve sustainable development, environmental protection shall constitute an integral part of the development process and cannot be considered in isolation from it".[15] As a consensus statement negotiated and signed by over 160 countries, this indicates that States agree that social and economic development should integrate environmental protection.[16] The Principle 4 argument that environmental protection cannot be considered in isolation advocates integrated consideration of these fields at the international level, in policy and in law. This view is supported by the language of Chapter 39 of *Agenda 21*, where States commit to focus on the "further development of international law on sustainable development, giving special attention to the delicate balance between environmental and developmental concerns"; and recognize an important

"need to clarify and strengthen the relationship between existing international instruments or agreements in the field of environment and relevant social and economic agreements or instruments, taking into account the special needs of the developing countries."[17]

After the Rio de Janeiro Earth Summit, integration of laws and policies in these areas was directly addressed in many global treaties, using different textual formulations depending on the context and purpose of the instruments. It is a keystone provision in two of the 1992 *Rio Conventions* (the *UN Framework Convention on Climate Change* and the *UN Convention on Biological Diversity*).[18] Most of the post-Rio environmental conventions contain specific substantive provisions which aim to address relevant social and economic considerations related to their purpose and object. Some even do it to the extent that they move away from being simply environmental conventions at all, and can be considered sustainable development conventions instead, whose integrated social, economic and environmental purpose focuses on the development of a resource or address a development challenge, in a sustainable way. Examples of such treaties might include the 1994 *United Nations Convention to Combat Desertification in Countries Experiencing Serious Drought and/or Desertification, Particularly in Africa*, and the 1997 *United Nations Convention on the Non-Navigational Uses of International Watercourses*.[19]

---

[15] *Rio Declaration, supra* note 1, Principle 4. See also the *Stockholm Declaration on the Human Environment*, UN Doc. A/C. 48/14 (1972), 11 ILM 1461 (1972) Principle 13 [hereinafter *Stockholm Declaration*].

[16] European Commission, *The Law of Sustainable Development* (Brussels: EC, 2001).

[17] *Agenda 21*, Report of the UNCED, I (1992) UN Doc. A/CONF.151/26/Rev.1, (1992) 31 ILM 874, para. 39.1 [hereinafter *Agenda 21*], ch. 39.1, Objectives (a) and (b).

[18] See the *Climate Change Convention, supra* note 2, Art. 3(4), with *Kyoto Protocol to the United Nations Framework Convention on Climate Change*, 10 Dec. 1997, 37 ILM 22 (1998), Art. 4(1)(f) [hereinafter *Kyoto Protocol*]; and the *Biodiversity Convention, supra* note 2, Art. 6.

[19] See the *Desertification Convention*, Art. 4(2) and the *Watercourses Convention, supra* note 2.

International scholarship in various fields notes a trend toward integration, at the international level. This refers to integration in the sense that economies and societies are becoming more integrated, on the international level (also some-times called the "globalization" phenomenon). For example, according to Alexandre Kiss:

"[e]vidence of global integration abounds: regional trading units; regional political and economic organizations... international regimes covering issues ranging from banking and trade to human rights, environmental protection, and arms control; and the spread of financial markets. The information revolution, the rapid technological advances, global environmental problems, liberalized trade, and other economic and other interdependencies compel greater interdependency and greater integration."[20]

Such a trend is clearly emerging. However, there is a second meaning to integration, one that seems closer to what is intended in the 1992 *Rio Declaration*, which looks to integration between economic and social law and policy, and environmental law and policy. This type of integration is not simply a trend or a "coming together", on the international level, but rather, a need to undertake development in a way that fully takes into account, and combines, its social, economic and environmental aspects. It is a challenging requirement for research, planning, law-making and judicial decision-making. Indeed, as noted by one commentator, "if there is no longer much doubt about whether integrative approaches to research are needed in support of a sustainability transition, how to achieve such integration in rigorous and useful programs remains problematic."[21]

Application of the principle

One of the particularly difficult conceptual aspects of the integration and interrelationship principle is that not all treaties, or other actions of states in international law, integrate social, economic and environmental considerations to the same extent, or in the same way. The norm is applied in ways that are extremely specific to the context and purpose of the international instrument or commitment in question. However, to assist in the analysis of integration, a conceptual "continuum" can be proposed, one which describes and tracks the degree to which international regimes integrate economic, social and environmental law. Four degrees of integration can be identified in particular. These range from regimes that envisage international economic, social and environmental law as separate, independent fields to regimes that fully integrate these

---

[20] A. Kiss, "The Implications of Global Change for the International Legal System" in E. Brown Weiss, ed., *Environmental Change and International Law* (Tokyo: United Nations University Press, 1992) 319, 345.

[21] W.C. Clark "A Transition towards Sustainability" (2001 Symposium: Environment 2000 – New Issues for a New Century, Sustainable Science for a Sustainable Environment) (2001) 27 *Ecology L.Q.* 1021.

three areas of law. These integrated instruments and principles, and their components in other regimes, form the corpus of international sustainable development law (ISDL).

Separate spheres

Many international economic, social and environmental regimes engage one field of law in particular, with little integration presently sought or expected. In this instance, the regime is not held to have particular significance for the other sustainable development priorities, and as such, there is little pressure to integrate the three spheres of economic, environmental and social law. For example, an important instrument for social law in the international criminal law instruments, the *Rome Statute of the International Criminal Court*,[22] does not include many significant environmental or economic provisions.

Parallel yet interdependent

At this degree of integration, a core agreement in one field of law exists in parallel with additional, complementary accords in the other areas of law. This parallel yet interdependent relationship exists in order to allow the whole package to proceed on a policy level, but interlinkages between the elements can be weak or almost non-existent. For example, environment and labour agreements can run parallel to trade liberalisation agreements, as does the *North America Free Trade Agreement* (NAFTA) and its North American Commission for Environmental Cooperation and North American Labour Cooperation Agreement,[23] as well as the Environmental Side Agreements to the Canada-Chile and the Canada-Costa Rica Free Trade Accords.[24]

Partially integrated spheres

Certain international legal rules are progressing toward greater integration, whereby instruments emerging primarily in one field of law are slowly taking into account and integrating social, economic or environmental priorities. In these instances, the changing views of developing or developed country governments, sometimes due to pressure from civil society or industry, are forcing a gradual integration of the missing elements of sustainable development into the

---

[22] *Rome Statute of the International Criminal Court*, 17 July 1998, UN Doc. A/CONF.183/9 (1980).

[23] *North America Agreement on Environmental Cooperation* (Washington, Ottawa, Mexico City), 8, 9, 14 September 1993, in force 1 Jan. 1994; 32 ILM (1993) 1480 [hereinafter *NAAEC*]. For commentary, see M.-C. Cordonier Segger and M. Leichner Reynal, eds., *Beyond the Barricades: An Americas Trade and Sustainability Agenda* (Aldershot: Ashgate Press, 2005, forthcoming).

[24] For an exploration of these regional relationships, and their contribution to sustainable development in the Americas, see M.-C. Cordonier Segger *et al.*, *Ecological Rules and Sustainability in the Americas* (Winnipeg: IISD/UNEP, 2002); and M.-C. Cordonier Segger *et al.*, *Social Rules and Sustainability in the Americas* (Winnipeg: IISD/OAS, 2004). See also M.-C. Cordonier Segger, "Sustainable Development in the Negotiation of the Free Trade Area of the Americas" (2004) 27 *Fordham Int'l. L. J.* 1118.

regime. Thus, actors in international legal regimes once thought to be isolated or concerned only with a particular domain are becoming cognizant of linkages with other areas, and designing particular, context-specific manners to take these linkages into account. An example of this process is the integration of environmental considerations and health issues into trade laws, such as those of the World Trade Organization (WTO), through recent decisions of the WTO Appellate Body.[25] These "partially integrated" instruments may use or mandate the use of "inter-locking" institutions or "integrative" mechanisms, such as specific impact assessment processes, inspection panels, information exchange devices or units whose responsibility it is to liaise with and report to the other regimes. In another instance, one regime, meant specifically to address priorities in one field, might use instruments or measures developed and tested in other fields to achieve its purposes. There are many examples, including the successful use of trade measures for the purpose of environmental protection in the 1987 *Montreal Protocol on Substances that Deplete the Ozone Layer*[26] and the 1985 *Vienna Convention for the Protection of the Ozone Layer*,[27] or the linkage between human rights and environmental matters in the 1998 UN/ECE *Aarhus Convention on Access to Information, Public Participation in Decision-making and Access to Justice in Environmental Matters*, which also acknowledges an obligation to future generations and seeks to achieve sustainable development through the involvement of all stakeholders.

Highly integrated new regimes

Finally, certain highly integrated sustainable development law treaties and instruments are now emerging. Such integrated regimes include consideration of social, economic and environmental aspects of a problem, often in the negotiations process, the provisions of the final accord, and eventually in the decisions of their dispute settlement mechanisms. Few complete examples exist, but perhaps one of the treaties worth further review is the 1994 *United Nations Convention to Combat Desertification in Countries Experiencing Serious*

[25] See e.g. *European Communities – Measures Affecting Asbestos and Asbestos-Containing Products (Complaint by Canada)* (18 Sept. 2000), WTO Doc. WT/DS135/R (Panel Report) [hereinafter *Asbestos*]. For commentary, see M.-C. Cordonier Segger and M. Gehring, "The WTO Asbestos Cases and Precaution: Sustainable Development Implications of the WTO Asbestos Dispute" (2003) 3 *Oxford Journal of Environmental Law*. See also *Shrimp Turtle*, *supra* note 3 and *EC – Measures Concerning Meat and Meat Products (Hormones) (Compliance USA and Canada)* (13 Feb. 1998), WTO Doc. WT/DS26/AB/R,WT/DS48/AB/R (Appellate Body Report) [hereinafter *Hormones*], online: World Trade Organization http://docsonline.wto.org. For commentary on how the WTO is integrating social concerns, such as health, into its interpretation of its obligations, see M.-C. Cordonier Segger and M. Gehring, "Precaution, Health and the World Trade Organization: Moving Toward Sustainable Development" (2003) *Queen's Law Journal* 29:1 at 133–140.

[26] *Montreal Protocol on Substances that Deplete the Ozone Layer*, 16 Sept. 1987, 26 I.LM 154 (entered into force 1 Jan. 1989), as amended by the *London Amendments to the Montreal Protocol on Substances that Deplete the Ozone Layer*, 29 June 1990, UNEP/OZ.L.Pro.2.3 (Annex II) [hereinafter *Montreal Protocol*]. See also the Protocol's *Noncompliance Procedure*, 29 June 1990, 30 ILM 537.

[27] *Vienna Convention for the Protection of the Ozone Layer*, 22 March 1985, UNEP Doc. 1G.53/5/Rev.1, 26 ILM 1529 (entered into force 22 Sept. 1988) [hereinafter *Vienna Convention*].

Drought and/or Desertification, Particularly in Africa,[28] which attempts to slow the advance of encroaching deserts often created by environmental and economic pressures, primarily for social development goals, especially health and community well-being. Another example is the 2000 *Cartagena Protocol on Biosafety* to the 1992 *Convention on Biological Diversity*,[29] which entered into force in 2003, and contains provisions regulating trade in genetically modified products for social and environmental objectives. A third example is the 2001 *International Plant Genetic Resources Treaty*.[30] International and regional fisheries regimes, which seek to ensure sustainable use of a particular fish stock or protection of the marine environment, may also be examples of sustainable development law though further study is needed in this area.[31]

This conceptual continuum raises a number of questions, particularly in the most highly contested "degree", that of partially integrated international laws or legal instruments. Further examination of practical legal instruments or treaties is provided in Part IV of this book, where case studies of the process of integration are provided.

THE DUTY OF STATES TO ENSURE SUSTAINABLE USE OF NATURAL RESOURCES

States have sovereign rights over their natural resources. However, these rights are not absolute. Their sovereignty is restricted by a second objective well recognized in international environmental law, namely, that States must not cause irreparable damage to the territories of other States. Increasingly, this is extended to the principle that States cannot cause irreparable damage to the global environment. Leaving aside the practical challenges often involved in demonstrating the links of "causality" between an action, and irreparable

---

[28] *Desertification Convention, supra* note 2.

[29] *Cartagena Protocol on Biosafety*, 15 May 2000, 39 ILM 1027, online: http://www.biodiv.org [hereinafter *Cartagena Protocol*]. See K. Garforth, *When Biosafety Becomes Binding: A Decision-Maker's Guide* (Montreal: CISDL, 2004).

[30] *International Treaty on Plant Genetic Resources for Food and Agriculture* (3 Nov. 2001) (Rome) available online at www.fao.org/biodiversity/cgrfa.

[31] See the *Southern Bluefin Tuna Provisional Measures, (New Zealand and Australia v. Japan)*, Cases 3 and 4, Order of 27 Aug. 1999, online: <http://www.un.org//Depts/los/ITLOS/Tuna_cases. htm>. See also the 2002 *Convention for Cooperation on the Protection and Sustainable Development of the Marine and Coastal Environment of the Northeast Pacific* at Art. 3(1)(a), where the parties adopted the following definition: "... [S]ustainable development means the process of progressive change in the quality of life of human beings, which places them as the center and primary subjects of development, by means of economic growth with social equity and transformation of production methods and consumption patterns, sustained by the ecological balance and life support systems of the region. This process implies respect for regional, national and local ethnic and cultural diversity, and full public participation, peaceful coexistence in harmony with nature, without prejudice to and ensuring the quality of life of future generations." 2002 *Convention for Cooperation in the Protection and Sustainable Development of the Marine and Coastal Environment of the Northeast Pacific* (18 Feb. 2002), City of Antigua, Guatemala (author's translation). Available online at www. cep.unep. org/services/nepregseas/Convention_English_NEP.doc.

damage to the global environment, this precept is quite reasonable. However, a further implication is also gaining currency. It can now be argued that this negative obligation ("not to cause damage"), when applied to the management of shared natural resources, has evolved into a positive obligation, namely, "to ensure that shared natural resources are used in a sustainable manner". This norm, which can be formulated in different ways in specific treaties, is not unproblematic. It depends on certain conditions being met. For instance, as a principle of international law, it is likely that the natural resources to which the principle refers must not be purely domestic resources. The harm must have some international, or at least transboundary implications. Another condition with relation to this principle is the need to be able to identify what is "sustainable use", and this will differ in relation to each natural resource, and the "use" that is proposed. Other questions also flow from the specifics of application, the nature of the particular international natural resource and the particular intended use. What are the limits? When is a manner of use clearly unsustainable? When would another State be permitted to object? And finally, of course, should States make a commitment to ensure "sustainable use", how to ensure that this is being done, when science is often unable to make accurate predictions? However, the challenges of application do not negate the value of the principle itself, which helps to identify the obligation, and encourage States to seek appropriate instruments and practices to resolve them. For example, long-term natural resource planning and management systems, modelling to estimate or predict "sustained yield", and thresholds for resource collapse, and joint international monitoring systems might all be put in place to help meet the obligation posed by this principle.

Emergence of the principle

An early form of this principle emerged from environmental law, as in Principle 21 of the *Stockholm Declaration*, whereby:

[s]tates have, in accordance with the Charter of the United Nations and the principles of international law, the sovereign right to exploit their own resources pursuant to their own environmental policies, and the responsibility to ensure that activities within their jurisdiction or control do not cause damage to the environment of other States or of areas beyond the limits of national jurisdiction.

Subsequently, the 1992 *Rio Declaration* reaffirmed Principle 21 of the *Stockholm Declaration*, with one addition. Principle 2 declares, while reaffirming the responsibility not to cause damage to the environment of other States or areas beyond the limits of national jurisdiction, that the States have "the sovereign right to exploit their own resources pursuant to their own environmental *and development* policies" (emphasis added). Principle 21 of the *Stockholm Declaration* and Principle 2 of the *Rio Declaration* each comprise two fundamental elements. The first element reaffirms the sovereign right of States to exploit their own natural resources. The second element, however, limits the first, by introducing the responsibility, or an obligation, not to cause damage to the environments of other States. Taken together, in the context of scientific advancements in many resource sciences which indicate much greater degrees of connection between natural systems over distances, these can be interpreted to extend a basic obligation of sustainable use, so as not to damage the environment and natural resources of other States.[32]

The principle of State sovereignty provides that States, within limits established by international law, will act according to their own laws about natural resources within their territory. This includes activities that may result in negative effects on their own environment. This is rooted in the principle of permanent sovereignty over natural resources as formulated in various resolutions of the UN General Assembly regularly adopted after 1952.[33] A landmark resolution was adopted by the UN General Assembly in 1962, when it was agreed that the "rights of peoples and nations to permanent sovereignty over their natural wealth and resources must be exercised in the interest of their national development of the well-being of the people of the state concerned".[34] The resolution reflects the right to permanent sovereignty over natural resources. In this formulation that right also seems limited by a duty to exercise their rights in the interest of development for their people. Sovereignty in this area has been accepted by tribunals as reflecting customary international law.[35] This was made more specific in 1972, before the Stockholm Conference, when the UN General Assembly also declared that "each country has the right to formulate, in accordance with its own particular situation and in full enjoyment of its national sovereignty, its own national policies on the human environment".[36] Later, the UN Resolution on Permanent Sovereignty over Natural Resources would "strongly reaffirm [...] the inalienable rights of States to permanent sovereignty over all their natural resources, on land within their international boundaries".[37]

The importance placed by States on permanent sovereignty over natural resources is also reflected by its frequent invocation, in various forms, in international agreements. The 1971 *Ramsar Convention* emphasized that the inclusion of national wetlands sites in its List of Wetlands did "not prejudice the exclusive sovereign rights of [...] the party in whose territory the wetland is

---

[32] Referred to below as the rule in Principle 21/Principle 2.

[33] See, for example, UNGA Res. 523, UN GAOR, 6th Sess., UN Doc. A/RES/523 (VI) (1952); UNGA Res. 626, UN GAOR, 7th Sess., UN Doc. A/PV.411 (VII) (1952); UNGA Res. 837, UN GAOR, 9th Sess., 512th plen. mtg., Supp. No. 21, at 21, UN Doc. A/2890 (1954); UNGA Res. 1314, UN GAOR, 13th Sess. Doc. A/RES/1314 (XIII) (1958); and UNGA Res. 1515, UN GAOR, 15th Sess., 948th plen. mtg., Supp. No. 16, at 9, UN Doc. A/4648 (1960).

[34] UNGA Res. 1803, UN GAOR, 17ª Sess., Supp. No. 17.

[35] *Texaco Overseas Petroleum Co. & California Asiatic Oil Co. v. Libya*, 53 ILR 389 (1977) at para. 87; *Kuwait v. American Independent Oil Co.*, 21 ILM 976 (1982).

[36] UNGA Res. 2849, UN GAOR, 26th Sess., UN Doc. A/RES/2849 (1972).

[37] UNGA Res. 3171, UN GAOR, 28th Sess., Supp. No. 30, at 52, UN Doc. A/9400 (1973).

situated".[38] The 1983 *International Tropical Timber Agreement* recalled "the sovereignty of producing members over their natural resources".[39] Recent treaties also refer to the sovereign rights of States over natural resources in their territory. The preamble to the 1992 *Climate Change Convention* reaffirmed "the principle of sovereignty of States in international co-operation to address climate change". And the 1992 *Biodiversity Convention* more specifically reaffirmed that States have "sovereign rights [...] over their natural resources" and that "the authority to determine access to genetic resources rests with the national governments and is subject to national legislation".[40]

Nevertheless, as early as the 1970s, limits to the application of the principle of State sovereignty over natural resources emerged as the international community recognized the need for co-operation for sustainable development. Both protection of the environment, and respect for universal human rights, emerged as limits to sovereignty. Consequently, the second element of the principle of permanent sovereignty over natural resources reflects the view that States are subject to social and environmental limits in the exercise of their rights. Beyond its specific relevance in sustainable development law, it has also been persuasively demonstrated that the responsibility not to cause damage to the environment of other States or of areas beyond national jurisdiction has been accepted as an obligation by all States, a central tenet of international environmental law.[41]

The principle resonates in human rights laws, given the reference in Article 2.1 of the *International Covenant on Economic, Social and Cultural Rights* to the essential role of international cooperation for the realization of economic, social and cultural rights. In particular, States parties to the Covenant are required to respect these rights in other countries, including through refraining from embargoes or similar measures, and to ensure that their own citizens or companies do not violate rights of persons in other countries.[42]

Nicholas Schrijver has commented that the rights of States in international law under the principle of permanent sovereignty over natural resources, bound as they are by the other conditions, imply the following duties: (i) to ensure that the whole people (including indigenous peoples and future generations), benefit from the exploitation of resources and the resulting national development; (ii) to have due care for the environment, which incorporates the customary obligation to prevent harm to areas beyond national jurisdiction, as well as the

[38] *Convention on Wetlands of International Importance, Especially as Waterfowl Habitat*, 2 Feb. 1971, TIAS No. 11,084, 996 UNTS 245, Art. 2(3) [hereinafter *Ramsar Convention*].

[39] *International Tropical Timber Agreement*, 18 Nov. 1983, UN Doc. TD/TIMBER/11, Art. 1.

[40] *Biodiversity Convention, supra* note 2, Art. 15(1). See also the *Food and Agriculture Organization Undertaking on Plant Genetic Resources* (1983) and the 1989 Agreed Interpretation, recognizing that plant genetic resources are a "*common* heritage of mankind" at ch. 10, 410.

[41] P. Sands, *Principles of International Environmental Law: Frameworks, Standards and Implementation*, 2nd edn. (Cambridge: Cambridge University Press, 2003) [hereinafter Sands, *International Environmental Law*].

[42] For example, Committee on Economic, Social and Cultural Rights, *General Comment No.15: The Right to Water* UN ESCOR, 2002, UN Doc. E/C.12/2002/11, paras. 30–34.

nascent responsibility to manage natural resources to ensure sustainable production and consumption.[43] The second limb of this duty is, according to Nicholas Schrijver, discernible from both UN resolutions and treaty law relating to matters of common concern to both present and future generations.

The responsibility of States not to cause damage in areas outside their jurisdiction is related to the obligation of all States to protect within their territory the rights of other States, in particular their right to integrity and inviolability in peace and war.[44] This obligation was subsequently relied upon, and elaborated, by the Arbitral Tribunal in the *Trail Smelter* case, which stated that:

"[u]nder the principles of international law [. . .] no state has the right to use or permit the use of territory in such a manner as to cause injury by fumes in or to the territory of another or of the properties or persons therein, when the case is of serious consequence and the injury is established by clear and convincing evidence."[45]

Most writers have accepted this formulation as a rule of customary international law, and it was cited by H.E. Justice Castro in his dissent in the *Nuclear Tests* case.[46]

Consistent State practice and *opinio juris* are not easy to discern. Legal analysis is confounded by the many different formulations and contexts in which the principle is used. While there are relatively few claims brought by States relying upon this principle there are many treaties and "soft law" declarations which do reflect the rule in various formulations, related to respect for the territory, heritage, environment *and* natural resources of other States. This principle may have originated as one of the principles of good neighbourliness in international law. The general principle relied upon in the *Trail Smelter* case, discussed above, can be seen to extend from good-neighbourliness. While the *UN Charter* does not expressly address sustainable development as such, Article 74 reflects the agreement of the UN's members that their policy in their metropolitan areas must be based on the general principles of good neighbourliness and take account of "the interests and well-being of the rest of the world, in social, economic and commercial matters." The principles of good-neighbourliness underlie the doctrine of the ICJ that the principle of sovereignty includes "the obligation of every state not to allow its territory to be used for acts contrary to the rights of other States."[47] In the *Lac Lanoux* arbitration, involving the proposed diversion

---

[43] N. Schrijver, *Permanent Sovereignty over Natural Resources: Balancing Rights and Duties* (Cambridge: Cambridge University Press 1997) 390–392 [hereinafter *Schrijver*].

[44] *Palmas* case, 2 H.C.R. (1928) 84 at 93.

[45] *Trail Smelter Arbitration (United States v. Canada)*, 3 R. Int'l Arb. Awards 1911 (1938), reprinted in 33 *AJIL* 182 (1939), 3 R. Int'l Arb. Awards 1938 (1941), reprinted in 35 *AJIL* 684 (1941).

[46] *Case Concerning Nuclear Tests (New Zealand and Australia v. France)* (1974) ICJ Rep. 457 [hereinafter *Nuclear Tests*]. Judge Castro stated: "If it is admitted as a general rule that there is a right to demand prohibition of the emission by neighbouring properties of noxious fumes, the consequences must be drawn, by an obvious analogy, that the Applicant is entitled to ask the Court to uphold its claims that France should put an end to the deposit of radio-active fall-out on its territory."

[47] *Corfu Channel* case *(UK v. Albania)*, (1949) ICJ Rep. 4 at 22 [hereinafter *Corfu Channel*].

of an international river by an upstream state, the Arbitral Tribunal reaffirmed that a State has an obligation, when exercising its rights, to consider the interests and respect the rights of another state. The tribunal stated that "France is entitled to exercise her rights; she cannot ignore the Spanish interests. Spain is entitled to demand that her rights be respected and that her interests be taken into consideration."[48] The principle was further recognized, in a context of respect for present and future generations, in 1961, when the UN General Assembly declared, specifically in relation to radioactive fallout, that "[t]he fundamental principles of international law impose a responsibility on all States concerning actions which might have harmful biological consequences for the existing and future generations of peoples of other States, by increasing the levels of radioactive fallout."[49] In 1972, shortly before the Stockholm Conference, the General Assembly directed that the Conference must "respect fully the exercise of permanent sovereignty over natural resources, as well as the right of each country to exploit its own resources in accordance with its own priorities and needs and in such a manner as to *avoid producing harmful effects for other countries*"[50] (emphasis added).

The development of the second element of the principle, an obligation not to damage the territory or natural resources of other States – can also be traced to several early treaties. The 1951 *International Plant Protection Convention* expressed the need to prevent the spread of plant pests and diseases across national boundaries.[51] The 1963 *Nuclear Test Ban Treaty* prohibits nuclear tests if the explosion would cause radioactive debris "to be present outside the territorial limits of the state under whose jurisdiction or control such explosion is conducted",[52] and the 1968 *African Conservation Convention* requires consultation and co-operation between parties where development plans are "likely to affect the natural resources of any other state".[53] Under the 1972 *World Heritage Convention* the parties agreed that they would not take deliberate measures which can damage heritage which is "situated on the territory" of other parties.[54]

This principle has also been affirmed in many General Assembly resolutions and acts of other international organisations. In international environment law, Principle 21 is well established. Shortly after the Stockholm Conference, Principle 21 was expressly stated by the UN General Assembly resolution 2996

---

[48] *Lac Lanoux Arbitration (Spain v. France)*, 12 R.I.A.A. 281, 23 ILR 101, 123 (1957).

[49] UNGA Res. 1629, UN GAOR, 15th Sess., Supp. No. 16A, at 241–242, UN Doc. A/4684/Add.1 (1961).

[50] UNGA Res. 2849, UN GAOR, 26th Sess., UN Doc. A/RES/2849 (1972) (emphasis added).

[51] *International Plant Protection Convention*, 6 Dec. 1951, 150 UNTS 67, Preamble, Art. VII.

[52] *Nuclear Test Ban Treaty*, 5 Aug. 1963, 14 U.S.T. 1313, T.I.A.S. 5433, 480 UNTS 43 (entered into force 10 Oct. 1963), Art. I(1)(b).

[53] *African Convention on the Conservation of Nature and Natural Resources*, 15 Sept. 1968, 1001 UNTS 3, Art. XVI(1)(b) [hereinafter *African Convention*].

[54] *Convention Concerning Protection of World Cultural Property and Natural Heritage*, 23 Nov. 1972 U.S.T. 40, Art. 6(3), [hereafter *World Heritage Convention*].

to lay down the "basic rules" governing the international responsibility of States in regard to the environment. It was also the basis of Article 30 of the *Charter of Economic Rights and Duties of States*, which provides that: "[a]ll States have the responsibility to ensure that activities within their jurisdiction or control do not cause damage to the environment of other States or of areas beyond the limits of national jurisdiction."[55] Principle 21 is also endorsed by the 1975 Final Act of the Helsinki Conference on Security and Co-operation in Europe,[56] Principle 3 of the 1978 UNEP *Draft Principles*, which requires States to ensure that "activities within their jurisdiction or control do not cause damage to the natural systems located within other States or in areas beyond the limits of national jurisdiction",[57] and the 1982 *World Charter for Nature*, which declares the need to "safeguard and conserve nature in areas beyond national jurisdiction".[58]

More recently, the respect for sovereignty and the requirement for sustainable use, has been referred to or incorporated[59] in the preamble to several treaties. The principle appears in the operational part of a treaty at Article 3 of the 1992 *Biodiversity Convention*, and in the Preamble of the 1992 *Climate Change Convention*.

Language similar to the second element of this principle also appears in treaties. The 1978 *Amazonian Treaty* declares that the exclusive use and utilization of natural resources within their respective territories is a right inherent in the sovereignty of each State and that "the exercise of this right shall not be subject to any restrictions other than those arising from international law".[60] The 1981 *Lima Convention* requires activities to be conducted so that "they do not cause damage by pollution to others or to their environment, and that pollution arising from incidents or activities under their jurisdiction or control does not, as far as possible, spread beyond the areas where [they] exercise sovereignty and jurisdiction".[61] The 1982 *UNCLOS* transforms the responsibility into a duty. Under Article 193 of *UNCLOS*, States have the sovereign right to exploit their natural resources pursuant to their environmental policies and in accordance with their duty to protect and preserve the marine environment.

---

[55] UNGA Res. 3821, UN GAOR, 29th Sess., Supp. No. 31, at 50, UN Doc. A/9631 (1974).

[56] 14 ILM (1975), 1292; 1 Aug. 1975 [hereinafter *Helsinki Final Act*].

[57] UNEP *Draft Principles of Conduct in the Field of the Environment for Guidance of States in the Conservation and Harmonious Utilization of Natural Resources Shared by Two or More States*, UN Doc. UNEP/1G12/12 (1978), 17 ILM 1097, 1099 (1978).

[58] *World Charter for Nature*, UNGA Res. 37/7, UN GOAR, 37th Sess., Supp. No. 51, UN Doc. A/37/51 (1983); 23 ILM 455. para. 21(e) [hereinafter *World Charter for Nature*].

[59] *Convention on the Prevention of Marine Pollution by Dumping of Wastes and Other Matter*, Nov. 13, 1046 UNTS 120, 11 ILM 1294 (1972) [hereinafter *London Convention*]; *Convention on Long-Range Transboundary Air Pollution*, 13 Nov. 1979, T.I.A.S. No. 10,541 [hereinafter *LRTAP Convention*]; and the *Vienna Convention for the Protection of the Ozone Layer*, *supra* note 7.

[60] *Amazonian Treaty* (3 Jul. 1978), Art. IV.

[61] *Lima Convention for the Protection of the Marine Environment and Coastal Area of the South-East Pacific*, 12 Nov. 1981 UN Doc UNEP/GC/INF.11, 185, Art. 3(5) [hereinafter *Lima Convention*].

UNCLOS shifts the emphasis from a negative obligation to prevent harm to a positive commitment to preserve and protect the marine environment. To that end, however, Article 194(2) provides that States "[s]hall take all measures necessary to ensure that activities under their jurisdiction or control are so conducted as not to cause damage by pollution to other States and their environment, and that pollution arising from incidents or activities under their jurisdiction or control does not spread beyond the areas where they exercise sovereign rights in accordance with [the] Convention."[62] The 1985 *ASEAN Convention* goes further, by recognizing the second element of Principle 21 as a "generally accepted principle of international law".[63]

On this basis, certain scholars have observed that the support given to a principle on sustainable use of transboundary natural resources by States and other members of the international community over the past twenty years establishes a compelling basis for the view that it now reflects a general rule of customary international law.[64] And indeed, the need to focus on "protecting and managing the natural resource base of economic and social development" was given highest priority, as the focus of Chapter IV in the 2002 *World Summit on Sustainable Development Johannesburg Plan of Implementation*.[65] This places international legal limits on the right of States in respect of activities carried out within their territory or under their jurisdiction.[66]

Application of the principle

As mentioned above, application of the obligations implied by this principle is not unproblematic. One way that this is attempted is through the adoption of a "sustainable management approach", whereby the States or managers set standards governing the rate of use or exploitation of specific natural resources. Particularly for marine living resources, exploitation is required to be conducted at levels that are "sustainable" or "optimal". The 1946 *International Whaling Convention*, for example, had as its stated objective the achievement of an "optimum level of whale stocks", restricting whaling operations "to those species best able to sustain exploitation in order to give an interval for recovery

---

[62] *United Nations Convention on the Law of the Sea*, 10 December 1982, UN Doc. A/CONF.62/122 21 ILM 1245 (entered into force 16 November 1994) [hereinafter *UNCLOS*].

[63] *Association of South East Asian Nations (ASEAN) Agreement on the Conservation of Nature and Natural Resources*, (1985) 15 Envtl Pol'y. & L. 64, 68, Art. 20 [hereinafter *ASEAN Convention*].

[64] Schrijver, *supra* note 43.

[65] In the JPOI, while the legal duty is not recognized as such, its importance is underlined. Chapter IV focuses on natural resources, and states that "[m]anaging the natural resources base in a sustainable and integrated manner is essential for sustainable development". See *Johannesburg Declaration*, and JPOI, *supra* note 14.

[66] See L.B. Sohn, "The Stockholm Declaration on the Human Environment" [1973] *Harv. Int'l L.J.* 423 at 485–93.

to certain species of whales now depleted in numbers."[67] Similar commitments to limit catches or productivity to "maximum sustained" levels have been agreed for other marine species such as tuna,[68] North Pacific fish,[69] Pacific fur seals,[70] and living resources in the Exclusive Economic Zone.[71] Other treaties limit catches to "optimum sustainable yields" or subject them to a required standard of "optimum utilization". This applies in relation to Antarctic seals,[72] high seas fisheries,[73] and some highly migratory species.[74]

Sustainable use is an equally applicable principle for non-marine resources. The 1968 *African Conservation Convention* provides that the utilization of all natural resources "must aim at satisfying the needs of man according to the carrying capacity of the environment".[75] Similarly, the 1983 *International Tropical Timber Agreement* encourages "sustainable utilisation and conservation of tropical forests and their genetic resources".[76] The *ASEAN Convention* was one of the first treaties to require Parties to adopt a standard of "sustainable utilisation of harvested natural resources [...] with a view to attaining the goal of sustainable development".[77] Further applications of sustainable use or management may be found in the 1987 *Zambezi Action Plan Agreement*,[78] the *Climate Change Convention*,[79] the *Biodiversity Convention*,[80] and the 1992 *OSPAR Convention*.[81]

---

[67] *International Convention for the Regulation of Whaling*, 2 Dec. 1946, 62 Stat. 1716, 161 UNTS 72 at Preamble. See also Art. V(2).

[68] *Convention for the Establishment of an Inter-American Tuna Commission*, 31 May 1949, 1 U.S.T. 230, 80 UNTS 3 [hereinafter *Tuna Convention*], at Preamble; *International Convention for the Conservation of Atlantic Tunas*, 14 May 1966, 20 U.S.T. 2887, 673 UNTS 63, Art. IV(2)(b) [hereinafter *Atlantic Tuna Convention*].

[69] *International Convention for the High Seas Fisheries of the North Pacific Ocean*, 9 May 1952, United States-Canada-Japan, 4 U.S.T. 380, T.I.A.S. No. 2786, Preamble and Art. IV(1)(b)(ii) [hereinafter *North Pacific Fisheries Convention*].

[70] *Ibid.* at preamble, Arts. II(1)(a), V(2)(d), and XI.

[71] UNCLOS, *supra* note 62, Art. 61(3).

[72] *Convention for the Conservation of Antarctic Seals*, 1 June 1972, 29 UST 441, TIAS No. 8826, Preamble.

[73] *High Seas Fishing and Conservation Convention* (29 Apr. 1958), which defines conservation at Art. 2 as "the aggregate of the measures rendering possible the optimum sustainable yield from those resources so as to secure a maximum supply of food and other maritime products".

[74] UNCLOS, *supra* note 62, Art. 64(1).

[75] *African Convention*, *supra* note 53, Preamble.

[76] *International Tropical Timber Agreement*, 10 Jan. 1994, UN Conference on Trade and Development, UN. Doc. TD/TIMBER.2/Misc.7/GE.94–50830 (1994), Art. 1(h).

[77] *Supra* note 63, Art. 1(1); see also Art. 9 on the protection of air quality, and Art. 12(1) in respect of land use, which is to be based "as far as possible on the ecological capacity of the land".

[78] *Zambezi Action Plan Agreement* (28 May 1987), Preamble.

[79] *Supra* note 2, Art. 3(4).

[80] *Supra* note 2, Preamble and Arts. 1, 8, 11, 12, 16, 17, 18. The Convention defines "sustainable use" in Art. 2 as "the use of components of biological diversity in a way and at a rate that does not lead to long-term decline of biological diversity, thereby maintaining its potential to meet the needs and aspirations of present and future generations".

[81] *Convention for the Protection of the Marine Environment of the North-East Atlantic*, 22 Sept. 1992, *reprinted in* 32 ILM 1069 (1993) (entered into force 25 March 1998), Preamble [hereinafter

In the same vein, international legal instruments have aimed for measures and programmes which are rational,[82] proper,[83] wise[84] or a combination of the above.[85] Other standards introduced by international agreements use analogous terms such as "judicious exploitation",[86] "sound environmental management",[87] "appropriate environmental management",[88] and "ecologically sound and rational" use of natural resources.[89] The significance of these terms is that

OSPAR Convention]. The Convention defines sustainable management as the "management of human activities in such a manner that the marine ecosystem will continue to sustain the legitimate uses of the sea and will continue to meet the needs of present and future generations".

[82] See, for example, 1986 *WCED Legal Principles*, para. (i); *Convention on Nature Protection and Wildlife in the Western Hemisphere*, 12 Oct. 1940, 56 Stat. 1354, 161 UNTS 193 (entered into force 30 April 1942) Art. VII; [hereinafter *Western Hemisphere Convention*], *Danube Fishing Convention* (1958), Preamble and Art. VIII; *North-East Atlantic Fisheries Convention*, 24 Jan. 1959, T.I.A.S. No. 7078, 486 UNTS 158, Preamble and Art. V(1)(b); *Black Sea Fishing Convention* (1959), Preamble and Arts. 1 and 7; *Southeast Atlantic Fisheries Convention* (1969), Preamble; *Convention on Fishing and Conservation of the Living Resources in the Baltic Sea and Belts*, 12 ILM 1291 (1973) Arts. I and X(h), [hereinafter *Baltic Fishing Convention*]; *Convention on Future Multilateral Co-operation in the Northwest Atlantic Fisheries*, opened for signature 24 Oct. 1978, Art. II(I), [hereinafter *Northwest Atlantic Fisheries Convention*]; *Convention for the Conservation of Salmon in the North Atlantic*, 2 March 1982, 1338 UNTS 33, TIAS No. 10789, Preamble [hereinafter *North Atlantic Salmon Convention*]; *African Convention on the Conservation of Nature and Natural Resources*, 15 Sept. 1968, 1001 UNTS 3, Art. II; *Amazonian Treaty* (1978), Arts. I, V and VII; *Convention for the Conservation of Antarctic Seals*, 1 June 1972, 29 UST 441, TIAS No. 8826, Art. 3(1); *North Pacific Fur Seals Convention* (1976), Art. II(2)(g). They are the required standards called for by Principles 13 and 14 of the *Stockholm Declaration*. and the 1980 *Antarctic Marine Living Resources Convention* defines "conservation" objectives as including "rational use" (Arts. II(1) and (2)) as does the *Jeddah Protocol Concerning Regional Co-operation in Combating Pollution by Oil and Other Harmful Substances in Cases of Emergency*, 14 Feb. 1982 , Art. 1(1) [hereinafter *Jeddah Protocol*].

[83] *General Fisheries Council for the Mediterranean* (1949), Preamble and Art. IV(a); *Latin American Forest Institute* (1959), Art. III(1)(a).

[84] *African Convention, supra* note 53, Art. VII(1); *Stockholm Declaration, supra* note 15, Principle 4; *South Pacific Natural Resources Convention* (1986), Art. V(1); *Ramsar Convention, supra* note 38, Arts. 2(6) and 6(2)(d); *Convention on the Conservation of Migratory Species of Wild Animals*, 23 June 1979, 19 ILM 15 (1980), Preamble [hereinafter *Bonn Convention*].

[85] The use of various terms in a single instrument is illustrated by *UNCLOS*; it requires conservation at "maximum sustainable yield" for the living resources of the territorial and high seas; the "optimum utilization" of the living resources found in the EEZ, and the "rational management" of the resources in the Area in accordance with "sound principles of conservation". See *UNCLOS, supra* note 62, Preamble and Arts. 61(3), 62(1), 119(1)(a) and 150(b).

[86] *Act regarding Navigation and Economic Cooperation between the States of the Niger Basin*, Act of 26 October 1963, Preamble [hereinafter *Niger Basin Act*].

[87] *Convention for Co-operation in the Protection and Development of the Marine and Coastal Environment of the West and Central African Region*, UN Doc. UNEP/1G.22/7 (31 March 1981), 20 ILM 746 [hereinafter *Abidjan Convention*], Arts. 4(1) and 14(3); *Cartagena de Indias Convention*, 5 December 1985, 25 ILM 529 (1986), Art. 4(1) [hereinafter *Cartagena de Indias Convention*]; *Convention for the Protection, Management and Development of the Marine and Coastal Environment of the Eastern African Region*, 21 June 1985, I.E.L.M.T. 985:46, Art. 4(1) [hereinafter *Nairobi Convention*].

[88] *Lima Convention, supra* note 61, Art. 3(1).

[89] *Convention on the Protection and Use of Transboundary Watercourses and International Lakes*, 17 March 1992, 31 ILM 1312, Art. 2(2)(b) [hereinafter *Transboundary Watercourses Convention*].

each recognizes limits placed by international law on the rate of use or manner of exploitation of natural resources. In this way, this terminology integrates development and environmental protection, extending the two distinct concepts represented by Principle 21 of the *Stockholm Declaration* and Principle 2 of the *Rio Declarations*.

This tension between the right to utilize resources and the international duty to "use them sustainably" is at the core of the debate over resources recognized as a "common concern of humanity" and, more recently, "global public goods". Both the "concept of common heritage of humankind" and "common concern of humankind" relate to the use of common resources. State sovereignty and the principles and rights that derive from it have historically been applied to the natural resources contained within the national borders of a State. Yet, a large percentage of the world's surface area lies outside the sovereignty of any one State. Consequently, the first concept of "the common heritage of mankind" emerged at the end of the 1960s to challenge older concepts of *res nullius* and *res communis* as a legal approach to common resources. *Res nullius*, which in most systems included wild animals and plants, belongs to no one and can be freely appropriated and used. The concept of *res communis*, however, includes common ownership that precludes individual appropriation, but allows common use of the resources. Examples include water, air, and light.

The concept of "common heritage of mankind" is distinct from both *res nullius* and *res communis*, in part because of its inclusion of the word "heritage", thereby introducing a temporal aspect to the communal safeguarding of areas incapable of individual State ownership. Special legal regimes have been created for the deep seabed and its subsoil,[90] Antarctica,[91] the Moon,[92] the geostationary orbit of satellites,[93] and areas, sites, and monuments that form essential parts of the cultural heritage of humanity.[94] The nature of the common heritage is a form of trust whose principal features include non-appropriation,[95]

---

[90] See *UNCLOS, supra* note 62.

[91] *Antarctic Treaty*, 1 Dec. 1959, 402 UNTS 71 [hereinafter *Antarctic Treaty*].

[92] *Agreement Governing the Activities of States on the Moon and Other Celestial Bodies*, 5 Dec. 1979 [hereinafter *Moon Treaty*]

[93] *Treaty on Principles Governing the Activities of States in the Exploration and Use of Outer Space, Including the Moon and Other Celestial Bodies*, 27 Jan. 1967 18 U.S.T. 2410, 610 UNTS 205 (entered into force 10 Oct. 1967) [hereinafter *Outer Space Treaty*].

[94] *World Heritage Convention, supra* note 54. See generally United Nations, Division for Ocean Affairs and the Law of the Sea, *The Law of the Sea, Concept of the Common Heritage of Mankind* (New York: United Nations, 1996).

[95] The "ownership" of the global commons can be said to remain with all of humanity. Claims by any State that it could assert territorial sovereignty over these areas are rejected by the international community.

international management,[96] shared benefits,[97] and the exclusive use for peaceful purposes.[98]

The "common heritage of mankind" or "humanity" has been applied in attempts to develop an international regulatory regime for resources in the global commons. However, the concept has not been widely accepted when it comes to resources or activities located within sovereign countries. At the same time, a growing consensus has emerged that the planet is ecologically interdependent and that humanity may have a collective interest in certain activities that take place wholly within State boundaries. The compromise reached with respect to the *Biodiversity Convention* and the *Climate Change Convention* is that these treaties address common "concerns" of humankind.[99] During the drafting of the *Biodiversity Convention*, some States criticized the concept of common heritage of mankind. States having rich biological diversity opposed including such resources as parts of the common heritage of mankind, the benefit of which should be shared with others. These views can be understood in historical context. Ashish Kothari, a leading Indian scholar, has argued that the opposition to common heritage, and its eventual abandonment in favour of "common concern" during the CBD negotiations, was due to the historical exploitation of (mainly) developing country biological resources by pharmaceutical companies (mainly) based in developed countries, and that as few processes and mechanisms had been set in place for the equitable sharing of benefits arising out of such exploitation, developing countries were understandably concerned. This historical exploitation was made possible by adherence to the principle of common heritage. It will be recalled that it was out of fidelity to the common heritage principle that the FAO *Undertaking on Plant Genetic Resources*

[96] National management by one country of the areas covered by common heritage is viewed as undermining the concept that no country should be allowed to appropriate the commons. As a result, the *Law of the Sea Convention* established an elaborate system for the management of the deep seabed, including the creation of a Seabed authority. The *Moon Treaty* also makes general reference to the desirability of an international management system once economic development of the moon is feasible. Antarctica, too, is managed co-operatively by a group of States through an elaborate system of treaties and protocols. Finally, it can be administered by individual States under the supervision of an international body, as with the cultural and natural heritage designed by the 1972 *UNESCO Convention for the Protection of the World's Cultural and Natural Heritage*. The last example shows that, in contrast to the concept of *res communis*, the common heritage of mankind can comprise elements under national sovereignty, like protected cultural areas in Egypt or nature reserves in Kenya, and can even be owned by private persons.

[97] Benefits from the use and exploitation of natural resources in the deep seabed and the moon are to be shared among all countries. This is critical for developing countries who do not have access to the technology required to take advantage of these resources. Rather than all benefits going to those who "capture" the resource first, some mechanism is required for making an equitable allocation of the benefits. See *Moon Treaty, supra* note 92, Art. 11(7)(d) which requires an "equitable sharing" of the benefits received from the moon's resources.

[98] The *Outer Space Treaty* as well as the subsequent *Moon Treaty* specified that these areas could only be used for peaceful purposes.

[99] The *Biodiversity Convention's* preamble affirms that "the conservation of biological diversity is a common concern of humankind", even though most biodiversity is found within individual States. Likewise, the *Climate Change Convention's* preamble acknowledges that "change in the Earth's climate and its adverse effects are a common concern of humankind".

provided that such resources shall be the common heritage of mankind.[100] The insistence of biodiversity-rich countries that biological resources should be governed by the countries in which they are situated, and that while their preservation is of common concern to humanity, they do not belong to humanity as a whole, directly stems from the open-access implications of the common heritage principle. Up until negotiations began in the CBD, such access had not resulted in any material benefits to the centuries-old stewards and custodians of the resources.[101] In the end, the *Biodiversity Convention* entrusts States with the conservation and sustainable use of biological diversity on their territories.[102] The *Biodiversity Convention* explicitly proclaims the common concern of humanity for these resources[103] by stating "the importance of biological diversity for evolution and for maintaining life sustaining systems in the biosphere" and by "affirming that the conservation of biological diversity is a common concern of mankind". Its Preamble affirms that the conservation of biological diversity is a common concern of humankind and declares that the contracting parties are determined to conserve and sustainably use biological diversity for the benefit of present and future generations. The 7th Conference of the Parties in Kuala Lumpur, Malaysia, in 2004, launched negotiations for an international regime on access to the benefits of genetic resources, and benefit sharing, to operationalize these provisions.[104]

The *Climate Change Convention* follows the same conception by proclaiming in the first paragraph of its Preamble that "change in the Earth's climate and its adverse effects are a common concern of humankind".

The term "common interest" has also been used. This term appeared early in international treaties concerning the exploitation of natural resources. The *Convention for the Regulation of Whaling* recognizes in its preamble the "interest of the world in safeguarding for future generations the great natural resources represented by the whale stocks" and that it is in the common interest to achieve the optimum level of whale stocks as rapidly as possible.[105] The depletion of fish

---

[100] See FAO Res 8/83 (1983), Art. 1.

[101] A. Kothari, "Beyond the Biodiversity Convention: A View from India" in V. Sanchez and C. Juma eds., *Biodiplomacy: Genetic Resources and International Relations* (Nairobi: ACTS, 1994) 67 at 72. For an example of the historical exploitation referred to above, see the controversy over the neem tree patent granted to the US pharmaceutical company Grace and Co. For a discussion of that controversy and its effect on the "common concern"/"common heritage" debate, see E. Marden, "The Neem Tree Patent: International Conflict over the Commodification of Life" (1999) 22 *Boston Col. Int'l & Comp. L Rev.* 2, 279.

[102] *Biodiversity Convention, supra* note 2, Arts. 6–10.

[103] See *Schrijver, supra* note 43 at 246 on the replacement of the concept of "common heritage of mankind" by "common concern".

[104] See 2004 *Kuala Lumpur Declaration,* adopted at the Meeting of the Parties of the UN *Convention on Biological Diversity,* 19 Feb. 2004, available online: http://www.biodiv.org/doc/ref/cop-07/cop-07-md-01-en.pdf, which states: "*Commit* ourselves in a decisive manner to the development of an effective international regime on Access and Benefit Sharing and support relevant capacity building efforts;" and ... "*Commit* our Governments to integrate biodiversity conservation and sustainable use of its components into socio-economic development ... ".

[105] *International Convention for the Regulation of Whaling,* 2 Dec. 1946, 62 Stat. 1716, 161 UNTS 72 [hereinafter *Whaling Convention*].

resources began as a local problem, but in the second half of the twentieth century it took on much larger dimensions, and States then recognized that it was in their common interest to take measures to ensure sustainable yield. The 1952 *Tokyo Convention for the High Seas Fisheries of the North Pacific Ocean* expresses the conviction of the parties that it will best serve the common interest of mankind, as well as the interests of the contracting parties, to ensure the maximum sustained productivity of the fishery resources of the North Pacific Ocean.[106] A major step in international recognition of the term "common interest" of humanity came in the conclusion of the 1959 *Antarctic Treaty*.[107] Its preamble affirmed that "it is in the interest of all mankind that Antarctica shall continue forever to be used exclusively for peaceful purposes". The *Antarctic Treaty* system further developed with the adoption of the *Canberra Convention on the Conservation of Antarctic Marine Living Resources* which made express reference to the "interest of all mankind to preserve the waters surrounding the Antarctic continent for peaceful purposes only".[108] The most recent addition to the *Antarctic Treaty*[109] achieved full recognition of the common interest. Its preamble expresses the conviction that the development of a comprehensive regime for the protection of the Antarctic environment and dependent and associated ecosystems is in the interest of mankind as a whole and for this purpose it denominates Antarctica a nature reserve, devoted to peace and science.[110]

The principle of sustainable use of natural resources demonstrates an integrative potential – it weaves together economic, environmental and social concerns by mediating between resource use and environmental protection, bearing in mind a collective "concern", or "interest" for the management of resources that extend beyond the territory of single States, based on the obligation not to damage their interests.

THE PRINCIPLE OF EQUITY AND THE ERADICATION OF POVERTY

Equity and poverty eradication are key principles of international sustainable development law. These principles have been mentioned in a consistent manner in international instruments in the fields of social, economic and environmental law. Many of the references to equity and poverty eradication in international

---

[106] *Tokyo Convention for the High Seas Fisheries of the North Pacific Ocean*, 9 May 1952, Emu. T. 52:35.

[107] *Supra* note 91.

[108] *Convention on the Conservation of Antarctic Marine Living Resources*, 20 May 1980, 19 ILM 841 (1980), preamble. See also D. Vignes, "Protection of the Antarctic Marine Fauna and Flora: The Canberra Convention and the Commission Set Up by It" in F. Francioni and T. Scovazzi, eds., *International Law for Antarctica* (The Hague: Kluwer Law International, 1996).

[109] 4 Oct. 1991, 30 ILM 1461 (1991).

[110] See also UN General Assembly *Resolution on the Question of Antarctica*, UNGA Res. 46/41, UN GAOR, 46th Sess. Supp. No 49 UN Doc. A/46/49 (1992) at 83, which implicitly recognizes that Antarctica constitutes a common concern of all States.

instruments on environment and development are influenced by the definition of "sustainable development" provided by the World Commission on Environment and Development in the report, *Our Common Future*. The report states that "overriding priority" should be given to the "concept of "needs", in particular "the essential needs of the world's poor" as a key component of sustainable development.[111] This principle was strongly reinforced and highlighted in the 2002 *World Summit on Sustainable Development*.[112] Indeed, Chapter II of the *Johannesburg Plan of Implementation* focuses on the eradication of poverty for sustainable development. Equity also has an inter-generational dimension, in that States and other actors have an obligation to take into account the long-term impact of all activities on future generations of humankind.

The imperative of equity and clear legal obligations upon states to establish poverty eradication programmes, at the national and international level, have a clear legal basis in various human rights treaties such as the *International Covenant on Economic, Social and Cultural Rights*,[113] the *Universal Declaration on Human Rights*, the *Declaration on the Right to Development*, the *Convention on the Elimination of all forms of Discrimination against Women*, and the *Convention on the Rights of the Child*. The legal basis for these obligations are addressed in further detail below on the role of economic, social and cultural rights in international sustainable development law.

Emergence of the principle

The principle of equity and the eradication of poverty finds its roots in Chapter IX of the *Charter of the United Nations*, where the United Nations has the role of promoting higher standards of living, full employment, conditions of economic and social progress and development, respects for human rights, among others.[114] Various multilateral declarations have followed on this objective, some of which are mentioned below. Principle 5 of the *Rio Declaration* recognized the indispensable role of poverty alleviation in achieving sustainable development.[115] The imperative of the eradication of hunger and poverty was given key importance in *Agenda 21*.[116]

[111] World Commission on Environment and Development, *Our Common Future* (Oxford: Oxford University Press, 1987) at 13 [hereinafter *Our Common Future*].

[112] In the *Johannesburg Declaration on Sustainable Development*, states committed themselves to "building a humane, equitable and caring global society, cognizant of the need for human dignity for all". In the JPOI, this recognition also appears in numerous instances, for example at para. 1 stating the objectives of the JPOI, recognizes that "Poverty eradication [and other aims] ... are overarching objectives of, and essential requirements for, sustainable development." See *Johannesburg Declaration*, and JPOI, *supra* note 14.

[113] See in particular, the statement of the Committee on Economic, Social and Cultural Rights, *Poverty and the International Covenant on Economic, Social and Cultural Rights*, UN ESCOR, 2001, UN Doc. E/C.12/2001/10 [hereinafter *CESCR Poverty Statement*].

[114] *Charter of the United Nations*, 26 June 1945, Can. T.S. 1945 No. 7, Arts. 55–56 [hereinafter *UN Charter*].

[115] *Rio Declaration*, *supra* note 1, Principle 5.

[116] See *Agenda 21*, *supra* note 17, ch. 3, esp. s. 3.1.

One of the key components of the principle of equity is the concept of inter-generational equity, which is defined as "that principle of ordering of the community of mankind which will make it possible for every generation, by virtue of its own effort and responsibility, to secure a proportionate share in the common good of the human species".[117] Over the last decade, it has been widely accepted that, for the first time in the history of humankind, human activity has the potential to irreversibly alter the world on a massive scale. This concern has emerged in the context of future generations in particular; as noted in the *Brundtland Report*:

"Many present efforts to guard and maintain human progress, to meet human needs, and to realize human ambitions are simply unsustainable – in both the rich and poor nations. They draw too heavily, too quickly, on already overdrawn environmental resource accounts to be affordable far into the future without bankrupting those accounts... We act as we do because we can get away with it: future generations do not vote, they have no political or financial power; they cannot challenge our decisions. But the results of the present profligacy are rapidly closing the options for future generations."[118]

According to the *Brundtland Report*:

"[f]uture generations are disadvantaged with respect to the present generation because they can inherit an impoverished quality of life... Future generations are disadvantaged because they are mute, have no representatives among the present generation. Consequently, their interests are often neglected in present socio-economic and political planning. They cannot plead or bargain for reciprocal treatment since they have no voice and nothing they do will affect the current situation."[119]

It should be recalled however, that at the root of sustainable development is the belief that the resources of the earth belong to all generations. It follows, therefore, that the present generation has no right to intervene irreversibly and exhaustively so as to deprive future generations of environmental, social and economic opportunities of well-being. No country, continent or generation has an exclusive right to the natural resources of the earth. The principle suggests that just as these resources have been handed over from past generations, the present generation has an obligation to transmit them in good and even enhanced conditions to posterity.[120] Inter-generational equity, as employed in current international instruments, calls for States to "ensure a just allocation in the utilisation of resources between past, present and future generations". It requires attaining a balance between meeting the consumptive demands of existing societies and ensuring that adequate resources are available to meet the needs of future generations.[121]

---

[117] E. Agius, "Obligations of Justice Towards Future Generations: A Revolution on Social and Legal Thought" in E. Agius, ed., *Future Generations and International Law* (London: Earthscan Publications, 1998) at 10.

[118] *Our Common Future, supra* note 111.   [119] *Ibid.*   [120] *Ibid.*

[121] See O. Schachter, *Sharing the World's Resources* (Bangalore: Allied, 1977) at 11–12 [hereinafter Schachter]. See also, E. Brown Weiss, *In Fairness to Future Generations: International Law, Common*

A corollary concept is intra-generational equity. This term can be formulated as the obligation "to ensure a just allocation of the utilisation of resources among human members of the present generation, both at the domestic and global levels".[122] Intra-generational equity is directed at the serious socio-economic asymmetry in resource access and use within and between societies and nations that has exacerbated environmental degradation and the inability of a large part of humanity to adequately meet its most basic needs. At its bare minimum, intra-generational equity entails "that everyone is entitled to the necessities of life: food, shelter, health care, education, and the essential infrastructure for social organization".[123]

Schachter has suggested that intra-generational equity had become a *de facto* legal norm for developing countries and generally for many industrialized countries:

What is striking is not so much its espousal by the large majority of poor and handicapped countries but that the governments on the other side, to whom the demands for resources are addressed, have also by and large agreed that the need is a legitimate and sufficient ground for preferential distribution [. . .] It is undeniable that the fulfilment of the needs of the poor and disadvantaged countries has been recognized as a normative principle which is central to the idea of equity and distributive justice.[124]

Proponents of equity as a legal norm have emphasized that equitable utilization, including its intergenerational dimension, regarding management and utilisation of global resources, is the primary factor defining sustainable development. The WCED characterized sustainable development in inherently intergenerational terms that distinguished it from other previous types of development that focused merely on economic growth.[125] Indeed, Edith Brown Weiss argues that, "the notion that future generations have rights to inherit a robust environment provides a solid normative underpinning for environmentally sustainable development. In its absence, sustainable development might depend entirely on a sense of *noblesse oblige* of the present generation."[126]

Patrimony, and Intergenerational Equity (New York: Transnational, 1989); and T.M. Franck, *Fairness in International Law and Institutions* (Oxford: Oxford University Press, 1995).

[122] A more controversial view seeks to extend "intra-generational equity" beyond the human species to include fairness toward other life forms. See A. D'Amato and S.K. Chopra, "Whales: Their Emerging Right to Life" (1991) 85 *Am. J. Int'l. L.* 1. See also C.D. Stone, *Should Trees Have Standing? Legal Rights for Natural Objects* (Los Altos, California: William Kaufmann, Inc., 1974); *Sierra Club v. Morton*, 405 US 727, 92 S.Ct. 1361 (1972) (Douglas J. dissenting); C. Giagnocavo & H. Goldstein, "Law Reform or World Reform: The Problem of Environmental Rights" (1990) 35 *McGill L. J.* 345.

[123] See Schachter, *supra* note 121 at 11–12.

[124] "This agreement is evidenced [. . .] by their concurrence in many international resolutions and by their own policy statements [and] more convincingly, by a continuing series of actions to grant assistance and preferences to those countries in need." *Ibid.* at 8.

[125] *Our Common Future, supra* note 111 at 8, 43, 47, 156–157, 160 (focusing on ensuring equitable sharing of natural resources and their benefits with the world's poor).

[126] E. Brown Weiss, "Environmentally Sustainable Competitiveness: A Comment" (1993) 102 *Yale L.J.* 2123.

There is no doubt that some kind of responsibility towards future generations exists. This is increasingly reflected in a number of international agreements and treaties. The *UN Charter*, in the preamble states a purpose to "to save succeeding generations from the scourge of war". More specifically, the 1946 *International Convention for the Regulation of Whaling* recognizes the "interest of the nations of the world in safeguarding for future generations the great natural resources represented by the whale stocks".[127] The 1992 *Convention on the Protection and Use of Transboundary Watercourses and International Lakes* states that "water resources shall be managed so that the needs of the present generation are met without compromising the ability of future generations to meet their needs".[128] The *Treaty on Good Neighbourly Relations and Friendly Cooperation between the Republic of Hungary and the Slovak Republic*, concluded on 19 May 1995,[129] stated at Article 9 that:

[t]he contracting parties, motivated by their interest concerning care for the natural environment and preservation of acceptable living conditions for future generations, shall cooperate in environmental and nature protection, aiming at preventing and reducing environmental pollution, especially as regards trans-frontier pollution.

Support for this principle is also found in recent "soft law" declarations.

Principle 3 of the *Rio Declaration* provides that "the right to development must be fulfilled so as to equitably meet developmental and environmental needs of present and future generations". The IUCN *Draft International Covenant on Environment and Development* provides that "inter-generational and intra-generational responsibility, as well as solidarity and cooperation among the peoples of the Earth, are necessary to overcome the obstacles of sustainable development,"[130] and that "the freedom of action of each generation in regard to the environment is qualified by the needs of future generations".[131] Respect for future generations is linked to equity in many treaties. Article 3 of the *United*

---

[127] *Whaling Convention, supra* note 105, preamble.

[128] *Transboundary Watercourses Convention, supra* note 89, Art. 2, para. 6(c).

[129] *Treaty on Good Neighbourly Relations and Friendly Cooperation between the Republic of Hungary and the Slovak Republic*, concluded on 19 May 1995.

[130] IUCN, *Draft International Covenant on Environment and Development*, (Gland, Switzerland: IUCN, 1995), preamble [hereinafter *IUCN Draft Convention*].

[131] *Ibid.*, principle 4. For other examples, see the *Pacific Fur Seal Arbitration* (1893) 1 Moore's Int'l Arb. Awards 755 [hereinafter *Pacific Fur Seal*], the *African Convention, supra* note 53 (the preamble provides that natural resources should be conserved, utilized and developed "by establishing and maintaining their rational utilization for the present and future welfare of mankind"); the 1972 *World Heritage Convention, supra* note 54 (where the parties agree, at Art. 4, to protect, conserve, present and transmit cultural and natural heritage to "future generations"); *Convention on International Trade in Endangered Species of Wild Fauna and Flora*, 3 March 1973, 993 UNTS 243, T.I.A.S. No. 8249, 12 ILM 1085 (1973), preamble [hereinafter *CITES*]; *Kuwait Regional Convention for Cooperation on the Protection of the Marine Environment from Pollution*, 24 April 1978, 17 ILM 511 preamble, [hereinafter *Kuwait Convention*]; *Cartagena de Indias Protocol, supra* note 87, preamble; the *Jeddah Protocol, supra* note 82, Art. 1(1); the 1976 *South Pacific Nature Convention*, preamble; the *Bonn Convention, supra* note 84, preamble; the *Nairobi Convention, supra* note 87, Art. 16(1); the *ASEAN Convention, supra* note 63, preamble; the *Transboundary Waters Convention, supra* note 89, Art. 2(5)(c); and the *Biodiversity Convention, supra* note 2, preamble.

Nations Framework Convention on Climate Change states that: "Parties should protect the climate system for the benefit of present and future generations of humankind, on the basis of equity and in accordance with their common but differentiated responsibilities."[132] A few hortatory and soft-law texts such as the *Goa Guidelines on Intergenerational Equity*[133] and the *Declaration Universelle des droits de L'Homme des Generations Futures* adopted at a Laguna, Canary Islands, February 1994,[134] seek to develop a normative framework for protecting the interests of future generations. Finally, Principle 4 of the *Draft Principles on Human Rights and the Environment*, recognizes a right to an environment "adequate to meet equitably the needs of present generations [. . .] that does not impair the rights of future generations to meet equitably their needs".[135]

Outside of treaty law and other multilateral instruments, the International Court of Justice has addressed intergenerational aspects of state activities in at least one domestic court case – albeit in a separate opinion. In the *Maritime Delimitation in the Area between Greenland and Jan Mayen (Denmark v. Norway)*,[136] Judge Weeramantry discussed the historico-cultural framework for intergenerational equity in global legal traditions in his extensive separate opinion on the issue of "equity". He also has insisted upon the recognition of equity as an international legal principle in his dissents in *Nuclear Tests (New Zealand v. France)* 1995[137] and *Advisory Opinion on the Legality of the Threat or Use of Nuclear Weapons (Nuclear Weapons Advisory Opinion)*.[138]

In *Denmark v. Norway*, Judge Weeramantry referred to intergenerational equity and specifically to "the concept of wise stewardship [of natural resources] [. . .] and their conservation for the benefit of future generations".[139] These statements were included in his separate concurring opinion as dicta, and were not decisive in the Court's decision regarding delimitation of a maritime boundary. In his dissenting opinion in *Nuclear Tests*, he stated: "[t]he case before the

---

[132] *Climate Change Convention, supra* note 2, Art. 3(1).

[133] Intergenerational equity is referred to as a "principle" that "requires that we avoid actions with harmful and irreversible consequences for our natural and cultural heritage". See *Goa Guidelines on Intergenerational Equity* adopted by the Advisory Committee to the United Nations University Project on "International Law, Common Patrimony and Intergenerational Equity", 15 Feb. 1988, reprinted in E. Brown Weiss, "Our Right and Obligations to Future Generations for the Environment" (1990) 84 *AJIL* 198 at 293–294.

[134] The declaration was drawn up at a meeting of experts under UNESCO auspices held at L'Institut Tricontinental et la Democratie Parlementaire et des Droits de l'Homme of the University of La Laguna, Canary Islands.

[135] This is a draft text attached as Annex I, to the UN ESCOR, Commission on Human Rights, Sub-commission on Prevention of Discrimination of Minorities, *Review of Further Developments in Fields with which the Sub-Commission has been concerned, Human Rights and the Environment*: Final Report prepared by Mrs. Fatma Zohra Ksentini, Special Rapporteur, UN Doc. E/CN. 4/Sub.2/1994/9 (1994), principle 4.

[136] See *Case Concerning Maritime Delimitation in the Area Between Greenland and Jan Mayen (Denmark v. Norway)* [1993] ICJ Rep. 38 (Separate Opinion of Judge Weeramantry) 211–279 [hereinafter *Denmark v. Norway*].

[137] See *Nuclear Tests, supra* note 46 (dissenting opinion by Judge Weeramantry) 341–342.

[138] *Nuclear Weapons, supra* note 3 at 888.

[139] *Denmark v. Norway, supra* note 136 (separate opinion of Judge Weeramantry) 274.

court raises, as no case before the court has done, the principle of intergenerational equity – an important and rapidly developing principle. [. . .] The court has not thus far had occasion to make any pronouncement on this rapidly developing field. [. . .] [The case] [. . .] raises in pointed form the possibility of damage to generations yet unborn."[140] The Court in *Nuclear Tests* rendered its decision on other grounds before it had the opportunity to address the normative status of intergenerational equity. In *Nuclear Weapons Advisory Opinion*, in which the ICJ was asked to hold whether the threat or use of nuclear weapons by a state was unlawful *per se* under international law, Judge Weeramantry found that:

> At any level of discourse, it would be safe to pronounce that no one generation is entitled, for whatever purpose, to inflict such damage on succeeding generations [. . .] This Court, as the principal judicial organ of the United Nations, empowered to state and apply international law [. . .] must, in its jurisprudence, pay due recognition to the rights of future generations. [. . .] The rights of future generations have passed the stage when they were merely an embryonic right struggling for recognition. They have woven themselves into international law through major treaties, through juristic opinion and through general principles of law recognized by civilized nations.[141]

In the main opinion, the Court determined that it could not hold that based on existing international law, in all circumstances use of nuclear weapons would be unlawful, and it also did not discuss the legal status of intergenerational equity. However, it did acknowledge the catastrophic implications for future generations due to environmental harm from nuclear weapons.[142]

It is noteworthy that intergenerational equity as a legal norm has been included in the case law of the International Court of Justice, albeit in separate opinions. Separate and dissenting opinions, such as those provided by Judge Weeramantry in the above cases, are useful in offering alternative interpretations on the subject matter and contribute to what many regard as the ICJ's role in developing and clarifying international law on controversial issues.[143] It is likely that the ICJ will be called upon to directly address the normative status of intergenerational equity in the future.

The concept of generational equity, in both its "intra-" and "inter-" generational dimensions, was also at issue before the Philippine Supreme Court in *Minors Oposa v. Secretary of the Department of Environment and Natural Resources (DENR)*.[144] This case addressed intergenerational equity in the context of state management of national forests. In a novel situation under Philippine law, the Philippine Supreme Court permitted a class action brought by Filipino children acting as representatives for themselves and future generations. The petitioners sought to halt cutting by government licensees of remaining

---

[140] *Nuclear Tests, supra* note 46 (dissenting opinion by Judge Weeramantry) 341–342.
[141] *Nuclear Weapons, supra* note 3 at 888.   [142] *Ibid.* at 821.
[143] See H. Lauterpacht, *The Development of International Law by the International Court* (London: Stevens, 1958).
[144] See *Minors Oposa v. Secretary of the Department of Environment and Natural Resources (DENR)*, 33 ILM 173 (1994).

national forests. They alleged that present and continued logging violated their right to a healthy environment under the Philippine Constitution and would entail irreparable harm to them and future generations of the nation. The Court expressly considered the issue of intergenerational responsibility[145] and recognized that plaintiffs had *locus standi* for their class action on behalf of present and future generations in the Philippines.

In rendering its ruling, the Court accepted the petitioners' statistical evidence regarding the amount of forest cover required to maintain a healthy environment for present and future generations.[146] The Court's recognition of the utility of this kind of evidence for determining resource use needs for future generations is a bold attempt at realizing the demands posed by intergenerational equity. A subsequent critique of the decision in *Minors Oposa* has argued that references to intergenerational equity were not decisive in the Court's ruling and that reliance on this issue was a political matter on the part of the deciding Justices.[147] However, this case is significant as a reported ruling by a nation's highest court to openly address intergenerational equity as a factor in rendering its decision[148] and specifically recognizing that future generations have standing to bring an action regarding degradation of natural resources.

Application of the principle

One of the most concrete applications of equity is found in the social law aspect of sustainable development, which commits to the eradication of poverty. In the *Programme of Action of the World Summit for Social Development*, States identified the needs relating to poverty eradication, and committed to a programme to resolve these needs.[149] The *Millennium Declaration* commits States to a series of particular means and targets, including the commitment to halve by 2015 the proportion of the world's people whose income is less than one dollar a day, who suffer from hunger and do not have access to clean water.[150] The *Monterrey Consensus on Financing for Development* sets out a number of objectives relating to poverty eradication, and indicates their importance in the areas of the mobilization of domestic financial resources, foreign direction investment, trade, international cooperation, external debt and the overall

---

[145] *Ibid.* at 185.   [146] *Ibid.* at 177.

[147] See D.B. Gatmaytan, "Half a Landmark Case: Reflections on *Oposa v. Factoran*" (1994) 6 *Philippine Natural Resources Law Journal* 30.

[148] The US Government has previously alleged consideration of future interests in arguments before its own lower courts. See *United States v. 18.2 Acres of Land*, 442 F. Supp. 800, 806 (E.D. Cal. 1977). Additionally, in *Cape May County Chapter, Inc., Isaak Walton League of America v. Macchia*, 329 F. Supp. 504 (D.N.J. 1971), a US federal court permitted a local conservation NGO to bring an action in both its own right and as a representative of future generations to block conversion of a marshland.

[149] *World Summit for Social Development Programme of Action*, UN Doc. A/CONF.166/9 (1995), ch. 2.

[150] *Millennium Declaration*, GA Res. 55/9, UN GAOR, 2000, ch. III [hereinafter *Millennium Declaration*].

monetary, financial and trading system.[151] The principle, primarily with regard to poverty and intra-generational equity, is also reflected in human rights instruments relevant to sustainable development, discussed in one case study below.

While application of an inter-generational equity is problematic, it is not impossible. Regular references to the rights and interests of "present and future generations" in contemporary international legal instruments[152] dealing with sustainable development suggest that the international community has come to recognise the use of natural resources in an inter-temporal context. These references also indicate that generational equity has become integral to international law dealing with environmental protection, resource utilization and socio-economic development.[153] In both its "intra-" and "inter-" generational dimensions, equity constitutes a bridge for recognized mutual interests between environmental protection, socio-economic development and human rights law. This evolving complementarity is a new phenomenon, as suggested by proponents of environmental justice in general[154] and indigenous peoples' rights in particular.[155]

In their efforts to protect the interests of indigenous communities, the human rights movement has begun to find allies in the environmental and development[156] communities. The interdependent relationship between intergenerational equity and sustainable development of natural resources is highlighted in situations involving protection of fragile ecosystems inhabited by long-term occupant communities. Well-publicized examples of co-operation between

---

[151] *Monterrey Consensus on Financing for Development*, 22 March 2002, UN Doc. A/AC.257/32, para. 1 refers to poverty eradication as an overall objective, and poverty eradication is referred to in each chapter as a guiding principle (with the exception of ch. C, Trade, paras. 26–36). However, the latter section refers, *inter alia*, to the need to increase market access for least developed countries, and in light of the overall objective of the Consensus, is clearly directed in part at the eradication of poverty.

[152] See *Climate Change Convention*, *supra* note 2, para. 23, preamble; *Biodiversity Convention*, *supra* note 2, para. 23, preamble; *Desertification Convention*, *supra* note 2, para. 26, preamble.

[153] G.F. Maggio, "Inter/intra-Generational Equity: Current Applications under International Law for Promoting the Sustainable Development of Natural Resources" (1997) 4 *Buff. Envt'l. L.J.* 161. A UNEP Expert Group on International Environmental Law identified intergenerational equity as among the "Concepts and Principles in International Law". See Final Report of the Expert Group Workshop on International Environmental Law Aiming at Sustainable Development, UNEP/IEL/WS/3/2, (1996) at 10–14.

[154] See D.A. Sarokin and J. Schulkin, "Environmental Justice: Coevolution of Environmental Concerns and Social Justice" (1994) 14 *The Environmentalist* 121 [hereinafter *Sarokin & Schulkin*].

[155] See M. Colchester, *Salvaging Nature Indigenous Peoples, Protected Areas and Biodiversity Conservation*, (Discussion Paper 55, United Nations Research Institute for Social Development, World Rainforest Movement and WWF, 1994). See also R.K. Hitchcock, "International Human Rights, the Environment, and Indigenous Peoples" (1994) 5 *Colo. J. Int'l Envtl. L. & Pol'y* 1 and B. Rich, *Mortgaging the Earth: The World Bank, Environmental Impoverishment, and the Crisis of Development* (Boston: Beacon Press, 1994).

[156] See, for example, Second Ibero-American Summit of Heads of State and Government, *Proposal for the Establishment of the Fund of the Indigenous Peoples of Latin America and the Caribbean, Final Version* (New Haven: Yale Law School, 1992). See also Human Rights Watch And Natural Resources Defense Council, *Defending The Earth: Abuses Of Human Rights And The Environment* (1992); and Yale Law School, *Earth Rights And Responsibilities: Human Rights And Environmental Protection Conference Report* (1992).

human rights and conservation advocates in enhancing this relationship include recent concerns about the effects of pollution by domestic and multinational oil companies in indigenous tribal areas in Ecuador's biologically rich Amazon region. The issue is the subject of two recent class action suits brought by Amazonian communities in US federal courts.[157]

Integration of environment, development and human rights objectives is also manifest in recent instruments concerning indigenous peoples, such as the United Nations[158] and Inter-American Commission on Human Rights[159] draft declarations on indigenous peoples. These documents reflect a new awareness by human rights proponents that securing the rights of indigenous communities entails protection of their cultural values and knowledge as well as their genetic and other biological/environmental resources for future generations. The international conservation community now recognizes this issue as a practical necessity.

The 1992 *Biodiversity Convention*, for example, shifts from a so-called "defensive posture" in protecting nature from the impacts of development, to a more proactive effort seeking to use biological resources to meet the needs of people, while ensuring the long-term sustainability of the earth's biotic wealth.[160]

In addition to the inter-State dimension, intra-generational equity also encompasses what is now referred to as "environmental justice" or "intra-generational justice".[161] This principle refers to fairness in utilization and enjoyment of resources including the cost of degradation, disposal and rehabilitation of resources, among all persons and groups both domestically and internationally. Environmental justice has become a significant legal issue in the United States as

---

[157] See *Aguinda v. Texaco, Inc.*, 93 CIV 7527 S.D.N.Y. (3 Nov. 1993). For examples of collaboration between human rights and environmental groups to protect long-term human occupants and biodiversity, see B.R. Johnston, *Who Pays the Price? The Socio-cultural Context of Environmental Crisis*, (Corelo, California: Island Press, 1994); and L. Udall, "Irian Jaya's Heart of Gold. Natural Resource Extraction Takes a Heavy Toll on Indonesian Island's Peoples and Habitats" (1995) 10 *World Rivers Review* 10.

[158] *Draft United Nations Declaration on the Rights of Indigenous Peoples*, 26 Aug. 1994, 31 ILM 541 (1995) [hereinafter *Indigenous Peoples Declaration*].

[159] Organization of American States, Inter-American Commission on Human Rights, *Draft of the Inter-American Declaration on the Rights of Indigenous Peoples*, OEA/Ser/L/V/II. 90 Doc. 9 rev. 1. (21 Sept. 1995), Art XX.

[160] This observation has also been confirmed in studies by the World Resources Institute (WRI) and other organizations. See esp. World Resources Institute, *Global Biodiversity Strategy* (Washington: WRI, 1992); and R.A. Sedjo, "Ecosystem Management: An Unchartered Path for Public forests" (1995) 10 *Resources for the Future* at 10.

[161] See L.A. Thrupp, "Social Justice as a Key Element of Sustainable Development", text of Presentation Given at International Congress "Down to Earth" San Jose, Costa Rica (1994). See also generally *Sarokin & Schulkin, supra* note 154. The *Brundtland Commission* also advocated environmental justice as a prerequisite for sustainable development: "Meeting essential needs requires not only a new era of economic growth for nations in which the majority are poor, but an assurance that those poor get their fair share of the resources to sustain that growth." Specifically regarding conserving biodiversity, it maintained that industrialized nations seeking to reap economic benefits from flora, fauna and other genetic resources located in developing countries "should seek ways to help tropical nations – and particularly the rural people most directly involved with these species – realize some of the economic benefits of these resources". See *Our Common Future, supra* note 111 at 63.

a result of allegations that areas inhabited by indigenous peoples and other socio-economically marginalized groups have shouldered a disproportionate amount of the nation's waste disposal facilities and other environmentally dangerous activities.[162]

The examples considered above demonstrate that the two aspects of generational equity – between generations and within generations – are useful tools for integrating human rights with economic and environmental priorities.

As with the other principles of international law on sustainable development, the recognition and use of a particular "principle" in treaty laws and their regimes does not necessary mean that the principle has been recognized and is formally binding in customary law.

States are increasingly willing to recognize that sustainable development must be equitable and must aim to progressively eradicate poverty. In the present case, the obligation to progressively eradicate poverty is an important principle of international law on sustainable development, found in many widely ratified international human rights, economic and environmental treaties, as well as international declarations such as the 1992 *Rio Declaration*. While some components of the obligation to eradicate poverty, such as the prohibition of racial discrimination and torture, are entrenched in international customary law, other components, reflected in international treaties, may not yet constitute part of international customary law.

The principle of inter-generational equity and intra-generational equity is less clearly represented in international customary law at present, due in part to difficulties in identifying with certainty the needs of future generations, and the lack of consensus between States on the obligation to ensure distributional justice between States. However, State commitments to the objectives of greater inter-generational equity, and to increased intra-generational equity at the global level, have been increasingly reflected in international treaties, declarations, and decisions of courts. As such, it appears that at present, equity can be recognized as a principle that guides a significant number of international treaties related to sustainable development, and a potential future customary norm.

THE PRINCIPLE OF COMMON BUT DIFFERENTIATED RESPONSIBILITIES

Emergence of the principle

As a nascent principle of international law related to sustainable development, "common but differentiated responsibility" evolved from the notion of the "common heritage of mankind" and is a particular manifestation of general

---

[162] See J.A. Hernandez, "How the Feds are Pushing Nuclear Waste on Reservations" [1994] *Cultural Survival Quarterly* 40 at 40–42.

principles of equity in international law.[163] This principle recognizes historical differences in the contributions of developed and developing States to global environmental problems, and addresses their respective economic and technical capacity to tackle these problems. Clearly, despite their common responsibilities, important differences exist between the stated responsibilities of developed and developing countries.[164] Accordingly, the *Rio Declaration* provides:

In view of the different contributions to global environmental degradation, States have common but differentiated responsibilities. The developed countries acknowledge the responsibility that they bear in the international pursuit of sustainable development in view of the pressures their societies place on the global environment and of the technologies and financial resources they command.[165]

This principle, an important one for developing countries, appears six times in the *Johannesburg Plan of Implementation*.[166] Similar language exists in the *Climate Change Convention*, which provides that the parties should act to protect the climate system "on the basis of equality and in accordance with their common but differentiated responsibilities and respective capabilities".[167]

The principle of common but differentiated responsibility includes two fundamental elements. The first concerns the common responsibility of States for the protection of the environment, or parts of it, at the national, regional and global levels. The second concerns the need to take into account the different circumstances, particularly in relation to each State's contribution to the evolution of a particular problem and its ability to prevent, reduce and control the threat.

Application of the principle

In practical terms, the application of the principle has at least two consequences. First, it entitles and may require all concerned States to participate in international response measures aimed at addressing environmental problems. Secondly, it leads to environmental standards that impose differing obligations on States. Despite its recent emergence in the current formulation, the principle of common but differentiated responsibility finds its roots prior to UNCED and is supported by State practice at the regional and global levels.[168]

Common responsibility describes the shared obligations of two or more States towards the protection of a particular environmental resource. Natural resources

---

[163] Sands, *International Environmental Law, supra* note 41 at 217.

[164] J.C. Dernbach, "Sustainable Development as a Framework for National Governance" (1998) 49 *Case W. Res.* 1 [hereinafter *Dernbach*]. See also for an overview of this issue, D. French, "Developing States and International Environmental Law: The Importance of Differentiated Responsibilities" (2000) 49 *International & Comparative Law Quarterly* 35.

[165] *Rio Declaration, supra* note 1, Principle 7.

[166] See JPOI, *supra* note 14, e.g. at para. 2 where States commit "to undertaking concrete actions and measures at all levels and to enhancing international cooperation, taking into account the Rio principles, including the principle of common but differentiated responsibilities as set out in Principle 7 of the Rio Declaration on Environment and Development".

[167] *Climate Change Convention, supra* note 2, Art. 3(1).

[168] Sands, *International Environmental Law, supra* note 41 at 155.

can be shared, subject to a common legal interest, or the property of no State. Common responsibility is likely to apply where the resource is not the property of, or under the exclusive jurisdiction of, a single State. The concept of common responsibility evolved from the legal rules governing resources labelled "common heritage of mankind".

As early as 1949, tuna and other fish were described as being "of common concern" to the parties by reason of their continued use by those parties.[169] Outer space and the moon, on the other hand, are the "province of all mankind",[170] waterfowl is "an international resource",[171] natural and cultural heritage are "part of the world heritage of mankind as a whole",[172] the conservation of wild animals is "for the good of mankind",[173] resources of the seabed, ocean floor and subsoil are "the common heritage of mankind",[174] and plant genetic resources have been defined as "a heritage of mankind".[175] Recent State practice supports the emergence of the concept of "common concern" as reflected in the *Climate Change Convention*, which acknowledges that "change in the Earth's climate and its adverse effects are a common concern of humankind",[176] and the *Biodiversity Convention* which affirms that "biological diversity is a common concern of humankind".[177] While each of these formulations differ, and must be understood and applied in the context of the circumstances in which they were adopted, the attributions of "commonality" to a shared common consequence. Although State practice is inconclusive as to the precise legal nature of each formulation, certain legal responsibilities are attributable to all States with respect to these environmental media and natural resources under treaty or customary law as the case may be. While the extent and legal nature of that responsibility will differ for each resource and instrument, the responsibility of each State to prevent harm, in particular through the adoption of environmental standards and international environmental obligations, can also differ.

Differentiated responsibility of States for the protection of the environment is widely accepted in treaty and other State practices. It translates into differentiated environmental standards set on the basis of a range of factors, including special needs and circumstances, future economic development of countries, and historic contributions to the creation of an environmental problem. The 1972 *Stockholm*

---

[169] *Tuna Convention, supra* note 68, Preamble.

[170] *Outer Space Treaty, supra* note 93, Art. 1

[171] *Ramsar Convention, supra* note 38, Preamble.

[172] *World Heritage Convention, supra* note 54, Preamble.

[173] *Bonn Convention, supra* note 84, Preamble.

[174] *UNCLOS, supra* note 62, Preamble; see also UNGA Res. 2749, 25 UN GAOR, 25th Sess. Supp. (No. 28) at 24, UN Doc. A/8028 (1970).

[175] *Food and Agriculture Organization Undertaking on Plant Genetic Resources* (1983), Art. 1.

[176] *Climate Change Convention, supra* note 2, Preamble. See also UNGA Res. 43/53, UN GAOR, 43rd Session, Agenda Item 148, UN Doc. A/RES/43/53 (1989), 28 ILM 1326; UNGA Res. 44/207, UN GAOR, 2d Comm., 44th Sess., Agenda Item 85, UN Doc. A/Res/44/207 (1989); and UNGA Res. 45/212, UN GAOR, 2d Comm., 45th Sess., Supp. No. 49A at 147, UN Doc. A/45/49 (1991), acknowledging that climate change is a "common concern of mankind" and rejecting the original proposal in the draft prepared by Malta which describes the global climate as the "common heritage of mankind".

[177] *Biodiversity Convention, supra* note 2, Preamble.

Declaration emphasized the need to consider "the applicability of standards which are valid for the most advanced countries but which may be inappropriate and of unwarranted social cost for the developing countries".[178] The 1974 *Charter of Economic Rights and Duties of States* expresses the same principle, only in more precise terms: "The environmental policies of all States should enhance and not adversely affect the present and future development potential of developing countries."[179] In the *Rio Declaration*, the international community agreed that "environmental standards, management objectives and priorities should reflect the environmental and developmental context to which they apply", that "the special situation of developing countries, particularly the least developed and those most environmentally vulnerable, shall be given special priority", and that standards used by some countries "may be inappropriate and of unwarranted economic and social cost to other countries, in particular developing countries".[180]

The differentiated approach is also reflected in many treaties. The 1972 *London Convention* required measures to be adopted by parties "according to their scientific, technical and economic capabilities".[181] The special needs of developing countries are expressly recognized at Article 11(3) of the 1976 *Barcelona Convention* and in the preamble to *UNCLOS*, where account is to be taken of their "circumstances and particular requirements", of their "specific needs and special circumstances", or of their "special conditions" and "the fact that economic and social development and eradication of poverty are the first and overriding priorities of the developing country parties". Other treaties identify the need to take account of States' "capabilities",[182] "economic capacity", the "need for economic development",[183] or the "means at their disposal and their capabilities".[184]

The principle of differentiated responsibility has also been applied to treaties and other legal instruments for developed countries. Examples include the 1988 EC *Large Combustion Directive*, which sets different levels of emission reductions for each member state,[185] the 1991 *VOC Protocol*, which allows parties to specify one of three different ways to achieve reduction,[186] and the 1992 *Maastricht Treaty* which provides that: "Without prejudice to the principle that the polluter should pay, if a measure [. . .] involves costs deemed disproportionate for the public authorities of a member state, the Council shall, in the act adopting

---

[178] *Stockholm Declaration*, *supra* note 15, Principle 23.

[179] *Charter of Economic Rights and Duties of States*, UNGA Res. 3281 (XXIX) (12 Dec. 1974), Art. 30; See also UNGA Res. 3201, UN GAOR, 6th Spec. Sess., Supp. No. 1, at 3, UN Doc. A/9559 (1974).

[180] *Rio Declaration*, *supra* note 1, Principles 11 and 6; see also the *Climate Change Convention*, *supra* note 2, Preamble.

[181] *London Convention*, *supra* note 59, Art. II.

[182] *Abidjan Convention*, *supra* note 87, Art. 4(1)

[183] *UNCLOS*, *supra* note 62, Art. 207

[184] *Vienna Convention for the Protection of the Ozone Layer*, *supra* note 27, Art. 2(2)

[185] Council Directive 88/609/EEC, 1988 OJ (L 336) 1 (on limitation of emissions from large combustion plants).

[186] *Protocol to the 1979 Convention on Long Range Transboundary Air Pollution Concerning the Control of Emissions of Volatile Organic Compounds and Their Transboundary Fluxes*, 18 Nov. 1991, 31 ILM 568, Art. 2, para. 2.

that measure, lay down appropriate provisions in the form of temporary deroga-
tions and/or financial support from the Cohesion Fund."[187]

Differential responsibility promotes substantive equality between developing
and developed States within a regime, rather than mere, formal equality. The aim
is to ensure that developing countries can come into compliance with particular
legal rules over time – thereby strengthening the regime in the long term.
Practically speaking, however, differential responsibility does result in different
legal obligations. The techniques available in differentiated responsibility include "grace periods" or delayed implementation, less stringent commitments
and international assistance, including financial aid and technology transfer.

Under the 1987 *Montreal Protocol* the special situation of developing countries entitles them, provided they meet certain conditions, to delay their compliance with control measures.[188] Under the *Kyoto Protocol* to the *UN Framework
Convention on Climate Change*, the principle of common but differentiated
responsibilities requires specific commitments only for developed country
parties, and allows for differentiation in reporting requirements.[189]

Other means of implementing the concept of differentiated responsibility
include international environmental funds from such institutions as the UNEP
Environmental Fund and the World Heritage Fund in the 1970s. A key example
of implementation in this context is in relation to the ozone layer and the
Multilateral Fund for the Montreal Protocol. Financing mechanisms, partly
implemented by the Global Environmental Facility,[190] are established under the
UN *Framework Convention on Climate Change*, the UN *Convention on Biological Diversity* and the UN *Convention to Combat Desertification*. These
mechanisms provide financial grants to implement environmental projects
and environmentally sound technology. An emerging aspect of common but
differentiated responsibility is differentiation within developing countries on
the basis of particular situations. For example, the *UN Framework Convention
on Climate Change* recognizes the "special needs and special circumstances of
developing country parties, especially those that are particularly vulnerable to the
adverse effects of climate change".[191] Similarly, the UN *Convention to Combat
Desertification* requires that "Parties [. . .] give priority to affected African country parties, in the light of the particular situation prevailing in that region, while
not neglecting affected developing country parties in other regions."[192]

Recognition of common but differentiated responsibilities strengthens the
integrative potential of international law relating to sustainable development
by addressing the balance between global environmental problems and eco-

---

[187] *European Union Treaty*, 1 Feb. 1992, 31 ILM 247 (1992), Title XVI, Art. 130 s(5) [hereinafter
Maastricht Treaty].
[188] *Vienna Convention for the Protection of the Ozone Layer*, *supra* note 27, Preamble.
[189] *Kyoto Protocol*, *supra* note 18, Arts. 4.1, 4.2.
[190] The GEF provides resources in the areas of climate change, biodiversity, pollution of international watercourses and depletion of the ozone layer. In 2002, desertification was added as a focus
for GEF funding.
[191] *Climate Change Convention*, *supra* note 2, Art. 3
[192] *Desertification Convention*, *supra* note 2, Art. 7.

nomic development.[193] It is therefore closely related to the principle of poverty eradication and equity. As developed countries have played the greatest role in creating most global environmental problems, and have superior ability to address them, they are expected to take the lead on environmental problems. As a result, in addition to moving toward sustainable development on their own, developed countries are urged to provide financial, technological, and other assistance to help developing countries fulfil their sustainable development responsibilities.[194] In *Agenda 21*, developed countries reaffirmed their previous commitments to reach the accepted United Nations target of contributing 0.7 per cent of their annual gross national product to official development assistance. These contributions were expected to fund, *inter alia*, technical assistance, facilitate the use of environmental technologies in developing countries, and help developing countries improve their capacity to govern in a responsible and sustainable manner.[195]

As the above analysis demonstrates, States have common responsibilities to protect the environment and promote sustainable development, but because of different social, economic, and ecological situations, countries must shoulder different responsibilities. The principle of common but differentiated responsibilities therefore provides for asymmetrical rights and obligations regarding environmental standards. This approach appears to be a workable way of inducing broad State acceptance of treaty obligations, while avoiding the type of problems typically associated with a lowest common denominator approach. The principle also reflects the core elements of equity, placing more responsibility on wealthier countries and those more responsible for causing specific global problems. Perhaps more importantly, the principle also presents a conceptual framework for compromise and co-operation in meeting environmental challenges since it allows countries that are in different positions with respect to specific environmental issues to be treated differently.

The principle after Johannesburg

The principle of common but differentiated responsibilities is referenced six different times in the *Johannesburg Plan of Implementation* (JPOI), emphasizing

---

[193] See S.R. Chowhury, "Common but Differentiated State Responsibility in International Environmental Law: From Stockholm (1972) to Rio (1992)" in K. Ginther *et al.*, *Sustainable Development and Good Governance* (The Hague: Martinus Nijhoff, 1995) at 322, 331 (argues that the right to formulate development policies is indisputably tied to the right to self-determination).

[194] *Climate Change Convention, supra* note 2, Art. 3(2), stating that policies and measures "should be appropriate for the specific conditions of each Party and should be integrated with national development programs". See also *Biodiversity Convention, supra* note 2, Arts. 20, 21, stating that developing-country implementation of convention "will depend on the effective implementation by developed country Parties of their commitments under the Convention related to financial resources and transfer of technology and will take fully into account the fact that economic and social development and poverty eradication are the first and overriding priorities of the developing country Parties"; *London Amendments to the Montreal Protocol on Substances that Deplete the Ozone Layer, supra* note 26, Art. 10.

[195] See *Agenda 21, supra* note 17, paras. 33.13, 33.18 (where the Secretariat of the Conference estimated the average annual costs of implementing *Agenda 21* between 1993 and 2000 at $600 billion).

its importance in the commitments of the States.[196] Specifically, it is raised in the Introduction where governments agree to "undertaking concrete actions and measures at all levels and to enhancing international cooperation, taking into account the Rio principles, including the principle of common but differentiated responsibilities as set out in Principle 7 of the *Rio Declaration on Environment and Development*". This commitment to "concrete actions and measures" refers to specific priorities, as mentioned in the JPOI in connection with issues such as unsustainable consumption and production, energy, greenhouse gas stabilization, air pollution, and means of implementation. It also refers to international treaties where specific sustainable development obligations and measures are being developed and financed.

The principle emerged strengthened, broadened and invigorated by the WSSD in several ways. In the JPOI, most references to the Rio Principles singled out the principle of common but differentiated responsibilities[197] and it was also specifically mentioned as a principle to guide efforts relating to: the enhancement of international cooperation;[198] unsustainable patterns of consumption and production;[199] transboundary air pollution,[200] and energy and climate change.[201] Perhaps mostly importantly, the JPOI indicates that the principle of common but differentiated responsibility should be taken into account in implementing *Agenda 21* and the internationally agreed development goals.[202] This statement suggests that the principle does not apply only to environmental protection, but also to social development goals such as poverty eradication. This interpretation is novel, since the principle was previously seen to focus on environmental responsibilities. However, although Rio Principle 7 begins by mentioning the need to protect Earth's ecosystem as well as the differential contributions to global environmental degradation, it indicates that responsibilities for developed countries relate to the "international pursuit of *sustainable development*". The pursuit of sustainable development includes non-environmental goals such as equity, poverty eradication and development. The broad interpretation of the principle is justified for two reasons. First, as recognized since the UNCED, at least in theory, the environment cannot be protected in isolation from the social and economic context. Secondly, and more importantly, although the principle is grounded on the greater contribution of developed countries to global *environmental* degradation, environmental degradation often has negative social and

---

[196] See M.-C. Cordonier Segger, A. Khalfan, M. Gehring, & M. Toering, "Prospects for Principles of International Sustainable Development Law after WSSD: Common but Differentiated Responsibilities, Precaution and Participation" (2003) *RECIEL* 12:3 at 54.

[197] See JPOI, *supra* note 14 above, paras. 2, 4, and 81. Each of these references to the Rio Principles, expressly state that these Principles include the principle of common but differentiated responsibilities, thereby highlighting its relevance to sustainable development actions. However, in para 81, in the chapter dealing with financing and trade measures, the reference to the principle of common but differentiated responsibilities is preceded by the term "in particular...". It is instructive that the principle of common but differentiated responsibilities is given the greatest importance in the chapter on financing.

[198] *Ibid.*, at para. 2.   [199] *Ibid.*, at para. 14.   [200] *Ibid.*, at para. 39.

[201] *Ibid.*, respectively at paras. 20 and 38.   [202] *Ibid.*, at para. 81.

economic effects. Remedial measures therefore need to be taken in each of the three pillars of sustainable development.

The above interpretation of the principle is consistent with the overall theme of integration of the three pillars of sustainable development reflected in the WSSD *Johannesburg Declaration* and JPOI. A broadening of the principle expands the responsibility for sustainable development. This emphasizes that all sustainable development issues (such as poverty eradication) are a common responsibility, rather not primarily those of developing countries.[203]

After Johannesburg, the challenge is to ensure that the principle of common but differentiated responsibilities is applied in a concrete manner in sustainable development decision-making. One opportunity provided in a draft of the JPOI required the UNCSD to consider modalities to operationalize the principle so as to enhance the capabilities of developing countries to implement *Agenda 21* and the outcomes of the WSSD.[204] However, consensus was not found on this proposal, and it was removed in the final days at Johannesburg. On the other hand, the WSSD clearly signalled the relevance of the principle in a wide range of sustainable development issues. It is therefore likely that negotiators and civil society organizations will take greater account of the principle in further negotiations, and decision-making in specialized treaty bodies.

It will be necessary to track the implementation of these Johannesburg commitments in regard to three aspects in particular: commitments to financial aid must be increased and met; practical mechanisms facilitating the principle of common but differentiated responsibilities must be applied in specific treaty regimes; and the principle must be thoroughly applied in the contexts of economic development and social development.

First, as became clear in the Johannesburg debates, a particularly important aspect in the operationalization of this principle is international assistance, including financial aid and technology transfer. In addition to moving toward sustainable development on their own, developed countries are expected to provide financial, technological, and other assistance to help developing countries fulfil their sustainable development responsibilities. In *Agenda 21*, developed countries reaffirmed their previous commitments to reach the accepted UN target of contributing 0.7 per cent of their annual gross national product to official development assistance. These contributions were expected to fund technical assistance, facilitate the use of environmental technologies in developing countries, and help developing countries improve their capacity to govern in a responsible and sustainable manner.[205] This commitment has not been met, in almost all cases, with the exception of the Nordic countries and the Netherlands.

---

[203] Cordonier Segger, Khalfan, Gehring and Toering "Prospects", *supra* note 196.

[204] Draft Plan of Implementation of the *World Summit on Sustainable Development*, Fourth Preparatory Commission Meeting (Bali, 7 June 2002), A/CONF.199/PC/L.5/Rev.1, at para. 138(c).

[205] This wording was crafted in order not to apply to the United States and Switzerland, which had not committed to reaching the 0.7 per cent target. See *Agenda 21*, *supra* note 17, at paras. 33.13 and 33.18 where the Secretariat of the Conference estimated the average annual costs of implementing *Agenda 21* between 1993 and 2000 at US$600 billion.

The JPOI urges developed States that have not already done so to make concrete efforts towards the target of 0.7 per cent of gross national product as official development assistance. The use of the term "the target" in the JPOI indicated that there had been no movement away from the UN target accepted in *Agenda 21*.[206] To ensure implementation of the principle of common but differentiated responsibility, a significant redoubling of efforts will be required. In the WSSD process, steps were taken in the right direction, both for increased development financing through financial commitments made at the 2002 UN Conference on Financing for Development in Monterrey, Mexico, and in the Summit itself through a series of announcements by the European Union, the United States, Norway, Canada, Switzerland, and others. For example, at the Monterrey Conference, the EU committed its members to devote 0.39 per cent of Gross National Product (GNP) to official development assistance with the aim of reaching the UN target of 0.7 per cent. Each individual EU member was to commit at least 0.33 per cent of its individual GNP towards official development assistance. This was estimated to represent an estimated increase of 7 billion dollars a year. The United States committed to increase its assistance by 50 per cent per year, from approximately 0.1 per cent of its GNP to 0.15 per cent, representing an estimated increase of 5 billion dollars a year.[207] In addition, the Johannesburg Summit's aims benefited from the replenishment of the Global Environment Facility (GEF) by a total of US$3 billion. Although these commitments do not indicate that the 0.7 per cent target will be universally achieved in the next decade, they clearly would halt and reverse the reduction in international assistance levels that occurred in the 1990s. Although such figures are promising, they may be put into context by noting that the United Nations estimates that to reach, by 2015, the international development goals in the *Millennium Declaration* would require a doubling of existing aid from approximately US$50 billion annually to US$100 billion.[208] The cost of fully implementing the JPOI, which includes a number of goals in addition to the Millennium Development Goals, would be much higher. The 0.7 per cent commitment on its own is not legally binding, but the increasing status of the principle of common but differentiated principle may develop toward further legal obligations relating to financing of sustainable development.[209]

Secondly, the principle can also be specifically applied through practical mechanisms in each international treaty regime. As mentioned above, and was

---

[206] See JPOI *supra* note 14, at para. 85(a). However, the United States made a statement after the adoption of the Plan indicating that it considered this target non-binding.

[207] See the website of the UN Conference on Financing for Development, online: www.un.org/esa/ffd.

[208] *Millennium Declaration, supra* note 150, at para. 19. The estimate is contained in the Report of the High-Level Panel on Financing for Development to the Secretary General (26 June 2001), UN Doc. A/55/1000, at 68–72. It is not an exact estimate, but is intended to indicate the magnitude of the financial need.

[209] It should be noted, however, that there are strong arguments that human rights laws create international cooperation obligations relating to sustainable development issues. See A. Khalfan, "International Human Rights Law and Levels of Financing for Development" in M.-C. Cordonier Segger and C.G. Weeramantry, eds., *Sustainable Justice: Reconciling Economic, Social and Environmental Law* (Leiden: Martinus Nijhoff, 2004).

highlighted in Johannesburg, treaties on climate change, biodiversity, and the protection of the ozone layer provide for such mechanisms implemented by the Global Environment Facility (GEF).[210] A key example of implementation in this context is related to innovative financing mechanisms, which provide financial grants to developing countries for the implementation of related projects and the development of more sustainable technology. The *Kyoto Protocol* to the *United Nations Framework Convention on Climate Change* received a strong boost in Johannesburg, with ratification initiatives announced from Russia and Canada which would be sufficient to bring the Protocol into force. The full and effective implementation of the proposed financing mechanisms for the Protocol will be of particular importance in the follow-up to the Summit in light of the principle. The *United Nations Convention to Combat Desertification* (UNCCD) also received a needed increase in support through the WSSD commitments. In the lead-up to the Summit, the GEF Council recommended the addition of land degradation (desertification and deforestation) as a focal area of the GEF. The Summit called on the GEF Assembly to act on this recommendation and to consider making the GEF a financial mechanism of the Convention.[211] This decision will provide tangible financial resources to combat desertification, but also has the symbolic effect of designating desertification as an issue of global concern, entailing global responsibilities. The JPOI also firmly indicated the need for adequate and predictable resources to implement the UNCCD.[212] This Convention, due to its high priority to developing countries, particularly in Africa, is perceived to be a key indicator of success or failure to live up to international sustainable development law obligations. It will be essential to ensure that these new financing mechanisms are effectively implemented.

Thirdly, the WSSD's recognition that the principle of common but differentiated responsibilities applies to the whole range of sustainable development concerns leaves the door open to the application of the principle in decision-making on social and economic issues, such as the human rights, labour and trade regimes, at least when sustainable development concerns arise. For example, the principle could be taken into account when human rights bodies consider responsibility for human rights violations caused by climate change or desertification, and obligations to address these issues. In the trade regime, there already is movement in the application of WTO law towards an obligation upon developed countries to consider the particular economic, social and environmental situation of developing countries when adopting environmental measures that would have an effect on these developing countries. The WTO dispute settlement panel in the *US – Shrimp Turtle* case expressly applied this principle to explain the need to recognize differential priorities for conservation. This principle was also recognized in the 2001 *EU – Asbestos* case, where exemption

---

[210] See *Climate Change Convention, supra* note 2, Art. 3(2). See also *Biodiversity Convention, supra* note 2, Arts. 20 and 21; and see London Amendments to the *Montreal Protocol on Substances that Deplete the Ozone Layer, supra* note 27, Art. 10.

[211] See JPOI, *supra* note 14 above, at para. 41(f).

[212] *Ibid.*, at para. 7(l).

of measures necessary to protect human health were reviewed with due consideration given to Members' practical ability to implement alternatives.[213]

The application of common but differentiated responsibilities in social and economic regimes will not be a revolutionary change. It would not, for example, reduce the extent of State sovereignty, nor conversely would it create entirely new exceptions to international human rights or trade law. This is primarily because it is similar to principles that are indigenous to these regimes. For example, in the human rights field, there is a strong focus on universality of human rights obligations.[214] At the same time, human rights law accepts that the extent to which some economic, social and cultural rights are realized is dependent upon the resources available to the State – although even when resources are scarce, there is an obligation upon each State to distribute them in order that at least minimum core rights, such as primary education and primary health care are realized for all persons within its jurisdiction.[215] Essentially, this means that developed countries (and middle-income developing countries) will be held to a higher standard of achievement. In addition, references to international cooperation have been interpreted by the UN treaty body supervising the implementation of economic, social and cultural rights, as imposing an obligation upon developed States and other countries in a position to assist developing countries to maintain an international minimum threshold of rights such as the right to an adequate standard of living.[216] The labour regime similarly reflects compromises between universal obligations and some level of differentiation. For example, the *ILO Convention concerning Minimum Age for Admission to Employment*, accepts that children above the age of 13 are permitted to carry out light work that will not harm their education or development, but the minimum age of 12 is prescribed for "insufficiently developed economies". However, regardless of levels of development, in no case may children engage in types of employment, which by its nature or circumstances will jeopardize their health, safety or morals.[217] In the WTO regime, special and differential treatment for developing country members has been the most recognized principle of this sort. This was usually taken only to mean extending timelines or occasionally reducing the amount of obligations. However, WTO members have agreed to review all special and differential treatment provisions with a view to strengthening them and making them more precise, effective and operational.[218]

---

[213] *US – Shrimp Turtle* case, *supra* note 3, 2001 *EU – Asbestos* case, *supra* note 25.

[214] *Universal Declaration of Human Rights* (10 December 1948), UNGA Res. 217 A, UN GAOR, 3d Sess., pt. I, Resolutions, at 71, UN Doc. A/810 (1948), Preamble, Arts. 2 and 28. See also World Conference on Human Rights: Vienna Declaration and Programme of Action (25 June 1993), A/CONF.157/23, Art. 5.

[215] *International Covenant on Economic Social and Cultural Rights*, 19 Dec. 1966, 993 UNTS 3, (entered into force 3 Jan. 1976), Arts. 2(1) and 2(3). On the nature of State obligations under the treaty, see Committee on Economic, Social and Cultural Rights, *General Comment No. 3*, UN ESCOR, 1990, UN Doc. E /1991/23, paras. 1 and 2.

[216] *CESCR Poverty Statement*, *supra* note 113.

[217] (Geneva, 26 June 1973), 1015 UNTS. 297 (No. C138), Arts. 3, 7.

[218] See World Trade Organization, *Ministerial Declaration* (Doha, 14 Nov. 2001), WT/MIN(01)/DEC/W/1, para. 44.

The WSSD's application of the principle of common but differentiated responsibilities to sustainable development decision-making in general will play a great part in fostering coherence in the manner in which developed and developing countries divide responsibilities in the environment, economic and social regimes. This being said, the principle of common but differentiated responsibilities is not identical to similar principles in human rights, labour and trade regimes. In particular, the latter regimes do not include a critical aspect of the common but differentiated responsibilities principle – the *explicit* acceptance of greater responsibility by developed countries on the basis of greater contributions to global problems. In contrast, developed countries have not accepted that they hold greater responsibility for ensuring social protection and economic development.[219] Many developing countries have claimed that developed countries have greater responsibilities, on the basis of unequal benefits from the world economy, or as compensation for the effects of colonialism and certain countries have viewed international assistance obligations in human rights treaties as fulfilling such obligations.[220] But developed countries have so far been unwilling to join in any international consensus on such interpretations. Given the reality of inter-sectoral concerns, as recognized by the WSSD, the principle of common but differentiated responsibilities should be used to interpret, and strengthen other corresponding principles of sustainable development law in situations of overlap or conflict between social, economic and environmental regimes.

PRECAUTION REGARDING HUMAN HEALTH, NATURAL RESOURCES AND ECOSYSTEMS

Emergence of the principle

The origins of precaution[221] appear to lie in national law, notably the German law, where the precautionary principle (termed as *Vorsorgeprinzip*) is considered

---

[219] See M. Drumble, "Poverty, Wealth and Obligation in International Environmental Law" (2002) 76 *Tul. L. Rev.* 843 at 926 & 936.

[220] A useful summary of these discussions, in the context of the negotiation of the ICESCR is provided in P. Alston and G. Quinn, "The Nature and Scope of States Parties' Obligations under the International Covenant on Economic, Social and Cultural Rights" (1987) 9 *Human Rights Quarterly* 156, at 187–191. The authors conclude that States are more likely to assume a greater level of obligation in *practice* than *in writing*. However, since the publication of this article, the UN Committee that supervises the Covenant has advanced the understanding of the treaty, by indicating that there are concrete international assistance obligations, as discussed in Part III, Chapter 6 on the role of economic, social and cultural rights in sustainable development law. The statements of the Committee are authoritative interpretations of the Covenant. The ability of a human rights treaty body to significantly extend the understanding of a multilateral treaty does not have a parallel in the environment field, and provides an interesting lesson for environmental governance.

[221] There is significant debate on the connotations of normativity of the term "precautionary principle" as compared with "precautionary approach" – the "principle" being seen as suggesting a binding law while the "approach" implies a non-binding guideline. We adopt the neutral term "precaution" in this publication.

the most important principle of German environmental policy.[222] Within international law, the concept is enshrined in Article 15 of the 1992 *Rio Declaration on Environment and Development* where the most widely accepted elaboration of the concept of precaution is found. It states: "In order to protect the environment, the precautionary approach shall be widely applied by States according to their capabilities. Where there are threats of serious or irreversible damage, lack of scientific certainty shall not be used as a reason for postponing cost-effective measures to prevent environmental degradation."[223] Precaution responds to an important problem in decision-making, namely, the absence of complete scientific information concerning the environmental consequences of a particular activity. If decisions are made based only on available information, it is highly likely that they will damage the environment, perhaps severely or irreparably. Because the impetus for economic development tends to be strong, the environment has been protected only to the extent that scientific information exists.[224] Consequently, precaution has received widespread support by the international community as a valuable tool to integrate development, both economic and social, with environmental protection.[225]

Simply put, precaution means the proponent of activities which might lead to either significant, serious or irreversible harm is obliged to take measures (or permit measures to be taken) to prevent this damage (including halting the proposed activities), even if there is a lack of full scientific certainty as to the existence and severity of the risk. In essence, precaution switches the burden of proof necessary for triggering policy responses (see Table 5.1). It is not a panacea, nor is it intended for use in all situations. It is, however, a useful tool for a more systematic response to the problem of scientific uncertainty in environment and health decision-making. Essential elements include the magnitude, distribution and probability of damage needed to trigger the principle, as well as an aspect of proportionality between the magnitude of potential harm, and its likelihood of occurring. The distribution of risk is also important, as harms rarely fall equally on those affected. Perhaps most important, precaution also means a reversal of the burden of proof.[226]

---

[222] P.L. Gündling, "The status in International Law of the Principle of Precautionary Action" in D. Freestone and T. Ijlstra, eds., *The North Sea: Perspectives on Regional Environmental Co-operation*, (London: Graham & Trotman, 1990) at 23–30; K. von Moltke, "The *Vorsorgeprinzip* in West German Policy", Appendix 3, Royal Commission on the Environment, Twelfth Report (1988); A. Nollkaemper, "The Precautionary Principle in International Environmental Law: What's New Under the Sun?" (1991) 22 *Marine Pollution Bulletin* 3 [hereinafter *Nollkaemper*]; J. Cameron and J. Abouchar, "The Precautionary Principle: A Fundamental Principle of Law and Policy for the Protection of the Global Environment" (1991) 14 *B.C. Int'l & Comp. L. Rev.* 1.

[223] *Rio Declaration, supra* note 1.   [224] *Dernbach, supra* note 164.

[225] For a detailed review of the origins and history of precaution see A. Trouwborst, *Evolution and Status of the Precautionary Principle in International Law* (The Hague: Kluwer Law International, 2002).

[226] In more detail, these include proportionality; non-discrimination; consistency; examination of the benefits and costs of action or lack of action; and examination of scientific developments. Proportionality means that measures are proportional to the desired level of protection. Non-discrimination means that comparable situations should not be treated differently and different situations should not be treated in the same way, unless there are objective grounds for doing so.

Table 5.1: Precautionary Thresholds[227]

Status	Soft law	Treaty law
standard & year	"possibly damaging effects of most dangerous substances" *Final Declaration of the Second International North Sea Conference*, 1987	"may cause harm to humans or the environment" *Bamako Convention*, 1991
	"potentially damaging impacts" *Final Declaration of the Third International North Sea Conference*, 1990	"threat of significant reduction or loss of biological diversity" *Biodiversity Convention*, 1992
	"serious or irreversible damage" *Rio Declaration Principle 15*, 1992	"reasonable grounds for concern [that . . .] may bring about hazards to human health, harm living resources and marine ecosystems" *OSPAR Convention*, 1992
	"significant adverse effects" *WSSD Johannesburg Declaration*, 2002	"potential adverse effects" *Cartagena Protocol* to *Biodiversity Convention*, 2000

The degree of harm needed to trigger the principle depends on the provisions of the relevant law or treaty. Further, the magnitude of damage is usually inversely proportionate to the likelihood of risk, for precaution to be triggered. Precaution can be recommended when there is a *high* risk of "possible harm", or when there is a *lower* risk of "serious and irreversible harm". They are balanced by proportionality. On one hand, whether the likelihood of a risk is high or low, and on the other, whether the magnitude or severity of consequences, should the harm occur, is high or low. If the weight of the legal "good" in danger is very high (such as human lives), the correlating potential for it to occur may be minimal but could still pass over the threshold, triggering the need for precaution.[228]

Consistency means being consistent with measures already adopted in similar circumstances or using similar approaches. Examination of the benefits and costs of action and lack of action means making a comparison between the most likely positive or negative consequences of the envisaged action and those of inaction in terms of the overall cost to proponents, both in the long and short term. Examination of scientific developments means maintaining measures adopted for as long as the scientific data are inadequate, imprecise or inconclusive, and as long as the risk is considered too high to be imposed on society. Two aspects are balanced against each other. First, it matters whether the likelihood of a risk is high or low. Secondly, should the harm occur, it matters whether the magnitude (severity) of the harm is high or low. Scientific research is carried out with a view to obtaining a more advanced or more complete scientific assessment. In this context, measures are subjected to regular scientific monitoring, so that they can be re-evaluated in the light of new scientific information.

[227] Communication from the European Commission on the Precautionary Principle, EC COM 1 (2000) WTO document WT/CTE/W/147G/TBT/W/137 27 June 2000, and F. Perrez, *Precaution: From Rio to Johannesburg* (Geneva: Geneva Environment Network/Swiss Agency for Environment, Forests and the Landscape, 2002).

[228] *Ibid. Precaution: From Rio to Johannesburg.*

Table 5.2 demonstrates the rough balancing relationship between both considerations.

Table 5.2: Precaution and Proportionality

Degrees of Certainty (Probability) about Threat	Relevant Degrees (Magnitude) of Potential Harm
Threat almost unknown	Serious *and* irreversible harm
Highly uncertain of threat	Serious *or* irreversible damage
Fairly uncertain of threat (possibly)	Significant harm
Uncertain of threat (potentially)	Potentially damaging impacts/effects
Highly certain of threat	Potential adverse effects

This rough equilibrium seems to play out in international law related to environment and health. Risks of a serious hazardous waste spill might be very, very harmful but fairly unlikely. Precautionary action would be justified, since should the event occur, the harms would be so high.[229]

It was first explicitly introduced into international negotiations in the *North Sea Ministerial Conferences*. As early as 1980, the German Council of Experts in Environmental Matters found that the principle was a "requirement for a successful environmental policy for the North Sea ecosystem".[230] The principle was included in the *Final Declaration of the Second International North Sea Conference* in 1987, where the ministers noted: "Accepting that, in order to protect the North Sea from possibly damaging effects of the most dangerous substances, a precautionary approach is necessary which may require action to control inputs of such substances even before a causal link has been established by absolutely clear scientific evidence."[231]

Precaution was repeated at the third *North Sea Conference* in 1990, where the participants agreed to: "continue to apply the Precautionary Principle, that is to take action to avoid potentially damaging impacts of substances that are persistent, toxic, and liable to bioaccumulate even where there is no scientific evidence to prove a causal link between emissions and effects."[232] Eventually this process led to the principle's inclusion in the 1992 *OSPAR Convention*.[233]

---

[229] M.-C. Cordonier Segger and M. Gehring, "Precaution, Health and the World Trade Organization: Moving Toward Sustainable Development" (2003) *Queen's Law Journal* 29:1 at 133–140.

[230] See D. Freestone and E. Hey, eds., *The Precautionary Principle and International Law: The Challenge of Implementation* (The Hague: Kluwer Law International, 1996) generally, see also P.L. Gündling, "The Status in International Law of the Principle of Precautionary Action" (1990) 5 *Int'l J. of Estuarine & Coastal L.* 23 at 24.

[231] *Second International Conference on the Protection of the North Sea: Ministerial Declaration Calling for Reduction of Pollution*, 25 Nov. 1987, 27 ILM 835 (1988), Art. VII.

[232] *Declaration of the Third International Conference on Protection of the North Sea*, 7–8 Mar. 1990, reprinted at 1 *Yb. I.E.L.* 658 at 662–73.

[233] OSPAR Convention, *supra* note 81, Art. 2(2)(a).

Although the text of the 1973 *Convention on the International Trade in Endangered Species of Wild Flora and Fauna* (*CITES*) does not explicitly invoke the principle, in 1994, the Conference of the Parties has since clearly endorsed it. In fact, at the Ninth Meeting of the Conference of the Parties to *CITES*, States adopted a resolution to incorporate the precautionary principle in the procedure for listing species in need of protection. The resolution reads:

Recognizing that by virtue of the precautionary principle, in cases of uncertainty, the Parties shall act in the best interest of the conservation of the species when considering proposals for amendment of Appendices I and II; [. . .] resolves that when considering any proposal to amend Appendix I or II the Parties shall apply the precautionary principle so that scientific uncertainty should not be used as a reason for failing to act in the best interest of the conservation of the species.[234]

The *Vienna Convention* and its *Montreal Protocol*, concerning protection of the ozone layer, also provide important examples of the precautionary principle. The preamble to the *Montreal Protocol* explicitly states that Parties to this protocol are "determined to protect the ozone layer by taking precautionary measures to control equitably total global emissions of substances that deplete it, with the ultimate objective of their elimination on the basis of developments in scientific knowledge, taking into account technical and economic considerations."[235] The *Protocol* and its subsequent revisions are considered as taking a precautionary approach because they adopt strict policy measures despite uncertainty.

By 1992, UNCED significantly furthered the consensus around the precautionary principle. As noted above, Principle 15 of the *Rio Declaration* was adopted. In addition, UNCED delegates also invoked the precautionary principle in both the *Biodiversity Convention*[236] and the *Climate Change Convention*,[237] as well as *Agenda 21*.[238]

The precautionary principle has also appeared in regional declarations and treaties. In Europe, in addition to the *North Sea Conferences* noted above, the *Bergen Ministerial Declaration on Sustainable Development* in the Economic Commission for Europe Regions, stated: "In order to achieve sustainable development, policies must be based on the precautionary principle. Environmental measures must anticipate, prevent and attack the causes of environmental degradation where there are threats of serious or irreversible damage. Lack of full scientific certainty should not be used as a reason for postponing measures to prevent environmental degradation."[239]

---

[234] Resolution of the Conference of the Parties, Criteria for Amendment of Appendices I and II, Ninth Meeting of the Conference of the Parties, Fort Lauderdale (USA), 7–18 Nov. 1994, Com.9.24. See also J. Cameron and J. Abouchar, "The Status of the Precautionary Principle in International Law" in D. Freestone and E. Hey, eds., *The Precautionary Principle and International Law: The Challenge of Implementation* (The Hague: Kluwer Law International, 1996) at 46.

[235] *Montreal Protocol, supra* note 26, preamble.

[236] *Biodiversity Convention, supra* note 2, preamble.

[237] *Climate Change Convention, supra* note 2, Art. 3(3).

[238] *Agenda 21, supra* note 17, ch. 17, 18 and 35.

[239] *Bergen Declaration on Sustainable Development in the ECE Region*, 16 May 1990, UN Doc. A/CONF. 151/PC/10), reprinted at 1 *Yb. I.E.L.* 424 (1990) at para. 7.

Early the following year, over fifty African countries negotiated the *Bamako Convention*, which provides:

[e]ach Party shall strive to adopt and implement the preventive, precautionary approach to pollution problems which entails, *inter alia*, preventing the release into the environment of substances which may cause harm to humans or the environment without waiting for scientific proof regarding such harm. The parties shall cooperate with each other in taking the appropriate measures to implement the precautionary principle to pollution through the application of clean production methods, rather than the pursuit of a permissible emissions approach based on the assimilative capacity assumptions.[240]

In Asia, the 1991 *Ministerial Conference on the Environment of the United Nations Economic and Social Commission for Asia and the Pacific* invoked the precautionary principle: "[I]n order to achieve sustainable development, policies must be based on the precautionary principle."[241]

In 1993, the European Union officially adopted the precautionary principle as a basis for all community environmental policy. According to Article 130r(2) of the *Treaty Establishing the European Economic Community*, as amended by the *Treaty on European Union* (the *Maastricht Treaty*): "Community policy on the environment shall aim at a high level of protection taking into account the diversity of situations in the various regions of the Community. It shall be based on the precautionary principle and on the principles that preventive action should be taken, that environmental damage should as a priority be rectified at the source and that the polluter should pay." As a "constitutional" document of the European Union, the *Maastricht Treaty* will guide future adoption of EU environmental policy.

Since the early 1990s many European regional agreements have also included the precautionary principle, including the *ECE Transboundary Watercourses Convention*,[242] the *Baltic Sea Convention*,[243] and the *North-East Atlantic Convention*.[244] Several of the protocols to the *Convention on Long-Range*

---

[240] *Bamako Convention on the Ban of Import into Africa and the Control of Transboundary Movement and Management of Hazardous Wastes within Africa*, 29 Jan. 1991, 30 ILM 775 (1991), Art. 4(3)(f) [hereinafter *Bamako Convention*].

[241] Report of the United Nations Economic and Social Commission for Asia and the Pacific (ESCAP) Ministerial Meeting in the Environment, Bangkok, *Declaration on Environmentally Sound and Sustainable Development in Asia and the Pacific* (1990) at para. 19

[242] See *Transboundary Watercourses Convention*, *supra* note 89, which provides at Art. 2(5)(a) that "the Parties shall be guided by the [. . .] precautionary principle, by virtue of which action to avoid the potential transboundary impact of the release of hazardous substances shall not be postponed on the ground that scientific research has not fully proved a causal link between those substances, on the one hand, and the potential transboundary impact, on the other hand."

[243] See *Convention on the Protection of the Marine Environment of the Baltic Sea Area*, 9 April 1992, stating at Art. 3(2) that "the Contracting Parties shall apply the precautionary principal [*sic*], i.e., to take preventative measures when there is reason to assume that substances or energy introduced, directly or indirectly, into the marine environment may create hazards to human health, harm living resources and marine ecosystems, damage amenities or interfere with other legitimate uses of the sea even when there is no conclusive evidence of a causal relationship between inputs and their alleged effects."

[244] See OSPAR Convention, *supra* note 81, Art. 2(2)(a)

Transboundary Air Pollution also specifically invoke the precautionary principle.[245] Finally, in 1995, fifty-nine countries signed the *Straddling Stocks Agreement*.[246] Article 6 of the Agreement deals entirely with application of the precautionary approach:

1. States shall apply the precautionary approach widely to conservation, management and exploitation of straddling fish stocks and highly migratory fish stocks in order to protect the living marine resources and preserve the marine environment. 2. States shall be more cautious when information is uncertain, unreliable, or inadequate. The absence of adequate scientific information shall not be used as a reason for postponing or failing to take conservation and management measures.[247]

Article 6 thus includes explicitly the affirmative requirement to be "more cautious" in the face of uncertainty.

Precaution has also appeared in international trade law. The World Trade Organizations's *Agreement on the Application of Sanitary and Phytosanitary Measures* (SPS Agreement) provides that Members may "provisionally" adopt SPS measures "where relevant scientific evidence is insufficient". In full, Article 5.7 provides:

In cases where relevant scientific evidence is insufficient, a Member may provisionally adopt sanitary or phytosanitary measures on the basis of available pertinent information, including that from the relevant international organizations as well as from sanitary or phytosanitary measures applied by other Members. In such circumstances, Members shall seek to obtain the additional information necessary for a more objective assessment of risk and review the sanitary or phytosanitary measure accordingly within a reasonable period of time.

In the *Hormones* case[248] the Appellate Body explicitly discussed the relationship of the precautionary principle to the SPS Agreement. It noted that "the precautionary principle finds reflection in Article 5.7".[249] It also found that the principle is reflected in the sixth paragraph of the preamble and in Article 3.3, which "explicitly recognize the right of Members to establish their own appropriate level of sanitary protection, which level may be higher (i.e., more cautious) than that implied in existing international standards, guidelines and recommendations".[250]

---

[245] *Protocol to the Convention on Long-Range Transboundary Air Pollution on Persistent Organic Pollutants*, 25 June 1998, UN Doc. EB.AIR/1998/2, preamble. See also *Protocol to the 1979 Convention on Long-Range Transboundary Air Pollution on Further Reduction of Sulphur Emissions*, 14 June 1994, UN Doc. EB.AIR/R.84, 33 ILM 1542 (1994), which provides in the preamble that parties are "[r]esolved to take precautionary measures to anticipate, prevent or minimize emissions of air pollutants and mitigate their adverse effects"; *Protocol to the Convention on Long-Range Transboundary Air Pollution on Heavy Metals*, 25 June 1998, UN Doc. EB.AIR/1998/1, stating in the preamble that parties are "[r]esolved to take measures to anticipate, prevent or minimize emissions of certain heavy metals and their related compounds, taking into account the application of the precautionary approach, as set forth in Principle 15 of the *Rio Declaration on Environment and Development*".

[246] *Agreement for the Implementation of the Provisions of the UN Convention on the Law of the Sea of 10 December 1982 relating to the Conservation and Management of Straddling Fish Stocks and Highly Migratory Fish Stocks*, 4 Aug. 1995, UN Doc A/CONF.164/38 (1995) 34 ILM 1542, Art. 5(c) [hereinafter *Straddling Stocks Agreement*].

[247] *Ibid.*, Arts. 6(1) and (2).

[248] *Supra* note 25.   [249] *Ibid.*, at para. 124.   [250] *Ibid.*

In the *Asbestos* case, the WTO Appellate Body used precautionary reasoning, though not explicitly, to uphold a French ban on chrysotile asbestos due to its carcinogenic effects, though the parties' science was uncertain whether the substitutes could be used safely, or whether a "controlled use" was not an option.[251] Moreover, while the *Agreement on Technical Barriers to Trade* (TBT Agreement) does not explicitly incorporate a precautionary approach in its text, it does provide in the Preamble that:

"no country should be prevented from taking measures... for the protection of human, animal or plant life or health [or] of the environment,... at the levels it considers appropriate, subject to the requirement that they are not applied in a manner which would constitute a means of arbitrary or unjustifiable discrimination between countries where the same conditions prevail or a disguised restriction on international trade, and are otherwise in accordance with the provisions of this Agreement."

This statement acknowledging the right of a WTO Member to set the level of protection "at the level it considers appropriate" parallels that in the SPS Preamble and Article 3.3, which the Appellate Body has stated are reflections of the precautionary principle.

On the basis of the aforementioned evidence, some claim that there is sufficient evidence of state practice to justify the conclusion that the principle, as elaborated in the *Rio Declaration*, the *Climate Change* and the *Biodiversity Conventions*, is receiving sufficiently broad support to allow a good argument to be made that it reflects an emerging principle of customary international law.[252]

Application of the principle

The value of precaution lies primarily in its assumption that natural systems are vulnerable, as opposed to being resilient or invulnerable,[253] thereby giving the benefit of the doubt to environmental protection when there is scientific uncertainty. In its application, then, precaution shifts the burden of proof from those supporting natural systems to those supporting development.[254] The principle is premised on the preference of preventing pollution to subsequent remediation,

---

[251] The AB took toxicity and health risks into account in like-product analysis, reversing the burden of proof from Canada to France in demonstrating comparative health risks of substitutes versus asbestos itself, and including an element of proportionality in their analysis. See M. Gehring and M.-C. Cordonier Segger, "The WTO Asbestos Cases and Precaution: Sustainable Development Implications of the WTO Asbestos Dispute" [2003] 3 *Oxford Journal of Environmental Law*.

[252] Sands, *International Environmental Law*, *supra* note 41 at 112. Support for the emerging customary law status of precaution has been expressed by national courts; see e.g. *114957 Canada Ltée (Spraytech, société d'arrosage)* v. *Hudson (Town)*, [2001] 2 S.C.R. 241 (Supreme Court of Canada, *per* Judge L'Heureux-Dubé).

[253] See A.M.H. Clayton and N.J. Radcliffe, *Sustainability: A Systems Approach* (London: Earthscan Publications, 1996) at 213.

[254] See B. Weintraub, "Science, International Environmental Regulation, and the Precautionary Principle: Setting Standards and Defining Terms" (1992) 1 *N.Y.U. Envtl. L.J.* 173 at 178–180; D.A. Wirth, "The Rio Declaration on Environment and Development: Two Steps Forward and One Back, or Vice Versa?" (1995) 29 *Ga. L. Rev.* 599 at 634.

the relevance of scientific data to governmental decision-making and the obligation to take precautionary measures that are in proportion to the potential damage.[255]

Nevertheless, much of the confusion surrounding the interpretation of precaution relates to the distinction between precaution and more traditional preventive standards. Precaution, both at its conceptual core and its practical implications, is preventive. However, not all preventive standards are precautionary. More precisely, any particular preventive standard may be either non-precautionary or precautionary in various degrees. By contrast, any given precautionary standard may be preventive in various degrees, but cannot be non-preventive.[256]

For example, according to the terms of the 1990 *International Maritime Organization International Convention on Oil Pollution Preparedness, Response and Cooperation*,[257] parties to it, "recognising the serious threat posed to the marine environment by oil pollution incidents involving ships, offshore units, sea ports and oil handling facilities", noted that they were "mindful of the importance of the precautionary measures and prevention in avoiding oil pollution in the first instance".[258] Despite the presence of precautionary language, there are few precautionary elements within the standards set. The threats posed to the marine environment are clear. Measures are being taken to prevent such known threats from being realized. The certainty of the environmental damage that would result from a failure to adhere to those standards, means that the Convention is not precautionary, but rather, preventive, in its intention. The terms of the Convention may be contrasted with those of the *Conference for the Protection of Coasts and Waters of the North East Atlantic Against Pollution Due to HydroCarbons or Other Harmful Substances*. The Conference's final Act declared the need for measures designed to prevent discharges of "[o]ther harmful substances, where the latter were defined as substances the release of which into the marine environment *may* lead to injury to human health, to eco-systems or living resources, or to the coasts or related interests of the Parties".[259] The risks to be reduced in this case are of an unknown nature. It is unclear what environmental damage the release of these "other harmful substances" into the marine environment would cause. The standard set is obviously preventive in

---

[255] See J.E. Hickey, Jr., & V.R. Walker, "Refining the Precautionary Principle in International Environmental Law" (1995) 14 Va. Envtl. L.J. 423 at 436. The principle does not answer certain questions, however: the level of potential damage, the level of certainty required, and the circumstances under which the government would act (as opposed to the circumstances under which it would refrain from acting).

[256] J. Cameron, W. Wade-Gery & J. Abouchar, "Precautionary Principle and Future Generations" in E. Agius, ed., *Future Generations and International Law* (London: Earthscan Publications, 1998).

[257] *Final Act of the Conference on Oil Pollution Preparedness, Response and Cooperation*, London, 30 Nov. 1990, 30 ILM 733 (1991).

[258] *Ibid.*, at 735.

[259] *Final Act of the Conference for the Protection of Coasts and Waters of the North East Atlantic Against Pollution Due to HydroCarbons or Other Harmful Substances, and Accord of Cooperation*, Lisbon, 17 Oct. 1990, 30 ILM 1227 (1991) (emphasis added).

intent, since it clearly seeks to prevent environmental damage, but it is also precautionary, in that the standards set are a response to the uncertainty surrounding the environmental effects of particular discharges. Of crucial importance, of course, is the term "may". This example provides us with the key element of the conceptual core of precaution.

A lack of certainty about the cause and effect relationships, or the extent of possible environmental harm, does not allow the delaying of some kind of regulatory mechanism over the activity in question. Precaution means that where the environmental risks of regulatory inaction are in some way uncertain but non-negligible, regulatory inaction is unjustified. Andre Nollkaemper rightly inquires "whether or not [precaution] distinguishes itself in the already dense normative scenery in this field".[260] The conceptual core of precaution, discussed above, suggests that the concept does contribute, rather than obfuscate this normative scenery.

Precaution is especially important for sustainable development because the carrying capacity of the global environment as well as regional ecosystems is mostly unknown, or at least uncertain.[261] Although it is generally agreed that the environment can tolerate some abuse, there is a tendency to believe and act as if the environment can tolerate a particular human activity or set of activities unless scientific information demonstrates otherwise. Because the quality of human life ultimately depends on these natural resources, we must be careful to protect them. As such, the precautionary principle provides a useful tool that to ensure that development trends do not have a detrimental effect on the environment, particularly those caused by unknown risks.[262]

Precaution after the Johannesburg Summit

In Johannesburg, while there was not universal acceptance of a broad new formulation for the principle, understanding of precaution was advanced, myths were broken, and States developed better understandings of how the legal concept of precaution could be applied in specific instances. Precaution is neither a solution to all environmental problems, nor an end to all economic activities. The contribution of the WSSD was to re-focus thinking away from debates on the precise status of precaution in international law (is it customary law, or simply an approach),[263] and toward its affirmation, recognition of its relevance as a complement to science-based decision-making, and with regard to social and development agendas (such as human health and the need for

---

[260] *Nollkaemper, supra* note 222 at 107. Note that Nollkaemper responds differently to this question.

[261] See D.H. Meadows *et al., Beyond the Limits* (New York: Universe Books, 1972) at 1–14.

[262] G. Maggio and OJ Lynch, *Human Rights, Environment, and Economic Development: Existing and Emerging Standards in International Law and Global Society* (World Resources Institute, 1996) at 75.

[263] See OECD, *Policies to Enhance Sustainable Development* (Paris: OECD, May 2001).

assistance to strengthen developing country capacities).[264] To the credit of many governments from the Group of 77 and China and leading developed countries, civil society organizations, including legal and academic institutions participated from the start in these debates.[265]

Looking forward requires a brief analysis of the WSSD outcomes themselves, in their ordinary meaning as a consensus of the governments represented at the Summit. Precaution is raised in the *Johannesburg Plan of Implementation*, in Chapter X on Means of Implementation, as part of a commitment to improve "policy and decision-making at all levels through, *inter alia*, improved collaboration between natural and social scientists, and between scientists and policy makers".[266] States call for urgent actions at all levels to promote and "improve science-based decision-making and reaffirm the precautionary approach as set out in Principle 15 of the Rio Declaration on Environment and Development" after which the version of the principle set out in the *Rio Declaration* is restated.[267] The reference to precaution complements and balances the reference to the need for science-based decision-making. Both are valid and important priorities, and they work together. Wherever science-based decision-making is possible, it can make a significant contribution to sustainable development. As stated in Principle 15, lack of full scientific certainty should not be used as a reason for postponing cost effective measures to prevent environmental degradation. As such, in the areas where there is a risk of environmental degradation, but not yet scientific certainty that damage will occur, precautionary actions may be needed.

Precaution is also raised in the *Johannesburg Plan of Implementation* in regard to the *Agenda 21* commitment to sound management of chemicals and hazardous wastes. This commitment aims to achieve, by 2020, "the use and production of chemicals in ways that lead to the minimization of significant adverse effects on human health and the environment". In order to do this, States agree to use "transparent science-based risk assessment procedures and science-based risk management procedures, taking into account the precautionary approach, as set out in Principle 15 of the Rio Declaration on Environment and Development".[268] Again, precaution complements the use of science-based

---

[264] A more detailed overview of the development on precaution between Rio and Johannesburg is provided in the Geneva Environment Network (GEN)/Swiss Agency for the Environment, Forests and Landscape (SAEFL) publication, *Precaution from Rio to Johannesburg* (GEN/SAEFL, 2002) available online at: <http://www.environmenthouse.ch/Roundtables/pp%20report/pp%20 report%20e.pdf>. See also F.X. Perrez, "The World Summit on Sustainable Development: Environment, Precaution and Trade – A Potential for Success and/or Failure" (2003) RECIEL 12:3.

[265] Early in the ECE negotiations, the Centre for International Sustainable Development Law (CISDL) released a legal brief on precaution in international sustainable development law, advising of the need for a balanced legal agenda. See M.-C. Cordonier Segger and M. Gehring, "Precaution in International Sustainable Development Law", *CISDL Legal Brief* Aug. 2002, found online at <http:// www.cisdl.org/pdf/ brief_precaution.pdf>. In the Johannesburg Summit itself, a study on precaution in five UN languages, which gave background for discussions in the Rio Principles working group, was contributed by Switzerland and the Geneva Environment Network. Both studies focused on practical applications and demonstrated the much broader use of precaution since the 1992 Rio Earth Summit.

[266] JPOI, *supra* note 14 at Chapter X.   [267] See *Rio Declaration, supra* note 1.

[268] JPOI, *supra* note 14 at para. 109(f).

procedures. In addition, this reference suggests that significant adverse effects on human health can be a "trigger" for the principle. The concern for human health, coupled with a commitment to provide support for developing countries, gives a clearer social and development side to the concept of precaution.

As such, the WSSD advanced acceptance of the principle in three ways. It clarified the debates; it took developing country perspectives further into account; and it resulted in broader recognition of the principle as a part of international law.

First, negotiations surrounding the principle served to clarify myths. In preparations for the WSSD, legal and scientific debates took place, and reports of their results were released at the Summit.[269] States raised questions on how the legal concept of precaution has evolved since the 1992 UNCED, examining the nature of precaution with reference to its place in legal methodology and policy making, and considering its role as a complement to science-based decision-making. Precaution has developed further in specialized treaty regimes and priority areas of international action for sustainable development. In some fields, such as straddling fish stocks, it has clear relevance and utility. It is also relevant to issues such as human health in the context of chemicals and hazardous wastes management. In these areas, formulations of the principle should take into account progress on its modalities since 1992. These were carefully negotiated in the context of particular sustainable development problems and should be used where appropriate in specific international regimes.[270]

Secondly, at Johannesburg developing countries became engaged on this issue. In the Plan of Implementation States commit to "support developing countries in strengthening their capacity for the sound management of chemicals and hazardous wastes by providing technical and financial assistance".[271] For developing countries, slow progress at the WSSD on this issue was not about precaution itself. Indeed, several leading developing countries have deliberately incorporated precaution into their domestic law, or even into their constitutions, recognizing the principle as a useful legal tool.[272] In the past decade, developing countries have often fought hard for precaution, in order to cope with lack of full scientific knowledge and certainty about environmental and social impacts, as well as other related issues, in their national contexts. For example in the field of biodiversity and biotechnology, certain developing countries have been

---

[269] Geneva Environment Network (GEN)/Swiss Agency for the Environment, Forests and Landscape (SAEFL), *Precaution from Rio to Johannesburg, supra* note 261, M.-C. Cordonier Segger and M. Gehring, "Precaution in International Sustainable Development Law", *supra* note 262.

[270] See A. Trouwborst, *Evolution and Status of the Precautionary Principle in International Law* (The Hague: Kluwer Law International, 2002). And see T. O'Riordan, A. Jordan & J. Cameron (eds.), *Reinterpreting the Precautionary Principle* (London: Cameron May, 2001).

[271] JPOI, *supra.* note 14 at para. 23.

[272] See M.-C. Cordonier Segger and M.W. Gehring, "Precaution in International Sustainable Development Law", *supra* note 265.

greatly concerned about the need for precaution in relation to trade in and release of genetically modified organisms.[273] They have also sought recourse in precautionary measures to make decisions on trade in domestically prohibited goods, expressing concern about the environment and health impacts of international trade in chemicals and hazardous substances.[274] However, financial and technical assistance are needed to build legal capacity for sound management, risk assessment and capacity building on implementation of precautionary analysis. Careful implementation in accordance with the priorities of developing countries will be necessary, to further acceptance of the principle.

Thirdly, at the Summit, the question of the legal validity of the precautionary principle *per se* became less relevant internationally. Discussions focused more specifically on the scope and nature of precaution, such as, for example, in relation to the use and production of chemicals.

Precaution is a principle at the intersection of three areas of law, within the broader rubric of international law for sustainable development. It can foster useful and legitimate environmental law and policy, it has legitimate application in social (especially health) law, and certain formulations are increasingly recognized by economic (trade) law. This holds the potential to reconcile sometimes clashing interests for constructive, long-term solutions to challenging policy dilemmas. Governments could have gone further than what was agreed in Johannesburg. Developments since Rio could have been underlined, and more specific guidelines for the application of precaution could have been detailed. The WSSD reaffirmed the importance of precaution, in its 1992 *Rio Declaration* formulation at Principle 15. In most areas, including where environmental law intersects with international economic or social development law, this concept appears to be *lex ferenda*, a principle in the process of becoming international customary law, with persistent objectors properly on record.[275] The debates at the Johannesburg Summit on precaution may well foster and enhance implementation because instead of focusing on an abstract legal concept, debates now consider how the principle actually works and can be applied in a transparent and fair way. In the future, the manner of application and implementation will be crucial to both its acceptance and utilization.

---

[273] See *Cartagena Protocol on Biosafety, supra* note 29. For information on the negotiations of the Protocol see: <http:// www.biodiv.org/biosafety/protocol.asp>.

[274] World Health Organization and World Trade Organization, *WTO Agreements and Public Health: A Joint Study by the WHO and the WTO Secretariat* (Geneva: WTO/WHO, 2002). See also J. Cameron and J. Abouchar, "The Precautionary Principle: A Fundamental Principle of Law and Policy for the Protection of the Global Environment" (1991) 14 *Boston CICLR*, 1; and J.E. Hickey, Jr., and V.R. Walker, "Refining the Precautionary Principle in International Environmental Law", (1995), 14 *Va. Envtl. L.J.* 423, at 436.

[275] For further information about the process, see J. Cameron, "International Law and the Precautionary Principle" in T. O'Riordan, J. Cameron & A. Jordan, *Reinterpreting the Precautionary Principle* (London: Cameron May, 2001) 123.

The principle of public participation and access to information and justice

Public participation, supported by transparency and access to justice, is one of the most recognised principles of sustainable development.[276] In this regard, the emerging norm may take a formulation such as "states will ensure broad public participation in initiatives for sustainable development, through access to information and access to justice."[277] This is based on social laws, such as respect for the human rights to assembly, freedom of speech and expression. The State ensures that all persons have effective access to relevant information held by public and private actors regarding sustainable development issues. Effective participation also depends on attention to disparities within society and removal of obstacles to participation by vulnerable groups such as minorities, or the poor. A corollary to this requirement is the need for access to justice for individuals and groups, comprising effective judicial or administrative procedures to redress allegations of violations of entitlements or rights.

Emergence of the principle

Early manifestations of the right to participate at national levels are recognized in several major international human rights instruments, foremost among them being Article 25 of the *International Covenant on Civil and Political Rights* and Article 21 of the *Universal Declaration of Human Rights*.[278] One of the first major international documents to recognize public participation as central to equitable socio-economic development, was the 1986 United Nations General Assembly *Declaration on the Right to Development*. Its preamble recognises that "development is a comprehensive economic, social, cultural and political process, which aims at the constant improvement of the well-being of the entire population and of all individuals on the basis of their active, free and meaningful participation in development and in the fair distribution of benefits arising there from." Article 1 of the Declaration, which defines the "right to development," recognises universal public participation as essential for the expression of this right. It asserts that the "right to development is an inalienable human right by

---

[276] See Principle 10, 1992 *Rio Declaration, supra* note 1. See also the 1998 *Aarhus Convention on Access to Information, Public Participation and Access to Justice in Environmental Matters* (25 June 1998) (in force 30 Oct. 2001) 38 *ILM* 517. For discussion, see S. Charnovitz, "Two Centuries of Participation: NGOs and International Governance" (1997) 18 *Mich. J. of Int'l. L.* 183 and see Cordonier Segger, Khalfan, Gehring and Toering, "Prospects", *supra* note 196.

[277] See *Agenda 21, supra* note 17 at para. 8.3(d), 8.4(e), and 23.2, providing that sustainable development requires "broad public participation in decision-making." See also Principle 10, 1992 *Rio Declaration, supra* note 15.

[278] See the *Universal Declaration of Human Rights*, 10 Dec. 1948, G. A. Res. 217 A, U. N. GAOR, U. N. Doc. A/810 (1948). And see the *International Covenant on Civil and Political Rights*, 19 Dec. 1966, 999 UNTS 171 (entered into force 23 Mar. 1976).

virtue of which every human person and all peoples are entitled to participate in, contribute to, and enjoy social, cultural and political development, in which all human rights and fundamental freedoms can be fully realized".

The role of public participation as a necessary means for achieving sustainable development was clearly identified in the *Brundtland Report*, which found that:

in the specific context of the development and environment crisis [. . .], which current national and international political and economic institutions have not and perhaps cannot overcome, the pursuit of sustainable development requires: [. . .] a political system that secures effective citizen participation in decision-making.

The Brundtland Commission identified "effective participation" as a necessary component of sustainable development. The Commission refers particularly to the significance of participation in promoting sustainable development by specific groups of the public, namely indigenous people and NGOs.

Although *Agenda 21* and related texts do not refer to "participation" as a right, they do indicate that participation is vital in the process of sustainable development.

The preamble to the *Rio Declaration* calls for the establishment of a "new and equitable global partnership" which will be realised through new levels of co-operation among States and with non-state actors, namely "key sectors of societies and people." This new form of co-operation is based on the right to participation. *Agenda* 21 provides that "one of the fundamental prerequisites for the achievement of sustainable development is broad public participation in decision-making."

Agenda 21 emphasizes the desirability of direct participation in governance by identifying important roles for women, youth, indigenous people and their communities, non-governmental organizations, local authorities, workers and their trade unions, business and industry, the scientific and technological community, and farmers.[279] Public participation in the development and implementation of environmental and other laws is also encouraged.[280]

The Johannesburg Summit strongly reconfirmed this principle, at almost all levels. As well as reflecting its importance for international environmental decision-making, provisions on the importance of public participation can be found in almost all sections of the *Johannesburg Plan of Implementation*.[281] Legal

---

[279] *Ibid.*, chs. 23–32, and para. 8.3(c), recommending that governmental processes "facilitate the involvement of concerned individuals, groups and organizations in decision-making at all levels".

[280] See also *Agenda 21, ibid.* at para. 23.2, stating "One of the fundamental prerequisites for the achievement of sustainable development is broad public participation in decision-making." In addition, citizens should have "effective access to judicial and administrative proceedings, including redress and remedy". *Rio Declaration, supra* note 1, Principle 10; see also *Agenda 21* at para. 27.13, recommending that non-governmental organizations have the right to protect the public interest by law.

[281] *Johannesburg Declaration, supra* note 14 at 26 which states "[w]e recognize that sustainable development requires a long-term perspective and broad-based participation in policy formulation,

scholars have discussed participation by affected groups in areas of environment and development decision-making as a right.[282]

International instruments concerning indigenous peoples have been explicit in referring to participation as a right. In these texts, participation is expressed as instrumental to the realisation of other rights and values. For example, the International Labour Organizations's (ILO) 1989 *Convention on Indigenous and Tribal Peoples* recognizes "[t]he rights of the peoples concerned to the natural resources pertaining to their lands...[T]hese rights include the right of these peoples to participate in the use, management and conservation of these resources." The 1994 *Draft UN Declaration on Indigenous Peoples* likewise recognizes a right of indigenous peoples to participate "in the political, economic, social and cultural life of the State [Article 4] [...] if they so choose, at all levels of decision-making in matters which may affect their rights, lives and destinies [Article 19] [...] if they so choose, through procedures determined by them, in devising legislative or administrative measures that may affect them [Article 20]."

The right to participation is treated as a means for facilitating the realisation of other human rights in the 1994 *Draft Principles on Human Rights and the Environment*. It maintains that "[a]ll persons have the right to active, free and meaningful participation in planning and decision-making and processes that may have an impact on the environment and development. This includes a right to a prior assessment of the environmental, developmental and human rights consequences of proposed actions." The IUCN *Draft Covenant on Environment and Development* also refers to the right to public participation as a facilitating right, stating that "[a]ll persons [...] have [...] the right to participate in relevant decision-making processes."

Application of the principle

Since the *United Nations Conference on Environment and Development* (UNCED), there has been widespread agreement in international legal agreements dealing with the environment and socio-economic development that active "participation" by affected groups is not only desirable but necessary if sustainable development objectives are to be met. These instruments reflect the emergence of three dimensions to the concept of "public participation".

First, people should be accorded the opportunity to participate in official socio-economic development decision-making processes and activities that directly affect and impact their lives and well-being.

---

decision-making and implementation at all levels. As social partners, we will continue to work for stable partnerships with all major groups, respecting the independent, important roles of each of them."

[282] See A. Kiss and D. Shelton, *International Environmental Law*, 2nd edn. (New York: Transnational Publishers, 1994) at 67 [hereinafter *Kiss & Shelton*].

Secondly, in order to participate fully, the public must be provided with, or at least have access to, adequate information concerning the decisions and activities of government.

Agenda 21 recommends that governments ensure that non-State actors have access to information necessary for effective participation.[283] By including diverse groups as necessary participants for achieving sustainable development, *Agenda 21* and the other UNCED materials challenged longstanding assumptions regarding the role of government as the only legitimate player in developing and implementing international standards and legal rights and obligations. Recognising a place for non-State actors in the drafting and amending of international legal instruments for environmental protection and sustainable development is one of the major developments to come out of the UNCED.

Thirdly, those whose rights are affected by State decisions should have a right of access to justice. This aspect of public participation has developed significantly within Europe and is discussed further below.

The UN Committee on Economic, Social and Cultural Rights has indicated that this principle is essential to the realization of economic, social and cultural rights, such as, *inter alia*, the rights to health and water. It states that the right of individuals and groups to participate in decision-making processes, which may affect their development, must be an integral component of any policy, programme or strategy developed to discharge governmental obligations under the right to health. Furthermore, promoting health must involve effective community action in setting priorities, making decisions, planning, implementing and evaluating strategies to achieve better health.[284] It indicates that one component of these rights is "information accessibility" including the right to seek, receive and impart information concerning such issues.[285]

On the issue of access to justice, the Committee, in General Comment No. 9 on the *Domestic Application of the Covenant*, states that legally binding international human rights standards should operate directly and immediately within the domestic legal system of each State party, thereby enabling individuals to seek enforcement of their rights before national courts and tribunals. International remedies are also important as a supplementary measure. Such remedies need not always have a judicial dimension:

Administrative remedies will, in many cases, be adequate and those living within the jurisdiction of a State party have a legitimate expectation, based on the principle of good

---

[283] *Agenda 21, supra* note 17, para. 40.17–40.30, recommending more effective public dissemination of data related to sustainable development.; Sands, *International Environmental Law, supra* note 41, at 596–628, offering detailed explication of types of environmental information required under *Agenda 21* and other international agreements. National governments also are urged to educate the public about the challenges and opportunities of sustainable development. See *Agenda 21*, para. 8.11, 36.10.

[284] Committee on Economic, Social and Cultural Rights, *General Comment No.14: The Right to the Highest Attainable Standard of Health*, UN ESCOR, 2000, UN Doc. E/C.12/2000/4, at para. 54.

[285] *General Comment No. 15, supra* note 42 at para. 12 (c) (iv), *General Comment No. 14, supra* note 284 at, para. 12 (b) (iv).

faith, that all administrative authorities will take account of the requirements of the Covenant in their decision-making. Any such administrative remedies should be access-ible, affordable, timely and effective. An ultimate right of judicial appeal from adminis-trative procedures of this type would also often be appropriate. By the same token, there are some obligations, such as (but by no means limited to) those concerning non-discrimination, in relation to which the provision of some form of judicial remedy would seem indispensable in order to satisfy the requirements of the Covenant. In other words, whenever a Covenant right cannot be made fully effective without some role for the judiciary, judicial remedies are necessary.

Interestingly, in *General Comment No. 15* on the right to water, the Committee cites Principle 10 of the *Rio Declaration* to note the importance of effective remedies.[286] Therefore, the human rights system provides strong support and recognition of the sustainable development principle of participation and access to information and justice.

The 1998 *Aarhus Convention on Access to Information, Public Participation in Decision-making and Access to Justice in Environmental Matters*[287] *(Aarhus Convention)* has developed the principle of public participation significantly. Concluded under the auspices of the United Nations Economic Commission for Europe (UNECE) at its fourth "Environment for Europe" Convention in Aarhus, Denmark in June 1998.[288] The Convention is one of the first binding inter-national instruments to recognize "the right of every person of present and future generations to live in an environment adequate to his or health and well-being". The preamble to the Convention links this right of access to justice in environ-mental matters, stressing that "effective judicial mechanisms should be access-ible to the public, including organizations, so that its legitimate interests are protected and the law is enforced". This right is guaranteed by three types of procedural rights that each Party undertakes to provide: (1) access to infor-mation; (2) public participation in decision-making; and (3) access to justice in environmental matters. Article 9 of the 1998 *Aarhus Convention* provides for access to justice in environmental matters.[289]

---

[286] *General Comment No. 15, supra* note 42, para. 55.

[287] This regional convention is open to participation by members or consultative members of the UNECE (including North America and the former Soviet States of Central Asia). An annex lists the activities and installations in respect of which public participation provisions apply, including refiner-ies, power stations, nuclear reactors and installations, smelters, chemical plants, mines and waste management installations. It applies not just to transboundary activities, but also to national activities.

[288] Relevant background material includes important case-law of the European Court; see esp. Case C–25/62, *Plaumann v. Commission* [1963] ECR 95 at 107. See also Case C–231/82, *Spijker v. Commission* [1983] ECR 2559; Case C–97/85, *Deutsche Lebensmittelwerke v. Commission* [1987] ECR 2265; Case C–198/91, *Cook v. Commission* [1993] ECR I–2487; Case C–225/92, *Matra v. Commission* [1993] ECR I–3203; Case T–2/93, *Air France v. Commission* [1994] ECR II–323; Case T–465/93, *Consorzio Gruppo di Azione Locale "Murgia Messapica" v. Commission* [1994] ECR II–361.

[289] Article 9 requires Parties to ensure access to justice in three circumstances: (1) Parties must ensure access to a review procedure before a court or another independent and impartial body

The provisions of Article 9(2) and 9(3) offer the greatest potential for civil society organisations (CSOs) seeking to bring enforcement actions against Community institutions. Article 9(2) of 1998 *Aarhus Convention* obligates the Parties to provide access to justice to members of the public having either a "sufficient interest" in a matter or "maintaining impairment of a right".[290] Whether the language of Article 9(2) creates an obligation to provide a remedy to CSOs in matters involving activities subject to Article 6 is still in question. Decisions encompassed by Article 6 (and hence potentially challengeable under Article 9(2)) are only those debated to permit the proposed activity. Generally, permitting decisions falls within the jurisdiction of the member States rather than Community institutions. Therefore, a decision concerning funding to support the construction of power stations, such as the *Greenpeace* case, would most likely not be considered to rest "on whether to permit" the activity.[291]

The most far-reaching of the access to justice provisions are those contained in Article 9(3).[292] Access to justice for members of the public to enforce environmental laws was a hotly debated issue in the negotiations leading up to the Aarhus Conference. The result of this debate is reflected in the terms of Article 9(3), which provides: "In addition and without prejudice to the review procedures referred to in [Articles 9(1) and (2)] above, each Party shall ensure that,

established by law for any person who considers that his or her information request has been ignored, wrongfully refused, inadequately answered, or otherwise not dealt with in accordance with the Convention's access to information provision under Art. 4; (2) Parties must ensure access to a review procedure before a court or another independent and impartial body established by law for "members of the public concerned" to challenge "the substantive and procedural legality of any decision, act or omission subject to the provisions of Art. 6" (dealing with public participation in decision-making), and "where [review is] so provided for under national law...of other relevant provisions of this Convention"; and (3) Parties must ensure access to administrative or judicial procedures for "members of the public...to challenge acts and omissions by private persons and public authorities which contravene provisions of its national law relating to the environment."

[290] Parties must determine whether an applicant has sufficient interest or maintains an impairment of a right in accordance with the requirements of national law and consistent "with the objective of giving the public concerned wide access to justice within the scope of the Convention." Many environmental CSOs will meet the definition of "the public concerned" in Art. 2(5) of the Convention. Moreover, CSOs may also have rights capable of being impaired for the purposes of invoking Art. 9(2).

[291] Case C–321/95 P *Greenpeace Int'l v. Commission* [1998] ECR I–1651 [hereinafter *Greenpeace Case*]. The case was brought by a number of individuals claiming to be affected by the decision of the European Commission, two local environmental associations based in the Canary Islands (Tagoror Ecologista Alternativo (TEA) and Comision Canaria Contra la Contaminacion (CIC)), and Greenpeace Spain. The individual applicants sought to justify their claims on a number of bases, including residence in the area of the works in question, ownership of real estate in the area, the carrying on of occupational activity within the area and alleged negative impacts on health, tourism, fishing, farming, education of the young, local flora and fauna, and occupations connected with windsurfing in the islands. At para. 28, the ECJ upheld the decision of the Court of First Instance denying the individual applicants standing on the basis that "where...the specific situation of the applicant was not taken into consideration in the adoption of the act, which concerns him in a general and abstract fashion and, in fact, like any other person in the same situation, the applicant is not individually concerned by the act".

[292] See P. Sands, "European Community Environmental Law: The Evolution of a Regional Regime of International Environmental Protection" (1991) 100 *Yale L.J.* 2511 at 2519.

where they meet the criteria, if any, laid down in its national law, members of the public have access to administrative or judicial procedures to challenge acts and omissions by private persons and public authorities which contravene provisions of its national law relating to the environment."[293] Rather than preserving the *status quo*, however, the 1998 *Aarhus Convention* may provide a basis for the European Court of Justice to reconsider its application of the "direct and individual concern" criterion in environmental cases.[294] Effective judicial recourse is mainly achieved within the domestic legal order of the Member States, as both the European Court of Justice in Luxembourg and the European Court of Human Rights in Strasbourg involve a slow, cumbersome and costly procedure of redress. However, recent judicial activism at the level of these courts, securely grounded on the basic principles of the founding treaties and the protection of human rights worldwide, has significantly advanced openness. In the European Court of Justice, the perceived "democratic deficit" created by its ruling in the *Greenpeace* case may be remedied by implementing the *Aarhus Convention's* access to justice provisions. As such, the 1998 *Aarhus Convention* may give CSOs standing to bring their own suit to the European Court of Justice to challenge acts of Community institutions that allegedly violate Community environmental law. As the European Community proceeds to ratify the treaty, the European Court of Justice may need to reconsider its interpretation of the "direct and individual concern" criteria of Article 173 to allow the public and CSOs to vindicate the environmental rights expressed in the treaty.

The need to broaden the type of participants recognized as necessary for sustainable development has transformed international law-making. Public participation in the design and implementation of objectives in international law relating to sustainable development has become standard in both hard and soft law. One of the most innovative instruments in this regard, the 1994 UN *Desertification Convention*, includes participation among the objectives and obligations of States.

Article 3 of the *Desertification Convention*, provides that "[i]n order to achieve the objectives of this Convention and to implement its provisions, the Parties shall be guided *inter alia*, by the following: (a) the Parties should ensure that decisions [. . .] are taken with the participation of populations and local

---

[293] As members of the "public", NGOs are entitled to challenge the actions of public authorities that contravene environmental laws. Prospective challengers, however, must "meet the criteria, if any, laid down in [a Party's] national law". In the EU context, where NGOs seek to challenge the actions of Community institutions that allegedly contravene provisions of Community environmental laws, these criteria would seem to include the Art. 173 requirements of "direct and individual concern".

[294] The appellants in *Greenpeace* relied on the judgments of the ECJ in Case C-240/83 *Procureur de la Republique* v. *Association de Defense des Bruleurs d'Huiles Usagees* [1985] ECR 531, and Case C-131/88 *Commission* v. *Denmark* [1988] ECR 4607, which declared environmental protection to be one of the Community's essential objectives; Case C-361/88 *Commission* v. *Germany* [1991] ECR I-825 and I-2567, which found that Community environmental legislation can create rights and obligations for individuals, and Case C-431/92 *Commission* v. *Germany* [1995] ECR I-2189, which holds that Directive 85/337 creates individual rights of participation in the environmental impact assessment procedure.

communities" In Article 5, signatories to the Convention commit themselves to "[u]ndertake to [...] promote awareness and facilitate the participation of local populations, particularly women and youth with the support of non-governmental organisations, in efforts to combat desertification". In Article 9, they promise that "[i]n carrying out their obligations [...] affected country Parties [...] shall, as appropriate, prepare, make public and implement national action programmes. [...] Such programmes shall be updated through a continuing participatory process."

Participation within international law relating to sustainable development also embodies a framework in which critical decisions can be made at the level most consistent with effectiveness. *Agenda 21* calls on national governments to delegate sustainable development responsibilities "to the lowest level of public authority consistent with effective action".[295] This is well known within the European Community as the principle of subsidiarity.[296] In federal systems, for example, national governments would delegate to states or provinces responsibilities for sustainable development that would be most effectively carried by those levels, whereupon these governments would delegate those responsibilities best managed locally to local governments. Subsidiarity attempts to ensure that national policies are carried out in a manner that fosters self-determination and accountability at a local level, including political liberty, flexibility, preservation of community identity, social and cultural diversity, and respect for distinct communities within States.[297]

In most States, the application of subsidiarity equates with a decentralization of power and increased local decision-making. Indeed, it may be that interconnections between the environment, the economy and social conditions are more readily visible at the local level, typically less complex, easier to understand and thus often easier to address.[298] In short, the public's dependence on the resources and particular ecosystems in question provides its own regulatory framework. Decentralization on the whole is seen to bring the government closer to the people and in one commentator's words has the ability "to release the energies of ordinary people, enabling them to take charge of their lives".[299]

The debate over sustainable use of biologically diverse resources provides a useful example for the role of public participation. For non-State actors, participation leading to sustainable development requires that affected groups, such as local communities inhabiting and utilising biologically rich areas, play an active role in shaping and implementing laws for the protection of local species and

---

[295] *Agenda 21, supra* note 17, at para. 8.5(g).
[296] GA Bermann, "Taking Subsidiarity Seriously: Federalism in The European Community and the United States" (1994) 94 *Colum. L. Rev.* 331 at 338.
[297] *Ibid.*, at 339–44. See also *Dernbach, supra* note 164.
[298] See J.S. Adams and T.O. Mcshane, *The Myth of Wild Africa: Conservation Without Illusion*, (New York: Norton, 1996) (stating that wildlife conservation can succeed only if it is directly related to rural economic development).
[299] J. Holmberg, *Defending the Future: A Guide to Sustainable Development* (London: Earthscan Publications, 1988).

ecosystems. Increased participation in the institutions and processes of international law is often a prerequisite for the successful design and implementation of socio-economic and environmental objectives. Neither environmental nor developmental strategies are likely to be sustainable unless all affected actors, both State and non-State, and particularly those with special dependencies on the resources at issue, are involved in decision-making.

Participation after the Johannesburg Summit

The *Johannesburg Declaration* states that countries "recognize that sustainable development requires a long-term perspective and broad-based participation in policy formulation, decision-making and implementation at all levels".[300] They commit, as social partners, to "continue to work for stable partnerships with all major groups, respecting the independent, important roles of each of them".

A coalition of civil society organizations, called the "Access Initiative", worked hard at the Johannesburg Summit to further support for the principles of the *Aarhus Convention* and other commitments to public participation.[301] Efforts to gain the Summit's support for global multilateral guidelines on the implementation of Rio Principle 10 were unsuccessful. However, in the JPOI governments agreed to "[e]nsure access, at the national level, to environmental information and judicial and administrative proceedings in environmental matters, as well as public participation in decision-making, so as to further principle 10 of the Rio Declaration on Environment and Development, taking into full account principles 5, 7 and 11 of the Declaration."[302] This is a clear vote of support for the work of the Access Initiative, and indeed, a project has been organized to follow up from this process, in the form of a "Type II Outcome" of the WSSD which will be tied to the Plan of Implementation and the *Johannesburg Declaration.*[303] Principles 5, 7 and 11 of the Declaration concern principles regarding poverty eradication, common but differentiated responsibilities, and the need for standards to reflect specific contexts, particularly for developing countries. These principles qualify the commitment to ensure access to information and justice for public participation by taking into account the specific needs of different regions.

While the specific reference to national level access and Principle 10 of the *Rio Declaration* seems focused on the environment alone, provisions on public participation, access to information and access to justice are found throughout the JPOI referring to public participation in areas such as poverty eradication, which focuses on the participation of traditionally marginalized groups, such as women and indigenous peoples, in the development and implementation of

---

[300] Johnnesburg Declaration, *supra* note 14 at para. 26.
[301] See World Resources Institute and partners, found online at <www.wri.org>. And see 1992 Rio Dedaration, Principle 10.
[302] See JPOI, note 14, at para. 128.
[303] For more information on the Type II and Type I Outcomes of the Summit, see *World Summit for Sustainable Development* Type II Initiatives, available online: www.un.org.

poverty reduction strategies.[304] In the area of ensuring more sustainable production and consumption patterns, public participation and consultation of stakeholders is specifically mentioned in sections committing to further efforts for energy and waste management. In addition, in the section focused on protecting and managing the natural resource base of economic and social development, references are made to ensuring public participation in different ways in terms of water, agriculture, mountains, biodiversity, forestry and mining. The Plan even provides for increased participation (in markets) of small and medium-sized enterprises, and special provisions regarding the need to ensure public participation in the development of national strategies for sustainable development as a means of implementation. Finally, in the Plan of Implementation, at Chapter XI on the Institutional Framework for Sustainable Development, there are provisions for the need to ensure the participation of civil society, major groups, and the public at different levels of sustainable development governance.[305]

In the end, the principle of participation received significant support and was taken into account in many different aspects of the sustainable development agenda. Follow-up will require a sustained and concerted effort on the part of civil society, including major groups. The procedures followed by the WSSD Bureau and UN Secretary General certainly point towards good possibilities for effective implementation of the principle.[306]

Perhaps the WSSD provisions for so-called "Type II" outcomes of the Summit were most interesting in this respect. These partnership initiatives for sustainable development can be directly undertaken by civil society groups in partnership with governments, as part of Summit follow-up activities. One such initiative in this area is the partnership undertaken by the "Access Initiative" and others – the PP10 (Partnership for Principle 10), which seeks to further develop concrete national and regional strategies to ensure public participation, access to information and justice in economies in transition, developing countries, and other areas.[307] As another example, a coalition of institutions led by the Centre for International Sustainable Development Law, the International Development Law Organization and the International Law Association (Committee on International Law on Sustainable Development) launched the "International Law for Sustainable Development" partnership at WSSD.[308] Further work is needed to ensure that in the context of sustainable development, the principle of public participation becomes better recognized. The challenge will be the need to set

---

[304] See JPOI, *supra* note 14, at para. 7.

[305] See *ibid.*, at para. 164, which states: "[a]ll countries should also promote public participation, including through measures that provide access to information regarding legislation, regulations, activities, policies and programmes. They should also foster full public participation in sustainable development policy formulation and implementation. Women should be able to participate fully and equally in policy formulation and decision-making."

[306] In the lead-up to the WSSD, these included stakeholder dialogues, experts' sessions and round-tables, and major efforts for outreach to civil society events. See www.johannesburgsummit.org.

[307] See Partnership for Principle 10 (PP10), available online: www.pp10.org.

[308] The International Law for Sustainable Development partnership's objectives are threefold. First, the partners will carry out legal research and capacity building in international sustainable development law to assist developing country governments, Inter-Governmental Organizations,

sustained efforts in place to better implement the principle in national, regional and international legal and policy contexts, over the course of the next decade.

THE PRINCIPLE OF GOOD GOVERNANCE

The challenge for all societies is to create a system of governance that promotes, supports and sustains human development – especially among the poorest and most marginalized peoples. Governance can be described as the exercise of economic, political and administrative authority to manage a country's affairs at all levels and on all issues. It comprises the mechanisms, processes and institutions through which citizens and groups articulate their interests, exercise their legal rights, meet their obligations and mediate their differences.[309] Good governance has been proposed by the ILA as a principle, one which requires governments to ensure reliable institutions for coherent, effective decision-making, and, respect for the rule of law. It is closely related to the principle of participation, access to information and justice. The term "good governance" though widely used and well popularized, is yet to be formally defined. Aside from the above-mentioned components, there is significant debate as to its scope (e.g. to inter-state decision-making) and the range of actors to which it applies (e.g. to private actors).

The importance of this principle was strongly recognized in the *Johannesburg Declaration*, with a commitment to "undertake to strengthen and improve governance at all levels for the effective implementation of *Agenda 21*, the Millennium development goals and the Plan of Implementation of the Summit".[310] Aspects of the good governance are dealt with in international institutions such as the New Partnership for Africa's Development "Peer Review Mechanism" and in the *United Nations Convention to Combat Corruption*.

In its original formulation, good governance was used mainly by international financial and development institutions to depict the need to review improper or unsatisfactory functioning of governmental machinery or the need for more efficient administration.[311] There have been varied, if perfunctory definitions of the term "governance". The World Bank states that "Governance [is] the

judges, parliamentarians, local communities, and the media to effectively address inter-linked environmental, economic and social challenges. Second, they seek to produce a series of policy and educational publications on international sustainable development law, particularly to be used in training seminars/workshops, which shall be made widely accessible to scholars, decision-makers and civil society, in particular those in developing countries (and countries in transition). Third, they aim to develop a user-friendly web-based legal resource centre, engaging developed and developing country jurists, to assess, promote and implement integration of international social, economic, and environmental law. A network of developed and developing country sustainable development law faculties will support this legal resource centre. See CISDL, ILA and IDLO Type II Partnership initiative, found online at <http://www.un.org>.

[309] P. Uvin and I. Biagiotti, "Global Governance and the 'New' Political Conditionality" (1996) 2 *Global Governance: A Review of Multilaterism and International Organizations* 377.

[310] *Johannesburg Declaration, supra* note 14 at 30.

[311] For example, in explaining Africa's development problems, the World Bank stated that "Underlying the litany of Africa's development problems is a crisis of governance." See World Bank, *Sub-Saharan Africa: From Crisis to Sustainable Growth* (Washington: World Bank, 1989) at 60.

exercise of political power to manage a nation's affairs."[312] Another articulation, more descriptive than definitional, sees governance as "the conscious management of regime structures with a view to enhancing the legitimacy of the public realm".[313] There are a number of reasons why attempts at a solid definition of good governance may have failed. Clearly, the concept is heavily value-laden. It is also very general in its orientation. Moreover, the elements of "good" governance are not incontestable in themselves. This section addresses these issues.

Emergence of the principle

The use of the term "governance", in its contemporary form, is attributed to the World Bank.[314] In a foreword to the 1989 *World Development Report*, the President of the Bank stated that "private sector initiative and market mechanisms are important, but they must go hand-in-hand with good governance".[315] Indeed, the entire report contained extensive references to the substance of "governance". In 1992, the World Bank published a report entitled *Governance and Development*, which in many respects represented the promulgation of good governance as a major variable in economic development. It discussed in more detail some of the signposts of "good governance" as perceived by the institution. These include public sector management, legal framework, accountability and transparency. Following the 1992 publication closely, the World Bank described in 1994 some of its experiences with a team working in concrete situations.[316] In that material, the World Bank indicated its sensitivity to the political dimensions of governance and its restraint in that regard. It did, however, confirm the consultative role it must play with governments and other funding agencies in "governance matters". Finally, in an acknowledgement of the critical role the State plays in economic development, the World Bank in 1997 announced that an effective State apparatus, combined with "good governance" is a necessary condition for development.[317]

A number of other development-oriented institutions have paid attention to the issue of governance. For example, in 1997 the International Monetary Fund (IMF) decided to incorporate governance as a criterion for assistance.[318] However, given

---

[312] See World Bank, *Sub-Saharan Africa: From Crisis to Sustainable Growth* (1989) [hereinafter World Bank, *Africa*].

[313] G. Hyden and M. Bratton, eds., *Governance and Politics in Africa* (Boulder: Lynne Rienner Publishers, 1993) at 7.

[314] See A. Tolentino, "Good Governance Through Popular Participation in Sustainable Development" in K. Ginther *et al.*, *Sustainable Development and Good Governance* (The Hague: Martinus Nijhoff, 1995) at 142; World Bank, *Governance: The World Bank's Experience* (Washington: World Bank, 1994) at vii [hereinafter World Bank, *Governance*].

[315] See World Bank, *Africa*, *supra* note 312 at xii.   [316] *Ibid.*

[317] See World Bank, *The State in a Changing World* (Washington: World Bank, 1997). Besides these publications, the World Bank also released materials dealing with governance at various times. Examples include L. Frischtak, *Antinomies of Development: Governance Capacity and Adjustment Responses* (Washington: World Bank, 1993); L. Mills and I. Serageldin, *Governance and the External Factor* (Washington: World Bank, 1992).

[318] See generally International Monetary Fund, *Good Governance: The IMF's Role* (Washington: IMF, 1997); International Monetary Fund, *Code of Good Practices on Fiscal Transparency – Declaration of Principles*, 16 April 1998, 37 ILM 942 (1998) at 942 [hereinafter IMF, *Governance*].

its preoccupation with macroeconomic management issues, the IMF has been less conspicuous in its interest in "good governance". Nevertheless, it proposed to co-ordinate its concerns on governance with other bilateral and multilateral funding sources.[319] Furthermore, the United Nations Development Program (UNDP) has stated that "it is only with good governance that we can find solutions to poverty, inequity and insecurity".[320] The Organization for Economic Co-operation and Development (OECD) also stated its preparedness to rely on governance as a test for assistance to poor countries.[321] The African Development Bank, the Asian Development Bank, bilateral development agencies such as the British Overseas Development Agency, the Danish Development Agency, the United States Development Agency and others, have all, at various times and occasions since the late 1980s, stressed the importance of governance as a critical factor in development.[322]

It is hardly challenged that the concept of good governance, in its modern form, owes its popularity to the international financial and development institutions. The substance of governance, however, has earlier origins.[323] In the early twentieth century, for example, Max Weber outlined the functions of a bureaucracy that would facilitate development.[324] He called for the strict observance of rule of law and legal rationality and advised against the mixture of private interests with the public responsibilities of the bureaucrat.[325]

Application of the principle

There appear to be two key approaches to current discussions on governance. The first emphasizes the domestic dynamics of good governance, while the second focuses on the international dimensions of governance. The domestic approach argues for stringent reforms in developing countries that are seen to lack sufficient progress towards good governance.[326] The international approach points to an emerging requirement of democratic governance under international law.[327] This

---

[319] IMF, *Governance, ibid.*

[320] United Nations Development Program, *Governance Policy Paper* (New York: UNDP, 1997) at 1 [hereinafter UNDP, *Governance*].

[321] The European Union also resolved in 1991 to condition its development relationships with poor countries on good governance. See P.J.I.M. de Waart, "Securing Access to Safe Drinking Water through Trade and International Migration", in E. Brans *et al.*, eds., *The Scarcity of Water: Emerging Legal and Policy Responses* (New York: Kluwer Law International, 1997) at 116–17.

[322] See T.M. Franck, *Fairness in International Law and Institutions* (Oxford: Oxford University Press, 1995) [hereinafter *Franck*].

[323] The works of classical philosophers such as Thomas Hobbes, Jean J. Rousseau, Montesquieu, Machiavelli, Plato, Confucius, J.S. Mill, Adam Smith, Karl Marx and many others, have all hinged on the idea of proper governance of society. See G.H. Sabine, *A History of Political Theory* (New York: Holt, Rinehart and Winston, 1961); D. Held, *Models of Democracy* (Stanford: Stanford University Press, 1987).

[324] For a relevant discussion of Weber, see W.J. Mommsen, *The Age of Bureaucracy: Perspectives on the Political Sociology of Max Weber* (Oxford: Oxford University Press, 1974).

[325] See generally G. Roth & C. Wittich, eds., *Max Weber, Economy and Society: An Outline of Interpretive Sociology* (Berkeley: University of California Press, 1968).

[326] P. McAuslan, "Good Governance and Aid in Africa" (1996) 40 *J. Afr. L.* 168 at 168–82.

[327] *Franck, supra* note 322 at 83. In 1994, the UN and the Organization of American States refused to recognize the military junta that overthrew the democratically elected government of Haiti and

approach calls for greater participation of developing countries in international institutions, particularly international economic institutions such as the Bretton Woods institutions, where developed countries hold majority voting power, and the World Trade Organization, where developed countries have historically dominated negotiations. Debate on both approaches were predominant in the 2002 *World Summit for Sustainable Development* and in the Monterrey Conference on Financing for Development.

Indeed, the *Johannesburg Plan of Implementation* states that:

[g]ood governance within each country and at the international level is essential for sustainable development. At the domestic level, sound environmental, social and economic policies, democratic institutions responsive to the needs of the people, the rule of law, anti-corruption measures, gender equality and an enabling environment for investment are the basis for sustainable development.[328]

In Chapter XI on Institutional Framework for Sustainable Development, as is discussed below in greater detail, the importance of good international governance, in particular global economic governance and a rules-based multilateral trading system, is recognized. In addition, Chapter XI goes on to offer specific guidance to countries on a national level, stating (at para. 162) that countries must:

[c]ontinue to promote coherent and coordinated approaches to institutional frameworks for sustainable development at all national levels, including through, as appropriate, the establishment or strengthening of existing authorities and mechanisms necessary for policy-making, coordination and implementation and enforcement of laws

and (at para 163) that:

[a]ll countries should promote sustainable development at the national level by, *inter alia*, enacting and enforcing clear and effective laws that support sustainable development. All countries should strengthen governmental institutions, including by providing necessary infrastructure and by promoting transparency, accountability and fair administrative and judicial institutions.[329]

---

called for the forcible removal of the junta. See P. Uvin and I. Biagiotti, "Global Governance and the 'New' Political Conditionality" (1996) 2 *Global Governance: A Review of Multilaterism and International Organizations* 377 at 384–88. The international wing of the governance discourse can be seen beyond the political or individual countries' or regional responses to events in any one country. The UN, the ICJ, the WTO, the World Bank, IMF and regional organizations such as the EU, MERCOSUR, OAU, OAS, the Commonwealth, and ECOWAS, may all be seen as institutions of global governance seeking to facilitate the harmonization of national policies in various fields. See M.J. Trebilcock, "What Makes Poor Countries Poor?: The Role of Institutional Capital in Economic Development" in E. Buscaglia, W. Ratliff & R. Cooter, eds., *The Law and Economics of Development* (London: JAI Press Inc., 1997) at 15. See also *Charter of Paris for a New Europe*, 21 Nov. 1990, 30 ILM 190 at 193.

[328] JPOI, *supra* note 14 at para. 4. There are also specific references to the need to improve governance and the rule of law with regard to forests (para. 45 (f)), and sustainable development in Africa with reference to human rights and urban management (paras. 62 and 71).

[329] See JPOI, *supra* note 14, at paras. 162–163.

This underlines one of the most critical tasks in sustainable development law for the next decade – to support domestic implementation of global sustainable development principles and agreements. This focus depends not only on new resources, technical assistance and capacity building programmes, but also on legal and institutional reform: governance.

Integrating these two approaches, the UNDP has identified a set of character-istics for good governance.[330] They include: participation,[331] rule of law,[332] transparency,[333] responsiveness,[334] consensus orientation,[335] equity,[336] effect-iveness and efficiency,[337] accountability,[338] and strategic vision.[339] These core characteristics are interrelated and mutually reinforcing – they cannot stand alone. For example, accessible information means more transparency, broader participation and more effective decision-making. Broad participation contrib-utes both to the exchange of information needed for legitimate decision-making. Legitimacy, in turn, means effective implementation and thus further participa-tion. Responsive institutions must therefore be transparent, and function according to the rule of law if they are to be equitable. The UNDP has later indicated that such principles as equity, transparency and accountability must equally apply to the international as national level, especially to trade and financial intergovernmental institutions.[340] While these aspects are all essential for the adoption and promulgation of the principles of international law relating to sustainable development, and many are reflected in international treaties and customary law, it remains to be seen whether "good governance" as a distinct legal obligation can be developed into a customary legal principle in its own right.

---

[330] UNDP, *Governance, supra* note 320. An exception to this trend towards assessment of charac-teristics is A. Seidman *et al.*, "Building Sound National Frameworks For Development and Social Change" (1999), 4 *CEPML & P. J.* 1.

[331] All men and women must have a voice in decision-making, either directly or through legitimate intermediate institutions that represent their interests. Such broad participation is built on freedom of association and speech, as well as capacities to participate constructively.

[332] Legal frameworks must be fair and enforced impartially, particularly the laws on human rights.

[333] Transparency is built on the free flow of information. Processes, institutions and information are directly accessible to those concerned with them, and enough information is provided to under-stand and monitor them.

[334] Institutions and processes must try to serve all stakeholders.

[335] Good governance mediates differing interests to reach a broad consensus on what is in the best interests of the group and, where possible, on policies and procedures.

[336] All men and women must have opportunities to improve or maintain their well-being.

[337] Processes and institutions should produce results that meet needs while making the best use of resources.

[338] Decision-makers in government, the private sector and civil society organizations must be accountable to the public, as well as to institutional stakeholders. This accountability differs depending on the organization and whether the decision is internal or external to an organization.

[339] Leaders and the public must have a broad and long-term perspective on good governance and human development, along with a sense of what is needed for such development. There is also an understanding of the historical, cultural and social complexities in which that perspective is grounded.

[340] United Nations Development Programme, *Human Development Report 2002: Deepening Democracy in a Fragmented World* (Oxford: Oxford University Press, 2000) at 112–122.

GENERAL OBSERVATIONS FROM THE SURVEY OF PRINCIPLES

The Principles of International Law Related to Sustainable Development, as proposed by the International Law Association in the 2002 New Delhi Declaration, have clear resonance in emerging treaty regimes, decisions of tribunals and in the Johannesburg outcomes themselves. They represent a useful first step in analysis. However, in most cases, these are as yet emerging principles of international law. Further study, precise analysis of their normative (rule-setting) formulations and above all, evidence of acceptance as binding custom by States, is still required to make a convincing case for their normative, binding character. Principles such as integration, precaution, equity and poverty eradication, sustainable use of natural resources, common but differentiated responsibility, public participation and good governance, along with others that may be proposed, appear with increasing frequency and operational relevance in many social, economic and environmental regimes. It will be important, over the next decades, to monitor their development, operationalization and recognition by States as sustainable development law becomes better defined and implemented.

PART III

THE PRACTICES

6

Case Studies of Innovative Instruments

These case studies provide examples of international legal instruments and regimes at the various degrees of integration. They illustrate the manner in which integration can occur in a practical sense, and to varying extents, also demonstrate instances where the principles of sustainable development law discussed in Part III have become operational.

The four degrees of integration, again, are:

- separate, non-integrated social, economic and environmental regimes,
- parallel yet interdependent regimes,
- partially integrated environmental, economic and social regimes, and
- innovative, fully-integrated instruments within regimes.

The first case study, of Sustainability Impact Assessment (SIA), is examined as an example of an integrated tool of sustainable development law, describing stakeholder participation strategies and recent innovations in integrated assessment procedures. The second case study surveys Regional Integration Agreements (RIAs) in the Americas for the use of innovative instruments (at different degrees of integration) to address environmental and social concerns in diverse economic integration arrangements, with notes on mechanisms to ensure increased openness. Finally, a third case study focuses on the application of international human rights instruments relating to economic, social and cultural rights in order to address international economic and environmental concerns.

SUSTAINABILITY IMPACT ASSESSMENTS (SIAs)

Impact assessment procedures have become one of the most obvious examples of "integrated thinking" in the international arena.[1] The whole terrain, originally

---

[1] Although international law may not currently require development to be sustainable, international law can require development decisions to be the outcome of a process which promotes sustainable development – including the carrying out of SIAs on the correct levels and ensuring public

centred upon environmental impact assessments (EIAs) of specific projects, has broadened dramatically. There have been significant increases in the range of activities to which assessments are applied, and a widening of the scope of assessment criteria beyond the purely environmental.[2] At the same time increasing attention is being given to public participation and decision-making on different levels.

This case study presents impact assessment as an instrument initially at the "third degree" of integration, but which is evolving towards the "fourth degree", becoming a highly integrated mechanism in which economic, social and environmental objectives and instruments are woven together.

Environmental impact assessment

An environmental impact assessment is a procedure that is carried out to determine possible effects of a proposed activity on the environment. It usually includes a preliminary scientific or information-gathering phase and a report, which is then followed by a decision to proceed or not with a full study, sometimes in tandem with additional measures such as full investigations and studies, public meetings or consultations and the publication of extensive studies with recommended mitigation measures. The earliest mandatory EIA procedures were introduced in the 1970s by the US *National Environmental Protection Act*.[3] The impetus behind such laws has been changing, but originally the motivation stemmed from a need to balance different domestic agendas. As with certain other emerging themes in contemporary international law, the idea of EIA arose in national policy and was then adopted into the international arena.[4] EIA norms have then "filtered back" from international to national and regional laws in three ways:

---

participation in decision-making. See D. Devuys, "Sustainability Assessment: the Application of a Methodological Framework" (1999) 1 *Journal of Environmental Assessment Policy and Management* 4 at 459–87.

[2] Early EIA procedures were not as integrated. According to M. Lee and C. Kirkpatrick, in M. Lee and C. Kirkpatrick, eds., (Manchester: Manchester University Press, 2000) [hereinafter *Lee & Kirkpatrick*], at 2 "[t]he US National Environmental Protection Act (NEPA) was not an example of integrated appraisal," rather choosing to establish a specialised environmental appraisal separate from and largely additional to the technical, financial and economic appraisals that were in practice and encouraged by legal requirements." See also UNEP, *Goals and Principles of Environmental Impact Assessment* (Nairobi: UNEP, 1987). And see the 1991 Convention on Environmental Impact Assessment in a Transboundary Content (25 Feb. 1991) 30 *I.L.M.* 800.

[3] 42 U.S.C. § 4321–47. The Act applies only to US Federal Government projects.

[4] See EC, Commission, *Communication from the European Commission on the Precautionary Principle*, COM 1 (2000), WTO doc. WT/CTE/W/147G/TBT/W/ 137 (27 June 2000); and Bundesimmissionsschutzgesetz—BImSchG, Art. 5.2: "Installations subject to authorization are to be constructed and operated in such a manner that...2. Precaution is taken against damaging environmental effects..." and G. Feldhaus, "Der Vorsorgegrundsatz des Bundes-Immissionsschutzgesetzes" [1980] *Deutsches Verwaltungsblatt*, at 133–139; Rat von Sachverständigen für Umweltfragen, *Umweltprobleme der Nordsee* (Stuttgart: Kiepenheuer & Witsch, 1980) at 444–446; and G. Hartkopf and E. Bohne, *Umweltpolitik, vol. 1: Grundlagen, Analysen, und Perspektiven* (Opladen: Westdeutscher Verlag, 1983) at 112–113, where it is noted that the precautionary principle originated in Germany.

- through the influence of "soft law"
- under State obligations to implement specific international law instruments
- to some extent at least, under obligations in customary international law.[5]

There is now a general international acknowledgement of the growing importance of EIA as a national instrument, and there are currently regulations for project level EIA in over 100 countries. There are also tremendous variations in the numbers of assessments carried out in each country. According to a 1993 European Commission study, in France, 5,500 assessments were carried out per annum; in the United Kingdom, 189; in Italy there were 28; and in Denmark, six. There were also considerable variations in the types of projects assessed, particularly with regard to situations where assessment was discretionary. In Flanders, for example, 71 per cent of the projects assessed were in agriculture. All projects assessed in Italy were infrastructure projects. This was also the highest category for the United Kingdom at 49 per cent. The highest number in Spain, also at 49 per cent, was in mining. The increasing recognition of its utility on a national level is reflected in Principle 17 of the 1992 *Rio Declaration*, which provides: "Environmental impact assessment, as a national instrument, shall be undertaken for proposed activities that are likely to have a significant adverse impact on the environment and are subject to a decision of a competent national authority."[6] Indeed, in some cases, civil society groups wielding demands for EIAs have been able to appeal to courts for enforcement of their requests, obliging governments to comply with EIA requirements.[7]

At the international level, obligations in international environmental law to conduct EIAs arose first in the context of the potential transboundary impacts of particular projects, and were largely the cumulative corollary of a State's international environmental law obligations. These include obligations under customary international law first described in the early US-Canada *Trail-Smelter* dispute, to ensure that activities within State jurisdiction or control do not damage the environment of other States.[8] The International Court of Justice has also found a

---

[5] For a survey of hard and soft legal obligations to conduct EIAs, see P.N. Okowa, "Procedural Obligations in International Environmental Agreements" [1996] *Brit. Y.B. of Int'l L.* 275.

[6] *Rio Declaration on Environment and Development*, Report of the *United Nations Conference on Environment and Development*, UN Doc. A/CONF.151/6/Rev.1, (1992), 31 ILM 874 (1992), Principle 17 [hereinafter *Rio Declaration*].

[7] In *Quebec v. Canada* [1994] S.C.J. No. 13 (online: QuickLaw), a group of parties, including local aboriginal communities, successfully applied for an injunction to suspend the transportation of produced hydroelectric power to the United States until an EIA of the operation was completed.

[8] This principle follows the well-established legal maxim: "*sic utere tuo ut alienum non laedas*". The obligation to refrain from injuring other States is recognized as a fundamental norm of international customary law. See *Corfu Channel Case (UK v. Albania)* (1949) ICJ Rep. 4 at 22 [hereinafter *Corfu Channel*], and *Trail Smelter Arbitration (United States v. Canada)*, 3 R. Int'l Arb. Awards 1911 (1938), reprinted in 33 *AJIL* 182 (1939), 3 R. Int'l Arb. Awards 1938 (1941), reprinted in 35 *AJIL* 684 (1941) at 699 "[n]oting that a state was held internationally responsible for causing transboundary harm". For "soft" law to this effect, see the *Rio Declaration*, *supra* note 6, Principle 2. See also the *Stockholm Declaration on the Human Environment*, UN Doc. A/C. 48/14 (1972), 11 ILM 1461 (1972) [hereinafter *Stockholm Declaration*].

duty to conduct EIAs before proceeding with serious transboundary projects under customary international law as well as treaty and customary obligations to consult and cooperate in implementation of projects which might affect other States' interests.[9] Debatably, there is also a need to act in accordance with the precautionary principle and the principle of prevention.[10] The same underlying international environmental law obligations in relation to areas beyond the limits of national jurisdiction has similarly led to EIA obligations when activities are proposed to take place in areas of common concern or heritage of humanity. Obligations to conduct a variety of EIA procedures are found in the 1991 *Protocol to the Antarctic Treaty on Environmental Protection,*[11] and under the 1982 *UN Convention on the Law of the Sea* (UNCLOS).[12] It is also likely that there is a customary international law obligation to do an EIA in such circumstances.

EIA has often been considered an essential tool in the implementation of other emerging legal obligations. With the growing recognition of international inter-

[9] For an expression of the customary principle, see *Case Concerning the Gabčíkovo-Nagymaros Project (Hungary/Slovakia)* (1997), ICJ Rep. 7 at 206. Judge Schwebel, speaking for the majority, took judicial notice of the vulnerability of the environment and the importance of having risks assessed on a continuous basis. These provisions were construed by Judge Weeramantry in a minority opinion as "building in" the principle of EIA. He added that a duty of EIA is to be read into treaties whose subject can reasonably be considered to have a significant impact upon the environment. See also the discussion of the Court in the *1995 Request for an Examination of the Situation in Accordance with Paragraph 63 of the Court's Judgment of 20 December 1974 Case Concerning Nuclear Tests (New Zealand v. France)* [1995] 106 ILR 1 [hereinafter *Nuclear Tests II*]. In the earlier dispute in 1973, France publicly declared its intention to cease atmospheric tests, which led to a resolution of their dispute with New Zealand and Australia concerning the legality of the tests in the South Pacific. See *Case Concerning Nuclear Tests (New Zealand and Australia v. France)* (1974) ICJ Rep. 457 [hereinafter *Nuclear Tests I*]. The Experts Group on Environmental Law of the World Commission on Environment and Development then identified EIA as an emerging principle of international law. For examples of treaty obligations in this respect, see the *United Nations Convention on the Non-Navigational Uses of International Watercourses,* UN Doc. A/51/869 (1997) [hereinafter *Watercourses Convention*], and the *Convention on the Protection and Use of Transboundary Watercourses and International Lakes,* 17 March 1992, 31 ILM 1312, [hereinafter *Transboundary Watercourses Convention*], at Art. 3 (1)(h), where States are required to develop, adopt, implement, and, as far as possible, render compatible relevant measures to ensure that an EIA is applied. See also the International Law Commission (ILC) *Draft Articles on the Non-Navigational Uses of International Watercourses,* UN Doc. A/46/10 (1991) at 161 and UN Doc. A/CN.4/L.492 & Add. 1 (1994).

[10] *Rio Declaration, supra* note 6 at Principle 15: "In order to protect the environment, the precautionary approach should be widely applied by States according to their capabilities. Where there are threats of serious or irreversible damage, lack of full scientific certainty shall not be used as a reason for postponing cost-effective measures to prevent environmental degradation."

[11] See the *Antarctic Environmental Protocol,* 30 ILM 1461 (1991), Art. 23(1). Nine parties have ratified the Protocol to date but all Antarctic Treaty Consultative Parties, amounting to 26, are required to bring it into force. See also *Convention on the Conservation of Antarctic Marine Living Resources,* 20 May 1980, T.I.A.S. No. 10240, 1329 UNTS 48 (1980).

[12] *United Nations Convention on the Law of the Sea,* 10 Dec. 1982, UN Doc. A/CONF.62/122 21 ILM 1245 (entered into force 16 Nov. 1994), preamble, Arts. 192, 194, [hereinafter *UNCLOS*]. See also *Agreement for the Implementation of the Provisions of the UN Convention on the Law of the Sea of 10 December 1982 relating to the Conservation and Management of Straddling Fish Stocks and Highly Migratory Fish Stocks,* 4 Aug. 1995, UN Doc A/CONF.164/38 (1995) 34 ILM 1542, preamble and Arts. 2, 5, [hereinafter *Straddling Stocks Agreement*], addressing issues such as the inadequate management of high seas fisheries, the over-utilization of fishing resources, and the inadequate regulation of fishing vessels. UNCLOS states, at Art. 206: "When States have reasonable grounds for believing that planned activities under their jurisdiction or control may cause substantial pollution

dependence, and of the significance of certain largely domestic activities for issues of concern to the international community at large, international obligations to conduct EIAs have arisen for certain sustainable development challenges, such as biodiversity[13] and climate change.[14] Here again, arguments have been made for international customary law obligations in these respects, especially in relation to sustainable use of biodiversity.[15]

Extension of EIAs to include social criteria

In the early years of EIA, environmental impacts were considered to be only changes which affected the natural, biophysical environment. However the institutionalization of EIA, with its public disclosure and consultation processes, acted as a magnet for individuals, groups and agencies that wanted other potential impacts to be incorporated into decision-making processes. It was not long before that at the national project level, the inclusion of social and health impacts in EIAs was standard, either as part of the EIA itself or alongside it. This was due to a fairly wide agreement that these considerations should be necessary and logical components of EIAs.[16]

Some international instruments relating to EIA focus only on potential effects of a proposed activity on the specific environmental issue covered by the instrument, such as the 1991 *Antarctic Treaty Protocol* and the 1982 *UNCLOS*.[17] This may be because it is implicit that the reason for concluding these Conventions and their EIA aspects stems only from those concerns, or because given the subject matter they are arguably less likely to involve direct social effects. In other international

of or significant and harmful changes to the marine environment, they shall, as far as practicable, assess the potential effects of such activities on the marine environment and shall communicate reports of the results of such assessments in the manner provided in Art. 205."

[13] See *United Nations Convention on Biological Diversity*, 5 June 1992, 31 ILM 822 [hereinafter *Biodiversity Convention*]. Flexible language defining the international EIA requirement is evident at Art. 14 (1)(a), that requires parties "as far as possible and as appropriate...[to]...introduce appropriate procedures...[requiring environmental impact assessment of proposed projects that are]...likely to have significant adverse effects on biological diversity".

[14] *United Nations Framework Convention on Climate Change*, 9 May 1992, 31 ILM 849, Art. 9 [hereinafter *Climate Change Convention*].

[15] See, for example, arguments in the *Case Concerning the Island of Kasikili-Sedudu* (*Botswana v. Namibia*) [1999] ICJ Rep. 14 (13 December 1999), available online at http://www.icj-cij.org/icjwww/idocket/ibona/ibonaframe.htm (separate opinion of Judge Weeramantry).

[16] C. Kirkpatrick, *The Impact of the Uruguay Round on Least Developed Countries' External Trade: Strengthening the Capacity of LDCs to Participate Effectively in the World Trade Organisation and to Integrate into the Trading System* (Manchester: Manchester University Press, 1998); UNCTAD and GATT, *An Analysis of the Proposed Uruguay Round Agreement with Particular Emphasis on Aspects of Interest to Developing Countries* (Geneva: GATT Secretariat, 1993), MTN.TNC/W/122; World Bank, *Social Indicators of Development* (Washington DC: World Bank, 1995); World Bank, *World Development Report. Knowledge for Development* (Oxford: Oxford University Press, 1999); World Bank, *World Development Indicators*, CD-ROM (Washington DC: The International Bank for Reconstruction and Development/The World Bank, 1999). See also UNEP, *Environmental Impact Assessment; Issues, Trends and Practice* (Geneva: UNEP, 1996) at paras. 4.24–5, Appendix I.

[17] *UNCLOS, supra* note 12, Part XII, Art. 206.

treaty law, the "human factor" is becoming more explicit. This can be seen both in the general framework of the 1992 *UN Biodiversity Convention* and the 1994 *UN Convention to Combat Desertification*,[18] and in specific assessment related provisions of particular treaties. For example, Article 4(2)(f) of the 1989 *Basel Convention on the Control of Transboundary Movements of Hazardous Wastes and their Disposal* specifically requires information on effects on human health and the environment.[19] Article 4(1) of the 1992 *UN Framework Convention on Climate Change* refers to "impact assessments formulated with a view to minimising adverse effects on the economy, on public health and on the quality of the environment". The 1991 *Espoo Convention*, on which the European Communities EIA Directive is modelled, refers in Article 1(vii) to "any effect... on the environment including human health and safety [and] includes effects on cultural heritage or socio-economic conditions".

International development banks and financial institutions also include social assessment aspects both in their EIA procedures and separately. Indeed, the World Bank was the first to introduce environmental impact assessment requirements in 1991, and this initiative has since been replicated in other international organizations. The World Bank's current EIA requirements require that EIAs should address a number of issues including indigenous peoples and socio-cultural aspects of development.[20] As such, in EIAs across the board, social impacts are increasingly being considered alongside environmental impacts. Debate continues regarding the benefits and drawbacks of integrated as compared to thematic parallel assessment. Recent proposals for sustainability assessments are giving an innovative perspective to these discussions. Sustainability assessments are discussed below.

Strategic assessment: from projects to policies, plans and programmes

Over the last 25 years, EIA has evolved into a comprehensive and versatile instrument. However, several authors suggest that it has not yet been able to

---

[18] *Biodiversity Convention, supra* note 13, *Convention to Combat Desertification in Those Countries Experiencing Serious Drought and/or Desertification, particularly in Africa,* 17 June 1994, 33 ILM 1328, Arts. 4 & 5 [hereinafter *Desertification Convention*].

[19] *Basel Convention on the Control of Transboundary Movements of Hazardous Wastes and Their Disposal,* 22 Mar. 1989, UN Doc. EP/IG.80/3, 28 ILM 649 (1989) [hereinafter *Basel Convention*].

[20] See D. Bradlow, "A Test Case for the World Bank" (1996) 11 *Am. U.J. Int'l L. & Pol'y* 247 at 262. For an up-to-date summary of Inspection Panel decisions, see the report by the Center for International Environmental Law, online: http://www.ciel.org/wbip.html. See I.F.I. Shihata, "The World Bank and the Environment: Legal Instruments for Achieving Environmental Objectives" in I.F.I. Shihata, *The World Bank in a Changing World, Vol. II* (Cairo: Martinus Nijhoff Publishers, 1995), and I.F.I. Shihata, "The World Bank and the Environment: A Legal Perspective" (1992) 16 *Maryland Journal of International Law and Trade* 1. See also World Bank, *The World Bank Inspection Panel, Resolution 93-10,* online: World Bank http://www.worldbank.org/html/ins-panel/operatingprocedures.html, "An 'affected party' is any party that is not a single individual, whose rights or interests have been directly affected in the course of a Bank operation. It can also be a local representative or another representative, such as a foreign NGO, in exceptional cases where appropriate representation is not locally available and the Executive Directors agree. The eligibility requirement for bringing a complaint has been narrowly interpreted by World Bank counsel."

play a significant role in reducing the serious global and regional environmental problems caused by economic growth.[21] Scales and rates of environmental deterioration and resource depletion are more significant now than when EIA was introduced in the 1970s. EIAs conventionally applied to projects, represent a limited response to these problems. It has been recognized that there is a need to adopt more proactive, integrated approaches that deal with the multiple causes of deterioration in quality of life and related environmental conditions. Often, problems are caused by initiatives such as government macro-economic policies, energy and transport plans which fail to adequately integrate sustainable development priorities.[22] On the international level, there are other non-project level actions that can have significant environmental consequences, such as structural and sectoral adjustment programmes, international trade liberalization agreements and fundamental policy initiatives (for example, privatization).[23] In addition, structural, scale, technology and product effects of trade and investment liberalization policies can impact on environmental and social systems.[24]

A response to this situation has been to supplement project level EIAs with cumulative or strategic environmental assessment procedures (SEAs). "Project" usually means the execution of particular construction works or of other particular interventions in the natural surroundings and landscape including those involving the extraction of minerals. At the national and international level, project-level assessment is primarily carried out in relation to development concerns, and increasingly in relation to investment or loan decisions for such particular initiatives. Strategic-level assessments are more complex. They extend the scope of project-level regulatory provisions, sometimes by less formal arrangements, to cover earlier stages in planning cycles, in particular, policies, plans and programmes (PPPs).[25] For example, strategic assessments can apply to rolling national, regional or local development plans, or sectoral investment strategies. According to the European Commission, which recently commissioned a study into the relationship between project-level EIA and strategic-

---

[21] E. Brown Weiss, "International Environmental Law: Contemporary Issues and the Emergence of a New World Order" (1993) 81 *Geo. L.J.* 675 [hereinafter *Brown Weiss*, New World Order]; See also B. Clark, "Environmental Impact Assessment (EIA): Scope and Objectives" in *Perspectives on Environmental Impact Assessment* (Dordrecht: D. Reidel Publishing Co, 1984) 3.

[22] UNEP, *Environmental Impact Assessment: Issues, Trends and Practice* (Geneva: UNEP, 1996), para. 6.1 [hereinafter UNEP, *EIA*].

[23] *Lee & Kirkpatrick, supra* note 2 at 2.

[24] The North American Commission for Environmental Cooperation (NACEC) has designed a framework for assessing environmental effects of the *North American Free Trade Agreement* (NAFTA), NACEC, *Assessing Environmental Effects of the North American Free Trade Agreement (NAFTA): An Analytic Framework (Phase II) and Issue Studies* (Montreal: NACEC, 1999). See also D.C. Esty, *Greening the GATT* (Chicago: Institute for International Economics, 1994) [hereinafter *Esty*]; UNCTAD *Newly Emerging Environmental Policies with a Possible Trade Impact: A Preliminary Discussion – Report by the UNCTAD Secretariat*, (New York: United Nations, 1995); and UNCTAD, *Trade and the Environment: Issues of Key Interest to the Least Developed Countries*, (New York: United Nations, 1997).

[25] UNEP, *supra* note 22, paras. 6.30–6.47.

level assessment (SEA), SEA does not replace project-level EIA, but rather complements it. By definition SEA addresses alternatives not addressed at project level. It also often results in reducing the time and cost needed at the lower project level.[26] As such, while there is no internationally agreed definition of what either the narrow project or broader strategic assessments should cover, there is a consensus on the need for both EIAs and SEAs, and a view that the benefits will outweigh the costs.

Currently, several international instruments provide for strategic environmental assessment, and this view appears to be gaining strength. A leading effort is made in the 1991 *Espoo Convention on Environmental Impact Assessment in a Transboundary Context*.[27] While this Convention is limited to cases of effects that are transboundary rather than global, and applies to member States, it is one of the most complete and progressive examples of EIA requirements in international environmental law.

The 1991 *Espoo Convention*, at Article 2(7) provides that "environmental impact assessments as required by this convention shall, as a minimum requirement, be undertaken at the project level of the proposed activity". In less binding language, "to the extent appropriate, the Parties also commit to apply the principles of environmental impact assessment to policies, plans and programmes". According to Karin Gray, the 1991 *Espoo Convention* provides for EIA requirements in a transboundary context.[28] It was negotiated under the auspices of the United Nations Economic Commission of Europe and over 28 parties have ratified the Agreement. The Treaty creates obligations to take all appropriate and effective measures to prevent, reduce, and control significant adverse transboundary environmental impact from proposed activities, and ensures that affected parties are notified of a proposed activity, listed in Appendix I, that is likely to cause a significant adverse transboundary impact. States are required to establish an EIA procedure for so-called "Appendix I" activities. Where a project does not fall under the projects enumerated in the Appendix, an affected party can request an EIA if the project may cause significant adverse transboundary impact. A decision by the affected party not to participate in an EIA gives the party of origin the freedom not to carry out an assessment subject to its national law. Where the parties are unable to agree whether the impact is likely, the question can be submitted to an inquiry commission. Providing for the arbitration of such disputes is crucial because it avoids any reliance on a dubious EIA done by the state of origin.[29] The affected

---

[26] S. Nooteboom, *Strategic Decisions and Project Decisions: Interactions and Benefits* (Ministry of Housing Spatial Planning and the Environment of The Netherlands, with the support of the European Commission DGXI, 1999) at 5–6.

[27] *Espoo Convention on Environmental Impact Assessment in a Transboundary Context*, 25 Feb. 1991, 30 ILM 800 [hereinafter *Espoo Convention*].

[28] K.R. Gray, "International Environmental Impact Assessment" (2000) 11 *Colo. J. Int'l Envtl. L. & Pol'y* 83.

[29] See A. Weale, "Ecological Modernisation and the Integration of European Environmental Policy" in J.D. Lieferink *et al.*, eds., *European Integration and Environmental Policy* (Cambridge: Cambridge University Press, 1993) 196 at 208.

state may have different standards, thresholds, or past experiences that contribute to the characterization of the environmental impact. Thus, the *Espoo Convention* creates conditions for dialogue and for the exchange of cultural perceptions of the environment.

Key provisions of the 1991 *Espoo Convention* relate to public participation. The public in the affected area has a right to be informed of and to participate in the EIA procedure, even though the procedure takes place in another country. Public participation in making comments or objections to the competent authority of the party of origin is permitted during interstate discussions concerning the significance of the trans-boundary environmental impact. The level of participation is equivalent to what is offered to the public in the party of origin, with a baseline requirement that the public is informed and provided with possibilities for making comments or objections on the proposed activity. Although novel in principle, a great challenge for the 1991 *Espoo Convention* regime will be how the responsibilities for facilitating cross-boundary consultation will be allocated. The 1991 *Espoo Convention* does not expressly resolve which party is under the obligation. Having two consultation/decision-making processes operating simultaneously can be problematic because public participation commences at different stages in the EIA process amongst the parties. In addition, the scoping process – establishing the scope of the assessment – may differ in relation to public access, there may be temporal or substantive inconsistencies for information provided to the public, post-project analysis obligations can vary and there may be contrasting levels of public participation and available remedies. This could lead to abuse as affected parties may engage another State's judicial system simply because it facilitates public participation more favourably. There are also jurisdictional problems associated with one State conducting public hearings in another State. The development of a coordinated procedure that reflects the political and cultural elements of government decision-making of the neighbouring States will be critical to the proper functioning of trans-frontier public participation in the 1991 *Espoo Convention*. The treaty does not usurp the application of the parties' existing EIA legislation. A process is outlined in the 1991 *Espoo Convention* but its substantive details are left to the discretion of the parties. The outcome of an EIA must be taken into account, including public comments and the results of consultations between the parties, when decisions are arrived at concerning a proposed activity. However, the wording falls short of mandating action recommended in the EIA.

Generally, the EIA procedure of the party of origin applies thereby respecting existing procedures in the particular State.[30] However, the balance is tipped away from State discretion when significant transboundary effects flow from a project. It reviews scientific information and assesses risk, and development is permitted following the completion of an EIA and the undertaking of potential

---

[30] D.R. Brown, "Transboundary Environmental Impacts in a European Context" (1997) 3 *Eur. Env't* 80.

mitigating measures. The acceptance of EIA reveals a common outlook of industrialized countries that projects having significant environmental impacts in another country must be reviewed.[31]

The European Community has adopted *Directives on Strategic Environmental Assessment*, which apply fully to plans and programmes, and also take development policies into account.[32] The 1991 *Espoo Convention* and the 1998 *Aarhus Convention*[33] secretariats are also currently working together on a protocol to the 1991 *Espoo Convention* dealing with SEA. In addition, certain particularly comprehensive treaties, while not specifically obliging Parties to undertake SEAs, require or recommend that appropriate arrangements are made along those lines. The 1992 *UN Convention on Biological Diversity* provides in Article 14(b) that each Contracting Party, as far as possible and where appropriate, shall introduce appropriate arrangements to ensure that the environmental consequences of its programmes and policies that are likely to have significant adverse impacts on biological diversity are duly taken into account.[34] As will be seen below, there have also been voluntary initiatives to assess certain strategic-level activities in the international arena.

Sustainability impact assessments

The potential value of EIA as an instrument to promote sustainable development was recognized in Principle 17 of the 1992 *Rio Declaration*. More recently however, there have been innovative efforts in cooperation with civil society organizations, on the domestic and international levels to devise and apply "sustainability impact assessments" (SIAs) which take environmental, social

---

[31] See also the EC, *Council Resolution 93/138 on the European Community's Fifth Environmental Action Programme*, [1993] OJ C. 138/1 at 3, which recognized that continued human activity and further economic and social development depended upon the quality of the environment and its natural resources.

[32] The Council has adopted two EIA Directives. The first measure amends the original EC *Directive 85/337* on EIAs, while EC *Directive 97/C 129/08* extends the EIA requirements to plans and programmes on the environment, better known as strategic environmental assessment (SEA). The amended Directive, which is now in force, moves several Annex II projects to Annex I, consistent with Annex I projects listed in the 1991 *Espoo Convention*. EC *Directive 97/C* was proposed to pre-empt project decisions where alternatives could not be pursued, while allowing for an assessment of the cumulative environmental impacts of a series of projects. Since plans and programmes anticipate a series of consent decisions, there was a need to set a framework for future decisions subject to minimal procedural requirements ensuring a high level of environmental protection and progress towards sustainable development. Plans and programmes are restricted to those prepared and adopted by a competent authority or subject to preparation and adoption by such authority, pursuant to a legislative act, and which set a framework for future development consents of projects making reference to their size, location, nature or operating conditions. This advances the EIA requirement to an earlier stage in accordance with a precautionary approach to environmental regulation. Under this proactive EIA strategy, environmentally risky decisions can be precluded before any impact is sustained. EC *Directive 97/C* sets out only broad principles leaving the procedural details to the member States.

[33] *Convention on Access to Information, Public Participation in Decision-making and Access to Justice in Environmental Matters*, 25 June 1998, 38 ILM 517, online: UNECE <http://www.unece.org/env/ pp> [hereinafter *Aarhus Convention*].

[34] *Biodiversity Convention, supra* note 13.

and economic factors into consideration.[35] The new SIA instruments apply to policies, plans and programmes as well as projects, and seek strategies which will result in long term sustainability.[36] They are based on procedural innovations, such as the recent identification of combined international sustainability indicators,[37] and are being formulated using dynamic, developing expertise from many sectors of society. However sustainable development is conceptualized, the task remains of translating this concept into operational appraisal criteria and then into law. A broad distinction can be drawn between *target-related indicators* and *process-related indicators*. The former involves expressing sustainable development goals in terms of a set of targets to be achieved at a specified future point in time, and developing a corresponding set of indicators to measure progress (performance-based indicators). Sustainable development process indicators relate to the soundness of the institutional planning and management processes including mechanisms for the meaningful involvement of the appropriate stakeholders, thereby strengthening institutional capacity and decision-making along sustainable development lines (management or systems-based indicators).[38] This concern with process is increasingly being taken on board. Access to information and public participation are considered essential and efforts are made to involve civil society organizations in all aspects of the SIA process.[39]

While there are still few existing concrete international legal obligations with regard to SIAs, leading international efforts have been undertaken to formulate sustainability assessment procedures, indicators and appraisal criteria. One of the best examples is the Sustainability Impact Assessment Study of the proposed *Millennium Round* negotiations in the World Trade Organization (WTO), which was commissioned by the European Commission. The first phase of the SIA included a review of literature on trade-related assessments (covering economic, social and environmental impacts relevant to sustainable development),

---

[35] Sustainability Impact Assessments have recently been done on a national level by governments and NGOs in the Netherlands, Philippines, Indonesia and in the USA. See for example Oxfam, *Trade Liberalisation as a Threat to Livelihoods: the Corn Sector in the Philippines* (Oxford: Oxfam, 1998) online: http://www.oxfam.org.uk/policy/research/corn.htm; A. Strutt & K. Anderson "Estimating Environmental Effects of Trade Agreements with Global CGE Models: A GTAP Application to Indonesia" (Paper presented at Workshop on *Methodologies for Environmental Assessment of Trade Liberalization Agreements*, OECD, Paris, October 1999). They have been conducted at the level of Europe in the EC, for example in relation to transport strategy, see OECD, *Freight and the Environment: Effects of Trade Liberalisation and Transport Sector Reforms* (Paris: OECD, 1997).

[36] M. Perrin, "Sustainability Assessment of Trade Liberalisation Agreements" (Paper presented at Workshop on *Methodologies for Environmental Assessment of Trade Liberalization Agreements*, OECD, Paris October 1999).

[37] B. Moldan & S. Billharz, *Sustainability Indicators: Report of the Project on Indicators of Sustainable Development* (Chichester: John Wiley, SCOPE 58, 1997).

[38] D.W. Pearce & G.D. Atkinson, "Capital Theory and Measurement of Sustainable Development: an Indicator of 'Weak' Sustainability" [1993] 8 *Ecological Economics*, 103–8. See also C. Milner & O. Morrissey, *"Measuring Trade Liberalisation"*, in M. McGillivray and O. Morrissey (eds.), *Evaluating Economic Liberalization* (New York: Macmillan, 1999).

[39] OECD Secretariat, "Timing and Public Participation Issues in Undertaking Environmental Assessments of Trade Liberalisation agreements" (Paper presented at Workshop on *Methodologies for Environmental Assessment of Trade Liberalization Agreements*, OECD, Paris, Oct. 1999).

an examination of relevant cases where these assessment methodologies have been applied with an evaluation of their effectiveness, and a proposal for a fully defined sustainable impact assessment methodology.[40]

The second phase was quite comprehensive, involving an examination of the potential sustainability impact of each measure that might have been covered within the WTO negotiations. Impacts, positive and negative, were assessed for four groups of countries – the European Union, developing countries, least developed countries, and the world as a whole. The findings distinguished those areas where negotiations were likely to have a relatively limited impact and those where the impact might have been greater. Additionally, proposals were formulated for mitigation and enhancing measures. In particular, the study examined "core sustainability indicators" (including economic factors such as average real income, net fixed capital information and employment; social factors such as equity and poverty; health and education, and gender inequalities; and environmental factors such as ecological quality (covering air, water and land), biological diversity; and other natural resource stocks. This was done in the context of "significance criteria" (including the extent of existing economic, social and environmental stress, in affected areas; direction of changes to baseline conditions; nature, order of magnitude, geographic extent and duration of changes; and regulatory and institutional capacity to implement mitigation measures). As such, the SIA consisted of four main phases:

- *screening*: to determine which measures require SIA because they are likely to have significant impacts,
- *scoping*: to establish the appropriate coverage of each SIA,
- *preliminary sustainability assessment*: to identify potentially significant effects, positive and negative, on sustainable development, and
- *mitigation and enhancement analysis*: to suggest types of improvements which may enhance the overall impact on sustainable development of New Round Agenda measures.

There were also extensive procedures for public participation and consultation with civil society organizations. Numerous workshops and consultations were held at each phase of reports, and a website was designated with reports, timely publications and informal mechanisms for involvement during the process.[41] Though political factors resulted in the delay or cancellation of the proposed

---

[40] C. Kirkpatrick, N. Lee & O. Morrissey, *WTO New Round: Sustainability Impact Assessment Study (Phase One Report)*, online: Manchester University <http://fs2.idpm.man.ac.uk/sia/Phase1/phase1.html>.

[41] C. Kirkpatrick, N. Lee & O. Morrissey, *WTO New Round: Sustainability Impact Assessment Study (Phase Two Report)*, online: Manchester University <http://fs2.idpm.man.ac.uk/sia/Phase2/EXSUMFINAL.htm>. The Study examined changes to agreement on agriculture, changes to the General Agreement on Trade in Services [hereinafter GATS], development of a multilateral framework of rules relating to international investment, development of a multilateral framework of rules relating to competition, measures relating to trade facilitation, further measures relating to tariffs on non-agricultural products, clarification of the relationship between WTO rules and trade measures taken pursuant to multilateral environmental agreements and other environmental policy initiatives,

trade liberalization negotiations,[42] this innovative attempt to undertake a comprehensive international SIA of the proposed WTO trade liberalization programme certainly provides an excellent example of the most highly integrated impact assessment instruments in the field of sustainable development law and policy.

The SIA shows evidence of being a fully integrated instrument, which takes into consideration economic, social and environmental concerns at the level of methodology and indicators. While the original mechanism, EIA, developed out of a rapidly evolving aspect of international environmental law, the more it was used, the more pressure was generated to include social criteria in this instrument designed to evaluate economic development initiatives. This new form of instrument, the SIA, may be an example of the "fourth degree of integration" mentioned above, and appears to be a successful way to address sustainable development concerns. Its normative elements, including its incorporation into domestic and international laws, remain to be further developed and explored.

REGIONAL INTEGRATION AGREEMENTS (RIAs)

The nexus between trade, environment and social law is one of the sharpest areas of potential conflict in the evolving tapestry of sustainable development law.[43] On regional and sub-regional levels, pressure is mounting to find innovative mechanisms which integrate environmental and social considerations into economic integration instruments, particularly into trade law.[44] This case study

changes to the agreement to strengthen the global protection of intellectual property rights [hereinafter TRIPS], measures to improve market access in government procurement policies and practices, measures relating to technical barriers to trade [hereinafter TBT], measures relating to the protection of human health, measures relating to the use of trade defence instruments (anti-dumping, subsidies, agreement on safeguards), horizontal measures to promote development, various trade and core labour standard issues, various other issues relating to treatment of products of least developed countries, transparency, coherence of policies between WTO and other international organizations, the dispute settlement mechanism, and electronic commerce.

[42] For a brief description of debates and events surrounding the proposed "WTO Millennium Round", see G. Sampson, *Trade, Environment and the WTO: The Post-Seattle Agenda*, Overseas Development Council Policy Essay No. 27 (Washington: ODC, 2001) [hereinafter *Sampson*]. See also P. Grady and K. Macmillan, *Seattle and Beyond: The WTO Millennium Round* (Ottawa: Global Economics Ltd and International Trade Policy Consultants Inc., 1999) and *Brown Weiss, New World Order, supra* note 21.

[43] T. Schoenbaum, "International Trade and Protection of the Environment: The Continuing Search for Reconciliation" (1997) 91:2 *American Journal of International Law* 281. See also F. Francione, *Environment, Human Rights and International Trade* (Oxford: Hart, 2001).

[44] M.-C. Cordonier Segger *et al.*, *Beyond the Barricades: An Americas Trade and Sustainability Agenda* (Aldershot: Ashgate, 2005). See also K. von Moltke, *International Environmental Management, Trade Regimes and Sustainability* (Winnipeg: International Institute for Sustainable Development, 1996). And see P. Konz, C. Bellmann, L. Assuncao & R. Melendez-Otiz, *Trade, Environment, and Sustainable Development Views from Sub-Saharan Africa and Latin America: A Reader* (Geneva: UNU/IAS & ICTSD, 2000). See also R. Meléndez-Ortiz and C. Bellmann, *Commerce international et développement durable: Voix africaines et plurielles* ICTSD, (Paris: Editions Charles Léopold Mayer, 2002).

surveys regional economic integration agreements (RIAs) in the Americas, those which engage both developed and developing countries from diverse political and economic contexts. The study will focus on key aspects of the regional treaties which underpin the regional integration processes, and survey how environmental cooperation instruments are being established as part of (or parallel to) the economic integration package.[45] Social cooperation instruments are also being established as part of (or parallel to) economic integration processes, but these aspects are beyond the scope of this brief case study.[46]

As is seen in the survey below, some regional (or sub-regional, if the Americas were to be considered one region) cooperation instruments, especially those governed mainly by "Free Trade Area" agreements, utilize a clear "parallel yet interdependent" strategy of integration (environment and labour accords running as protocols or side agreements to the economic integration agreements). Others have integrated environment and social considerations into institutional structures and mechanisms of their overall economic cooperation project, especially those sub-regional integration processes that seek mainly to become "customs unions" or "common markets". In addition, certain economic cooperation treaties, particularly those which govern new economic relationships between developed and developing States, actually incorporate substantive provisions on social and environmental issues in the text of their trade agreement itself. The lessons learned in these sub-regional legal experiments are useful for sustainable development law in general, and for the construction of any new regimes for the Western Hemisphere.

The Americas: a region seeking models for integration

A process has been initiated which could significantly re-structure the "architecture" of international economic and environmental cooperation in the Americas over the course of the next decade. At the "Santiago Summit of the Americas" in April 1998, 34 governments launched negotiations for a new Free Trade Area of

---

[45] M.-C. Cordonier Segger, "Sustainable Development in the Free Trade Area of the Americas – Negotiations" (2004) 27 *Fordham Int'l L. J.* 1118. See also M.-C. Cordonier Segger *et al.*, "A New Mechanism for Hemispheric Cooperation on Environmental Sustainability and Trade" (2002) 27:2 *Columbia Journal of Environmental Law* 613. See also D.C. Esty and D. Geradin, "Market Access, Competitiveness, and Harmonization: Environmental Protection in Regional Trade Agreements" (1997) 21 *Harv. Envtl. L. Rev.* 265. And see M.-C. Cordonier Segger and N. Borregaard, "Sustainability and Hemispheric Integration: A Review of Existing Approaches" in D. Esty and C. Deere, *Greening the Americas*, eds. (Boston: MIT Press, 2002).

[46] M.-C. Cordonier Segger *et al.*, *Social Rules and Sustainability in the Americas* (Winnipeg: IISD/OAS, 2004). See A.C. Reynaud, *Labour Standards and the Integration Process in the Americas* (Geneva: ILO, 2001). See also O. Uriarte, "La ciudadanía laboral en el MERCOSUR" *Derecho Laboral*, Montevideo 1998, Tomo XLI N° 190. K. Banks "Civil Society and the *North American Agreement on Labor Cooperation*" in *Linking Trade, Environment and Social Cohesion: NAFTA Experiences, Global Challenges*, J. Kirton and V. Maclaren, eds. (Aldershot: Ashgate, 2002). See also *Human Rights: How to Present a Petition in the Inter-American System* (Washington: OAS, 2000).

the Americas (FTAA), which aspires to link almost 800 million people, with a combined GDP of up to 9 trillion US dollars, by 2005. The 1998 *Declaration of Trade Ministers of the Americas* cited the need for mutually supportive environmental and trade policies, improvements in quality of life, and increased participation of civil society, and the 2001 *Quebec City Summit of the Americas Declaration* made sustainable development a goal of hemispheric integration.[47] Meetings of the Summit of the Americas process, including the 2001 *Buenos Aires Meeting of Trade Ministers*, the 2001 *Montreal Meeting of Environment Ministers*, the 2001 *Quebec City Summit of the Americas*, the 2002 *Quito Meeting of Trade Ministers*, the 2003 *Miami Meeting of Trade Ministers*, and the 2004 *Monterrey Special Summit of the Americas*, were expected to advance the sustainable development agenda. Encouraging signals were generated by the trade ministers through the release of the FTAA negotiating text, institutionalization of civil society consultation mechanisms, and commitments for participation of smaller economies in the process. Environment ministers of the Americas, after their first meeting, committed to "maximise the potential for mutually supportive policies regarding economic integration and environmental protection . . . " and stated an intention "to work, in particular, to ensure that the process of economic integration supports [their] ability to adopt and maintain environmental policy measures to achieve high levels of environmental protection".[48] Such cooperation will be built on existing environmental law and policies in the Americas.[49] However, after the 2001 *Summit of the Americas* in Quebec City, trade and sustainability issues still constitute challenges that must be addressed by the summitry process and key hemispheric or sub-regional institutions.

Regional accords and mechanisms have been developed, recently, to address shared environmental challenges in geographically contiguous areas. According to recent studies, these sub-regional environmental cooperation regimes tend to run parallel to sub-regional trade agreements or common markets, can be integrated to different degrees into their structures, and were formed to address concerns requiring trans-boundary policy coordination, in particular shared

---

[47] *Third Summit of the Americas Declaration*, Quebec City, 22 April 2001, available online: www.oas.org.

[48] *Declaration of Ministers of Environment of the Americas*, 28–29 March 2001, Montreal, available online: www.ec.gc.ca.

[49] See M.-C. Cordonier Segger *et al.*, *Ecological Rules and Sustainability in the Americas* (Winnipeg: UNEP/IISD, 2002) [hereinafter *Ecological Rules*]. This study divides current international environmental regimes in the Americas into four categories. These are: 1) Species-specific accords – those which protect particular migratory or transboundary species and populations, 2) Natural resources accords – those which ensure that the productive capacity of certain natural resources is respected, restored or managed, 3) Ecosystem areas accords – those which encourage conservation of a particular ecosystem, habitat or heritage area, and 4) Ecological cooperation accords – those new comprehensive environmental agreements formed as part of a broader integration package. Many use trade measures for environmental purposes (TMEPs), and in several, TMEPs may be vital to agreement implementation.

ecological regions.[50] (An eco-region can be defined, at varying scales, as "a geographically distinct assemblage of natural communities that share a large majority of their species, ecological dynamics, and similar environmental conditions...".[51]) Experience is also revealing that effective public participation in these processes can lead to greater accountability and long term support for these accords, as well as better rules.[52] These sub-regional environmental cooperation structures have broad mandates, can include institutional or dispute settlement aspects, and exist primarily to promote environment and sustainable development co-operation on many levels between and within the Parties.[53] Below, two of the best-known examples are described, the proposed *Framework Agreement on the Environment* for the MERCOSUR, and the *North American Agreement for Environmental Cooperation,* and in addition, less publicized but equally interesting models from accords among smaller economies of the region such as the *Central American Alliance for Sustainable Development*, the efforts of the Andean *Consejo de Autoridades Ambientales de la Comunidad Andina*, and the recent Canada–Chile and *Canada–Costa Rica Free Trade Agreements*, or the *Chile–USA Free Trade Agreement*. Many of these accords recognize the "promotion of sustainable development" as an objective in their preamble.

The Southern Cone, and the 2001 MERCOSUR Framework Agreement on the Environment

The Southern Common Market includes Brazil, Argentina, Uruguay and Paraguay, with Bolivia and Chile as associate members. The MERCOSUR is a combined market composed of more than 207 million people with a GDP of about US$1,163.4 billion. In spite of recent economic challenges, this customs union has become a new model of integration in Latin America, with intra-regional exports totalling 21.5 per cent of total at US$19,967 million, and a common external tariff, averaging 11.4 per cent, arranged in 11 tiers from 0 to 20 per cent.[54] The market aims to become a community, committed to democratic principles and the stabilization of their economies.[55] The MERCOSUR

---

[50] See E. Leff & M. Bastida, (eds.) *Comercio, Medio Ambiente y Desarollo Sustentable: Perspectivas de America Latina y el Caribe* (Mexico: UNEP, 2002). See also M.-C. Cordonier Segger *et al.*, *Ecological Rules and Sustainability in the Americas* (Winnipeg: UNEP/IISD, 2002).

[51] E. Dinerstein *et al.*, *A Conservation Assessment of the Terrestrial Ecoregions of Latin America and the Caribbean* (Washington DC: WWF & World Bank, 1995) at 4.

[52] In the North-South Institute *Engaging with Civil Society* (2000) study, lessons from the OAS, FTAA and Summits of the Americas are surveyed. Strategies for public consultation are recommended.

[53] M. Cordonier Segger *et al.*, *Trade Rules and Sustainability in the Americas* (Winnipeg: IISD, 2000). See also S. Charnovitz, "Regional Trade Agreements and the Environment" (1995) 37:5 *Environment* 95 and D. Tussie & P.I. Vasquez, "The FTAA, MERCOSUR and the environment" (1997) 9:3 *International Environmental Affairs: A Journal for Research and Policy*.

[54] In Jan. 1995, MERCOSUR members agreed on a list of more than 8,700 products to be exempted from import duties.

[55] T.A. O'Keefe, "An Analysis of the MERCOSUR Economic Integration Project from a Legal Perspective" (1994) 28:2 *The International Lawyer* 28, 439–448.

structure, though still developing, displays various innovative environment and trade mechanisms, which began as integrated components in the structure of the MERCOSUR, and are now described as a quasi-independent framework regime for environmental cooperation.

Several resolutions of the *"Grupo Mercado Comun"* and decisions of the *"Consejo de Mercado Comun"* touched upon environmental protection issues, including rules to regulate the levels of pesticide residues acceptable in food products, the levels of certain contaminants in food packaging, eco-labelling and regional transportation of dangerous goods.[56] Linkages between trade and the environment were recognized early in the process, and the 1992 *Canela Declaration* created an informal working group, the *Reunion Especializada en Medio Ambiente* (REMA), to study environmental laws, standards and practices in the four countries. This forum evolved into the creation of a *"Sub-Grupo No.6"* on the environment, one of the recognized technical working bodies of the MERCOSUR. This group examines issues such as environment and competitiveness, non-tariff barriers to trade, and common systems of environmental information. It negotiated the 2001 *MERCOSUR Framework Agreement on the Environment* which, as a decision of the Common Market Council (*Consejo del Mercado Comun*), is added to the *Treaty of Asunción* of the MERCOSUR.[57]

A comprehensive stand-alone treaty, the 2001 *MERCOSUR Framework Agreement on the Environment,* at Chapter 2, Article 4, establishes a shared objective of "sustainable development and environmental protection through the development of economic, social and environmental dimensions, contributing to a better quality of environment and life for the people".[58] This objective establishes the integrative tendencies of this accord. The text of the agreement provides for upwards harmonization of environmental management systems and increased co-operation on shared ecosystems, in addition to mechanisms for social participation and the protection of health. At Chapter 3, it commits States to cooperation on the development of instruments for environmental management including quality standards, environmental impact assessment methods, environmental monitoring and costs, environmental information systems and certification processes. At Chapter 4, Articles 8 to 11, there are provisions for the settlement of any disputes (by reference to the existing MERCOSUR dispute settlement process) and other general mechanisms for implementation of the

[56] Inter-American Development Bank, *Integration and Trade in the Americas* (Washington: IDB, 1996).

[57] *Acuerdo Marco sobre Medio Ambiente del MERCOSUR*, Approved Text from the XX Reunión del Consejo Mercado Común, 22 June 2001, Asunción, MERCOSUR/CMC/DEC.N°2/01. To be annexed, upon ratification by member States, to *El Tratado de Asunción, el Tratado de Ouro Preto, la Resolución* N° 38/95 del Grupo Mercado Común y la Recomendación N° 01/01 del SGT N° 6 "Medio Ambiente".

[58] See *Acuerdo Marco sobre Medio Ambiente del MERCOSUR*, Approved Text from the XX Reunión del Consejo Mercado Común, 22 de junio de 2001 en Asunción MERCOSUR/CMC/DEC.N°2/01, at Art. 4 where the objective is stated to be "desarrollo sustentable y la protección del medio ambiente, mediante la articulación de las dimensiones económicas, sociales y ambientales, contribuyendo a una mejor calidad del ambiente y de la vida de la población".

Framework Agreement.[59] The Annex provides a framework for the future development of protocols in three areas: sustainable management of natural resources (such as protected areas, biological diversity, biosafety, wildlife management, forests, and hydrological resources); quality of life and environmental management (such as hazardous waste management, urban planning, renewable energy, and improvement of soil and atmosphere/air quality); and environmental policy (such as environmental impact assessment, economic instruments, environmental information exchange, environmental awareness programmes).

Though the regime has much work to do to ensure that the promise of the 2001 *Framework Agreement on the Environment* is realized, important elements seem present, and key civil society actors have expressed cautious optimism in this linkage at a sub-regional level.[60] It is interesting to note that the 2001 *Framework Agreement on the Environment* was generated by the consideration of both sustainable development and environmental issues from within the structures of the customs union. In this instance, it appears that the international economic negotiations took these priorities into account, then created an integrated instrument for cooperation as part of the general sub-regional economic integration process for convenience and to ensure continued political will.

The Andean Community and the *Consejo de Autoridades Ambientales* of the ANCOM

The Andean Community consists of Bolivia, Colombia, Ecuador, Peru and Venezuela. The CAN dates from 1969, has a total population of 106 million and a GDP of about 226 billion dollars. Chile was a founding member, but withdrew with differing investment strategies in 1976.[61] The intra-regional trade expanded by an average of 29 per cent a year between 1990 and 1995, in 1996 accounting for 16 per cent of total non-oil exports, and reached 5,403 million dollars by 1997. Common external tariffs range from 5 to 35 per cent in five tiers. The Andean Group is a customs union. Once doubtful in its efficacy,[62] it has recently gained strength as an integration strategy.[63]

Scant information is available about embryonic environmental cooperation in the Andean Zone, but it can be noted that a new *Comite Andino de Autoridades Ambientales* (CAAAM) has been developed and is creating a biodiversity strat-

---

[59] *Protocolo Adicional Al Tratado De Asuncion Sobre Medio Ambiente'*, Draft, Capitulo XXVI, Montevideo, Uruguay.

[60] M. Leichner, "The MERCOSUR Framework Agreement on the Environment" (2001) ICTSD *Bridges*, Fall Edition.

[61] M. Thornton, "Since the Breakup: Developments and Divergences in ANCOM's and Chile's Foreign Investment Codes" (1983) 1 *Hastings International and Comparative Law Review* 7.

[62] S. Horton, "Peru and ANCOM: A Study in the Disintegration of a Common Market" (1982) 1 *Texas International Law Journal* 17.

[63] M. Rodriguez-Mendoza, "The Andean Group's Integration Strategy" in A. Julia Jatar and S. Weintraub eds. *Integrating the Hemisphere – Perspectives from Latin America and the Caribbean* (Bogota: Inter-American Dialogue, 1997) 10.

egy for the ANCOM.[64] The Decision 391 also empowers the national authority and indigenous Afro-American and local communities in each country as the custodians of traditional knowledge and resources, to grant prior informed consent to potential users in return for equitable returns.[65] The biodiversity strategy integrates and joint Andean Declaration on phytosanitary measures, which includes provisions on biosafety. This implies that environmental cooperation measures are being developed as part of the Andean integration processes.

Central or Mesoamerica, and the Central American Alliance for Sustainable Development

The Central American Common Market (CACM) consists of Guatemala, El Salvador, Nicaragua, Costa Rica and Honduras. CACM is a customs union of about 42 million people and a GDP of about 54 billion dollars. Inter-CACM trade accounts for roughly 20 per cent of total exports, an increase of 4 per cent from 1990. In mid-1993, Guatemala, Honduras, El Salvador and Nicaragua formed the customs union, joined by Costa Rica and Panama in 1995. Common external tariffs average 15 per cent (tiered from 5 to 20 per cent). Mexico and Belize are now engaged in negotiating a single treaty covering the whole of the region.[66]

The CACM clearly adopted a parallel course in the development of sub-regional environmental laws. Their sub-regional institutions are not linked to the regional common market agenda, and appear more interesting to foreign donors this way. Although environmental progress by individual countries has been uneven, harmonization and coordination of national activities on sustainable development is increasing. The environment became a significant issue in 1989, following the signature of the 1989 *Central American Convention for the Protection of the Environment* (CPC), and the subsequent creation of the *Central American Commission for the Environment and Development* (CCAD). The signature of the Alliance for Sustainable Development (ALIDES) in 1994 was even more significant, in that it generated a conceptual and operational framework

---

[64] See ICTSD, "Comercio y medio ambiente en los acuerdos regionales" (1999) 2:1 *Puentes Entre el Comercio y el Desarollo Sostenible* (Online: http://www.ictsd.org./monthly/puenarc.htm). See also M.-C. Cordonier Segger and N. Borregaard, "Sustainability and Hemispheric Integration: A Review of Existing Approaches" in D. Esty and C. Deere, eds., *Greening the Americas*, (Boston: MIT Press, 2002).

[65] See S. Prakash, "Towards a Synergy Between Intellectual Property Rights and Biodiversity" (1999) *Journal of World Intellectual Property*. According to the 1992 *Convention on Biological Diversity* (CBD), access to resources is subject to the prior informed consent (PIC) of the provider of such resources. This means that any company or individual seeking access to genetic resources must first seek and receive the consent of the custodian of these resources, before procuring any genetic resources from the provider's jurisdiction. Therefore, access must be granted on mutually agreed terms, as defined by the seeker and provider.

[66] E.V. Iglesias, *El nuevo rostro de la integracion regional en America Latina y el Caribe* (Washington: Inter-American Development Bank, 1997); see also OAS, *Acuerdos de comercio e integracion en las Americas – Un compendio analitico* (Washington: OAS, 1997).

for sub-regional and national goals and strategies. The ALIDES is a comprehensive sub-regional initiative that addresses political, moral, economic, social, and environmental issues that might otherwise have fallen to trade negotiators to resolve. National Councils on Sustainable Development were established, and act as instruments for implementation. ALIDES was seen as a potential foundation from which to strengthen environmental protection and other development priorities. It was a starting point for the 1994 CONCAUSA (CONvenio CentroAmérica – USA), a partnership for sustainable development which provided funding to the region for a list of concrete commitments including environmental measures such as the conservation of biodiversity, development of renewable energy, environmental legislation standards and eco-friendly industrial processes.

Two tangible achievements from this linkage can be noted. First, in 1992, the CCAD coordinated the development of a joint position ("Agenda 2000") for the region at UNCED. After UNCED, CCAD supported the creation of the Central American Inter-Parliamentary Commission on the Environment. Central America has experienced high levels of deforestation and forest degradation over the last decade. Costa Rica's annual deforestation rate was 2.6 per cent between 1980 and 1990; the deforestation rates in El Salvador and Honduras (2.1 and 1.9 per cent per year) also increased over the same period. This commission, consisting of members of parliament from the seven Central American countries, was instrumental in getting these countries to sign a regional Forests Convention that is now being implemented by the regional Central American Forest Council created exclusively for this purpose. Following the high-level call to address deforestation, CCAD created a regional forestry unit to work on a Tropical Forestry Action Program for the region during the period 1990–91. One result of the TFAP process was adoption of common guidelines for forestry concessions, largely in response to poor concession management in Guatemala, Honduras, and Nicaragua.[67] CCAD's success stems partly from its transparent and participatory decision-making process: civil society organizations, representatives of indigenous peoples, and businesses all participate in CCAD's quarterly meetings and other sponsored events. Another key element is its regional rather than global approach. Because only a small number of member countries with clear common interests are involved, progress on sensitive issues is possible.

Secondly, a Mesoamerican Biological Corridor (MBC), has been proposed as Central American network of protected areas to serve as an effective biological link between North and South America. Any mechanisms and institutions whereby the Central American Integration System could conceivably establish an effective MBC are of worldwide interest, given that few models presently exist of multilateral cooperation in natural resource management on the scale

---

[67] Guidelines include commitments to establishing a forestry policy based on zoning of permanent forestry, the adoption of a contractual system for the long-term use of forests, and the even-handed application of laws regulating forestry activities to national and foreign concessionaires.

required to achieve such a corridor. The MBC concept was supported in the 1992 *Central American Convention for the Conservation of Biodiversity and the Protection of Priority Natural Areas,* which states, at Article 21, the six countries' intention: to create, associated to the Central American Commission for Environment and Development, CCAD, the Central American Council for Protected Areas, with personnel and institutions related to the World Commission on Protected Areas, CNPPA, and financed by the Regional Fund for Environment and Development, as the main entity charged with coordinating regional efforts towards harmonizing policies related to and for the development of the Regional Protected Area System as an effective MBC. The World Bank fully endorses an MBC, supporting 75 major projects and studies out of the approximately 450 development activities related to the concept. At their Regular Meeting during the 19th Central American Summit (1997), the region's presidents approved the Central American Council on Protected Areas' (CCAP) proposal for implementation of an MBC.

It appears that the CACM will, for the present, continue to develop environmental protection as a separate agenda to the trade integration process. As the Central American trade liberalization process appears less likely to bring major changes to the sub-region, and indeed, developments in policy seem to focus more toward Mexico and the North, the political need for a trade and environment agenda is embryonic and perhaps more connected to foreign donor interests than a proper agenda for the sub-region.

NAFTA and the North American Agreement for Environmental Cooperation

NAFTA is one of the more developed models of a free trade zone in the hemisphere, with a population of 393 million people and an estimated GDP of 8,495.9 million dollars. It is a free trade area, and became effective in 1994. In 1996, intra-block exports reached almost 50 per cent as a proportion of total exports, expanding nine per cent per year. There is no common external tariff. The NAFTA is the classic example of the parallel yet politically interdependent degree on integration in international sustainable development law. Labour and environment side agreements exist between the three countries, and these are clearly designated as separate, non-trade agreements. The *North American Agreement for Environmental Cooperation* (NAAEC) is by far the most extensive trade-related environmental agreement of the hemisphere. It creates an institutional framework for continental environmental cooperation and civil society participation through the creation of the *North American Commission for Environmental Cooperation* (NACEC).[68] The NACEC is governed by a Council composed of the three countries' environment ministers and has a secretariat established in Montreal, Canada. After seven years in existence, the

---

[68] Available online: www.cec.org.

NAAEC has developed an extensive environmental cooperation programme and considerable expertise in the fields of trade and environment, biodiversity, environmental law, the sound management of chemicals, and others.

The CEC facilitated the involvement of civil society in trade and sustainability dialogues through the inclusion of NGOs in the development and implementation of its projects, and through the work of its Joint Public Advisory Committee (JPAC) that provides the commission with advice on various issues related to its mandate. Public outreach has been at the centre of the CEC's mission from its inception. This has fostered the development of a small but active continental environmental community addressing trade issues, in North America.[69]

The NAAEC focuses on effective enforcement of environmental standards in the three countries. Enforcement provisions are the only part of the agreement, which is itself subject to a dispute resolution process. The most innovative part of the agreement, however, is a procedure by which civil society groups can file in a complaint to the NACEC alleging that a country is failing to effectively enforce its environmental laws and regulations. This process can lead to the elaboration of a factual record, which is a summary of the facts that serves to highlight a pattern of noncompliance. At the end of the process, the NACEC cannot force a country to comply with its environmental law. However, the complaints procedure can certainly be a source of embarrassment for countries. In addition, it has been of capital importance in maintaining support for the work of the NACEC in civil society.

As in the MERCOSUR, the trade community of NAFTA itself also grappled with certain environmental aspects of their work, in this case within the text of the NAFTA accord itself and its working groups. Sustainable development is recognized in the Preamble as a goal of the Agreement, as is the right of each country to establish its own level of environmental protection. Perhaps one of the most interesting innovations in the NAFTA is the explicit reference to environmental agreements. NAFTA Article 104 lists seven such accords, and agrees that they will trump the NAFTA in the case of disagreement. The seven include the *Montreal Protocol*, the *Basel Convention*, the *Convention on International Trade in Endangered Species of Flora and Fauna*, and four bilateral environmental treaties. On investment, in NAFTA (Chapter 11), the parties promise not to try to attract investment by relaxing or ignoring domestic health, safety or environmental regulations. Other parts of Chapter 11 strive to ensure that foreign NAFTA investors will be safe from harassment by host governments, ideally creating a secure and predictable framework for the unencumbered flow of North American investment. The regime disallows expropriation

---

[69] G. Alanis, "Public Participation within NAFTA's Environmental Agreement: The Mexican Experience" in J. Kirton and V. Maclaren, eds. *Linking Trade, Environment and Social Cohesion: NAFTA Experiences, Global Challenges* (Aldershot: Ashgate, 2002). See also M.-C. Cordonier Segger and J. Cabrera, "Public Participation in Americas Trade and Environment Regimes" in M.-C. Cordonier Segger and C.G. Weeramantry, *Sustainable Justice: Reconciling Economic, Social and Environmental Law* (Leiden: Martinus Nijhoff, 2004).

without due process, for example, and in general holds host governments to the same standards for foreign investors as for domestic ones. Recent research has shown that these provisions have been used in unintended ways, where investors have filed a number of spurious suits against the three governments alleging that their investment interests are damaged by new environmental regulations or community decisions.[70] Governments are only just beginning to respond to these suits. As a result of these challenges, the governments prepared an interpretative statement, and its objection to the incorporation of such an investor-state dispute resolution procedure in the FTAA.[71]

NAFTA and the NAAEC emphasize national autonomy. However, their environmental provisions create a North American environmental framework with mild harmonization effects. This harmonization does not come from mandated NAFTA standards but from requirements imposed on the three countries: health and safety regulations based on sound science and risk assessment; recognition of standard-setting bodies and equivalency of standards; enforcement of environmental laws; and acceptance of a tri-State dispute settlement mechanism for enforcement matters. Between Canada and the US, convergence in environmental policy is apparent. This results from parallel domestic pressures, international environmental agreements, increased economic integration, and emulation. The US is the largest trading partner of Canada and Mexico and in most cases has higher environmental standards than those of NAFTA partners. The NAFTA, by increasing economic integration, allows greater interaction between policymakers and NGOs, magnifying the pressure for convergence. It is clear that without the environment and labour side agreements, the NAFTA would not have been approved in the political processes of the United States, and might even have faced more ferocious opposition in Canada. It remains to be seen how these parallel yet interdependent aspects of social, economic and environmental law develop cooperative links and work together. Perhaps the most interesting (and least explored) linkages in this arrangement to date will be the issues where the mandates of the social and environmental accords overlap.[72]

Bilateral environmental accords and other groupings

Countless bilateral environmental accords also exist in the Americas. An estimation in 1998 counted over 106 bilateral agreements in force or being

---

[70] H. Mann and K. von Moltke, *NAFTA's Chapter 11 and the Environment – Addressing the Impacts of the Investor-State Process on the Environment* (Winnipeg: International Institute for Sustainable Development, 1999).

[71] See NAFTA Free Trade Commission, *Notes of Interpretation of Certain Chapter 11 Provisions* (31 July 2001). See also Canada, "Pettigrew Welcomes NAFTA Commission's Initiatives to Clarify Chapter 11 Provisions" Press Release No. 116 (1 Aug. 2001).

[72] P.L. Stenzel, "Can NAFTA's Environmental Provisions Promote Sustainable Development?" (1995) 59 *Alb.L. Rev.* 43 [hereinafter *Stenzel*].

negotiated in the Americas.[73] Some are simple tariff elimination agreements, or selective strategic objectives, and others seem geared toward bilateral common markets. This is rapid proliferation – in 1994, there were only 26 bilateral or trilateral free trade agreements or customs unions in the hemisphere. Agreements have continued to develop, including on bilateral investment treaties.[74]

In terms of the environment/trade linkage, three bilateral trade agreements use innovative mechanisms which integrate economic and environmental priorities to some degree. First, under the framework of the NAFTA, a technical assistance programme has been established between Mexican authorities and the US Environmental Protection Agency to provide an *Integrated Border Environmental Plan* and an action agenda of collaborative projects with strong social and environmental components to improve health, working conditions and polluted areas on the border with the *maquiladora* factories.[75]

Secondly, the *Chile–Canada Free Trade Agreement, and its parallel Chile–Canada Agreement on Environmental Cooperation* (CCAEC) bears special mention. The Chile–Canada FTA explicitly recognizes the promotion of sustainable development as an objective, in its preamble. The CCAEC provides a framework for bilateral cooperation on environmental issues, committing the Parties to effectively enforce their environmental laws and work cooperative to protect and enhance the environment and promote sustainable development.[76] Modelled on the NAAEC, the CCAEC provides a commission for environmental cooperation, the provision of environmental information and a joint public advisory council process.[77] It also obliges parties to consider implementing limits to specific pollutants and prohibiting the export of domestically prohibited substances, to notify each other of domestic limits or restrictions, ensure transparency through publication and access to justice, including procedural guarantees. It also has provisions for private access to remedies, establishes national secretariats to implement its mandate, and recognizes any prior commitments under other environmental accords. The annexes, which phase-in the application of the agreement to Chilean environmental law, led to a comprehensive and

---

[73] C.S. Morton, *Progress toward Free Trade in the Western Hemisphere since 1994* (La Jolla: Institute of the Americas, 1998) Appendix E.

[74] In 2000, discussions were progressing between Chile and CARICOM, Chile and CACM, CACM and MERCOSUR, the Andean Community and MERCOSUR, Venezuela and MERCOSUR, Mexico and MERCOSUR, Mexico and the northern triangle countries in Central American, Mexico and Nicaragua, Mexico and CACM as a whole, Mexico and Peru, Mexico and Ecuador. Trinidad and Tobago expressed interest in joining the NAFTA, and Chile and Mexico explored the potential for a NAFTA-plus agreement.

[75] *Esty, supra* note 24 at 376–378.

[76] A. Bowcott, Manager, Environment Canada, International Relations, 10 Wellington Street, Hull, Quebec, Canada, and Canada's chief negotiator for the Canada–Chile, Canada–Costa Rica, and Canada–Central America environmental side agreements. Series of interviews, Jan.–Apr., 2003. Notes on file with author.

[77] W. Durbin, *A Comparison of the Environmental Provisions of the NAFTA, the Canada-Chile Trade Agreement and the Mexican-European Community Trade Agreement* (New Haven: Yale Centre for Environmental Law and Policy, 2000).

valuable revision of environmental law in Chile.[78] A similar environmental cooperation accord was signed between Canada and Costa Rica in Quito, Ecuador, at the FTAA Ministers of the Americas meeting in 2002.[79] It focuses more upon environmental information exchange and capacity building in the area of environmental enforcement and monitoring.[80] This agreement contains similar provisions to the CCCAE, but has a stronger focus on access to environmental information, and capacity building for environmental policy or law makers.[81] The agreement recognizes the relevance of transparency and public participation in the development of environmental laws and policies.[82] One objective is the promotion of public participation in the process of developing environmental laws.[83] Other provisions of the accord also deal with public participation and access to justice for violations of environmental laws, such as the right of citizens to request authorities to investigate potential violations of environmental laws,[84] the development of cooperation programmes which may involve the public and experts,[85] the right of any citizen or non-governmental organizations to request information from any party on the effective implementation of environmental law in its territory and the duty to respond to this request, including making summaries of the question and response publicly available,[86] the appointment of focal point for the communication between any party and the public on matters related to the implementation of the cooperation agreement, [87] the development of mechanisms to inform the public of the activities carried out under the agreement and to involve the public in such activities, as appropriate.[88]

Thirdly, the Free Trade Agreement between Chile and the United States presents a slightly different model. As with other recent US trade agreements, this accord actually includes environmental provisions, not as a side agreement but rather within the text of the FTA itself. The promotion of sustainable development is recognized by the parties as a common objective. Chapter 19 (Environment) establishes an Environmental Affairs Council. According to the Agreement, this Council shall ensure a process for promoting public participation in its work and shall seek opportunities for the public to participate in the development and implementation of environmental activities.[89] Each party shall

---

[78] *Agreement on Environmental Cooperation Between the Government of Canada and the Government of the Republic of Chile*, Art. 2, and 10, Sections 1 and 2, web: <http://www.sice.oas.org/trade/chican_e/env1e.stm#art1>.

[79] A. Bowcott, Manager, Environment Canada, International Relations, 10 Wellington Street, Hull, Quebec, Canada, and Canada's chief negotiator for the Canada–Chile, Canada–Costa Rica, and Canada–Central America environmental side agreements. Series of interviews, Jan.–Apr., 2003. Notes on file with author.

[80] E. Gitli and C. Murillo, "A Latin American Agenda for a Trade and Environment Link in the FTAA" in C. Deere and D. Esty, eds. *Greening the Americas: NAFTA's Lessons for the Western Hemisphere* (Boston: MIT Press, 2002).

[81] See *Environmental Cooperation Agreement between Canada and Costa Rica*, published in *La Gaceta of Costa Rica*, No. 127, 3 July of 2002, available online: www.ec.gc.ca.

[82] Ibid.

[83] *Environmental Cooperation Agreement between Canada and Costa Rica*, at Art. 1. (d), *ibid.*

[84] See Art. 5.   [85] See Art. 8.   [86] See Art. 9.   [87] See Art. 10.   [88] See Art. 11.

[89] See *US-Chile Free Trade Agreement*, available online at www.ustr.gov, at Art. 19.3.

provide receipt and consideration of public communications on matters related to the Chapter and shall make available to the other party and its public all the communications it receives and shall review in accordance with its domestic procedures.[90] In addition each party may also convene or consult an existing, advisory committee to advise on the implementation of the Chapter, comprising members of its public (representatives of business and NGO).[91] Also under the procedural matters, access to justice is provided for violation of environmental laws.[92] While these innovations are certainly of interest to the environmental community, it remains to be seen whether such a chapter could be agreed in the context of 34 countries of the Americas. If it could, a side agreement which provides for capacity building and other arrangements might also be part of the package, or all concerns might be addressed in the "Environmental Chapter".

These new bilateral agreements, as they are more flexible, may have room for innovation in integrated social, environmental and economic legal instruments that they employ. They bear observation for models that could be useful for larger processes.

As in the first case study, this brief survey of RIA processes in the Americas, and the manner in which they have integrated environmental concerns, raises a number of questions, and illustrates certain key characteristics of the RIA as a potential instrument of sustainable development treaty law. In terms of "degrees of integration" in these sub-regional trade agreements, we observed that none of the five presently in operation in the Americas have reached the full level of supra-national integration present in a highly developed regional organization like the European Union. Some, such as NAFTA, with its parallel environment and labour side agreements, are examples of the "second degree" of integration, but do not truly begin to integrate environmental, economic and social considerations through the principles of sustainable development. Others, such as the MERCOSUR which grants a right of access to the overall dispute settlement mechanism in the 2001 *Framework Agreement on the Environment* for environmental and social concerns and provides space for environmental debates in the general institutional structure through *Sub-Grupo No. 6*, are in the process of becoming more integrated (the "third degree"). It remains to be seen whether these issues will continue to be added as an "afterthought" or if they can become part of the agenda-setting process (though usually on unequal footing in domestic legal and political debates). While at present, several RIAs seem to give low priority to environmental or social-legal cooperation (preferring to leave these issues for domestic instruments) if the accords lead to deeper integration between the economies of these nations, it is possible that political expediency may force at least parallel, if not integrated and institutionalized structures in the future. This cooperation may simply consist of mutual recognition of health and environmental standards, for the purposes of a more level playing field in trade decision-making.

---

[90] See Art. 19.4.1.   [91] See Art. 19.4.3.   [92] See Art. 19.8.

On a broad conceptual level, the RIAs surveyed are based on an unspoken assumption that trade is an essential part of economic development which, parallel to appropriate social development and environmental protection, will lead toward the goal of sustainable development. Another view would be that RIAs can provide a platform for inter-linked economic growth, social justice and environmental protection objectives, as sustainable development accords. From this perspective, just as environmental cooperation may use economic instruments, so may social and environmental provisions be included in essentially economic cooperation processes. For the hemispheric cooperation process as a whole, and the progressive goals set by the 1994 Miami Summit of the Americas, the 1996 Santa Cruz de la Sierra Summit of the Americas, the 1998 Santiago Summit of the Americas, and the 2001 Quebec City Summit of the Americas, it remains to be seen whether this second framework can be adopted. It will be a challenge for the hemispheric trade agreement and its counterparts to choose between five very diverse models, each using a distinct degree of integration and each showing its own agenda or priorities for the trade/environment/social interface. The intricate nature of a new arrangement with 34 countries at very different levels of development promises interesting policy debates if the FTAA follows the dominant trend, and recognizes suitable development as one of its goals.

Economic, Social and Cultural Rights (ESCRs)

This case study will address the application of human rights in sustainable development, which gives effect to various principles of sustainable development law, and will illustrate the intersection of human rights law with international economic and environmental law. In particular, this study focuses on the *International Covenant on Economic, Social and Cultural Rights (ICESCR)*, which is in the process of becoming a "highly integrated" instrument, primarily due to its increasingly broad interpretation by its supervising treaty body,[93] as well as efforts by a variety of States and non-State actors to invoke its provisions in environmental and economic contexts.

International human rights law is increasingly being brought into play in sustainable development debates.[94] In the context of treaty bodies, civil society actors have begun raising issues of environmental degradation and impoverishment, as such dynamics have affected vulnerable communities, with the result that such treaty bodies have produced concluding observations and general

[93] See, for example, *Statement of the UN Committee on Economic, Social and Cultural Rights to the Third Ministerial Conference of the World Trade Organisation* (Seattle, 30 Nov. to 3 Dec. 1999) UN Doc. E.C.12/1999/ 9.

[94] One excellent overview is provided by S. Giorgetta, "The Right to a Healthy Environment, Human Rights and Sustainable Development" Kluwer Academic Publishers *International Environmental Agreements: Politics, Law and Economics* 2, 2 2002, 209–216, available online: http://www.kluweronline.com/issn/1567-9764/current.

comments that address issues relating to the environmental and economic pillars of sustainable development. Similarly, institutions such as the Office of the High Commissioner for Human Rights (OHCHR) have begun dialogues with economic and environmental organizations. In January 2002, a group of experts was jointly convened by the OHCHR and UNEP to set out principles to guide the integration of human rights and environment, in the context of sustainable development.[95]

The UN Committee on Economic, Social and Cultural Rights sent a public message to the organizing committee of the *World Summit for Sustainable Development* drawing attention to the role of the *ICESCR* in the issues up for discussion at the Summit.[96] In the *Johannesburg Plan of Implementation*, States committed to:

realize the right to a standard of living adequate for the health and well-being of themselves and their families, including food, including by promoting food security and fighting hunger in combination with measures which address poverty, consistent with the outcome of the World Food Summit and, for States Parties, with their obligations under article 11 of the International Covenant on Economic, Social and Cultural Rights.[97]

The JPOI also calls on States to take steps with a view to avoid and to refrain from "any unilateral measure not in accordance with international law and the Charter of the United Nations that impedes the full achievement of economic and social development by the population of the affected countries, in particular women and children, that hinders their well-being and that creates obstacles to the full enjoyment of their human rights, including the *right of everyone to a standard of living adequate for their health and well-being and their right to food, medical care and the necessary social services.*"[98]

The JPOI reflects a compromise over a hotly contested dispute on the relationship between human rights and environmental protection acknowledging "the consideration being given to the possible relationship between environment and human rights, including the right to development, with full and transparent participation of Member States of the United Nations and observer States".[99] This statement reflects concerns of many member States that support for human rights in an environmental context would be tantamount to recognizing the right

---

[95] UN High Commissioner for Human Rights and the United Nations Environmental Programme, *Meeting of Experts on Human Rights and the Environment, 14–15 Jan. 2002: Conclusions*, online: OHCHR www.unhchr.ch/environment/conclusions [hereinafter OHCHR, *Conclusions*].

[96] See Statement of the United Nations Committee on Economic, Social and Cultural Rights to the Commission on Sustainable Development acting as the Preparatory Committee for the *World Summit for Sustainable Development*, 24 May 2002.

[97] *Johannesburg Plan of Implementation*, para. 40 [hereinafter JPOI] (a) in Report of the *World Summit on Sustainable Development*, Johannesburg, South Africa, 26 Aug. to 4 Sept. 2002. See *Johannesburg Declaration on Sustainable Development*, in Report of the *World Summit on Sustainable Development*, Johannesburg, South Africa, 26 Aug.–4 Sept. 2002, A/CONF.199/20 (New York: United Nations, 2002). See also *Johannesburg Plan of Implementation*, Report of the *World Summit on Sustainable Development*, Johannesburg, South Africa, 4 Sept. 2002, UN Doc. A/CONF.199/20: <http://www.un.org/esa/sustdev/documents/WSSD_POI_PD/English/POIToc.htm>.

[98] JPOI, *ibid.*, para. 102.   [99] JPOI, *ibid.*, para. 169.

to a healthy environment – currently not contained in global human rights treaties, as well as the fact that it would open new doors to political conditionality on developing countries. However, as will be indicated below, internationally recognized and widely ratified human rights instruments have practical application in sustainable development, without necessarily postulating the emergence of the right to a healthy environment. In addition, as will be noted below, human rights principles include obligations that restrict as well as broaden the options of developing countries vis à vis developed countries.

This case study illustrates the manner in which international human rights instruments intersect with international economic and environmental law, focusing on desertification and climate change. Human rights laws constitute pre-existing imperatives upon States. They have been invoked with the following effects:

- to provide further support for and generate further compliance with certain economic and environmental agreements;
- to fill gaps in these treaties;
- to indicate "core" and other obligations that require immediate implementation;
- to provide mechanisms to monitor sustainable development obligations, including the international human rights system, judiciaries and human rights commissions;
- to spur the development of environmental and economic law and policy.[100]

The broad manner in which human rights are drafted mean that they can be applied in circumstances unforeseen when the treaties were originally drafted. In addition, human rights add unique elements to sustainable development governance. The rights focus carries connotations of unacceptability and necessarily requires the casting of responsibility. According to Alan Boyle and Micheal Anderson, where a human right is put forward, it connotes a claim to an absolute entitlement that is "theoretically immune to the lobbying and trade-offs which characterize bureaucratic decision-making. Its power lies in its ability to trump individual greed and short-term thinking."[101]

However, the transfer is not only one-way, as economic and environmental concepts have been applied by human rights bodies in their recommendations to States on the means to implement human rights obligations. As discussed above, aspects of "good governance" such as transparency are seen as a corollary to the right to due process and necessarily to realize economic, social and cultural rights. Human rights bodies are increasingly drawing on environmental

---

[100] A. Khalfan and M.-C. Cordonier Segger "Human Rights and International Sustainable Development Law" Aug. 2002, CISDL Legal Brief, released at the WSSD, available online: <http://www.cisdl.org/pdf/WSSD_HR&SD.pdf>.

[101] M. Anderson, "Human Rights Approaches to Environmental Protection: An Overview" in A. Boyle and M. Anderson, eds. *Human Rights Approaches to Environmental Protection* (Oxford: Clarendon, 1996) at 21.

principles, as well as instruments addressing environmental and sustainable development issues. For example, *General Comment No. 15 on the Right to Water*, released by the UN Committee on Economic, Social and Cultural Rights, explicitly directs States to take into account instruments such as the *Watercourses Convention*, the *Climate Change Convention*, the *Biodiversity Convention* and the *Desertification Convention* in addressing water availability, water quality and the distribution of shared water resources between States.[102]

Human rights law provides a substantive legal basis for key principles of sustainable development. The International Law Association's *Declaration on Principles of International Law related to Sustainable Development* states, "The realization of the international bill of human rights, comprising economic, social and cultural rights, civil and political rights and peoples' rights, is central to the pursuance of sustainable development."[103] Similarly, the conclusions of the OHCHR-UNEP experts session on human rights and environment, in the context of sustainable development state: "Poverty is at the center of a number of human rights violations and is at the same time a major obstacle to achieving sustainable development and environmental protection. A rights-based approach can enhance the impacts of policies and programmes at the national and international levels on this matter."[104]

Human rights law related to the right to participation provides support to the principle of public participation, and by extension to the principle of eradication of poverty. The right to participation is notably enshrined in the *International Covenant on Civil and Political Rights*, as well as the UN Declaration on the Rights of Ethnic, National and Linguistic Minorities (1992),[105] among other instruments.

The rights in the *ICESCR* provide direct legal support particularly for the principle of equity and the eradication of poverty. Economic, social and cultural rights, in general, have been historically neglected by States, intergovernmental organizations and civil society organizations.[106] However, towards the end of the 1990s, there was significant growth in the level of international attention given to economic, social and cultural rights, in particular by organisations such

---

[102] Committee on Economic, Social and Cultural Rights, *General Comment No.15: The Right to Water* UN ESCOR, 2002, UN Doc. E/C.12/2002/11. For further description of the relevance of environment treaties for the right to water, see M. Langford, A. Khalfan, C. Fairstein & H. Jones, *Legal Resources for the Right to Water: International and National Standards* (Geneva: COHRE, 2004), Section 4.3 (International Environmental and Labour Treaties).

[103] International Law Association (ILA) Resolution 3/2002: *New Delhi Declaration Of Principles Of International Law Relating to Sustainable Development*, Preamble, in ILA, Report of the Seventieth Conference, New Delhi (London: ILA, 2002). Available online: http://www.ila-hq.org and excerpted above.

[104] OHCHR, *Conclusions*, *supra* note 95, at para. 18.1.

[105] United Nations General Assembly Resolution 47/135 of 18 Dec. 1992, available online: http://www.unhchr.ch/html/menu3/b/d_minori.htm.

[106] P. Alston, "The Fortieth Anniversary of the Universal Declaration" in J. Berting *et al*, eds. *Human Rights in a Pluralist World, Individuals and Collectivities* (Westport, Conn: Greenwood Press, 1990) at 12.

as the Office of the High Commissioner for Human Rights,[107] the World Health Organization, the World Bank, and the United Nations Development Programme.[108] A key institution that has provided much of the new thinking around such rights is the ECOSOC Committee on Economic, Social and Cultural Rights, an expert body that monitors the implementation of the *ICESCR*. At the domestic level, virtually all constitutions enacted in the 1990s and thereafter in developing countries include economic, social and cultural rights.[109]

The *ICESCR* recognizes a number of key rights that address the equity and poverty eradication dimension of sustainable development. It recognizes, *inter alia*, the following rights:

- The right to an adequate standard of living for every person, including adequate food, clothing and housing, and to the continuous improvement of living conditions.[110] Under Article 11.2, the Covenant recognizes the fundamental right of freedom from hunger. The latter obligation requires that States "individually and through international co-operation carry out measures to improve methods of production, conservation and distribution of food, [. . .] by developing or reforming agrarian systems in such a way as to achieve the most efficient development and utilization of natural resources; and to ensure an equitable distribution of world food supplies in relation to need".[111]
- The right to everyone to the enjoyment of the highest attainable standard of physical and mental health.[112] The *ICESCR* specifies a number of steps to be taken by states to achieve this right, including, for example, the improvement of all aspects of environmental and industrial hygiene.[113] The right to health is also recognized in a number of related conventions.[114]
- The right to education.[115]

---

[107] See, for example, *Statement by Mary Robinson, High Commissioner for Human Rights,* Preparatory Committee for the International Conference on Financing for Development, Third Session, 16 Oct. 2001. The Human Rights Commissioner's role is to be the UN's principal spokesperson on human rights, to act as the "world's moral conscience", and to link and strengthen the various UN human rights mechanisms.

[108] United Nations Development Programme, *Human Development Report – 2000* (New York: Oxford University Press, 2000) at 73 *ff*.

[109] See for example, the Constitutions of South Africa, Namibia, Ethiopia, Ghana and the draft constitutions of Kenya and Sri Lanka.

[110] *International Covenant on Economic, Social and Cultural Rights,* 19 Dec. 1966, 993 UNTS 3, (entered into force 3 Jan. 1976), Art. 11 [hereinafter *ICESCR*]. The right to an adequate standard of living is also recognized in the *Universal Declaration of Human Rights,* 10 Dec. 1948, GA Res. 217 A, UN GAOR, UN Doc. A/810 (1948), Art. 25.1 [hereinafter *UDHR*].

[111] *ICESCR*, Art. 11(2)(b).   [112] *ibid.,* Art. 12.1.   [113] *Ibid.,* Art. 12.2.

[114] *UDHR, supra* note 110, Art. 25.1, *International Covenant on Civil and Political Rights* 19 Dec. 1966, 999 UNT.S 171 (entered into force 23 March 1976), Art. 6(1) (The right to life) [hereinafter *ICCPR*]. In addition, as noted above, the right to life, as part of the ICCPR, requires positive measures, which, according to the Human Rights Committee, should include measures to eliminate epidemics, Human Rights Committee, *General Comment No. 6,* UN GAOR, 1982, Supp. No. 40, UN Doc. A/37/40 at para. 5.

[115] *ICESCR, supra* note 110, Art. 13, see also *UDHR, supra* note 110, Art. 26.

Obligations under the *ICESCR* exist in three forms:

- first, States have an obligation to *respect* these rights, by not taking any action to prevent individuals access to their rights;
- secondly, they must *protect* the rights by taking measures to ensure that enterprises or individuals do not deprive individuals of their rights;
- thirdly, States have an obligation to *fulfil* these rights, by pro-actively taking steps to strengthen peoples' access to resources and means to secure their livelihood, and by providing such resources directly where an individual or group, for reasons beyond their control, cannot enjoy their rights.[116]

It should be noted that the obligations of States are extensive – for example, effective implementation of the right to food requires full compliance with principles, *inter alia*, of people's participation, decentralization, transparency, independence of the judiciary, etc.[117] Since these processes are not related to resource constraints, they are to be implemented immediately.

The *ICESCR* requires that State parties: "take steps, individually and through international assistance and co-operation, especially economic and technical, to the maximum of its available resources, with a view to achieving progressively the full realization of the rights recognized in the present Covenant by all appropriate means, including particularly the adoption of legislative measures economic, social and cultural rights be realised progressively, to the maximum of available resources."[118] Such "progressive obligations" nevertheless consist of certain immediate requirements: that there not be discrimination in implementation of the rights, and that policies be implemented immediately with a view to progressively realizing the rights contained in the *ICESCR*.

In addition, the content of "progressive obligations" has been clarified and developed by international organizations, in particular the Committee on Economic, Social and Cultural Rights (CESCR), the United Nations ECOSOC body of independent experts that monitors the Covenant. The concept of "minimum core obligations" as set out by the CESCR, is key:

a minimum core obligation to ensure the satisfaction of, at the very least, minimum essential levels of each of the rights is incumbent upon every State party. Thus, for example, a State party in which any significant number of individuals is deprived of essential foodstuffs, of essential primary care, of basic shelter and housing or of the most basic forms of education is *prima facie* failing to discharge its obligations under the *ICESCR* ... In order for a State party to be able to attribute its failure to meet at least its minimum core obligations to a lack of available resources, it must demonstrate that

---

[116] Committee on Economic, Social and Cultural Rights, *General Comment No. 12: The Right to Food* at para. 15 [hereinafter CESCR, *General Comment 12*].

[117] *Ibid.*, para. 23.

[118] *ICESCR, supra* note 110, Art. 2.1. A similar limitation on economic, social and cultural rights, albeit broader, exists in the Universal Declaration on Human Rights, which states in Art. 22; "Persons are entitled to realization of their economic and social rights through national effort and international co-operation and in accordance with the organization and resources of each State."

every effort has been made to use all resources that are at its disposition in an effort to satisfy, as a matter of priority, those minimum obligations.[119]

A key point that should be noted is that economic, social and cultural rights apply in conjunction with other rights related to civil and political rights, and the right to development. Poverty must be addressed at its roots by overcoming the constraints that give rise to it rather than merely treating the symptoms of poverty through welfare transfers.[120] On this point, the CESCR has indicated that non-discrimination and the broad range of human rights, including the right to meaningful participation, are critical to the successful realization of any anti-poverty programme.[121]

The Covenant therefore consists of principles that have extremely significant and broad-ranging implications for State parties, as they relate to "social" law on poverty eradication.[122] The broad range of economic, social and cultural rights lend themselves to application outside the realm of social law, where environmental or economic issues intersect with basic economic, social and cultural rights.

Although the focus of this case study is on the *ICESCR*, substantive economic, social and cultural rights related to sustainable development are also found in international treaties such as the *Convention on the Rights of the Child*[123] and the *Convention on the Elimination of Discrimination Against Women*,[124] and regional instruments, notably the *European Convention on Human Rights*,[125]

---

[119] United Nations Committee on Economic, Social and Cultural Rights, *General Comment No.3, The Nature of States Parties' Obligations* UN ESCOR, 1990, UN Doc. E/1991/23 at para. 10 [hereinafter CESCR, *General Comment 3*]. See also the list of obligations in Committee on Economic, Social and Cultural Rights, *General Comment No.14: The Right to the Highest Attainable Standard of Health*, UN ESCOR, 2000, UN Doc. E/C.12/2000/4, at para. 43–44 [hereinafter CESCR, *General Comment 14*]. In this comment, at para. 47, the CESCR has stated that such core obligations are "non-derogable" and that a State party cannot, under any circumstances whatsoever, justify its non-compliance with core obligations. The General Comments of the CESCR are authoritative interpretations of the *ICESCR*. The Committee was encouraged in ECOSOC Resolution 1990/45 to "continue using that mechanism to develop a fuller appreciation of the obligations of State Parties under the Covenant".

[120] N. Singh and R. Strickland "Sustainable Development, Poverty Eradication and Macro/Micro Policy Adjustments: An Overview" in N. Singh and R. Strickland, eds., *From Legacy to Vision: Sustainability, Poverty and Policy Adjustment* (Winnipeg: International Institute for Sustainable Development, 1996) at 33.

[121] Statement of the Committee on Economic, Social and Cultural Rights, *Poverty and the International Covenant on Economic, Social and Cultural Rights*, UN ESCOR, 2001, UN Doc. E/C.12/2001/10, paras. 10–13, [hereinafter CESCR *Poverty Statement*].

[122] In addition, the rights it upholds are referred to in other treaties, such as the *Convention on the Elimination of all Forms of Racial Discrimination*, the *Convention on the Elimination of Discrimination Against Women* and the *Convention on the Rights of the Child*, as well as in General Assembly Declarations, in particular the *UDHR*.

[123] *UN Convention on the Rights of the Child*, GA Res. 44/25, UN GAOR, 44th Sess., Annex, Supp. No. 49, UN Doc. A/44/49 (1989) 167 (entered into force 2 Sept. 1990).

[124] *Convention on the Elimination of All Forms of Discrimination Against Women*, 4 Jan. 1969, Can. T.S. 1982 No. 31.

[125] *European Convention for the Protection of Human Rights and Fundamental Freedoms* 4 Nov. 1950, 213 UNTS 222 (entered into force 3 Sept. 1953).

the *European Social Charter*,[126] the *Inter-American Convention on Human Rights*[127] and the *African Charter on Human and People's Rights*.[128]

A number of judicial and arbitral decisions have applied such human rights provisions in reviewing environment and social protection measures by States. For example, in *Social and Economic Rights Action Center and the Center for Economic and Social Rights* v. *Nigeria*, the African Commission on Human and People's Rights found that the disposal of oil wastes into the environment and local waterways in violation of applicable environmental standards amounted to a violation of the rights to life, health, property, the right to free disposal of natural resources, freedom from discrimination and the right to a healthy environment.[129] In *Lopez-Ostra* v. *Spain*, the European Court of Human Rights found that pollution from a tannery that resulted in health problems for neighbouring residents violated the Convention. Although the European Convention does not comprise the right to health, the pollution was held to violate Article 8 of the Convention on the right to respect for the home and for private and family life. In making this decision, the Court noted the need for a fair balancing of economic and human rights interests, in this case, between the rights of the individual person and the economic well-being of a municipality. The Court ruled that the proper balance gave priority to individual human rights.[130]

The right to life in the Indian Constitution has been given broad application in the constitutional jurisprudence of India, where it has allowed Courts to require States to address cases of environmental pollution of water and air.[131] The Court has also ordered the State to ensure provision of basic services such as sanitation in particular circumstances.[132] In the *Grootboom* case, the South African Constitutional Court required the State to revise its housing programme, on the basis that the programme did not pass a test of "reasonableness" in that it did not make sufficient provision for the persons whose housing needs were the most serious. In that decision, the Court was faced with a programme that allotted significant amounts of funding to meeting medium- and long-term needs, but did not make provision for even temporary relief for persons living in intolerable conditions due to natural disasters or evictions.[133] In the *Treatment Action*

---

[126] *European Social Charter*, 18 Oct. 1961, Eur. TS No. 35, 529 UNTS 89.

[127] *Inter-American Convention on Human Rights*, 22 Nov. 1969, 1144 UNTS 123.

[128] *Banjul Charter on Human and Peoples' Rights*, 27 June 1981, O.A.U. Doc. CAB/LEG./67/3/Rev.5. reprinted 21 ILM 59 (1982)

[129] Communication 155/96.

[130] Case 41/1993, Judgment of 9 Dec. 1994; Ser. A No.303C (1994).

[131] The application of this right to require various forms of environmental protection as seen in Indian cases such as *Subhash Kumar* v. *State of Bihar*, AIR 1991 SC 420, Supreme Court of India. See also *Charan Lal Sadhu* v. *Union of India* AIR 1990 SC 1480 and *Koolwal* v. *Rajasthan* AIR 1998, Raj. 2, referring to environmental pollution as "slow poisoning" of humans, cited in M. Anderson, "Individual Rights to Environmental Protection in India" in A. Boyle and M. Anderson, eds. *Human Rights Approaches to Environmental Protection* (Oxford: Clarendon, 1996) at 211–21.

[132] *Municipal Council Ratlam* v. *Vardhichand and others*, AIR 1980 SC 1622.

[133] *Government of the Republic of South Africa and others* v. *Grootboom and others*, 2001 (1) SA 46 (CC), South African Constitutional Court, http://www.concourt.gov.za/judgment.php?case_id =11987.

Campaign case, the Constitutional Court of South Africa held that the right to health required the State to provide anti-retroviral drugs to pregnant HIV-positive women.[134]

The *ICESCR* and international economic law

Human rights obligations ratified by States apply domestically as well as internationally. According to Article 28 of the Universal Declaration of Human Rights: "Everyone is entitled to a social and international order in which the rights and freedoms set forth in this Declaration can be fully realised." Similarly, under the *ICESCR*, State obligations are joint since States commit to take steps "individually and through international assistance and co-operation".[135] In particular, the *ICESCR* requires States to "ensure an equitable distribution of world supplies in relation to need".[136]

According to the Committee on Economic, Social and Cultural Rights (CESCR), "international cooperation for development and thus for the realization of economic, social and cultural rights is an obligation of all States. It is particularly incumbent upon those States that are in a position to assist others in this regard."[137] However, while the existence of some legal obligation in relation to international cooperation is therefore clear, the particular content of this obligation has been the object of much controversy and requires further analysis.[138]

International obligations, although different from domestic obligations, may similarly be classified according to obligations *to respect, to protect* and *to fulfil* economic, social and cultural rights. The latter, the obligation "to fulfil", is particularly controversial. It is difficult to show that these clauses create a legally binding obligation upon any particular state to provide any particular form of assistance to another.[139] Nevertheless, in certain circumstances, it may be

---

[134] *Minister of Health* v. *Treatment Action Campaign*, Constitutional Court of South Africa, Case CCT 8/02, decided 5 July 2002.

[135] *ICESCR, supra* note 110, Art. 2 (1).   [136] *Ibid.*, Art. 11 (2) (b).

[137] CESCR, *General Comment 3, supra* note 119 at para. 14. This commitment exists in Arts. 2(1), 11, 15, 22 & 23 of the *ICESCR*.

[138] M. Craven, *The International Covenant on Economic, Social and Cultural Rights: A Perspective on its Development* (Oxford: Clarendon, 1995) at 147 & 149 [hereinafter *Craven*].

[139] See *ibid.* at 149, and P. Alston and G. Quinn, "The Nature and Scope of States Parties' Obligations under the International Covenant on Economic, Social and Cultural Rights" (1987) 9 *Human Rights Quarterly* 156 at 186–191. The countries that negotiated the *Covenant* stated that developing countries could not claim aid as a legal right, which is relevant as a supplementary means of interpreting the terms of the Covenant. However, other factors are relevant. Under the *Vienna Convention on the Law of Treaties*, the *ICESCR* should be interpreted in good faith with regard to its ordinary meaning, the object and purpose, the preparatory work and the relevant practice. See *Limburg Principles on the Implementation of the Covenant on Economic, Social and Cultural Rights*, (1987), UN Doc. E/CN.4/1987/17, para. 4 [hereinafter *Limburg Principles*]. *Vienna Convention on the Law of Treaties*, 23 May 1969, 1155 UNTS 331, 8 ILM 679 (entered into force 27 Jan. 1980) [hereinafter *Vienna Convention on the Law of Treaties*]. The *Vienna Convention on the Law of Treaties*, at Arts 31–33, also permits account to be taken of any relevant rules of international law applicable in relations between the parties (such rules could include the *UN Charter* and the *UDHR*), and any subsequent practice in its application that establishes the agreement of the parties regarding its interpretation.

possible to identify obligations to cooperate internationally that would appear to be mandatory.[140] For example, it has been suggested that a State could be viewed as not complying with its *ICESCR* obligations if the amount of aid it provided to other countries declined over a number of years.[141] Finally, the text of the *ICESCR* clearly mandates international cooperation to ensure an equitable distribution of world food supplies in relation to need.[142]

The CESCR's statement on poverty and the *ICESCR* elaborate on this notion by adding the concept of an "international minimum threshold", stating that:

[w]hen grouped together, the core obligations establish an international minimum threshold that all developmental policies should be designed to respect. In accordance with General Comment No. 14, it is particularly incumbent on all those who can assist, to help developing countries respect this international minimum threshold. If a national or international anti-poverty strategy does not reflect this minimum threshold, it is inconsistent with the legally binding obligations of the State party.[143]

This suggests a process to delineate the extent of international obligations relative to domestic obligations. If international anti-poverty strategies must "enable" developing countries to meet their core obligations under the *ICESCR*, the international community would be responsible for raising the resources that developing countries – in particular the lesser developing countries – clearly require in addition to their available domestic resources in order to meet such core obligations. The *ICESCR* does not impose any particular obligation on any one country to provide aid to another, nor does it require any specific policy choices. However, it does require that the State parties to the Covenant individually and collectively take necessary actions consistent with the Covenant to ensure, as stated in the *UDHR*, that international co-operation and assistance be directed towards the establishment of a social and international order in which the rights and freedoms set forth in the *ICESCR* can be fully realized.[144]

[140] Alston and Quinn, *supra* note 139 at 191.

[141] *Craven* also suggests that standards could be set by the CESCR with reference to the resources required to meet the challenge of global poverty, *supra* note 138 at 150.

[142] Art. 11.2 requires that States "individually and through international co-operation, [undertake] the measures, including specific programmes, which are needed ... to ensure an equitable distribution of world food supplies in relation to need".

[143] *CESCR Poverty Statement, supra* note 121 at para. 20. Minimum core obligations in the domestic context were explained as necessary since: "If the Covenant were to be read in such a way as not to establish such a minimum core obligation, it would be largely deprived of its *raison d'être*" (see CESCR, *General Comment 3, supra* note 119 at para. 10). An analogical argument may apply at the international level. Unless international obligations do not exist to compensate for the inability of a domestic party to meet its core obligations, references to international cooperation in the *ICESCR* would be of little relevance in light of the *ICESCR's* purpose, which is to ensure the realization of economic, social and cultural rights for all in accordance with the commitments in the *UN Charter* and the *UDHR*. Preambulatory para. 3 of the *ICESCR* states, "Recognizing that, in accordance with the Universal Declaration of Human Rights, the ideal of free human beings enjoying freedom from fear and want can only be achieved if conditions are created whereby everyone may enjoy his economic, social and cultural rights, as well as his civil and political rights."

[144] As stated in the *Limburg Principles, supra* note 139 at para. 30. See also International Council on Human Rights Policy, *Duties sans Frontieres: Human Rights and Global Social Justice* (Geneva: ICHRP, 2003), www.ichrp.org.

An inter-related obligation is the requirement that – in the same manner as domestic resources – international assistance (aid and/or debt relief) corresponding to *ICESCR* obligations be targeted towards the most vulnerable populations.[145] This obligation is of significant concern since it has been estimated that historically and presently, international assistance is not focused on the most needy States, and even less toward the most needy populations within them.[146] The obligation upon developed countries is particularly clear since failures to target aid may not be excused by claiming a "lack of available resources".

In contrast to obligations to fulfil economic, social and cultural rights, duties to respect and protect the rights of persons in other countries are probably the most easily justified aspects of international obligations. International lending institutions are required to respect economic, social and cultural rights in the context of their imposition of structural adjustment programmes.[147] Similarly, it has been suggested that States have a duty to ensure that all bodies subject to their control respect the enjoyment of rights in other countries. This would apply to the voting of States in international organizations and the regulation of multinational companies based in their countries.[148]

In addition, the obligations under the *ICESCR* require that measures be urgently taken to remove global structural obstacles, such as unsustainable foreign debt.[149] For example, the right to food requires that international lending agencies pay attention to the right to food in their lending and credit agreements, and in international measures to address the debt crisis.[150]

The *ICESCR*, along with other human rights conventions, declarations and customary law, thus represents a significant body of law that exists in uneasy contradiction with international financial and trade law and practice. The

---

[145] The CESCR has stressed, for example in the context of the right to housing, that international assistance should be focused on the most disadvantaged groups. *General Comment No. 4: The Right to Adequate Shelter*, E/1992/23-E/C.12/1991/4.annex III at para. 19. The *Limburg Principles*, *supra* note 139, state: "international cooperation must be directed towards the establishment of a social and economic order in which the rights and freedoms in the Covenant can be fully realized (cf. Art. 28, *UDHR)*".

[146] In 1995, it was estimated that twice as much overseas development assistance (ODA) per capita went to countries including the wealthiest 40% of people in the developing world as opposed to the poorest 40%. Less than 7% of bilateral ODA was directed to human development concerns – primary health care, basic education, safe drinking water, etc. M. Ul-Haq, *Reflections on Human Development* (New York: Oxford University Press, 1995) at 35.

[147] Committee on Economic, Social and Cultural Rights, *General Comment No.2, International Technical Assistance Measures* UN ESCOR, 1990, UN Doc. E/1990/23, at para. 9 [hereinafter CESCR, *General Comment No. 2*].

[148] *Craven*, *supra* note 138 at 148. In relation to membership in international organizations, see *General Comment No. 2, ibid.*

[149] CESCR *Poverty Statement, supra* note 121 at para. 21. In addition, CESCR *General Comment No. 2, supra* note 147, refers to the possible need for debt relief initiatives. Debt repayments have at times amounted to between 69% to 200% of their combined health, education and social expenditure, as has been the case of Zambia, as stated in Commission on Human Rights, *Joint Report by the Independent Expert on Structural Adjustment Programmes and the Special Rapporteur on Foreign Debt*, UN ESCOR, 2000, UN Doc. E/CN.4/2000/51 at para 17.

[150] CESCR, *General Comment 12, supra* note 116 at para. 41.

decade of the 1990s has seen some sporadic attempts by intergovernmental bodies, and non-governmental organizations to begin addressing the relationship between human rights and international economic law. Growing receptiveness of some international financial institutions to such legal resources may give way to greater development of the intersections between these two domains.

The *ICESCR* and International Environment Law

The *ICESCR* has broad applications to environmental issues. According to the CESCR, the notion of sustainability is intrinsically linked to the right to food, or food security, implying that food must be accessible for both future and present generations.[151] The drafting history and wording of these two articles acknowledge that the right to health includes a wide range of socio-economic conditions that promote conditions in which people can lead a healthy life, and also extends to the underlying determinants of health, including a healthy environment.[152] In particular, Article 12.2(b) which refers to "the improvement of all aspects of environmental and industrial hygiene" is understood by the Committee to require the reduction of all detrimental environmental conditions that directly or indirectly impact upon human health.[153] The Human Rights Committee has taken a similar approach in relation to the *ICCPR*. The Committee has consistently sought information on specific measures in the field of public health, including environmental matters such as the registration and transportation of nuclear waste.[154] Certain forms of environmental degradation and environmental policies will violate the right to non-discrimination.

In relation to health, the CESCR has identified a number of acts that may constitute violations including: "the failure to enact or enforce laws to prevent the pollution of water, air and soil by extractive and manufacturing industries".[155] It should be noted that the right to health also includes international obligations. State parties have to respect the right to health in other countries and have the obligation to prevent third parties from violating the right to health in other countries, if they have legal or political influence over such parties. State parties also have the obligation to ensure that the right to health is given due attention in international instruments.[156]

One may argue that the *ICESCR* constitutes the juridical basis for the right to a healthy environment. Phillip Alston suggests that there is little to support the

---

[151] *Ibid.*, at para. 7.   [152] *Ibid.*, at para. 4.   [153] *Ibid.*, at para. 14.

[154] However, there remain doubts as to whether such rights are to be realized immediately or progressively, R. Churchill, "Environmental Rights in Existing Human Rights Treaties" in A. Boyle and M. Anderson, eds. *Human Rights Approaches to Environmental Protection* (Oxford: Clarendon, 1996) at 90.

[155] CESCR, *General Comment No.14, supra* note 119 at para. 51. The CESCR states (at para. 39) that States must prevent third parties from violating the right to health in other countries, if they are able to influence these third parties by way of legal or political means. However, it further states (at para. 51) that a State violates its obligations when it fails to take all necessary measures to safeguard *persons within their jurisdiction* from infringements of the right to health.

[156] *Ibid.*, at para. 39.

claim that the right to a healthy environment, as currently formulated, goes beyond rights that are protected under existing treaties. Indeed, many scholars go further to note that the right to a healthy environment *could not* significantly move beyond existing rights.[157] Without delving into this controversial issue too deeply, this indicates that the *ICESCR* constitutes at the least a key resource in addressing environmental issues. Its application to climate change and to desertification, discussed below, indicates its concrete effects.

Applications of the *ICESCR* to climate change

This sub-section indicates the effects of climate change in exacerbating poverty and in causing further impoverishment. It suggests that human rights instruments can provide a mechanism to support and monitor the mitigation of climate change. Such instruments also indicate approaches to support the growing awareness of the need to address vulnerable communities that are most likely to be affected by climate change. Furthermore, human rights instruments require that measures to combat climate change take full account of the needs of the poor.

Climate change will result in a general reduction in crop yields for most projected increases in temperature, in most tropical and sub-tropical regions.[158] It will also lead to an increase in food prices. Furthermore, there is evidence (which still requires further research) that climate change will lower the incomes of vulnerable populations and increase the absolute number of people at risk of hunger. For example, it has been established, though incompletely, that climate change will worsen food security in Africa.[159]

Some of the processes that would affect agriculture include soil erosion, increased flooding, landslides, avalanches and mudslide damage as a result of more intense precipitation, heat waves,[160] decreased water availability in many water-scarce regions, particularly in the sub-tropics.[161] Climatic variations are expected to exacerbate desertification caused by human activities.[162]

In addition, one of the likely consequences of climate change is an increase in the number of people exposed to vector-borne diseases such as malaria and water-borne diseases, such as cholera.[163] In general, the impacts of climate extremes are expected to fall disproportionately on the poor. This is because

[157] P. Alston, "Peoples' Rights: Their Rise and Fall" in P. Alston, ed., *Peoples' Rights* (Oxford: Oxford University Press, 2001) at 282–283. See also on this point, D. Shelton, "Environmental Rights" in P. Alston, ed., *Peoples' Rights* (Oxford: Oxford University Press, 2001) at 233–236.

[158] Intergovernmental Panel on Climate Change, Third Assessment Report, Working Group II, *Climate Change 2001: Impacts, Adaptation and Vulnerability*, 13–16 Feb. 2001, online: http://www.ipcc.ch at 5. The IPCC's formulations include projections for the upper and lower estimated ranges of possible temperature increases [hereinafter IPCC, *Impacts*].

[159] *Ibid.*, at 11.   [160] *Ibid.*, at 7.   [161] *Ibid.*, at 5.

[162] United Nations Environmental Programme, Report of the Executive Director, *Status of Desertification and Implementation of the United Nations Plan of Action to Combat Desertification*, UNEP/GCSS.III/3. at 3 [hereinafter UNEP, *Desertification*].

[163] IPCC, *Impacts*, *supra* note 158 at 5.

tropical regions, and primarily Africa will be the most affected by climate change, and further because poorer peoples and States are less able to adapt to climate change.[164] Flooding over the next 80 years could displace between 75 million to 200 million people, in most cases destroying their shelter and means of livelihood.[165]

Climate change therefore clearly impacts on key human rights, such as the rights to health, food and an adequate standard of living. International law on climate change has been relatively conservative in protecting such rights. The *United Nations Framework Convention on Climate Change* (UNFCCC) envisages a reduction in carbon emissions to prevent dangerous anthropogenic interference with the atmosphere as an ultimate objective.[166] However, both the *Climate Change Convention* and *Kyoto Protocol* clearly do not come close to this target.[167] The *Kyoto Protocol*'s key commitment is to achieve stabilization for developed States at 5 per cent below 1990 levels between 2008 and 2012,[168] a goal later reduced to 2–3 per cent reductions for State parties. However, according to the Intergovernmental Panel on Climate Change (IPCC), stabilization would require a very significant reduction in world carbon emissions levels from 1990 levels.

If considered in the context of climate change, the *ICESCR* would impose obligations upon States to be responsible for the damage they cause to the rights of persons in other States (i.e. they will have violated their obligation to *protect* the rights of persons in other States from the actions of persons within their jurisdiction). In relation to both of the above decisions, the greater resources of more economically advanced States will place much of the burden on them.[169] The result is similar to that which would have been achieved by the principle of common but differentiated responsibilities.[170]

Human rights imperatives related to poverty eradication will require that some care be taken in the design of laws relating to climate change. Some reduction in emissions may negatively affect the right to an adequate standard of living, for the poor. For example, the State parties to the *Kyoto Protocol* commit to the "progressive reduction or phasing out of market imperfections, fiscal incentives, tax and duty exemptions and subsidies in all greenhouse gas

---

[164] *Ibid.*, at 6–8.   [165] *Ibid.*, at 13.

[166] *Climate Change Convention*, *supra* note 14, Art. 2.

[167] Third Assessment Report, Working Group III, *Climate Change 2001: Mitigation*, online: htttp://www.ipcc.ch at 5 [hereinafter IPCC, *Mitigation*].

[168] *Kyoto Protocol to the United Nations Framework Convention on Climate Change*, 10 Dec. 1997, 37 ILM 22 (1998), Art. 3.1. [hereinafter *Kyoto Protocol*].

[169] It is estimated that the costs of meeting the proposed Kyoto commitments for Annex B States would be between 0.1% and 1.1% of GDP. IPCC, *Mitigation*, *supra* note 167, at 8. Even with a doubling of such costs, the funds could be raised through a modest increase in taxes on wealthier groups.

[170] See for more information on this principle as an element of ISDL, Part II, Chapter 5. The principle is reflected in Art. 3.1 of the *Climate Change Convention*, *supra* note 14, which requires States to protect the atmosphere on the basis of "equity and in accordance with their common but differentiated responsibilities and respective capabilities".

emitting sectors that run counter to the objective of the Convention and application of market instruments".[171] The reduction of energy subsidies could be very significant for lower income groups, especially in relation to transport and heating costs. This effect can be prevented or minimized by structuring emissions reductions programmes so that they do not unduly impact upon the standard of living of the poor[172] and by instituting employment programmes for displaced workers and other such affected persons, at least to the extent permitted by the availability of resources. The human rights approach therefore requires that States move away from subsidizing the population in general, and instead target subsidies to those who would be unable to afford energy costs needed for a decent life, consistent with the "priority to the poor" focus of sustainable development. It should be noted, in this vein, that cost recovery pricing policies are necessarily increasingly being used to ensure sustainable use of scarce resources such as water and energy, as well as to internalize costs of pollution control. Such policies will only be sustainable if they ensure that basic needs are respected. Human rights standards provide a policy tool as well as moral basis for targeting social protection subsidies in a manner consistent with environmental protection.

The *Protocol* does not refer to poor-friendly strategies; though this would have been useful. However, the *Protocol* does not take away from the ability of countries to provide appropriate exemptions for vulnerable groups – and instead to shift the costs elsewhere. This exclusion may become more problematic in the future when developing countries commit to emissions reduction targets. A growing contributor to greenhouse gases is methane produced by animal husbandry and rice cultivation.[173] Developing countries can argue that they may not be in a position to compensate for methane emissions with reductions in other parts of their economies, and would therefore have to limit the "survival emissions" of rural producers – which would impoverish rural communities, undermining food security.

The second poverty eradication element to be considered in climate change involves how to support vulnerable communities adapt to climate change and to mitigate the effects of climate change upon them. Prevention of extensive climate change could be considered *prima facie* to constitute a minimum core obligation under the *ICESCR*, given that the poorer sectors of society are likely to be the first affected by climate change and will also be affected to the greatest extent. However, it is clear that adaptation and mitigation strategies are an element of a State's core obligations under the *ICESCR*, particularly given that climate

---

[171] *Ibid.* Art. 2(v).

[172] An example would be to use the proceeds from carbon taxes to compensate negatively affected low-income groups. IPCC, *Mitigation, supra* note 167 at 9.

[173] About 75% of the increase in emissions since 1750 has been caused by industrial emissions and the rest by changes in land-use patterns, such as deforestation: Intergovernmental Panel on Climate Change, Third Assessment Report, Working Group I, *Climate Change 2001: The Scientific Basis,* available online: <http://www.ipcc.ch at 7>.

change has already begun to cause damage which cannot be reversed, at least in the short term. To make this statement does not imply a simple endorsement of adaptive measures as an alternative to prevention of climate change. From a pragmatic point of view, the need for adaptive and mitigating measures will be of growing importance given that greenhouse gas emissions are rising and will continue to rise in most States in the near future. It is therefore important to focus on adaptation as a means to protect human rights in the context of climate change.

The need for a focus on adaptation is reflected in the *Climate Change Convention*, which requires developed countries to assist developing countries that are particularly vulnerable to the adverse effects of climate change to meet the cost of adaptation to these adverse effects.[174] This assistance is not based on set amounts. However, a good faith interpretation of the *Climate Change Convention* would require that some substantial assistance be given.[175] The application of human rights law to this issue would bolster and even extend the obligations of States in relation to climate change. Internationally, the *ICESCR* places a general responsibility on developed States to assist developing States in times of emergency.[176] In addition, under the *ICESCR*, the more developed States – who have disproportionately contributed to climate change, could be held to have violated the economic and social rights of individuals and groups in poorer countries who are affected by climate change. The logical step is to state that each of these States would be required, under article 2.1 of the *ICESCR*, to take action to repair the damage that it had caused.

The human rights approach would also require remedial actions to be taken domestically. Climate change impacts particularly upon the poorer States and the most economically vulnerable within each State. Under the *ICESCR*, it is precisely such groups who must be prioritized by States in situations where such conditions occur. The Committee on Economic, Social and Cultural Rights states in relation to the right to food: "even where a state faces severe resource constraints, whether caused by [...] climatic conditions or other factors, measures should be taken to ensure that the right to adequate food is especially fulfilled for vulnerable population groups and individuals".[177] Such obligations certainly apply to the other rights related to poverty, such as the right to an adequate standard of living and the right to health.

---

[174] *Climate Change Convention, supra* note 14, Art. 44.

[175] Such an obligation may be seen in light of the principle not to cause environmental harm (or disproportionate harm), the violation of which could lead to the invocation of State responsibility, thereby requiring compensation. As recognized by the Permanent Court of International Justice in *Chorzow Factory Case (Indemnity) (Germany v. Poland)* (1928), P.C.I.J. (Ser. A), No. 17 at 29. The obligation to interpret treaties in good faith is contained in the *Vienna Convention on the Law of Treaties, supra* note 139, Art. 31.

[176] CESCR, *General Comment No. 14, supra* note 119, para. 40.

[177] CESCR, *General Comment No. 12, supra* note 116, para. 28.

The analysis of the *ICESCR* and climate change is an example of the potential integration of social law, in particular human rights law, with environmental issues.

Applications of the *ICESCR* to desertification

As with climate change, desertification is a phenomenon that has a critical impact on the existence of poverty. The United Nations Environment Programme estimates that 70 per cent of the world's dryland is threatened by desertification. These drylands account for one-fifth of the world's population[178] and generate one-fifth of the world's agricultural output.[179] Desertification will undermine the access to food of families that depend on farming, either as a source of their food or as a source of core income.

About $42 billion annually is lost as a result of desertification, primarily in Africa (of which 70 per cent of the land is dryland) and Asia. Most of this loss is borne by people at the lower end of the income spectrum.[180] It is unfortunate that it is least developed countries that are the most threatened by desertification. Those States with annual per capita incomes of less than $500 make up 20 per cent of the total land area of developing countries, yet comprise 63 per cent of the drylands of all developing countries.[181] Desertification forces farmers to give up their property, their housing and social networks and to relocate. It is estimated that 135 million people may get displaced due to desertification in this way, including at least one-sixth of the population of Niger and Burkina Faso.[182]

As with climate change, addressing desertification will require sensitivity to the interests of the poor. In contrast, however, the eradication of poverty is probably a prerequisite to addressing desertification. The *Desertification Convention*[183] can be identified as a good example of an attempt to address questions of marginalization within the sphere of environmental protection.

The *Desertification Convention* explicitly requires that States pay special attention to the socio-economic factors contributing to the desertification process,[184] that they integrate strategies for poverty eradication into efforts to combat desertification[185] and that they improve national economic environments with a view to eradicating poverty and ensuring food security.[186]

---

[178] UNEP, *Desertification, supra* note 162 at xiii.

[179] R. Heathcote, *The Arid Lands: Their Use and Abuse* (Tokyo: United Nations University, 1983) at 296

[180] H. Dregne *et al.*, "A New Assessment of the World Status of Desertification" (1991) 20 *Desertification Control Bulletin* 6.

[181] R. Kates & V. Haaman, "Where the Poor Live" (1992) 33 *Environment* 1 at 5,7.

[182] K. Danish "International Environmental Law and the 'Bottom-Up' Approach: A Review of the Desertification Convention" (1995) 3 *Ind. J. Global Leg. Stud.* 133 at 138 [hereinafter *Danish*].

[183] *Desertification Convention, supra* note 18.

[184] *Ibid.*, Art. 5 (c).   [185] *Ibid.*, Art. 2 (c).   [186] *Ibid.*, Art. 10.4.

The Convention addresses the imperative of ensuring greater participation in decision-making.[187] This characteristic reflects the lessons of previous experiences where large government desertification programmes had attempted to organize and educate rather than to cooperate with affected communities.[188] The Implementation Annex for Africa in the *Desertification Convention* goes further than the Convention itself, as it encourages "a policy of active decentralization, devolving responsibility for management and decision-making to local authorities".[189] In the Annex for Africa, States also commit to adjusting regulatory frameworks of natural resources management to provide security of land tenure for local populations.[190] Furthermore, they commit to putting in place "price and tax polices and commercial practices that promote growth".[191]

In relation to ensuring adequate financing for desertification programmes, the *Desertification Convention* requires that parties "taking into account their capabilities, shall make every effort to ensure that adequate financial resources are available for programmes to combat desertification and combat the effects of drought".[192] Under the terms of the Convention, developed countries undertake to mobilize "substantial financial resources including grants and concessional loans"[193] and to facilitate the transfer of technology.[194] The first of these, as a matter of treaty interpretation does appear to be a concrete obligation, since the use of the term "substantial" would have to be interpreted in good faith.[195] It should be noted, however, that in the Annex related to Africa, developed States undertake to *increase* resources granted to the continent for desertification initiatives, although the exact amount is not stated.[196]

Developed States also undertake "to promote the mobilization of adequate, timely and predictable financial resources, including new and additional financing from the Global Environmental Facility of the agreed incremental costs of those activities concerning desertification that relate to its four focal areas"[197] (i.e. ozone layer, greenhouse gas emissions, protection of biodiversity and protection of international waters). There is a tangible link between these issues because desertification leads to the loss of indigenous wild plant species. The loss of such species will in turn undermine the survival of other species that rely upon them as habitat or food supply.[198] Consequently, the loss of plant life occasioned by desertification will increase climate change, though at a lesser level than processes such as deforestation.[199]

---

[187] *Ibid.*, Arts. 5 (d), 10 (f).   [188] *Danish, supra* note 182, at 143–148.

[189] *Desertification Convention, supra* note 18, Annex 1: Regional Implementation Annex for Africa, [hereinafter *Desertification Convention, Africa Annex*], Art. 5.1 (b).

[190] *Desertification Convention, Africa Annex, ibid*, Art. 8 (c) (iii).

[191] *Ibid.*, Art. 8 (a) (ii).   [192] *Ibid.*, Art. 20.1.   [193] *Ibid.*, Art. 20.2 (a).

[194] *Ibid.*, Art. 20.2 (c).

[195] See *Vienna Convention on the Law of Treaties, supra* note 139, Art. 31.

[196] *Desertification Convention, Africa Annex, supra* note 189, Art. 5.1 (b).

[197] *Desertification Convention, supra* note 18, Art. 20.2 (b).

[198] *Danish, supra* note 182, at 149.

[199] *Ibid.*, at 139.

However, desertification programmes will have to compete with other initiatives for a relatively small amount of money. In comparison to the $10–22 billion estimated by UNEP to be necessary to combat desertification annually,[200] the annual budget of the GEF in 1997 was roughly about $2 billion,[201] and has only recently been replenished to more adequate levels. The *Desertification Convention* establishes a Global Mechanism dedicated to financing. It does not, in itself, provide for funding, but rather is intended to promote the mobilization of resources for desertification programmes.[202]

In relation to international dynamics, the *Desertification Convention* requires that the State parties, in pursuing the objectives of the Convention, "give due attention, within the relevant international and regional bodies, to the situation of affected developing country Parties with regard to international trade, marketing arrangements and debt, with a view to establishing an enabling economic environment conducive to the promotion of sustainable development".[203] While the recognition that international economic systems impact on desertification is welcome, the obligation to give attention to this is framed in loose terms and transfers actual measures to be taken to unspecified other bodies, thereby making it extremely difficult to hold developed States accountable for this obligation.

From the viewpoint of poverty eradication, the *Desertification Convention* is a useful instrument. However, it can be critiqued on a number of grounds, in which human rights obligations, in particular those of the *ICESCR* can apply to some extent to "fill the gap". The *ICESCR* is a useful complement to the *Desertification Convention* in four ways:

- First, it would mandate for all States the actions that are reflected in the African Annex, but left out in the other Annexes; these actions are decentralization[204] and non-discrimination between rural and urban areas.
- Secondly, while the *Desertification Convention* requires States to fund these programmes "according to their capabilities", the language in the *ICESCR* is tighter, requiring action from a State "to the maximum of its available resources . . . by all appropriate means".[205] Although a State would have competing resource demands relating to other human rights obligations, desertification would receive significant priority as it normally affects the most vulnerable communities.
- Thirdly, application of the *ICESCR* would support the social justice element of reform measures. It would, for example, require the redressing of discrimination against rural areas rather than the development of "appropriate pricing policies" for agricultural produce. The *Desertification Convention* only refers

---

[200] W. Burns, "The International Convention to Combat Desertification: Drawing a Line in the Sand?" 1995 16 *Mich. J. Int'l L.* 831 at 863–864.

[201] *Danish, supra* note 182 at 159.

[202] *Desertification Convention, supra* note 18, Art. 21.4.   [203] *Ibid.*, Art. 2 (b).

[204] A component of the right to food, see CESCR, *General Comment 12, supra* note 116 at para. 23.

[205] *Desertification Convention, supra* note 18, Art. 20.3, ICESCR, *supra* 110, Art. 2.1.

to providing "security of tenure" for local populations, which is not as extensive as the land reform, coupled with financial and technical assistance required to properly eradicate poverty (as indicated in Part I). The *ICESCR* may be understood to require such action as part of its requirement to address the provision of rights "by all appropriate means". The right to food comprising guarantees of full and equal access to economic resources, particularly for women.[206]

• Finally, while the *Desertification Convention*'s approach to international economic dynamics is weak, as discussed above, the *ICESCR*, as interpreted by the CESCR, clearly indicates the need for debt relief and changes to the international trading system where core economic and social rights are threatened.[207]

CONCLUSION: PROSPECTS FOR FURTHER INTEGRATING HUMAN
RIGHTS LAW IN SDL

Human rights law provides significant elements of binding international law corresponding to the "social" pillar of sustainable development. This case study has noted that human rights institutions provide significant resources, mechanisms and legal support for actions that implement the "priority to the poor" element of sustainable development. In addition, environmental and economic development concerns are increasingly being addressed by human rights institutions. Human rights law, as indicated in the example of the *ICESCR*, has broad intersections with international environmental and economic law, in many cases creating obligations that significantly affect their design, scope and implementation. It is precisely due to the broad scope of human rights law and discourse, its imperative character, and its subversive nature, that there has been resistance to the mainstreaming of human rights in international sustainable development law and policy. Resistance to human rights is of two main varieties. One position, specific to economic, social and cultural rights, is from governments that resist the justiciability of such rights, including at the international level. Another more common position is that of many developing countries who argue that human rights language opens to the door to political conditionality. As explained above, these concerns do not negate the utility of a rights-based approach in sustainable development law, but rather provide impetus for a more open, international debate on the manner in which it should be applied.[208]

---

[206] CESCR, *General Comment No. 12, supra* note 116, at para. 26.

[207] *Ibid.*, para. 9.

[208] This issue is discussed further in A. Khalfan, "Human Rights and Development Financing" in M.-C. Cordonier Segger and C.G. Weeramantry, *Sustainable Justice: Reconciling Economic, Social and Environmental Law* (Leiden: Martinus Nijhoff, 2004). See also K. Tomasevksi, who argues that sanctions for human rights have often been inconsistent, relying on legal fictions of trickle-up effects, carried out for appearances sake and often benefiting the sanctioning State, in *Responding to Human Rights Violations 1946–1999* (The Hague: Martinus Nijhoff, 2000).

There are indications of growing international practice that accepts the human rights law as a basis for sustainable development. Human rights law is not necessarily a synonym for the social aspects of sustainable development, such as development, poverty eradication, gender awareness and equity. Nevertheless, it constitutes a significantly developed body of law in the social realm that has been embraced by a growing number of states, intergovernmental organizations and civil society organizations. It is therefore poised to become a key aspect of sustainable development law.

7

General Observations from the Case Studies

Several principal observations can be made with regard to the case studies of integrated instruments canvassed above.

In the first case study, Sustainability Impact Assessment procedures are examined. These processes provide an example of an integrated sustainable development legal tool which emerged from the environmental law field, and can be applied both internationally and at the domestic levels. Sustainability impact assessment is done by carefully considering, through a series of steps, the potential social, economic and environmental consequences of a decision, with spaces provided for public participation. It is expressly future-oriented, attempting to define and provide for the limits of human capabilities and the environment. As such, it provides a useful instrument which, whether required by domestic laws and regulations, international treaties, or the policies of international organizations, holds great potential to implement the principle of integration in sustainable development law.

In the second case study, several Regional Integration Agreements are surveyed. It is found that each accord uses different strategies and instruments to address environmental concerns through their links to economic integration arrangements. Focusing on the environmental provisions in each regional arrangement, it becomes clear that often, comprehensive cooperation mechanisms run parallel to trade treaties and are backed by institutions or commissions to provide a forum to facilitate public participation and address future issues as they arise. It is found that these regional integration agreements and processes are worthy of much greater scholarly scrutiny, so that their emerging potential as tools for sustainable development become clearer.

Finally, the third case study focuses on the role of human rights law in sustainable development law. It demonstrates the utility of cross-fertilization between human rights, economic and environmental regimes, and shows how social, economic and cultural rights enshrined in the *International Covenant on Economic, Social and Cultural Rights* are relevant and can strengthen international treaties relating to the environment and the economy, and therefore to sustainable development.

To draw together these distinct case studies, several cross-cutting observations can be made. In all of the international sustainable development law instruments surveyed, the principles of international law relating to sustainable development identified in Part II come into play. These principles are reflected in many of the instruments reviewed, although not consistently. The more rigorous application of these principles in the further development and implementation of instruments addressing sustainable development concerns would strengthen governance at the international and national level.

The principle of integration and interrelationship, in particular in relation to human rights and social, economic and environmental objectives, is reflected throughout the case studies. The sustainable development law instruments examined all appear to take into account social, economic and environmental obligations, though each does it in different ways. This book does not argue that all international instruments governing economic, environment and social issues are moving towards greater full integration. Not all circumstances or situations necessarily require integration. However, the instances of integration are multiplying both in terms of their objectives, and the mechanisms used to achieve them. "Environmental" treaties use economic instruments to encourage compliance, human rights institutions orient natural resource management and economic development policies toward the needs of the most vulnerable, and economic treaties provide mechanisms to identify and avoid undue social and environmental impacts of trade liberalization.

All the integrated instruments in question address the principle of the duty of States to manage natural resources in a rational, sustainable and safe way. Human rights instruments necessarily require that natural resources be managed in a manner does not impact upon basic human rights such as the right to health, a point illustrated in the decisions of the Indian Supreme Court and the African Commission on Human and People's Rights. The regional integration agreements can and increasingly do provide mechanisms for cooperation on transboundary problems which might result from unsustainable levels of exploitation of natural resources. The instruments examined also reveal sensitivity to the principle of inter-generational and intra-generational equity, though not all instruments fully take into account the duty to cooperate for the eradication of poverty. All of the case studies uncover a concern for future sustainability of policies and programmes. In particular, the SIA seeks to identify future impacts, and define flanking measures or otherwise mitigate impacts on future generations from policies, programmes and projects of today.

The integrated instruments examined above also attempt to provide for the principle of common but differentiated responsibilities of States and other relevant actors. In particular, the principle is critical to implementing and making compliance with sustainable development instruments possible. The principle is reflected in the two tracks to achieve compliance identified in the *United Nations Convention to Combat Desertification,* whereby one group of parties has an obligation to provide financing, and another to implement national action plans. The human rights instruments addressed similarly provide strong support for differentiated obligations for better resourced States, while simultaneously insisting on respect for universal human rights obligations.

A number of the integrated instruments address the principle of precaution by providing for the uncertainty of science in their anticipatory, future-oriented approach. Sustainability impact assessment is essentially a precautionary procedure – it seeks to identify impacts, and can provide a tool assessing whether States should regulate or restrict actions that could harm the environment, health or ecosystems.

The integrated instruments all illustrate the importance of the principle of public participation, access to information and justice, expressly providing for transparency and the active engagement of citizens, civil society and other actors. Human rights law provides a legal basis on which all States are obliged to ensure public participation, access to information and remedies for violations as a right in themselves, as well as means to realize economic, social and cultural rights. Many sustainable development treaties, including the *Biosafety Protocol* to the *United Nations Convention on Biological Diversity* explicitly recognize the need for broad public participation as a tool to achieve their aims. In addition, the need to implement the principle of good governance is revealed in the cases, affecting the potential for progressive development and codification of international law relating to sustainable development. In particular, the regional economic integration agreements established environmental bodies to resolve issues that might arise from closer economic cooperation, and in several cases, required greater respect for the rule of law by requiring that domestic environmental laws would be enforced in the context of economic cooperation.

The three case studies further indicate that integration is "demand-driven" and iterative. It is rare for an integrated instrument to emerge in a pre-fabricated form. Rather, the instrument, or a precursor to it, gradually emerged from a self-contained regime and then took on integrative features, or was applied in innovative ways. For example, there is a shift underway from environmental impact assessments to sustainability impact assessments. There is a similar shift through the inclusion of environment and social issues in regional economic integration agreements. Similarly, human rights instruments are being applied to address environmental and economic processes in a manner that could not have been foreseen when the treaties were enacted.

This evolutionary process has occurred because States have absorbed sustainable development lessons from recent experiences. In addition, important political and social groups have anticipated that their interests would not be served through a one-dimensional approach, as illustrated by the development of environmental and labour side agreements to the *North American Free Trade Agreement* (NAFTA), and have exerted pressure, or developed capacity, to ensure a more integrated or balanced approach.

It is therefore rare for those designing international regimes to self-consciously aim towards ensuring integration. Such an approach may indeed be unnecessary.

However, as the demands of environmental protection, social improvement and economic development become increasingly intertwined, the designers of instruments addressing sustainable development issues should consider whether it is appropriate in the international or national circumstances to implement an integrated legal approach based on the concept of sustainable development. Should they decide to do so, the emerging principles of sustainable development law and a wealth of practical experience can form part of their legal and regulatory toolbox.

8

Addressing Implementation
Challenges

International law on sustainable development is evolving at a rapid pace, as
are international laws in the fields of economic and social development, and
environmental protection. New treaties are being negotiated and ratified, customary principles are in the process of recognition, international organizations
are brokering agreements between states on priorities and action. International
courts and tribunals are increasingly asked to reconcile environmental, human
rights and economic interests.[1] International law is being influenced by a body of
international instruments, institutions and policy-making processes which, while
perhaps not formally binding, shape the options and guide the conduct of states.[2]
It is an exciting and demanding time for sustainable development jurists.

However, in the 1992 Rio Earth Summit, the 1997 Earth Summit+5 Special
Session, and 2002 *World Summit for Sustainable Development*, and in the
United Nations Commission on Sustainable Development, concerns have been
raised that perhaps international law has moved too far ahead of real progress on
the ground. Hundreds of sustainable development-related treaties have
been ratified and come into force, the majority in the past two decades. The

---

[1] In the International Court of Justice, see especially the *Case Concerning the Gabčíkovo-
Nagymaros Project (Hungary/Slovakia)* (1997), ICJ Rep. 7; in the International Tribunal on the
Law of the Sea, see the *Case Concerning Land Reclamation by Singapore in and around the Straits
of Johor* 12 (Malaysia/Singapore) Order of 8 Oct. 2003 (Request for Provisional Measures); the
Southern Bluefin Tuna Cases (Australia and New Zealand/Japan) Order of 27 Aug. 1999, *The MOX
Plant Case*, Order of 3 Dec. 2001; and the *Case Concerning the Conservation and Sustainable
Exploitation of Swordfish Stocks in the South-Eastern Pacific Ocean* 7 (Chile/European Community)
Order 2003/2 of 16 Dec. 2003. In the World Trade Organization, see, e.g., *European Communities –
Measures Affecting Asbestos and Asbestos-Containing Products* (5 April 2001) WT/DS135/AB/R
(Appellate Body Report), WT/DS135/R (Panel Report), and the *United States – Import Prohibition
of Certain Shrimp and Shrimp Products* (20 Sept. 1999) WT/DS58/AB/R (Appellate Body Report),
WT/DS58/R (Panel Report).

[2] See R. Jennings, "What Is International Law and How Do We Tell It When We See It?" (1981) 37
ASDI 59. And see C. Parry, *The Sources and Evidences of International Law* (Manchester: Manchester University Press, 1965). See also E. Brown Weiss, "The Emerging Structure of International
Environmental Law" in N.J. Vig and R.S. Axelrod, eds., *The Global Environment: Institutions,
Law, and Policy* (Washington: Congressional Quarterly, 1999) 98, where it is argued that "[i]nterna-
tional law now consists of other important legal instruments in addition to binding agreements and
rules of customary international law, namely, legally non-binding or incompletely binding norms, or
what has been called 'soft law.' These instruments exist in all areas of international law, although they
appear to be more abundant in human rights, environment, and financial dealings."

Johannesburg Plan of Implementation, alone, refers directly to over 30 relatively new international treaties, and highlights more than 400 accords that have developed in the context of particular regimes.[3] Many of these treaties are regional in scale and scope, or aim to use regional mechanisms for their implementation. One of the most challenging issues facing all three fields of economic, environmental and human rights law today involves the "implementation gap". Much international law in the field of sustainable development is not yet being adequately implemented. Indeed, many developing countries lack even the resources and capacity to participate in the myriad Conferences of the Parties for existing conventions. There is a need to overcome existing challenges and strengthen implementation of sustainable development law. There are two particularly important implementation challenges.

First, as the International Law Commission has expressed, there are general concerns about the risk of *fragmentation* of international law.[4] This broader trend appears quite evident in the area of sustainable development law. As was recognized when negotiations for the JPOI were launched, there is a significant need to clarify, strengthen and enhance the international institutional architecture of sustainable development. International laws and policies have been designed to implement policy objectives in the three separate spheres of sustainable development – the economic, environmental and social – with insufficient attention to coherence or even co-ordination between them. As mentioned in the first chapter of this book, as international regimes become more complex, and new institutions are constituted to implement obligations, States may even find that they have overlapping or conflicting obligations. This situation is most challenging for developing countries. Valuable resources, political will and capacity are squandered in the attempts to harmonize policies that were never meant to conflict. The challenge is about governance.

Secondly, while many treaties have been negotiated and ratified, there is still far too little implementation, enforcement and monitoring: compliance. Due in part to a lack of understanding of their modalities, as well as a lack of political will for their use, cooperative instruments can become inefficient, cumbersome, or slow to deliver on commitments. Their nascent compliance and enforcement mechanisms can be perceived as ineffective or weak. This can lead treaties and institutions charged with sustainable development mandates to suffer lack of respect and credibility in international circles.

This chapter will focus on ways to address these challenges. It presents an analysis of the clarified global sustainable development governance system that

[3] See WSSD Tables, above, which include the treaties and protocols of the International Maritime Organization (IMO), the 1994 Agreements establishing the World Trade Organization (which includes 12 specific treaties, each of which having implications for sustainable development), more than 180 Conventions of the International Labour Organization (ILO), over 45 diverse international and regional treaties addressing fisheries and oceans, and the various Agreements establishing multilateral and regional financing institutions.

[4] G. Hafner, "Risk Ensuing from Fragmentation of International Law", *I.L.C. Report on the Work of its 52nd Session* United Nations General Assembly Official Records, 55th Session, Supp. 10 (A/55/10) 321.

emerged in the 2002 WSSD negotiations,[5] and, with Salim Nakhjavani, an analytical survey of innovative international approaches to compliance-building in sustainable development law.

SUSTAINABLE DEVELOPMENT GOVERNANCE

The *World Summit on Sustainable Development* (WSSD) in Johannesburg attracted 45,000 people from over 180 countries. Sustainable development is clearly a world priority. But it still appears hard to implement in a straightforward way. This should not be surprising. Sustainable development is a global goal rather than just one project. From formulation to implementation and monitoring, in law and in policy, three interrelated international spheres of action – economic, environmental and social – are shaped by the sustainable development goal. This conceptual dilemma has one very practical result. Systems of governance and international cooperation for sustainable development are incredibly complex, and not very coherent.

Global systems of sustainable development governance have changed after the 2002 *World Summit for Sustainable Development*.[6] The *Johannesburg Plan of Implementation* (JPOI) attempted to address coherence challenges, in Chapter XI on the institutional framework for sustainable development.[7] In the WSSD processes, negotiators struggled to review existing, rather inchoate international governance structures within and outside the United Nations and gain a detailed understanding of their interrelations. While the final text of the JPOI did not make as much progress as many had hoped,[8] much of the current system was clarified and some important steps were taken. In Chapter XI negotiations, several key proposals to improve sustainable development governance were accepted.[9] This section starts with a summary of how the JPOI actually changes existing sustainable development governance, then highlights several specific aspects of the new system of institutional arrangements for sustainable development that are relevant to international law.

---

[5] The chapter shares thoughts with the article, M.-C. Cordonier Segger, "Significant Developments in Sustainable Development Law and Governance: A Proposal" (2004) *United Nations Natural Resources Forum* 28:1.

[6] This process was initiated pursuant to a mandate from the United Nations General Assembly, Ten-year Review of Progress Achieved in the Implementation of the Outcome of the *United Nations Conference on Environment and Development*, UNGA Res A/RES/55/199 20 Dec. 2000.

[7] See the *Johannesburg Plan of Implementation*, Report of the *World Summit on Sustainable Development*, Johannesburg (South Africa) (4 Sept. 2002) UN Doc. A/CONF.199/20: <http://www. un.org/esa/sustdev/documents/WSSD_POI_PD/English/POIToc.htm>.

[8] UN University, *Sustainable Development Governance: The Question of Reform: Key Issues and Proposals*. (Tokyo: United Nations University Institute for Advanced Studies, 2002).

[9] See "Sustainable Development Governance" (Paper prepared by the *World Summit for Sustainable Development* Governance Working Group Vice-Chairs Ositadinma Anaedu and Lars-Goran Engfeldt). Available online: <www.johannesburgsummit.org/html/documents/prepcom3docs/governance30.3.rev1.doc>.

Sustainable development governance and the results of the 2002 WSSD

The 2002 JPOI, at Chapter XI, sheds some light on the current global institutional[10] architecture for sustainable development. Institutions related to sustainable development are linked by the governance system as a whole and are responsible for the implementation of the 1992 *Agenda 21*[11] and the 2002 WSSD outcomes. They also identify and address emerging sustainable development challenges. And they have a role in implementing other internationally agreed development goals, including the objectives contained in the 2000 *United Nations Millennium Declaration*, the 2002 *Monterrey Consensus on Financing for Development*,[12] and the relevant outcomes of other major UN conferences and international agreements since 1992.[13] According to the JPOI, there is a need for all actors to strengthen commitments to sustainable development, and integrate the economic, social and environmental dimensions of sustainable development in a balanced manner. There is also a need to enhance implementation of *Agenda 21*,[14] strengthen coherence, coordination and monitoring, promote the rule of law and strengthen governmental institutions. Finally, the JPOI highlights the need to increase effectiveness and efficiency;[15] enhance participation and effective involvement of civil society and other relevant stakeholders;[16] strengthen capacities for sustainable development at all levels;[17] and strengthen international cooperation.

To meet these wide-ranging objectives, the JPOI defines an international sustainable development governance system. It sets out an international framework that is meant to enhance and link the work of different institutions dealing

[10] In this book, an institution is defined as *"a network of organizations and other actors that are working towards a common mandate, supported by a common organizsational structure"*. This definition encompasses the goals and rules, those devising them, and the coordination mechanisms and structures that are used to achieve the goals within the rules. See UNDP, *Capacity Development for Governance for Sustainable Human Development* (New York: UNDP, 1996). See also M. Lovei, and P. Pillai, *Assessing Environmental Policy, Regulatory and Institutional Capacity: A World Bank Policy Note* (Washington, DC: World Bank, 2003).

[11] *Agenda 21*, Report of the UNCED, I (1992) UN Doc. A/CONF.151/26/Rev.1, (1992) 31 ILM 874 [hereinafter *Agenda 21*]. References to *Agenda 21*, in the JPOI, also include the 1992 *Rio Declaration on Environment and Development*, *Report of the United Nations Conference on Environment and Development*, UN Doc. A/CONF.151/6/Rev.1, (1992), 31 ILM 874 (1992) and the 1997 *Programme for the Further Implementation of Agenda 21* GA Res. A/RES/S-19/2, UN GAOR, 19th Sess., UN Doc. A/Res/S-19/2 (1997).

[12] Further information on the International Conference on Financing for Development, held in Monterrey, Mexico 18–22 Mar. 2002, can be found at the ECOSOC website, online: <http://www.un.org/esa/ffd>.

[13] Further information on the international series of conferences from 2002 can be found at the ECOSOC website, online: <http://www.un.org/esa>.

[14] This includes the mobilization of financial and technological resources as well as capacity-building programmes, particularly for developing countries.

[15] Through limiting overlap and duplication of activities of international organizations, both within and outside the United Nations system, based on their mandates and comparative advantages.

[16] As well as promoting transparency and broad public participation, to further implement *Agenda 21*, *supra* note 11.

[17] Including the local level, in particular those of developing countries.

with economic, social and environmental issues. This global framework for sustainable development governance is complex and multi-tiered. It can be described as an inter-linked system of institutions, and the international, regional and national regimes in which they operate. This regime is shaped on three principal levels:

- international (including the United Nations General Assembly, the United Nations Economic and Social Council (ECOSOC), and the United Nations Commission for Sustainable Development (UNCSD),[18] but also other agencies and international organizations),
- regional (including the UN Regional Commissions and other regional and sub-regional bodies, including the regional development banks), and
- national (which includes sub-national bodies and local authorities).[19]

Economic, social and environmental pillars of sustainable development governance

Integration was recognized as an essential element of global sustainable development governance. Many different institutions have sprung up, on several levels, to implement mandates from all three pillars of sustainable development. The WSSD JPOI recognizes the need to strengthen and better integrate the social, economic and environmental dimensions of sustainable development into policies and programmes at all levels. As such, sustainable development governance is not simply about international environmental governance – indeed, those discussions are being carried out elsewhere.[20] Rather, in the new sustainable development governance system, it is recognized that all three fields of sustainable development law and policy – economic, social and environmental – need to be strengthened. And where there is overlap or intersection between the fields, including for cross-cutting or emerging issues, several forums have been charged to facilitate more coordinated and coherent implementation activities.[21]

First, the JPOI identifies a clear need for further collaboration between the WTO and the United Nations Conference on Trade and Development

---

[18] Further information on the United Nations Commission on Sustainable Development and its relationship to other international organizations can be found at the UN CSD website, online: <http://www.un.org/esa/sustdev/csd.htm>.

[19] Further information on the United Nations Commission on Sustainable Development and its relationship to other international organizations can be found at the UN CSD website, online: <http://www.un.org/esa/sustdev/csd.htm>. Further information on the broader United Nations system of agencies, and their relationship to other international organizations, can be found at the UN website, online: <http://www.un.org>.

[20] See UNEP/GCSS.VII/6, Annex I. The United Nations Environment Programme Governing Council, the Global Ministers of Environment Forum, and the international environmental governance (IEG) process are discussed earlier in this book, at Part I – The Foundations.

[21] This is particularly important for developing countries with newly designed national development strategies (including those for economic growth, or poverty reduction). These countries are often facing simultaneous pressures from international agencies, different treaty commitments and global markets.

(UNCTAD), the International Labour Organization (ILO), the United Nations Development Programme (UNDP), the UNEP and other relevant organizations and agencies. The exact nature of this link, as well as calls for trade and financing institutions to take sustainable development goals more seriously, were highly controversial points in negotiations leading up to the WSSD. In the international economic area, debates centred on the need to further enhance the contribution of trade and finance institutions to sustainable development. There were strong demands, especially from developing countries, to go beyond the provisions of the *Monterrey Consensus* for more concrete commitments on financing for sustainable development.

The JPOI calls for trade and financial agencies to enhance the integration of sustainable development goals into their activities and take full account of national programmes to achieve sustainable development. It also calls on countries to take concrete action to implement the *Monterrey Consensus* at all levels. It further indicates the need to ensure a "dynamic and enabling international economic environment" and the importance of promoting global economic governance through "addressing the international finance, trade, technology and investment patterns that have an impact on the development prospects" of developing countries.[22] As such, in the international economic pillar, three priorities emerge. There is a need to re-focus trade and financial policies toward sustainable development, to deliver on commitments made in Monterrey on financing for development, and to deal with international finance, trade, technology and investment patterns that have impacts on (or block) development prospects.

The JPOI also recognizes that the social dimension of sustainable development needs to be strengthened. It recognizes the need to promote the full integration of sustainable development objectives into programmes and policies of bodies that have a primary focus on social issues. It also emphasizes the need to strengthen follow-up to the outcomes of the World Summit for Social Development and its five-year review, and take into account their reports. In the negotiations, it was important to several developing countries that the social agenda be recognized as broader than simply labour rights, and that the work of the ILO[23] was placed in the broader context of social development. The consensus, in the end, to refer to "bodies that have a primary focus on social issues" proved to bridge this gap.

---

[22] In this respect, the JPOI recommends that the international community ensure support for structural and macroeconomic reform, a comprehensive solution to the external debt problem and increasing market access for developing countries. It also observes that efforts to reform the international financial architecture need to be sustained with greater transparency and the effective participation of developing countries in decision-making processes. Finally, it is stated that a universal, rules-based, open, non-discriminatory and equitable multilateral trading system, as well as meaningful trade liberalization, can substantially stimulate development worldwide, benefiting countries at all stages of development.

[23] Further information on the International Labour Organization can be found at the ILO website, online: <http://www.ilo.org>.

International environmental governance will be mainly done through the implementation of the outcomes of UNEP's Governing Council Seventh Special Session, Decision I: International Environment Governance (IEG).[24] This decision was the result of a ministerial-level intergovernmental process, established by the UNEP governing council, addressing issues and options for strengthening international environmental governance.[25] In the negotiations for the JPOI, some actors sought to re-open the IEG process. As environmental governance is only one part of sustainable development governance (and as the IEG decision had been the result of very difficult negotiations), this idea was rejected. The IEG process clarified and streamlined the global system of environmental governance, helped to stabilize UNEP financing arrangements through a modified system of assessed contributions, recognized the Environmental Management Group within the UN system, helped to "group" MEAs along programmatic lines, and re-focused attention on the UNEP Governing Council/UNEP Global Ministerial Environment Forum as the hub of a global network of environmental institutions. As did the IEG, the JPOI left outstanding one controversial point, for resolution by vote in the United Nations General Assembly. Specifically, it invited the "General Assembly... to consider the important but complex issue of establishing universal membership for the Governing Council/Global Ministerial Environment Forum" (GMEF). Universal membership in the GMEF may be the first step in a movement toward the establishment of a global environmental organization or mechanism.

The role of the international community in sustainable development governance

On the international level, the JPOI set in place a system of cooperation centred on the role of the broader international community and three specific international institutions: the United Nations General Assembly (UNGA), the United Nations Economic and Social Council (ECOSOC), and the United Nations Commission for Sustainable Development (UNCSD), with cooperation from other international organizations.

It also encourages collaboration within and between the UN system, the International Financial Institutions, the Global Environment Facility and the World Trade Organization (WTO). To do this, a rather complex grouping of institutions, including the United Nations Chief Executive Board (CEB), the UN Development Group and the Environment Management Group (EMG) and

---

[24] Further information on the United Nations Environment Programme, and the international environmental governance negotiations, can be found at the UNEP website, online: <http://www.unep.org/IEG>.

[25] See also M.-C. Cordonier Segger, A. Khalfan & M. Gehring, *International Environmental Governance for Sustainable Development: A Legal Brief* (Montreal: CISDL, 2001) available online: <http://www.cisdl.org>.

other inter-agency coordinating bodies are directed to coordinate.[26] This cooperation does not just mean more meetings – rather, it will be mainly operational, in partnership with others at all levels.

In three slightly new points, the JPOI also mentions the need for timely completion of the negotiations on a comprehensive *United Nations Convention against Corruption*,[27] recommends that the international community promote corporate responsibility and accountability,[28] and encourages multi-stakeholder dialogue. There was a trade-off between an explicit recognition of the need for international law, very much desired by the EU, many developing countries and others, and global support for an Anti-Corruption Convention, very much desired by the USA. Interestingly, in the end, it appears that both groups achieved their goal. The JPOI emphasizes that "a vibrant and effective United Nations system is fundamental to the promotion of international cooperation for sustainable development and to a global economic system that works for all." It notes the importance of a firm commitment to "the ideals of the United Nations, the principles of international law and those enshrined in the Charter of the United Nations" (a clear recognition that the principles of international law have evolved beyond those specifically mentioned in the Charter). It also commits to strengthening the United Nations system and other multilateral institutions and promoting the improvement of their operations.

The role of the UN General Assembly, ECOSOC and the UNCSD

The General Assembly of the United Nations (UN GA) was asked to adopt sustainable development as a key element of the overarching framework for UN activities, particularly for achieving the internationally agreed development goals, including those contained in the *Millennium Declaration*. It is also to give overall political direction to the implementation of *Agenda 21* and its review. This sets a global mandate in place, so that all other UN Agencies will support sustainable development objectives.

But on the international level, the UN GA's Economic and Social Council (ECOSOC)[29] and its Commission on Sustainable Development (UN CSD)[30] will play key roles.

---

[26] Further information on the United Nations system of agencies, and their relationship to other international organizations, can be found at the UN CSD website, online: <http://www.un.org/esa/sustdev/csd.htm>.

[27] Including the question of repatriation of funds illicitly acquired to countries of origin and promoting stronger cooperation to eliminate money laundering.

[28] For further proposals on how this could be done, see M.-C. Cordonier Segger, "Sustainability and Corporate Accountability Regimes: Implementing the Johannesburg Summit Agenda" (2003) 12 *RECIEL* 3.

[29] Explicit provisions regarding the United Nations Economic and Social Council (ECOSOC), and the General Assembly Resolutions 48/162 and 50/227, reaffirmed ECOSOC as the central mechanism for coordination of the UN system in this aspect, and its specialized agencies and supervision of subsidiary bodies, in particular its functional commissions (such as UN CSD). See *Charter of the United Nations*, 26 June 1945, Can. T.S. 1945 No. 7. See also *Agenda 21*, *supra* note 11. Further information on the United Nations Economic and Social Council can be found at the UN ECOSOC website, online: <http://www.un.org/esa/coordination/ecosoc>.

[30] The role, functions and mandate of the United Nations Commission on Sustainable Development (UN CSD) were set out in *Agenda 21*, *supra* note 11, and adopted in General Assembly

First, the JPOI grants a stronger role to the UN ECOSOC, especially in matters of coordination. ECOSOC is mandated to increase its role in overseeing system-wide coordination and the balanced integration of economic, social and environmental aspects of United Nations policies and programmes aimed at promoting sustainable development. It is to organize periodic consideration of sustainable development themes in regard to the implementation of *Agenda 21*, including the means of implementation. (Recommendations in regard to such themes could be made by the Commission on Sustainable Development.) It is to make full use of its high-level, coordination, operational activities and its general meetings to take into account all relevant aspects of the work of the United Nations on sustainable development.[31] It is also to promote greater coordination, complementarity, effectiveness and efficiency of activities of its functional commissions (such as the Commission on Sustainable Development, the Commission on Social Development, and others) and other subsidiary bodies; and ensure that there is a close link between the role of the Council in the follow-up to the Summit and its role in the follow-up to the *Monterrey Consensus*.[32] It is requested to intensify its efforts for gender mainstreaming.[33]

Secondly, the JPOI also recognizes that the UN CSD, as a Commission of the ECOSOC, will continue to be the high-level forum within the UN system for consideration of issues related to integration of the three dimensions of sustainable development. The UN CSD is only one forum among many involved in sustainable development law and policy,[34] but – as the focus for the UN system on these issues – it remains an important one. It is directed to place more emphasis on actions that enable implementation at all levels, including promoting and facilitating partnerships involving Governments, international organizations and relevant stakeholders for the implementation of *Agenda 21*. Implementation means more work for policy bodies, but a different kind of work.

To understand how this changes sustainable development governance, a little history is needed. The role, functions and mandate of the UN CSD were set out in *Agenda 21* and adopted in General Assembly Resolution 47/191.[35] In the 1992

Resolution 47/191. Further information can be found at the UN CSD website, online: <http://www.un.org/esa/sustdev/csd.htm>.

[31] In this context, the Council is directed to encourage the active participation of major groups in its high-level segment and the work of its relevant functional commissions, in accordance with the respective rules of procedure.

[32] To that end, the Council is asked to explore ways to develop arrangements relating to its meetings with the Bretton Woods Institutions and the World Trade Organization, as set out in the *Monterrey Consensus*.

[33] The JPOI also streamlined a little – the Committee on Energy and Natural Resources for Development was terminated, and its work transferred to the UN CSD.

[34] In the JPOI, the UN CSD continues to be the high-level commission on sustainable development within the United Nations system. It serves as a forum for consideration of issues related to integration of the three dimensions of sustainable development. The JPOI recognizes that although the role, functions and mandate of the Commission set out in *Agenda 21*, *supra* note 11, and adopted in the UN General Assembly Resolution 47/191 continue to be relevant, the UN CSD needs to be strengthened and other relevant institutions and organizations taken into account.

[35] Further information on the United Nations Commission on Sustainable Development can be found at the UN CSD website, online: <http://www.un.org/esa/sustdev/csd.htm>.

Earth Summit preparatory process, a follow up mechanism was needed for the United Nations to track progress toward sustainable development. In the end, it was agreed that a new functioning Commission would be set up, under the auspices of the United Nations ECOSOC.[36] At Chapter 38, *Agenda 21* states that:

... to ensure the effective follow-up of the Conference, as well as to enhance international cooperation and rationalization the intergovernmental decision-making capacity for the integration of environment and development issues and to examine the progress of the implementation of *Agenda 21* at the national, regional and international levels, a high level Commission on Sustainable Development should be established in accordance with Article 68 of the Charter of the UN.[37]

After the Earth Summit in 1992, the UN General Assembly agreed that the ECOSOC would establish a high-level Commission as a functional council body, and elect representatives of 53 States to serve for up to three-year terms. As such, the UN CSD is made up of 53 members, a third of which are up for election each year.[38] One of the interesting aspects of elections to the UN CSD is that these have been actively pursued by countries, unlike many other UN Commissions. Between 1992 and 2002, the UN CSD met once a year for two or three weeks, as a functional ECOSOC Commission with a full-time secretariat based in New York, and it was given a clear identity within the UN system. The Secretariat is located within the Department for Social and Economic Affairs (DESA). DESA also has secretariats for the Commissions on Population, Status of Women and Social Development, offering a good opportunity for collaboration. Relevant intergovernmental organizations and specialized agencies (UNEP, WHO, UNDP and others, including financial institutions) designated representatives to advise and assist the Commission, serving as focal points between sessions. The 1992 Earth Summit had also seen an unprecedented involvement of stakeholders in the preparatory process and the Summit itself. *Agenda 21* contains nine chapters dealing with the role of Major Groups.[39] In its first ten years of work, the UN CSD established innovative formal and informal procedures which gave major groups extremely high involvement in their work, and excellent access to deliberations.

The UN CSD's mandate was originally fairly broad.[40] It was to monitor progress on the implementation of *Agenda 21* and activities related to the integration of environmental and developmental goals by governments, NGOs, and other UN bodies; to monitor progress towards the target of 0.7% GNP from

---

[36] *Supra* note 29.

[37] *Agenda 21, supra* note 11 at Chapter 38. See also the *Charter of the United Nations, supra* note 29, at Art. 68.

[38] The allocation of seats is 13 from Africa, 11 from Asia, 6 from Eastern Europe, 10 from Latin America and the Caribbean and 13 from Western Europe and North America.

[39] The Major Groups in *Agenda 21* are Youth, Women, Farmers, NGOs, Local Government, Business, Academics, Indigenous People, and Trade Unions. See *Agenda 21, supra* note 11, at ch. 24–32.

[40] See UNGA Res. 1993/207.

developed countries for Overseas Development Aid; to review the adequacy of financing and the transfer of technologies as outlined in *Agenda 21*; to receive and analyse relevant information from competent NGOs in the context of *Agenda 21* implementation; to enhance dialogue with NGOs, the independent sector, and other entities outside the UN system, within the UN framework; and to provide recommendations to the General Assembly through the Economic and Social Council (ECOSOC).

The UN CSD did not negotiate treaties. If an issue required a stronger legal framework, initial discussions took place at CSD, but were then designated to an appropriate body to negotiate legally binding actions. In the years between 1992 and 2002, several critiques were raised by developing countries and others.[41] However, the CSD also developed a track record of certain achievements for international sustainable development policy, as a "soft law" forum.[42] In international law on sustainable development, so-called soft law instruments[43] are common.[44] Mainly, the UN CSD provided space for dialogue, coordination and

[41] They had expected the UN CSD to provide an effective body to monitor progress towards the target of 0.7% GNP, ensuring adequate financing and the transfer of sustainable development-related technologies, but this was not perceived to have happened. The UN CSD looked at finance and technology transfer themes in isolation from issues that might have enabled an effective argument for new funds. In addition, while occasionally development, transport, energy or agriculture Ministers would attend if their sector was being discussed, UN CSD was rarely attended by Ministers with budgets to deliver additional financing for sustainable development. Other critiques were also raised, including the UN CSD being described as a "talk shop" with too many environmental interests, not enough development Ministries, too many northern NGOs, and no machinery for implementation.

[42] According to Felix Dodds, these have included recommendations to codify Prior Informed Consent procedures (1994); the establishment of an Inter Governmental Panel on Forests (1995) and an International Forum on Forests (1997); supporting the Washington Global Plan of Action on protecting the marine environment from land-based activities (1996), agreeing to the replenishment of Global Environmental Facility (GEF) (1997); setting a firm date of 2002 for governments to produce their National Sustainable Development Strategies (1997); establishing a new process in the General Assembly to discuss oceans (1999); agreeing that new consumer guidelines would include sustainable development (1999); and developing an International Work Programme on Sustainable Tourism (1999). See F. Dodds, "Reforming the International Institutions" in F. Dodds, ed., *Earth Summit 2002: A New Deal* (London: Earthscan, 2002), online: <http://www.earthsummit2002.org/es/issues/Governance/governance.htm#Sustainable%20Governance>.

[43] The 1972 *Stockholm Declaration*, the 1992 *Rio Declaration* and the 2002 *Johannesburg Declaration* are all non-binding instruments, as are the 1992 *Forest Principles* adopted at UNCED. While not binding in the traditional sense, many statements of principles, guidelines, and codes of practices are influential international instruments. For example, the 2002 *Bonn Guidelines on Access to Genetic Resources and Fair and Equitable Sharing of their Benefits*, the 1990 FAO *Guidelines on the Operation of Prior Informed Consent*, the 1987 UNEP *London Guidelines for the Exchange of Information on Chemicals in International Trade*, the 1985 FAO *International Code of Conduct on the Distribution and Use of Pesticides* have been widely respected, although they are non-binding.

[44] See P. Sands, "Environmental Protection in the Twenty-First Century: Sustainable Development and International Law" in N.J. Vig and R.S. Axelrod, eds., *The Global Environment: Institutions, Law, and Policy* (Washington: Congressional Quarterly, 1999) 120. There are various reasons that States sometimes prefer non-binding documents. The negotiation of legally non-binding instruments is seen as more likely to be successful than the negotiation of formal international conventions, especially in controversial areas of international policy. Agreement appears easier to achieve, the transaction costs seem lower, the opportunity to detail cooperation strategies seems greater, and often, such norms can be made to respond better to rapid economic changes in scientific understanding or economic or social conditions. However, these instruments often serve as precursors to binding treaties.

eventual cooperation which leads to international instruments. It has made some progress in the past decade, but also faced many challenges.[45] The involvement of major groups at the UN CSD has increased each year, with formal and informal procedures being developed.[46]

The new UN CSD mandate focuses on reviewing and monitoring the progress in implementation of *Agenda 21*, and fostering coherence of implementation, initiatives and partnerships.[47] The UN CSD will still develop recommendations, but negotiations in the UN CSD will be limited to every two years, and the number of themes addressed in each session will be more constrained. As such, the UN CSD has been limited to a few clarified and strengthened functions.

It will review and evaluate progress, address new challenges and opportunities, and promote further implementation of sustainable development. It will focus on the cross-sectoral aspects of specific issues, provide a forum for better integration of policies.[48] In relation to its role in facilitating implementation, the UN CSD is directed to emphasize various aspects. It will review progress and promote the further implementation of *Agenda 21*, identifying constraints on

---

[45] For more civil society and expert reviews of the functioning of the United Nations Commission on Sustainable Development, see the International Institute for Environment and Development (IIED) series on the *World Summit for Sustainable Development*, online: <http://www.iied.org/wssd/index.html>. See also the International Institute for Sustainable Development (IISD), online: <http://www.iisd.org> and the Centre for International Sustainable Development Law (CISDL), online: <http://www.cisdl.org>. For the official structure, see *Johannesburg Plan of Implementation*, *supra* note 7.

[46] These included being let into informal and formal meetings and invited to speak (1993); being given the opportunity to ask their governments questions on their national presentations in front of their peer group (1994); the introduction of the Dialogue Sessions – as a series of 5 half-day Major Group presentations (1997); being invited to speak at the Heads of State meeting of the UN General Assembly Special Session for the first time (1997); and the inclusion of Dialogue Session outcomes as part of the materials for Ministerial discussion and part of official UN CSD Intersessional documents for governments to draw on by the UN CSD Chair (1999). The involvement of civil society organizations and Major Groups in the WSSD process has been unprecedented, with concrete steps being taken to ensure participation at each level. See Dodds, *supra* note 42. The 1992 Earth Summit had also seen an unprecedented involvement of stakeholders in the preparatory process and the Summit itself. *Agenda 21* contains nine chapters dealing with the role of major groups. The Major Groups in *Agenda 21* are Youth, Women, Farmers, NGOs, Local Government, Business, Academics, Indigenous People, and Trade Unions. See *Agenda 21*, *supra* note 11, at Ch. 24. In ten years of work from 1992 to 2002, the UN CSD established innovative formal and informal procedures which gave major groups extremely high involvement in their work, and excellent access to deliberations.

[47] The JPOI states that the UN CSD can promote and facilitate partnerships involving governments, international organizations and relevant stakeholders for the implementation of *Agenda 21*. The UN CSD will continue to review and evaluate progress and promote further implementation of *Agenda 21*, but will look to cross-sectoral aspects of specific sectoral issues. It will ensure better integration of policies through the interaction of Ministers dealing with the various dimensions and sectors of sustainable development. It will address new challenges and opportunities related to the implementation of *Agenda 21*, including the identification of constraints and ways these can be overcome. It will review issues related to financial assistance and transfer of technology for sustainable development as well as capacity building while making full use of existing information, such as national reports and regional experience.

[48] Including through interaction among Ministers dealing with the various dimensions and sectors of sustainable development through the high-level segments.

implementation and making recommendations to overcome those constraints. It will also serve as a focal point for the discussion of partnerships that promote sustainable development, including sharing lessons learned, progress made and best practices. In addition, it will review issues related to financial assistance and transfer of technology for sustainable development, as well as capacity-building. This was a significant point for developing countries – many felt that members of UN CSD had not lived up to their UNCED commitments on development assistance. It will provide a forum for analysis and exchange of experience on measures that assist sustainable development planning, decision-making and the implementation of sustainable development strategies. Finally, it will take into account significant legal developments in the field of sustainable development, with due regard to the role of relevant intergovernmental bodies in promoting the implementation of *Agenda 21* relating to international legal instruments and mechanisms.[49]

The UN CSD's new work programme is mandated to reflect these developments.[50] At its eleventh session, the Commission on Sustainable Development decided that its multi-year programme of work beyond 2003 would be organized on the basis of seven two-year cycles, with each cycle focusing on selected thematic clusters of issues. In 2004–2005, the CSD will address Water, Sanitation and Human Settlements. In 2006–2007, it will address Energy for Sustainable Development, Industrial Development, Air Pollution/Atmosphere and Climate Change. In 2008–2009, it will address Agriculture, Rural Development, Land, Drought, Desertification and Africa. In 2010–2011, it will address Transport, Chemicals, Waste Management and Mining, and a Ten-Year Framework of Programmes on Sustainable Consumption and Production Patterns. In 2012–2013, it will address Forests, Biodiversity, Biotechnology, Tourism and Mountains. And in 2014–2015, it will address Oceans and Seas, Marine Resources and Small Island Developing States. In each of these areas, it will take into account significant legal developments in the field of sustainable development. In each cycle, the thematic clusters of issues will be addressed

---

[49] For a proposal on sustainable development governance, the role and future mechanisms for the UN CSD to facilitate implementation taking into account significant legal developments in the field of sustainable development see M.-C. Cordonier-Segger, "Creating a New Network of Inquiry into Sustainable Development Law? A proposal for a new "network of inquiry" of experts to track significant legal developments in the field of sustainable development as follow up from the 2002 Johannesburg *World Summit for Sustainable Development*" (Symposium on Environmental Law for Judges, Johannesburg Summit Next Steps: The Role of the Judiciary in the Implementation and Enforcement of Environmental Law, Rome Italian Council of the Judiciary, 9–10 May 2003). Available online: <http://www.xcom.it/icef> and also <www.cisdl.org>.

[50] The work programme was directed to continue to provide for more direct and substantive involvement of international organizations as well as major groups in its work; give greater consideration to the scientific contributions to sustainable development; further the contribution of educators to sustainable development including, where appropriate, in the activities of the UN CSD; and promote best practices and lessons learned in sustainable development, as well as use of contemporary methods of data collection and dissemination, including broader use of information technologies. In regard to the practical modalities and work programme of UN CSD, specific decisions were made later, in the UN CSD 11 Meeting, when the Commission's thematic work programme was elaborated.

in an integrated manner with regard to the economic, social and environmental dimensions of sustainable development. The Commission further agreed that means of implementation should be addressed in every cycle and for every relevant issue, action and commitment. Linkages to other cross-cutting issues are also to be addressed in every cycle.[51] Finally, the CSD is mandated to share best practices and lessons learned in sustainable development, using contemporary methods of data collection and dissemination, especially information technologies.

The role of other international institutions

In terms of the role of other international institutions, the new sustainable development governance framework stresses the need for international institutions both within and outside the UN system to enhance their contribution to sustainable development.[52] The Secretary-General of the United Nations is encouraged to use the Chief Executive's Board for Coordination to further promote system-wide inter-agency cooperation and coordination on sustainable development, to take appropriate measures to facilitate exchange of information, and to keep ECOSOC and CSD informed of different actions being taken to implement *Agenda 21*. A report by the Secretary-General on the "Follow-up to Johannesburg and the Future Role of the CSD"[53] shed some clarity on this constellation of actors, and outlined new roles for various different aspects of the system.[54] Myriad other roles were also recognized in the JPOI, and it refers directly to the contributions of different UN Agencies to sustainable

---

[51] These include: Poverty eradication, Changing unsustainable patterns of consumption and production, Protecting and managing the natural resource base of economic and social development, Sustainable development in a globalizing world, Health and sustainable development, Sustainable development of SIDS, Sustainable development for Africa, Other regional initiatives, Means of implementation, Institutional framework for sustainable development, Gender equality, and Education.

[52] These include international financial institutions (IFIs), the World Trade Organization (WTO) and the Global Environment Facility (GEF), and the JPOI directs them to enhance, within their mandates, their cooperative efforts to promote effective and collective support to the implementation of *Agenda 21* at all levels. This is to be done with enhanced collaboration, not only on *Agenda 21* but also for the outcomes of the *World Summit on Sustainable Development*, relevant sustainable development aspects of the Millennium Declaration; the Monterrey Consensus; and the outcomes of the Fourth WTO Ministerial Meeting (Doha).

[53] 18 Feb. 2003 E/CN.17/2003/2.

[54] It purports a shift in focus from reporting and supporting normative discussions to implementation with a greater emphasis on specific thematic areas and goals/objectives; support for the follow-up mechanisms by other UN Conferences held during the last decade; promotion of stronger linkages between global intergovernmental deliberations and implementation measures at a country level; institution of more flexible, action-oriented, innovative and inclusive approaches with UN Agencies and non-UN actors; and promotion of overall integration of the three components of sustainable development. The report also points to the need for strengthening the UN CSD and expanding its resources so as to enable it to fulfil its original mandate of a coordinating body within the UN system and its new post-Johannesburg mandate for implementation of the WEHAB agreements.

development.[55] The need to streamline and open the international sustainable development governance system was also recognized.[56]

Other international aspects of the new sustainable development governance agenda should also be highlighted. The JPOI agreed to strengthen UNDP capacity-building programmes for sustainable development. It committed to strengthen cooperation among UNEP and other UN bodies and specialized agencies, the Bretton Woods Institutions and the WTO, within their mandates. The UNEP, UN-Habitat, UNDP and UNCTAD were also requested to strengthen their contribution to sustainable development programmes and the implementation of *Agenda 21* at all levels, particularly in the area of promoting capacity building. Finally, in a welcome step, governments established that the 1994 *United Nations Convention to Combat Desertification and Drought*, like other Rio Conventions, will have a dedicated, specific and permanent financial mechanism. Land degradation became a GEF focal area, through the decisions of the GEF Second Assembly in October 2002, in accordance with the recommendations in the JPOI.

Sustainable development governance at the regional (and sub-regional) levels

According to the JPOI, regional sustainable development governance must also be strengthened. The United Nations Regional Commissions, as well as other regional and sub-regional institutions and bodies, are given a special role in the implementation of *Agenda 21* and the outcomes of the *World Summit on Sustainable Development*.[57] Their role, in particular, is to facilitate and promote a balanced integration of the economic, social and environmental dimensions of sustainable development into the work of regional, sub-regional and other bodies. They will facilitate exchange of experiences related to best practices, case studies and partnerships. They will also assist in the mobilization of technical and financial assistance, as well as facilitate the provision of adequate financing for sustainable development programmes and projects, including

---

[55] The JPOI stresses that UNDP has capacity-building programmes for sustainable development. It commits to strengthen cooperation among UNEP and other UN bodies and specialized agencies, the Bretton Woods Institutions and the WTO, within their mandates. The UNEP, UN-Habitat, UNDP and UNCTAD are also expected to strengthen their contribution to sustainable development programmes and the implementation of *Agenda 21* at all levels, particularly in the area of promoting capacity building. *Johannesburg Plan of Implementation, supra* note 7.

[56] Governments also agreed to streamline the international sustainable development meeting calendar, reducing the number of meetings, the length of meetings and the amount of time spent on negotiated outcomes in favour of more time spent on practical matters related to implementation. They will encourage partnership initiatives for implementation by all relevant actors, making full use of developments in the field of information and communication technologies, though the modalities of these partnerships were still unclear.

[57] This includes improving intra-regional coordination and cooperation on sustainable development the regional commissions, United Nations Funds, programmes and agencies, regional development banks and other regional and sub-regional institutions and bodies. It also includes support for development, enhancement and implementation of agreed regional sustainable development strategies and action plans, reflecting national and regional priorities.

those related to poverty eradication. They will also continue to promote multi-stakeholder participation and encourage partnerships to support implementation of *Agenda 21* at the regional and sub-regional levels. Finally, the JPOI specifically recognizes the need to support the sustainable development programmes of certain groups.[58]

Sustainable development governance at the national, sub-national and local levels

Sustainable development governance also has a very important national dimension. The JPOI states that countries should continue to promote coherent and coordinated approaches to institutional frameworks for sustainable development (domestic authorities and mechanisms necessary for policy-making, coordination and implementation and enforcement of laws). It also commits countries to take immediate steps to make progress in the formulation and elaboration of national strategies for sustainable development and begin their implementation by 2005.[59] In WSSD negotiations, even this concrete target was viewed as a significant step forward by most countries.[60] The JPOI reiterated that each country has the primary responsibility for its own sustainable development, and encouraged countries to promote sustainable development at the national level by, *inter alia*, enacting and enforcing clear and effective laws. It also suggested that countries should strengthen governmental institutions, including by providing necessary infrastructure and by promoting transparency, accountability and fair administrative and judicial institutions.

In addition, the JPOI recognizes that all countries should also promote public participation, including through measures that provide access to information regarding legislation, regulations, activities, policies and programmes.[61] It calls for support for developing country (and economy in transitions) efforts to enhance national and local institutional arrangements for sustainable

---

[58] For example, the New Partnership for Africa's Development (NEPAD) and the inter-regional aspects of the globally agreed Barbados Programme of Action for the Sustainable Development of Small Island Developing States

[59] To this end, as appropriate, strategies should be supported through international cooperation, taking into account the special needs of developing countries, in particular the least developed countries. Such strategies, which, where applicable, could be formulated as poverty reduction strategies that integrate economic, social and environmental aspects of sustainable development, should be pursued in accordance with each country's national priorities.

[60] However, the Norwegian delegation noted that such a statement could also weaken earlier *Agenda 21* commitments, and sought to strengthen it.

[61] It states that they should also foster full public participation in sustainable development policy formulation and implementation. Women should be able to participate fully and equally in policy formulation and decision-making. It also commits to further promote the establishment or enhancement of sustainable development councils and/or coordination structures at national and local levels, in order to provide a high-level focus on sustainable development policies, and mentions multi-stakeholder participation.

development,[62] and highlights the need to enhance the role and capacity of local authorities, and the potential, in this respect, to strengthen links to the 1996 *United Nations Conference on Human Settlements (UN Habitat II) Agenda.*

As such, much of the mandate to implement international law on sustainable development has been directly referred to national governments, which are to enact clear and effective domestic laws, to promote fair administrative and judicial institutions, and to provide access to information on legislation and regulations.

Participation of major groups

The JPOI recognized the need for governments to enhance partnerships between governmental and non-governmental actors, including all major groups, as well as volunteer groups, on programmes and activities for the achievement of sustainable development at all levels. It also acknowledged the need for consideration to be given to the possible relationship between environment and human rights, including the right to development (with full and transparent participation of Member States of the United Nations and observer States). And it commits to promote and support youth participation in programmes and activities relating to sustainable development.[63]

Governments and intergovernmental agencies will not be alone in their efforts. As Stephen Toope and others have recently observed, international law is being broadened to include actors other than States as norm-generating actors.[64] With their emphasis on consultation and public participation, the 1972 Stockholm UNCHE, the 1987 World Commission on Environment and Development, the 1992 Rio UNCED, and the 2002 *World Summit on Sustainable Development* contributed significantly toward the development of this new, cooperative approach. Non-State actors now help to develop, implement and comply with norms.

An important factor has been the emergence of international and regional organizations within which government officials and experts, as well as non-governmental individual and group actors, interact and consider alternative policy options for the emerging problem.[65] The emerging international regimes

---

[62] This could include promoting cross-sectoral approaches in the formulation of strategies and plans for sustainable development, such as, where applicable, poverty reduction strategies, aid coordination, encouraging participatory approaches and enhancing policy analysis, management capacity and implementation capacity, including mainstreaming a gender perspective in all those activities.

[63] For example, supporting local youth councils or their equivalent, and encouraging their establishment where they do not exist.

[64] See J. Brunée and S.J. Toope "International Law and Constructivism: Elements of an Interactional Theory of International Law" (2000) 39(1) *Col. J. Trans'l. Law* 19 at 48 [hereinafter J. Brunée and S.J. Toope, *Interactional Theory*]. The writers refer to lawmaking as a mutually generative activity, and the dual function of States as both makers and observers of international law.

[65] On the role of international organizations as sites of interaction and arenas for coalition building at the international level, See H. Breitmeier, "International Organizations and the Creation of Environmental Regimes" in O. Young, ed., *Global Governance: Drawing Insights From the Environmental Experience* (Cambridge: MIT Press, 1997) at 87–114.

consist of networks, partnerships between States and these non-State actors (including intergovernmental organizations, civil society and private sector associations).

Traditional international law is healthy in the sense that there are more international agreements than ever, and States continue to serve important roles in the international system. It is no longer, however, the sole focus of international legal efforts. While the sovereign state remains the principal actor, its freedom to make decisions unilaterally appears increasingly restricted. Today, numerous non-State entities influence international decisions, and perform complex tasks for the implementation of international norms and treaties. By allowing a large group of non-governmental actors to attend the conferences as observers, the UN established a new standard of decision-making at the international level.[66] At Stockholm, non-governmental organizations (NGOs) presented their own statement of principles to the conference, in Rio the NGO Forum developed "alternative" accords among civil society groups,[67] and in Johannesburg, roundtable dialogues were held between heads of states and other experts, and non-State actors committed to "Type II Partnerships" to implement the intergovernmentally agreed outcomes of the Summit.

The JPOI, and subsequent re-organizations of international cooperation related to sustainable development, have not provided all the answers. However, governments have clarified existing relationships and laid out the rudimentary elements of a plan to facilitate sustainable development, focusing on key global priorities appropriate for the coming decade. Each issue addressed in the JPOI combines environmental, social and economic imperatives. Coordination and coherence, in this context, means that global sustainable development governance structures can, and will, focus on facilitating integration and implementation.

SUSTAINABLE DEVELOPMENT COMPLIANCE-BUILDING

with Salim Nakhjavani*

The integration of economic, environmental and social objectives is evident not only in the principles of sustainable development law, but also in their implementation, monitoring and enforcement. New, integrated approaches to compliance can contribute to the "clear and effective" implementation of sustainable development law. In this section, innovative approaches are discussed with examples from several highly integrated treaty-based regimes. An analysis

---

[66] An estimated 2000 NGOs were said to be in attendance at the UNCED Conference. L.K. Caldwell, *International Environmental Policy* (Durham: Duke University Press, 1996) 106. See also A. Kiss and D. Shelton, *International Environmental Law*, 2nd edn. (New York: Transnational Publishers, 1994) at 23 [hereinafter *A. Kiss and D. Shelton*].

[67] Caldwell, *supra* note 66, at 66.

* Salim Nakhjavani, LL.B, B.C.L. (McGill), Great Distinction, LL.M. (Cambridge, First Class) is lead counsel for cross-cutting issues with the CISDL.

follows of the theory and the practical effects of a *self-reinforcing dynamic* in highly integrated sustainable development treaty regimes. The section concludes by identifying four important trends in innovative approaches to compliance in sustainable development.

Throughout this discussion, two recurring themes are apparent. The first is a broad tension between respect for national sovereignty and the protection of common interests.[68] This tension is acute in new approaches to compliance, and shapes decisions about the appropriate role for external, expert bodies in implementation, monitoring and enforcement. In this chapter, the tension is addressed by suggesting that States are incrementally becoming more comfortable with the delegation of national sovereignty to international, independent, expert institutions where this seems necessary to advance the protection of common interests.[69]

The second tension is dispersal versus centralization of compliance-coordination. Innovative sustainable development law approaches to compliance rely on the enhancement of networks – as international, regional, national and sub-national governance mechanisms – both horizontally and vertically.[70] What is the most appropriate level for implementation, monitoring and enforcement measures, in sustainable development law? It is possible that regional agreements – implemented, monitored and enforced regionally or sub-regionally – are less

---

[68] This includes the concept of *common heritage of mankind*, which recognizes an essentially fiduciary responsibility over areas incapable of national appropriation such as the seabed and cultural heritage sites; as well as *common concern of humanity*, a more general concept that identifies spheres of action in which all nations share a common interest, such as preservation of fish stocks, conservation of migratory wild animals and, more recently, the conservation of biodiversity generally. See A. Kiss and D. Shelton, *supra* note 66 at 251–52.

[69] Recognition of this tension in relation to the growing reliance on "epistemic communities" is at least implicit in J. Brunée and S.J. Toope, "Environmental Security and Freshwater Resources: Ecosystem Regime Building" (1997) *Am. J. Int'l. Law* 26 at 40–44 [hereinafter J. Brunée and S.J. Toope, *Ecosystems*]. But see E. Benvenisti, "Domestic Politics and International Resources" in M. Byers, ed., *The Role of Law in International Politics: Essays in International Relations and International Law* (Oxford: Oxford University Press, 2000) at 109 [hereinafter *Benvenisti*], highlighting the key role of domestic politics – rather than delegation of sovereignty – in the protection of international resources; and A.-M. Slaughter, "Governing Through Government Networks" in M. Byers, ed., *The Role of Law in International Politics: Essays in International Relations and International Law* (Oxford: Oxford University Press, 2000) at 177 [hereinafter *Slaughter*], emphasizing that transgovernmental regulation is a manifestation of *disaggregation of the State* and the rise of *government networks* rather than delegation of sovereignty to international bodies.

[70] The consequences and theoretical implications of this integrated approach to compliance are both wide-ranging and exciting, and will be highlighted throughout this section. In particular, this model may be an illustration of transnationalism in international law, and particularly the "transmission belt" whereby "norms created by international society infiltrate into domestic society"; see H.H. Koh, "Why do Nations Obey International Law?"(1997) 106 *Yale L.J.* 2599 at 2651 [hereinafter *Koh*]. If this approach successfully builds compliance, it may also reflect J. Brunée and S.J. Toope's interactional theory of international law, insofar as this approach evolves norms through "processes of mutual construction by a wide variety of participants in a legal system" and relies on the deployment of reasoned argument within a predefined institutional framework to effect regime change. See J. Brunée and S.J. Toope, *Interactional Theory, supra* note 64.

prone to polarization along geo-political lines. By limiting the number of States Parties, regional agreements tend to give greater voice to developing country concerns and favour collaborative solutions that better respond to regional – though not always ecosystemic – needs.[71] In these contexts, compliance can be quite effective. However, centralized international compliance-coordination can also facilitate systematic efforts in fields where "artificial" national or regional boundaries impede effective global action. The concept that helps to address this tension is "subsidiarity", that is, "governance at the appropriate scale", at the level most consistent with effectiveness.[72]

As such, new approaches see compliance as both a *process* and an *attitude* that emerges when a treaty or customary rule is *implemented, monitored* and *enforced* effectively. Both the compliance-coordinating role of international bodies, and the linkage mechanisms that network implementation, monitoring and enforcement efforts are important for effective compliance. Innovations that facilitate linkages include provisions for public participation, education, openness, capacity-building, unification of scientific methodologies, sharing raw data, sharing knowledge analysis, sharing technology, and sharing financing. These linkages allow the regime to adapt quickly to address non-compliance, generating a self-reinforcing dynamic. Weaknesses within a particular mechanism of a highly-integrated sustainable development law regime are corrected through appropriate adjustments to the entire regime.

Genesis of integrated compliance mechanisms

As independent fields, different compliance mechanisms and processes are used in the fields of international environmental, economic and social law. These mechanisms are seen as most appropriate to the aims and interests of each field. For example, the regulation of international trade, from 1948 onwards, was focused on the reduction of tariff barriers and, more recently, non-tariff barriers.[73] Throughout this graduated transition, but especially during the 1970s, the unbalancing effects of trade distortions were a major cause for concern within the regulatory regime. Accordingly, anti-dumping and

---

[71] The best examples of promising regional agreements would be the proposed *Environmental Protocol* to the MERCOSUR and the *North American Agreement for Environmental Cooperation*; see above.

[72] M.-C. Cordonier Segger *et al.*, *Ecological Rules and Sustainability in the Americas* (Winnipeg: UNEP/IISD, 2002) at 64. This principle developed in the context of environmental protection measures in the European Union (see *Single European Act*, 17 Feb. 1986, 25 ILM 503 (entered into force 1 July 1987), Art. 130r(4)) and was expanded to apply to all Community action in the *Maastricht Treaty*, at Art. 3 (b). See P. Sands, *Principles of International Environmental Law: Frameworks, Standards and Implementation*, vol. 1 (Manchester: Manchester University Press 1996) at 546, 549 [hereinafter Sands, *International Environmental Law*]. The challenge for sustainable development law will be to incorporate the principle of subsidiarity in integrated environmental, economic and social law regimes.

[73] J.G. Castel, A.L.C. de Mestral & W.C. Graham, *The Canadian Law and Practice of International Trade* (Toronto: Montgomery, 1991) at 21.

countervailing duties[74] were used as remedies to re-establish equilibrium in trade flows.[75] That is, situations of non-compliance were addressed through proportional, targeted, "restorative" non-compliance. In comparison, post-war approaches to compliance in the field of human rights tended to favour judicial and quasi-judicial, "rights-based" approaches. So, among many examples, the 1947 *Genocide Convention* allows questions of State responsibility for genocide to be submitted to the International Court of Justice.[76] The Inter-American Commission on Human Rights, established in 1959, is competent to hear individual petitions and inter-State disputes, as well as conduct investigations *in situ* with State consent.[77] In contrast, compliance-building in early environmental law regimes relied principally on "soft law" mechanisms; knowledge sharing, collaborative mechanisms, and the marshalling of rhetoric. For example, the non-binding *World Charter for Nature* imposes broad duties of implementation on Member States, but provides no concrete mechanisms for monitoring.[78] Rather, the text stresses public education, dissemination of scientific knowledge, ongoing research, cooperation among various international actors, public disclosure of planning and environmental assessment information and public consultation and participation therein.[79]

In sustainable development law that addresses social, economic and environmental problems in an integrated way, early approaches to compliance have begun to weave together judicial and quasi-judicial dispute settlement, trade measures, promotion of scientific research, sharing of information and technology, public education and public participation. A distinctive, innovative, sustainable development law approach to compliance is emerging, but it is not without challenges. The 1992 *Rio Declaration on Environment and Development* and *Agenda 21* provide good examples. Neither document establishes a comprehensive framework for compliance. However, the 1992 *Rio Declaration* contributes principles and a sense of aspiration, and *Agenda 21* proposes a broad range of mechanisms and processes that can contribute to building compliance, if

[74] That is, duties levied in response to dumping of imports that "causes of threatens material injury" to domestic industry, or duties "levied to offset government subsidies to production"; see *ibid.* at 30–31. The re-balancing effect of these duties is apparent in that they could not exceed the initial margin of dumping or amount of subsidy.

[75] *Ibid.*, at 30–33. See General Agreement on Tariffs and Trade, 30 Oct. 1947, 55 UNTS 194, (1948) CTS No. 31, (provisionally entered into force 1 Jan. 1948), Arts. VI–VII.

[76] Convention on the Prevention and Punishment of the Crime of Genocide, 9 Dec. 1948, 78 UNTS 277, (entered into force 12 Jan. 1951). See A.L. Jernow, "*Ad Hoc* and Extra-conventional Means for Human Rights Monitoring" in P.C. Szasz, ed., *Administrative and Expert Monitoring of International Treaties* (New York: Transnational, 1999) at 21.

[77] The IACHR was established by the Organization of American States; see OAS Res. VIII, OEA/ Ser. F/111.5 (1959); see R.A. Painter, "Human Rights Monitoring: Universal and Regional Treaty Bodies" in P.C. Szasz, ed., *Administrative and Expert Monitoring of International Treaties* (New York: Transnational, 1999) at 58–59.

[78] The World Charter, as a General Assembly Declaration, not strictly binding in international law; however, it contains expressions of customary international law and strongly normative language. See E. Brown Weiss, P.C Szasz and D.B. Magraw, *International Environmental Law: Basic Instruments and Reference* (New York, Transnational, 1992).

[79] See Sands, *International Environmental Law*, *supra* note 72 at 42–43.

structured effectively. Together, and in combination with relevant economic, social and environmental legal instruments, these lay the groundwork for an integrated approach to compliance.

The focus of the 1992 *Rio Declaration* is essentially on *cooperation between nations* in areas such as protecting ecosystems,[80] strengthening capacity-building,[81] exchanging scientific knowledge and technology,[82] promoting a "supportive and open international economic system",[83] discouraging transfer or relocation of environmental degradation,[84] providing assistance in cases of environmental disasters,[85] and developing international law in the field of sustainable development.[86] According to Philippe Sands, Chapter 39 of *Agenda 21* – while "short on substance" – represents the closest we have to "a blueprint for the development of international law of sustainable development".[87] Alexandre Kiss and Dinah Shelton are also unequivocal about the significant implications of Chapter 39 for the development of international law. Since Rio, they note, almost every multilateral agreement has included environmental protection aspects.[88] Every paragraph of Chapter 39 on International Legal Instruments and Materials is relevant to the question of compliance. But Chapter 39 also highlights specific, innovative compliance-building mechanisms: building expertise in international law on sustainable development, environmental protection measures based on consensus, setting global, regional and sub-regional priorities, data and information exchange, elaboration of international standards, technical and financial assistance for developing countries, differential obligations were appropriate, balanced, transparent and open regime governance, trade measures to reinforce environmental policies, notification of potential disputes, consultation in dispute settlement, peaceful settlement of disputes including recourse to the International Court of Justice, timely reporting, review, assessment and, vitally, ongoing revision and adjustment of regimes.[89]

However, Chapter 39 is also lacking in several key areas. While emphasizing treaty-based regimes, little reference is made to customary principles of international law on sustainable development.[90] Philippe Sands refers to the "limited progress" on issues of dispute settlement at Rio, and finds that the emphasis on further study of "the range of techniques available at present"[91] is disappointing, especially as recourse to judicial dispute settlement in the area, in 1992, had been rare at best.[92] In sum, while both the *Rio Declaration* and *Agenda 21* offer insights into potential

---

[80] See Sands, *International Environmental Law*, *supra* note 72 at 42–43, Principle 7.
[81] *Ibid.*, Principle 9.   [82] *Ibid.*   [83] *Ibid.*, Principle 12.
[84] *Ibid.*, Principle 14.   [85] *Ibid.*, Principle 18.
[86] *Ibid.*, Principle 27.   [87] Sands, *International Environmental Law*, *supra* note 72 at 57.
[88] A. Kiss and D. Shelton, *supra* note 66 at 72–74.
[89] *Agenda 21*, *supra* note 11 para. 39.1–39.10.
[90] There is reference to the "progressive development and codification of international law on sustainable development", especially regarding the work of the International Law Commission; see *ibid.*, para. 39(1)(e).
[91] *Agenda 21*, *ibid.*, at para. 39.10.
[92] See A. Kiss and D. Shelton, *supra* note 66 at 603. Although the International Court of Justice established a seven-member Chamber for Environmental Matters in July 1993, it has been underutilized.

compliance-building mechanisms, they do not provide a comprehensive framework for combining and deploying those mechanisms, or coordinating their interaction.

Global policy debates in the 1987 World Commission on Environment and Development, the 1992 Rio UN Conference on Environment and Development, the 1997 United Nations General Assembly Special Session on Sustainable Development and the 2002 *World Summit on Sustainable Development* have emphasised the importance of effectiveness in every aspect.[93] For sustainable development law to be effective, innovative approaches to compliance and coordination are needed. These approaches can weave together mechanisms and processes drawn from economic, environmental and social law to offer a range of options for building compliance and addressing non-compliance. These options can be flexible and versatile; they are often tailored to have either a general or a highly specific impact. In sustainable development law, the innovative approaches to compliance often rely on networks, and benefits from a particular *self-reinforcing dynamic* that will be explored below.

First, what does compliance actually mean? The notion of compliance itself is elusive – underlying theories of law and international relations are needed to clarify it.[94] One suggestion, "correspondence of behaviour with legal rules", fails to capture the totality of experience in international law for realists, rationalists, liberals and constructivists alike. Perspectives both *external* (objective) and *internal* (subjective) to the actors in sustainable development related legal regimes may assist in defining compliance.

A regulatory "enforcement pyramid" model singled out by legal analysts[95] can be illustrated by explaining the compliance-building mechanisms of the *Montreal Protocol on Substances that Deplete the Ozone Layer* and its *Non-compliance Procedure*[96] as an innovative, complex, regulatory regime. The *Montreal Protocol* has attracted attention for its "positive and creative stance on the issue of compliance ... encourag[ing] and facilitat[ing] compliance".[97] It provides an

---

[93] *Rio Declaration, supra* note 11, Principles 10, 11, 14; *Agenda 21, supra* note 11, esp. para. 39.2, see also paras. 39.3, 39.5, 39.9, 39.10.

[94] B. Kingsbury, "The Concept of Compliance as a Function of Competing Conceptions of International Law" (1998) 19 *Mich. J. Int'l Law* 345 [hereinafter *Kingsbury*].

[95] I. Ayres and J. Braithwaite, *Responsive Regulation: Transcending the Deregulation Debate* (Oxford: Oxford University Press, 1992).

[96] *Montreal Protocol on Substances the Deplete the Ozone Layer*, 16 Sept. 1987, 26 I.LM 154 (entered into force 1 Jan. 1989), as amended by the *London Amendments to the Montreal Protocol on Substances that Deplete the Ozone Layer*, 29 June 1990, UNEP/OZ.L.Pro.2.3, Annex II [hereinafter *Montreal Protocol*]. See also the Protocol's *Non-compliance Procedure*, 29 June 1990, 30 ILM 537.

[97] S.J. Toope, "Emerging Patterns of Governance" in M. Byers, ed., *The Role of Law in International Politics: Essays in International Relations and International Law* (Oxford: Oxford University Press, 2000) 91 at 106 [hereinafter *S.J. Toope*]. From a divergent, even opposite perspective, Martii Koskenniemi agrees that the *Non-compliance Protocol* is "unprecedented", and notes that the regime's collective approach to addressing "breaches", a procedure that parties "buy into"; his concerns with the Implementation Committee seem to rest on early fears of bureaucratic inefficiency, partiality and overbroad discretion which, according to *Kingsbury*, have not arisen in practice; see M. Koskenniemi, "Breach of Treaty or Non-Compliance? Reflections on the Enforcement of the Montreal Protocol" (1992) 3 *Y.B. Int'l. Env'tl. L.* 123 [hereinafter *Koskenniemi*]; see *Kingsbury, supra* note 94 at 365.

example of "the intricate interactions of different types of norms and institutional structures" that characterize most of international law in the field of sustainable development,[98] as noted above. The significant scientific authority and effectiveness of the Protocol's Implementation Committee within the *Montreal Protocol* regime, suggest that "even the narrow 'legal' concepts of 'compliance' and 'non-compliance' would be better described in terms of a *process* involving relevant international institutions, the regulated States and other States".[99] Initially a creature of international environmental law, the *Montreal Protocol* is in the process of integrating economic concerns, particularly through the use of trade measures. Further analysis of emerging highly integrated sustainable development treaty regimes, below, supports this conception of *compliance as process.*

Compliance can be recognized as process, rather than a static label for one activity. This distances compliance from a vain hope of enforcement of abstract norms,[100] it recognizes that violation of norms cannot be the "beginning, middle, and end of the compliance story".[101] The emphasis on State cooperation and interdependency that pervades the 1992 Rio documents, alone, is inconsistent with a dogged expectation that compliance is necessarily and immediately extinguished by the fact of violation.[102] Approaching compliance as process enables a compliance framework to reinforce itself by adapting to address non-compliance, rather than self-destructing or losing legitimacy in the face of breach.

Seeing compliance as process is an *external view*; it comes from outside the actors within the regime. The *internal view* of compliance, from within the regime; the perspective of actors involved in a treaty, is also important. An innovative internal approach to compliance involves an attitude that goes beyond mere implementation of treaty obligations and hard rules; one of adherence to the "spirit of the treaty".[103] This depends on the treaty having legitimate, broadly understood provisions. For effective compliance, rules of international law "should first possess an internal force or dynamic that *makes sense* to the

---

[98] *Kingsbury, supra* note 94 at 367–68.   [99] *Ibid.* at 367 (emphasis added).

[100] J. Brunée and S.J. Toope, *Interactional Theory, supra* note 64 at 68. See also *S.J. Toope, supra* note 97, at 107. Both authors argue elsewhere that even the term "compliance" promotes the crystallization of "disputes", and see the term "implementation" as sufficient to cover development of norms and adherence thereto; see J. Brunée and S.J. Toope, *Ecosystems, supra* note 69 at 44. While the present publication adopts the terminology of implementation, monitoring, enforcement, these are employed merely as organizational elements in the analysis of the innovative "compliance-building" approach. The term "compliance" is employed without connotations of "dispute", but rather as both a *process* and an *attitude.*

[101] F. Kratochwil and J.G. Ruggie, "International Organization: a State of the Art on an Art of the State" (1986) 40(4) *Int'l. Org.* 753 at 768.

[102] On the counterfactual validity of norms, see *ibid.* at 766–79.

[103] H.K. Jacobson and E. Brown Weiss, "Strengthening Compliance with International Environmental Accords: Preliminary Observations from a Collaborative Project" (1995) 1 *Global Governance* 119 at 123–25 [hereinafter *Jacobson and Brown Weiss*].

parties and invokes an *attitude of compliance* rather than non-compliance".[104] Taking this reasoning further, these two conceptions of *compliance as attitude* and *as process* within sustainable development are strongly resonant with new theories of "inter-actionalists" thesis that "thick acceptance" of norms emerges through processes of "self-binding legitimization".[105] Such a self-reinforcing dynamic can be key to the effectiveness of sustainable development regimes.

In international environmental law, innovative approaches to compliance emphasize the importance of using rules and institutions operating on distinct levels, or through key phases in time ("phasing-in" measures). Legal scholars have identified three important elements of compliance. First, there are the means of *implementation* of international obligations – these include enabling national legislation, State monitoring of compliance by actors within each State, and international reporting obligations. Secondly, in cases of non-compliance, there are means of *international enforcement* of international obligations, by other States and international actors. Thirdly, there are the means of *international conflict resolution* through diplomatic and legal means, emphasizing effective access to justice.[106]

While valuable, this framework seems to place too much emphasis on coercive and contentious approaches to compliance. Sustainable development does not often rely on such approaches due to its focus on integration of a wide variety of social, environmental and economic laws. Sustainable development law calls for an innovative approach that is largely concerned with the prevention, rather than remediation of non-compliance, by drawing upon what has variously been called "monitoring", "compliance-control", "supervision", "surveillance",[107] "implementation review" and "compliance verification"[108] as a phase of the compliance-building process.

Such monitoring functions are important, and have seen extensive development over the past few decades.[109] Rather than identifying and punishing violators of the law, monitoring is designed to improve and enhance compliance,[110] typically through several steps:

---

[104] L. Guruswamy and B. Hendricks, *International Environmental Law* (St. Paul, Minn.: West, 1997) at 48 (emphasis added) [hereinafter *Guruswamy and Hendricks*].

[105] J. Brunée and S.J. Toope, *Interactional Theory, supra* note 64 at 72–73. Many aspects of the interactionalist thesis find expression in this innovative "sustainable development law" approach to compliance: a shift away from adjudicative processes in favour of building compliance through ongoing interaction between actors within the regime that, in turn, shapes the regime; a focus on self-government; ensuring "equity", "openness" and "transparency" in the governance of the regime as a means of building compliance. However, the application of this theory to customary regimes is challenging, especially in light of the adjudicative context in which disputes over customary law are usually (if rarely) brought. Overall, this theoretical orientation holds great promise for ongoing sustainable development law research in the field of compliance.

[106] Sands, *International Environmental Law, supra* note 72 at 141–178.

[107] See W. Lang, ed., *Sustainable Development and International Law* (London: Martinus Nijhoff & Graham Trotman, 1995) at 255 [hereinafter *Lang*].

[108] See A. Kiss and D. Shelton, *supra* note 66 at 588.

[109] P. Szasz, "Introduction" in P.C. Szasz, ed., *Administrative and Expert Monitoring of International Treaties* (New York: Transnational, 1999) at 1 [hereinafter *Szasz*].

[110] *Ibid.*, at 15.

- the designation of a reporting agency within each national government, raising "domestic bureaucratic conscience";
- formal and informal dialogue between national reporting agencies and international monitoring agencies, promoting a common understanding of norms within a regime, and can quickly identify difficulties faced by nations in implementing their obligations;[111]
- the publicity or threat of publicity of State non-compliance – the "discipline of shame";[112] and
- preventative inspections (which have been extensively used in the context of environmental protection).[113]

Finally, as suggested by Paul Szasz, monitoring is also important within "soft law" regimes. It can spur ongoing State compliance with non-binding instruments out of a "sense of quasi-obligation". Over the long term, these obligations might even form the basis for emerging customary norms.[114]

Innovative "sustainable development law" approaches to compliance can best be characterized by three phases: implementation, monitoring and "enforcement". While the latter term is not ideal, as mentioned earlier, it is used here to encapsulate the range of coercive and cooperative, formal and informal, diplomatic and legal measures that can be deployed by a sustainable development regime in response to non-compliance. It conveys a sense of action rather than sanction.

In order to draw out distinctive, innovative approaches to compliance in sustainable development law, three treaty-based regimes will be analysed below. The first provides an example of a regime in the process of integration – the *Montreal Protocol*, including its *Non-compliance Procedure* and provisions governing its Multilateral Fund.[115] The second is a relatively early example of a fully integrated regime, the 1994 *Convention to Combat Desertification in Countries Experiencing Serious Drought and/or Desertification, particularly in Africa*.[116] The third regime provides perhaps the best example of a highly-integrated sustainable development regime to date – the 2000 *Cartagena Protocol on Biosafety to the Convention on Biological Diversity*.[117] The use of compliance-coordinating bodies and linkage mechanisms between the implementation, monitoring and enforcement phases will also be considered.

---

[111] On the normative effect of "shared understandings", see J. Brunée and S. Toope, *Interactional Theory, supra* note 64, at 52–53.

[112] Such as the "1235 Procedure" and "1503 Procedure" for raising human rights violation within ECOSOC; see D.A. Silien, "Human Rights Monitoring: Procedures and Decision-Making of Standing United Nations Organs" in P.C. Szasz, ed., *Administrative and Expert Monitoring of International Treaties* (New York: Transnational, 1999) 83 at 94ff. [hereinafter *Silien*].

[113] See Szasz, *supra* note 109 at 15–17.

[114] *Ibid.* at 17.

[115] *Terms of Reference for a Multilateral Fund*, Annex IV, UN Doc. UNEP/OzL.Pro.4/15, (1992) YB Int'l L. 824 [hereinafter *Multilateral Fund Terms of Reference*].

[116] 17 June 1994, 33 ILM 1328, [hereinafter *Desertification Convention*].

[117] *Cartagena Protocol on Biosafety*, 15 May 2000, 39 ILM 1027, online: http://www.biodiv.org [hereinafter *Cartagena Protocol*].

The implementation phase

In sustainable development law, implementation is often coordinated internationally, but on multiple levels. This raises two interrelated questions. First, what are the mechanisms for international *coordination* of implementation? And secondly, what are the mechanisms for actual regional, sub-regional, national and local implementation of a treaty? These will be considered in turn, with reference to other features of implementation such as the use of networks to support implementation, and mechanisms for differentiated implementation that does not thwart the underlying purposes of the regime.

Centralization of coordination

All three example treaties establish intergovernmental bodies to play a coordinating role in implementation. Approaches to implementation within the *Montreal Protocol* display many compliance-building mechanisms mentioned earlier, such as cooperation, financial and technical support for developing countries, and "clearing-house" repositories of expertise and assistance. However, it is hard to gain a cohesive picture of how these mechanisms will specifically facilitate implementation. Although the initial text of the *Montreal Protocol* creates a Secretariat, this body is not designed to coordinate implementation, but rather, to provide administrative support.[118] The governing body of the Protocol is the Meeting of the Parties (MOP) which, while responsible for reviewing the implementation of the Protocol, is not charged with a facilitative role in initial implementation of the Protocol.[119] The MOP retains a broad discretion to "consider and undertake any action" for the achievement of the purposes of the Protocol, which could conceivably target implementation.[120] Amendments brought to the Protocol in 1990 prescribe a role for the Protocol's Multilateral Fund in financing co-operation, but these do not specifically envisage financing to facilitate implementation.[121] And the mandate of the "Implementation Committee" within the *Non-compliance Procedure*, despite the name, is better described as an "enforcement phase" tool for compliance-building.[122] Overall, the *Montreal Protocol* places primary responsibility for implementation on the Parties themselves. While Parties should "cooperate" in promoting technical assistance for the purposes of implementation,[123] no institution within the regime is charged with facilitating or targeting technical expertise. Parties

---

[118] *Montreal Protocol, supra* note 96, Art. 12.   [119] *Ibid.*, Art. 11(4).
[120] *Ibid.*, Art. 11(4)(j).   [121] *Montreal Protocol, supra* note 96, Art. 10.
[122] The Implementation Committee is to receive submissions on situations of non-compliance, report thereon to the Meeting of the Parties, and secure "amicable solutions" on the basis of "respect for the provisions of the Protocol"; see *Non-compliance Procedure, supra* note 96, Art. 7. The text of the *Non-compliance Procedure* uses the term "implementation" as J. Brunée and S.J. Toope do; see J. Brunée and S.J. Toope, *Ecosystems, supra* note 69.
[123] *Montreal Protocol, supra* note 123, Art. 10.

themselves "request" technical assistance from the Secretariat when required for implementation purposes.[124]

The role of intergovernmental bodies in implementation of the *Desertification Convention* is more explicit. First, all Parties and the "international community" are called upon to cooperate to "ensure the promotion of an enabling international environment in the implementation of the Convention".[125] Responsibility for "decisions necessary to promote...effective implementation" is explicitly granted to the Conference of the Parties (COP);[126] this body is also empowered to establish "such subsidiary bodies as are deemed necessary for the implementation of the Convention".[127] The treaty also expressly envisages a general facilitative role for its Permanent Secretariat, especially with regard to developing countries, but not specifically facilitation of implementation.[128] The principal mechanism for implementation within the Convention is the elaboration of national action programmes, as discussed below. But the Permanent Secretariat acts as a repository of these programmes, rather than an active facilitator in their elaboration.[129] While the Convention does not envisage an integrated, international compliance-coordination body, it is explicit in promoting the use of networks to "support the implementation of the Convention".[130]

The intergovernmental bodies in the *Cartagena Protocol*, in comparison, play quite a strong role in implementation. First, the treaty goes further than calling for an "enabling environment" for implementation. Instead, it immediately makes parties subject to a general *obligation of implementation* – each party "*shall* take necessary and appropriate legal, administrative and other measures to implement its obligations under the Protocol".[131] The Biosafety Clearing-House – an intergovernmental body conceived as playing a vital role in the implementation phase – is established at Article 20, and is quite distinct from the Conference of the Parties and Secretariat, which are institutions of the *Convention on Biological Diversity*, not the Protocol itself.[132] The Biosafety Clearing-House is networked to clearing-house mechanisms envisaged throughout the Convention regime as a whole. The *Cartagena Protocol* expressly recognizes that the Clearing-House will "assist Parties to implement the Protocol", it is to do so in a manner that integrates the environmental law interest in biosafety and genetic diversity, with the economic and developmental needs of least developed nations, small island developing nations, developing nations and economies in transition generally.[133] The Meeting of Technical Experts on the Biosafety Clearing-House, a preparatory body, has already pinpointed specific activities of the Clearing-House with regard to implementation. It will:

---

[124] *Ibid.*, Art. 10(2).
[125] *Desertification Convention, supra* note 116, Art. 12.   [126] *Ibid.*, art 22(2).
[127] *Ibid.*, Art. 22(2)(c).   [128] *Ibid.*, Art. 23(1)(c).   [129] *Ibid.*, Arts. 9–13.
[130] *Ibid.*, Art. 25(1).   [131] *Cartagena Protocol, supra* note 117, Art. 2 (emphasis added).
[132] *Ibid.*, Arts. 20, 29, 31.   [133] *Ibid.*, Art. 20(1)(b).

- provide improved and integrated access to existing information sources;
- promote the exchange of information, knowledge, experience and best practices;
- provide a forum for the exchange of views on biosafety between countries, scientists, non-governmental and intergovernmental organizations and the private sector; and
- provide access to a roster of government-nominated experts for advisory and other support, and risk assessment upon request.[134]

Another distinctive feature of the Protocol not found in the two other regimes is that the international Secretariat liaises with multiple national "focal points" to share primary responsibility for administration of the regime.[135] In sum, the *Cartagena Protocol* can be distinguished for explicitly assigning a coordinating role in implementation to an international body that is more highly specialized, adaptable and active than a Conference of the Parties. This is distinct from a Secretariat, as it has the authority to advance implementation rather than merely administer the process. This body respects the horizontal ordering of international actors, however, being composed of States Parties who play a facilitative role in the implementation of regimes by their peers.[136] Furthermore, expanding on the approach to implementation in the *Desertification Convention*, the *Cartagena Protocol* uses networks to support the work of specific *implementing bodies*, rather than means of supporting *implementation* in the abstract. This centralized coordination is balanced by a second innovative aspect – the dispersal of implementation.

Dispersal of implementation

A challenge for international environmental cooperation is that national concurrence with international norms as a formality is insufficient to ensure that effective cooperation will occur.[137] As suggested by Lynton Keith Caldwell, the way to resolve this paradox is to establish "institutional structures capable of operating with limited autonomy apart from the governments that created

---

[134] "Establishment of the Biosafety Clearing-House" (Note by the Executive Secretary of the Intergovernmental Committee on the *Cartagena Protocol*), Provisional Agenda Item 3.1, UN Doc. UNEP/CBD/BS/TE-BCH/1/2 (2000), online: Convention on Biological Diversity <http://www.biodiv.org> [hereinafter *Establishment Note*].

[135] *Cartagena Protocol, supra* note 117, Art. 19.

[136] We must be wary of idealism in this regard. As Konrad von Moltke noted in 1988, the proliferation of international environmental institutions should not lead to misconceptions of reality: these institutions are "very closely controlled by the States which have set them up, and they are very small. More often than not, members of the commissions ... will tend to be high-level civil servants answerable to their country of origin. This is no revolutionary departure ... Nevertheless, these commissions form a vital, and poorly understood, link in the current international system ..."; see K. von Moltke, "International Commission and Implementation of Law" in J.E. Carroll, ed., *International Environmental Diplomacy* (Cambridge: Cambridge University Press, 1988) at 90. Analysis of implementation starts to show why such commissions play an increasingly vital role in the international management not only of the environment, but development and social rights as well.

[137] L.K. Caldwell, "Beyond Environmental Diplomacy" in J.E. Carroll, ed., *International Environmental Diplomacy* (Cambridge: Cambridge University Press, 1988) at 16.

them".[138] However, effective implementation requires not only autonomous coordination to ensure effective cooperation, but also a link between domestic decision-making and international legal norms, ensuring something beyond "mere national concurrence".[139] For more effective compliance, in addition to centralized coordination of implementation, there is a need for vertical "dispersal" of implementation across regional, sub-regional, national or local levels.[140]

The *Montreal Protocol* and its companion documents do not appear to contain such "dispersal mechanisms". The *Desertification Convention*, however, offers promising and novel approaches in this regard. General principles of cooperation on multiple levels abound within the Convention text.[141] As mentioned above, the elaboration of *national action programmes* is the principal mechanism for implementation of obligations within this regime.[142] These programmes are the means by which dispersal of implementation is accomplished by the regime. They serve to link parties' international obligations on combating desertification to "the respective roles of government, local communities and land users".[143] They should also provide for cooperation and coordination "between the donor community, government at all levels, local populations and community groups"[144] and the "effective participation at the local, national and regional levels of non-governmental organizations and local populations" in "policy planning, decision-making and implementation...of national action programmes".[145] Thus, within one international regime, actors as specific as "farmers and pastoralists" on a village level are recognized as active partners in the fight against desertification. The Convention also uses regional and sub-regional action programmes of a similar character to national programmes.[146] Integrating the beginnings of an ecosystem orientation with sound economic and social reasons for regional implementation mechanisms, it further provides for *regional implementation annexes* "adapted to the socio-economic, geographical and climatic factors" of particular regions and sub-regions.[147] Within the highly comprehensive annex for Africa, national action programmes must

---

[138] L.K. Caldwell, "Beyond Environmental Diplomacy" in J.E. Carroll, ed., *International Environmental Diplomacy* (Cambridge: Cambridge University Press, 1988) at 16.

[139] *Koh, supra* note 70, at 2654. See esp. V. Lowe, "The Politics of Law-Making: Are the Method and Character of Norm Creation Changing?" in M. Byers, ed., *The Role of Law in International Politics: Essays in International Relations and International Law* (Oxford: Oxford University Press, 2000) at 224 *ff.*, referring to a process of diffusion within international law whereby "the techniques and principles of public international law are being borrowed... and applied... in the internal legal orders of States".

[140] See generally, for the Americas, J.L. Varela, "Regional Trends in International Law and Domestic Environmental Law: the Inter-American Hemisphere" in S.J. Rubin and D.C. Alexander, eds., *NAFTA and the Environment* (The Hague: Kluwer Law International, 1996).

[141] See *Desertification Convention, supra* note 116, esp. Arts. 3(c), 4(2)(e).

[142] *Ibid.*, Art. 9 *ff.* The Convention introduces the concept of national action programmes in the specific context of parties "carrying out their obligations" under the Convention.

[143] *Ibid.*, Art. 10(2).   [144] *Ibid.*, Art. 10(2)(e).   [145] *Ibid.*, Art. 10(2)(f).

[146] *Ibid.*, Art. 11.

[147] *Ibid.*, Art. 15. These annexes are binding insofar as they constitute integral parts of the Convention; see Art. 29(1). The Convention includes regional implementation annexes for Africa (Annex I), Asia (Annex II) and Latin America and the Caribbean (Annex III). Each establishes, *inter alia*, highly specific focus areas for national action programmes.

be tracked via "pertinent, quantifiable and readily verifiable" implementation indicators.[148] The concept of *capacity-building* is introduced, with 11 specific means for its promotion, though it is not explicitly linked to effective implementation in the treaty.[149] This regional annex also shows how the principle of subsidiarity is operative within the regime – the scope of regional and sub-regional capacity-building, education and public awareness programmes is a function of which specific activities "are better carried out or supported" at that level.[150]

The *Cartagena Protocol* is less detailed regarding mechanisms for dispersal of implementation; nevertheless, the concept is certainly operative, and may be best framed within this regime. By emphasizing *capacity-building* on many levels as a means of effective implementation,[151] the Protocol captures both the concept of dispersal of implementation (capacity-building *among all actors in the biosafety field*)[152] and the nature of implement as a process (capacity-*building*). Rhetorically, there is also greater force behind an obligation to consider, within funding arrangements, the financial needs of developing countries for capacity-building[153] rather than abstract calls for "activities pursuant to relevant provisions of the Convention".[154] Vitally, capacity-building begins at the implementation phase, with the Protocol specifically identifying "scientific and technical training" in biotechnology management, risk assessment and risk management and enhancement of technological and institutional capacities.[155] This training is important to ensure the elaboration of effective national implementing legislation; it has a direct impact on the implementation of the norms of the Protocol.

The preceding analysis points to the combination of *centralized coordination* with *dispersed implementation* as one innovative aspect for implementation of sustainable development law regimes. Essentially, this is a manifestation of subsidiarity, that is, implementation on the most appropriate scale (flexibly dispersal across multiple levels) consistent with effectiveness (through centralized, expert facilitation of implementation).

Implementation support networks

Networks, described by some as the "optimal form of organization in the information age",[156] are important for implementation. Their supporting roles are

---

[148] *Ibid.*, Annex I, Art. 9(d).   [149] *Ibid.*, Art. 19.   [150] *Ibid.*, Annex I, Arts. 11(d), 13(b).

[151] *Cartagena Protocol, supra* note 117, at Art. 22(1).

[152] The article on capacity-building has an extensive scope: capacity-building should strengthen both human resources and institutional capacities, should consider the needs of least developed countries, small island developing countries, developing countries in general and economies in transition, and should drawn on global, regional, sub-regional, national institutions and organizations, including the private sector.

[153] *Cartagena Protocol, supra* note 117, at Arts. 28(3), 28(4).

[154] *Desertification Convention, supra* note 116, at Art. 21(1)(a).

[155] *Cartagena Protocol, supra* note 117, Art. 22(2). The Intergovernmental Committee on the *Cartagena Protocol on Biosafety* (ICCP), a preparatory body, has requested Parties, non-governmental, private sector and scientific organizations to submit "suggestions on capacity-building for the implementation of the Protocol" by Mar. 2001; see "Capacity-building", online: Convention on Biological Diversity <http://www.biodiv.org>.

[156] For example *Slaughter, supra* note 69 at 204.

implicit in the *Montreal Protocol*, which calls for cooperation between Parties and through "competent international bodies" to promote research, development and exchange of information on best technologies for managing controlled substances, alternatives to controlled substances and cost-benefit analysis of control strategies.[157] Key "implementing agencies" are identified in the *Multilateral Fund Terms of Reference*, such as UNEP, UNDP and the World Bank, in order to facilitate compliance with the Protocol.[158] However, the Protocol does not adopt the language of "networks" and does not explicitly identify the scientific community and civil society organizations as key network partners, even though both the scientific community and larger civil society organizations already work through well-developed institutional networks.

The *Desertification Convention*, in comparison, provides for broad participation in "cooperative mechanisms", with a view to supporting implementation. In particular, organs, funds and programmes of the United Nations system, relevant intergovernmental organizations, academic institutions, the scientific community and "non-governmental organizations in a position to collaborate" are encouraged to participate in the implementation of action programmes under the Convention.[159] Local cooperative mechanisms are also envisaged.[160] The Convention also explicitly adopts the language of "networking" to "support the implementation of the Convention" and assigns authority to form such a network to a technical experts' group, the Committee on Science and Technology.[161] The Convention uses networks to bridge between international, regional, sub-regional and national "units", it requires that their operation be facilitated and strengthened by the Conference of the Parties.[162] Thus, the Convention nests multiple networks, on diverse levels, within the coordinating framework of an international regime.[163]

In the *Cartagena Protocol*, and throughout the *CBD*, this "nesting of networks" is systematized through the *clearing-house mechanism*,[164] of which the Biosafety Clearing-House forms one component.[165] The clearing-house mechanism is conceived as "a global network of Parties and partners working

---

[157] *Montreal Protocol, supra* note 96, Art. 9.

[158] *Supra* note 115, Arts. 2(a), 4.

[159] *Desertification Convention, supra* note 116, Art. 9(3).

[160] *Ibid.*, Art. 13(1)(b).

[161] *Ibid.*, Art. 25. While the Committee on Science and Technology is composed of government representatives "competent in the relevant fields of expertise", it is envisaged as taking a multi-disciplinary approach and receiving "information and advice" from panels of independent experts; see Art. 24.

[162] *Ibid.*, Art. 25(2). The role of networks on multiple levels is especially evident in the regional implementation annexes; see esp. Annex I, Art. 10(1)(a) on sub-regional focal points for information exchange, Art. 13(e) on regional networks for "systematic observation and assessment" that are integrated into "world-wide networks".

[163] On "nesting networks" and certain challenges posed by networking, see *Slaughter, supra* note 69, esp. at 204–5.

[164] *United Nations Convention on Biological Diversity*, 5 June 1992, 31 ILM 822, Art. 18(3).

[165] *Cartagena Protocol, supra* note 144, Art. 20(1).

together to facilitate implementation".[166] The functions of this mechanism include to:

- promote and facilitate scientific and technical cooperation;
- develop a global mechanism for exchanging and integrating biodiversity information;[167]
- develop the network, through clearing-house mechanism focal points and their partners.[168]

The impetus for the clearing-house mechanism is, once again, the tension between centralization and dispersal; this tension is addressed by measures to:

- centralize the facilitation role, the dissemination of experience and knowledge, and the identification and targeted networking of international, regional, sub-regional, national centres of expertise, governmental and civil society organizations and the private sector; as well as
- disperse the "process of gathering and organizing the information that feeds into the clearing house mechanism network" to national focal points "coordinating efforts among themselves".[169]

The consequences of this integrated approach to networking stretches across the implementation, monitoring and enforcement phases; simply put, it enables the entire regime to "learn from ... shared experience". As a principal distinctive feature of innovative approaches to compliance in general, this will be discussed in depth under *Effective Compliance*, below.

Differentiated implementation

The principle of common but differentiated responsibility in international environmental law arises from principles of equity within general international law.[170] Differentiated responsibility is a means to take into account each State's ability to implement the relevant international obligation and its contribution to the particular problem. Relevant factors include needs and circumstances, level of economic development, financial capacity and past acts causing harm.[171]

Differentiated responsibility within the implementation phase of the *Montreal Protocol* takes the form of delayed implementation for certain developing

---

[166] *Establishment Note, supra* note 134, at para. 8.

[167] The Parties have already begun to implement a pilot phase of the Biosafety Clearing-House on the Internet. See "Operation of the Biosafety Clearing-House" (Note by the Executive Secretary of the Intergovernmental Committee on the *Cartagena Protocol*), Provisional agenda item 3.2, UN Doc. UNEP/CBD/BS/TE-BCH/1/3 (2000), online: Convention on Biological Diversity <http://www.biodiv.org>. Pilot phase, available online: <www.biodov.org>.

[168] *Establishment Note, supra* note 134, at para. 9.

[169] *Ibid.* at para. 11.

[170] Sands, *International Environmental Law, supra* note 72 at 217.

[171] *Ibid.* at 219. Phillipe Sands' statement that "in practical terms, differentiated responsibility results in different legal obligations", while strictly true, is unhelpful as it downplays the processual nature of implementation. Highly-integrated regimes strike a careful balance between achievement of the objectives of the regime and implementation mechanisms to ensure that differentiated

countries – "grace periods"[172] – to exempt them from compliance with control measures for ozone-depleting substances for 10 years.[173] The regime attempts to balance achievement of its ends with equitable obligations in several ways: first, developing countries must not exceed a certain threshold of consumption of controlled substances in order to initially invoke and continue to benefit from delayed implementation;[174] secondly, any State becoming a Party to the protocol must immediately and continually provide extensive statistical data to the Secretariat, so delayed implementation of control measures does not entail a "holiday" from the regime;[175] and thirdly, channels exist for those developing countries invoking delayed control measures to receive adequate financial and technical support to further the fulfilment of their obligations.[176] Within the *Montreal Protocol*, then, differentiated implementation is not framed in terms of the obligations of Parties, rather, it is apparent in the specific control measures used.

The approach of the *Desertification Convention* is to more explicitly introduce the concept of differentiated responsibility, immediately following the statement of general obligations of Parties. Articles 5 and 6, respectively, provide for specific "Obligations of affected country Parties" and "Obligations of developed country Parties" within the regime. Recognizing the prevalence of desertification and drought in poorer nations, the text notes the "central importance of financing to the achievement of the objective of the Convention".[177] Hence, differentiated responsibility operates to place increased financial responsibility on developed nations, especially through innovative mechanisms such as debt swaps, facilitating the fight against desertification while relieving economic burdens on developing countries.[178] This is an example of how differentiated responsibility within sustainable development regimes is a useful tool to address both environmental and economic aspects of a problem in an integrated manner.

The promotion of economic development and respect for social rights can also be integrated through differentiated responsibility. A good example is the specific obligations of affected country Parties within the Convention. Affected country Parties specifically undertake to "address the underlying causes of desertification and pay special attention to the *socio-economic factors* contributing to desertification processes";[179] and "promote awareness and facilitate the *participation* of local populations, especially *women and youth* . . . in efforts to combat desertification and mitigate the effects of drought".[180]

The *Desertification Convention* does not emphasize differentiated *implementation* in light of the specific context of each Party; rather, it principally differentiates between "affected" and "developing" countries, in terms of overall

---

implementation will act as a *means* to ensure the fuller attainment of the objectives of the regime. In this sense, differentiated responsibility does not imply less responsibility. The principle of common but differentiated responsibility is discussed in detail in Part II, Chapter 5.4 above.

[172] *Ibid.*, at 220.   [173] *Montreal Protocol, supra* note 96, Art. 5.
[174] *Ibid.*, Arts. 5(1)–(2).   [175] *Ibid.*, Art. 7.   [176] *Ibid.*, Arts. 5(4)–(9).
[177] *Desertification Convention, supra* note 116, Art. 20(1).   [178] See *ibid.*, Arts. 6, 20(d).
[179] *Ibid.*, Art. 5(c) (emphasis added).   [180] *Ibid.*, Art. 5(d) (emphasis added).

obligations, and emphasizes the use of financial mechanisms. This may be well suited to the fight against desertification and drought specifically, but a more flexible, integrated approach to implementation is apparent in the *Cartagena Protocol*.

The appeal and distinctiveness of the *Cartagena Protocol* is based on the flexibility of its differentiated implementation mechanisms. First, it provides strong financial mechanisms, and these are specifically required to address important contextual variables, such as extent of economic development of States Parties. For example, the allocation of financial resources, "for the purposes of implementation", to developing countries in general, and least developed and small island developing States in particular, is a key aspect of the Protocol's financial mechanism.[181] This financial mechanism for implementation operates on an *international* level, guided by the Conference of the Parties.

Secondly, the Protocol recognizes that each Party's *national* implementing legislation may consider the socio-economic impact of import of living modified organisms (LMOs) on conservation and the sustainable use of biodiversity (especially its value to indigenous and local populations).[182] Therefore, implementation can be tailored in a manner that is sensitive to the socio-economic, environmental and even cultural context of each Party. However, implementation is not made discretionary through this sensitivity, as only enumerated, relevant considerations can be used in tailoring national implementing legislation.

Thirdly, the Protocol anticipates situations of deficient national implementation through the creation of a "backup" regulatory framework, a redundant system engaged in the absence of domestic regulatory frameworks within developing countries and economies in transition. Using this backup framework, developing countries and economies in transition may begin importing LMOs "for direct use as food or feed, or for processing" – meeting urgent economic development or even humanitarian needs – without frustrating the objectives of the Protocol.[183] This differentiated implementation mechanism is thus able to effectively integrate environmental, economic development and humanitarian objectives. The Parties concerned interact with the Biosafety Clearing-House in this regard, as opposed to the Conference of the Parties. As a repository of expertise on implementation, and charged with a general facilitative role therein, the Clearing-House is presumably well-placed to coordinate this "backup" regulatory framework.[184]

In sum, this analysis has shown the innovative approaches used by sustainable development treaties to preserve overall legitimacy and effectiveness. These include using differentiated implementation (and differentiated responsibility in general) to reinforce attainment of their objectives. The regimes are flexible

---

[181] *Cartagena Protocol, supra* note 117, at Art. 28.   [182] *Ibid.*, Art. 26.

[183] Such import is subject to the minimum of a risk assessment under the Protocol and a predictable timeframe for decision-making. See *ibid.*, Art. 11(6).

[184] See *ibid.*, Art. 20(1)(b).

enough to vary the means and degree of implementation according to contextual variables. Finally, coordination of implementation – especially through the clearing-house mechanism – ensures that differentiation is managed on an international scale by an appropriate body.

The monitoring phase

In the past 50 years, many intergovernmental organizations have taken on a strong role as compliance monitors. As Paul Szasz notes, "the monitoring of State compliance with normative multilateral treaties has become almost exclusively the province of IGOs...".[185] The promise of monitoring is not the prospect of sanctioning treaty "violators", but rather the ability to "improve and enhance compliance with treaty obligations".[186] A comparison of monitoring processes within the *Montreal Protocol, Desertification Convention* and *Cartagena Protocol* confirms that for sustainable development regimes, monitoring is seen as a "plastic and growing enterprise" by which those regimes are "almost invariably broadened and strengthened".[187] In this way, the monitoring phase contributes to the self-reinforcing dynamic of these regimes, it is important for effectiveness.

Two key features of sustainable development law emerge within the monitoring phase: the *broad scope* of reporting obligations and the emphasis on *horizontal and vertical monitoring*.

Broad scope of reporting

The effective flow of information is important for monitoring, both horizontally (between States) and vertically (through all levels of implementation). Thus, reporting obligations can broaden to supply clearing-house mechanisms with sufficient information to ensure that the aims of the regime are being met, and to quickly identify areas that require further compliance-building.

Within the *Montreal Protocol*, reporting obligations are regular and ongoing, from the moment of ratification or accession onwards. Given the focus of the regime on reduction of ozone-depleting substances, it is no surprise that initial reporting obligations – within three months of ratification or accession – encompass statistical data on production, destruction, import and export, as well as specific data on trade in controlled substances with Parties and non-Parties.[188] The *London Amendments* to the Protocol require reporting of further statistical data on the use of both controlled and transitional substances, including use for feedstock, on an annual basis.[189] Parties are also required to submit "summaries of activities" on other enumerated aspects of implementation every two years – specifically, activities relating to exchange of information on best technologies,

---

[185] *Szasz, supra* note 109 at 12.   [186] *Ibid.,* at 15.
[187] *Ibid.,* at 17.   [188] *Montreal Protocol* (original text), *supra* note 96, Art. 7.
[189] *Montreal Protocol* (as amended), *ibid.* Art. 7(2)–(3).

alternatives and cost-benefit analyses of control strategies as well as public-awareness projects.[190] However, the Protocol does not impose a general reporting obligation covering all aspects of implementation, and actual compliance with reporting obligations has been "problematic".[191]

The *Desertification Convention*, in comparison, does impose a general obligation on Parties to report to the Conference of the Parties according to a timetable set by that body, although this is framed within an article on "Communication of Information".[192] The scope of reporting is broadened in three ways. First, reporting extends to all measures taken for the implementation of the Convention.[193] Consistent with the Convention's bifurcated approach to differentiated implementation, both "affected country Parties" and "developed country Parties" must report on the implementation of their specific obligations.[194] Secondly, the scope of reporting is broadened through reporting on multiple levels. While Parties report to an international body on their national action programmes, regional and sub-regional coordinating bodies report to Parties within that region under the provisions of regional implementation annexes.[195] Once again, a balancing of centralization and dispersal is evident.

The obligation to report within the *Cartagena Protocol* is unequivocal. Article 33, "Monitoring and Reporting", provides that "Each Party shall monitor the implementation of its obligations under the Protocol, and shall ... report ... on measures that it has taken to implement the Protocol."[196] While this report is directed to the Meeting of the Parties, the report must be provided to the Biosafety Clearing-House as well – this reinforces the key role of the Clearing-House as a repository and network focal point for information.[197] Two distinctive aspects of the scope of reporting within the Protocol attract attention. First, beyond reporting on implementation, Parties must provide the Clearing-House with any non-confidential "laws, regulations and guidelines" for the implementation of the Protocol, as well as those applicable to the import of LMOs for direct use as food or feed, or processing.[198] Thus, the Clearing-House can review country reports in parallel with concrete legislative efforts, identify strengths and weaknesses of particular modes of implementation, and better fulfil its capacity-building role by transmitting its analysis to other Parties and across the Biosafety network. Secondly, Parties have an ongoing obligation to report to the Clearing-House any information on cases of illegal transboundary movement of LMOs

---

[190] *Ibid.*, Art. 9(3). All reports and summaries are submitted to the Secretariat.

[191] See S. Thomas-Nuruddin, "Protection of the Ozone Layer: the *Vienna Convention* and the Montreal Protocol", in P.C. Szasz, ed., *Administrative and Expert Monitoring of International Treaties* (New York: Transnational, 1999) 113 at 120–21 [hereinafter *Nuruddin*]. The author notes that by Oct. 1990, only 29 of the 65 Parties had submitted complete reports. See *contra* Phillipe Sands, *International Environmental Law*, *supra* note 72 at 148, noting the Protocol's "strong record", as the 29 Parties submitting complete reports represented 85% of world consumption of controlled substances.

[192] *Desertification Convention*, *supra* note 116, Art. 26(1).   [193] *Ibid.*, Art. 26(2).

[194] For affected country Parties, *ibid.*, Art. 26(2)–(3); for developed country Parties, *ibid.*, Art. 26(5).

[195] See e.g. *ibid.*, Annex I, Art. 18(5)(b).   [196] *Cartagena Protocol*, *supra* note 117, Art. 33.

[197] *Ibid.*, Art. 20(3)(e).   [198] *Ibid.*, Arts. 20(3)(a), 11.

pertaining to it – presumably because such illegal movement is detrimental to the integrity and aims of the regime.[199] This may signal a shift in the focus of reporting obligations in highly-integrated regimes from a State focus to a regime focus; rather than encompassing the content of international obligations of Parties, the scope of reporting may eventually come to include any information *relevant to the effectiveness of the regime.*

Horizontal and vertical monitoring

The three regimes under analysis all show awareness of a multiplicity of monitoring actors and, in more highly-integrated regimes, promise to integrate these actors into both horizontal and vertical monitoring mechanisms.

The *Non-compliance Procedure* of the *Montreal Protocol* seems to suggest that three actors within the regime have an interest in (although not a responsibility for) monitoring, insofar as these actors can trigger the non-compliance procedure of the regime. First, the Secretariat, presumably upon reviewing country reports, can seek further information and refer unresolved situations of possible non-compliance to the Meeting of the Parties.[200] These is also a role for Parties in monitoring each others' compliance, by referring their "reservations regarding another Party's implementation of its obligations" to the Secretariat with corroborating information, for eventual referral to a non-compliance body.[201] Finally, there is express recognition of the responsibility of Parties for self-monitoring.[202] Where a Party has failed to comply fully with its obligations despite *bona fide* efforts, it may invoke the non-compliance mechanism by communicating with the Secretariat.[203] Overall, then, monitoring actors are dispersed *horizontally* within the regime: non-complying Parties, other Parties, and intergovernmental bodies are involved. However, there is little suggestion of how the monitoring phase should be coordinated within the *Montreal Protocol* itself, except generally regarding the role of the Secretariat as recipient of national reports and summaries of activities. The focus is the detection and addressing of non-compliance – in a cooperative manner – rather than conceiving of the monitoring phase *itself* as a capacity-building exercise that reinforces compliance.

---

[199] *Cartagena Protocol, supra* note 117, Art. 25(3).

[200] *Non-compliance Procedure, supra* note 96, Art. 3.   [201] *Ibid.,* Arts. 1–2.

[202] *Ibid.,* Art. 4.

[203] Incentives for self-monitoring and reporting are clearly present in the *Non-compliance Procedure:* Parties are assured that the Implementation Committee will first seek an "amicable solution" and that Parties involved in the non-compliance mechanism will be able to participate in the consideration of the situation by the Implementation Committee. Finally, the list of measures that may be taken by the Meeting of the Parties in respect of non-compliance includes the rendering of "appropriate assistance", including technical and financial assistance. In practice, the use of financial assistance to address non-compliance is by far the most common measure applied by the Meeting of the Parties. See "Development of compliance procedures and mechanisms under the Cartagena Protocol on Biosafety" (Note by the Executive Secretary of the Intergovernmental Committee on the *Cartagena Protocol*), Provisional agenda item 4.5, UN Doc. UNEP/CBD/ICCP/1/7 (2000)), online: Convention on Biological Diversity <http://www.biodiv.org>at para. 19 [hereinafter *Compliance Note*].

The dispersal of implementation in the *Desertification Convention*, through regional and sub-regional coordinating bodies, operates in parallel to the dispersal of monitoring on these levels.[204] Monitoring actors are thus dispersed *vertically* within this regime. The Convention is also relevant here in addressing the need for external facilitation of reporting, as a means of enhancing the effectiveness of monitoring. Coordinating responsibility is given to the Conference of the Parties to provide technical and financial assistance to affected country Parties in meeting their reporting obligations.[205]

The *Cartagena Protocol* identifies Parties as the principal monitors of their own compliance.[206] The non-compliance procedure of the *Cartagena Protocol* is still under development, so it is not clear whether other Parties and actors within the regime will be able to invoke the non-compliance procedure. Hence, it is difficult to determine whether these actors will have an interest in monitoring compliance, based on currently-available documents.[207] However, it is likely that the Biosafety Clearing-House will act as the focal point for monitoring, through the extensive rules on information-exchange within the regime.[208] Parties are required to provide some twenty types of information to the Clearing-House, regarding their actions, the operation of the Protocol, the "advanced informed agreement" procedure for import of LMOs, and means of facilitating the exchange of information for the purposes of capacity-building.[209] The Clearing-House is thus vital to the monitoring phase, but the Protocol gives little guidance on the mechanisms by which information gathered in monitoring is to be distilled and addressed within the regime.

The emphasis of the *Cartagena Protocol* on the language of "information exchange" in describing the role of the Biosafety Clearing-House may assuage the ongoing discomfort of governments with third-party scrutiny of their international obligations. The designation of national central authorities and focal points[210] encourages ongoing interaction with the Clearing-House; thus, monitoring will likely be strengthened as institutional relationships – and institutional "dialogue" – continue to develop.[211] However, as Philippe Sands rightly notes, "information exchange" and "reporting" are two distinct concepts.[212] A key

---

[204] *Ibid.*, Annex I, Art. 18(5)(b).   [205] *Desertification Convention, supra* note 116, Art. 26(7).

[206] *Cartagena Protocol, supra* note 117, Art. 33.

[207] In a review of compliance mechanisms in several recent MEAs, the Executive Secretary of the Intergovernmental Committee for the *Cartagena Protocol* notes the reticence of government delegates to allow civil society and individuals to trigger the non-compliance mechanism of the *Montreal Protocol*. However, draft UNEP guidelines on the implementation of, and compliance with, multilateral environmental agreements prepared in Dec. 1999 do envisage a role for civil society, the private sector and individuals in assisting the monitoring of compliance. See *Compliance Note, supra* note 203, at paras. 27, 44.

[208] *Cartagena Protocol, supra* note 117, Art. 20. It is unlikely, however, that the Clearing-House will be responsible for administering the non-compliance mechanism. This possibility is not even considered in the *Compliance Note, supra* note 203.

[209] See *Establishment Note, supra* note 134, at paras. 19–33.

[210] *Cartagena Protocol, supra* note 117, Art. 19.   [211] See *Szasz, supra* note 109, at 15.

[212] Sands, *International Environmental Law, supra* note 72 at 598.

challenge will thus be to ensure that both information-exchange and firm reporting obligations are satisfied – an innovative approach might address this challenge by gradually transforming institutional "dialogue" into a tool for capacity-building.[213] In essence, compliance-coordinating bodies such as the Clearing-House would seek out every opportunity to strengthen the regime in their interaction with States by, for example, promulgating more effective surveillance, data-gathering and reporting techniques. Eventually, principles of participation and openness could be used to advocate for a role in monitoring for individuals and civil society organizations beyond their current role in implementation networks.[214]

The enforcement phase

The traditional understanding of "enforcement" in international law is strictly a question of which international actors can enforce the obligations of a State internationally, when that State has "failed to implement an international environmental obligation".[215] However, enforcement of international environmental obligations *after the fact* of harm, and especially the attribution of State responsibility, may well be "irrelevant" once the breach of obligation, and subsequent harm, have come about.[216] As argued by Martti Koskenniemi, damage to the environment is often irreparable and allocation of responsibility is not likely to encourage prevention. Also, the "quantification" of damages for liability is unable to properly capture "the value of nature as a spiritual amenity, its value to future generations and even *less nature* as a value in itself" regardless of its instrumental use to humans.[217] The complex rules on State responsibility may, therefore, provide an incomplete means of addressing situations of non-compliance within sustainable development regimes.[218] In this instance, the

---

[213] Further research is required on the issue of how consistently-implemented compliance-building mechanisms can gradually build towards the emergence of binding sustainable development norms. For discussion of this dynamic type of dynamic structure, as exemplified in freshwater resources regimes, see *S.J. Toope, supra* note 97, at 105 and J. Brunée and S.J. Toope, *Ecosystems, supra* note 69.

[214] Such arrangements exist under both the NAFTA Environmental Side Agreement and the Canada–Chile Environmental Side Agreement. On the importance and effectiveness of civil society participation in international environmental treaty regimes, see generally *A. Kiss and D. Shelton, supra* note 66, at 590.

[215] Sands, *International Environmental Law, supra* note 72, at 148.

[216] *Koskenniemi, supra* note 97 at 126.

[217] *Ibid.,* (emphasis added). He also points out that causal links are often difficult to establish in the context of transboundary environmental harms, and the rarity of actual judicial remedies.

[218] On the potential for conflict between rules of state responsibility and general international law with the *Non-compliance Procedure* of the *Montreal Protocol,* see *ibid.* Regarding the utility of state responsibility, we must note certain recent, remarkable developments in the work of the International Law Commission's *Articles on State Responsibility,* especially in the definition of an "injured State", that could have wide-ranging consequences for enforcement of sustainable development law. The 1996 *Report of the International Law Commission* contains draft language that allows any Party to a multilateral treaty to gain standing as an injured State if a right infringed is stipulated as being "in the collective interest" of the Parties (Art. 40). In the final version of the *Articles,* the Commission notes that the great difficulties in drafting a comprehensive meaning for "injured State", owing to the

focus of "enforcement" in sustainable development law shifts from reaction (punitive measures) to pro-action (protective or preventive measures), and from the specific relief to individual actors (as embodied in obligations of cessation, restitution and compensation) to systematic relief that enhances the effectiveness of the entire regime. One of the innovative aspects of compliance, for "enforcement" of sustainable development regimes, is the need for action rather than sanction.

As such, a spectrum of enforcement measures can address possible non-compliance – cooperative and coercive, formal and informal, preventative and remedial, diplomatic and legal measures. This spectrum affords a certain *flexibility* to these regimes to address varied cases of non-compliance in light of the particular context of nonconforming Parties. Furthermore, sustainable development regimes facilitate the *rapid and preventive deployment* of enforcement options. Finally, procedural values of *transparency* and *participation* are especially apparent. The three regimes under discussion display very similar characteristics in the enforcement phase – this is largely due to the innovative *Non-compliance Procedure* of the *Montreal Protocol*, a model that has been copied and adapted in the other highly-integrated regimes.[219] Various enforcement measures in the *Montreal Protocol* and possibilities for the *Cartegena Protocol* are surveyed here.

A spectrum of enforcement measures

The *Non-compliance Procedure* of the *Montreal Protocol* is "an intra-regime, nonjudicial, nonadversarial enforcement mechanism".[220] As such, it aims not to "establish guilt, but to identify solutions".[221] The enforcement measures available upon a finding of non-compliance by the Meeting of the Parties are established in an indicative list of measures. The first, and by far the most common in practice, is the rendering of "appropriate assistance", including:

- assistance for collection and reporting of data,
- technical assistance,
- technology transfer,
- information transfer and training, and
- financial assistance.

---

technical and legal complexity of the subject matter, not based solely on customary law. Therefore, the Commission recommends a general, inclusive definition rather than the extensive, enumerated definition found in previous drafts. The new Art. 43, seems to exclude a requirement of "injury". To summarize roughly, where an obligation is owed to a group of States or to the "international community as a whole", any State in that group or community "specifically affected" by a breach has standing. Where the breach of an obligation affects the "enjoyment of rights or performance of obligations" of that group of States or the "international community as a whole" any State in the group or community has standing. See J. Crawford, *The International Law Commission's Articles on State Responsibility: Introduction, Texts and Commentaries* (Cambridge: Cambridge University Press, 2002) 29–31 [hereinafter *Crawford*]. This requires further research; see below.

[219] See *Compliance Note, supra* note 203, at para. 14 *ff.*
[220] *Nuruddin, supra* note 191, at 124.   [221] *Ibid.*, at 125.

Financing of cooperative measures falls within the mandate of the *Multilateral Fund*.[222] Addressing a shortcoming in the original text, the *London Amendments* to the Montreal Protocol require that transfer of technology to developing countries occur under "fair and most favorable conditions".[223] This shows an awareness of the situational monopoly that exists when economically developed countries transfer technology to developing countries. These cooperative measures can all be seen as manifestations of capacity-building, and provide a framework to *enhance* compliance from the very existence of non-compliance, rather than simply terminate the non-compliance.

The introduction of an Implementation Committee within the *Montreal Protocol* regime is a novel approach: one body (made up of State representatives) to receive, consider and report on cases of non-compliance and mediate "an amicable solution" where possible, before referring cases to the full Meeting of the Parties for disposition.[224] This model is now widely applied.[225]

Other innovative measures specifically listed include issuing cautions and suspension of specific rights and privileges under the Protocol, for example, those associated with industrial rationalization, consumption, trade, and use of the financial mechanism.[226] There is also a possibility of action under Article 4 of the *Montreal Protocol*, which bars trade in controlled substances with non-Parties. However, these drastic measures have not normally been applied by the Implementation Committee. It more commonly sees economies in transition failing to meet phase-out targets for controlled substances.[227] However, the value of potential coercive sanctions should not be underestimated. In recent decisions of the Meeting of the Parties on cases of non-compliance, the threat of coercive sanctions has been expressly invoked to address situations where Parties must attempt to comply in good faith.[228] This is not an "empty threat" but rather, judicious use of another compliance tool to shape the behaviour of States.[229]

The *Cartagena Protocol* does not yet have a non-compliance mechanism and the Intergovernmental Committee is currently studying various options.[230] Enabling provisions in the text envisage "cooperative procedures and institutional mechanisms".[231] The broadest spectrum of enforcement options being studied is found in the *Draft Guidelines* of the UNEP Working Group of Experts on Enforcement and Implementation of Environmental Conventions.[232] These are consistent with the innovative approaches to compliance described in this

---

[222] *Montreal Protocol, supra* note 96, Art. 10.   [223] *Ibid.*, Art. 10A.

[224] *Non-compliance Procedure, supra* note 96, Arts. 5, 7, 8.

[225] See e.g. the Multilateral Consultative Process of the *Climate Change Convention*, the UN-ECE *Convention on Long-Range Transboundary Air Pollution* and its various protocols, as well as the emerging approach of the Basel Convention and the Kyoto Protocol.

[226] *Non-compliance Procedure*, Annex V, *supra* note 96, at para. A.

[227] *Compliance Note, supra* note 203, at para. 19.   [228] *Ibid.*

[229] See J. Brunée and S.J. Toope, *Interactional Theory, supra* note 64, at 64 *ff.*   [230] See *ibid.*

[231] *Cartagena Protocol, supra* note 117, Art. 34.

[232] See *Compliance Note, supra* note 203, at para. 27.

section, and should be given further attention. Drawing on these proposals, enforcement options could include:

- standard protocols for the reporting of data; as discussed below, this should be expanded to standardized methodologies throughout the regime, including scientific assessments;
- targeted investigations *in situ*; allowing for a fuller appreciation of country context and particular needs;
- technical and financial assistance and supply of equipment;
- economic incentives to encourage and reward ongoing compliance;
- a "suite of sanctions" including exclusion from benefits of the regime;
- formal and informal *fora* for accountability to peer nations, using diplomacy and rhetoric; and
- inclusion of Implementation Committees in treaties, with provisions for specific non-compliance procedures.

Rapid and preventative deployment

The experience of the *Non-compliance Procedure* of the *Montreal Protocol*, has shown that in practice, the use of cautions and suspensions is avoided in cases of *bona fide* attempts at compliance.[233] This is especially the case when the *Non-compliance Procedure* has been invoked by the non-complying Party itself, thus creating incentives for self-monitoring and rapid reporting. The Secretariat is required to report cases of "possible" non-compliance – this low threshold also shows the preventative focus of the *Non-compliance Procedure*.[234] The procedure also sets strict timelines to ensure efficiency in addressing non-compliance.[235]

The *Cartagena Protocol* envisages a number of subtle enforcement measures that are well integrated in the overall regime and designed for preventative deployment. The first is the promotion of standardized methodologies in scientific assessment and reporting. The requirement of standard methodologies is another example of capacity-building. For example, risk assessment must be carried out "in a scientifically sound manner...taking into account recognized risk assessment techniques [and] available scientific evidence".[236] Annexes detail the principles, methodologies and issues to consider in risk assessments, as well as listing specific information required for notifications of transboundary movement of LMOs.[237] These requirements reflect the requisite degree of precaution required to prevent lasting and devastating harm through uninformed transboundary movement. Parties are thus able to evaluate whether their internal

---

[233] *Nuruddin, supra* note 191, at 126.

[234] The threshold could also exist to avoid the discomfort of an unrepresentative entity prejudging the existence of non-compliance on the part of a State. Conclusive findings of non-compliance are almost exclusively the domain of political *fora* – in this case, the Meeting of the Parties.

[235] For example, the Secretariat must convey submissions from other Parties regarding a Party's non-compliance to that Party within two weeks, and the Implementation Committee must make its report within six weeks; *Non-compliance Procedure, supra* note 96, Arts. 2, 9.

[236] *Cartagena Protocol, supra* note 117, Art. 15.   [237] *Ibid.*, Annexes I, II, III.

regulatory framework is able to satisfy the requirements of standardized methodologies, and draw on centralized facilitation and assistance to improve that framework. This is a good example of a creative but unobtrusive means of *preventing* non-compliance that is both rigorous and supportive of the aims of the regime.

Another example of a preventative and rapid mechanism to address possible non-compliance is the introduction of the default, "backup" regulatory framework for countries lacking domestic regulation, as highlighted earlier.[238] This establishes a minimum standard of regulation as a *component* of the international regime agreed to by the Parties, ensuring that the means are in place to prevent non-compliance from the moment of ratification, even in the absence of full implementation. Thus, the linearity of implementation, monitoring and enforcement phases breaks down – these processes are largely contemporaneous.

Transparency and participation

Values of transparency and participation are especially vital in enforcement, to avoid creating mistrust or impressions of partiality that can de-legitimize the regime. This is manifest in the conciliatory approach of the Implementation Committee within the *Non-compliance Procedure* and the allocation of the decision-making function to the fully representative Meeting of the Parties.[239] These values are also operative in the express right of Parties involved in the procedure to make submissions and representations to the Implementation Committee,[240] and the subsequent bar on the participation of involved Parties in the elaboration of recommendations in the report on their case.[241] The report of the Implementation Committee is public, except for any confidential information therein.[242] The Protocol does, therefore, promote a good degree of transparency; participation extends to non-State stakeholders, and as such, would allocate a participatory role for civil society, the private sector and individuals within the *Non-compliance Procedure*.

The Executive Secretary of the ICCP has emphasized that "principles of timeliness, fairness, predictability, transparency and due process are deemed as essential underpinnings to...non-compliance regimes."[243] In elaborating a transparent and participatory non-compliance mechanism for the *Cartagena Protocol*, it may be appropriate to place an Implementation Committee as an independent section of the clearing-house mechanism of the Protocol. As the repository of implementation and monitoring information, focal point of the global biosafety network, and source of expertise on biosafety, the Biosafety Clearing-House would be well-suited to house an effective and rapidly deployable non-compliance mechanism.

---

[238] *Cartagena Protocol, supra* note 117, Art. 11(6).
[239] *Non-compliance Procedure, supra* note 96, Art. 14, Annex V.
[240] *Ibid.*, Art. 10.   [241] *Ibid.*, Art. 11.   [242] *Ibid.*, Art. 16.
[243] *Compliance Note, supra* note 203, at para. 38.

The phenomenon of Implementation Committees manifests a trend towards non-judicial, non-adversarial, cooperative enforcement mechanisms, drawing on measures aimed principally at capacity-building and thus well suited to enhancing compliance with the regime.[244] These non-compliance mechanisms are exclusively intra-regime bodies, specializing them to the particular types of non-compliance and means for addressing non-compliance that suit the regime. This approach does, however, face two challenges. First, there is a need to structure the interaction between specialized non-compliance mechanisms, dispute settlement mechanisms in more general framework convention, and principles of State responsibility and reparation for harm in general international law.[245] Secondly, there is a need to delineate a clearer role for the International Court of Justice in the enforcement of sustainable development law, in light of a trend away from judicial dispute settlement, especially given the recent openness of the Court to the concept of sustainable development as an interstitial norm.[246]

Effective compliance

Effectiveness of international regimes can be judged by analysing whether they (a) address *stated objectives*; and (b) address the *problems that led to the treaty* (to generalize, the *problems that led to the regime*).[247] The approach to compliance discussed above manifests a third element of effectiveness, namely a capacity within the regime to address *changing situations* by (a) developing new substantive norms within the regime, and (b) adapting its compliance framework as appropriate. Thus, the key benchmark of effective compliance is the operation of a *self-reinforcing dynamic* within the regimes themselves. This is the main innovation that can be highlighted in this chapter. Essentially, it involves how international legal regimes can reinforce themselves, through integrated approaches to compliance-building. Several principal mechanisms can be identified.

First, *parallel implementation, monitoring and enforcement mechanisms* are needed, to ensure that implementation obligations are provided with the associated monitoring and enforcement tools to make them work. So, for example, the bifurcated obligations of implementation in the *Desertification Convention* for "affected country Parties" and "developed country Parties" are paralleled in specialized reporting obligations for each of those groups of actors. Specific cooperative enforcement mechanisms such as financial and technical assistance are also tailored to the capacities of the various Parties. By ensuring that

---

[244] See A. Kiss and D. Shelton, *supra* note 66, at 588–89; *Compliance Note, supra* note 203, at para. 37.

[245] See Koskenniemi, *supra* note 97.

[246] The *Gabčíkovo-Nagymaros* case, *supra* note 1, is a recent example of the key role of the ICJ in elaborating guiding concepts and principles of sustainable development law, such as the rights of future generations, and, in a concurring opinion, the precautionary principle and ongoing obligation of environmental impact assessments. On the transformational power of interstitial norms as applied in the *Gabčíkovo-Nagymaros* case, see Lowe, *supra* note 139.

[247] Jacobson and Brown Weiss, *supra* note 103.

implementation, monitoring and enforcement mechanisms parallel one another, the regime sends a consistent and persistent message that reinforces the fact that affected country Parties and developed country Parties are subject to specialized norms. This reinforces the regime in that compliance with these specialized norms will eventually reduce imbalances in available technology and resources between affected country and developed country Parties without advocating the unidirectional flow of aid.

Secondly, *capacity-building* must be recognized as a principal tool of compliance-building. The normative influence of capacity-building is actually essential to this self-reinforcing dynamic. Within the *Cartagena Protocol*, capacity-building is promoted across the implementation, monitoring and enforcement stages. When the risk of non-compliance and actual non-compliance are addressed through capacity-building mechanisms, highly integrated regimes are not restoring a *status quo ante* (as in obligations of restitution), but rather strengthening themselves through effective non-compliance procedures. This indicates a self-reinforcing dynamic.

Thirdly, there is a role to be played by *comprehensive regime review*. In particular, the *Cartagena Protocol* expressly requires that the Meeting of the Parties undertake "an evaluation of the effectiveness of the Protocol, including an assessment of its procedures and annexes" every five years.[248] Contrasted with the piecemeal development of elements of the *Montreal Protocol* regime, the *Cartagena Protocol anticipates change* within the original framework of the regime. Another example would be the use of Annexes for particularly dynamic requirements such as notifications and risk-assessment procedures – "annexing for change" is a phenomenon that emerged in CITES and has contributed extensively to the adaptability of that regime. This space for comprehensive regime review underscores the organic nature of many sustainable development regimes – as Brunée and Toope suggest, interaction within a regime, building shared experience and understanding may lead to the elaboration of more binding norms.[249] The *Cartagena Protocol* builds in a mechanism for that process to take place, and exemplifies the operation of a self-reinforcing dynamic.

CONCLUSION

In conclusion, based on the survey of treaties, and the analysis of innovative approaches present above, it is possible to highlight several general trends in compliance-building for sustainable development law. These trends indicate the future direction of compliance in this area, and draw attention to the innovative approaches that are being adopted, drawing on diverse experiences from economic, social and environmental law, to build an attitude of compliance.

---

[248] *Cartagena Protocol, supra* note 117, Art. 35.
[249] J. Brunée and S.J. Toope, *Interactional Theory, supra* note 64.

First, there has been movement from "balanced governance" to self-governance. *Agenda 21* called for the "balanced governance" of instruments and agreements to reflect the concerns and interests of developing countries.[250] Progressing from "developing countries" as a homogenous category, individual country contexts are now recognized as a key variable, to be addressed through flexible regimes. The *Cartagena Protocol* distinguishes between developing, less developed, small island developing countries and economies in transition where such distinctions are important to the effectiveness of the regime, and demonstrates an awareness of the need to take into account country context aside from developmental status. The *Desertification Convention* encourages regions, subregions, nations and local communities to identify and implement an integrated sustainable development agenda on multiple levels, while reinforcing international coordination. This is a key example of application of the subsidiarity principle to resolve the centralization/dispersal tension noted in the Introduction. Secondly, there has been movement from treaty-monitoring bodies to compliance-coordinating bodies. Regimes such as the *Montreal Protocol* mark a shift towards a role for IGOs in the coordination of compliance rather than the passive monitoring of treaty obligations. Thirdly, *compliance-coordinating bodies* are now used. These independent, intergovernmental institutions draw on a level of authority as the designated implementers and monitors, grounded in growing de-politicization of enforcement and overall legitimacy. In this process, sovereignty of States is simultaneously attenuated by the role given to compliance-coordinating bodies and safeguarded through the use of non-coercive mechanisms and assistance provided to States in order to implement their voluntary commitments. Fourthly, there has been a shift from individualized relief to systematic relief. A further trend can be observed, in the movement away from limited, claim-dependent and claim-specific measures (generally coercive and by definition remedial in nature) towards flexible, systematized and generally cooperative measures that consistently approach non-compliance by reinforcing the regime as a whole. Finally, and perhaps most inspiring, there is clearly a movement from reaction to proaction. *Ex post facto* enforcement of obligations of cessation, restitution and compensation have been recognized as inadequate to address non-compliance in sustainable development regimes. Distinctive, innovative approaches to compliance can shift the paradigm from correction of harm through remedial sanctions to prevention of harm through information exchange and cooperative measures.

---

[250] *Agenda 21, supra* note 11 at para. 39.1(c).

PART IV

THE PROSPECTS

Integrated principles and practices of sustainable development law are rapidly emerging in many areas. This book now turns to the prospects for future developments in this area.

There have been numerous innovations and recent "significant legal developments" in domestic and international law.[1] Many of these developments are specifically related to the priorities identified in the 2002 *Johannesburg Plan of Implementation*, and in recent international sustainable development negotiations, treaties and other cooperative initiatives. Much can be gained from enhanced efforts to build legal awareness, capacity and education for policy makers, judiciaries, jurists, civil society and other actors. Within each economic, social or environmental pillar of sustainable development, some of these tasks have been undertaken by the relevant intergovernmental agencies, international instruments or *ad hoc* cooperation arrangements. However, there is a need for further work to address over-arching legal aspects of sustainable development, and to analyse emerging, integrated new legal issues and instruments. Such integrated elements may not fall into the legal mandates of either social, economic, or environmental institutions.

Further juridical inquiry, investigation and analysis are needed: a new legal research agenda. A focus on the needs of developing countries is essential to this

---

[1] For a good survey of recent international agricultural and natural resource management instruments relating to sustainable development, see FAO, *Law and Sustainable Development Since Rio: Legal Trends in Agriculture and Natural Resource Management* (Rome: FAO, 2002). For an excellent analysis of developments in international law of the sea and marine resource management, see A. Boyle and D. Freestone, *International Law and Sustainable Development: Past Achievements and Future Challenges* (Oxford: Oxford University Press, 1999), extensively cited earlier in this book. For an in-depth discussion of cross-cutting human rights and environmental aspects of the international trade law agenda, see F. Francioni, *Environment, Human Rights and International Trade* (Oxford: Hart, 2001). And for a collection of papers by leading scholars and judges on reconciling social, economic and environmental laws, see M.-C. Cordonier Segger and C.G. Weeramantry, eds., *Sustainable Justice: Reconciling Economic, Social and Environmental Law* (Leiden: Martinus Nijhoff, 2004).

agenda. This section will explore the emerging elements of a sustainable development law research agenda.

Increased analysis and knowledge building can focus on the significant legal and regulatory innovations and legal developments related to sustainable development. It can investigate and analyse general developments in legal principles, treaties, intergovernmental organizations and other instruments. It can research juridical innovations and developments in the general areas highlighted in the 2002 *World Summit for Sustainable Development* (such as consumption and production, poverty, natural resources, health, globalization), and their means of implementation. It can also focus on the issues that were identified for urgent attention and further development in the United Nations Secretary-General's papers at the Summit. These included water, energy, health, agriculture and biodiversity: the so-called "WEHAB" issues.[2] The legal implications of recent developments in these priority areas can be tracked and further analysed by legal scholars and practitioners. This research can assist the states and epistemic communities which surround international action on these issues, allowing them to learn from recent experience and challenges in domestic, sub-regional, regional and global implementation of the law. And as noted in the 2002 *Johannesburg Plan of Implementation*, there is also a significant need for facilitation and coordination to ensure coherence. New research can investigate ways to strengthen the legal foundations of such coherence.

There are several hundred bilateral, regional and global treaties as well as "soft law" instruments and guidelines related to sustainable development, most of which have been ratified or agreed in recent decades. Such instruments are emerging principally from three areas: economic law (including new trade, investment, financing and potentially, competition agreements and principles); social law (including treaties, jurisprudence and declarations on human rights, labour, humanitarian and social development law); and environmental law (such as treaties on waste management, endangered species and trans-boundary pollution). Further research and analysis is needed to understand and develop the recent developments in these exciting, evolving areas of international law, how they link to other international laws and policies and how they can shape the work of international and domestic institutions. In addition, at the intersections between economic, social and environmental law, there are new international conventions, negotiated after the 1992 Rio de Janeiro Earth Summit, which contain explicit sustainable development goals and provisions. These include, as will be further explored below, the 1994 UN *Convention to Combat Desertification*, the 1992 *Convention on Biological Diversity* (CBD) and its 2001 *Cartagena Protocol on Biosafety*, as well as negotiations in the CBD, launched in 2004, for an international regime on access genetic resources and benefit

---

[2] United Nations Secretary General, *World Summit on Sustainable Development WEHAB Framework Papers* (New Haven: Yale School of Forestry and Environmental Studies, 2002). Available online: www.johannesburgsummit.org/html/documents/wehab_papers.html.

sharing. They also include the 1992 UN *Framework Convention on Climate Change* with its 1998 *Kyoto Protocol*, as well as domestic law regulations and international carbon finance contracts which are developing to support this agenda. There are several other more recent treaties in environmental, economic or human rights fields of law, such as the 1998 *Rotterdam Convention on the Prior Informed Consent Procedure for Certain Hazardous Chemicals and Pesticides in International Trade*, the 2001 *Stockholm Convention on Persistent Organic Pollutants*, priority issues identified in the United Nations Human Rights Commission, and the 2001 *International Treaty on Plant Genetic Resources for Food and Agriculture* adopted in the Food and Agriculture Organization (FAO), which profess sustainable development objectives, and would benefit from further analysis from an integrated legal research perspective. Most of these treaties have Conferences of the Parties which meet on a regular basis, providing important places for legal research to inform and support legal and policy development agendas. Of particular interest in this respect are the new "inter-regional" economic cooperation agreements, such as the 2000 *Cotonou Partnership Agreement between the Members of the African, Caribbean and Pacific Group and the European Community and its Member States*, and negotiations for the (projected) 2005 *Free Trade Area of the Americas*, which also explicitly recognize sustainable development among their goals.

Recent decisions of the International Court of Justice, the World Trade Organization Appellate Body and Panels, the International Tribunal on the Law of the Sea, and the International Centre for the Settlement of Investment Disputes procedures, as well as many regional courts and tribunals, seek to reconcile or balance social and economic development with environmental protection toward a development that can last in the interest of present and future generations. Many of these judicial and quasi-judicial decisions, as well as the treaties mentioned above, reflect the emerging principles of international law relating to sustainable development identified earlier in this book, albeit not consistently. Rigorous research into the application of these principles in the further development and implementation of instruments addressing sustainable development concerns would strengthen governance at the international and national level.

However, a significant unresolved challenge cuts across all these treaties, instruments and judicial decisions. How best to implement international sustainable development law? More work is needed to investigate and analyse more effective and efficient ways to design, implement and monitor international sustainable development legal instruments. Sustainable development accords are often negotiated in an *ad hoc* manner, on the basis of solving specific problems. Their mandates can and do overlap or even conflict in key areas. Many such conflicts can be addressed within the existing rules of public international law.[3] However, such rules do not apply to all conflicts or overlaps

---

[3] See generally J. Pauwelyn, *Conflict of Norms in Public International Law: How WTO Law Relates to Other Rules of International Law* (Cambridge: Cambridge University Press, 2003).

between international regimes (which include, *inter alia*, legal norms and instruments, hard and "soft" legal principles, and acts of international organizations). They shed even less guidance if the issue is one of interpretation or application of overlapping mandates. Where possible, it is preferable for such intersections to be addressed through a principled, coherent approach appropriate to international law in the field of sustainable development, rather than through a rigid application of formal or technical rules alone.

As addressed above, the problem is not always the laws themselves, but their governance. International legal regimes require coordination and consensus between extremely diverse perspectives, cultures and geographies. Although many sustainable development treaties are starting to achieve their goals, in most areas the pace is still very slow. In addition, many developing countries (and several developed countries) still lack the resources, capacity and knowledge to put effective regimes in place for effective treaty negotiation and compliance. This exacerbates the potential for confusion. New international legal knowledge can assist in addressing these challenges. It can be broadly shared by developed and developing countries. It can inform the deliberations of the UN Commission on Sustainable Development. It can also be made available to the international organizations and treaty secretariats in social, economic and environmental fields,[4] and to domestic-decision-makers.

The final section of this book, focused on "the prospects" for sustainable development law, provides proposals for a future legal research agenda. It does not attempt to draw broad conclusions, but seeks to define future sustainable development law issues and agendas in key areas, and discusses the international regimes that seek to address them. In essence, it proposes further directions for legal research by those interested in advancing the understanding, development and implementation of international sustainable development law.

In six short chapters, it maps out prospects for development of future legal research agendas in priority areas of evolving integration between economic, social and environmental law. In these six areas of focus, where important overlaps exist, sustainable development principles may be particularly relevant, and new instruments are being developed and tested. These areas include trade, investment and competition law, and international natural resources law (from the field of economic law); international health law and international human rights and poverty eradication law (from the field of social law); and climate change law and biodiversity law (from the field of environmental law).

This section also highlights themes that crosscut these emerging legal research agendas. There are important cross-cutting questions to be addressed in research on the areas of intersection between social, economic and environmental law. Recent progress in areas such as foreign direct liability, responsibility and compensation mechanisms, advance informed consent procedures and corporate

---

[4] M.-C. Cordonier Segger, "Significant Developments in Sustainable Development Law and Governance: A Proposal" (2004) *United Nations Natural Resources Forum* 28:1.

social and environmental responsibility should be examined. International sustainable development law also needs to be effectively financed, if its goals are to be realized, and these mechanisms require investigation. There is an essential procedural aspect to international sustainable development law: consultations, impact assessment, transparency, public participation and access to justice are key characteristics that require more research. Finally, international sustainable development law is only successful when it can count on full and meaningful compliance. More research is needed into how innovative co-operative mechanisms for effective monitoring, implementation and enforcement can be designed to support the goals of international sustainable development law.

Finally, in a final brief concluding chapter, the authors summarize the proposals of this book on the principles, practices and prospects for sustainable development law.

9

Sustainable International Trade, Investment and Competition Law

with MARKUS W. GEHRING[1]

How can international trade, investment and competition law better support, and not frustrate, sustainable development goals? What is the future legal research agenda in this area?

This chapter identifies emerging issues in international sustainable development law (SDL), primarily from recent developments in international economic law.[2] The expansion of international economic law could lead to greater cooperation between economies, and also provide global and regional safeguards and balancing mechanisms similar to those already found on a domestic level in many countries. Different economic instruments at global and regional levels integrate economic law with environmental and social provisions. For example, while the proposed International Trade Organization was designed to integrate social and economic policy in one treaty instrument,[3] the 1947 *General Agreement on Tariffs and Trade* (GATT) was provisionally enacted and thought to be limited to trade issues.[4] However the GATT's agenda was soon expanded into neighbouring economic issues, such as trade-related investment measures,[5] and in 2001 at Doha, Qatar, governments launched

---

[1] Markus W. Gehring, LL.M. (Yale), PhD (Hamburg), is Lead Counsel in Sustainable International Trade, Investment and Competition Law at the CISDL, and works as a researcher in international public law with Professor Vaughan Lowe, All Soul's College, Oxford University Faculty of Law. He tutors at University College, Oxford University and is author of several reports, articles and books on sustainable developments in international trade, investment and competition law, and an expert adviser in the Concerted Action on Trade and Environment research consortium funded by the European Commission.

[2] For a more in-depth survey of certain issues, on global level, see M. Gehring and M.-C. Cordonier Segger, *Sustainable Developments in World Trade Law* (London: Kluwer Law International, 2004). See also F. Francioni, *Environment, Human Rights and International Trade* (Oxford: Hart, 2001). And see WTO Secretariat, *Trade, Development and the Environment* (New York: Kluwer Law International, 2000). For an excellent perspective on the policy aspects of a trade and sustainable development research agenda, see D. Runnalls and A. Cosbey, *Trade and Sustainable Development: A Survey of the Issues and a New Research Agenda* (Winnipeg: IISD, 1992) or more recently, the work of the IISD and the ICTSD in the Trade Knowledge Network, and the Southern Agenda on Trade and Environment Project, available online: <http://www.tradeknowledgenetwork.net/> and <http://www.iisd.org/trade/ldc/sate.asp>.

[3] See *Havana Charter for an International Trade Organization*, 24 March 1948, UN Doc. E/Conf. 2178.

[4] See J. H. Jackson, *The World Trading System*, 2nd edn. (Boston: MIT Press, 1997).

[5] On the history of the Agreement on Trade Related Investment Measures (TRIMs) see R.H. Edwards and S.N. Lester, "Towards a More Comprehensive World Trade Organization Agreement on Trade Related Investment Measures" [1997] *Stanford Journal of International Law* 169.

282 *with Markus W. Gehring*

international negotiations in the World Trade Organization (WTO) which reach far beyond a "trade only" agenda into important social and environmental issues.

The linkages between international economic law and the other two pillars of sustainable development have just begun to be seriously explored,[6] and these are the focus of a legal research agenda in sustainable trade, investment and competition law. But with the new approach offered by sustainable development law, it is possible to re-examine the areas of intersection, leading even to integration. This legal research agenda focuses on how important aspects of international economic law[7] can support sustainable development, and become part of the emerging international law on sustainable development.

This section provides a survey of a new sustainable development law research agenda in this area. As indicated by the title "trade, investment and competition law", debates have extended beyond traditional trade liberalization agenda items. Research and debate is needed to carefully examine the evolving fields of investment law, and competition law, both of which pose their own challenges and opportunities for sustainable development. New economic rules and institutions are also emerging to govern government procurement, intellectual property rights, services, agriculture and standards, all of which hold potential to either foster or frustrate sustainable development.

SUSTAINABLE DEVELOPMENTS IN ECONOMIC LAW

Recent global developments in trade, environment and development debates

International trade is one of the oldest areas governed by international law.[8] Multiple levels and forms of international trade rules exist, and are considered binding by the parties to these agreements. These bodies of rules are governed by an almost hierarchical set of intersecting regimes, which stretch from the global to regional, sub-regional and even bilateral levels, taking form as free trade areas, customs unions or common markets.

Vibrant debates have sparked the emergence of a vigorous sustainable development discourse in international trade research, focused primarily on two areas

---

[6] See P. Trepte, *Regulating Procurement – Understanding the Ends and Means of Public Procurement Regulation* (Oxford: Oxford University Press, 2004). And see G. Handl, *Multilateral Development Banking: Environmental Principles and Concepts Reflecting General International Law and Public Policy* (The Hague: Kluwer Law International, 2001). See also M.A. Echols, *Food Safety and the WTO: The Interplay of Culture, Science and Technology* (The Hague: Kluwer Law International, 2001). And see R.A. Westin, *Environmental Tax Initiative & International Trade Treaties* (The Hague: Kluwer Law International, 1997).

[7] On discussions between GATT "clinical isolation" and its discontinuity after the WTO see *United States – Standards for Reformulated and Conventional Gasoline* (*US – Gasoline*), Appellate Body, AB-1996-1, WTO-Document WT/ DS2/AB/R, adopted 20 May 1996; and see D. Palmeter and P.C. Mavroidis, "The WTO Legal System: Sources of Law" (1998) 92 *AJIL* 398.

[8] K. Ziegler, *Völkerrechtsgeschichte* (München: Beck, 1994).

of linkages: trade and environment, and trade and development. Both discussions are part of a growing body of scholarship, and are subject to increasing legal analysis.[9]

For example, just before the 1992 Earth Summit in Rio, academia and the public started to discuss the trade and environment link. Daniel Esty, in "Greening the GATT", was one of the first lawyers to seriously consider the legal implications and call for reforms of the GATT system.[10] The international community began to recognize the potential for conflicts between trade and environment regimes. Policies were sought to reinforce the role that trade could play as an instrument in sustainable development. Chapter 2 in *Agenda 21* suggests ways to promote sustainable development through trade, and provides proposals for making trade and environment mutually supportive. It states that:

[a]n open, equitable, secure, non-discriminatory and predictable multilateral trading system that is consistent with the goals of sustainable development and leads to the optimal distribution of global production in accordance with comparative advantage is of benefit to all trading partners. Moreover, improved market access for developing countries' exports in conjunction with sound macroeconomic and environmental policies would have a positive environmental impact and therefore make an important contribution towards sustainable development.[11]

Unsurprisingly, this broad statement did not resolve the debate. Indeed, a decade later, trade and finance aspects were still some of the most highly controversial issues in the negotiations for the *Johannesburg Plan of Implementation* at the 2002 WSSD.[12]

The WTO 2001 Doha Development Agenda can be seen as a first step into the direction of more serious integration between trade, environment and development issues. Trade ministers agreed to initiate negotiations on trade and environment issues and gave high priority – at least in the text – to development. The 2001 *Doha Declaration* explicitly encourages efforts to promote cooperation

[9] On trade and environment see *e.g.* S. Shaw and R. Schwartz "Trade and Environment in the WTO – State of Play" (2002) 36 *JWT* 129; D. Brack, ed., *Trade and Environment: Conflict or Compatibility* (London: Earthscan, 1998) and J. Cameron, P. Demaret and D. Geradin, eds., *Trade & The Environment: The Search For Balance* (London: Cameron May, 1994). On trade and development see for example B. Lal Das, *The WTO Agreements: Deficiencies, Imbalances and Required Changes* (Kuala Lumpur: Third World Network, 1998); J. M. Djossou, *L'Afrique, le GATT et l'OMC: Entre Territoires Douaniers et Régions Commerciales* (Sainte-Foy: Yvon Blais, 2000). See also M.A. Echols, *Food Safety and the WTO: The Interplay of Culture, Science and Technology* (The Hague: Kluwer Law International, 2001).

[10] See D. Esty, *Greening the GATT: Trade, Environment and the Future* (Washington: Institute for International Economics, 1994).

[11] *Agenda 21*, Report of the UNCED, I (1992) UN Doc. A/CONF.151/26/Rev.1, (1992) 31 ILM 874, para. 2.5 [hereinafter *Agenda 21*].

[12] See *Johannesburg Declaration on Sustainable Development*, in Report of the *World Summit on Sustainable Development*, Johannesburg, South Africa, 26 August to 4 Sept 2002, A/CONF.199/20 (New York, United Nations, 2002). See also *Johannesburg Plan of Implementation*, Report of the *World Summit on Sustainable Development*, Johannesburg (South Africa) (4 Sept. 2002) UN Doc. A/CONF.199/20: <http://www.un.org/esa/sustdev/documents/WSSD_POI_PD/English/POIToc.htm>.

between the WTO and relevant international environmental and developmental organizations, especially in the 2002 *World Summit on Sustainable Development* in Johannesburg, South Africa.[13] Unfortunately the *Doha Declaration* became somewhat of a stumbling block for negotiations in Johannesburg, as some delegations felt that the JPOI should not add to, or as some saw it, amend the *Doha Declaration*. Subsequent negotiations in the WTO have proven challenging, as experienced, for example, in the 2003 WTO Ministerial Conference in Cancun, Mexico, and it remains to be seen how the debate on trade, development and environment, which dates back over a decade, will be decided.

At the global level, not only do the WTO Agreements govern trade, but many Multilateral Environmental Agreements (MEAs) also contain trade provisions. The International Labour Organization (ILO) Conventions also have an impact on trade relations. Trade-related environmental measures (TREMs) continue to be used to deliver environmental and increasingly, sustainable development objectives in multilateral agreements,[14] and trade-related development measures (TRDMs) are also advocated and in some cases, adopted.[15] Several such measures are arguably key to prevent "free-riders" and ensure effectiveness and compliance[16] in treaties that have higher levels of membership than the WTO itself. More research is required to analyse and evaluate these instruments, within the context of sustainable development development law.

Sustainable development in international economic "jurisprudence"

Of further interest to sustainable law research, trade, investment and competition are influenced, and increasingly governed, by a growing body of jurisprudence and decisions of international tribunals and courts. On the global level, formal tribunals or court-like institutions used by this area of law include the WTO dispute settlement mechanism,[17] especially the WTO Appellate Body decisions. While not formally subject to *stare decisis* (binding precedent for subsequent cases), the WTO Appellate Body and Panels are very respectful of

---

[13] See WTO, Ministerial Declaration, Ministerial Conference Fourth Session, Doha, 9–14 Nov. 2001, WT/MIN(01)/DEC/W/1, online: WTO <www.wto.org>.

[14] A. Kiss, D. Shelton & K. Ishibashi *Economic Globalization and Compliance with International Environmental Agreements* (The Hague: Kluwer Law International, 2003).

[15] P. Gallagher, *Guide to the WTO and Developing Countries* (The Hague: Kluwer Law International, 2000).

[16] See, e.g., D. Brack, *International Trade and the Montreal Protocol* (London: Earthscan, 1996).

[17] Three of the most significant cases engaging sustainable development issues are *United States – Import Prohibition of Certain Shrimp and Shrimp Products*, 20 September, 1999, WTO Doc. WT/DS58/AB/R (Appellate Body Report) [hereinafter *Shrimp Turtle*], *European Communities – Measures Affecting Asbestos and Asbestos-Containing Products (Complaint by Canada)* (18 September 2000), WTO Doc. WT/DS135/R (Panel Report) [hereinafter *Asbestos*] and *EC – Measures Concerning Meat and Meat Products (Hormones) (Complaint by USA and Canada)* (13 February 1998), WTO Doc. WT/DS26/AB/R,WT/DS48/AB/R (Appellate Body Report) [hereinafter *Hormones*], online: World Trade Organization http://docsonline.wto.org.

former judgments.[18] Other institutions include the International Court of Justice and the International Tribunal of the Law of the Seas (ITLOS).[19] In investment law, increasingly, the decisions of the International Chamber of Commerce (ICC) dispute settlement procedures, and the awards of the International Centre for Settlement of Investment Disputes (ICSID) are also leading to a body of practice which provides guidance to future arbitrators of investment disputes.[20]

International economic subsidiarity? Sustainable regional integration agreements

Considerable research and analysis is also needed to investigate new and evolving regional integration agreements. Ranging from free trade areas to customs unions and common markets,[21] these regimes provide diverse innovative examples of how economic accords can contribute to (or detract from) sustainable development objectives. Regional examples of trade, investment and competition rules include the European Union (EU),[22] the Asia Pacific Economic Community and the Free Trade Area of the Americas (FTAA),[23] currently under negotiation. Each of these accords may have impacts on sustainable development, and increasingly, regional treaties recognize the promotion of sustainable development as a purpose or objective.

Many sub-regional economic integration regimes also include treaties and institutions of great relevance to sustainable development law research. These include, for example, the MERCOSUR, where an environmental framework agreement has been recently ratified and socio-laboural commission has been established, the Andean Community (ANCOM) with its parallel Committee of

---

[18] See W.J. Davey, "The WTO Dispute Settlement System" [2000] *JIEL* 3; J. H. Jackson, *The Jurisprudence of GATT and the WTO* (Cambridge: Cambridge University Press, 2000) at 113 *ff.*; E. Petersmann, "From the Hobbesian International Law of Coexistence to Modern Integration Law: The WTO Dispute Settlement" [1998] *JIEL* 1 at 175 *ff.*

[19] See *e.g.* the *Chile–EU Swordfish Dispute*. The ITLOS Special Chamber in the "Case concerning the Conservation and Sustainable Exploitation of Swordfish Stocks in the South-Eastern Pacific Ocean" suspended proceedings until 1 January 2004, ITLOS, Case No. 7 – Order 2001/1 of 15 March 2001, Chile/European Communities, para. 6, online: ITLOS <www.un.org/Depts/los/ITLOS/>.

[20] See International Centre for the Settlement of Investment Disputes, online: ICSID <http://www.worldbank.org/icsid/>. For commentary see M. Sornarajah, *The International Law on Foreign Investment* 2nd edn. (Cambridge: Cambridge University Press, 2004).

[21] J. Mathis, *Regional Trade Agreements in the GATT/WTO Article XXIV and the Internal Trade Agreement* (The Hague: T.M.-C. Asser Press, 2002). See also D.C. Esty & D. Geradin, "Market Access, Competitiveness, and Harmonization: Environmental Protection in Regional Trade Agreements" (1997) 21 *Harv. Envtl. L. Rev.* 265.

[22] See the informative website of the Director General Trade of the European Commission, DG Trade online: <http://trade-info.cec.eu.int/ europa/index_en.php>.

[23] Free Trade Area of the Americas Draft Agreement (21 November 2003) FTAA.TNC/w/133/Rev.3 (2003) <http://www.ftaa-alca.org/FTAADraft03/Index_e.asp> (18 May 2004). For commentary, see M.-C. Cordonier Segger and M. Leichner Reynal, *Beyond the Barricades: The Americas Trade and Sustainability Agenda* (Aldershot: Ashgate, 2005, forthcoming). See also M.-C. Cordonier Segger, "Sustainable Development in the Negotiation of the Free Trade Area of the Americas" Issues and Visions for the Future Interamerican Perspectives (2004) 27 *Fordham Intl L J* 1118.

Andean Environmental Authorities and Social Forum, the Caribbean Community (CARICOM) with its parallel social and environmental cooperation arrangements, the *North American Free Trade Agreement* (NAFTA) with its parallel labour and environment agreements.[24] Other interesting arrangements include the Southern African Development Community (SADC),[25] and the Association of South East Asian Nations (ASEAN) with its environmental[26] and social cooperation arrangements.

A further emerging area of legal research concerns inter-regional trade agreements, their sustainability impacts and their potential contribution to sustainable development law. Examples of such accords include the increasingly relevant *Cotonou Partnership Agreement between the Members of the African, Caribbean and Pacific Group and the European Community and its Member States,*[27] the inter-regional aspects of the potential *Free Trade Area of the Americas* agreement (which is being negotiated between countries party to five sub-regions in the Americas), and negotiations for a series of economic agreements between the European Union and the MERCOSUR in South America.[28] Finally, there are also numerous bi-lateral treaties worthy of examination. Commitments to "promote sustainable development" and innovative social and environmental mechanisms were included in the *Canada–Chile Free Trade Agreement* and its side agreements, the *Canada–Costa Rica Free Trade Agreement* and its side-agreements, the *USA–Jordan Free Trade Agreement*, and the *USA–Chile Free Trade Agreement.*[29]

---

[24] Regarding sub-regional agreements in the Americas, see M.-C. Cordonier Segger *et al., Trade Rules and Sustainability in the Americas* (Winnipeg: IISD, 1999); M.-C. Cordonier Segger *et al., Ecological Rules and Sustainability in the Americas* (Winnipeg: IISD/UNEP, 2002); and M.-C. Cordonier Segger et al., *Social Rules and Sustainability in the Americas* (Winnipeg: IISD/OAS, 2004).

[25] See SADC, Mandate of the South African Development Community Food, Agriculture and Natural Resources Directorate, which includes "Development, promotion and harmonization of policies and programmes aimed at effective and sustainable utilization of natural resources such as Water, Wildlife, Fisheries and Forestry." Available online: <http://www.sadc.int/fanr.php?lang= english&path= fanr&page=index>.

[26] K. Kheng-Lian & N.A. Robinson, "Strengthening Sustainable Development in Regional Inter-Governmental Governance: Lessons from the 'ASEAN Way'" (2002) *Singapore Journal of International & Comparative Law* 6, 640–682.

[27] *Partnership Agreement between the Members of the African, Caribbean and Pacific Group of States (ACP) of the one part, and the European Community and its Member States, of the other part* 2000/483/EC (Cotonou, 23 June 2000) *Official Journal* L 317 of 15.12.2000.

[28] *Interregional Framework Cooperation Agreement between the European Community and its Member States, of the one part, and the Southern Common Market and its Party States, of the other part* (Madrid, 15 December 1995) *Official Journal* L 069, 19/03/1996 pp. 0004–0022 – L 112 29/04/ 1999 p. 0066.

[29] See, e.g., *Canada – Chile Free Trade Agreement* (Canada-Chile) (entered into force 2 June 1997) (1997) 36 ILM 1079; *Canada – Chile Agreement on Environmental Cooperation* (Canada-Chile) (entered into force 2 June 1997) (1997) 36 ILM 1196; *Canada – Chile Agreement on Labor Cooperation* (Canada-Chile) (entered into force 2 June 1997) (1997) 36 ILM 1216. And see *Environmental Cooperation Agreement between the Government of Canada and the Government of the Republic of Costa Rica* (Canada-Costa Rica) (Canada-Costa Rica Agreement on Environmental Cooperation) (adopted 23 April 2001, entered into force 1 November 2002) published in *La Gaceta of Costa Rica*, No 127 (3 July 2002). See also *Free Trade Agreement between Canada and Costa Rica* (Canada-Costa Rica) (adopted 23 April 2001, entered into force 1 November 2002) published in *La Gaceta of Costa*

FUTURE RESEARCH IN TRADE, INVESTMENT AND COMPETITION LAW

For a future sustainable development law research agenda, it is possible to focus on three main areas. First, research can focus specifically on the environment and development issues prominent in recent and upcoming negotiat^l, implementation and dispute settlement of international trade, investment and competition law. Secondly, research can focus on the use of trade, investment and competition-related instruments in international environmental and social law. Thirdly, cross-cutting issues such as intellectual property rights and health, market access, standards and environmental or "fair trade" labelling, public participation in the WTO dispute settlement procedures, and the environmental, health and social impacts of trade agreements ("sustainability impact assessments") also have a strong legal dimension and deserve more research attention.[30]

Below, certain cutting-edge aspects of this agenda are highlighted to provide examples of new research issues in international sustainable trade, investment and competition law.

Sustainable government procurement

Government procurement is an important economic force. According to rough estimates, government procurement spending can account for between 10 and 15 per cent of national GDPs, some hundred billion USD worldwide.[31] There is a global government procurement discipline but the Agreement on Government Procurement is a plurilateral agreement of the WTO and as such only binding on the 29 WTO members that are also parties to the agreement.[32]

Changes in government procurement policies or rules can have a significant impact upon sustainable development and they are in many cases the only way to let preferences for the environment or social concerns take precedence over pure efficiency in an economic decision. For example, a decision that all government bureaucracies will use only recycled paper generates immediate economic opportunities for the recycling industries. However, should such a new law target a country as unsuitable for provision of the paper simply to protect domestic producers, this could violate the principle of non-discrimination in international

---

Rica, No 127 (3 July 2002). And see *United States – Chile Free Trade Agreement* (USA-Chile) (adopted 6 June 2003, entered into force 1 January 2004) <http://www.ustr.gov/new/ fta/chile. htm> (18 May 2004) at Chapters 18 and 19. Finally, see *Agreement Between the United States of America and the Hashemite Kingdom of Jordan on the Establishment of a Free Trade Area* (USA – Jordan) (adopted 24 October 2000, entered into force 17 December 2001). < http://www.jordanusfta. com/> at Chapters 5 and 6. The texts of these treaties are available online: <http://www.sice.oas.org/ TRADEE.ASP>.

[30] See Centre for International Sustainable Development Law, online: <www.cisdl.org> and International Centre for Trade and Sustainable Development (ICTSD), online: <www.ictsd.org>.

[31] See WTO, *Annual Report 1997*, (Geneva: WTO, 1997) at 142.

[32] Negotiations for a binding agreement for all WTO members could begin after the Cancun Ministerial Conference. See WTO, Government Procurement Gateway, online WTO: <http:// www.wto.org/english/tratop_e/ gproc_e/gproc_e.htm#plurilateral>.

trade law. Social and environmental criteria for governmental procurement are under discussion in several fora.[33]

Proponents argue that as taxpayer monies are being spent, more responsibility can be assumed and government procurement policies can be subject to sustainable development rules. Others fear that disguised protectionism, including "sweetheart deals", could be struck under the guise of social or environmental considerations. In another example, some wish to see countries demonstrate observance of basic human rights in order for their industries to be permitted to compete for procurement-related contracts. The recent *Burma* case dealt with such a law in the State of Massachusetts, which banned companies from trading with Myanmar to meet government procurement contracts. The US Supreme Court struck it down as unconstitutional.[34] The EC and Japan asked for consultations in the WTO dispute settlement mechanism, and methods of drafting a valid law are still under discussion. In the WTO, government procurement is part of the Singapore issues of the Doha Development Agenda. The potential for new negotiations has generated increased interest in the issues.

Sustainable trade in agricultural products

Trade in agricultural products has several sustainable development implications. Agricultural production is naturally linked with the environment and for many developing countries, is still a principal source of income. Hence, any change in agricultural trade is very likely to affect sustainable development goals.

The legal debate focuses on issues such as the multi-functional nature of agricultural policies, and whether current levels and mechanisms of support by developed countries for their agricultural industries is legitimate, or protectionist. Other important questions arise in connection with genetically modified organisms (GMOs) and the WTO *Agreement on Sanitary and Phyto-sanitary Measures* (SPS). The EC recently notified a regulation on GMOs, leading to heavy criticism from Canada and the USA, and ultimately to consultations with several countries.[35]

Trade in agricultural products also has strong equity implications. The new EU–APC Agreement attempted to address the issue, but according to development NGOs, still falls short. The treatment of perverse agricultural subsidies which can overstimulate exploitation of fisheries, forests and other potentially renewable resources is also under discussion in the WTO and in regional trade

---

[33] See G. Van Calster, "Green Procurement and the WTO – Shades of Grey" (2002) 11 (3) *RECIEL* 298 and C. McCrudden, "International Economic Law and Human Rights: A Framework for Discussion of the Legality of 'Selective Purchasing' Laws under the WTO Government Procurement Agreement" (1999) 2:1 *J. Int'l Econ. L.* 3.

[34] *Crosby v. National Foreign Trade Council*, 120 S. Ct. 2288 (US Mass., 2000).

[35] *Bridges Weekly Trade News Digest* 6:10 (19 March 2002) and *European Communities – Measures Affecting the Approval and Marketing of Biotech Products – (Request For Consultations by the United States)* WTO Doc. WT/ DS291/1, G/L/627, G/SPS/GEN/397, G/AG/GEN/60, G/TBT/ D/28, 20 May 2003.

agreements. For example, the Doha Development Agenda transfers fishery subsidies to the WTO Committee on Trade and Environment for discussions, but a ban on those harmful subsidies has not yet been won.

Sustainable services liberalization

Services liberalization has been called into question in terms of environmental and social services. On one hand, liberalization of services in certain sectors can stimulate better provision of services for populations, and lead to greater development and technology transfer. However, in other sectors, such as health and education, these may qualify as genuinely governmental and sensitive to national priorities, causing them to be exempted from the General Agreement on Trade in Services (GATS). This area has generated less controversy, however, as the GATS is formulated as a "reverse liberalization" procedure, whereby services must be deliberately listed to be liberalized and distinct categories permit different levels of treatment. Regional trade agreements that have chosen a "positive list" approach may attract higher levels of scholarly and NGO attention.

Other sustainable development questions related to this agenda include the human rights implications of limits on the movement of natural persons, and of migration, specifically in the services sectors. Service liberalization is also seen as a means of slowing or addressing the growing digital divide, particularly in terms of incentives to ensure more global provision of telecommunications services. Other issues include the liberalization of financial and legal services, which, if it led to greater access to credit or justice, could provide sustainable development benefits.

As mentioned above, international economic law intersects with other areas of law, both within and outside the agendas of official trade liberalization negotiations. Seeking solutions and legal principles to guide conflicts or overlaps, within and outside existing international institutions, is an essential aspect of sustainable development law.

Trade and environment in sustainable development law

Trade and environment in fact and in law do need to become mutually supportive, and still need legal analysis or new accords to ensure that conflicts of obligations are avoided. The United Nations Environment Programme has done some excellent work in this area, and the WTO Committee on Trade and Environment has held fruitful sessions with representatives from several MEAs to ensure coherence between the way trade measures are implemented, and the overall goals of the international trading system. Recent WTO negotiations on the intersection between WTO and MEAs have suffered from a very limited mandate. Nevertheless a contribution can still be made to clarify these overlaps.[36]

---

[36] M. Gehring and M.-C. Cordonier Segger, ed., *Sustainable Developments in World Trade Law* (The Hague: Kluwer Law International, 2005, forthcoming).

The integration potential of sustainable development law has not yet been used to its fullest extent. By making integration the determining principle, some of the potential conflicts have a better chance to be resolved. One possibility to evaluate MEAs and their trade measures could be to divide them into agreements with mainly environmental features and those with a clear sustainable development focus. Especially some of the newer MEAs can hardly be described as simply environmental accords. For example, the *UN Convention on Biological Diversity* aims both to protect the environment but also to encourage certain uses and share their benefits equitably. If conceptual sustainable development characteristics count, trade concerns can most likely be properly addressed by the integration features of the MEA itself.

Trade and human rights in sustainable development law

Trade and human rights are framed by an interdependent relationship. Human rights can no longer be ignored in an international trade regime based on the rule of law, and respect for existing international obligations. While several voices suggest that trade restrictions are particularly blunt instruments to use to influence domestic respect for human rights, and also fear the effects on their comparative advantage with regard to core labour rights, many others now argue that violations of basic human rights are deeply related to international trade, and that related measures already have serious positive or negative impacts.[37] These proponents, many of whom are lawyers, suggest that international negotiations leading to rules-based approaches would have a positive effect, helping to limit disguised protectionism and forward legitimate concerns.[38] Some commentators feel that the debate is somewhat ideological, but when it comes to the heart of the intersection between trade and human rights, one can identify several legal challenges.[39] Vibrant discussions are occurring, for example in debates on the enforcement of trade-related intellectual property rights (TRIPs) law in developing countries, and health concerns regarding access to medicines.[40] Similarly,

---

[37] See S. Charnovitz, "The Globalization of Economic Human Rights" [1999] *Brook. J. Int'l L.* 25, 113–124. See also E. Cappuyns, "Linking Labor Standards and Trade Sanctions: An Analysis of their Current Relationship" [1997/98] *Colum. J. Transnat'l L.* 36, 659–686. For a survey of these debates in the Americas regional context, see K. Banks "Civil Society and the North American Agreement on Labour Cooperation", in J. Kirton and V. Maclaren (eds.), *Linking Trade, Environment, and Social Cohesion: NAFTA Experiences, Global Challenges* (Aldershot: Ashgate Press, 2002) and A. Blackett, "Toward Social Regionalism in the Americas" (2002) 23 *Comp. Labor Law and Policy J.* 901.

[38] See C. McCrudden and A. Davies, "A Perspective on Trade and Labour Rights", in F. Francioni, ed., *Environment, Human Rights and International Trade* (Oxford: Hart Publishing, 2001) at 179–197. See also A. Blackett, "Whither Social Clause? Human Rights, Trade Theory and Treaty Interpretation" [1999/2000] *Columbia Human Rights Law Review* 31, 1–80. And see M. Dessing, *The Social Clause and Sustainable Development* (Geneva: ICTSD, 2001). And see, generally, D. Weissbrodt, J. Fitzpatrick and F. Newman, *International Human Rights: Law, Policy and Process* (Cincinnati: Anderson, 2001).

[39] See M. Robinson, "Shaping Globalization: The Role of Human Rights" online: Ethical Globalization Initiative <http://www.eginitiative.org/index.html>.

[40] See the International Health and Sustainable Development Law, Chapter 12 below.

the effect of service liberalization on social services is being viewed from a human rights perspective.[41] Issues of market access for developing countries are increasingly being considered as constituent elements of the right to an adequate standard of living and the right to development.

Sustainable investment law

International investment law is only developing as an international field, but has significant sustainable development implications – both social and environmental. Most international instruments are bilateral, or remain matters of private international law. A recent attempt to conclude a multilateral investment agreement (MAI) in the OECD failed. The legal aspects of sustainable development rights and responsibilities for investors and the best ways to ensure their observance is a particularly relevant subject matter as international investment laws continue to be negotiated, and principles developed through ad hoc tribunals increase in regularity. In addition, formal investment regimes such the WTO Trade-Related Investment Measures (TRIMS) agreement, and the rapidly proliferating bi-lateral investment treaties (BITS), urgently require further examination as to their sustainability implications. Some pioneering legal and policy research considers "more sustainable international investment regimes".[42] These considerations are particularly relevant in the light of recent NAFTA Chapter 11 tribunal decisions. Current examinations of these issues, from a sustainable development perspective, are still embryonic, and much work remains to be done.

Sustainable competition law

An international competition law regime is being developed in this decade, and its implications for sustainable development law require further investigation. As the economic impact of anti-trust and other competition decisions is increasing, the number of countries with competition legislation continues to rise.

Legal rules to ensure fair competition for environmental and social goods and services are just beginning to emerge. For example, one of the most serious social challenges in South African society has been to overcome the racial distribution of economic wealth and activity, based on historical disadvantages. South African competition law requires the competition authorities to consider the impact of a proposed merger on historically disadvantaged people and their ownership.

---

[41] See *Economic, Social and Cultural Rights: Liberalisation of Trade in Services and Human Rights: Report of the High Commissioner*, 25 June 2002, E/CN.4/Sub.2/2002/9. See also Chapter 6 for a discussion of the effects of linking human rights to international economic law. See also, *Statement of the UN Committee on Economic, Social and Cultural Rights to the Third Ministerial Conference of the World Trade Organisation* (Seattle, 30 November to 3 December, 1999). UN. Doc. E.C.12/1999/9.

[42] K. von Moltke, *An International Investment Regime? Implications for Sustainable Development* (Winnipeg: IISD, 2000).

with Markus W. Gehring

Such mechanisms, in South Africa, have gained considerable success and provide a striking example of how competition law can integrate social issues.[43]

The environmental dimension of competition law is somewhat more complicated. It has been argued that competition has nothing to do with the environment.[44] While social consciousness has long been part of economic debates, the environment has only recently gained attention by a broader economic audience.[45] Laws dealing with economic activity have received some criticism but "command and control"-style environmental law has been mainly perceived as separate from economic measures based on providing incentives for industrial actors. There was, perhaps, some degree of overlap in the area of health protection, but the two spheres were otherwise seen as separate. Only during the last ten years has it become more and more apparent that intelligent environmental laws also contain economic measures and vice versa. On the international level, this has led to a body of literature which can be described as the trade and environment debate.[46] The considerations for competition law are analogous to the trade and environment debate. Competition law is neither good nor bad for the environment.[47] It mainly depends on the accompanying environmental rules, and the level of sensitivity of competition authorities in the application of competition law in cases related to environmental law and policy.

There are several areas where strong enforcement of competition law has a very positive effect on environmental goals. For example, with relation to provision of energy, access to a secure localized market can have interesting effects.[48] Existing market conditions in the energy sector have allowed for huge energy conglomerates to emerge. This led the German government not to apply competition law vigorously, but rather to introduce a market share guarantee for small producers of renewable energy (the windmills in northern Germany).[49] The prevailing energy company in the area, Preussen Electra, contested the law

---

[43] D. Lewis, Chairperson, SA Competition Tribunal, "The Role of Public Interest in Merger Evaluation", online: SACT <http://www.comptrib.co.za/Publications/Speeches/ICN%20Naples.htm>.

[44] The authors thank Russell Pittman for his guidance and advice with regard to several major concerns in this area.

[45] For an overview of history see R.N. Stavins, ed., *Economics of the Environment*, 4th edn. (New York: W.W. Norton & Company, 2000).

[46] D. Esty, *Greening the GATT: Trade, Environment and the Future* (Washington DC: Institute for International Economics, 1994).

[47] On trade and environment see H. Nordström & S. Vaughan, *Trade and Environment*, WTO *Special Study 4* (Geneva: WTO, 1999) at 13.

[48] P.D. Cameron, *Competition in Energy Markets: Law and Regulation in the European Union* (Oxford: Oxford University Press, 2002); W. Jaeger, *Regulierter Wettbewerb in der Energiewirtschaft* (Baden-Baden: Nomas, 2002) and G. Hermes, *Staatliche Infrastrukturverantwortung: rechtliche Grundstrukturen netzgebundener Transport- und Übertragungssysteme zwischen Daseinsvorsorge und Wettbewerbsregulierung am Beispiel der leitungsgebundenen Energieversorgung in Europa* (Tuebingen: Mohr Siebeck, 1998).

[49] For opinion that the law violates EU competition rules see K. Gent, "Deutsches Stromeinspeisungsgesetz und Europäisches Wettbewerbsrecht" [1999] *Energiewirtschaftliche Tagesfragen – Zeitschrift für die Elektrizitäts- und Gasversorgung* 854–858.

as violating EU competition and subsidies provision.[50] The ECJ was ultimately called upon to decide, and proceeded to rule that while the law violated these provisions, it was doing so for the legitimate goal of protecting the environment.[51] Competition law can also have harmful effects. For example, in the area of waste management, statutory obligations to enter into agreements with the producing industry are used to ensure "cradle-to-grave" product responsibility. However, these could also raise competition concerns.[52] In another example, competition law problems could emerge from certain types of environmental labelling requirements, as well.[53] Finally, the application of strict interpretations of competition law to environmental information and communication could have an impact,[54] and would be worthy of further research.

At the area of integrated sustainable development law related to competition, further aspects of a future legal research agenda emerge. The sustainable development implications of monopolies, such as the international vitamins cartel, deserve increased scrutiny. Intellectual property rights' regimes can also include certain competition rules. The impact of incomplete competition when IPRs are guaranteed is of particular interest in TRIPS and health policy debates. Sustainable development aspects of bilateral cooperation agreements (and future multilateral agreements) concerning competition policy, in particular the establishment and strengthening of anti-trust authorities, require further examination.

The WTO is currently consulting as to the potential for negotiations on international anti-trust rules. Legal research and analysis in this area has barely scratched the surface of the agenda.

CONCLUSIONS

In this chapter, there is no attempt to provide a comprehensive overview of a future legal research agenda for more sustainable international trade, investment and competition law. Rather, the chapter signals certain key issues, seeking to give a flavour for the debate including the treaties, international institutions and in some cases, regional and even present domestic legal implications.

---

[50] Case C-379/88 *PreussenElektra AG v. Schleswag AG*, ECR I–2099 [2002] Celex No. 698J0379, 13 March 2001.

[51] In particular, the ECJ ruled that "[t]he use of renewable energy sources for producing electricity, which a statute such as the amended Stromeinspeisungsgesetz is intended to promote, is useful for protecting the environment in so far as it contributes to the reduction in emissions of greenhouse gases which are amongst the main causes of climate change which the European Community and its Member States have pledged to combat." *Ibid.* at para. 73.

[52] G. Posser, *Grundfragen des Abfallrechts: Abgrenzung von Produkt/Abfall und Verwertung/ Beseitigung* (München: Beck, 2001).

[53] T. Klindt, "Die Umweltzeichen 'Blauer Engel' und 'Europäische Blume' zwischen produktbezogenem Umweltschutz und Wettbewerbsrecht" [1998] *Betriebsberater* 545.

[54] I. Roth, *Umweltbezogene Unternehmenskommunikation im deutschen und europäischen Wettbewerbsrecht* (Frankfurt/Main: Lang, 2000).

There are strong indications that a sustainable development law approach to trade law can be helpful in overcoming some of the trade and environment and trade and development deadlocks. Different legal economic instruments, existing or in the process of negotiation, bear potential to integrate social and environmental considerations to varying degrees, or simply to support and take into account existing legal obligations in the other fields. In the areas of human rights and environment laws, legal economic measures and provisions are being increasingly used as incentives, or as protection against "free riders" and "backsliding", to the benefit of the regimes. As such, much further investigation is necessary, and it can be concluded that sustainable trade, investment and competition law is a fascinating new area of legal study, with significant potential as an intervention point to encourage sustainable development.

10

Sustainable International Natural Resources Law

with CAROLYN DEERE[1]

To protect and manage the natural resource base of economic and social development is a fundamental priority for sustainable development, especially human livelihoods. Put simply, life depends on natural resources. As noted at the recent *World Summit on Sustainable Development*, held in Johannesburg 2002:

"Human activities are having an increasing impact on the integrity of ecosystems that provide essential resources and services for human well-being and economic activities. Managing the natural resources base in a sustainable and integrated manner is essential for sustainable development. In this regard, to reverse the current trend in natural resource degradation as soon as possible, it is necessary to implement strategies which should include targets adopted at the national and, where appropriate, regional levels to protect ecosystems and to achieve integrated management of land, water and living resources, while strengthening regional, national and local capacities."[2]

Despite their importance, the world's natural resources – unlike the climate or biodiversity – escape the reach of any single, overarching international legal framework. Instead, they are covered by a patchwork of different rules. These include a range of sector- and resource-specific laws at the global, regional and national level. In addition to legal instruments, governments, non-governmental organizations (NGOs) and businesses have expanded the corpus of guidelines, best practices, principles and voluntary codes of conduct related to the management of natural resources. The scope of these hard and soft law efforts is vast.[3] They address both renewable (fisheries, oceans, marine resources and seas, freshwater resources, soils and desertification, forests, plant biodiversity, wetlands) and non-renewable resource issues (mineral and energy resources, and

---

[1] Carolyn Deere, M.A. (Johns Hopkins University, SAIS), B. Econ (Hons I) (Sydney) is Lead Research Fellow for Sustainable Natural Resources Law at the CISDL. She is currently also a researcher at the Global Economic Governance Programme at Oxford University. She was formerly the Assistant Director, Global Inclusion, at the Rockefeller Foundation in New York, USA and is the Founder of the Funders Network on Trade and Globalization and Intellectual Property Watch.

[2] *Johannesburg Plan of Implementation* Report of the *World Summit on Sustainable Development*, Johannesburg, South Africa, 4 Sept. 2002, UN Doc. A/CONF.199/L.1. www.un.org/esa/sustdev/documents/WSSD_P01_PD/English/P01 Toc.htm>.

[3] Priority areas of natural resources law include: laws related to fresh water, oceans, seas, islands and coastal areas – especially fisheries; agriculture and soils; plant biodiversity; wetlands; deserts and drylands; forestry; energy resources and mining and minerals development. These issues were highlighted in the JPOI, *ibid.*, at Chapter IV.

world heritage sites).[4] Given the complexity of issues specific to each particular resource, this chapter focuses its attention primarily on cross-cutting issues and on the international level.

While the challenges and issues vary from sector to sector, certain general observations can be made about laws concerning natural resources. Natural resources laws commonly include provisions to regulate: the distribution and ownership of natural resources among nations or groups within them; access to common lands and resources; and the allocation of rights to natural resource use. Many laws contain provisions on dispute resolution, enforcement, sustainable management of natural resources, and the joint financing of conservation. Natural resources laws also generally assert the need to protect and manage the natural resource base of economic and social development and to balance economic, social and environmental objectives. Given that many natural resources can be considered "global public goods" and the impacts of their use extend across national borders, most international agreements emphasize the importance of international cooperation.

This chapter offers a forward-looking legal research agenda for the next decade using an international sustainable development law (SDL) approach – one that works to integrate economic, social (including human rights and cultural), and environmental dynamics and laws. This sustainable development law agenda focuses on development and implementation of laws relevant to natural resources – targeting accountability as a thematic focus for which lawyers are particularly well positioned. In developing such an agenda, this chapter does not attempt to tackle the myriad natural resource issues that warrant analysis nor the spectrum of all worthy legal questions. Rather, the emphasis is on critical gaps in analysis and effort which escape attention, despite urgent need, and which the legal community has a particular comparative advantage or niche to address.

To set the context, this chapter begins by reviewing why natural resources law and legal analysis is important *now*, highlighting the emphasis on natural resources at the 2002 *World Summit on Sustainable Development* (WSSD), the

---

[4] Examples include the *United Nations Convention on the Law of the Sea*, 10 Dec. 1982, UN Doc. A/CONF.62/122 21 ILM 1245 (entered into force 16 Nov. 1994) [hereinafter UNCLOS], *Agreement for the Implementation of the Provisions of the UN Convention on the Law of the Sea of 10 December 1982 relating to the Conservation and Management of Straddling Fish Stocks and Highly Migratory Fish Stocks*, 4 Aug. 1995, UN Doc A/CONF.164/38 (1995) 34 ILM 1542 [hereinafter *Straddling Stocks Agreement*], *Convention on Wetlands of International Importance, Especially as Waterfowl Habitat*, 2 Feb. 1971, TIAS No. 11, 084, 996 UNTS 245 [hereinafter *Ramsar Convention*], *Convention to Combat Desertification in Those Countries Experiencing Serious Drought and/or Desertification, particularly in Africa*, 17 June 1994, 33 ILM 1328 [hereinafter *Desertification Convention*], drafts of Freshwater and Forest Conventions, and various international commodity agreements (e.g., the international copper agreement and OPEC). Regional and resource specific environmental agreements include the *International Convention for the Conservation of Atlantic Tunas*, 14 May 1966, 20 U.S.T. 2887, 673 UNTS 63 [hereinafter *Atlantic Tuna Convention*], the Commission on the Conservation of Southern Bluefin Tuna (CCSBT), the Commission for the Conservation of Antarctic Marine Living Resources (CCAMLR); and EU-West Africa fisheries agreements.

constraints to implementation of natural resources law and persistent trends of natural resource degradation. Then, the foundations for the proposed sustainable development law research agenda are further elaborated, by emphasizing the intersection of economics, society and the environment and the need to consider, in an integrated fashion, the dynamics and laws in these three realms. In the final part, four key areas are proposed for the attention, analysis and action of the legal research community.

WHY IS NATURAL RESOURCES LAW IMPORTANT NOW?

The area of natural resources law is important *now* for several reasons. First, the WSSD provided an agenda for action that features many commitments and targets specific to natural resources (see Table 10.1). The continuing, rapid degradation, often irreversible, of the world's renewable and non-renewable natural resource base has dire social and economic consequences for many countries, and particularly the most vulnerable or impoverished communities within them. This persistent trend serves as a timely reminder that more effort is required on all fronts.

Table 10.1

Natural Resource	WSSD Commitments
Energy	• Increase eco-efficiency, with financial support for capacity building, technology transfer and exchange of technology with developing countries and countries with economies in transition; • promote the internalization of environmental costs and the use of economic instruments; • establish domestic programmes for energy efficiency; • accelerate the development, dissemination and deployment of affordable and cleaner energy efficiency and energy conservation technologies; • recommend that international financial institutions and other agencies' policies support countries to establish policy and regulatory frameworks that create a level playing field; • support efforts to improve the functioning, transparency and information about energy markets with respect to both supply and demand; • strengthen and facilitate, as appropriate, regional cooperation arrangements for promoting cross-border energy trade; • implement transport strategies for sustainable development; and • promote investment and partnerships for the development of sustainable, energy efficient multi-modal transportation systems.
Biodiversity	• achieve by 2010 a significant reduction in the current rate of biodiversity loss;

(*Continued*)

Table 10.1 (Continued)

Natural Resource	WSSD Commitments
	• negotiate an international regime to promote and safeguard the fair and equitable sharing of benefits arising from the utilization of genetic resources.
Mining	• support efforts to address the environmental, economic, health and social impacts of mining, minerals and metals and calls for fostering sustainable mining practices.
Soils and Desertification	• calls on the GEF to designate land degradation as a focal area of GEF and to consider making GEF a financial mechanism for the CCD.
Water	• halve the proportion of people without access to sanitation by 2015 (linked to the Millennium Declaration Goal to halve the proportion without access to safe drinking water by 2015); • mobilize international and domestic financial resources, transfer technology, promote best practices and support capacity building; • promote and provide new and additional financial resources and innovative technologies to implement Chapter 18 of Agenda 21; • develop integrated water resource management and water efficiency plans by 2005.
Oceans/ Fisheries	• maintain or restore depleted fish stocks, where possible, to maximum sustainable yield levels not later than 2015; • eliminate subsidies contributing to illegal, unreported and unregulated fishing and to over-capacity; • implement the Ramsar Convention; • establish a regular process under the UN for global reporting and assessment for the state of the marine environment by 2004; • establish a representative network of marine protected areas by 2012; • undertake initiatives by 2004 to implement the Global Programme of Action for the protection of the Marine Environment from Land Based Sources.
Air	• improve access by developing countries to alternatives to ozone-depleting substances by 2010.
Forests	• take immediate action on domestic forest law enforcement and illegal international trade in forest production.
Consumption	• development of production and consumption policies using where appropriate, science based approaches such as life-cycle analysis, and for the development and adoption, on a voluntary basis, consumer information tools to provide information relating to sustainable consumption and production.

Secondly, the WSSD emphasized the importance of international cooperation and the urgent need for more focused engagement by the international legal research community. In particular, the WSSD Declaration and Plan of Implementation placed natural resources management clearly on the international agenda. Indeed, heads of state in Johannesburg recognized that among other priorities, "...managing the natural resource base for economic and social development are overarching objectives of and essential requirements for sustainable development." In many areas, sound laws exist on paper to manage these resources, but implementation, including compliance, enforcement and monitoring, is sadly lacking. While existing natural resources laws have played a crucial role in identifying environmental challenges, setting out steps for mitigation, and articulating the collective and individual duties of governments to act, the international community will rely on input from the legal research community, amongst others, to address the challenges for implementation. These challenges, it is suggested, include:

- Inadequate political will and financial commitments to promote compliance and enforcement (particularly with respect to non-Parties of agreements);
- Technical constraints due to inadequate data and incomplete understanding of the complex interactions of ecological, political and social systems that impact natural resources;
- Confusion about the plethora of overlapping agreements, fora and obligations, and the compatibility of the objectives of economic and environmental legal regimes;
- Lack of appropriate means for the resolution of natural resource-related disputes; and
- Seemingly endless negotiations on technical issues in lieu of concrete progress on the ground.

Not all of these are challenges can be addressed by the legal community alone. However, the legal community has much to offer in several significant areas – including interpretation of laws, clarifications of obligations, new thinking on dispute resolution, and creative, cost-effective legal approaches to compliance, monitoring and enforcement (particularly for developing countries with limited budgets).

Thirdly, a series of "neglected" challenges – such as the six discussed below – can be brought into the mainstream of legal analysis. A vanguard of legal groups and other NGOs have led the way with innovative legal advocacy, research and action.[5] Yet in much of the world's mainstream legal scholarship and teaching, analysis of these issues remains marginal. Future legal research must address this deficit.

---

[5] The Center for International Environmental Law <www.ciel.org>, the Foundation for International Environmental Law and Development <www.field.org>, EarthJustice <www.earthjustice.org> and EarthRights International <www.earthrights.org> are some of the NGOs that have pioneered the field of advocacy and action on international natural resource issues. The Centre for International Sustainable Development Law <www.cisdl.org> is not an advocacy organization, but is working to advance the cutting edge of sustainable development law through research, legal advice and capacity building.

Legal approaches to improving the credibility of scientific evidence

The provision of scientific evidence and analysis – vital to the lawmaking process – has often become a profit-driven activity. Efforts to improve compliance with principles regarding conflict of interest and funding disclosure among scientists in academia, research foundations and in the private sector is vital if laws and policies are to maintain the public's confidence.[6]

The relationship between human rights violations and natural resource use

The human rights community and media have drawn increasing attention to human rights violations and civil conflict that can accompany natural resource use. Many hundreds of tense, local stand-offs exist – particularly in the minerals and forestry sectors – where local communities raise a range of concerns about the extraction activities of companies on the lands upon which they rely for their livelihoods. Common complaints related to problems of erosion, increased vulnerability to natural disasters, and contamination of groundwater and rivers. A growing movement of NGOs focused on the intersection of human rights and environment also calls for greater attention to the protection of natural resource companies by national military or other security forces.[7]

Corporate responsibility and accountability

The need for greater corporate responsibility and accountability has gained increasing recognition in international policymaking, including in the WSSD itself. Large corporations form incredibly powerful and influential forces. In many areas of natural resource exploitation and management, they are the only lawmakers, and enforcers, operating in ways that enable them to control resource sectors and dominate markets. Some companies bring to developing

---

[6] The *Journal of Philosophy, Science and Law* regularly includes articles addressing the intersection of the scientific community, public policy and the law, including many articles relevant to the areas of human health, environment and social policy. A critical review of the implementation of environmental assessments by Sierra Club Canada highlights a range of problems associated with the challenge of gathering and reviewing scientific evidence on natural resource issues. See A. Nikiforuk, *The Nasty Game: The Failure of Environmental Assessment in Canada* (Canada: Sierra Club, 1997). The Center for Science and the Public Interest <www.cspinet.org> also provides ongoing analysis targeting policymakers of critical issues related to science and public regulation in natural resources, health, consumer safety, and the environment.

[7] Examples include: The Centre for Human Rights and Environment (CEDHA) in Argentina; the new Economic, Social and Cultural Rights Network; Project Underground – an NGO which challenges the conduct of resource extraction companies, particularly mining companies, whose activities threaten the human rights of indigenous communities. Their website contains numerous reports detailing links between natural resource companies and security forces. Also, Human Rights Watch – an international human rights organization – has recently expanded the scope of its work to include consideration of the connections between human rights abuse and natural resource use, see <www.hrw.org>. In the human rights community, public campaigning to restrict the marketing of "blood" diamonds – where profits are used to finance civil wars – has generated new industry-wide standards for the diamond sector, see <www.conflictdiamonds.ca>.

countries higher corporate social and environmental standards than local companies, but they also bring the power to negotiate the terms of their investment in the country – sometimes putting them at odds with the interests of local communities. As the legal community helps promulgate voluntary principles, standards and codes, there is also a need to address directly the power of the corporate sector in the natural resources arena – harnessing it for good where possible and ensuring adequate regulation where potential damage looms.[8]

Consumption law and policy

Since before the Earth Summit, the question of how to change unsustainable patterns of consumption has been among the most contentious in the international arena. There is no doubt that developed countries must take the lead in formulating more sustainable approaches to consumption. The reality, however, is that, while their record of success is steadily improving, voluntary and mandatory initiatives to promote sustainable consumption of the world's minerals, oil, gas and other energy resources, forests and fisheries remain the exception rather than the rule.[9] Further legal research in this area could focus on the lessons learned in the use of current instruments particularly at the intersections of law economics, science and technology.

Where powerful economic interests are absent

The problems that can emerge from the absence of powerful international economic interests warrant attention from lawmakers. The inter-related challenges of desertification and sustainable livelihoods in dryland areas provide a case in point. Both issues suffer overwhelming neglect by the international community and are prime candidates for assistance from the legal community in terms of ways to ensure the delivery of capacity building, technical assistance, and financial aid (promised, for example, by the UN *Convention to Combat Desertification*), even in instances where the economic or political stakes for the international community, especially developed countries, appear low.[10]

---

[8] See *e.g.* M.-C. Cordonier Segger "Sustainability and Corporate Accountability Regimes: Implementing the Johannesburg Summit Agenda" (2003) 12 *RECIEL* 295.

[9] A 10-Year Programme of Action on Promoting Sustainable Consumption Patterns was recently approved at the WSSD. This programme is being led by the United Nations Environment Programme <www.unep.org>, the Organization of Economic Cooperation and Development <www.oecd.org> and the International Trade Center <www.itc.org> have each conducted considerable research evaluating the effectiveness and economic viability of environmental and social labelling schemes as ways to promote more sustainable consumption and production.

[10] Desertification issues are generally discussed under the auspices of the *Desertification Convention* <www.unccd.int>, and through partnerships such as the Drylands Development Centre's Global Drylands Imperative <www.undp.org/dpa/frontpagearchive/2002/february/25feb02/>.

The challenge of State non-cooperation

Three kinds of behaviour warrant particular concern in the natural resources field. First, corruption is a concern.[11] Secondly, cases of non-compliance of a number of States parties to international agreements (particularly in terms of provision of capacity building and financial support) causes consternation.[12] Thirdly, there must be ways to address the impacts of non-Party actions, when these threaten the very goals of a treaty that seeks to manage global public goods.[13]

Each of these six challenges provides an example of how the failure to address underlying tensions can frustrate both international negotiations or progress with implementation. Even where these issues are acknowledged as important, they tend to lack concerted attention and focused resources by governments or international agencies. Instead, they are often left to "languish" in the "too hard" basket – only to receive a fleeting nod of acknowledgement at intergovernmental conferences. At best, allusions to these problems are usually discretely hidden between the lines of upbeat preambles, declarations and legal texts. On the one hand, this tendency to "paper over" difficult points is sometimes necessary to make any progress at all in international meetings. On the other hand, the problems often simply re-emerge later to frustrate the implementation and monitoring of law and policy.

LAW AND INTEGRATION: PEOPLE, PLANET AND PROSPERITY

Past efforts to promote conservation and sustainable use of natural resources instruct us that law alone is not enough. Too often, legal scholars and advocates focus on interpreting and evaluating laws without sufficient consideration of the broader economic framework or the real-world social and political dynamics that lie at the heart of natural resource issues.

First, the legal community has much work to do, to systematically incorporate the root causes of natural resource degradation into international legal research. Economic policies and dynamics are key drivers impacting both the pace of

---

[11] Struggles over natural resources often lie at the heart of corruption and civil strife. NGOs like Global Witness have documented the clandestine ties between large resource companies and resource traders, smugglers, local officials, arms dealers and mercenary companies. The Global Policy Forum website contains a range of documents with respect to corruption, conflict and natural resources (including oil and natural gas, water, timber, minerals). See online: <http://www. globalpolicy.org/security/docs/minindx.htm>.

[12] See "Making International Environmental Law Work: Improving Compliance and Resolving Disputes" in D. Hunter, J. Salzman, & D. Zaelke, *International Environmental Law and Policy* (New York: Foundation Press, 1998). For an example of recommendations for change see E. Dannenmeier and I. Cohen. "Promoting Meaningful Compliance with Climate Change Commitments" (Prepared for the Pew Center on Global Climate Change, 2000).

[13] The recent FAO *Agreement on Illegal, Unreported and Unregulated Fishing*, for example, is one recent step in the right direction. See C. de Fontaubert, *Achieving Sustainable Fisheries: Implementing the New International Regime* (Gland: IUCN, 2003).

natural resource use and the effectiveness of laws. The world's macro-economic policies – on trade, investment, exchange rate, interest rates, developing country debt – have a critical influence on prices and incentives for natural resources. The terms of international debt relief and trends in the world's commodity markets, for example, are two examples of dynamics that can have a crucial influence on the pace and pattern of natural resource extraction in developing countries.[14]

Where countries find themselves under intense pressure for debt servicing, the urge to generate foreign exchange through natural resource extraction drives overexploitation. Similarly, where governments lack the financing for effective management or tenure controls, the expansion of trade through liberalization policies can exacerbate overuse of resources, or result in the granting of concessions at low prices. International trade rules – such as rules to limit subsidies and tariffs – could also serve as a tool to promote more sustainable natural resource use.[15] In addition, poverty levels and income inequality are a major factor affecting the pace of natural resource use.[16] Most importantly, macro-economic policies incorporate a series of legal obligations with which governments must comply.[17] The legal obligations can either support sustainable management of natural resources, or do the opposite, and policies are only just beginning to be set in place to address this situation.[18] These topics need to be placed at the centre of

[14] See *e.g.* C. Tan, "Tackling the Commodity Price Crisis Should be WSSD's Priority" (online article on the Third World Network at www.twnside.org.sg/title/jb14.htm). See also P. Collier. "The Market for Civil War" *Foreign Policy* (May–June 2003). Collier argues that poverty and trade in natural resources, not historic ethnic tensions, are often the real culprits of civil wars.

[15] The stronger enforcement of trade rules on subsidies could, for example, force countries to reduce perverse government subsidies that contribute to environmental degradation (i.e. as subsidies to the fishing industry contribute to the overcapacity of fishing fleets and thus to overexploitation of fisheries). C. Deere, *Net Gains: International Trade, Sustainable Development and Fisheries* (Washington: IUCN, 1999). The elimination of tariff escalation could enable countries to export higher-value added processed natural resource products with the potential to reduce the amount of natural resource exploitation. See *e.g.* M. Gehring, "Sustainable International Trade, Investment and Competition Law", Chapter 9 in this volume. Policies with respect to foreign direct investment, competition and privatization all impact on the effectiveness of laws, availability of government resources for natural resource management and conservation purposes, resources, policy constraints/options.

[16] See *e.g.* the Overseas Development Institute Rural Policy and the Environment Group website on natural resources <http://www.odi.org.uk/RPEG/NR.html>. The website contains a series of working papers on intersections between various aspects of poverty, sustainable livelihoods and natural resources management in different sectors and countries.

[17] In developing countries, for example, project and sectoral loans, policy advice and debt relief arrangements from international financial institutions (such as the World Bank and IMF) and bilateral donors all involve some form of legal obligation. See G.K. Helleiner, "Developing Countries in Global Economic Governance and Negotiation Process", in D. Nayyar, ed., *The New Role and Functions for the United Nations and the Bretton Woods Institutions* (Tokyo: World Institute for Development Economics Research, University of the United Nations, 2000).

[18] The World Bank has, for example, put in place policies and monitoring mechanisms to ensure that social and environmental effects are considered in their loan agreements and other programmes. These policies are complemented by an Inspection Panel to promote accountability. See World Bank <www.worldbank.org>. For ongoing critical appraisals of the effectiveness and implementation of these policies see the Bank Information Centre <www.bicusa.org>. One example is L. Udall, *The World Bank Inspection Panel: A Three Year Review* (Washington: BIC, 1997). More generally, see

the purview of lawyers interested in natural resources. These obligations often determine the economic incentives and policy framework for natural resource use.

Secondly, in the natural resources arena, economic and social tensions frequently arise where different stakeholders have different priorities and interests with respect to the conservation, access, and use of particular resources. Indeed, natural resources generate significant economic returns to governments, local communities and to the private sector. For governments, natural resources are a source of export earnings, national income, tax revenue and employment generation. Some natural resources also have high strategic value (e.g., oil and minerals to meet security, energy and industrial manufacturing needs). And, in countries with abundant natural resources, officials who control access to natural resources often occupy positions of great power and influence (and at worst are susceptible to corruption).[19]

For local communities, natural resources can be a central source of income, food security and livelihoods, particularly in developing countries. National economic and political debates over issues such as land rights and land reforms thus have significant influence over natural resources. Similarly, cultural and ethical norms also complicate the task for lawyers. Traditional communities – on whose land significant natural resources reside – often consider themselves stewards of natural resources with spiritual and cultural responsibilities related to their use.[20] Tensions between different value-systems add to the complexity resulting from the range of possible short- and long-term end-uses for natural resources.

Finally, many laws reinforce rather than address the disconnection between economic, social and environmental dynamics and laws relevant to sustainable development. It is not enough, for example, that international "economic" or "environmental" treaties incorporate deceptively simple assurances that their provisions will not contradict each other. An integrated approach is needed, which actually considers and *responds* to intersecting issues. This will be vital to ensure sustainable management and protection of natural resources.

IMPROVING IMPLEMENTATION THROUGH ACCOUNTABILITY: A RESEARCH AGENDA FOR NATURAL RESOURCES LAW

Using a sustainable development law approach, this section proposes a natural resources law research agenda that focuses principally on improving *implementation* of laws through increased *accountability*.

J. Fox & L. Brown, *The Struggle for Accountability: The World Bank, NGOs, and Grassroots Movements* (Cambridge, Mass: MIT Press, 1998). The International Development Law Organization trains developing country lawyers in sustainable development law, so that they can also take these issues into account from their national interests when negotiating agreements with international economic institutions or complying with their obligations <www.idlo.int>.

[19] Tan, *supra* note 14. Collier, *supra* note 14.

[20] The journal *Cultural Survival* presents an ongoing series of articles on related topics <www.culturalsurvival.org>.

Legal analysis is needed to help advance many aspects of law relevant to natural resources. In several areas, studies are already underway. Some currently popular areas for investigation include studies of the implications of the precautionary principle in different areas of natural resources management, multi-stakeholder processes and instruments,[21] impact assessment, and ways to cost-effectively implement international laws on a domestic level (from marine resources to forestry and mining). In addition, the implementation of the natural resources priorities set forth by the WSSD will demand considerable input from the legal community (see Table 10.1). The focus of this sustainable development law research agenda is, however, to go beyond what is already on the table to draw together a creative, forward-looking agenda.[22]

Accountability should become a core element of a sustainable development law research agenda for natural resources. The struggle to improve accountability lies at the heart of international efforts for more effective implementation. Accountability is about compliance by State, citizens and private sector with the many rights, privileges, obligations, and duties they acquire voluntarily and through binding agreements. Accountability also requires transparency (about evidence, successes, failure), provision of explanations in times of failures, and commitments to improve performance where it has not fulfilled expectations. The challenge for managing the links between "people, planet and prosperity" is not so much to make new agreements but to hold groups accountable to existing ones. Improved accountability requires direct engagement with the many tensions and competing interests at stake. The call to accountability is a call for holding groups to account for derogation of social duties, moral responsibilities, and legal obligations and to reward them for constructive behaviour. The legal community is well-positioned to help make lasting improvements in the accountability of four core groups critical to sustainable development: business, citizens, government and scientists.

In terms of methodology, legal analysts have the opportunity to realize a more vibrant engagement in collaborative and participatory research, working more closely with policy analysts, economists, and sociologists. How can the work of leading scholars and analysts be linked more closely with efforts on the ground to change behaviour? What are the opportunities for different communities working on natural resource conservation and management to coalesce more effectively around analysis and advocacy?

---

[21] Multi-stakeholder processes are an important procedural element in sustainable development law. Potential research questions for this area include: What kinds of legal frameworks or processes best draw together the multiple stakeholders to deliberate upon appropriate natural resource management strategies and laws? What kinds of instruments can be developed to ensure that the voices of local communities, minority groups, and the poor are adequately heard in existing and future efforts to create new ground rules for corporations? How can the human rights, peace, indigenous peoples, labour rights and environmental communities share lessons?

[22] An overview of the current international environmental law agenda, with extensive consideration of economic, human rights, social and corporate issues, is provided by Hunter *et al.*, *supra* note 12.

In the discussion below, it is argued that the focus of scholarship should not be simply the production of legal journal articles, but legal briefs for vulnerable communities, information useful to advocacy campaigns, legal monitoring of environmental compliance, contributions to court proceedings, and case studies presented in a form that is accessible to policymakers and to local community organizations.

Business

The WSSD's call for "active promotion of corporate responsibility and account-ability, based on the Rio Principles" creates an important invitation to the legal community to bring forth specific expertise and analysis.

In recent years, NGOs, government and environmentally-aware business groups have initiated many important efforts to link business decision-making to sustainable development goals. Moreover, there is a growing body of research reviewing the objectives, track record and value of different approaches to corporate responsibility from voluntary principles, guidelines and codes of conduct that exist for many products and sectors and for different goals (including human rights, labour rights, environmental protection, and conflict prevention).[23]

The JPOI urged further progress, calling on businesses in the financial sector to incorporate sustainable development considerations into their decision-making processes. Taking up this mandate, the legal community can help to refine new legal approaches and principles that promote more sustainable practices among both individual and institutional investors (public and private) in the extraction, use and processing of natural resource extraction. Cutting edge issues for both theoretical and applied legal analysis include security commission disclosure requirements, government procurement procedures, and extending the responsi-bility of corporations to shareholders beyond fiduciary criteria. The legal com-munity may also wish to forge ahead, looking beyond the priorities set by the JPOI, to fill vital gaps of analysis and action in the following areas:

- How to improve the effectiveness and feasibility of initiatives to hold com-panies (from the North and the South) legally liable, including in their home countries and abroad, for investment decisions in natural resources;[24]
- What is the potential for the use of competition and anti-trust law to regulate the manner in which monopolies can influence patterns of natural resource extraction and use? (Particular issues worthy of investigation include: trends

---

[23] See e.g. Cordonier Segger, *supra* note 8.

[24] EarthRights International, for example, pursues litigation to provide remedies for earth rights abuses around the world. Working in partnership with other legal organizations and private lawyers, they are litigating several cases on behalf of victims of earth rights abuses and have filed *amicus curiae* ("friend of the court") briefs in several other cases. They seek to apply domestic and international law to hold corporations and others accountable for their actions, often using the *Alien Tort Claims Act (ATCA)*, which allows lawsuits in federal courts for violations of international law. EarthRights International's website contains summaries of recent ATCA cases against corporate defendants <www.earthrights.org>. See e.g. R.L. Herz, "Litigating Environmental Abuses Under the Alien Tort Claims Act: A Practical Assessment" (2000) 40 *Va. J. Int'l L.* 545.

in the vertical and horizontal integration of large natural resource companies; the impact of these companies on domestic natural resource policies and legislation; and options for regulating large public subsidies for activities that influence unsustainable patterns of natural resource use);

- How can legal principles and guidelines be used to regulate the role of multinational corporations in international treaty-making processes with respect to the management and use of natural resources?; and
- What are the options for an improved international regulatory framework for corporations? How should these be linked to international treaties which grant investor rights, and provide for dispute settlement?

Citizenry

The JPOI encourages and promotes the development of a 10-year framework for programmes supporting regional and national efforts to accelerate the shift towards sustainable consumption and production (see Table 10.1). This focus on the citizen as consumer is welcome. Citizens can be a vital instrument for reducing over-consumption, and promoting compliance with and implementation of natural resources law. Applied legal analysis and research has an important future role to define this agenda.

In recent years, NGOs, government agencies and the private sector have launched several initiatives to engage consumers in sustainability efforts. Examples include guidelines, principles, initiatives and national laws for certification and labelling of "sustainable" products and harvesting, extraction or production processes. Other examples include new rules on advertising rules and the use of boycotts as instruments for public awareness raising. In general, their common feature is to increase the information available to citizens hoping that they will exercise their purchasing power as a "vote" in the marketplace for either more sustainably produced products by: a) refraining from buying certain products; or b) selectively buying products.

The legal community can contribute to this area by exploring:

- What are the most effective ways to mitigate the regulatory burden on developing countries and low-incomes groups of certification processes?;
- What are the legal practicalities and associated costs and benefits of making some voluntary certification efforts mandatory?; and
- What are the prospects for legally-binding production and consumption targets in key areas?

Government

Governments play a key role in setting the frameworks for access to, and management of, natural resources. Transparency and accountability in government decision-making related to natural resources demands increased attention by legal researchers.

In terms of transparency, legal analysts can contribute to the promulgation of guidelines on public access to environmental information, decision-making as well as judicial and administrative proceedings. While considerable analysis of these issues takes place in developed countries, too little attention has been focused on promoting appropriate domestic laws in developing countries, and these may not be the same laws.

A much understudied aspect of transparency is the relationship between governments, armed groups, private companies and investors:

- What are the processes by which governments engage in the negotiation and granting of rights of access to natural resources, warrants for exploration, and granting of concessions, and how can these be improved?
- What are the legal guidelines in various countries for negotiating access to and use of natural resources, can cases of abuse and best practices be documented, can government misconduct be exposed, generating recommendations for reforms or legal action where appropriate?

Secondly, a range of government activities and laws – both in the developing and developed countries – frustrate the implementation of natural resources law. Beyond helping to articulate the positive duty of the governments to act, the legal research community can also help improve the accountability of governments by clarifying the duty of governments to abstain from measures that generate perverse economic incentives:

- What are the practical legal and economic solutions that will help governments to phase out subsidies that perversely promote overexploitation of natural resources and economic distortions in the fisheries, forests, energy and agriculture sectors?
- How can intergovernmental financial institutions (such as the World Bank and the IMF) and government export credit agencies improve evaluation and provision of their advice and loans? The goal of such analysis would be to reduce the incidence of policy advice, loan and project agreements, or export guarantees from these agencies which results in perverse economic incentives in terms of the pace of natural resource exploitation and the government support provided to natural resource management efforts? (A case study approach might also provide some insights about the way legal obligations embedded in policy and project loans and grants shape national approaches to natural resources and the differential social impacts that can result.)[25]

---

[25] Guidance on some of these issues, at least with regard to the environment-economic nexus, is provided by A. Kiss, D. Shelton & K. Ishibashi, *Economic Globalization and Compliance with International Environmental Agreements* (The Hague: Kluwer Law International, 2003), B.J. Richardson, *Environmental Regulation through Financial Organisations, Comparative Perspectives on the Industrialised Nations* (New York: Kluwer Law International, 2002) and G. Handl, *Multilateral Development Banking: Environmental Principles and Concepts Reflecting General International Law and Public Policy* (The Hague: Kluwer Law International, 2001).

Thirdly, legal research must focus on one of the most difficult issues related to accountability, namely compliance. Two practical, legal challenges to the implementation of international sustainable development treaties warrant particular attention:

- How to influence the effects of non-parties conduct on the success of sustainable development treaties. The use of trade-related measures in several regional fisheries arrangements has challenged many assumptions about the readiness of States to consider imposing trade measures against non-members of agreements. The legal aspects and implementation of such innovative models for promoting the compliance of non-parties warrants greater documentation, monitoring and analysis to test the applicability to other areas.
- How to ensure increased levels of developed country fulfilment of international legal obligations. Many developed countries fail to fulfil obligations for capacity building, finance and technology transfer embodied in a range of environment, economic and social agreements. Developing countries and the NGO sector could benefit from conceptual assistance from lawyers regarding the design of mechanisms for monitoring and documenting non-compliance, evaluating best practices among donors (e.g., best legal approaches to the transfer of environmental technologies to developing countries and delivery of legal, technical assistance related to natural resource regulation), and devising proposals of ways to increase legal and political pressure on developed countries to comply with international obligations.

Scientists

The availability and credibility of scientific data is critical to the implementation of natural resources law. Impact assessment and monitoring techniques similarly rely on the credibility of data and are critical to sustainable development. In practice, allegations of financial conflicts of interest and lack of scientific impartiality frequently conspire to undermine public confidence in regulations and frustrate efforts to improve both the management of natural resources (fisheries, forests, minerals, antarctic minerals, deep sea nodules) and their use (e.g., burning of fossil fuels and the climate change debate).

The legal community has been underactive in this important area and can contribute a great deal in coming years:

- What to do when there are fundamental differences of opinion about whether "sound science" judges certain activities to be sustainable or not?
- What kinds of principles can promote the objectivity of scientific research regardless of funding source?
- How can the law be more useful in reducing the incidence of conflicts of interest in scientific publishing, and how can these be enforced?
- What legal processes for public participation and transparency have proven most successful in generating publicly accepted data, impact assessments and monitoring, particularly where broad international consensus is often vital to prompt action?

CONCLUSIONS

The natural resources arena provides some of the clearest examples of the interplay between social, environmental and economic stakes, needs and priorities. Legal frameworks and implementation efforts need to reflect this reality. A sustainable development law approach can meet this challenge by encouraging a conscious engagement with the web of overlapping social, environmental, cultural and economic legal frameworks, as well as with the cultural considerations, economic policies, expectations, players and interests that shape natural resource use.

While much international environmental law appears most related to natural resource protection, the most relevant, and crucial, international law in relation to the use and management of natural resources, in fact, emerges in the economic domain. Here, significant changes need to be made, increasing integration with environmental and social laws must take place, and the future legal research agenda must focus.

Re-energizing the natural resources arena – as with so many other issues– requires that all communities – activists, policymakers, grassroots organizers, scientists and lawyers – focus their creative energy on addressing the *real* challenges to implementation (or, in the words of WSSD, "Making it Happen").[26]

---

[26] "Making it Happen" was the theme of Four Roundtables that were incorporated into the WSSD official agenda.

11

International Human Rights and Poverty Law in Sustainable Development

with SUMUDU ATAPATTU[1]

The need for both economic growth and social development to be treated as priorities was recognized by the international community more than 50 years ago when the UN Charter was adopted. One of the objectives of the Charter, as reflected in its Preamble, is "to promote social progress and better standards of life in larger freedom",[2] and toward that end "to employ international machinery for the promotion of the economic and social advancement of all peoples".[3] An Economic and Social Council was established under the Charter to initiate studies and reports with regard to international economic, social, cultural educational, health and related matters. Its mandate includes the promotion of human rights and fundamental freedoms for all.[4]

The UN Charter was closely followed by the Universal Declaration of Human Rights (UDHR),[5] which sought to expand on the basic rights referred to in the UN Charter. Albeit a non-binding instrument, the UDHR is widely acclaimed as laying the foundation for international human rights law. The UDHR contains both civil and political rights, and economic, social and cultural rights. The right relevant for the present discussion is contained in Article 25 which provides that "[e]veryone has the right to a standard of living adequate for the health and well-being of himself and of his family, including food, clothing, housing and medical care and necessary social services ... "

Twenty years later, state Parties recognized in a binding instrument "the right of everyone to an adequate standard of living for himself and his family, including adequate food, clothing and housing, and to the continuous improvement of living conditions."[6] Although access to water is not mentioned here, this

---

[1] Sumudu Atapattu LL.M (Cantab), PhD (Cantab), Attorney-at-Law (Sri Lanka); Lecturer, Adjunct Faculty, University of Wisconsin-Madison Law School, USA, is Lead Counsel, Human Rights and Poverty Eradication at the CISDL. She is also a Consultant, Law & Society Trust, Colombo, Sri Lanka; formerly, a Senior Lecturer at the Faculty of Law, University of Colombo, Sri Lanka; and a Visiting Fulbright Scholar, George Washington University Law School, Washington DC.
[2] United Nations Charter, Preamble.   [3] *Ibid.*
[4] Art. 62 of the UN Charter.   [5] Adopted in 1948.
[6] Art. 11 of the International Covenant on Economic, Social and Cultural Rights (ICESCR), 1966, 993 UNTS (entered into force 3 Jan. 1976).

void was filled in 2002 when the UN Committee on Economic, Social and Cultural Rights, through its General Comments, recognized the right to water as a basic human right under Article 11 of the ICESCR.[7] The General Comment provides that:

[t]he human right to water entitles everyone to sufficient, safe, acceptable, physically accessible and affordable water for personal and domestic use. An adequate amount of safe water is necessary to prevent death from dehydration, to reduce the risk of water-related disease and to provide for consumption, cooking, personal and domestic hygienic requirements.

Unfortunately, these basic rights have remained elusive to the majority of the world's population. Despite the developments in the human rights field, millions of people continue to live in poverty without adequate food and water and without adequate housing and sanitation. It is estimated that 1.2 billion people in the world today live on less than US$1.00 a day and about 2 billion live on less than US$2.00 a day.[8] Many people have become poorer and marginalized, with a degrading environment exacerbating the issue, and the reference to the "continuous improvement of living conditions" has become a non-starter as many millions of people in the world today continue to live in squalor and starvation.

POVERTY, HUMAN RIGHTS AND SUSTAINABLE DEVELOPMENT

Poverty is a primary concern of most disciplines in the social and natural sciences that address development issues. International law however, has traditionally given less attention to poverty eradication, as it was seen as an issue for national jurisdictions. However, there is a growing awareness that international legal arrangements, particularly on economic and environmental issues, have a significant impact on levels of poverty. It is already clear that the success of international economic and environmental institutions will be judged, in part, by whether they increase or reduce poverty. There has been a failure, over the past few decades, to eliminate poverty solely through national efforts (complemented by *ad hoc* international assistance). As such, more attention is being given to international law and its institutions. Those can provide tools for more predictable and fair international relations, and for the monitoring and strengthening of national efforts.

The World Commission on Environment and Development defined sustainable development as "Development that meets the needs of the present without

---

[7] See UN Committee on Economic, Social and Cultural Rights, General Comment No. 15 (2002) on "The Right to Water", UN Doc. E/C.12/2002/11, 26 Nov. 2002.

[8] See World Bank, *World Development Report 2000/01* (Oxford: Oxford University Press, 2001) and UN Secretary-General's *Millennium Report* (New York: UN, 2000) presented to the UN General Assembly's Millennium Summit.

compromising the ability of the future generations to meet their own needs."[9] As mentioned above, the report points out that this definition contains within it two key concepts:

- The concept of needs, in particular the essential needs of the world's poor, to which overriding priority should be given;
- The idea of limitations on the environment's ability to meet present and future needs.

The report further stresses that since poverty is a major cause and effect of global environmental problems, it is futile to attempt to deal with environmental problems without understanding the factors that underlie world poverty and international inequality.[10] Development in a broad sense requires dealing with these inequalities, demographic issues as well as trade issues which are closely related to economic development. Empowering the poor is another aspect that has received increasing attention by the international community,[11] this focuses on ways to lessen the sense of powerlessness that is experienced by poor people.

There is no doubt that poverty is the biggest violator of human rights. It leads to the deprivation of other rights enshrined in international human rights instruments, particularly the right to health, right to education, right to work, and the right to privacy. It also leads to the violation of other procedural rights such as the right to participate in the decision-making process and the right to information.[12] Moreover, it is a violation of the principle of equality, a fundamental tenet of international human rights law, and of the principle of intra-generational equity[13] which is generally considered as forming part of international environmental law and, as discussed in Part II, a principle of international law on sustainable development.[14]

Poverty is also one of the most significant polluters. Many people live in dire poverty,[15] which has exacerbated environmental degradation, as poor people often have no choice but to resort to unsustainable practices in order to eke out a meagre living. The link between poverty and environmental degradation is well recognized and constitutes, unfortunately, a vicious cycle: poverty leads to

---

[9] World Commission on Environment and Development, *Our Common Future* (Oxford: Oxford University Press, 1987) at 43 [hereinafter *Our Common Future*].

[10] *Ibid.*, at 3.

[11] UNDP, *Human Development Report 2000* (New York: Oxford University Press, 2000).

[12] See K.E. Mahoney & P. Mahoney (eds)., *Human Rights in the Twenty-first Century: A Global Challenge* (Norwell: Kluwer Academic Publishers, 1993). See also *Human Development Report 2000*, *supra* note 11, which, referring to the 1993 Vienna Declaration on Human Rights, affirmed that: "extreme poverty and social exclusion constitute a violation of human dignity".

[13] See the WCED report, *supra note 9*.

[14] See S. Atapattu, "Sustainable Development: Myth or Reality? A Survey of Sustainable Development under International Law and Sri Lankan Law" (2001) 14 *Georgetown International Environmental Law Review* 265.

[15] Various terms have been used to describe this – absolute poverty and extreme poverty are used often.

environmental degradation which, in turn, leads to more poverty which leads to even more environmental degradation. Desertification is a good example of this vicious cycle.[16]

The international community has also recognized the link between poverty and sustainable development[17] and proclaimed in the 1992 *Rio Declaration on Environment and Development* that:

[a]ll states and all people shall cooperate in the essential task of eradicating poverty as an indispensable requirement for sustainable development, in order to decrease the disparities in standards of living and better meet the needs of the majority of the people of the world.[18]

Poverty is also a developmental issue. Lack of economic development has contributed to the present problems associated with poverty. Thus, the *UN General Assembly Resolution on the Right to Development*[19] recognized: "[t]he right to development is an inalienable human right by virtue of which every human person and all peoples are entitled to participate in, contribute to, and enjoy economic, social, cultural and political development, in which all human rights and fundamental freedoms can be fully realized . . . ".

[16] The *Convention to Combat Desertification in those Countries Experiencing Serious Drought and/or Desertification, particularly in Africa*, (1994) 33 *ILM* 1328 recognizes the link between poverty and desertification. Its Preamble notes "Conscious that sustainable economic growth, social development and poverty eradication are priorities of affected developing countries, particularly in Africa, and are essential to meeting sustainability objectives. Mindful that desertification and drought affect sustainable development through their interrelationships with important social problems such as poverty, poor health and nutrition, lack of food security, and those arising from migration, displacement of persons and demographic dynamics . . . ".

[17] See A. Markandya, "Poverty alleviation and Sustainable Development: Implications for the Management of Natural Capital" and D. Morrow, "Poverty Reduction Strategy Papers and Sustainable Development" (Papers presented to the workshop on Poverty and Sustainable Development, Ottawa, Jan. 2001). See also, "Summary of the Workshop on Poverty Alleviation and Sustainable Development: Exploring the Links" *Sustainable Developments* 146:1 (23 Jan. 2001) online: <http://www.iisd.ca/sd/poverty/sdvo146num1.html> (date accessed: 25/4/2003).

[18] *Rio Declaration on Environment and Development*, Report of the *United Nations Conference on Environment and Development*, UN Doc. A/CONF.151/6/Rev.1, (1992) 31 ILM 874 (1992), Principle 5 [hereinafter *Rio Declaration*].

[19] UNGA Resolution 41/128 of 4 Dec. 1986. It must be recognized, however, that this Declaration is a soft law instrument and that the notion of right to development has attracted vigorous debate in the literature. See generally: S. Marks, "Emerging Human Rights: A New Generation for the 1980s?" (1980–1) 33 *Rutgers L. Rev.* 435; P. Alston, "Conjuring up New Human Rights: A Proposal for Quality Control" (1984) 78 *AJIL* 607; P. Alston, "A Third Generation of Solidarity Rights: Progressive Development or Obfuscation of International Human Rights Law?" (1985) 29 *Neth Int'l L. Rev.* 307; J. Crawford, ed., *Rights of Peoples* (Oxford: Oxford University Press, 1988); P. Alston, "Making Space for New Human Rights: The Case of the Right to Development" (1988) *Harv. Hum. Rts Y.B.* 3; A. Lindroos, *The Right to Development* (Helsinki: The Erik Castren Institute of International Law and Human Rights Research Reports, 1999). See also: U. Baxi, "The Development of the Right to Development", in J. Symonides, ed., *Human Rights: New Dimensions and Challenges* (Aldershot: Ashgate, 1998) at 99; C. Weeramantry, "Right to Development" (1985) *Indian JIL* 482; J.C.N. Paul, "The United Nations Family: Challenges of Law and Development: The United Nations and the Creation of an International Law of Development" (1995) 36 *Harv. Int'l L.J.* 307. It is also of concern that the debate on the right to development has not integrated the parallel developments in relations to sustainable development.

Thus, poverty has the ability to cut across a wide spectrum of issues – social, economic and environmental – requiring an integrated approach.[20] It is here that international sustainable development law – understood as the intersection between economic, social and environmental law[21] – plays a significant role.[22]

Many international instruments have grappled with the issue of poverty. *Agenda 21*, for example, devotes a separate chapter to "combating poverty". It echoes the *World Summit for Social Development Programme*, that "poverty is a complex multidimensional problem with origins in both the national and international domains".[23] It points out that a uniform global solution cannot be found and advocates for country-specific programmes with a parallel process of creating a supportive international environment. In order to achieve sustainable development, a specific anti-poverty strategy must be adopted. It further notes several conditions which should be included in such a strategy: focus on resources, production and people; cover demographic issues; enhance health care and education; provide for rights of women, youth and indigenous groups and local communities; democratic participation; and improved governance.

Agenda 21 further notes that while promotion of economic growth in developing countries is important, such growth must be both sustained and sustainable and must strengthen employment and income-generating programmes. The long-term objective is to achieve sustainable livelihoods (it should address development, sustainable resource management and poverty eradication). Empowering communities is important and sustainable development must be achieved at every level of society. *Agenda 21* estimates that the average annual cost of implementing this programme would be about $30 billion.[24]

An important milestone in relation to social issues was the World Summit for Social Development held in 1995 at which the Copenhagen Declaration was adopted. It devotes a separate chapter to poverty eradication. Commitment No. 2 of the Declaration deals with "the goal of eradicating poverty in the world, through decisive national actions and international cooperation, as an ethical, political and economic imperative of humankind".[25] The Declaration commits States to, *inter alia*, formulate national level policies to address the root

[20] J. Oloka-Onyango, "Human Rights and Sustainable Development in Contemporary Africa: A New Dawn, or Retreating Horizons?" (2000) 6 *Buff. Hum. Rts. L. Rev.* 39.

[21] Based upon the three pillars of sustainable development, see the *Johannesburg Plan of Implementation*, Report of the World Summit on Sustainable Development, Johannesburg, South Africa, UN Doc. A/CONF.199/20 at para. 2. See also the *Johannesburg Declaration on Sustainable Development* contained in the same Report.

[22] A. Cançado-Trindade, ed., *Human Rights, Sustainable Development and the Environment* (San José, Costa Rica: Instituto Interamericano de Derechos Humanos, 1992) and A. Boyle and D. Freestone (eds.), *International Law and Sustainable Development: Past Achievements and Future Challenges* (Oxford: Oxford University Press, 1999).

[23] Exact wording can be found in the Programme of Action of the World Summit for Social Development, 1995 online: <http://www.visionoffice.com/socdev/wssdpa-2.htm> (date accessed: 23/4/2003).

[24] See *Agenda 21*, ch. 3, para. 3.11.

[25] UN World Summit for Social Development, U.N.DOC.A/CONF.166/9 (1995).

causes of poverty and to provide for the basic needs of all, and to encourage international donors and multilateral development banks to support these efforts. The Declaration defines basic needs as: elimination of hunger and malnutrition; food security; education, employment and livelihood, primary health care services including reproductive health care, safe drinking water and sanitation, adequate shelter, and participation in social and cultural life.[26] In other words, basic needs means ensuring the protection of basic human rights enshrined in the International Bill of Rights. It further provides that special priority be given to the needs and rights of women and children and to the needs of vulnerable and disadvantaged groups and persons. Both the Declaration and the Program of Action call for national and international strategies to deal with the issue of poverty.

The most recent recognition of the need to combat poverty and global disparities appears in the *Johannesburg Declaration on Sustainable Development* of 2002. It calls upon States to "speedily increase access to such basic requirements as clean water, sanitation, adequate shelter, energy, health care, food security and the protection of biodiversity".[27] Again, like *Agenda 21*, the Plan of Implementation devotes a separate section to poverty eradication. It notes that "eradicating poverty is the greatest global challenging facing the world today and an indispensable requirement for sustainable development, particularly for developing countries".[28] It proposed the following:

- Halve by 2015 the proportion of people whose income is less than $1.00 a day, those who live in hunger and those without access to safe drinking water and basic sanitation,
- Establish a world solidarity fund to eradicate poverty (voluntary contributions),
- Develop national programmes for sustainable development,
- Promote women's access and full participation,
- Deliver basic health services,
- Ensure children have at least primary schooling,
- Combat desertification,
- Increase food availability and affordability,
- Improve the lives of at least 100 million slum dwellers.[29]

It can thus be seen that poverty encompasses much more than mere economic development.[30] It requires, *inter alia*, the promotion of women's rights, the provision of education, particularly primary education, good governance and democratic participation. In its report on Human Rights, Poverty Reduction and

---

[26] *Ibid.*

[27] *Johannesburg Declaration on Sustainable Development, supra* note 21, at para 18.

[28] JPOI, *supra* note 21, at para 7.   [29] *Ibid.*

[30] The *Human Development Report 2000* points out that "poverty is broader than lack of income". It is deprivation across many dimensions. Thus, the UNDP prefers the broader term "human poverty" rather than the narrower term "income poverty", *supra* note 11, at 73.

Sustainable Development, the Office of the High Commissioner for Human Rights notes that:

[i]t is now widely accepted that – on the one hand – poverty should not be seen only as a lack of income, but also as a deprivation of human rights, and – on the other hand – that unless the problems of poverty are addressed, there can be no sustainable development. It is equally accepted that sustainable development requires environmental protection and that environmental degradation leads directly and indirectly to violations of human rights.[31]

The report which advocates a human rights approach to poverty points out that such an approach focuses on empowerment of the poor, and that this occurs through their gaining access to their rights. In the report, "accountability, the principle of non-discrimination, equality, and participation, and the recognition of the interdependence of rights"[32] are the most relevant parts of the human rights normative framework.

While enormous theoretical and legal strides have been made in international protection of human rights, a significant gap exists in practice between civil and political rights, on the one hand, and economic, social and cultural rights, on the other.[33] This gap reflects the North–South divide on these issues, and contributes to the marginalization of the poor. The time has come to bridge the gap between these two sets of rights, and give effect to the official UN position that all rights are indivisible, interdependent and inter-related.[34]

The progressive realization of economic, social and cultural rights is imperative, if the present plight of the poor is to be ameliorated. The UNDP in its *Human Development Report* notes that all human rights are causally linked and can be mutually reinforcing: "They can create synergies that contribute to poor people's securing their rights, enhancing their human capabilities and escaping poverty. Because of these complementarities, the struggle to achieve economic and social rights should not be separate from the struggle to achieve civil and political rights. And the two need to be pursued simultaneously."[35] As explained by the *Report*, a decent standard of living, adequate nutrition, health care and other achievements are not just development goals – these are human rights inherent in human freedom and dignity.[36]

Furthermore, governance issues have exacerbated the problems faced by the poor. Societies in which governments are corrupt and do not respect the rule of law or fundamental rights of peoples can further marginalize the poor.[37]

---

[31] *Ibid.*   [32] *Ibid.*

[33] A. Eide, C. Krause & A. Rosas eds., *Economic, Social and Cultural* Rights, 2nd edn. (The Hague: Kluwer Law International, 2001).

[34] See Vienna Declaration and Programme of Action adopted at the World Conference on Human Rights, UN DOC.A/CONF.157/23, 12 July 1993, para. 5.

[35] *Supra* note 11, at 73.   [36] *Ibid.*

[37] K. Ginther, E. Denters & P.J.I.M. de Waart eds, *Sustainable Development and Good Governance* (Norwell: Kluwer Academic Publishers, 1995).

GOVERNANCE AND INSTITUTIONAL STRUCTURES

There are many international institutions in this field, including the World Bank, the UNDP, the UNEP, the Office of the UN High Commissioner for Human Rights and the various UN bodies involved in promoting human rights, the UN Commission on Sustainable Development, national governments and, of course, poor communities themselves.

While not originally established to deal with worldwide poverty, the World Bank has become an important actor. Its Operational Directive on Poverty Reduction states that sustainable poverty reduction is the Bank's overarching objective.[38] Environmental protection, institution building and investing in local capacity to assess poverty are essential to achieve this goal. The World Development Report, prepared annually by the Bank, provides useful information on poverty, economic growth, environmental protection and sustainable development.

The United National Development Program has become increasingly involved in sustainable human development linking poverty, environmental protection and human development through a paradigm of sustainable development. The Human Development Report published annually by the UNDP provides a wealth of material; its 1997 report focused on Poverty and its 2000 report on Human Rights and Human Development.

The Office of the UN High Commissioner for Human Rights deals with the issue of poverty through a human rights perspective. In 2002, it prepared a document entitled "Draft Guidelines: A human rights approach to poverty reduction strategies" which deals with poverty eradication through a human rights focus. In addition, its background paper on Human Rights, Poverty Reduction and Sustainable Development stresses the need to address issues related to poverty if sustainable development is to be achieved.[39] The Commission on Human Rights appointed a Special Rapporteur on the subject of human rights and extreme poverty[40] and an expert seminar on the subject was held in February 2001.[41]

The UN General Assembly declared 1997–2006 as the first UN Decade for the Eradication of Poverty and in his report on the implementation of the first decade, the Secretary-General notes that many obstacles to poverty eradication arise from political, economic and social conditions at the national level. While progress towards the millennium development goals has been uneven, the report

---

[38] *The World Bank Operational Manual on Poverty Reduction*, OD 4.15 (Washington: World Bank, 1991).

[39] *Human Rights, Poverty Reduction and Sustainable Development: Health, Food and Water* (Background paper prepared for the *World Summit on Sustainable Development*, 2002) available online at www.ohchr.org.

[40] The Special Rapporteur, Mr Leandro Despouy, submitted his final report to the Sub-Commission in June 1996 (E/CN.4/Sub.2/1996/13), 28 June 1996.

[41] See *Report of the Expert Seminar on Human Rights and Extreme Poverty*, UN Commission on Human Rights, 57th sess., UN DOC.E/CN.4/2001/54/Add.1, 21 March 2001.

points out that if international cooperation to achieve these is lacking, these goals will be unattainable by 2015. In addition, the UN Commission on Sustainable Development has also dealt with the issue of poverty eradication.[42]

A FUTURE LEGAL RESEARCH AGENDA

There is an important interrelationship between poverty, human rights and sustainable development. A human rights approach can frame and support sustainable development, and poverty eradication is both at the centre of sustainable development, and a necessary pre-condition to it. As such, a sustainable development law research agenda in this area should consider the following issues.

Economic, social and cultural rights, including rights to development and environment

The starting point of a legal research agenda in this area focuses on defining and investigating relevant international legal principles (including "soft law" documents) for instance, the seven principles covered in Part II of this volume. Such principles should help the economic, social and cultural rights, the right to development, and the right to environment, to be assessed and reconciled at the international level.[43] Research must also consider how these principles are reflected at the national level in human rights law, and any disconnections between international law and national law, as well as the reasons for such gaps.

Poverty eradication

The role of international sustainable development law in achieving poverty eradication, as well as the obstacles impeding such achievement, is important. Legal scholarship is moving forward to define new ways to use human rights tools to empower vulnerable individuals and groups to defend their livelihoods. It can also address issues of land tenure and examine the provision of credit and extension services, analyse and propose changes to tax reform measures, and reveal budgetary allocations for social expenditure. Legal research is also

---

[42] See *Report of the Secretary-General on Combating Poverty*, UN Commission on Sustainable Development acting as a preparatory committee meeting for the *World Summit on Sustainable Development*, Organizational Sess., UN DOC.E/CN.17/2001/PC/5, 14 March 2001.

[43] D. McGoldrick, "Sustainable Development and Human Rights: An Integrated Conception" (1996) 45 *Int'l & Comp. L.Q* 796; and A. Boyle & M. Anderson eds., *Human Rights Approaches to Environmental Protection* (Oxford: Clarendon Press, 1996); P. Sands, "International Law in the field of Sustainable Development" (1994) 65 *Br. Y.B. Int'l L.* 303; for a different view see M. Pallemaerts, "The Future of Environmental Regulation: International Environmental Law in the Age of Sustainable Development: A Critical Assessment of the UNCED Process" (1996) 15 *J. L. & Com.* 623.

necessary to develop measures to implement the concept of "minimum core obligations",[44] improve compliance with the ICESCR,[45] address legal aspects of vulnerability; and identify other mechanisms for more equitable distribution of wealth.

Good governance

It will be important to address the role of good governance and participatory rights, and to identify priority institutional structures at both national and international levels. This should include consideration of institutional development (legal and judicial reform) and anti-corruption approaches, and best practices in the devolution of power. Procedural human rights requirements are also relevant, including, as mentioned in Principle 10 of the *Rio Declaration* and discussed above in Part II, rights to information, access to justice and the right to democratic participation.

Financing mechanisms for poverty eradication

To reduce the gap between theory and practice, there is a need to consider financing mechanisms for poverty eradication and the role of development agencies.[46] Such work should canvass the application of the *Monterrey Consensus on Financing for Development* in the context of sustainable development. It will also be important to consider the particular roles of domestic sources, debt relief, trade and investment.

Civil society

Civil society participation is necessary to achieve human rights, and to ensure that programmes for poverty eradication can support sustainable development. There is a need for research on the most effective forms of legal advocacy, dissemination of information and training, especially in the context of the roles to be played by international organizations, States, and the media. When communities mobilize in order to realize human rights and poverty eradication, this can affect the sustainability of their livelihoods, leading to empowerment or

---

[44] A. Chapman and S. Russell, eds. *Core Obligations: Building a Framework for Economic, Social and Cultural Rights* (Antwerp: Intersentia, 2002). Another relevant concept is the concept of "reasonability" in State action. See the decision of the South African Constitutional Court as set out in *Treatment Action Campaign* v. *Minister of Health* [2002] 10 B. Const. L. R. 1033 (S. Afr. Const. Ct.).

[45] See, in this regard, S. Leckie, "Another Step Towards Indivisibility: Identifying the Key Features of Violations of Economic, Social and Cultural Rights" [1998] 20 *Human Rights Quarterly* and M. Langford, *Litigating Economic, Social and Cultural Rights: Achievements, Challenges and Strategies* (Geneva: COHRE, 2003), at <www.cohre.org/litigation>.

[46] D. Bradlow, "Social Justice and Development: Critical Issues Facing the Bretton Woods System: The World Bank, the IMF, and Human Rights" (1996) 6 *Transnat'l. L. & Contemp. Probs.* 47.

oppression. Participatory legal research, and action, will further advance these developments in the future.

Protection of vulnerable groups

How to give "priority to the poor" in sustainable development? The future legal research agenda in this area should examine State obligations to groups especially vulnerable to the adverse effects of economic policies, and to environmental degradation (including desertification and climate change). Such an agenda can also assess the question of liability for causing climate change and obligations and approaches for addressing environmental racism. It is important to consider approaches to provide for non-discrimination and mechanisms for improving the participation in decision-making of socially excluded groups including racial, ethnic and religious minorities, poor and less-educated people, women, etc. In this respect, the *Draft Guidelines: A Human Rights Approach to Poverty Reduction Strategies* prepared by the Office of the High Commissioner for Human Rights can be assessed for their practical implementation, particularly with regard to legal and institutional reforms.

CONCLUSIONS

This chapter does not attempt to provide a comprehensive overview of a future legal research agenda for human rights and poverty eradication as part of sustainable development law. Rather, the chapter signals certain key trends and issues, seeking to give a flavour for the debate including the treaties, international institutions and in some cases, domestic legal implications.

There is a strong indication that a human rights approach can be helpful in addressing sustainable development issues. There is a need to ensure that sustainable development law does, indeed, make poverty eradication a centre of its analysis, an "essential pre-condition" for the realization of its goals. Much further legal investigation is necessary, starting from the understanding that human rights and poverty eradication, including the analysis of financing for development, are essential to the achievement of sustainable development.

12

International Health and Sustainable Development Law

with MAYA PRABHU[1]

While health has long been central to the sustainable development agenda, academics and scholars are only just beginning to analyse the relevance of international health law to sustainable development law. This work requires a great deal of future development, and this chapter simply presents a starting point, the identification of a future legal research agenda. Such an agenda seeks to encourage public health practitioners and international legal specialists to consider health law from a genuinely global perspective. This chapter argues that the future legal research agenda in health law and sustainable development will focus on intersections between health regimes and others. To provide a flavour of recent debates, the chapter surveys recent trends in international health law, examining certain selected areas of law in more detail.

THE HISTORIC SCHISM BETWEEN INTERNATIONAL HEALTH AND INTERNATIONAL LAW

There is a historic disconnect between international health concerns and international law. There are a number of reasons for this intellectual disengagement.

First, until recently, neither public health practitioners nor lawyers saw international health law as an "outcome-determining factor" for public health progress. Health problems, in general, have been seen as "technical" or "scientific" problems to be solved, rather than social and political ones to be debated and negotiated. Accordingly it has been medical, pharmaceutical, engineering and technological breakthroughs which have been given credit for the greatest advances in twentieth-century health.[2] While this approach was appropriate in past decades when there seemed to be no limit to the scientific and antibiotic revolutions, for a number of reasons laid out below, this approach is no longer

[1] Maya Prabhu, A.B. (Social Studies, Harvard), M.Sc. (Political Economy, LSE), M.D. (Dalhousie Medical School), LL.B. (Law, McGill), is Lead Counsel for sustainable international health law at the CISDL. She wishes to give special thanks to Alicen Chow, Research Fellow, CISDL.
[2] D.P. Fidler, "The Future of the World Health Organization: What Role for International Law" (1998) 31 *Vand. J. Transnat'l, L.* 1079 [hereafter Fidler, *Future*]; A.L. Taylor, "Making the World Health Organization Work: A Legal Framework for Universal Access to the Conditions for Health",

viable; moreover, where "technical" has also come to mean static, nonpolitical and non-interdisciplinary, this is no longer sufficient.[3]

Secondly, any international health law which *has* developed is mainly the purview of public health experts, rather than legal experts. Much international public health policy emanates from health organizations, such as the World Health Organization (WHO), rather than from judicial decision-making bodies. And, despite the tremendous international legal powers given to the WHO,[4] including the authority to adopt treaties addressing any matter in its domain, health law has tended to be derived from soft law processes. Policy implementation and enforcement have operated through recommendations and regulations rather than through legally binding rules. Even the interpretation and dispute settlement of those recommendations have tended to be governed by informal processes. In the words of one author, this "ethos" has been based on the assumption that public health progress can be better achieved through cooperation and consensus building rather than through a hard legal approach.[5]

The International Health Regulations system (IHR) is a prime example of the present-day "soft law" approach to global health.[6] The IHR was one of the earliest attempts by WHO to act collectively with regard to world health. Its purpose was to ensure the "maximum security against the international spread of disease with minimum interference with world traffic".[7] The IHR creates a comprehensive surveillance programme for member states to monitor and respond to infectious disease in their respective countries – yellow fever, plague and cholera. However, neither the IHR nor the WHO Constitution permits action against States who fail to comply with a regulation. Moreover, the three diseases that are the focus of the IHR have been eclipsed by other infectious diseases in public attention and mortality. As such, the IHR have been increasingly criticized for being neither relevant to nor useful for addressing the public health problems of our time.

A final reason for the disjuncture between international law and health policy is illustrated by the IHR example. In addition to being without clear mechanisms to ensure compliance and enforcement, the WHO has sought to maintain a conscientiously "apolitical character".[8] Again, with the idea that global health is better addressed in a consensual manner, the WHO has eschewed the "strong-

(1992) 18 *Am. J. L. & Med.* 301; M. Ghezuhly *et al.*, "International Health Law" (1998) 32 *Int'l Law.* 539; D.P. Fidler, *International Law and Infectious Diseases* (Oxford: Clarendon, 1999) [hereafter Fidler, *International*].

    [3] *Ibid.*   [4] WHO, Art. 19.   [5] See generally Fidler, *International*, *supra* note 2.
    [6] World Health Org., "International Health Regulations" *International Health Regulations*, 3rd ann. edn, 91983, (25 July 1969). See also: World Health Org., "Revision of the International Regulations: Progress Report" 74 *Weekly Epidemiology Rec.* (Jan. 1999) at 25; World Health Org., 78 *Weekly Epidemiology Rec.* (July, 1998) at 23.
    [7] World Health Org., Foreword to International Health Regulations online: <http://policy.who.int/cgi-bin/om_isapi.dll?infobase=Ihreg&softpage=Brownse_frame_pg42> (date accessed: 30 May 2004).
    [8] H.F. Shattuck, Jr. *et al.*, "World Health Organization, Section Recommendation and Report of the American Bar Association" (1996) 30 *Ill. J. Int'l Law* 688; Fidler, *Future*, *supra* note 2.

arming and sweet-talking" that is the hallmark of negotiations of other international regimes. Consequently, international health law has not received extensive interest among lawyers, who have not seen their skills as necessary in its domain.

RATIONALE FOR THE DEVELOPMENT OF INTERNATIONAL SUSTAINABLE HEALTH LAW

However, a changing global context means that this division between the legalists and the medical experts is no longer practicable: international health concerns have been necessarily drawn closer to economic and social law. Conversely, those interested in economic and social development are more likely to appreciate the importance of investing in health.

There are a number of factors which capture the changing landscape. First, due to globalization, public health dangers now have a scale beyond the capacity of any single national health care system. Indeed, as the Centers for Disease Control (CDC) has suggested, any assertions about a distinction between national and international health are anachronistic.[9] A population-based approach is needed now, one that is transnational in orientation.

While there is a tendency to overstate how much globalization is a very recent phenomenon, it is undeniable that certain recent globalization processes have had particularly significant impacts on public health. These processes include increased travel, migration and cross-border trade; changes in individual behavior (especially sexual behavior); rapid urbanization (driven in part by the opportunities and constraints caused by economic globalization) and hastened environmental degradation. The critical element in these processes is the way in which cross-border channels have increased in numbers and speed.[10] Thus, populations have become vulnerable to disease-causing agents imported from elsewhere in a manner unprecedented since the beginnings of the colonial period in the Americas, Africa and Asia.

Globalization also has a negative "multiplier" effect on the impacts on health. For example, urbanization is associated with overcrowding and poor sanitation; environmental degradation is associated with changing weather patterns which affect habits and locales of disease-carrying insects and animals;[11] the

---

[9] Noting that the "concept of domestic as distinct from international health is outdated" see US Centers for Disease Control and Prevention, *Addressing Emerging Infectious Disease Threats: A Prevention Strategy for the United States* (Atlanta: Center for Disease Control and Prevention, 1994) at 12; observing that national health has become an international challenge see J.W. Le Deuc, "World Health Organization Strategy for Emerging Infectious Diseases" (1996) 275 *JAMA* 318.

[10] D. Fidler, "International Law and Global Public Health" (1999) 48 *U. Kan. L. Rev.* 1, 9 [hereafter Fidler, *Global*]; S. Lederberg, R.E. Shope & S.C. Oak (eds.) *Emerging Infectious Diseases: Microbial Threats to Health in the United States* (Washington, DC: Institute of Medicine, National Academy Press, 1992) at 77.

[11] *Ibid.* See also: D. Fidler, "Trade and Health: The Global Spread of Disease and International Trade" (1997) 40 *Germ. Y. B. Int'l L.* 300.

liberalization of international trade has contributed to the dissemination of disease-causing products such as tobacco; and cross-border travel has heightened the spread of Severe Acute Respiratory Disease (SARS) and HIV/AIDS. All of these circumstances confirm that the nature of public health is inherently global with causes related to the world's growing interconnectedness and with consequences that must be addressed by international solutions.

As a second element of the changing context, the past decade has seen a growth in the power and reach of non-State actors. These actors have an increasing role in public health policy, law and practice.[12]

One positive example, from the perspective of patients or consumers, is the newfound effectiveness of non-governmental organizations (NGOs). The best model is the campaign of NGOs against pharmaceutical companies over access to HIV/AIDS drugs in South Africa. *Medicins sans Frontières* (Doctors without Borders) in particular was instrumental in affecting international governance by forcing the "intellectual property rights vs. public health debate" higher on the intergovernmental agenda; the campaign also supported South Africa's exercise of public health sovereignty.

A less benign example, again from the consumer perspective, is the role of multinational corporations (MNCs), which appear to influence international agency and government health policies in the direction of minimal restrictions on unhealthy consumer products. Developing countries are under pressure to present attractive investment and trade environments, and appear particularly vulnerable. Examples around tobacco and pharmaceuticals have been well-documented.[13] A more recent case is that of the sugar industry in the United States, which threatened to challenge US funding for the WHO unless the WHO retracts its guidelines on healthy eating.[14]

The more actors and the greater their variety, the more important formal legal channels become. The informal, consensual negotiations of the past become less successful when the system becomes more complex.

A final reason to draw the two disciplines together in view of changing circumstances is that many of the most pressing health concerns are deeply political issues. Climate change, destruction of biodiversity, trade in hazardous wastes, for example, are all highly contentious areas at the intersection of health and the environment. Relevant human rights questions include whether there is a right to a healthy environment, independently of the right to health and other

---

[12] D. Fidler, "A Globalized Theory of Public Health Law" (2002) 30 *J. L. Med. & Ethics* 150.

[13] For tobacco see: Dr. G.H. Brundtland, "Response of the Director General to the Report of the Committee of Experts on Tobacco Industry Documents" WHO Doc. WHO/DG/SP (6 Oct. 2000) at 1, online: <http://tobacco.who.int/repoistory/stp58/inquiryDGres1.pdf> (last accessed: 30 May 2003); "Committee of Experts on Tobacco Industry Documents, Tobacco Industry Strategies to Undermine Tobacco Control Activities at the World Health Organization" (July, 2000) online at: <http://tobacco.who.int/repository/stp59/who_inquiry.pdf)> (last accessed: 30 May 2003); for pharmaceuticals see <http:// www.cptech.org>.

[14] S. Boseley, "Sugar industry threatens to scupper WHO" online: <http:// www.guardian.co.uk/international/story/0,3604,940287,00.html> (last accessed: 30 May 2003).

human rights recognized in international treaties or where the right to health brings a corresponding right to medications (such as for HIV/AIDS). Political conflicts occur especially when health concerns interfere with trade. The furore over trade in tobacco, beef growth hormones, asbestos and genetically modified organisms (GMOs) provide examples. As these disputes continue to grow in number and volume, there will be a greater need for international lawyers to provide solutions and for public health professionals to engage with legal issues.

AN OPENING FOR A NEW INTERNATIONAL SUSTAINABLE HEALTH LAW

Fortunately, the last ten years have seen a burgeoning interest, meetings and activities related to national and international public health law.[15] On the domestic front, States and health organizations have begun to use legal means to pursue public health concerns. For example, in Canada and the United States, State and provincial governments have pursued tobacco litigation to bolster public health measures. In South Africa and Thailand, governments have resisted pharmaceutical company pressure by asserting their legal rights under TRIPS to provide for generic drugs.

In December 1997, the WHO and the Indian Law Institute sponsored an International Conference on Global Health Law in New Delhi at which the delegates adopted the New Delhi Declaration on Global Health Law.[16] For the first time, the WHO has exercised its treaty-making powers, in order to pursue the first international health treaty in the area of tobacco control;[17] the WHO is also currently revising the International Health Regulations as a prelude to the development of a convention on infectious diseases.[18]

Finally, the WHO's "Health for All in the Twenty-First Century" policy emphasizes the importance of international law, stating that "WHO will develop international instruments that promote and promote health, will monitor their implementation, and will also encourage its member states to apply international laws related to health." The Health for All Policy demonstrates an appreciation of the importance of different international legal regimes to WHO's global work,

---

[15] A. Taylor, "Globalization and Public Health: Regulation, Norms and Standards at the Global Level" (Background Paper for the Conference on World Health Cooperation, Mexico City, 29 Mar. to 1 Apr. 1998. Unpublished manuscript on file with David Fidler) as quoted by Fidler, *Global, supra* note.

[16] New Delhi Declaration, 7 Dec. 1997 [hereafter *New Delhi Declaration*].

[17] See *International Framework Convention for Tobacco Control*, World Health Association Res. 49. 17., 49th Ass., 6th Plen. Mtg., WHO Doc. A49/VR/6 (26 May 1996).

[18] There are those who have articulated the need for a convention on infectious diseases, see D. Fidler, "Return of the Fourth Horseman: Emerging Infectious Diseases and International Law" (1997) 81 *Minn. L. Rev.* 771, 863–67. Others have seen this idea as unrealistic, see B.J. Plotkin, "Mission Possible: The Future of the International Health Regulations" (1996) 10 *Temp. Int'l & Comp. L. J.* 503 at 515.

including the three critical sustainable development regimes (human rights, international trade and environmental protection).[19]

International legal regimes represent both the solutions and additional complications for the global public health agenda. On one hand, international human rights laws provide powerful arguments for improving access to life-saving AIDS cocktails that are protected by international patent laws. On the other hand, liberalizing trade regimes only hasten the transnational flow of goods and peoples who serve as vectors for microscopic health threats. International environmental and health specialists may find themselves as part of a united front taking a precautionary approach to GMOs but may find resistance from within WTO and GATT rules which take different approaches to legislating risk. The relationship between the international finance and debt regimes and their implications for health are only just beginning to be explored. It is increasingly important to consider the linkages between "international health law" and the other legal regimes and to create methods to unravel the tensions between competing international agendas.

Without diminishing the WHO's special role in creating international health law, a new legal research agenda in this area suggests that international health law ought to be on the agenda of all those organizations involved with sustainable development law. Health is a multi-sectoral objective and must involve diverse legal regimes and organizations; international health law goes far beyond what the WHO may adopt under its international legal powers. There is a real need for a new and identifiable corpus of law that addresses the phenomenon of global public health in a way that existing laws are unable to do.

Elements of an international sustainable development law approach

There are three elements of international sustainable development law that have particular resonance for international health issues.

First, the precautionary principle, which has become intrinsic to international environmental policy, is important to international health law and policy. In a nutshell, the precautionary principle is innovative in that it changes the role of scientific data. It requires that once environmental damage is threatened, action should be taken to control or abate possible environmental interference even though there may still be scientific uncertainty as to the effects of the activities. As such it deviates from more traditional risk assessments based on a preponderance of available information; but it is not without foundation in medicine where the benefit of the diagnosis is often given to the patient ("Better Safe than Sorry"). As the precautionary principle solidifies its place in international law, it has the potential to be used as a mediating principle between equally laudable

---

[19] *Health for All in the Twenty-First Century*, World Health Assembly OR, 51st Sess., Annex, Agenda Item 19, WHO Doc. A51/5 (1998A) at paras. 2, 23, 25, 52 [hereafter *Health For All*]. See also A. L'Hirondel and D. Yach, "Develop and Strengthen Public Health Law" (1998) 51 *World Health Stat. Q.* 79, 83.

but conflicting goals in international law, especially in areas around health, trade and the environment.

The second principle is inter-generational and intra-generational equity and the eradication of poverty. This principle has particular implications for the health agenda related to both environmental pollution and infectious diseases. It asserts that the present generation has the obligation to refrain from depriving future generations of environmental, social and economic opportunities of well-being. Also, States should promote a fair utilization of resources among members of the present generation and should focus in particular on the needs of the poor, who have the greatest priority.

With regard to this principle's application to the environment and health, it can be noted that environmental pollution not only has health effects on present populations, but, by despoiling resources that contribute to health, it impairs the health of future generations. As more has been learned about the natural environment and its complexities, more has also been learned about the human body's sensitivity to apparently modest assaults and about the problems associated with the migration of pollutants, their transformation and the potential for accumulation over time; not only is the harm passed down between populations, but within families.[20]

The issue of infectious disease containment, in light of current drug use practices and antimicrobial resistance, also calls for an analysis of harm to future generations. In the 1970s, experts believed that the fight against infectious diseases was won. But during the last two decades, this opinion has been reversed. The spread of new diseases and the resurgence of diseases long considered under control has alarmed the medical community. Today, infectious diseases, particularly HIV/AIDS, have reversed hard-won gains in life expectancy in Africa and Asia. Moreover, the re-emergence of these epidemics has coincided with antimicrobial resistance. Until recently, science and medicine were able to stay ahead of the pathogens through the discovery of ever more potent classes of pharmaceuticals. This success has slowed markedly in no small part because of profligate use of antibiotics. The consequences of this question for present and future generations, both at home and in developing countries, will be important.

Finally, the sustainable development law principle of integration and inter-relationship, in particular in relation to human rights and social, economic and environmental objectives, has the potential to help elaborate the content of the right to health in relation to trade and environment regimes. The right to health

---

[20] There is a large body of evidence that shows many toxins are passed through breast milk. See *e.g.* E. Dewailly, A. Nantel, J.P. Weber and F. Meyer, "High levels of PCBs in breast milk of Inuit women from Arctic Québec" (1989) 43:5 *Bull. Environ. Contam. Toxicol.* 43, 641; S. Patandin *et al.*, "Dietary exposure to polychlorinated biphenyls and dioxins from infancy to adulthood: A comparison between breast-feeding, toddler, and long-term exposure" (1999) 107 *Environ. Health Perspect.* 45; J. Mörner, R.Bos & M. Fredrix, "Reducing and Eliminating the use of Persistent Organic Pesticides", online at www.who.int/.

had its first expression in the 1946 World Health Organization Constitution,[21] and its content has been elaborated with significant detail by the UN Committee on Economic, Social and Cultural Rights (CESCR) in its General Comment on the Right to Health. The Committee has noted that when concluding other international agreements, "States parties should take steps to ensure that these instruments do not adversely impact upon the right to health. Similarly, States parties have an obligation to ensure that their actions as members of international organizations take due account of the right to health."[22] Given the broad scope of the right to health, it will be relevant in considering many economic and environmental regimes.

A FUTURE LEGAL RESEARCH AGENDA

International health and trade

Public health and the liberalization of trade as concretized in the World Trade Organization (WTO) can provide most of the potent examples of laudable goals working at cross-purposes. The very goal of WTO law – to facilitate the increased cross-border movement of people and goods – only multiplies the vectors by which disease is spread across borders. All the benefits of liberalized trade (such as increased access to improved and cheaper consumer products) apply in reverse to goods which have adverse health impacts (such as tobacco, processed foods such as soft drinks). And where environmental health concerns interfere with trade, the conflict can be intense. While public health has focused most significantly on the control of infectious diseases (and will continue to do so), trade conflicts are also likely to arise with issues such as the standards for the safety, purity and potency of biological and pharmaceutical products; the regulation of the trade of blood and human organs; and the trade of health information, services, and products over the internet.[23]

The right to health is key when considering the health-trade nexus. The UN Committee on Economic, Social and Cultural Rights has previously advised the WTO to review its international trade and investment policies and rules in order to ensure that these are consistent with existing treaties, legislation and policies designed to protect and promote all human rights.[24] The UN Commission on Human Rights, the UN Special Rapporteur on the right to health and the Office

---

[21] "The enjoyment of the highest attainable standard of health is one of the fundamental rights of every human being without distinction of race, religion, political relief, economic or social condition."

[22] Committee on Economic, Social and Cultural Rights, *General Comment No.14: The Right to the Highest Attainable Standard of Health*, UN ESCOR, 2000, UN Doc. E/C.12/2000/4, para. 39.

[23] Fidler, *Future, supra* note 2, at 1109–1110.

[24] *Statement of the UN Committee on Economic, Social and Cultural Rights to the Third Ministerial Conference of the World Trade Organisation* (Seattle, 30 November to 3 December, 1999), UN. Doc. E.C.12/1999/9, para. 2.

of the UN High Commissioner for Human Rights have raised concerns about the impact of WTO rules, in particular those regarding intellectual property and services liberalization, on the right to health.[25]

The following areas are likely for future disputes around trade and health. First, States use public health rationales to restrict the imports of goods. States' rights to restrict trade on public health grounds remain a prominent feature of the international trading system for both developed and developing States. The contours of this protection have been articulated in Article XX(b) of GATT which extends protective measures to human, plant and animal life or health, in the SPS and TBT. It has also been extended by key WTO cases such as the dispute between the USA and Canada and the EU about hormone-treated beef, Britain's challenge to the EU's ban on beef because of concerns about bovine spongiform encephalopathy, and the Canada–France Asbestos disputes.[26] However, the international trade regime also attempts to constrain States' ability to misuse their power to protect public health by making the use of science integral. Thus, an important question in the context of international trade liberalization, specifically in the context of the round of WTO negotiations launched by the Doha Ministerial, is the extent to which government authorities are justified in taking a precautionary approach when they adopt unilateral health protection measures.[27]

In this area, certain questions should be considered in future legal research. First, how can market liberalization be pursued without undermining genuine national concerns about the transmission of infectious disease? How does the precautionary principle affect what constitutes an adequate risk assessment for an SPS challenge? Since mounting or defending challenges to health and safety measures requires scientific capabilities and resources, how can developing countries achieve parity with major industrial nations? How can the public's concerns about "foreign disease" threats (via the transmission of goods and people) avoid violations of individuals' rights in the name of "safety"?

---

[25] See *Economic, Social and Cultural Rights: Liberalisation of Trade in Services and Human Rights: Report of the High Commissioner*, 25 June 2002, E/CN.4/Sub.2/2002/9 and *Economic, Social and Cultural Rights: The impact of the Agreement on Trade-Related Aspects of Intellectual Property Rights on Human Rights*, 27 June 2001, E/CN.4/Sub.2/2001/13. Both reports are primarily concerned with the right to health. Together with related documents, they can be found at: http://www.unhchr.ch/development/globalization-02.html.

[26] See Case C–180/96, *United Kingdom v. Commission*, 1998 ECJ Celex Lexis 5270, at 3–4 (5 May 1998); WTO Arbitrator's Report on European Communities–Measures Concerning Meat and Meat Products (Hormones), WTO Doc. WT/DS26/ARB (12 July 1999); WTO Arbitrator's Report on EC Measures Concerning Meat and Meat Products (Hormones), WTO Docs. WT/DS26/15 and WT/DS48/13 (29 May 1998), WT/DS48/AB//R (16 Jan. 1998), WTO Doc. WT/DS26/R.USA (18 Aug. 1997).

[27] L. Ruessmann, "Putting the Precautionary Principle in its Place: Parameters for the Proper Application of a Precautionary Approach and the Implications for Developing Countries in Light of the Doha WTO Ministerial" (2002) 17 *Am. U. Int. L. Rev* 905.

Tobacco and trade

Tobacco use is an extraordinary threat both to human health and the environment. About one in every two long-term smokers dies from smoking. The WHO
estimates that tobacco products currently kill 4.2 million people each year; by
the year 2030, this annual toll will rise to nearly ten million deaths or one in six
adults globally per year.[28] In addition to the absolute human cost, there are
important regional variations. Country-specific analyses of the tobacco industry
by the World Bank in collaboration with the WHO found that tobacco addiction
imposes high opportunity costs on many poor households, who spend significant
proportions of their income on tobacco instead of on nutrition and other
needs.[29] Most of the projected deaths will occur in low and middle income
countries.[30] Moreover, as market share in industrialized countries decline, and
tobacco companies target developing countries and world youth, the disease
burden caused by tobacco usage will increase at an alarming rate.[31]

Thus, there is no greater area of structural conflict between trade liberalization
and public health than that of tobacco control. Empirical evidence confirms that
trade openness leads to increased tobacco consumption.[32] Tobacco control
measures such as tobacco tax increases, higher tariffs, smoking bans and health
warnings on packaging all substantively reduce tobacco consumption.[33]

Most countries have faced strong challenges to implementing comprehensive
control measures. Some might even argue that an international "social licence to
exist" must develop – and be denied to these companies. In this respect, an
entirely new area of contention may be opened by the WHO's *Framework
Convention on Tobacco Control* which was adopted on 21 May 2003.[34] The
FCTC is a comprehensive multilateral treaty that covers a wide range of issues

[28] Summarizing World Bank, *Curbing the Epidemic: Governments and the Economics of Tobacco
Control* (Washington, DC: World Bank, 1999), see WHO, "Economics of Tobacco Control" WHO
Doc. A/FCTC/WG1/2 (20 Aug. 1999) at 2 online: <http://www.who.int.gb.fctc.wg1/PDFwg1/
elt2.pdf> [hereinafter Economics of Tobacco Control]; Intergovernmental Negotiating Body of the
WHO Framework Convention on Tobacco Control, Activities Since the Previous Session, WHO Doc.
A/FCTC/INB5/4 (12 Sept. 2002) at 1 online: <http://www.who.int/gb/fctc/PDF/inb5/einb54.pdf>
[hereinafter Negotiating Body].

[29] Negotiating Body, *ibid.*, at 1.

[30] *Ibid.*, at 2.

[31] WHO, "Opening Statement by the Director-General", WHO Doc.A/FCTC/INB1/DIV/3 (16 Oct.
2000) at 1–2 online: <www.who.int/gb/fctc/inb1/PDFinb1/e1inbd3.pdf>, "Burden of Disease"
online: <www.tobacco.who.int/page/cf?sid=47>.

[32] A.L. Taylor and D.W. Bettcher, "WHO Framework Convention on Tobacco Control: A Global
'Good' For Public Health" (2000) 78:7 *Bulletin World Health Organization*, 920–9.

[33] J.P. Townsend, *Price, Tax and Smoking in Europe* (Copenhagen: World Health Organization,
1998); The World Bank, *Development in Practice Series: Curbing the Epidemic; Governments and the
Economics of Tobacco Control* (Washington DC: The World Bank, 1999); P. Jha & F.J. Chaloupka
eds., *Tobacco Control in Developing Countries* (New York: Oxford University Press, 2000).

[34] For a complete discussion of the use of international law in connection with tobacco control see
WHO, *World Heath Report 1999: Making a Difference* (Geneva: World Health Organization, 1999)
78; WHO Press release, "World Health Assembly Adopts Historic Tobacco Control Pact" (Press
Release, 21 May 2003) online: <http://www.who.int/mediacentre/releases/2003/prwha1/en/>.

such as tobacco smuggling, advertising, taxes, warning labels design and the extent of the liability of tobacco companies. The FCTC is a legally binding international treaty – an important step forward from the WHO's usual soft-law approach.

Tobacco control and trade promises to be an important area for the sustainable international health law agenda. Various questions need to be considered. First, what is the significance of TRIPS on trade mark protection and the disclosure of confidential product information? What are the implications of GATS in relation to restrictions on cigarette advertising? What is the affect of the TBT in relation to packaging and labelling? Does the WTO Agreement on Agriculture have implications for government support to tobacco production?

International health, access to medicines and intellectual property rights

Since the 1978 Alma-Ata conference, there has been recognition that access to essential drugs is vital for preventing and treating diseases affecting millions of people throughout the world. Indeed, most of modern medicine depends heavily on drugs and vaccines to treat illness.

However, the WHO estimates that currently one-third of the world's population lacks access to essential drugs, with this figure rising to over 50 per cent in parts of Africa and Asia. Reasons for lack of access to various medicines are complicated and beyond the scope of this chapter. But in the health and sustainable development law debates, the appropriate focus is on the pricing of drugs especially as a result of international trade and patent laws.

A key question for a sustainable health law research agenda is to what extent the intellectual property laws have contributed to the difficulty of global access to essential drugs. TRIPS requires that all member countries provide exclusive marketing rights to holders of patents on pharmaceutical products for a period of at least 20 years. TRIPS is an exception to the general liberalization tenets of the trade regime. TRIPS attempts to harmonize protection of IP rights among members; it imposes a positive duty on countries to implement intellectual property laws that draw on concepts found in United States intellectual property laws. However it provides some flexibility for States to address their public health needs by allowing several public interest exceptions to patent protection.[35]

Many developing countries and human rights activists claim that expensive drug prices are the result of strong patent protection.[36] What is unequivocal,

---

[35] "Significant public and private investment, particularly in the United States, converted this killer into a manageable chronic disorder for many in the developed world." J. Rein, "International Governance Through Trade Agreements: Patent Protection for Essential Medicines" (2001) 21 *NW. J. Int'l L. & Bus.* 379.

[36] See N. Ford & D. German, "AIDS and Essential Medicines and Compulsory Licensing" online: <http://www.cptech.org/March99-c1/report1/html>, Agreement on Trade-Related Aspects

however, is that the mere threat of legal action by pharmaceutical companies against countries shapes access as much as the actual patent laws. This inequality of resources and leverage is also a critical area for future research related to sustainable development. Law critics have pointed out, for example, that during the anthrax scare following the 11 September 2001 terrorist attacks in the USA, the US government considered the compulsory licensing of Cipro, an anthrax antibiotic.[37] Although, ultimately, the United States did not issue compulsory licences for Cipro, the US government has been accused of using the threat of compulsory licensing as leverage to negotiate favourable terms from Bayer, Cipro's patent holder. However, when faced with threats of compulsory licensing from countries which have sought to meet the pandemic needs of their own populations, the United States has sought to protect the IP rights of its pharmaceutical companies.[38]

Since the adoption of the *Declaration on the TRIPS Agreement and Public Health* at the WTO Ministerial Conference in Doha,[39] the fear of retaliatory action may have been somewhat minimized.[40] The *Doha Declaration* expressly recognizes that TRIPS "does not and should not prevent Members from taking measures to protect public health".[41] Further, the Declaration stresses that TRIPS "can and should be interpreted and implemented in a manner supportive of WTO Members' right to public health and, in particular, to promote access to medicines for all", and that member States have the right "to use, to the full, the provisions in the TRIPS Agreement, which provide flexibility for this purpose".[42] Although developing countries pushed for a legally binding interpretation of TRIPS, the *Doha Declaration* is a ministerial declaration and does not supersede TRIPS.[43] The status of the *Doha Declaration* is unclear, and interpretations of its import range from that of a "political statement" to that of "persuasive authority in the interpretation of TRIPS in the event of a

---

of Intellectual Property Rights, Including Trade in Counterfeit Goods, 15 Apr. 1994, *Marrakesh Agreement Establishing the World Trade Organization*, Annex 1C, Legal Instruments-Results of the Uruguay Round vol. 31, 33 ILM 81 (1994) [hereinafter TRIPS].

[37] S.K. Sell, "TRIPS and the Access to Medicines Campaign" (2002) 20 *Wis. Int'l L.J.* 481, 500–02.

[38] For a description of US pressure on South Africa and Thailand, on behalf of the US drug industry, to prevent the implementation of laws to make HIV/AIDS drugs cheaper see *ibid.*, at 515–16.

[39] Declaration on the TRIPS Agreement and Public Health, 20 Nov. 2001, WTO Res., 4th Sess., Ministerial Conference, WT/MIN(01)/DEC/2 [hereinafter *Doha Declaration*].

[40] Describing how countries who can barely meet the costs of purchasing drugs are not going to risk a legal challenge by an international pharmaceutical company see H. Walkowiaz, "AIDS in National and International Law" (2002) 96 *Am. Soc'y Int'l L. Proc.* 320 at 328.

[41] Declaration on the TRIPS Agreement, *supra* note 39, at para. 4.

[42] J.M. Bergerat, "Tripping over patents: aids, access to treatment and the manufacturing of scarcity" (2002) 17 *Conn. J. Int'l L.* 157 at 164.

[43] Sell, *supra* note 37, at 517–18; "ministerial declarations within the WTO are not legally binding in the dispute resolution process, and in the event of a dispute the language of the treaties as approved by national governments would prevail over any contradictory declaration by the ministers" A.O. Sykes, "Trips, Pharmaceuticals, Developing Countries, and the Doha 'Solution'" (2002) 3 *Chi. J. Int'l L.* 47, at 54.

dispute".[44] This may have affected the US position on the application of the *Doha Declaration*.[45]

The ways in which TRIPS impinges on access to medicine will continue to be a fertile area for legal research for many years. Various questions need to be answered. How can the *Doha Declaration* inform other provisions of the WTO? Can international finance regimes help national strategies finance the supply and increase the affordability of essential drugs in both the public and private sectors? How might developing countries structure intellectual property legislation in a way that respects both producing and consumer country concerns? How do the contours of the right to health interact with intellectual property regimes?

Health and GMOs[46]

Biotechnology and genetically modified organisms (GMOs) have ignited fierce debates over trade policy in the WTO, in TRIPS, and even amongst human rights thinkers. It touches every area of sustainable development law from trade to environment to health policy and as such will be a significant new area for legal research especially as the Doha Round moves forward. The Doha Development Round will address biotechnology through negotiations on issues such as agriculture, intellectual property rights, sanitary and phytosanitary standards, and the environment. Specific discussions on biotechnology and trade and IP policy promise to be extremely contentious. There are a number of elements of the conflict the most important of which is the tension between developing countries' access to food and medical security and their right to determine what safety standards to set for themselves in light of WTO rules.

This tension is exemplified by a dispute that has been brewing since the beginning of 2003, when the USA announced that it would bring a case before the WTO dispute settlement committee to persuade the EU to lift a ban on genetically modified (GM) foods. The situation is compounded when EU trading partners were pulled into the fray: importing GM products adversely affects their ability to export to the EU. This posed a major dilemma for developing countries such as Zimbabwe and Zambia, which had refused emergency food aid from the USA containing GM corn because they would no longer be able to export certain agricultural goods to the EU. Not only does this dispute capture concerns about the long-term health affects of GMOs, it raises new equity issues about what levels of safety ought to govern aid to developing countries.

The biotechnology debate extends beyond the trade and human rights concerns to the implications of extending intellectual property to living organisms. These concerns are linked to fears that biotechnology will transfer resources

---

[44] See Sell, *supra* note 37 at 54, and Sykes, *supra* note 43, at 54.
[45] Online: <http://www.cptech.org/ip/wto/p6/cptech03052003.html>.
[46] Online: <http://www.cid.harvard.edu/cidtrade/issues/biotechnology.html>.

from the public sphere to private ownership via the enforcement of intellectual property rights. Firms that have invested in the development of genetically modified varieties want to protect their proprietary knowledge, but many farmer groups have protested that enforcing intellectual property rights will disrupt their access to seed. These debates draw attention to the controversial TRIPS Article 27.3(b), which exempts advanced life forms from patentability but requires countries to establish some form of protection for plant varieties. This is also an area of concern for a new legal research agenda. It foresees the protection of indigenous plants and healing approaches as a flashpoint for developing vs. developed country tensions in the future.

GMOs and its implications for sustainable development law will be a rich and varied debate. Questions to be considered include: Will emerging understandings of the precautionary principle be used to justify the refusal of the transboundary movement of GMOs intended for direct use? How can developing country concerns about clearly defined liability be reconciled with developed countries' reluctance to assume liability for uncertain, foreseeable risk? How can long-term health concerns about the potential effects of GMOs be reconciled with the short-term food needs of developing populations?

International environmental law (IEL) and Health

The environment is a major health determinant and worthy of a full chapter to itself. Both "traditional" health hazards (such as lack of access to safe drinking water; inadequate basic sanitation; indoor air pollution from cooking and inadequate solid waste disposal) and "modern" hazards (such as water pollution from industry and intensive agriculture; air pollution from transportation or power stations, hazardous wastes, and other forms of transboundary pollution) contribute to about a quarter of human morbidity and mortality. Environmental changes too will increasingly affect human health. The fact that many people are not able to adapt to such circumstances, while others are forced to do so is the antithesis of sustainable development.

Fortunately much of international environmental law already does concern the protection of human health. A great deal of IEL focuses on shielding people from the health-damaging consequences of pollution and environmental degradation. IEL should be seen, therefore, as an important part of the international law that supports public health objectives.

Many questions need to be considered. How can public health practitioners and environmental experts work together to translate the inherent uncertainties around environmental hazards into concrete laws? How specifically does the international human rights regime add to the debate about the movement of hazardous wastes to low labour-cost environments, about the right to a healthy environment, about the tensions between what is seen as the developed world's focus on the environment and the developing world's desire for development?

How can the precautionary principle be reconciled with the desire for evidence-based policy in the area of health?

Health and human rights

There is a wealth of legal authority regarding the international human right to health.[47] But this legal authority must be developed to deal effectively with the implications of the right to health, especially for developing countries, in the face of scarce resources that can be allocated to health. One approach that may yield concrete answers is the emerging application of budget analysis techniques to human rights issues.[48] In particular, domestic courts in countries such as South Africa,[49] Colombia[50] and India[51] have reviewed resource allocations made by governments in the health sector.

Given the plethora of debates within health and human rights, it would be impossible to canvass them all in this prospectus. However further questions need to be considered. How is the Right to Health to be reconciled with TRIPS? How can access to basic health facilities be incorporated within international

---

[47] See *General Comment No. 14, supra* note 22, A. Chapman, "Core Obligations Related to the Right to Health" in A. Chapman and S. Russell, eds. *Core Obligations: Building a Framework for Economic, Social and Cultural Rights* (Oxford: Intersentia, 2002), B. Toebes, *The Right to Health as a Human Right in International Law* (Oxford: Intersentia, 1999) and *Report of the Special Rapporteur, Paul Hunt, submitted in accordance with Commission resolution 2002/31*, Commission on Human Rights, 59th Session, E/CN.4/2003/58, 13 February 2003.

[48] See for an empirical application of the right to health to public health budgets: H. Hofbauer, G. Lara and B. Martinez, *Health Care: A Question of Human Rights, Not Charity* (Mexico City: FUNDAR, Centro de Análisis e Investigación, 2002), http://www.fundar.org.mx.

[49] See *Minister of Health* v. *Treatment Action Campaign*, Constitutional Court of South Africa, 5 Jul. 2002, CCT Case 08102, in which the Court required the State to provide detailed treatments to reduce mother to child transmission of HIV. Conversely, the Court decided that the state's failure to provide free renal dialysis was justified after reviewing the resources available: *Soobramany* v. *Minister of Health, KwaZulu-Natal* [1998] 18 Const. LR 765 (S. Afr. Const. Ct.). The court stated: "to be reasonable, measures cannot leave out of account the degree and extent of the denial of the right they endeavour to realise. Those whose needs are the most urgent and whose ability to enjoy all rights therefore is at most peril must not be ignored by the measures aimed at achieving realisation of the right."

[50] The Colombian Constitutional Court stated that since provision of health care is subordinate to the existence of economic resources, and is partial and progressive in nature, available resources should be used in a rational and equitable fashion in cases in which the restoration of health is actually possible. It therefore approved the removal from hospital of a girl who was in a stable but irreversible condition on the basis that hospital beds and room should not be occupied by persons whose state of health was not expected to improve, so as to deprive other persons of care. Constitutional Court, Judgment No. T-484 of 11 Aug. 1992, *Revista Mensual, Jurisprudencia y Doctrina*, 1992, Vol. 21, pp. 1008-1109. Conversely, the State was required to provide treatment to an AIDS sufferer in a precarious economic state. Constitutional Court, Judgment No. T-505 of 28 Aug. 1992, *Revista Mensual, Jurisprudencia y Doctrina*, 1992, Vol. 21, pp. 1101-1106.

[51] The Indian Supreme Court held that the State is required to provide *at least the minimum conditions ensuring human dignity,* and ordered the government to provide suitable accommodation for a disabled woman living in a mental home. *Vikram Deo Singh Tomar* v. *State of Bihar,* (1988) Supp. SCC 734 at 736.

financial regimes, or, what new mechanisms need to be put into place to secure funding for basic health needs?

Complex humanitarian emergencies and sustainable development

An emerging area for sustainable health law includes the intersection between complex humanitarian emergencies and sustainable development law. Humanitarian emergency situations have become more frequent, more widespread, more complex and long lasting, combining interstate and internal conflicts, large-scale displacements of people, mass famine, disruption of economic, political and social institutions, and, in some cases, natural disasters. As seen in several locations recently (Kosovo, East Timor, Chechnya, Congo), these humanitarian crises can disrupt regional security and undermine efforts to promote sustainable development.

In virtually all post-emergency situations, resettlement of refugees, displaced persons and other disaster victims as well as the restoration of physical infrastructure are some of the major conditions for recovery. While peacekeeping, civilian, humanitarian, economic, social, and political activities are all part of the integrated process of post-crisis rebuilding, special attention should be given to the observance of the norms and principles of international law, including international sustainable development law. Failure to incorporate sustainable development can result in conflict over resources that lead to violent confrontation. Violent confrontations often have serious impacts on the vegetation, land, and water, undermining sustainable development still further. The period immediately post-conflict offers opportunities to make health law an integral part of national strategies and programmes for sustainable development.

There are several important questions to be considered. How can sustainable development law principles be incorporated into the restoration of national legal and judicial systems in post-conflict situations? How would a comprehensive and coordinated response to rehabilitation and reconstruction by the United Nations system, Bretton Woods Institutions, humanitarian agencies and Governments involve the application of sustainable development law principles at all stages of development?

Sustainable health processes and capacities

The New Delhi *Declaration on Global Health Law* states that "global health law" includes "strengthening institutional and human capacity for law"; developing regulatory and legislative approaches to support "health for all" and ensuring monitoring and implementation of health law.[52] These items do not represent principles of law but rather focus on processes and capabilities needed

---

[52] New Delhi Declaration, *supra* note 16.

to improve the contribution of national and international law to global public health.

One area of critical importance to a new legal research agenda in this area is an investigation of the new global institutions that support public health. What transnational authorities and procedures are needed for national governments to promote and protect public health, both within and without the WHO? Should the WHO have its own adjudicatory organ consistent with the World Health Assembly to settle political questions of significance to health? What executive-type enforcement power comparable to the WTO's dispute settlement system' threat of trade sanctions ought the WHO be endowed with?

CONCLUSIONS

While health has long been central to the sustainable development agenda, academics and scholars are only just beginning to analyse the relevance of international heath law to sustainable development law. Health laws and policies, as part of sustainable development law, are shaped by interconnections between social, environmental and economic law.

Legal scholarship in this area requires a great deal of future development, and this chapter simply presents a starting point, the identification of a future legal research agenda. Such research seeks to encourage public health practitioners and international legal specialists to consider health law from a genuinely global perspective. Globalization has rendered many distinctions between national and international policy objectives almost meaningless. Legal frameworks and implementation efforts need to reflect this reality. The traditional schism must be bridged between health policy and international law relating to sustainable development. A sustainable development law perspective can help meet this challenge by addressing cutting edge areas of sustainable development law related to health, especially in key policy areas where international treaties and principles are fast becoming part of the operating environment for all actors.

13

Sustainable International Biodiversity Law

with JORGE CABRERA MEDAGLIA and KATHRYN GARFORTH[1]

For the purposes of this chapter, the term biodiversity echoes the definition in the *Convention on Biological Diversity*[2] and include the variability among all life forms at the genetic, species and ecosystem levels.[3] Future research should uncover and highlight areas where the right balance has been struck between the social, environmental and economic aspects of biodiversity issues, and areas where more work is needed to integrate the three areas of sustainable development as they relate to biodiversity.

In particular, a future-oriented sustainable development law research agenda in international biodiversity law can focus on developing knowledge in two specific areas of inter-linkages. First, research is needed to define the linkages between different biodiversity-related policies and law in economic, environmental and social regimes. Secondly, research is needed to strengthen connections between biodiversity initiatives at the national, regional and international levels.

SUSTAINABLE BIODIVERSITY LAW IN ECONOMIC REGIMES

The relationship between trade and biodiversity protection has acquired increased significance over the past decade, as various multilateral agreements have been adopted by the international community.

In 1992 at the Earth Summit in Rio de Janeiro, world leaders agreed to the *Convention on Biological Diversity* which, for the first time, set out the principle of state sovereignty over natural resources in international treaty law.[4] This meant that access to genetic resources within a state's borders now required

---

[1] Jorge Cabrera Medaglia, B.C.L & LL.M (University of Costa Rica), is Lead Counsel for Sustainable International Biodiversity Law at CISDL, Professor at the University of Costa Rica Faculty of Law and the UNED University in Costa Rica and legal adviser to Costa Rica's National Biodiversity Institute. Kathryn Garforth, LL.B. (Osgoode Hall), M.E.S (York), is Research Fellow at the CISDL, and serves as a Consultant to the UNEP-GEF project on development of National Biosafety Frameworks.

[2] 5 June 1991, 31 ILM 818 (entered into force 29 Dec. 1993) [Biodiversity Convention].

[3] *Ibid.*, Art. 2.

[4] *Ibid.*, Art. 3; F. Yamin, "Biodiversity, Ethics and International Law" (1995) 71:3 *International Affairs* 529 at 540–541.

permission from the relevant state authority and brought biodiversity much closer to the international trading system. In 1994, world leaders met again, this time in Marrakesh, Morocco, and agreed to adopt a new set of trade rules and establish an international trade authority – the World Trade Organization. The new rules included agreements on minimum standards of intellectual property protection and allowable forms of sanitary and phytosanitary measures both of which affect the protection and conservation of biodiversity. Finally, in 2000, the Conference of the Parties to the CBD agreed to the *Cartagena Protocol on Biosafety*,[5] which fulfils the mandate established in article 19(3) of the CBD and sets out means to ensure "the safe transfer, handling and use of living modified organisms resulting from modern biotechnology that may have adverse effects on the conservation and sustainable use of biological diversity" in the context of international trade.[6] This multiplicity of agreements points to the need for research to explore the relationship between the legal regimes for trade and biodiversity as well as their implications for sustainable development. To this end, future research in this area must consider numerous aspects of the trade-biodiversity interface.

There are five parts from the Uruguay Round of trade negotiations that are particularly relevant to international biodiversity law: GATT 1994,[7] the Agreement on Agriculture,[8] the Agreement on the Application of Sanitary and Phytosanitary Measures,[9] the Agreement on Technical Barriers to Trade,[10] and the Agreement on Trade-Related Aspects of Intellectual Property Rights.[11] The first four of these can be discussed together and indeed all four are at issue in pending disputes between the United States and the European Community over the EC's moratorium on the approval of biotechnology products.[12] Such disputes raise a variety of broader questions concerning trade and biodiversity. What role should the precautionary principle have in the application of the SPS Agreement? To what extent are different states able to set culturally-appropriate levels of environmental and health protection? How will trade rules on sanitary or phytosanitary measures affect markets for genetically modified organisms or products thereof? Do laws requiring the labelling and traceability of GMOs constitute

---

[5] 29 Jan. 2000 (entered into force 11 Sept. 2003) [*Cartagena Protocol*, or Biosafety Protocol].

[6] *Ibid.*, Art. 1.

[7] *General Agreement on Tariffs and Trade 1994*, 15 April 1994, being part of Annex IA to the *Agreement Establishing the World Trade Organization*, 15 April 1994, 33 ILM 1144.

[8] *Ibid.*   [9] *Ibid.*   [10] *Ibid.*

[11] *Agreement on Trade-Related Aspects of Intellectual Property Rights*, 15 April 1994, 33 ILM 1197, being Annex 1C to the *Agreement Establishing the World Trade Organization*, 15 April 1994, 33 ILM 1144 [TRIPs].

[12] WTO, *European Communities – Measures Affecting the Approval and Marketing of Biotech Products: Request for Consultations by the United States*, WTO Doc. WT/DS291/1 (20 May 2003). Argentina and Canada have also launched parallel "requests for consultations" with the EC. For background information on the dispute, see Pew Initiative on Food and Biotechnology, *U.S. vs. EU: An Examination of the Trade Issues Surrounding Genetically Modified Food* (August 2003), online: Pew Initiative on Food Biotechnology <http://pewagbiotech.org/resources/issuebriefs/europe.pdf> (date accessed: 19 Sept. 2003).

technical barriers to trade? How will the entry into force of the *Cartagena Protocol* affect the application and interpretation of the WTO texts?

The last round of GATT trade negotiations also introduced *intellectual property rights* (IPRs) to the realm of international trade agreements.[13] The role of intellectual property regimes in the protection of biodiversity and the development of biotechnology has been the subject of substantial commentary.[14] IPRs have the potential to make important contributions to the promotion of technology and innovation, transfer of environmentally-sound technologies, health care, and access to medicines. The question remains, however, whether the current corpus of IPRs is sufficient to realize the environmental and social objectives that, together with the predominant economic motive of intellectual property regimes, underlie sustainable development.

A related concern is whether the TRIPs Agreement and the CBD are compatible or whether they are in conflict. One of the outcomes of the WTO Doha ministerial meeting in 2001 was that the TRIPs Council was mandated to examine the relationship between TRIPs and the CBD.[15] That said, the Secretariat of the CBD has yet to be granted observer status at the TRIPs Council. The WTO's Committee on Trade and Environment also received instructions in the *Doha Declaration* to give "particular attention" to the relevant provisions in TRIPs.[16] The sorts of questions these bodies could address in their work include whether IPRs promote research and development in areas relevant to the sustainable development of biodiversity. How do IPRs contribute to the protection or destruction of biodiversity? Should the origins of source material be disclosed in patent applications? How should indigenous knowledge be protected and biopiracy prevented? What are the scope and implications of the exclusions for plants and animals from intellectual property regimes? How can the benefits from patents based on biological resources be shared with the communities and countries of origin?

One type of intellectual property right is *plant variety protection*, the most widespread form of which is plant breeders' rights (PBRs) as embodied in the UPOV Conventions.[17] These Conventions grant exclusive rights to breeders who

---

[13] See D. Gervais, *The TRIPS Agreement: Drafting History and Analysis* (London: Sweet & Maxwell, 1998) for more information on the relationship between intellectual property rights and GATT.

[14] See e.g. G. Dutfield, *Intellectual Property Rights, Trade and Biodiversity*, (London: Earthscan Publications, 2000); and Crucible Group II, *Seeding Solutions, Volume 1. Policy Options for genetic resources, People, Plants, and Patents Revisited* (Ottawa: International Development Research Centre, Rome: International Plant Genetic Resources Institute, Uppsala: Dag Hammarskjöld Foundation, 2000).

[15] WTO, *Ministerial Declaration*, WTO Doc. WT/MIN(01)/DEC/1 at para. 19.

[16] *Ibid.*, at para. 32.

[17] The acronym "UPOV" is derived from the French name of the organization, *Union internationale pour la protection des obtentions végétales*. There have been three versions of the UPOV Convention, two of which are of concern here: *International Convention for the Protection of New Varieties of Plants*, 2 Dec. 1961, as revised on 23 Oct. 1978, U.K.T.S. 74 (1984) (entered into force 8 Nov. 1981); *International Convention for the Protection of New Varieties of Plants*, 2 Dec. 1961, as revised on 23 Oct. 1978 and 19 March 1991 (entered into force 24 April 1998).

develop distinct, uniform and stable varieties of plants.[18] They also allow farmers to save seeds from protected varieties to replant the following year and allow researchers to use protected varieties for research purposes.[19] The most recent version of the Convention increases the scope and strength of the breeder's right – bringing PBRs much closer to patent protection – while weakening the exemptions for farmers and researchers.[20]

The TRIPs Agreement does not specifically mention UPOV, however article 27(3)(b) requires members to "provide for the protection of plant varieties either by patents or by an effective *sui generis* system or by any combination thereof". This *sui generis* provision has been widely equated with the UPOV Convention but the issue has yet to be decided by a dispute settlement panel. Other bilateral trade agreements have been more explicit, requiring signatory states to join UPOV thus creating "TRIPs-plus" obligations for the countries involved.[21] The chapter on IPRs from the November 2002 draft text of the Free Trade Area of the Americas tentatively requires parties to implement parts of either the 1978 or 1991 version of the UPOV Convention, but the provision remains controversial.[22] Other relevant articles include a provision requiring parties to give effect to much of the CBD[23] and draft provisions that include the UPOV system of Plant Breeders' Rights as one possible definition of "effective *sui generis* system".

In addition to these international texts, there are several regional and national measures – such as the Andean Pact's Decision 345 and the Organization for African Unity's Model Plant Law – creating non-UPOV forms of plant variety protection.[24] The interplay of these different levels of law raises a variety of questions. What constitutes effective *sui generis* protection for plant varieties? Do TRIPs-plus agreements threaten biodiversity by requiring more stringent forms of intellectual property protection for life forms? Will the FTAA come into conflict with TRIPs if the former incorporates parts of the CBD?

The final economic issues to be explored by a research agenda on sustainable international biodiversity law are *competition and investment concerns*. Most of the research and development, patents, and market share in the life sciences industry is dominated by a handful of multinational corporations, predominantly

---

[18] Art. 6(1) of UPOV 1978. The 1991 version of the Convention requires that plant varieties be novel in addition to distinct, uniform and stable, Arts. 5(1) & 6.

[19] Art. 5(3) of UPOV 1978.

[20] UPOV 1991, Arts. 15(1), (2) & 14(5).

[21] Genetic Resources Action International, "'TRIPS-plus' Through the Back Door" (July 2001), online: GRAIN <http://www.grain.org/publications/trips-plus-en.cfm> (date accessed: 9 Nov. 2002). Some of these bilateral agreements go even further and require states to grant patent protection for plants.

[22] Free Trade Area of the Americas Draft Agreement, chapter on Intellectual Property Rights, document FTAA.TNC/w/133/Rev.2, online: FTAA <http://www.ftaa-alca.org/> (date accessed: 9 Nov. 2002), Part I, Art. 5.2(f).

[23] *Ibid.*, at Art. 5.2(p).

[24] See the website of Genetic Resources Action International <www.grain.org> and the section on biodiversity rights legislation in particular for texts of the various measures.

from Western industrialized countries.[25] In some cases, these MNCs have collaborated with government, universities or research institutions in developing countries, as encouraged under the CBD.[26] While the domination of the life sciences by a few multinationals is not necessarily problematic in itself, these companies may have research and market interests that do not coincide with the needs of developing countries or the conservation of biodiversity. The dominant position of these companies can make it hard for such other needs to be met. Further research is needed in this area.

International trade law is still grappling with how best to address competition and investment issues. There is no specific chapter from the Uruguay Round agreements that discusses competition law and the *Agreement on Trade-Related Investment Measures*[27] is very brief. TRIPs does contain provisions allowing member states to take action where intellectual property rights lead to anti-competitive behaviour but when and how these provisions should be applied is still in dispute.[28] At the Singapore Ministerial in 1996, the WTO created a Working Group on the Interaction between Trade and Competition Policy which continues to explore different topics related to these themes. To date, however, the Working Group has not been authorized to develop a text for inclusion in the Doha round of negotiations. The most recent draft text for the Free Trade Area of the Americas does include a chapter on competition policy but much of the wording remains in square brackets.[29]

In the context of sustainable international biodiversity law, issues for consideration relating to competition and investment include consolidation in the life sciences and agro-chemical industries; the effect of broad patent claims and their negative consequences for research and development; chain of control from seed to processing to distribution and marketing; and barriers to entry for new competitors, amongst others. Against this backdrop of the patterns of investment in the biotechnology industry, a sustainable development law research agenda could focus on discovering and testing new legal tools that may serve as incentives for technology transfer and research and development.

---

[25] ETC Group, Communiqué Issue #71, "Globalization, Inc. Concentration in Corporate Power: The Unmentioned Agenda" (July/Aug. 2001).

[26] *Biodiversity Convention, supra* note 2, Art. 15.

[27] *Agreement on Trade-Related Investment Measures*, 15 April 1994, being part of Annex 1A to the *Agreement Establishing the World Trade Organization*, 15 April 1994, 33 ILM 1144.

[28] See e.g. *Brazil – Measures Affecting Patent Protection* and the US request for a panel in relation to Brazil's domestic working and compulsory licensing scheme, WTO document WT/DS199/3 9 Jan. 2001; as well as *The Pharmaceutical Manufacturers' Association of America et al.* and *The President of the Republic of South Africa, The Honourable Mr. N.R. Mandela, N.O. et al.* which was the lawsuit by 39 pharmaceutical firms against the Government of South Africa and its 1997 *Medicines and Related Substances Control Amendment Act* which allows the use of compulsory licensing and parallel imports, online: The Consumer Project on Technology <http:www.cptech.org/ip/health/sa/pharma-v-sa.html> (last modified: 22 Aug. 2002).

[29] Free Trade Area of the Americas Draft Agreement, Chapter on Competition Policy, document FTAA.TNC/w/133/Rev.2, online: FTAA <http://www.ftaa-alca.org/> (date accessed: 9 Nov. 2002).

SUSTAINABLE BIODIVERSITY LAW IN ENVIRONMENTAL REGIMES

At first glance, it would appear as though the relationship between environmental regimes and sustainable international biodiversity law should be straightforward. In reality, however, this is not the case. The number of international organizations and multilateral agreements whose purposes pertain to the environmental dimension of biodiversity means that a great deal of cross-referencing must be done. In addition to the *Convention on Biological Diversity* (CBD) and the *Cartagena Protocol on Biosafety*, the international community has now agreed to the *International Treaty on Plant Genetic Resources for Food and Agriculture*.[30] This Treaty was created under the auspices of the Food and Agriculture Organization and its objectives are "the conservation and sustainable use of plant genetic resources for food and agriculture and the fair and equitable sharing of the benefits arising out of their use, in harmony with the Convention on Biological Diversity, for sustainable agriculture and food security".[31] While the treaty aims to be in harmony with the CBD, it takes quite a different approach from the sustainable use aspect of its mandate, and, as we shall see below, this creates friction between the two agreements. None of these agreements are purely environmental.[32] All involve both economic and social concerns, tying them to the other questions raised in the international biodiversity law research programme.

The first two objectives of the *Convention on Biological Diversity* are the *conservation of biodiversity* and the *sustainable use of its components*. The Convention sets out fairly detailed provisions on *in-situ* and *ex-situ* conservation[33] and rather general guidelines for sustainable use.[34] The first two objectives of the IT similarly concern conservation and sustainable use, although in the more limited category of plant genetic resources for food and agriculture. Articles 5 and 6 of the Treaty elaborate as to what sorts of measures may be taken to encourage conservation and sustainable use. The relatively brief nature of these articles raises a variety of questions. To what extent are the provisions of the CBD and the IT appropriate for the realization of two of their principal objectives? What legal mechanisms could be introduced to facilitate the realization of these objectives? What are some of the constraints? Do other legal regimes, such as TRIPs, for example, help or hinder the goals of conservation and sustainable use?

The third objective of the CBD is *access to genetic resources and benefit-sharing*. Article 15 of the Convention encourages state parties to enter into

---

[30] *International Treaty on Plant Genetic Resources for Food and Agriculture* (hereinafter IT) was adopted on 3 Nov. 2001.

[31] Art. 1.1.

[32] U.P. Thomas, "The CBD, the WTO, and the FAO: The Emergence of Phytogenetic Governance" in P.G. LePrestre, ed., *Governing Global Biodiversity: The Evolution and Implementation of the Convention on Biological Diversity* (Aldershot, Vi: Ashgate, 2002) 177 at 180.

[33] *Biodiversity Convention*, Arts. 8 & 9.   [34] *Biodiversity Convention*, Arts. 10 & 11.

bilateral agreements with other states or private parties in order to ensure access and benefit-sharing. These agreements are to be on mutually agreed terms and subject to prior informed consent. The provisions in article 15 have now been used to develop the *Bonn Guidelines on Access to Genetic Resources and the Fair and Equitable Sharing of the Benefits Arising out of their Utilization*.[35] While not legally binding, the Guidelines were unanimously adopted at the sixth Conference of the Parties to the CBD in April 2002. Subsequently, the Guidelines were noted in the Plan of Implementation of the *World Summit on Sustainable Development*. Paragraph 44 of the Plan focuses on biodiversity, and encourages the implementation and further development of the Guidelines. It also calls for action to "[n]egotiate within the framework of the Convention on Biological Diversity, bearing in mind the Bonn Guidelines, an international regime to promote and safeguard the fair and equitable sharing of benefits arising out of the utilization of genetic resources".

Access to genetic resources and benefit-sharing must also be examined in the context of the new IT. The Treaty attempts to establish a multilateral system of access to plant genetic resources as well as create a means to share the benefits arising from use of the resources in the system. Because of the principle of state sovereignty over natural resources, the Treaty contains an appendix listing the types of crops states were willing to include in the multilateral system. The possibility of separate, bilateral access and benefit-sharing agreements under the CBD, however, meant that some of the gene-rich countries were unwilling to include certain species in the multilateral system in the hope that these species could generate more revenue through bilateral contracts.[36]

The current status of access to genetic resources and benefit-sharing raises a number of questions. Is a bilateral or multilateral system of ABS a better approach or can the two co-exist harmoniously? What should an international regime on benefit-sharing look like? What sorts of benefit-sharing mechanisms should exist for the use of *ex-situ* collections?

According to the Secretariat of the Convention on Biological Diversity, the term biosafety is "used to describe efforts to reduce and eliminate the potential risks resulting from biotechnology and its products".[37] A variety of recent world events has focused attention on biosafety issues. In 2001, reports emerged that genetically modified corn had appeared in remote parts of Mexico despite a ban on planting GM corn in the country.[38] Mexico is a centre of diversity for corn and concerns focused on the potential for GM varieties to out-compete and

---

[35] Being the Annex to *Access and benefit-sharing as related to genetic resources*, CBD COP Dec. VI/ 24 A, 2002, UN Doc. UNEP/CBD/COP/ 6/20 [Bonn Guidelines].

[36] H.D. Cooper, "The International Treaty on Plant Genetic Resources for Food and Agriculture" (2002) 11 *RECIEL* 1 at 5.

[37] "Frequently Asked Questions on the Biosafety Protocol", online: Convention on Biological Diversity, <http://www.biodiv.org/biosafety/faqs.asp?area=biotechnology&faq=2> (date accessed: 19 Sept. 2003).

[38] D. Quist and I. Chapela, "Transgenic DNA Introgressed into Traditional Maize Landraces in Oazaca, Mexico" (2001) 414 *Nature* 541.

reduce the biodiversity of local varieties. If this did indeed come to pass, the repercussions would be felt well beyond Mexico as the country's corn biodiversity is used as a source of genetic variability by international crop breeders. A second event was the refusal of several southern African countries to accept American food aid to help relieve famine. The countries were concerned that the food would be genetically modified and they were not prepared to accept the perceived risks to public health or their access to European agricultural markets, which are largely closed to GM foods.

The *Cartagena Protocol on Biosafety* was meant to remedy some of these difficulties. The Protocol creates different procedures for notification and approval by both exporting and importing countries for different types of living modified organisms (LMOs).[39] The main division is between LMOs destined for intentional release into the environment, which are subject to an Advance Informed Agreement procedure,[40] and LMOs that are not intended for release into the environment and are instead to be used as food, feed or processing.[41] The Protocol allows importing states to make their own decisions about whether or not to allow the importation of specific types of LMOs. These decisions can be based on domestic regulatory frameworks or states can use the procedural requirements set out in the Protocol. Decisions are to be based on sound science and the use of precaution is allowed where the science is insufficient or non-existent.[42] States are also allowed to include some socio-economic considerations in their decision-making.[43]

The Protocol is very new, however, so many questions remain. Can the concepts of precaution in the Biosafety Protocol and the SPS Agreement be reconciled? How well can the Protocol function without the participation of the United States, the largest exporter of genetically modified organisms? Can states truly consider socio-economic factors in their decision-making about the importation of living modified organisms as allowed under the Protocol or will this bring them into conflict with provisions in the WTO Agreements?

The United Nations Environment Programme, with funding from the Global Environment Facility, is conducting three projects that will help developing countries with their implementation of the Biosafety Protocol. These projects are the Global Project on Development of National Biosafety Frameworks, the Project on Implementation of National Biosafety Frameworks, and the Biosafety Clearing-House Project.[44] The UNEP-GEF Development Project is designed to prepare countries for the entry into force of the Biosafety Protocol including through the creation of national biosafety frameworks.[45] The project currently

---

[39] For a thorough overview of the provisions of the Protocol see IUCN, *An Explanatory Guide to the Cartagena Protocol on Biosafety* (Cambridge: IUCN, 2003).

[40] Protocol, Arts. 7–10.   [41] *Ibid.*, Art. 11.   [42] IUCN, *supra* note 39, at para. 340.

[43] *Supra* note 5, Art. 26.

[44] For more information, see the projects' website, http://www.unep.ch/biosafety/.

[45] UNEP–GEF Global Project on Development of 100 National Biosafety Frameworks (Global Programme Document), online: http://www.unep.ch/biosafety/development/devdocuments/GPD.pdf.

includes 123 participating countries. Over the course of the Development Project, countries have had to face the uncertainty over the relationship between the Protocol and other international economic, environmental and social agreements. The reports from the series of three regional and sub-regional workshops that formed part of the project illustrate both the complexity of the field of biosafety and its inherently integrative nature.[46]

Sustainable biodiversity law in social regimes

The social aspect of sustainable international biodiversity law is probably the least developed in national and international law. It includes some areas that overlap with other research programmes of ISDL – the right to food, access to medicines, the right of access to innovations. It also includes relatively new concepts that have arisen largely in response to the growing commercialization of biodiversity – Farmers' Rights and protection of Traditional Knowledge. The newness of these areas means their content is still being developed, making them perfect subjects for future inquiry in sustainable international biodiversity law scholarship.

The protection of traditional knowledge has gained increasing importance in the face of ever expanding intellectual property rights regimes. Traditional knowledge includes things like information on the medicinal qualities of plants and animals, or the years of selective breeding that have produced particular varieties of crops. For the most part, traditional knowledge does not fit well within the Western systems of patents, copyrights, trade marks, etc. If the value of traditional knowledge is ignored, however, it gives the knowledge-holders little incentive to share, protect, and develop their insights.

The World Intellectual Property Organization (WIPO) has been actively working on three main issues in this area: folklore, protection of traditional knowledge, and genetic resources.[47] To date, no agreement has been reached to recommend to the next WIPO General Assembly that it initiate negotiations towards a legally-binding international treaty for the protection of traditional knowledge. In addition, the TRIPs Council has been unable to agree as to

---

[46] See, for example, UNEP-GEF Project on Development of National Biosafety Frameworks, *Synthesis Report of Regional Biosafety Workshops, 2002*, online: http://www.unep.ch/biosafety/development/devdocuments/RWsynthesis020802.pdf; UNEP-GEF Project on Development of National Biosafety Frameworks, *Report of the Sub-regional Workshops for Asian Countries on: Risk Assessment and Management and Public Awareness and Participation*, 21–24 January 2003, Kuala Lumpur, Malaysia, online: http://www.unep.ch/biosafety/development/devdocuments/2Malaysia WebReport.pdf; UNEP-GEF Project on Development of National Biosafety Frameworks, *Final Report of the Anglophone Africa Sub-regional Workshop on the Development of a Regulatory Regime and Administrative Systems for National Biosafety Frameworks*, 9–12 March 2004, Dar Es Salaam, United Republic of Tanzania, online: http://www.unep.ch/biosafety/development/devdocuments/3TanzanianWebReportEN.pdf.

[47] For an overview of the work to date, see WIPO, Intergovernmental Committee on Intellectual Property and Genetic Resources, Traditional Knowledge and Folklore, 5th sess., Doc. WIPO/GRTKF/IC/5/12 (2003).

whether it should discuss protection of traditional knowledge in the context of its work.[48]

This lack of agreement means there are many questions to be considered in the area of sustainable biodiversity law. How can the contributions of traditional communities be acknowledged and valued in the intellectual property system? Can and should there be an international regime for the protection of traditional knowledge? How do we address cultural values that baulk at the conceptualization of traditional knowledge as property?

Farmers' Rights have already been alluded to in other parts of this chapter. The concept arose in response to the development of the UPOV Convention and the idea of Plant Breeders' Rights. According to the IT, Farmers' Rights are based in "the past, present and future contributions of farmers in all regions of the world, particularly those in centres of origin and diversity, in conserving, improving and making available these resources".[49] Despite the IT's affirmation that the rights recognized in the Treaty to, amongst other things, "save, use, exchange and sell farm-saved seed and other propagating material" are fundamental to the realization of Farmers' Rights, the actual text of the Treaty leaves the implementation of Farmers' Rights up to national governments.[50]

As the concept of Farmers' Rights begins to take greater shape, the types of questions that need to be answered include whether the national recognition of Farmers' Rights is sufficient or whether an international treaty is necessary to assure their adequate protection. What is the relationship between Farmers' Rights and other international human rights treaties? To what degree are Farmers' Rights threatened by international trade and intellectual property agreements?

All of these questions provide important starting points for a timely, cutting-edge future legal research agenda in the area of sustainable international biodiversity law.

---

[48] J.A. Ekpere, "TRIPs, Biodiversity and Traditional Knowledge" (2003) 7:5 *Bridges* 11, at 11–12, online: International Centre for Trade and Sustainable Development at www.ictsd.org.
[49] IT, *supra* note 30, preamble, para. 7.   [50] *Ibid.*, Art. 9.

14

Sustainable International Climate Change Law

with XUEMAN WANG[1]

Climate change poses a serious challenge to the ability of international law to construct equitable global responses to shared problems. Emissions of greenhouse gases (GHGs) come disproportionately from industrialized countries. Some countries, again predominantly in the industrialized world, are better placed than others to pioneer the technologies, processes, and behavioural changes that will be necessary to mitigate their emissions. However, the most harmful consequences of climate change are likely to befall the poorest countries. In many cases, these countries are not only those least responsible for unleashing them, but also those least equipped to deal with them. Furthermore, in international climate negotiations, the same countries are often the least able to make their voices heard, or to assess the implications of any proposed outcome in light of their own interests.[2] A sustainable development law perspective in the area of climate change focuses on how climate change law is developed and implemented, with a focus on the needs of smaller economies, especially least-developed countries and new actors, including civil society and corporate citizens.

EQUITY AND CLIMATE CHANGE LAW

It is not surprising that the language of equity has permeated the international negotiations on climate change since they began in 1991. Different nations and groups of nations have offered different, and often conflicting, visions of what is equitable. Not surprisingly, these visions tend to coincide in most cases with

---

[1] Xueman Wang LL.M. (Wu Han, China), M.A. (Fletcher School, Tufts) is Lead Counsel for Climate Change and Vulnerability Law at CISDL. She works with the Secretariat of the Convention on Biological Diversity and previously worked for the UN Climate Change Secretariat and the Ministry of Foreign Affairs of China. This chapter shares thoughts with her chapter, with J. Ashton, "Equity and Climate: In Principle and Practice" in *Beyond Kyoto: Advancing the International Effort Against Climate Change* (Washington: Pew Foundation, 2003).

[2] *Ibid.* See also T. Heller and P.R. Shukla, "Development and Climate: Engaging Developing Countries" in *Beyond Kyoto: Advancing the International Effort Against Climate Change* (Arlington: Pew Center on Global Climate Change, 2003). And see Intergovernmental Panel on Climate Change, *The Regional Impacts of Climate Change: An Assessment of Vulnerability*, A Special Report of Working Group II, R.T. Watson, M.C. Zinyowera, R.H. Moss (eds.) (Cambridge: Cambridge University Press, 1997) [hereinafter *Vulnerability*].

perceived material interest of countries. The two major agreements to date, the 1992 *United Nations Framework Convention on Climate Change* (UNFCCC), and the 1997 *Kyoto Protocol*, reflect a rough calculus of equity at the early stages of the international climate effort.[3] The Convention commits parties to "protect the climate... on the basis of equity". It makes the fulfilment of obligations by developing countries conditional on assistance from the developed countries, while the Kyoto Protocol emissions constraints apply only to the latter. But the Convention and the Protocol are only first steps towards an international regime capable of neutralizing the impact of human activity on the climate. The withdrawal of the United States from the Kyoto Protocol has made them yet more tentative. A successor agreement will need to deliver stronger commitments further into the future. That will demand more effort and inevitably throw into sharper relief the links between climate change and equity. A deeper and more universal understanding of the equity considerations inherent in the climate problem will be needed. So will more powerful tools to resolve the conflicts and trade-offs between competing views of fair outcomes. In short, the success of the negotiation will hinge in large measure on the ability of parties to come to terms with the equity dilemmas they will face.

As discussed in recent studies, many different equity notions or claims have been put forward in the climate debate, and these can be described as five dimensions of equity.[4] Not all are universally held principles, but each has sufficiently broad appeal to have attained legitimacy in the eyes of many. First, in many circumstances, equity boils down to an allocation of responsibility. When interests are harmed, the question of who is to blame is usually among the first to arise.[5] An equitable agreement on climate would need somehow to reflect the relative degrees of responsibility for the problem arising in the first place. As noted above in Part III, the failure to limit greenhouse gas emissions can be seen as constituting a violation of human rights of others. A second approach to equity is based on the idea of rights or entitlements to certain goods or benefits. Equity becomes a question of how these entitlements should be distributed.[6]

---

[3] Ashton and Wang, *supra* note 1. The authors put the onus for early action on industrialized countries, citing common but differentiated responsibilities. They make clear that measures to deal with climate change should not limit the ability of developing countries to develop and pay special attention to the needs of the poorest and most vulnerable countries. They include provisions for the transfer of technology and financial resources and help in dealing with the impacts of climate change. See also B. Müller, *Equity in Climate Change: The Great Divide* (Oxford: OISE, 2002).

[4] Ashton and Wang, *supra* note 1. See also Müller, *supra* note 3.

[5] The notion of responsibility is hard to apply when the chain of cause and effect linking the initial action to the harm is long and uncertain; when the extent or distribution of the damage is difficult to quantify; when compensation for damage does not by itself solve the problem; or when the benefit arising from the harmful behaviour is spread beyond the party responsible for the harm, for example through trade in carbon-intensive goods. All these difficulties apply in the case of climate change. See Intergovernmental Panel on Climate Change, *Vulnerability*, *supra* note 2.

[6] Entitlements of this kind are well established in international law, not least in the United Nations Charter and the two international covenants covering civil, political, economic, social, and cultural rights.

Climatic stability can be seen as a global commons attribute: an equal share of the total "carbon space" should be available for human activity. On that basis, equity in any new climate agreement would be judged by the extent to which it carries us towards such an equal entitlements world. A third basic notion of equity relates to the capacity to act. The most able should contribute the most to the provision of a public good.[7] An equitable approach to climate would thus demand more from those most equipped to respond. A fourth component of equity is the idea that the strong and well endowed should help the weak and less well endowed in meeting their most basic needs and human rights.[8] Thus an equitable climate change agreement would help, and certainly not undermine, the efforts of the poorest countries to meet the basic needs of their people. There is a fifth dimension, relating to comparative equity. In assessing whether an outcome is equitable, parties will invariably compare the effort they are being asked to make with that required of other parties. The essence of this dimension lies in its *relational* quality: the effort demanded of a party not only has to seem fair as an absolute expression of its record and circumstances but also in light of the deals secured by others. Finally, climate change will restrict the choices of generations to come. Few would dispute that the next climate agreement should in some sense be fair to future generations. A crude way to assess this would be in terms of its overall impact on emissions. The faster climate change can be brought under control, the less it can damage the interests of successor generations.

There are, in essence, four separate but connected domains of choice to consider, and each leads to new directions for legal research on sustainable climate law. The first concerns what action should be taken, if any, to constrain *emissions* of greenhouse gases. The second concerns the *process* of negotiation on climate change. The third concerns the *consequences* of climate change, and the steps necessary to deal with them. The fourth concerns the help given to, or received from others, through *transfers* of resources.

New obligations for emissions constraints

First, with relation to equity and emissions, what obligations should a state in a given set of circumstances be expected to undertake to constrain its GHG

---

[7] Industrialized countries have more access to the technologies necessary to address such problems, and to the capital necessary to develop them and bring them to market. They are better able to put in place the necessary policies, including those linking domestic measures to international commitments, and to innovate in pursuit of national goals. See Intergovernmental Panel on Climate Change, *Climate Change 2001: Mitigation* Contribution of Working Group III to the Third Assessment Report, B. Metz, O. Davidson, R. Swart & J. Pan (eds.) (Cambridge: Cambridge University Press, 2001) [hereinafter *Mitigation*].

[8] Most countries at least aspire to offer a safety net to the helpless. Internationally, this is one impulse behind the effort to eradicate poverty. The Millennium Development Goals and international human rights instruments define a set of basic human requirements to be met through shared action and support from those rich enough to provide it. See Heller and Shukla, *supra* note 2.

emissions? Responsibility for human interference with the climate is distributed unevenly. So it might seem reasonable to assess how much different countries have contributed to the problem, and to apportion accordingly the responsibility for solving it. But in practice, the assignment of responsibility is hardly straightforward. There is uncertainty over the detailed connections between emissions at one time and climatic variation at another. One approach would be to distribute emissions according to the relative *historic responsibility* of different countries for the extent of the problem so far.[9] Or perhaps it would be fairer to allocate responsibility according to *current emissions*. Furthermore, should not those whose *future emissions* are likely to grow most rapidly assume some responsibility for the climate consequences of their chosen development path? In assessing responsibility, it is also reasonable to ask who benefits from the emissions caused by a particular activity, whereby those who receive the benefits from the emissions (or "embedded carbon") associated with the production of traded goods carry the cost. An entitlements approach circumvents these complexities by choosing a different starting point. Rather than responsibility, it assigns rights, in the form of equal entitlements to the atmosphere. This is the basis of the proposal known as "Contraction and Convergence".[10] As a practical framework for the next stage of the international negotiations, this proposal faces serious obstacles, not least in addressing concerns about the scale of resource transfers and domestic dislocation it might require of high emitters. However, the notion of *per capita emissions* remains central to any discussion of climate and equity. Taking all these arguments together, an equity perspective on emissions suggests that the more prosperous a country is, and the higher its total and per capita emissions, the stronger should be its obligations. That points in the near term to more vigorous action by industrialized than developing countries. It also suggests the need for differentiation of commitments and a mechanism for minimizing competitive stresses, perhaps linked to international frameworks for trade and investment. But it also follows that as the more advanced developing countries achieve a higher level of development, and as their emissions and

---

[9] Methodologies for doing this have been under discussion for several years, based on a proposal originally made by Brazil. See *United Nations Framework Convention on Climate Change*, "Implementation of the Berlin Mandate, Additional Proposals from Parties" (1997) UNFCCC Seventh Session of the Ad-Hoc Group on the Berlin Mandate, Bonn, Germany. Tangled legal and political problems for further research include: From what date should the accounting of responsibility begin? Should the clock start with industrialization, with scientific speculation about the link between human activity and climate change, or at some later date? Should the account include only direct GHG emissions, or should it also cover emissions and withdrawals as a result of changes in land use? Should it be based on total emissions over the chosen period, on the resulting changes in GHG concentrations in the atmosphere, or on the degree of climate change likely to have been caused or committed to as a result of the changed concentrations? And why in any case should parties be held responsible for what they did before the international community understood that human activity affects the climate?

[10] If everyone has an equal right to account for emissions, the next stage of the climate regime should bring per capita emissions closer together. So countries with high per capita emissions should reduce them; but those with low ones should have headroom within which to increase them.

income grow, they will over time have to assume an appropriate share of the responsibility for limiting and ultimately reducing global emissions.

Ensuring an open, transparent, participatory negotiating process

Secondly, the process by which climate agreements are reached should be open, transparent and participatory. Whether or not such procedural requirements are legally binding, there is no surer way to push an agreement out of reach than for a group of States to find that the negotiating process is biased against them. In the climate negotiations, the meeting in The Hague in 2000 of the Sixth Conference of Parties (COP6) collapsed partly because developing countries would not accept as a *fait accompli* any last-minute agreement between the European Union and the United States. Indeed, even the experience of the *Kyoto Protocol* negotiations illustrates the importance of a fair process.[11] The next climate negotiations (and hence, their outcomes) stand a better chance of being accepted if the process is transparent and open to all parties. In a negotiation with 168 parties clustered into disparate groups, each incorporating a range of conflicting interests, it is a challenge to establish these conditions, and further legal research is needed to discover mechanisms, and principles, which support the goal of open, transparent and participatory process.

In addition, the climate negotiations are among the most complex ever attempted, and some parties have far greater capacity to participate effectively in them. During any session, several dozen highly technical negotiations proceed simultaneously, covering issues as diverse as the rules of procedure and feedbacks between climate change and ozone depletion. Parties with enough skilled negotiators to engage effectively on each issue, and make the linkages between them, are at an advantage, so further legal and technical capacity development is highly necessary.[12] Finally, most debate about the future of the climate regime takes place among scholars, officials, activists, and others from the North. It

---

[11] There were no agreed criteria for assigning obligations. Some commitments were imposed by muscular chairmanship or gavelled through without reaction from exhausted negotiators. Developing countries were on that occasion pressed into accepting a deal made in their absence among their industrialized partners, fuelling their suspicions ever since about *faits accomplis*. The Kyoto Protocol might not have been agreed without such methods; but it has been fragile in part because of them. As the process becomes more demanding on more countries, it will become ever more important for all to feel that their voice in it will be heard. This imperative derives, in a sense, from the equity dimension of entitlements: all who believe they have interests at stake in any aspect of the negotiation are entitled to equal access to the process. See S. Oberthür and H.E. Ott eds., *The Kyoto Protocol: International Climate Policy for the 21st Century* (Berlin: Springer Verlag/Ecologic, 1999).

[12] The larger industrialized countries typically bring teams of several dozen – in some cases over a hundred – officials to a major negotiating session. Many of the poorest countries manage only to send a single representative. This is not just a question of the size or skills of the team a country can deploy in a negotiating session. To participate with confidence in the process as a whole, a government needs to be able to maintain an up-to-date assessment of its national interest in each of the many areas under discussion. It must understand the implications of the positions and underlying policies of others. It must maintain domestic systems to set climate goals, integrate them with other areas of policy,

would be worthwhile to provide opportunities for representatives of developing countries to play a fuller part in such dialogues, off line from the formal negotiations. Participation in such initiatives would help build confidence and shared perspectives on key issues before they arise in the more highly charged setting of the negotiations.

Economic aspects of climate change law

The three Kyoto market mechanisms, emissions trading, clean development mechanism (CDM) and joint implementation, were designed for maximum effectiveness while meeting social and economic needs. Research can focus on two features of the Kyoto Protocol that could, if extended, make an indirect yet critical contribution to implementing the principle of equity in future climate treaties. The first is the flexibility that the Protocol allows to parties in meeting their commitments: through action on different GHGs, through the sequestration of carbon in soil and vegetation, through projects to mitigate emissions elsewhere, and through trading in emissions permits. The aim of this flexibility is to enable parties to meet their commitments at the lowest possible cost, thereby delivering more mitigation for a given effort. In pursuit of an equitable outcome, regime flexibility is an ally. The second important feature of the Kyoto Protocol architecture is the way that it enshrines different treatment for different countries and groups of countries. Industrialized countries have individually negotiated emissions targets. Among them the economies in transition can choose the baseline year against which their targets are defined. Developing countries have no emissions commitments, and access to certain kinds of assistance, with further help available for the poorest. This differentiation is in some respects arbitrary. But it also opens up many possibilities to take account of equity considerations. In all likelihood, further differentiation will be critical to achieving an equitable outcome in the next phase of negotiations.

According to John Ashton and Xueman Wang, new legal instruments might make useful features of the next climate regime.[13] These have been analysed in recent studies and present important areas for the next generation of climate law research, which might focus on:

- *Investigating the nature of fixed Kyoto-like targets*   Fixed targets expressed in total national net emissions (or possibly limited to specific sectors) over a

monitor performance against them, and anticipate future developments. This requires a large investment in people and institutions. Many countries simply lack this capacity. The process has coped with this so far. The most pressing commitments have up to now largely been required from countries able to participate fully. But it may not be possible to broaden participation in the next phase without a major effort to broaden the capacity to participate. Various means are available. Training can be provided to negotiators and policymakers. Advice and financial support can be given to strengthen domestic institutions. Investment could be made in shared regional capacity among groups of countries with similar circumstances.

[13] Ashton and Wang, *supra* note 1.

given period could be the most equitable mechanism to slow climate change. Emissions could be allocated in light of a country's responsibility for current and past emissions as well as its per capita emissions, its capacity to act and the implications of its commitment for basic needs. Standard indicators could be developed to inform the assessment of each factor.

- *Investigating the utility of indexed targets*   Indexed targets express commitments not in terms of absolute emissions, but as an "indexed" or "relative" target set as a ratio between emissions and some indicator of economic performance. Options include emissions per unit of gross domestic product (GDP) (the "carbon intensity" of the economy), energy consumption per unit GDP, or analogous sector-specific indices. An alternative form of relative target could be expressed in terms of per capita emissions. This would build the entitlements approach into the regime, and many developing countries would see this as a step forward for equity.

- *Designing climate safety valves*   A maximum price for emissions permits would ensure that if the marginal cost of abatement rose above that price, parties would not have to pay more for additional emissions permits. The net effect would be less mitigation than would have been required without the price cap. This would give parties confidence that they would not be risking a degree of effort that they judged unfair. They might therefore be willing to take on more demanding commitments than they would in a regime without such a mechanism.

- *Analysing "no-lose" targets and graduation thresholds*   As a means of entry for developing countries into a regime of emissions commitments, stages can be adopted. These require first taking on softer, non-binding obligations. It might be possible to devise these to allow at least partial access to emissions trading and project investment beyond the CDM. New opportunities might be devised, building on the experience of the CDM, to attract investments that would provide benefits both for the global climate and for local sustainable development needs. These might include innovative forms of finance, mixing public and private capital. The aim in each case would be to offer the prospect of economic as well as climate benefit at low or zero risk.

From an equity perspective, such approaches offer a constructive response to the arguments put forward by developing countries. They could open the way for evolutionary progress towards more demanding commitments, linked to economic and social progress. But there is also a need to investigate criteria for determining who should enter the commitments regime in the first place and when they should do so: conditions, in effect, for graduating from the group of developing (or "non-Annex I") countries in its current form. This is a very sensitive area of research. The attractions of graduation would need to overcome the strong resistance, going well beyond the climate process, to any erosion of the principle that developing countries should wherever possible act as a single group. Developing countries have argued that emissions commitments should in fairness only apply to countries beyond a certain level of development. In a more flexible and varied system of commitments, there would be more room on equity grounds for an initial threshold that would allow some developing countries at least to take on "no-lose" commitments at an early stage. One way to approach this would be to design a threshold based on objective indicators. No single metric would be acceptable to all countries. The correct mix would be difficult to negotiate. But if a graduation criterion of this kind could be agreed, it would streamline the process by avoiding the need to negotiate all new commitments on a case-by-case basis. It would also contribute to confidence that those who achieve the capacity to act in line with their growing responsibility will do so. An alternative approach would simply be to create a mechanism whereby countries that felt comfortable about taking on commitments could have them recognized within the framework of the new regime. They would in effect decide to graduate, on the basis of their own assessment of where a reasonable threshold lies. Such a mechanism was under negotiation at Kyoto, but was not part of the final package.

All of these elements require further investigation and analysis, to allow countries to choose from a menu of possible options those about which they felt most comfortable. Such choices can extend the flexibility and differentiation reflected in Kyoto, though there would be a price in terms of greater complexity and therefore higher transaction costs. Countries have learned to live with complex regimes in other areas, and this may be an acceptable price for a regime that delivers more mitigation on a more equitable basis.

Many of the elements described above may be compatible with each other and also with the essential features of the Kyoto Protocol, such as project mechanisms, carbon trading, and standardized procedures for maintaining and reporting emissions inventories. Most of them are not alternatives to each other, but potential components of a more sophisticated climate regime.

Trade issues are also particularly relevant. The international climate regime is evolving alongside an international regime promoting trade liberalization, raising the potential links or conflicts between these two regimes.[14] Any allocation of mitigation burden – whether through rights or responsibility – is further complicated if comparability of effort is to be an objective: competitiveness. Any regime that puts some countries under tighter carbon constraints than others alters the terms of trade and conditions for investment between them. This can also be the case among countries with the same carbon constraints. Two countries might have identical emission, population, and income levels, but differences in other circumstances – such as natural endowment, energy mix, or energy efficiency – will translate into greater marginal abatement costs for one than for the other. Arguments about unfair competition from unconstrained

---

[14] W.B. Chambers, ed., *Inter-linkages: The Kyoto Protocol and the International Trade and Investment Regimes* (Tokyo: United Nations University Press, 2001).

economies are likely to intensify as the regime becomes more ambitious. As climate measures begin to affect energy markets and trade in energy-intensive goods, some countries may move to shield or subsidize vulnerable sectors. Trade measures against non-parties may be used. Future legal research is needed to analyse the relationship and interface of these two regimes. Related to trade, there is a need to investigate legal means to provide incentives for the promotion of cleaner energy development. For example, competition rules in the energy market can favour small and medium-size units on a local or regional level, including those producing clean energy. Further legal research is needed in this area.

Finally, there are commitments, under the Protocol and the Convention, to transfer technology and to help countries develop the capacity to engage on climate change. The existing instruments set up various mechanisms for the provision by industrialized countries of funds, technology, and knowledge to developing countries. Stronger assistance to developing countries for both mitigation and adaptation is an important component of equity, in particular the dimensions of responsibility and capacity. But as a practical matter, transfers of public funds are unlikely ever to meet the full needs of developing countries. The Kyoto Protocol establishes an instrument, the Clean Development Mechanism (CDM), for channelling private investment towards climate goals. The CDM is of particular interest to developing countries, and worthy of further research by legal scholars, among others.[15] The pilot phase of CDM has been launched. Clean energy technologies such as wind, solar, aqua and geo-thermic power are already available. Current debates centre on means of promoting these forms of energy, such as tax, energy or competition laws. Phasing out market imperfections in greenhouse gas emitting sectors is a key element of upcoming legal research, in particular under the *Kyoto Protocol* at Article 1(a). It will be important in the next phase to further explore the potential scope of private sector finance in strengthening the capacity both to mitigate emissions and to deal with the consequences of climate change. It can be hard to separate transfers driven by the climate regime from those that would take place anyway. Likewise, if funding for an activity with a climate benefit is provided through bilateral development assistance rather than a channel established under the climate regime, should that be reflected in the equity calculation? Furthermore, where do climate benefits end and others begin? Arguably, well-governed countries will be better able to implement successful policies to adapt to climate change. Does that mean that assistance outside the climate regime for general good governance should appear in the "equity account"?

---

[15] I.L. Worika and M. Brown, "Contractual Aspects of Implementing the Clean Development Mechanism and the Other Flexibility Mechanisms Under the Kyoto Protocol" in W.B. Chambers, ed., *Inter-linkages: The Kyoto Protocol and the International Trade and Investment Regimes* (Tokyo: United Nations University Press, 2001).

Vulnerability and social aspects of climate change law

For many countries, particularly the poorest, the most pressing requirement in any new agreement will be for help in dealing with the harmful consequences of climate change.[16] Consequences may arise from the impacts of climate change itself, and also from the measures taken in response to it. The principle of equity is particularly relevant for analysis of the legal aspects of these issues. Poorer countries are not only less responsible for the problem: they are also, by and large, less equipped to deal with its results, and more vulnerable to disruption of their ability to meet the basic needs of their people. They can be expected to press for assistance commensurate with the scale of the damage they are likely to suffer. They will seek this both through the climate negotiations and in other contexts.[17]

How will equity considerations affect their responses? Those who suffer harmful climate change impacts will wish to hold accountable in some way those whose emissions are largely responsible. But even more than in the case of emissions there is a practical difficulty in translating responsibility in principle into a quantitative allocation of obligations. It is extremely difficult if not impossible either to establish the precise causal connections between one country's emissions and the climatic impacts of those emissions on another, or to establish the exact additional costs of making an economy resilient to those impacts. Recent studies show that climate change will result in mass displacement of populations.[18] Human issues are raised as climate change will cause humanitarian disasters of unfathomable proportions. This raises the issue of the rights of persons affected by climate change. Might these individuals be able to invoke legal rights against States or other actors, for failure to undertake climate-saving action when required? State responsibility as well as individual rights to compensation, refugee law, and humanitarian law will come into play. Does the UN *Refugee Convention* cover all aspects of personal vulnerability?

The equity principle suggests that a new agreement will need to embody enhanced support for those countries facing harmful impacts of climate change. Natural Disaster Preparation and Relief includes international legal including

---

[16] Harmful climate-related impacts are projected to arise from rising sea level; changes in patterns of temperature, winds, cloudiness, precipitation, ocean chemistry, and perhaps ocean currents; more frequent and possibly more violent storms; and destabilization of natural biomes. The human consequences are expected to include displacement of people, disruption of agriculture and fisheries, more intense competition for water, enhanced threats from agricultural pests and human diseases, and possibly enhanced risks of conflict arising from the interplay between these and other stresses. See Intergovernmental Panel on Climate Change, *Vulnerability, supra* note 2.

[17] For example, if weather-related natural disasters continue to become more frequent, their victims can be expected to call not only for emergency humanitarian relief but also for more systematic compensation in the context of climate change. This kind of thinking could introduce strong currents of resentment into the climate debate, possibly flowing back into the wider dynamic of international affairs. One mechanism for this might be attempts to bring "class action" lawsuits for compensation against governments or energy companies. See D.A. Grossman, "Warming Up To a Not-So-Radical Idea: Tort-Based Climate Change Litigation" (2003) 28 *Colum. J. Envtl. L.* 1.

[18] Intergovernmental Panel on Climate Change, *Vulnerability, supra* note 2.

domestic and international control of aid, access to geographical information and data, and relevant technology transfer or investment law to mitigate possible effects of disasters.[19] But it does not offer a detailed prescription for the scale of that support, for how the burden of providing it should be equitably distributed, nor for how it should be shared among recipients. Developing countries may also argue that due to the global problem, a collective global response is needed through financial institutions such as the World Bank Group. Will the World Bank offer special grants for the prevention of direct climate change consequences, addressing vulnerability issues such as preparation, mitigation and relief strategies? The Bonn and Marrakech Accords that clarify the operation of the Kyoto Protocol establish designated funds to help vulnerable countries adapt to climate change and to meet the special needs of the least developed countries. There are three separate funds: a Special Climate Change Fund, a Least Developed Countries Fund, and an Adaptation Fund. Developed countries have pledged new support in part through these funds amounting to 450 million euro annually by 2005. Rules, procedures and modalities on these mechanisms have been developed at the seventh meeting of the Conference of the Parties. Research is needed to fully understand the functioning of these market mechanisms and assess their effectiveness.

Future legal research, from a sustainable development law perspective, should look to the particular aspects of the climate change issues that have international social, economic and environmental legal significance in an integrated manner (e.g. economic and social aspects of climate provisions or vulnerability to change). More work is necessary in the areas that integrate two of the three (e.g. emission trading/environment–economic). Future legal research should also focus on the need to define and clarify complex regimes, looking at the broader legal system in which measures are taken, with examples drawn from qualitative examination of case studies of legal instruments and their effects and contexts to complement analysis. A sustainable development law perspective should not ignore the increasing influence of private law, and can trace climate change and economic linkages between public international and private law spheres, as well as the interaction between the two (such as inter-corporate emission trading). A special focus should lay on insurance legislation especially regarding the social aspects of climate change. Finally, the compliance system is also critical in ensuring the credibility of the Kyoto Protocol. Future sustainable development law research agendas should focus on a three-step system: reporting, review of reporting conducted by the expert review teams under Article 8 and the procedures and mechanisms on compliance, with a view to assessing their roles in the climate change process. It can examine and analyse the rich *lex ferenda* in this area, and take new measures and modes of international law into account. While remaining aware of *Agenda 21* and other basic climate and SD documents, legal scholars should also reach beyond into new tools being tested on national or nascent international levels.

[19] Intergovernmental Panel on Climate Change, *Mitigation, supra* note 7.

15

Crosscutting Issues in Sustainable Development Law

with SALIM NAKHJAVANI and MARIA LEICHNER REYNAL[1]

International sustainable development law is characterized by creative, dynamic instruments and institutions with fresh potential for legal solutions that integrate environmental, economic and social dimensions of legal problems. In particular, sustainable development law often employs the most recent scientific methods, drawing upon indigenous and traditional knowledge, uses new measures for technology transfer, and provides for corporate responsibility and public–private partnerships.[2] Sustainable development law seeks more integrated, effective and efficient approaches to environment, social and economic regulation. In *Agenda 21*, States recognize as an objective for international law of sustainable development "[t]o improve the effectiveness of institutions, mechanisms and procedures for the administration of agreements and instruments...".[3] The 1997 *Programme for Further Implementation of Agenda 21*, and the *World Summit for Sustainable Development* call for innovative new approaches and partnerships for sustainable development, based on the most up-to-date scientific and technological information.

These procedural aspects of sustainable development law regimes are engaged by each of the research agendas discussed above. Understanding the effect of these "cross-cutting issues" on sustainable development law regimes helps to explain the integrative potential of sustainable development law principles, for these themes serve as vehicles for weaving together environmental, economic and social priorities.

These cross-cutting issues include:

---

[1] Salim Nakhjavani LL.B, B.C.L. (McGill, Great Distinction), LL.M (Cambridge, First Class) and Dr. Maria Leichner Reynal BCL (Buenos Aires), DCL (Montevideo), are lead counsels for cross-cutting issues with the CISDL.

[2] D. Vogel, *Trading Up: Consumer and Environmental Regulations in a Global Economy* (Cambridge: Harvard University Press, 1995); N. Roht-Arriaza, "Shifting the Point of Regulation: The International Organization for Standardization and Global Lawmaking on Trade and the Environment" (1995) 22 *Ecology L.Q.* 479. See also M. Cappelletti *et al.* (eds.), *Integration through Law* (Berlin: Walter de Gruyter, Inc, 1986); H. Collins, "The Voice of the Community in Private Law Discourse" (1997) 3 *Eur. L.J.* 407.

[3] *Agenda 21*, Report of the United Nations Conference on Environment and Development (1992), UN Doc. A/CONF.151/26/Rev.1, (1992) 31 *ILM* 874, ch. 39.3(f).

Accountability for Environmental and Developmental Damage

Future legal research should focus both through the regime of State responsibility premised on wrongful acts, and liability for international environmental and developmental damage in the absence of wrongdoing, legal implications of the polluter pays principle, methods for economic calculation of social and environmental damages, and international insurance regimes.

Socially and Environmentally Sound Investment

Future legal research should focus on how to ensure sustainable multilateral investment regimes, institutions which provide for development loans or promote foreign direct investment, and frameworks which lever or create incentives for corporate social responsibility.

Compliance in sustainable development law

Future legal research should investigate compliance and Dispute Settlement processes, including non-adversarial dispute settlement or environmental mediation; and distinctive features of dispute settlement in sustainable development law treaties, including the meshing of dispute settlement and dispute avoidance, the increased capacity of sustainable development law dispute settlement processes to address conflicting norms, and the dynamic interaction between dispute settlement processes and substantive rules within sustainable development law regimes.

Science and Precaution in sustainable development law

Future legal research should consider including use of international social, environmental and sustainability impact assessment methodologies, the developing precautionary principle, and the increasing reliance upon academic work, scientific standards and expert evidence in sustainable development law decision-making.

Transparency and Participation in sustainable development law

Future legal research should focus on openness in international law, such as processes to ensure openness in treaty drafting, implementation, monitoring and non-compliance procedures, participation in international processes for the evaluation of *Agenda 21* implementation, and standing and intervener rights in sustainable development law disputes for present and future generations.

Financing implementation of sustainable development law

Future legal scholarship is needed in the area of sustainable development financing, including mechanisms to generate new and additional resources, technology transfer agreements, and policy linkages between foreign debt, debt relief and the right to development.

Conclusions

This book has sought to advance understanding of the development and implementation of international sustainable development law. To this purpose it has led the reader through current concepts of sustainable development law, surveyed recent developments in the fields of international social, economic and environmental law, analysed the proposed principles of sustainable development law, provided practical case studies of sustainable development law instruments, analysed the challenges of sustainable development governance and implementation, and identified prospects for further legal research.

In these chapters, there has been no attempt to analyse all situations in which international economic, social, and environmental legal regimes relating to sustainable development intersect. Indeed, it is unlikely that these myriad instances could be satisfactorily analysed in one publication. However, the book provides a current guide to this emerging area, a framework and methodology for researching and implementing sustainable development law, illustrated by representative case studies. As a guide, it can be used in capacity-building programmes and courses for lawmakers, jurists, scholars, and educators in developed and developing countries, from environmental protection, economic progress, and social development communities. It can serve as a primary source for courses and seminars on sustainable development law, and on specific issue areas raising interconnected economic, social and environmental laws. The book can also provide a secondary resource for courses and seminars on environmental law, economic law, and human rights and development law.

As stated in the first part of the book, legal aspects of the concept of sustainable development can be identified, as can the formation of a body of "international law on sustainable development". Brief descriptions of the evolving fields of international social, economic, and environmental law demonstrate how quickly all three areas have developed in recent years, and serve as a basis to explain how sustainable development law is emerging at the areas of intersection. As was discussed, sustainable development law is both an emerging body of legal principles and instruments, as well as an "interstitial norm", a concept that serves to reconcile conflicting environmental, social and economic development norms in international law, in the interest of present and future generations.

As was seen in the second part, certain principles of international law related to sustainable development, proposed by the International Law Association Committee on the Legal Aspects of Sustainable Development, are useful to jurists and judges working in this area. Such Principles have been recently reflected in many international treaty instruments in the spheres of social, economic, and environmental law. A typology, describing the degree of integration between international social, economic, and environmental law, can assist in analysing these different instruments and regimes. The "continuum" identified a range of "states of integration" – from instruments displaying little or no integration to fully integrated international sustainable development law.

As observed in the third part of the book, representative illustrations of the practices of sustainable development law can be developed. In particular, three case studies of legal instruments at these various degrees of integration were used to illustrate challenges and innovative methodologies that have been implemented in recent years. First, the development and application of "sustainability impact assessment" was analysed, demonstrating an instrument for the integration of social and environmental concerns into economic development projects, programmes and policies. Secondly, "regional integration agreements" were examined from five sub-regions of the Americas, providing a brief survey of new social, economic, and environmental developments. Thirdly, the role of economic, social, and cultural rights in international sustainable development law was analysed, demonstrating the movement towards application of human rights law in economic and environmental governance.

In addition, the manner in which the international community is addressing the practical challenges of implementing sustainable development law is of high importance, as was canvassed in this book. The new institutional architecture of "sustainable development governance" was described and analysed. Further, in a chapter with Salim Nakhjavani, innovative aspects of "integrated compliance building" were identified, and analysis was provided on the way that these "compliance building mechanisms" are utilized in a number of international treaties and regimes that integrate environment, economic, and social concerns for sustainable development.

As identified in the final part of this book, cutting-edge legal research agendas can be pursued in six priority areas of intersection between international social, economic, and environmental law, and several themes which cross-cut these substantive agendas are also significant. Priority areas of intersection can be drawn, in a balanced way, from all three fields as was done above. First, a brief section with Markus W. Gehring identified emerging social and environmental issues in international trade, investment, and competition law; a second section with Carolyn Deere, examined economic and social issues in international natural resources law; a third section, with Maya Prabhu, examined emerging sustainable development issues in international health law; a fourth section, with Sumudu Atapattu, discussed economic and environmental applications of international human rights and poverty law; a fifth analysis, with Xueman Wang, discussed economic and social aspects of international climate change law, and a sixth section with Jorge Cabrera Medaglia and Kathryn Garforth, analysed emerging social and economic aspects of international biodiversity law. Then,

Salim Nakhjavani and Maria Leichner Reynal briefly examined cross-cutting issues.

The analysis and proposals contained in this book sought to shed light on this emerging area of law, and offer thoughts toward future developments in the field. To conclude, it is important to consider what general observations can be made at these early stages in the investigation and analysis of sustainable development law. Several points emerge.

While there is widespread acceptance of the concept and precepts of sustainable development, a significant obstacle to its realization is the "over-adoption" of sustainable development. Sustainable development almost seems to have come to mean all things to all people. The multiplicity of meanings, and consequent lack of clarity, has caused difficulties at national and international level.

For international law, this imprecision has been increasingly difficult to address, leading to fragmentation and contradiction. As international legal regimes become more complex, and institutions are established to implement obligations, countries are faced with overlapping and sometimes even conflicting legal rules. The problem lies not in the social justice, economic growth, and environmental protection objectives or rules themselves, but rather in their governance. Laws and policies have been designed to implement policy objectives in the three separate spheres of sustainable development (the economic, environmental, and social) without sufficient coherence or co-ordination between them.

As noted throughout this book, this situation has become particularly unmanageable for developing countries. Valuable resources, political will, and capacity are squandered in the attempts to harmonize programmes which were never meant to conflict. Furthermore, international treaties and institutions charged with sustainable development mandates begin to suffer from a lack of respect and credibility. The instruments for cooperation themselves, or their compliance and enforcement mechanisms, are called into question.

These problems have not gone unnoticed. As mentioned above, in 1992, in *Agenda 21*, governments called for "[t]he further development of international law on sustainable development, giving special attention to the delicate balance between environmental and developmental concerns"; and identified a "need to clarify and strengthen the relationship between existing international instruments or agreements in the field of environment and relevant social and economic agreements or instruments, taking into account the special needs of developing countries". Ten years later, the *Johannesburg Declaration on Sustainable Development*, and the Johannesburg Plan of Implementation, made a collective commitment to "advance and strengthen the interdependent and mutually reinforcing pillars of sustainable development – economic development, social development and environmental protection – at the local, national, regional and global levels". These commitments have become central tenets of the emerging international sustainable development law agenda.

Moving forward from the 2002 *World Summit on Sustainable Development*, it is necessary to develop the legal principles and techniques to coordinate and, where necessary, integrate international social, economic, and environmental regimes – including the design, strengthening and implementation of laws, instruments, and policies to address current sustainable development challenges at the global, regional, national, and local levels. It is an exciting area, and one that promises to grow exponentially in coming years, as the international legal community, through the International Law Commission and other bodies, seeks to address perceptions of "fragmentation" in its system.

International law is needed to govern the intersections between conflicting global priorities and norms in this field, to ensure a balanced outcome. This book has identified and begun to analyse the emergence of international law on sustainable development, or, in short, "sustainable development law" as a means to address this challenge. Sustainable development, in international law, can be understood through two complementary approaches.

First, it can be seen as an emerging area of international law in its own right. It is an emerging body of legal principles and instruments at the intersection of environmental, social, and economic law, those that aim to ensure development that can last. As such, sustainable development law describes a group of congruent norms, a corpus of international legal principles and treaties, which address the areas of intersection between international economic law, international environmental law, and international social law in the interests of both present and future generations. Procedural and substantive norms and instruments, which help to balance or integrate these fields, form part of this body of international law and play a role in its implementation.

And secondly, sustainable development may also serve as a special type of norm in its own right, one that facilitates and requires a balancing, an accommodation, or even "reconciliation" between conflicting legal norms relating to environmental protection, social justice, and economic growth. As an "interstitial norm", sustainable development is a concept that serves to reconcile conflicting environmental, social, and economic development norms in international law, in the interest of present and future generations. The substantive aspect of this "interstitial norm" is the requirement that all three sets of priorities be reflected in the substantive outcomes of a given dispute or conflict. As shown above, while there are few bright lines, and no hard and fast rules, it is not "sustainable" to allow one or the other priority to completely "fall off the table" in situations where common international concerns are at stake. Viewed in this way, sustainable development helps to curb the worst social and environmental excesses of nations in economic development activities; it coordinates the internalization of otherwise externalized common concerns. It can exert an immense gravitational pull when it is used by States as they negotiate treaties or by judges as they seek ways to reconcile other conflicting legal norms and principles.

In addition, as explained in this book, the changing structure of international law has allowed a multiplicity of actors, both State and non-State, to generate knowledge and participate in the development of sustainable development discourse through domestic and international legal systems. Greater international recognition of emerging norms and principles holds the potential to further strengthen sustainable development law. As "soft-law instruments", such as declarations and international statements, become better recognized and are used, for example to demonstrate good faith or generate "legitimate expect-ations" in international law, such principles are starting to assert certain persua-sive force. Still, much further work is needed to properly analyse and understand the implications and level of acceptance of each, in international law, even as increasing compliance with these norms contributes to the unfolding process of sustainable development.

Respect for human rights, environmental protection, and economic develop-ment are complementary rather than unrelated or opposing objectives. Measures to address them require balanced, integrated approaches. At the international level, there are a growing number of international instruments and declarations that indicate coordination and integration of economic, social, and environmen-tal laws and objectives. Sustainable development law can serve as the umbrella term to describe the collection of rights and norms that are beginning to be reflected in international treaties, custom, the decisions of international organ-izations. It is gaining recognition by international courts and tribunals and in national courts. However, much can also be gained from further elaboration of a more coherent legal concept of sustainable development.

This book has suggested ways that sustainable development law can help to make globalization more sustainable, and guide further integration at the inter-section of international environmental, social, and economic law. Its principles can also offer guidance where environmental, social, and economic norms and laws intersect and there is little clear precedence. In the *Brundtland Report* formulation, sustainable development is clearly a political and social construct, not a scientific blueprint that can be applied in the same way in each set of circumstances. But international law and policy have moved on. It is a principal conclusion of this book that sustainable development law can provide new insights and solutions to many of the important challenges of the next century, guiding relationships at the interstices of the three systems of international economic, social, and environmental law.

There will be a number of critical challenges for the further elaboration of sustainable development law. First, very few lawyers can realistically develop expertise in all of the diverse areas of law related to sustainable development, ranging from trade, to human rights, to environment law, among others. This reality requires those working on legal aspects of sustainable development to, at the very least, gain an overview of the various sub-components of sustainable development law. Lawyers in each related discipline must be alive to the need to collaborate with lawyers specialized in other fields in addressing sustainable development law. The present book, for example, could not have been written without the participation of legal scholars from diverse disciplines such as trade and investment, natural resources, health, human rights, and biodiversity conservation.

The second challenge is the need for coordination and integration between economic, social, and environmental law in the field of sustainable development to be carried out in a more systematized, principled, and balanced fashion. Where there is legal confusion due to conflicts between different legal instruments, there is a danger that disputes will be resolved on the basis of power differences and common denominator interests, rather than reasoned, consistent legal principles that can also protect the interests of those most vulnerable and the public. This poses both conceptual and political challenges. As noted in this book, coordination and integration was occurring between different areas of economic, social and, environment law, even before researchers and policy makers began to articulate the need for it. Such efforts have generally been *ad hoc*, driven by the particular context and positions taken by the participating actors. Often important goals were left off the table. In addition, reconciling and balancing economic, social, and economic objectives requires critical decisions to be taken, particularly with regard to the allocation of costs and the extent to which each goal is furthered. Emerging principles of international law related to sustainable development law can therefore provide a legal and moral basis to guide political decision-making and the work of judiciaries around the world in this area. However, they will need to be developed and further analysed to acquire optimal precision and application.

In relation to this challenge, a further reality must also be recognized. Political obstacles may prove to be more important than conceptual challenges in the long run. Ideally, sustainable development law provides a means by which actors from different issue groups can negotiate to reconcile their different goals. However, powerful and privileged groups may perceive benefits in reducing the importance given to one or more of the pillars of sustainable development. The most commonplace has been the subversion of social and environmental goals to economic goals. However, the converse is also true in other cases. Ignoring social and economic aspects of environmental protection has led to situations in which marine reserves, parks, and forests have been protected in a manner that has ignored or even negatively impacted upon local communities. In other cases, social goals such as the subsidization of scarce goods (such as water, energy) for upper-income groups in society has reduced the access of future generations to basic resources as well as depleting financing that could be allocated to poverty eradication.

Each of the principles of international law relating to sustainable development requires special attention to the needs of the most vulnerable communities and peoples, in relation to both present and future generations, at the national and international level. The principles of equity, poverty eradication, common but differentiated responsibilities, transparency, public participation and access to justice and good governance, effectively move in the direction of re-distribution of power in society, while the principles of sustainable use of natural resources and precaution will often relate to the needs of those unable to protect their own ecosystems from negative economic activity, either due to lack of knowledge or power or due to the fact of belonging to future generations. It can therefore be expected that there will be political resistance from powerful groups and States to a balanced development and application of sustainable development law. Such pressures will certainly affect policy-making by States, but they may also affect the priorities of researchers. It is hoped, however, that principles and practical rules of sustainable development law can be further developed and implemented, guiding policy and providing a resource for those representing vulnerable communities.

The third challenge relates to the likely opposition of those whose mandate or research interests relate to a single issue in sustainable development, whether it is in the area of economic growth, environmental protection, or social justice and human rights. There may be an understandable concern that the concept of sustainable development law risks submerging some important and neglected area of law. For example, some environmental lawyers have expressed concern to the writers of this book that pursuing sustainable development law would weaken environmental protection in the United Nations and in national systems. However, as described in this book, attempts to develop social, economic, or environmental law in isolation will often result in unworkable situations, thereby discrediting the goal being promoted, in all three areas. Coordination, and in many cases, integration, can actually strengthen each pillar, granting them further effectiveness and focus. Coherence does not weaken programmes and the achievement of important objectives; rather, it enhances the possibilities of successful implementation. It is necessary for single-issue individuals and institutions to advance their objectives in a manner cognizant of the overall goal of sustainable development. If sustainable development law is carried out in a principled and balanced manner, important goals will not be excluded, but rather, granted further legitimacy.

For policy makers, the challenges of developing and implementing sustainable development law will not be unfamiliar. Many governments and international institutions have established mechanisms to ensure coordination between different departments. For example, at the national level, sustainable development law would require the establishment of inter-departmental coordination bodies to develop laws and regulations on integrated issues of sustainable development, rather than leaving this task to any particular ministry or department. Yet, competing mandates, bureaucratic infighting and conflicts over boundaries often hamper cooperation, or conversely allow decision-makers to abdicate responsibility for difficult issues, leaving important gaps. Most international instruments and national laws and regulations continue to be developed under the aegis of one international organization or national ministry. Conceptual acceptance of sustainable development law approach may provide a basis for national and international institutions to establish a coordinating mechanism with the power to implement hard decisions across dispersed mandates.

For scholars and teachers, the need to encourage expertise in sustainable development law can require a new approach to skills development. For example, in universities, new courses on sustainable development law should aim to provide an overview of the more specialized areas of law and how they relate to each other, whether these be trade law, environmental law, or labour law. The temptation to simply combine environment law and sustainable development law should be avoided, as such an approach could be unbalanced. It risks ignoring important areas of environmental law that properly address mainly environmental goals, and distorting the concept of sustainable development by marginalizing important economic and social concerns in sustainable development. Another approach could be to ensure that each relevant course includes a segment addressing intersections with other areas of law, within the framework of sustainable development law.

As discussed in the part of this book on "Prospects", the intellectual challenges raised by sustainable development law are diverse, exciting, and extremely topical. They will no doubt occupy scholars for generations to come. Much remains to be done to refine, further analyse, and develop the emerging principles of international law related to sustainable development and to clarify their application. Their status in international law, in most cases, is not yet clear. Sustainable development law focuses on a contextual reconciling and balancing of social, economic, and environmental law rather than the application of formal and technical rules. This may be the path less travelled, but it is all the more interesting, as new discoveries await. Future legal scholars bear a significant responsibility to develop principled research analysis and recommendations in this regard. As with other areas of international and domestic law, the achievement of sustainable development objectives will depend to a great extent on the creativity, integrity, and rigour of jurists, researchers, and practitioners to come. Sustainable development law is clearly becoming one of the most important and intellectually challenging areas of international law and policy.

Table of Treaties

Year	Treaty	Pages
1969	*Agreement on Andean Subregional Integration*, Colombia-Venezuela-Bolivia-Ecuador-Peru, 26 May 1969, reprinted in S. Zamora & R. A. Brand eds, B.D.I.E.L at 597 (1990).	192–3
	Inter-American Convention on Human Rights, 22 November 1969, 1144 U.N.T.S. 123, O.A.S. TS No. 36 (entered into force 18 July 1978).	73
1971	*Convention on Wetlands of International Importance, Especially as Waterfowl Habitat*, 2 February 1971, 996 U.N.T.S. 245, T.I.A.S. No. 11084.	39, 111–12
1972	*Convention for the Conservation of Antarctic Seals*, 1 June 1972, 29 U.S.T. 441, T.I.A.S. No. 8826.	88
	Convention on the Prevention of Marine Pollution by Dumping of Wastes and other Matter, 13 November 1972, 1046 U.N.T.S. 120, 11 I.L.M. 1294.	135
	Convention Concerning Protection of World Cultural Property and Natural Heritage, 23 November 1972, 1037 U.N.T.S. 151, 11 I.L.M. 1358.	114
1973	*Convention on International Trade of Endangered Species and Wild Fauna and Flora*, 3 March 1973, 993 U.N.T.S. 243, T.I.A.S. No. 8249, 12 I.L.M. 1085 (1973).	85, 147
	International Labour Convention (No. 139) Concerning Minimum Age for Admission to Employment, 26 June 1973, 1015 U.N.T.S. 297 (entered into force 19 June 1976).	142
	Convention on Fishing and Conservation of the Living Resources in the Baltic Sea and Belts, 13 September 1973, 12 I.L.M. 1291 (entered into force 28 July 1974).	118 n82
	International Convention for the Prevention of Pollution from Ships (MARPOL), 2 November 1973, IMO Doc. MP/CONF/ WP.35, 12 I.L.M. 1319.	87
	Oslo Agreement on the Conservation of Polar Bears, 15 November 1973, 27 U.S.T. 3918, T.I.A.S. 8409.	85
1974	*Convention on the Protection of the Environment Between Demark, Finland, Norway and Sweden*, 19 February 1974, 13 I.L.M. 591.	82 n148
1975	*Treaty of Lagos*, 28 May 1975, 14 I.L.M 1200.	64 n68
1976	*Convention on Conservation of North Pacific Fur Seals*, 7 May 1976.	118 n82
1977	*Protocol Additional to the Geneva Conventions of 12 August 1949, and Relating to the Protection of Victims of International Armed Conflicts (Protocol I)*, 8 June 1977, 1125 U.N.T.S. 3 (entered into force 7 December 1978).	75
	Protocol Additional to the Geneva Conventions of 12 August 1949, and Relating to the Protection of Victims of Non-International Armed Conflicts (Protocol II), 8 June 1977, 1125 U.N.T.S. 609, (entered into force 7 December 1978).	75

Year	Treaty	Pages
1988	*Convention on the Regulation of Antarctic Mineral Resource Activities*, 2 June 1988, 402 U.N.T.S. 71, 27 I.L.M. 868.	88
	Protocol to the 1979 Convention on long-range transboundary air pollution concerning the control of emissions of nitrogen oxides or their transboundary fluxes, 31 October 1988, UN Doc. C.N.252.1985. Treaties.1 of December 1988 (entered into force 14 February 1991).	135 n186
	Additional Protocol to the American Convention on Human Rights in the Area of Economic, Social and Cultural Rights (Protocol of San Salvador), 17 November 1988, O.A.S. TS No 69 (1988) rep. *Basic Documents Pertaining to Human Rights in the Inter-American System*, OEA/Ser L V/II.82 Doc. 6 Rev 1 at 67 (1992) (entered into force 16 November 1999).	72
1989	*Basel Convention on the Control of Transboundary Movements of Hazardous Wastes and Their Disposal*, 22 March 1989, 1673 U.N.T.S. 57, 28 I.L.M. 649 (entered into force 5 May 1992).	180
	Convention concerning Indigenous and Tribal Peoples in Independent Countries (ILO No. 169), 27 June 1989, 28 I.L.M. 1382 (entered into force 5 September 1991).	158
	Convention on the Rights of the Child, 20 November 1989, 1577 U.N.T.S. 3 (entered into force 2 September 1990).	71
1990	*Montreal Protocol Non-compliance Procedure*, 29 June 1990, 30 I.L.M. 537.	249, 252–3, 264, 267–70
	Charter of Paris for a New Europe, 21 November 1990, 30 I.L.M. 190.	169 n327
	International Convention on the Protection of the Rights of All Migrant Workers and Members of their Families, 18 December 1990, GA Res. 45/158, annex, 45 UN GAOR, Supp. No. 49A, UN Doc. A/45/49 (1990).	73–5
1991	*Bamako Convention on the Ban of Import into Africa and the Control of Transboundary Movement and Management of Hazardous Wastes within Africa*, 29 January 1991, 30 I.L.M. 775.	145, 148
	United Nations Convention on Environmental Impact Assessment in a Transboundary Context, 25 February 1991, 1989 U.N.T.S. 309, 30 I.L.M. 800 (entered into force 10 September 1997).	180, 182–4
	Treaty of Asunción, 26 March 1991, 30 I.L.M. 1041 (entered into force 1 January 1995).	65–6, 191

Year	Treaty	Pages
1991	*Protocol to the Antarctic Treaty on Environmental Protection (with Schedule on Arbitration and four Annexes—Environmental Impact Assessment, Conservation of Antarctic Fauna and Flora, Waste Disposal and Waste Management, and Prevention of Marine Pollution)*, 24 April 1991, 30 I.L.M. 1455.	178–9
	Convention on Biological Diversity, 5 June 1991, 31 I.L.M. 818 (entered into force 29 December 1993).	341, 346
	Arctic Environmental Protection Strategy, 14 June 1991, 30 I.L.M. 1624.	88
	Agreement between the Government of the United States of America and the European Communities Regarding the Application of Their Competition Laws, 23 September 1991, 4 Trade Ref. Rep (CCH) 13,504.	61 n52
	1.d. Protocol to the 1979 Convention on Long-Range Transboundary Air Pollution Concerning the Control of Emissions of Volatile Organic Compounds or their Transboundary Fluxes, 18 November 1991, 2001 U.N.T.S. 187, 31 I.L.M. 568 (entered into force 29 September 1997).	135
1992	*Treaty on European Union (Maastricht Treaty)*, 7 February 1992, 1992 O.J. (C 191) 1, 31 I.L.M. 253.	65, 135–6, 148
	Convention on the Protection and Use of Transboundary Watercourses and International Lakes, 17 March 1992, UN Doc. ENVWA/R.53 and Add.1, 31 I.L.M. 1312 (entered into force 6 October 1996).	126
	Agreement on the Conservation of Small Cetaceans of the Baltic & North Seas, 17 March 1992, 1772 U.N.T.S. 217 (entered into force 29 March 1994) [ASCOBANS].	85
	Convention on the Protection of the Marine Environment of the Baltic Sea Area, 9 April 1992 (entered into force 17 January 2000).	87
	United Nations Framework Convention on Climate Change, 9 May 1992, 1771 U.N.T.S. 107, 31 I.L.M. 849 (entered into force 21 March 1994).	105, 112, 115, 120, 121, 126–7, 133, 134, 136, 147, 150, 180, 214, 216, 352
	United Nations Convention on Biological Diversity, 5 June 1992, 1760 U.N.T.S. 79, 31 I.L.M. 822 (entered into force 29 December 1993).	85, 105, 109, 112, 115, 120, 121, 131, 134, 136, 145, 147, 150, 180, 184, 225, 254, 290

Year	Treaty	Pages
1992	*Convention for the Protection of the Marine Environment of the North-East Atlantic*, 22 September 1992, reprinted in (1993) 32 I.L.M. 1069 (entered into force March 25, 1998).	145, 146
	North American Free Trade Agreement, 17 December 1992, Can. T.S. 1994 No. 2, 32 I.L.M. 289 (entered into force 1 January 1994).	59, 66, 107, 195–200, 225, 286, 291
	Terms of Reference for a Multilateral Fund, U.N. Doc. UNEP/OzL.Pro.4/15, (1992) Y.B. Int'l. L. 824.	86
1993	*North America Agreement on Environmental Cooperation*, 14 September 1993, 32 I.L.M. 1480 (entered into force 1 January 1994).	107, 195–8
1994	*International Tropical Timber Agreement*, 10 January 1994, U.N. Conference on Trade and Development, UN Doc. TD/TIMBER.2/Misc.7/GE.94-50830 (1994).	117 n76
	Marrakesh Agreement Establishing the World Trade Organization, 15 April 1994, 1867 U.N.T.S. 154 (entered into force 1 January 1995).	51, 52
	Agreement on Trade-Related Aspects of Intellectual Property Rights, Including Trade in Counterfeit Goods, 15 April 1994, 33 I.L.M. 1125.	55
	Agreement on Trade-Related Investment Measures, 15 April 1994, being part of Annex 1A to the *Agreement Establishing the World Trade Organization*, 15 April 1994, 33 I.L.M. 1144.	345
	Dispute Settlement Understanding, being Annex 2 to the Agreement Establishing the World Trade Organization, 15 April 1994, 33 I.L.M. 1125 (entered into force 1 January 1995).	56
	General Agreement on Tariffs and Trade, being part of Annex IA to the Agreement Establishing the World Trade Organization, 15 April 1994, 33 I.L.M. 1144.	281
	General Agreement on Trade in Services (GATS), 15 April 1994, 33 I.L.M. 44.	61
	Convention to Combat Desertification in Those Countries Experiencing Serious Drought and/or Desertification, particularly in Africa, 17 June 1994, 33 I.L.M. 1328.	39, 136, 141, 162–3, 180, 217–20, 224, 241, 252–65, 271, 273
	1.e. Protocol to the 1979 Convention on Long-Range Transboundary Air Pollution on Further Reduction of Sulphur Emissions, 14 June 1994, Doc. EB.AIR/R.84; 33 I.L.M. 1542 (entered into force 5 August 1998).	84–5

Table of Declarations

Table of Cases

Court	Case	Page
	Legal Consequences of the Construction of a Wall in the Occupied Palestinian Territory, [9 July 2004] I.C.J. List 131 (Advisory Opinion).	311–22
WTO CASES	*United States—Standards for Reformulated and Conventional Gasoline* (1996) WTO Doc. WT/DS2/AB/R, AB-1996–1 (Appellate Body Report).	282 n7
	European Communities—Measures Concerning Meat and Meat Products (Hormones) (1998) WTO Doc. WT/DS26/AB/R, WT/DS48/AB/R (Appellate Body Report), WT/DS26/R/USA, WT/DS48/R/CAN (Panel Report).	149
	Australia-Salmon Australia—Measures Affecting Importation of Salmon (1998) WTO Doc. WT/DS18/AB/R, AB-1998–5 (Appellate Body Report).	281–94
	Japan—Measures Affecting Agricultural Products (1999) WTO Doc. WT/DS76/AB/R, AB-1998–8, (Appellate Body Report).	281–94
	United States—Import Prohibition of Certain Shrimp and Shrimp Products (1999), WTO Doc. WT/DS58/AB/R (Appellate Body Report), WT/DS58/R (Panel Report).	48, 141
	European Communities—Measures Affecting Asbestos and Asbestos-Containing Products (2001), WTO Doc. WT/DS135/AB/R (Appellate Body Report), WT/DS135/R (Panel Report).	141–42, 150
	United States—Import Prohibition of Certain Shrimp and Shrimp Products: Recourse to Article 21.5 of the DSU by Malaysia (2001), WTO Doc. WT/DS58/AB/RW (Appellate Body Report), WT/DS58/RW (Panel Report).	48, 141
	Japan—Measures Affecting the Importation of Apples (2003), WTO Doc. WT/DS245/AB/R (Appellate Body Report), WT/DS245/R (Panel Report).	281–94
CANADIAN CASES	*114957 Canada Ltée (Spraytech, société d'arrosage) v. Hudson (Town)*, [2001] 2 S.C.R. 241 (Supreme Court of Canada).	150 n252
U.S. CASES	*Cape May County Chapter, Inc., Isaak Walton League of America v. Macchia*, 329 F. Supp. 504 (D.N.J. 1971), (United States).	129 n148
	Sierra Club v. Morton, 405 U.S. 727, 92 S.Ct. 1361 (1972), (United States).	125 n122
	United States v. 18.2 Acres of Land, 442 F. Supp. 800, 806 (E.D. Cal. 1977), (United States).	129 n148

Court	Case	Page
	Crosby v. National Foreign Trade Council, 120 S. Ct. 2288 (2000), (United States).	288
	Aguinda v. Texaco, Inc., 142 F. Supp. 2d 534 (S.D.N.Y. 2001), (United States).	131 n157
ASIAN CASES	*Municipal Council Ratlam v. Vardhichand and others*, AIR 1980 SC 1622 (Indian Supreme Court).	208 n132
	Vikram Deo Singh Tomar v. State of Bihar, (1988) Supp. SCC 734 at 736 (Indian Supreme Court)	337 n51
	Shehla Zia and others v. WAPDA, Case No 15–K of 1992 (Pakistan Supreme Court).	96 n4
	Subhash Kumar v. State of Bihar, AIR 1991 SC 420, (Indian Supreme Court).	208 n131
	Zia v. WAPDA, P L D 1994 Supreme Court 693 (Pakistan Supreme Court).	
	Minors Oposa v. Secretary of the Department of Environment and Natural Resources (DENR), 1994, 33 I.L.M. 173 (Philippines Supreme Court).	128–29
	Bulankulama v. The Secretary, Ministry of Industrial Development (2000) Vol. 7, No. 2 South Asian Environmental Law Reporter 1 (Sri Lankan Supreme Court).	96 n4
SOUTH AFRICAN CASES	*Soobramany v. Minister of Health, KwaZulu-Natal*, 1998 (1) SA 765 (Constitutional Court of South Africa).	337 n49
	Government of the Republic of South Africa and others v. Grootboom and others, 2001 (1) SA 46 (CC).	208
	Treatment Action Campaign v. Minister of Health, 2002 SA 8 (Constitutional Court of South Africa).	208–9
COLOMBIAN CASES	Constitutional Court, Judgement No. T-484 of 11 August 1992, *Revista Mensual, Jurisprudencia y Doctrina*, 1992, Vol. 21, PP. 1008–1109 (Colombia).	337 n50
	Constitutional Court, Judgement No. T-505 of 28 August 1992, *Revista Mensual, Jurisprudencia y Doctrina*, 1992, Vol. 21, PP. 1101–1106 (Colombia).	337 n50
AFRICAN COMMISSION ON HUMAN RIGHTS	*Social and Economic Rights Action Center and the Center for Economic and Social Rights v. Nigeria*, (2002) African Commission on Human Rights, Communication 155/96.	208

Court	Case	Page
COURT OF JUSTICE OF THE EUROPEAN COMMUNITIES	*Plaumann v. Commission*, C-25/62, [1963] E.C.R. I-95.	160 n288
	Spijker v. Commission, C-231/82, [1983] E.C.R. I-2559.	160 n288
	Procureur de la Republique v. Association de Defense des Bruleurs d'Huiles Usagees, C-240/83, [1985] E.C.R. I-531.	162 n294
	Deutsche Lebensmittelwerke v. Commission, C-97/85, [1987] E.C.R. 2265.	160 n288
	Commission v. Denmark, C-131/88, [1988] E.C.R. 4607.	162 n294
	Commission v. Germany, C-361/88, [1991] E.C.R. I-825 and I-2567.	162 n294
	Matra v. Commission, C-225/92, [1993] E.C.R. I-3203.	160 n288
	Cook v. Commission, C-198/91, [1993] E.C.R. I-2487.	160 n288
	Air France v. Commission, T-2/93, [1994] E.C.R. II-323.	160 n288
	Consorzio Gruppo di Azione Locale "Murgia Messapica" v. Commission, T-465/93, [1994] E.C.R. II-361.	160 n288
	United Kingdom v. Commission, C-180/96, [1996] E.C.R. I-3903.	331 n26
	Greenpeace International v. Commission, C-321/95 P, [1998] E.C.R. I-1651.	161
	R. v. Secretariat of State for the Environment, Transport and the Regions, ex parte First Corporate Shipping Ltd., C-371/98, [2000] ECR I-9235.	48 n12
	Preussen Elektra AG v. Schleswag AG, C-379/98, [2002] E.C.R. I-2099.	292–3
EUROPEAN COURT OF HUMAN RIGHTS CASES	*Lopez-Ostra v. Spain*, Case 41/1993, Judgment of 9 Dec. 1994; Ser. A., No.303C (1994).	208
ITLOS CASES	*Southern Bluefin Tuna (New Zealand and Australia v. Japan) Provisional Measures* (1999), Case 3 and 4, (International Tribunal of the Law of the Sea), online: <http://www.itlos.org>.	109 n31

Court	Case	Page
	Case concerning the Conservation and Sustainable Exploitation of Swordfish Stocks in the South-Eastern Pacific Ocean (Chile/European Community) (2001), Case 7—Order 2001/1, (International Tribunal of the Law of the Sea), online: ITLOS <http://www.itlos.org>.	285 n19
	The MOX Plant Case (Ireland v. United Kingdom) Provisional Measures (2001), Case 10 (International Tribunal of the Law of the Sea), online: <http://www.itlos.org>.	227 n1
	Case concerning the Conservation and Sustainable Exploitation of Swordfish Stocks in the South-Eastern Pacific Ocean (Chile/European Community) (2003), Case 7—Order 2003/2, (International Tribunal of the Law of the Sea), online: <http://www.itlos.org>.	285 n19
	Case concerning Land Reclamation by Singapore in and around the Straits of Johor (Malaysia v. Singapore), Provisional Measures (2003), Case 12—Order of 8 October 2003, (International Tribunal of the Law of the Sea), online: <http://www.itlos.org>.	227 n1
INTERNATIONAL ARBITRATION CASES	*Pacific Fur Seal Arbitration,* (1893) 1 R.I.A.A. 755.	79
	Trail Smelter Arbitration (United States v. Canada), (1938) 3 R.I.A.A. 1911, reprinted in (1939) 33 A.J.I.L. 182, (1941) 3 R. Int'l Arb. Awards 1938, reprinted in (1941) 35 A.J.I.L. 684.	79, 113, 117
	Island of Palmas Case, (1928) 2 R.I.A.A. 829.	113 n44
	Lac Lanoux Arbitration (Spain v. France), [1957] 12 R.I.A.A. 281, 23 I.L.R. 101.	113–14
	BP v. Libya, (1974) 53 I.L.R. 297.	88
	Texaco Overseas Petroleum Co. and California Asiatic Oil Co. v. Libya, (1977) 53 I.L.R. 389.	111 n35
	LIAMCO Award, (1981) 20 I.L.M. 1.	59 n25
	Kuwait v. American Independent Oil Co., (1982) 21 I.L.M. 976.	111 n35

Recommended Resources

Further recommended print and web-based resources on international sustainable development law are also available on the CISDL website (http://www.cisdl.org).

MONOGRAPHS AND PERIODICALS

J.S. Adams and T.O. Mcshane, *The Myth of Wild Africa: Conservation Without Illusion* (New York: Norton, 1996).

E. Agius, ed., *Future Generations and International Law* (London: Earthscan Publications, 1998).

P. Alston, "Conjuring up New Human Rights: A Proposal for Quality Control" (1984) 78 *AJIL* 607.

—— "Making Space for New Human Rights: The Case of the Right to Development" [1988] *Harv. Hum. Rts. Y.B.* 3.

—— "The Fortieth Anniversary of the Universal Declaration" in J. Berting *et al.*, eds. *Human Rights in a Pluralist World, Individuals and Collectivities* (Westport, Conn. Greenwood Press, 1990) at 12.

—— ed., *Peoples' Rights* (Oxford: Oxford University, 2001).

—— and G. Quinn, "The Nature and Scope of States Parties' Obligations under the International Covenant on Economic, Social and Cultural Rights" (1987) 9 *Hum. Rts. Q.* 156.

C.F. Amerasinghe, *Principles of the Institutional Law of International Organizations*, 2nd edn. (Cambridge: Cambridge University Press, 2004).

O. Anaedu and L. Engfeldt, "Sustainable Development Governance" (Paper prepared by the *World Summit for Sustainable Development* Governance Working Group Vice-Chairs Ositadinma Anaedu and Lars-Goran Engfeldt), online: <http://www. johannesburgsummit. org/html/documents/prepcom3docs/governance30.3.rev1.doc>.

S. Arrowsmith, *Government Procurement in the WTO* (The Hague: Kluwer Law International, 2002).

Aspen Institute, *The Alternative Path: A Cleaner, Cheaper Way to Protect and Enhance the Environment* (Washington DC: The Aspen Institute, 1996).

A.A. Asouzu, *International Commercial Arbitration and African States: Practice, Participation and Institutional Development* (Cambridge: Cambridge University Press, 2001).

S. Atapattu, "Sustainable Development: Myth or Reality? A Survey of Sustainable Development under International Law and Sri Lankan Law" (2001) 14 *Geo. Int'l Envtl. L. Rev.* 265.

J.E. Austin and C.E. Bruch, *The Environmental Consequences of War: Legal, Economic, and Scientific Perspectives* (Cambridge: Cambridge University Press, 2001).

M. Austen and T. Richards, *Basic Legal Documents on International Animal Welfare and Wildlife Conservation* (The Hague: Kluwer Law International, 2000).

I. Ayres and J. Braithwaite, *Responsive Regulation: Transcending the Deregulation Debate* (Oxford: Oxford University Press, 1992).

S. Baker, M. Kousis, D. Richardson & S. Young, eds., *The Politics of Sustainable Development* (London: Routledge, 1997).

K. Banks, "Civil Society and the *North American Agreement on Labor Cooperation*" in J. Kirton and V. Maclaren, eds., *Linking Trade, Environment and Social Cohesion: NAFTA Experiences, Global Challenges* (Aldershot: Ashgate, 2002).

K. Bastmeijer, *The Antarctic Environmental Protocol and its Domestic Legal Implementation* (The Hague: Kluwer Law International, 2003).

U. Baxi, "The Development of the Right to Development" in J. Symonides, ed., *Human Rights: New Dimensions and Challenges* (Aldershot: Ashgate, 1998).

C. Bellmann, G. Dutfield & R. Meléndez-Ortiz, *Trading in Knowledge: Development Perspectives on TRIPS, Trade and Sustainability* (London: Earthscan /ICTSD, 2003).

E. Benvenisti, "Domestic Politics and International Resources" in M. Byers, ed., *The Role of Law in International Politics: Essays in International Relations and International Law* (Oxford: Oxford University Press, 2000).

J.M. Bergerat, "Tripping over Patents: Aids, Access to Treatment and the Manufacturing of Scarcity" (2002) 17 *Conn. J. Int'l L.* 157.

G.A. Bermann, "Taking Subsidiarity Seriously: Federalism in the European Community and the United States" (1994) 94 *Colum. L. Rev.* 331.

M. Bowman and A. Boyle, *Environmental Damage in International and Comparative Law – Problems of Definition and Valuation* (Oxford: Oxford University Press, 2002).

—— and C. Redgwell, *International Law and the Conservation of Biological Diversity* (The Hague: Kluwer Law International, 1995).

A. Boyle and M. Anderson, eds., *Human Rights Approaches to Environmental Protection* (Oxford: Clarendon Press, 1996).

—— and D. Freestone, eds., *International Law and Sustainable Development: Past Achievements and Future Challenges* (Oxford: Oxford University Press 1999).

D. Brack, "Multilateral Environmental Agreements: An Overview" in H. Ward and D. Brack, eds., *Trade, Investment and the Environment* (London: Royal Institute of International Affairs and Earthscan, 2000).

D. Bradlow, "Social Justice and Development: Critical Issues Facing the Bretton Woods System: The World Bank, the IMF, and Human Rights" (1996) 6 *Transnat'l. L. & Contemp. Probs.* 47

—— "A Test Case for the World Bank" (1996) 11 *Am. U. J. Int'l L. & Pol'y* 247.

H. Breitmeier, "International Organisations and the Creation of Environmental Regimes" in O. Young, ed., *Global Governance: Drawing Insights from the Environmental Experience* (Cambridge: MIT Press, 1997) at 87–114.

J.L. Brierly, *Law of Nations*, 6th edn. (Oxford: Clarendon Press, 1963).

C. Brower and J. Brueschke, *The Iran-United States Claims Tribunal* (The Hague: Kluwer Law International, 1998).

D.R. Brown, "Transboundary Environmental Impacts in a European Context" (1997) 3 *Eur. Env't* 80.

E. Brown Weiss, *In Fairness to Future Generations: International Law, Common Patrimony, and intergenerational Equity* (New York: Transnational, 1989).

—— "Environmentally Sustainable Competitiveness: A Comment" (1993) 102 *Yale L.J.* 2123

—— "International Environmental Law: Contemporary Issues and the Emergence of a New World Order" (1993) 81 *Geo. L.J.* 675.

—— "The Emerging Structure of International Environmental Law" in N. J. Vig and R.S. Axelrod, eds., *The Global Environment: Institutions, Law, and Policy* (Washington: Congressional Quarterly, 1999) at 98.

—— P.C. Szasz & D.B. Magraw, *International Environmental Law: Basic Instruments and Reference* (New York: Transnational, 1992).

I. Brownlie, *Principles of Public International Law* (Oxford: Oxford University Press, 1998).

J. Brunée and S.J. Toope, "Environmental Security and Freshwater Resources: Ecosystem Regime Building" (1997) *AJIL* 26 at 40.

—— and —— "International Law and Constructivism: Elements of an Interactional Theory of International Law" (2000) 39 (1) *Colum. J. Transnat'l L.* 19.

W. Burns, "The International Convention to Combat Desertification: Drawing a Line in the Sand?" (1994) 16 *Mich. J. Int'l L.* 831.

L.K. Caldwell, *International Environmental Policy* (Durham, NC: Duke University Press, 1996).

J. Cameron, "International Law and the Precautionary Principle" in T. O' Riordan, J. Cameron & A. Jordan, eds., *Reinterpreting the Precautionary Principle* (London: Cameron May, 2001).

—— and J. Abouchar, "The Precautionary Principle: A Fundamental Principle of Law and Policy for the Protection of the Global Environment" (1991) 14 *B.C. Int'l & Comp. L. Rev.* 1.

—— and —— "The Status of the Precautionary Principle in International Law" in D. Freestone & E. Hey, eds., *The Precautionary Principle and International Law: The Challenge of Implementation* (The Hague: Kluwer Law International, 1996).

—— P. Demaret & D. Geradin, eds., *Trade & The Environment: The Search For Balance* (London: Cameron May, 1994).

—— W. Wade-Gery & J. Abouchar, "Precautionary Principle and Future Generations" in E. Agius, ed., *Future Generations and International Law* (London: Earthscan Publications, 1998).

P.D. Cameron, *Competition in Energy Markets: Law and Regulation in the European Union* (Oxford: Oxford University Press, 2002).

—— and D. Zillman, *Kyoto: From Principles to Practice* (New York: Kluwer Law International, 2001).

L. Campiglio, L. Pineschi & D. Siniscalco Treves, eds., *The Environment After Rio: International Law and Economics* (Boston: Graham & Trotman, 1994).

A.A. Cancado Trindade, ed., *Human Rights, Sustainable Development and the Environment* (San José, Costa Rica: Instituto Interamericano de Derechos Humanos, 1992).

M. Cappelletti, M. Seccombe & J. Weiler, eds., *Integration through Law* (New York: W. de Gruyter, 1986).

J.E. Carroll, ed., *International Environmental Diplomacy* (Cambridge: Cambridge University Press, 1988).

A. Cassese, *International Law* (Oxford: Oxford University Press, 2001).

J.G. Castel, A.L.C. de Mestral and W.C. Graham, *The Canadian Law and Practice of International Trade* (Toronto: Montgomery, 1991).

W.B. Chambers, ed., *Inter-linkages: The Kyoto Protocol and the International Trade and Investment Regimes* (Tokyo: United Nations University Press, 2001).

A. Chapman and S. Russell, eds., *Core Obligations: Building a Framework for Economic, Social and Cultural Rights* (Oxford: Intersentia, 2002).

S. Charnovitz, "Regional Trade Agreements and the Environment" (1995) 37:5 *Environment 95*.

W. Choi, *"Like Products" in International Trade Law – Towards a Consistent GATT/ WTO Jurisprudence* (Oxford: Oxford University Press, 2003).

S.R. Chowdhury, "Common but Differentiated State Responsibility in International Environmental Law: From Stockholm (1972) to Rio (1992)" in K. Ginther, E. Denters, R. Churchill & V. Lowe, *The Law of the Sea* (Oxford: Oxford University Press, 1999).

B. Clark, "Environmental Impact Assessment (EIA): Scope and Objectives" in *Perspectives on Environmental Impact Assessment* (Dordrecht: D. Reidel Publishing Co, 1984).

W.C. Clark, "A Transition towards Sustainability" (2001) 27 *Ecology L.Q.* 1021.

A.M.H. Clayton and N.J. Radcliffe, *Sustainability: A Systems Approach* (London: Earthscan, 1996).

M. Colchester, *Salvaging Nature Indigenous Peoples, Protected Areas and Biodiversity Conservation*, World Rainforest Movement and World Wildlife Fund Discussion Paper 55 (Geneva: United Nations Research Institute for Social Development, 1994).

H. Collins, "The Voice of the Community in Private Law Discourse" (1997) 3 *Eur. L.J.* 407.

H.D. Cooper, "The International Treaty on Plant Genetic Resources for Food and Agriculture" (2002) 11 *RECIEL* 1.

M.-C. Cordonier Segger "Sustainability and Corporate Accountability Regimes: Implementing the Johannesburg Summit Agenda" (2003) 12:3 *RECIEL*.

—— "Significant Developments in Sustainable Development Law and Governance: A Proposal" (2004) 28:1 *United Nations Natural Resources Forum.*

—— "Sustainable Development in the Negotiation of the FTAA – The Free Trade Area of the Americas: Issues and Visions for the Future, Interamerican Perspectives" (2004) 27 *Fordham. Intl. L. J.* 1118.

—— and N. Borregaard, "Sustainability and Hemispheric Integration: A Review of Existing Approaches" in C. Deere and D. Esty, eds. *Greening the Americas*, (Boston: MIT Press, 2002).

—— and J. Cabrera, "Civil Society in Americas Trade and Environment Negotiations" in M.-C. Cordonier Segger *et al.*, *Beyond the Barricades: A Trade and Sustainable Development Agenda for the Americas* (Aldershot: Ashgate, 2005).

—— and M. Gehring, "Precaution, Health and the World Trade Organisation: Moving toward Sustainable Development" (2003) 29 *Queen's L. J.* 133.

—— A. Khalfan, M. Gehring & M. Toering, "Prospects for Principles of International Sustainable Development Law after WSSD: Common but Differentiated Responsibilities, Precaution and Participation" (2003) 12:3 *RECIEL*

—— and M. Leichner Reynal, eds., *Beyond the Barricades: An Americas Trade and Sustainability Agenda* (Aldershot: Ashgate, 2004).

—— and C.G. Weeramantry, eds., *Sustainable Justice: Reconciling Economic, Social and Environmental Law* (Leiden: Martinus Nijhoff, 2004).

—— et al., *Trade Rules and Sustainability in the Americas* (Winnipeg: IISD, 1999).

—— *et al.*, "A New Mechanism for Hemispheric Cooperation on Environmental Sustainability and Trade" (2002) 27:2 *Columbia Journal of Environmental Law* 613.

—— *et al.*, *Ecological Rules and Sustainability in the Americas* (Winnipeg: IISD/UNEP, 2002).

—— *et al.*, *Social Rules and Sustainability in the Americas* (Winnipeg: IISD/OAS, 2004).

M. Craven, *The International Covenant on Economic, Social and Cultural Rights: A Perspective on its Development* (Oxford: Clarendon, 1995).

J. Crawford, ed., *Rights of Peoples* (Oxford: Oxford University Press, 1992).

—— *The International Law Commission's Articles on State Responsibility–Introduction, Texts and Commentaries* (Cambridge: Cambridge University Press, 2002).

A. D'Amato and S.K. Chopra, "Whales: Their Emerging Right to Life" (1991) 85 *Am. J. Int'l. L.* 1.

K. Danish, "International Environmental Law and the 'Bottom-Up' Approach: A Review of the Desertification Convention" (1995) 3 *Ind. J. Global Leg. Stud.* 133.

W.J. Davey, "The WTO Dispute Settlement System" (2000) 3:1 *J. Int'l Econ. L.* 15.

M. Decleris *The Law of Sustainable Development: General Principles, A Report for the European Commission* (Brussels: European Commission, 2000).

C. Deere, *Net Gains: International Trade, Sustainable Development and Fisheries* (Washington: IUCN – World Conservation, 1999).

K. de Feyter, *World Development Law: Sharing Resources for Development* (Antwerp: Intersentia, 2001).

C. de Fontaubert, *Achieving Sustainable Fisheries: Implementing the New International Regime* (Gland: IUCN, 2003).

P.J.I.M. de Waart, "Securing Access to Safe Drinking Water through Trade and International Migration", in E. Brans *et al.*, eds., *The Scarcity of Water: Emerging Legal and Policy Responses* (New York: Kluwer Law International, 1997) at 116–17.

J.C. Dernbach, "Sustainable Development as a Framework for National Governance" (1998) 49 *Case W. Res.* 1.

D. Devuys, "Sustainability Assessment: the Application of a Methodological Framework" (1999) 1:4 *Journal of Environmental Assessment Policy and Management* 459.

E. Dewailly, A. Nantel, J.P. Weber & F. Meyer, "High Levels of PCBs in Breast Milk of Inuit Women from Arctic Québec" [1989] *Bull. Environ. Contam. Toxicol.* 43.

E. Dinerstein *et al.*, *A Conservation Assessment of the Terrestrial Ecoregions of Latin America and the Caribbean* (Washington: WWF & World Bank, 1995).

J.M. Djossou, *L'Afrique, le GATT et l'OMC: Entre territoires douaniers et régions commerciales* (Sainte-Foy: Presses de l'Université Laval, 2000).

F. Dodds, "Reforming the International Institutions" in F. Dodds, ed., *Earth Summit 2002: A New Deal* (London: Earthscan, 2002).

C. Dommen and P. Cullet, *Droit International de L'Environment, Textes de base et reference* (The Hague: Kluwer Law International, 2001).

M. Drumble, "Poverty, Wealth and Obligation in International Environmental Law" (2002) 76 *Tul. L. Rev.* 843.

P. Dupuy, "Soft Law and the International Law of the Environment" (1991) 12 *Mich. J. Int'l L.* 420

W. Durbin, *A Comparison of the Environmental Provisions of the NAFTA, the Canada–Chile Trade Agreement and the Mexican–European Community Trade Agreement* (New Haven: Yale Centre for Environmental Law and Policy, 2000).

G. Dutfield, *Intellectual Property Rights, Trade and Biodiversity* (London: Earthscan, 2000).

M.A. Echols, *Food Safety and the WTO: The Interplay of Culture, Science and Technology* (The Hague: Kluwer Law International, 2001).

R.H. Edwards and S.N. Lester, "Towards a More Comprehensive World Trade Organisation Agreement on Trade Related Investment Measures" (1997) 33 *Stan. J. Int'l L.* 169.

A. Eide, C. Krause & A. Rosas, eds., *Economic, Social and Cultural Rights*, 2nd rev. edn. (The Hague: Kluwer Law International, 2001).

J.A. Ekpere, "TRIPs, Biodiversity and Traditional Knowledge: OAU Model Law on Community Rights and Access to Genetic Resources" (2003) 7:5 *Bridges* 11.

D. Esty, *Greening the GATT: Trade, Environment and the Future* (Washington: Institute for International Economics, 1994).

D.C. Esty and D. Geradin, "Market Access, Competitiveness, and Harmonization: Environmental Protection in Regional Trade Agreements" (1997) 21 *Harv. Envtl. L. Rev.* 265.

T.F.M. Etty and H. Somsen, *Yearbook of European Environmental Law* 4 (Oxford: Oxford University Press, 2004).

European Commission, *Communication from the European Commission on the Precautionary Principle* COM 1 (2000), WTO doc. WT/CTE/W/147G/TBT/W/137 (27 June 2000).

M. Evans and R. Murray, eds., *African Charter on Human and People's Rights: The System in Practice 1986–2000* (Cambridge: Cambridge University Press, 2002).

D.P. Fidler, "Trade and Health: The Global Spread of Disease and International Trade" (1997) 40 *Germ. Y. B. Int'l L.* 30.

—— "Return of the Fourth Horseman: Emerging Infectious Diseases and International Law" (1997) 81 *Minn. L. Rev.* 771.

—— "The Future of the World Health Organisation: What Role for International Law" (1998) 31 *Vand. J. Transnat'l, L.* 1079.

—— *International Law and Infectious Diseases* (Oxford: Clarendon Press, 1999).

—— "International Law and Global Public Health" (1999) 48 *U. Kan. L. Rev.* 1.

—— "A Globalized Theory of Public Health Law" (2002) 30 *J. L. Med. & Ethics* 150.

D. Fleck, ed., *Handbook of Humanitarian Law in Armed Conflicts* (Oxford: Oxford University Press, 2000).

C. Ford, "Judicial Discretion in International Jurisprudence: Article 38(1)(C) and 'General Principles of Law'" (1994) 5 *Duke J. of Comp. & Int'l Law* 35–86.

E. Fox, "Anti-trust and Regulatory Federalism: Races Up, Down and Sideways" (2000) 75 *NYUL Rev.* 1781.

—— "Competition Law" in A. Lowenfeld, *International Economic Law* (Oxford: Oxford University Press, 2002) at 340–83.

J. Fox and L. Brown, *The Struggle for Accountability: The World Bank, NGOs, and Grassroots Movements* (Cambridge, Mass: MIT Press, 1998).

F. Francione, *Environment, Human Rights and International Trade* (Oxford: Hart, 2001).

—— and T. Sovazzi, eds., *International Law for Antarctica* (The Hague: Kluwer Law International, 1996).

T.M. Franck, *Fairness in International Law and Institutions* (Oxford: Oxford University Press, 1995).

D. Freestone and E. Hey, eds., *The Precautionary Principle and International Law: The Challenge of Implementation* (The Hague: Kluwer International, 1996).

D. French, "Developing States and International Environmental Law: The Importance of Differentiated Responsibilities" (2000) 49 *International & Comparative Law Quarterly* 35.

L. Frischtak, *Antinomies of Development: Governance Capacity and Adjustment Responses* (Washington: World Bank, 1993).

P. Gallagher, *Guide to the WTO and Developing Countries* (The Hague: Kluwer Law International, 2000).

F.V. Garcia-Amador, "The Proposed New International Economic Order: A New Approach to the Law Governing Nationalization and Compensation" (1980) 12 *Lawyer of the Americas* 1.

K. Garforth, *When Biosafety becomes Binding: A Decision-Maker's Guide* (Montreal: UNCBD/CISDL, 2004).

D.B. Gatmaytan, "Half a Landmark Case: Reflections on Oposa v. Factoran" (1994) 6 *Philippine Natural Resources Law Journal* 30.

A.I. Gavil et al., *Antitrust Law in Perspective: Cases, Concepts and Problems in Competition Policy* (St. Paul: Thomson West, 2002) 38.

M. Gehring and M.-C. Cordonier Segger, "The WTO Asbestos Cases and Precaution: Sustainable Development Implications of the WTO Asbestos Dispute" (2003) 15 *Oxford J of Environmental L* 289.

—— and M.-C. Cordonier Segger, eds., *Sustainable Developments in World Trade Law* (The Hague: Kluwer Law International, 2004).

Geneva Environment Network (GEN)/Swiss Agency for the Environment, Forests and Landscape (SAEFL) publication, *Precaution from Rio to Johannesburg* (Geneva: GEN/SAEFL, 2002).

K. Gent, "Deutsches Stromeinspeisungsgesetz und Europäisches Wettbewerbsrecht" [1999] *Energiewirtschaftliche Tagesfragen – Zeitschrift für die Elektrizitäts- und Gasversorgung* 854–858.

D. Gerber, *Law and Competition in Twentieth-Century Europe – Protecting Prometheus* (Oxford: Oxford University Press, 2001).

D. Gervais, *The TRIPS Agreement: Drafting History and Analysis* (London: Sweet & Maxwell, 1998).

M. Ghezuhly et al., "International Health Law" (1998) 32 *Int'l Law* 539.

C. Giagnocavo & H. Goldstein, "Law Reform or World Reform: The Problem of Environmental Rights" 35 *McGill L.J.* 345.

K. Ginther, E. Denters & P.J.I.M. de Waart, eds., *Sustainable Development and Good Governance* (The Hague: Martinus Nijhoff, 1995).

E. Gitli and C. Murillo, in *Greening the Americas*, C. Deere & D. Esty eds., (Cambridge: MIT Press, 2002).

M. Goransson, "Liability for Damage to the Marine Environment" in A. Boyle and D. Freestone, eds., *International Law and Sustainable Development: Past Achievements and Future Challenges* (Oxford: Oxford University Press, 1999).

D.G. Goyder, *EC Competition Law* 4th edn. (Oxford: Oxford University Press, 2003).

P. Grady & K. Macmillan, *Seattle and Beyond: The WTO Millennium Round* (Ottawa: Global Economics Ltd and International Trade Policy Consultants Inc., 1999).

K.R. Gray, "International Environmental Impact Assessment" (2000) 11 *Colo. J. Int'l Envtl. L. & Pol'y* 83.

D.A. Grossman, "Warming Up To a Not-So-Radical Idea: Tort-Based Climate Change Litigation" (2003) 28 *Colum. J. Envtl. L.* 1.

P.L. Gündling, "The Status in International Law of the Principle of Precautionary Action" in D. Freestone & T. Ijlstra, eds., *The North Sea: Perspectives on Regional Environmental Co-operation* (London: Graham & Trotman, 1990) at 23–30.

L. Guruswamy and B. Hendricks, *International Environmental Law* (St. Paul, Minn.: West, 1997).

A. Guzman, "Why LDCs Sign Treaties that Hurt Them: Explaining the Popularity of Bilateral Investment Treaties" (1998) 38 *Va. J. Int'l Law* 639.

G. Hafner, "Risk Ensuing from Fragmentation of International Law", *I.L.C. Report on the Work of its 52nd Session*, United Nations General Assembly Official Records, 55th Session, Supp. 10 (A/55/10) 321.

G. Handl, *Multilateral Development Banking: Environmental Principles and Concepts Reflecting General International Law and Public Policy* (The Hague: Kluwer Law International, 2001).

——and R.E. Lutz, *Transferring Hazardous Technologies and Substances* (The Hague: Kluwer Law International, 1990).

X. Hanqin, *Transboundary Damage in International Law* (Cambridge: Cambridge University Press, 2003).

D. Harris and S. Livingstone, eds., *The Inter-American System of Human Rights* (Oxford: Clarendon, 1998).

G. Hartkopf and E. Bohne, *Umweltpolitik, vol. 1: Grundlagen, Analysen, und Perspektiven* (Opladen: Westdeutscher Verlag, 1983).

R. Heathcote, *The Arid Lands: Their Use and Abuse* (Tokyo: United Nations University, 1983).

D. Held, *Models of Democracy* (Stanford: Stanford University Press, 1987).

G.K. Helleiner, "Developing Countries in Global Economic Governance and Negotiation Process", in D. Nayyar, ed., *The New Role and Functions for the United Nations and the Bretton Woods Institutions* (Tokyo: World Institute for Development Economics Research, University of the United Nations, 2000).

K. Helmore and N. Singh, *Sustainable Livelihoods: Building on the Wealth of the Poor* (Bloomfield: Kumarian Press, 2001).

B. Hepple, ed., *Social and Labour Rights in a Global Context: International and Comparative Perspectives* (Cambridge: Cambridge University Press, 2002).

G. Hermes, *Staatliche Infrastrukturverantwortung: rechtliche Grundstrukturen netzgebundener Transport- und Übertragungssysteme zwischen Daseinsvorsorge und Wettbewerbsregulierung am Beispiel der leitungsgebundenen Energieversorgung in Europa* (Tuebingen: Mohr Siebeck, 1998).

J.A. Hernandez, "How the Feds are Pushing Nuclear Waste on Reservations" [1994] *Cultural Survival Quarterly* 40.

G. Herrmann, "The Role of UNCITRAL" in I. Fletcher, L. Mistellis & M. Cremona eds., *Foundations and Perspectives of International Trade Law* (London: Sweet & Maxwell, 2001) 28–36.

R.L. Herz, "Litigating Environmental Abuses Under the Alien Tort Claims Act: A Practical Assessment" (2000) 40 *Va. J. Int'l L.* 545.

J.E. Hickey, Jr., & V.R. Walker, "Refining the Precautionary Principle in International Environmental Law" (1995) 14 *Va. Envtl. L.J.* 423.

R.K. Hitchcock, "International Human Rights, the Environment, and Indigenous Peoples" (1994) 5 *Colo. J. Int'l Envtl. L. & Pol'y* 1.

H. Hofbauer, G. Lara & B. Martinez, *Health Care: A Question of Human Rights, Not Charity* (Mexico City: FUNDAR, 2002).

J. Holder, *Environmental Assessment – Legal Regulation of Decision-Making* (Oxford: Oxford University Press, 2003).

J. Holmberg, *Defending the Future: A Guide to Sustainable Development* (London: Earthscan, 1988).

S. Horton, "Peru and ANCOM: A Study in the Disintegration of a Common Market" (1982) 1 *Texas International Law Journal* 17.

Human Rights Watch & Natural Resources Defense Council, *Defending the Earth: Abuses of Human Rights and the Environment* (1992).

M. Humblett, *International Labour Standards: A Global Approach* (Geneva: International Labour Office, 2002).

D. Hunter, J. Salzman & D. Zaelke, *International Environmental Law and Policy*, 2nd edn. (New York: Foundation Press, 2003).

——J. Sommer & S. Vaughan, *Concepts and Principles of International Law* (Nairobi: UNEP, 1998).

G. Hyden and M. Bratton, eds., *Governance and Politics in Africa* (Boulder: Lynne Reinner Publishers, 1993).

IBRD, *The Convention on the Settlement of Investment Disputes: Documents Concerning the Origin and Formulation of the Convention* (Washington: IBRD, 1970).

E.V. Iglesias, *El nuevo rostro de la integracion regional en America Latina y el Caribe* (Washington: Inter-American Development Bank, 1997).

Inter-American Development Bank, *Integration and Trade in the Americas* (Washington: IDB, 1996).

International Council on Human Rights Policy, *Duties sans Frontieres: Human Rights and Global Social Justice* (Geneva: ICHRP, 2003), online: <www.ichrp.org>.

International Institute for Sustainable Development (IISD), *Impoverishment and Sustainable Development* (Winnipeg: IISD, 1996).

International Law Association, *2002 New Delhi Declaration on Principles of International Law Relating to Sustainable Development* (London: ILA, 2002).

International Law Commission (ILC), *Draft Articles on the Non-Navigational Uses of International Watercourses*, UN Doc. A/46/10 (1991) at 161 and UN Doc. A/ CN.4/ L492 & Add. 1 (1994).

International Monetary Fund, *Code of Good Practices on Fiscal Transparency – Declaration of Principles* (1998) 16 April 1998, 37 ILM 942.

International Union for Conservation of Nature and Natural Resources, *An Explanatory Guide to the Cartagena Protocol on Biosafety* (Cambridge: International Union for Conservation of Nature and Natural Resources and FIELD, 2003).

Iran-United States Claims Tribunal Reports (Cambridge: Grotius, 1981–1993).

J. Jackson, *The World Trading System: Law and Policy of International Economic Relations*, 2nd edn. (Cambridge: MIT Press, 1997).

J.H. Jackson, *The Jurisprudence of GATT and the WTO* (Cambridge: Cambridge University Press, 2000).

H.K. Jacobson, *Networks of Interdependence: International Organisations and the Global Political System*, 2nd edn. (New York: Knopf, 1984) 386.

H.K. Jacobson, and E. Brown Weiss, "Strengthening Compliance with International Environmental Accords: Preliminary Observations from a Collaborative Project" (1995) 1 *Global Governance* 119.

W. Jaeger, *Regulierter Wettbewerb in der Energiewirtschaft* (Baden-Baden: Nomos, 2002).

M. Janis, R. Kay & A. Bradley, *European Human Rights Law: Texts and Materials* (Oxford: Oxford University Press, 2000).

R. Jennings, "What Is International Law and How Do We Tell It When We See It?" (1981) 37 *ASDI* 59.

A.L. Jernow, "*Ad Hoc* and Extra-conventional Means for Human Rights Monitoring" in P.C. Szasz, ed., *Administrative and Expert Monitoring of International Treaties* (New York: Transnational, 1999).

P. Jha and F.J. Chaloupka eds., *Tobacco Control in Developing Countries* (Oxford: Oxford University Press, 2000).

B.R. Johnston, "Indigenous Rights" in B.R. Johnston, ed. *Who Pays the Price? The Socio-cultural Context of Environmental Crisis* (Corelo, California: Island Press, 1994).

P. Kahn, "Contrats d'Etat et Nationalisation – Les Apports de la Sentence Arbitrale du 24 Mars, 1982" (1982) 109 J. *Droit Int'l* 844.

A. Khalfan, "International Human Rights Development Financing", in M.-C. Cordonier Segger and C.G. Weeramantry, eds., *Sustainable Justice: Reconciling Economic, Social and Environmental Law* (Leiden: Martinus Nijhoff, 2004).

—— and M.-C. Cordonier Segger, *International Human Rights and International Sustainable Development Law* CISDL Legal Brief, 26 August 2002, online: <www.cisdl.org>.

B. Kingsbury, "The Concept of Compliance as a Function of Competing Conceptions of International Law" (1998) 19 *Mich. J. Int'l Law* 345.

E. Kinney, "AIDS in National and International Law" (2002) 96 *Am. Soc'y Int'l L. Proc.* 320 (American Society of International Law Proceedings 16 March 2002).

A. Kirchner, *International Marine Environmental Law: Institutions, Implementation and Innovations* (The Hague: Kluwer Law International, 2003).

C. Kirkpatrick, *The Impact of the Uruguay Round on Least Developed Countries' External Trade: Strengthening the Capacity of LDCs to Participate Effectively in the World Trade Organisation and to Integrate into the Trading System* (Manchester: Manchester University Press, 1998).

J. Kirton and V. Maclaren, eds., *Linking Trade, Environment, and Social Cohesion: NAFTA Experiences, Global Challenges* (Aldershot: Ashgate, 2002).

A. Kiss, "The Implications of Global Change for the International Legal System" in E. Brown Weiss, ed., *Environmental Change and International Law* (Tokyo: United Nations University Press, 1992) 319–25.

—— and D. Shelton, *International Environmental Law*, 2nd edn. (New York: Transnational Publishers, 1994).

—— and ——, *Judicial Handbook on Environmental Law (Draft)* (Nairobi: UNEP, 2004).

——, —— & K. Ishibashi, *Economic Globalization and Compliance with International Environmental Agreements* (The Hague: Kluwer Law International, 2003).

N. Klein, *Dispute Settlement in the UN Convention on the Law of the Sea* (Cambridge: Cambridge University Press, 2004).

H.H. Koh, "Why do Nations Obey International Law?"(1997) 106 *Yale LJ*. 2599.

P. Konz, C. Bellmann, L. Assuncao & R. Melendez-Otiz, *Trade, Environment, and Sustainable Development Views from Sub-Saharan Africa and Latin America: A Reader* (Geneva: UNU/IAS & ICTSD, 2000).

M. Koskenniemi, "Breach of Treaty or Non-Compliance? Reflections on the Enforcement of the Montreal Protocol" (1992) 3 *YB Int'l. Env'tl. L.* 123

A. Kothari, "Beyond the Biodiversity Convention: A View from India" in V. Sanchez and C. Juma, (eds.) *Biodiplomacy: Genetic Resources and International Relations* (Nairobi: ACTS, 1994) 67.

F.V. Kratochwil, *Rules, Norms and Decisions. on the Conditions of Practical and Legal Reasoning in International Relations and Domestic Affairs* (Cambridge: Cambridge University Press, 1989) 201.

—— and J.G. Ruggie, "International Organisation: a State of the Art on an Art of the State" (1986) 40(4) *Int'l. Org.* 753 at 768.

A.K. Kuhn, Comment, "The Trail Smelter Arbitration – United States and Canada" (1938) 32 *AJIL* 785.

K. Kummer, *International Management of Hazardous Wastes – The Basel Convention and Related Legal Rules* (Oxford: Oxford University Press, 1995).

J. Kurtz, "A General Investment Agreement in the WTO?: Lessons from Chapter 11 NAFTA and the OECD Multilateral Agreement on Investment" (2002) 23 *Journal of International Economic Law* 713–89.

W.M. Lafferty and J. Meadowcroft, *Implementing Sustainable Development – Strategies and Initiatives in High Consumption Societies* (Oxford: Oxford University Press, 2000).

B. Lal Das, *The WTO Agreements: Deficiencies, Imbalances and Required Changes* (London: Zed Books, 1998).

W. Lang, ed., *Sustainable Development and International Law* (London: Graham & Trotman/Martinus Nijhoff, 1995).

M. Langford, *Litigating Economic, Social and Cultural Rights: Achievements, Challenges and Strategies* (Geneva: COHRE, 2003).

——, A. Khalfan, C. Fairstein & H. Jones, *Legal Resources for the Right to Water: International and National Standards* (Geneva: COHRE, 2004).

H. Lauterpacht, *The Development of International Law by the International Court* (London: Stevens, 1958).

S. Leckie, "Another Step Towards Indivisibility: Identifying the Key Features of Violations of Economic, Social and Cultural Rights" [1998] 20 *Human Rights Quarterly*.

J.W. Le Deuc, "World Health Organization Strategy for Emerging Infectious Diseases" (1996) 275 *JAMA* 318.

S. Lederberg, R.E. Shope, S.C. Oak, eds., *Emerging Infectious Diseases: Microbial Threats to Health in the United States* (Washington DC: Institute of Medicine, National Academy Press, 1992).

A. L'Hirondel and D. Yach, "Develop and Strengthen Public Health Law" (1998) 51 *World Health Stat. Q.* 79.

A. Lindroos, *The Right to Development* (Helsinki: The Erik Castren Institute of International Law and Human Rights Research Reports, 1999).

M. Lovei and P. Pillai, *Assessing Environmental Policy, Regulatory and Institutional Capacity: A World Bank Policy Note* (Washington: World Bank, 2003).

V. Lowe, "Sustainable Development and Unsustainable Arguments" in A. Boyle and D. Freestone, eds., *International Law and Sustainable Development: Past Achievements and Future Challenges* (Oxford: Oxford University Press, 1999).

—— "The Politics of Law-Making: Are the Method and Character of Norm Creation Changing?" in M. Byers, ed., *The Role of Law in International Politics: Essays in International Relations and International Law* (Oxford: Oxford University Press, 2000).

A. Lowenfeld, *International Economic Law* (Oxford: Oxford University Press, 2002).

S. Lyster, *International Wildlife Law: An Analysis of International Treaties concerned with the Conservation of Wildlife* (Cambridge: Cambridge University Press, 1985).

R. Mackenzie *et al.*, *An Explanatory Guide to the Cartagena Protocol on Biosafety* (Cambridge: IUCN, 2003).

G.F. Maggio, "Inter/intra-Generational Equity: Current Applications under International Law for Promoting the Sustainable Development of Natural Resources" (1997) 4 *Buff. Envt'l. L.J.* 161.

—— and O.J. Lynch, *Human Rights, Environment, and Economic Development: Existing and Emerging Standards in International Law and Global Society* (World Resources Institute, 1996).

K.E. Mahoney and P. Mahoney, eds., *Human Rights in the Twenty-first Century: A Global Challenge* (Norwell: Kluwer Academic Publishers, 1993).

H. Mann and K. von Moltke, *NAFTA's Chapter 11 and the Environment – Addressing the Impacts of the Investor-State Process on the Environment* (Winnipeg: International Institute for Sustainable Development, 1999).

G. Marceau, *Anti-Dumping and Anti-Trust Issues in Free-Trade Areas* (Oxford: Clarendon Press, 1994).

E. Marden, "The Neem Tree Patent: International Conflict over the Commodification of Life" (1999) 22 *Boston Col. Int'l & Comp. L Rev.* 2:279.

S. Marks, "Emerging Human Rights: A New Generation for the 1980s?" (1980–1) 33 *Rutgers L. Rev.* 435.

J. Mathis, *Regional Trade Agreements in the GATT/WTO Article XXIV and the Internal Trade Agreement* (The Hague: T.M.C. Asser Press, 2002).

M. Matsushita, "International Cooperation in the Enforcement of Competition Policy" (2002) *Washington University Global Studies Law Review Vol.* 1:463.

——, T.J. Schoenbaum & P.C. Mavroidis, *The World Trade Organization – Law, Practice, and Policy* (Oxford: Oxford University Press, 2004).

P. McAuslan, "Good Governance and Aid in Africa" (1996) 40 *J. Afr. L.* 168 at 168–82.

S. McCaffrey, *The Law of International Watercourses – Non-Navigational Uses* (Oxford: Oxford University Press, 2003).

C. McCrudden, "International Economic Law and Human Rights: A Framework for Discussion of the Legality of 'Selective Purchasing' Laws under the WTO Government Procurement Agreement" (1999) 2:1 *J. Int'l Econ. L.* 3.

D. McGoldrick, "Sustainable Development and Human Rights: An Integrated Conception" (1996) 45 *Int'l & Comp. LQ.* 796.

H. McGoldrick, "Sustainable Development: The Challenge to International Law" [1994] *RECIEL* 3.

D.H. Meadows *et al.*, *Beyond the Limits* (New York: Universe Books, 1972).

R. Meléndez-Ortiz and C. Bellmann, *Commerce international et développement durable: Voix africaines et plurielles* ICTSD (Paris: Editions Charles Léopold Mayer, 2002).

L. Mills and I. Serageldin, *Governance and the External Factor* (Washington: World Bank, 1992).

C. Milner and O. Morrisey, "Measuring Trade Liberalization in Africa" in M. McGillvray and O. Morrisey, eds., *Evaluating Economic Liberalization. Case-Studies in Economic Development* 4 (New York: St. Martin's Press, 1999 / London: Macmillan Press, 1999).

B. Moldan and S. Billharz, *Sustainability Indicators: Report of the Project on Indicators of Sustainable Development* (Chichester: John Wiley, SCOPE 58, 1997).

W.J. Mommsen, *The Age of Bureaucracy: Perspectives on the Political Sociology of Max Weber* (Oxford: Oxford University Press, 1974).

M. Moore, *Doha and Beyond: The Future of the Multilateral Trading System* (Cambridge: Cambridge University Press, 2004).

B. Müller, *Equity in Climate Change: the Great Divide* (Oxford: OISE, 2002).

D.A. Munro and M.W. Holdgate, eds., *Caring for the Earth: A Strategy for Sustainable Living* (Geneva: IUCN, 1991).

S. Murphy, "The ELSI Case: An Investment Dispute at the International Court of Justice" (1991) 16 *Yale J. Int'l L.* 391.

E. Neumayer, "Multilateral Agreement on Investment: Lessons for the WTO from the Failed OECD Negotiations" (1999) 46 *Wirtschaftspolitische Blätter* 618–28.

E.C. Nieuwenhuys and M.M.T.A. Brus, *Multi-lateral Regulation of Investment* (The Hague: Kluwer Law International, 2001).

A. Nollkaemper, "The Precautionary Principle in International Environmental Law: What's New Under the Sun?" (1991) 22 *Marine Pollution Bulletin* 3.

S. Nooteboom and K. Wieringa, "Comparing strategic environmental assessment and integrated environmental assessment" (1999) 1 *Journal of Environmental Assessment Policy and Management* 4, 441.

M. Nordquist and J. Norton Moore, *Current Marine Environmental Issues and the International Tribunal for the Law of the Sea* (Leiden: Martinus Nijhoff, 2001).

H. Nordström and S. Vaughan, *Trade and Environment, WTO Special Study 4* (Geneva: WTO, 1999).

North American Commission for Environmental Cooperation, *Assessing Environmental Effects of the North American Free Trade Agreement (NAFTA): An Analytic Framework (Phase II)* and *Issue Studies* (Montreal: NACEC, 1999).

OAS, *Acuerdos de comercio e integracion en las Americas – Un compendio analitico* (Washington: OAS, 1997).

—— *Human Rights: How to Present a Petition in the Inter-American System* (Washington: OAS, 2000).

S. Oberthür and H.E. Ott, eds., *The Kyoto Protocol: International Climate Policy for the 21st Century* (Berlin: Springer Verlag Ecologic, 1999).

OECD, *Freight and the Environment: Effects of Trade Liberalisation and Transport Sector Reforms* (Paris: OECD, 1997).

—— *Policies to Enhance Sustainable Development* (Paris: OECD, May 2001).

P.N. Okowa, "Procedural Obligations in International Environmental Agreements" [1996] *Brit. YB of Int'l L.* 275.

—— *State Responsibility for Transboundary Air Pollution in International Law* (Oxford: Oxford University Press, 2000).

T.A. O'Keefe, "An Analysis of the MERCOSUR Economic Integration Project from a Legal Perspective" (1994) 28:2 *The International Lawyer* 28, 439.

J. Oloka-Onyango, "Human Rights and Sustainable Development in Contemporary Africa: A New Dawn, or Retreating Horizons?" (2000) 6 *Buff. Hum. Rts. L. Rev.* 39.

M.K. Omalu, *NAFTA and the Energy Charter: Treaty Compliance with, Implementation and Effectiveness of International Investment Agreements* (The Hague: Kluwer Law International, 1999).

T. O'Riordan, A. Jordan & J. Cameron, eds., *Reinterpreting the Precautionary Principle* (London: Cameron May, 2001).

T. Padoa-Schioppa, *Regulating Finance – Balancing Freedom and Risk* (Oxford: Oxford University Press, 2004).

R.A. Painter, "Human Rights Monitoring: Universal and Regional Treaty Bodies" in P.C. Szasz, ed., *Administrative and Expert Monitoring of International Treaties* (New York: Transnational, 1999).

M. Pallemaerts, "The Future of Environmental Regulation: International Environmental Law in the Age of Sustainable Development: A Critical Assessment of the UNCED Process" (1996) 15 *Journal of Law & Com.* 623

D. Palmeter and P.C. Mavroidis, "The WTO Legal System: Sources of Law" (1998) 92 *AJIL* 398.

—— and P.C. Mavroidis, *Dispute Settlement in the World Trade Organization: Practice and Procedure* 2nd edn. (Cambridge: Cambridge University Press, 2004).

C. Parry, *The Sources and Evidences of International Law* (Manchester: Manchester University Press, 1965).

J.C.N. Paul, "The United Nations Family: Challenges of Law and Development: The United Nations and the Creation of an International Law of Development" (1995) 36 *Harv. Int'l L.J.* 307.

S. Patandin, P.C. Dagnelie, P. Mulder, E. Op de Coul, J.E. Van der Veen, N. Weisglas-Kuperus & P.J.J Sauer, "Dietary exposure to polychlorinated biphenyls and dioxins from infancy to adulthood: A comparison between breast-feeding, toddler, and long-term exposure" (1999) 107 *Environ. Health Perspect.* 45.

D.W. Pearce and G.D. Atkinson, "Capital Theory and Measurement of Sustainable Development: An Indicator of "Weak" Sustainability" (1993) 8 *Ecological Economics* 103–8.

F. Perrez, "The Relationship Between Permanent Sovereignty and the Obligation Not to Cause Transboundary Environmental Damage" (1996) 26 *Environmental Law* 1187.

—— *Cooperative Sovereignty: From Independence to Interdependence in International Environmental Law* (The Hague: Kluwer Law International, 2000).

—— "The World Summit on sustainable Development: Environment, Precaution and Trade – A Potential for Success and/or Failure" (2003) 12:3 *RECIEL*

E.U. Petersmann, "From the Hobbesian International Law of Coexistence to Modern Integration Law: The WTO Dispute Settlement" (1998) 1:2 *J. Int'l Econ. L.* 175.

B.J. Plotkin, "Mission Possible: The future of the International Health Regulations" (1996) 10 *Temp. Int'l & Comp. L. J.* 503.

G. Posser, *Grundfragen des Abfallrechts : Abgrenzung von Produkt/Abfall und Verwertung/Beseitigung* (München: Beck, 2001).

S. Prakash, "Towards a Synergy Between Intellectual Property Rights and Biodiversity" (1999) *Journal of World Intellectual Property* 2:5.

R. Pritchard, *Economic Development, Foreign Investment and the Law* (The Hague: Kluwer Law International, 1996).

R. Provost, *International Human Rights and Humanitarian Law* (Cambridge: Cambridge University Press, 2002).

D. Quist and I. Chapela, "Transgenic DNA Introgressed into Traditional Maize Landraces in Oazaca, Mexico" (2001) 414 *Nature* 541.

Rat von Sachverständigen für Umweltfragen, *Umweltprobleme der Nordsee* (Stuttgart: Kiepenheuer & Witsch, 1980).

J. Razzaque, *Public Interest Environmental Litigation in India, Pakistan and Bangladesh* (The Hague: Kluwer Law International, 2004).

J. Rein, "International Governance through Trade Agreements: Patent Protection for Essential Medicines" (2001) 21 *N.W. J. Int'l L. & Business* 379.

A.C. Reynaud, *Labour Standards and the Integration Process in the Americas* (Geneva: ILO, 2001).

B. Rich, *Mortgaging the Earth: The World Bank, Environmental Impoverishment, and the Crisis of Development* (Boston: Beacon Press, 1994).

B.J. Richardson, *Environmental Regulation through Financial Organisations, Comparative Perspectives on the Industrialised Nations* (The Hague: Kluwer Law International, 2002).

M. Rodriguez-Mendoza, "The Andean Group's Integration Strategy" in A. Julia Jatar and S. Weintraub eds. *Integrating the Hemisphere – Perspectives from Latin America and the Caribbean* (Bogota: Inter-American Dialogue, 1997).

G. Roth and C. Wittich, eds., *Max Weber, Economy and Society: An Outline of Interpretive Sociology* (Berkeley: University of California Press, 1968).

I. Roth, *Umweltbezogene Unternehmenskommunikation im deutschen und europäischen Wettbewerbsrecht* (Frankfurt: P. Lang, 2000).

N. Roht-Arriaza, "Shifting the Point of Regulation: The International Organisation for Standardization and Global Lawmaking on Trade and the Environment" (1995) 22 *Ecology L.Q.* 479.

A.R. Rosencranz, R. Campbell & D.A. O'Neil, "Rio Plus Five: Environmental Protection and Free Trade in Latin America" [1997] *Georgetown International Environmental Law Review* 9.

L. Ruessmann, "Putting the precautionary principle in its place: Parameters for the proper application of a precautionary approach and the implications for developing countries in light of the Doha WTO ministerial" (2002) 17 *Am. U. Int'l L. Rev.* 905.

N. de Sadeleer, *Environmental Principles – From Political Slogans to Legal Rules* (Oxford: Oxford University Press, 2002).

M. Salazar Xirinchas, *Towards Free Trade in the Americas* (Washington: OAS /Brookings Institute, 2002).

G. Sampson, *Trade, Environment and the WTO: The Post-Seattle Agenda*, Overseas Development Council Policy Essay No. 27 (Washington: ODC, 2001).

P. Sands, "European Community Environmental Law: The Evolution of a Regional Regime of International Environmental Protection" (1991) 100 *Yale L.J.* 2511.

—— "International Law in the field of Sustainable Development" (1994) 65 *Br. Yrbk. of I.L.* 303.

—— *Principles of International Environmental Law: Frameworks, Standards and Implementation* 1st edn. (Manchester: Manchester University Press, 1996).

P. Sands, "Environmental Protection in the Twenty-First Century: Sustainable Development and International Law" in N.J. Vig & R.S. Axelrod, eds., *The Global Environment: Institutions, Law, and Policy* (Washington: Congressional Quarterly, 1999) 116.

—— *Principles of International Environmental Law* 2nd edn. (Cambridge: Cambridge University Press, 2003).

D.A. Sarokin and J. Schulkin, "Environmental Justice: Co-evolution of Environmental Concerns and Social Justice (1994) 14 *The Environmentalist* 121.

O. Schachter, *Sharing the World's Resources* (Bangalore: Allied, 1977).

T. Schoenbaum, "International Trade and Protection of the Environment: The Continuing Search for Reconciliation" (1997) 91:2 *American Journal of International Law* 281.

C.H. Schreuer, *The ICSID Convention: A Commentary* (Cambridge: Cambridge University Press, 2001).

N. Schrijver, *Permanent Sovereignty over Natural Resources: Balancing Rights and Duties* (Cambridge: Cambridge University Press 1997).

—— and F. Weiss, "Editorial" in Kluwer Academic Publishers 2 *International Environmental Agreements: Politics, Law and Economics* 2 2002, 105 – 108.

R.A. Sedjo, "Ecosystem Management: An Unchartered Path for Public Forests" (1995) 10 *Resources for the Future* 1.

I. Seidl-Hohenveldern, *International Economic Law*, 3rd edn. (The Hague: Kluwer Law International, 1999).

A. Seidman *et al.*, "Building Sound National Frameworks for Development and Social Change" (1999) 4 *CEPML & P. J.* 1.

S.K. Sell, "TRIPS and the Access to Medicines Campaign" (2002) 20 *Wis. Int'l L.J.* 481.

M. Sepulveda, *The Nature of the Obligations Under the International Covenant on Economic, Social and Cultural Rights* (Antwerp: Intersentia, 2003).

H.F. Shattuck, Jr. *et al.*, "World Health Organisation, Section Recommendation and Report of the American Bar Association" (1996) 30 *Ill. Int'l Law.* 688.

S. Shaw & R. Schwartz "Trade and Environment in the WTO – State of Play" (2002) 36 *JWT* 129.

I.F.I. Shihata, "The World Bank and the Environment: A Legal Perspective" (1992) 16 *Maryland Journal of International Law and* Trade 1.

—— "The World Bank and the Environment: Legal Instruments for Achieving Environmental Objectives" in I.F.I. Shihata, *The World Bank in a Changing World, Vol. II* (Leiden: Martinus Nijhoff Publishers, 1995).

D.A. Silien, "Human Rights Monitoring: Procedures and Decision-Making of Standing United Nations Organs" in P.C. Szasz, ed., *Administrative and Expert Monitoring of International Treaties* (New York: Transnational, 1999) 83.

N. Singh and R. Strickland, eds., *From Legacy to Vision: Sustainability, Poverty and Policy Adjustment* (Winnipeg: International Institute for Sustainable Development, 1996).

A.-M. Slaughter, "Governing Through Government Networks" in M. Byers, ed., *The Role of Law in International Politics: Essays in International Relations and International Law* (Oxford: Oxford University Press, 2000) at 177.

L.B. Sohn, "The Stockholm Declaration on the Human Environment" [1973] *Harv. Int'l L.J.* 423

M. Sornarajah, *The International Law on Foreign Investment* 2nd edn. (Cambridge: Cambridge University Press, 2004).

R.N. Stavins, ed., *Economics of the Environment*, 4th edn. (New York: W.W. Norton & Company, 2000).

H. Steiner and P. Alston, *International Human Rights in Context: Law, Politics, Morals* 2nd edn. (Oxford: Oxford University Press, 2000).

P.L. Stenzel, "Can NAFTA's Environmental Provisions Promote Sustainable Development?" (1995) 59 *Alb.L. Rev.* 43

J. Stiglitz, *Globalization and its Discontents* (London: Penguin Books, 2002).

O. Stokke, *Governing High Seas Fisheries – The Interplay of Global and Regional Regimes* (Oxford: Oxford University Press, 2001).

C.D. Stone, *Should Trees Have Standing? Legal Rights for Natural Objects* (Los Altos, California: William Kaufmann, Inc., 1974).

A.O. Sykes, "Trips, Pharmaceuticals, Developing Countries, and the Doha 'Solution'" (2002) 3 *Chi. J. Int'l L.* 47.

P.C. Szasz, "Introduction" in P.C. Szasz, ed., *Administrative and Expert Monitoring of International Treaties* (New York: Transnational, 1999).

A.L. Taylor, "Making the World Health Organization Work: A Legal Framework for Universal Access to the conditions for Health" (1992) 18 *Am. J. L. & Med.* 301.

—— *An International Regulatory Strategy for Global Tobacco Control* (1996) 21 *Yale J. Int'l Law* 257.

—— and D.W. Bettcher, "WHO Framework Convention on Tobacco Control: A Global 'Good' For Public Health" (2000) 78:7 *Bulletin World Health Organization*, 920–9

J.C. Thomas, "Investor-State arbitration under NAFTA Chapter 11" (1999) 37 *The Canadian Yearbook of International Law* 99–137.

S. Thomas-Nuruddin, "Protection of the Ozone Layer: the Vienna Convention and the Montreal Protocol", in P.C. Szasz, ed., *Administrative and Expert Monitoring of International Treaties* (New York: Transnational, 1999) 113.

U.P. Thomas, "The CBD, the WTO, and the FAO: The Emergence of Phytogenetic Governance" in P.G. LePrestre, ed., *Governing Global Biodiversity: The Evolution and Implementation of the Convention on Biological Diversity* (Aldershot: Ashgate, 2002) 177.

M. Thornton, "Since the Breakup: Developments and Divergences in ANCOM's and Chile's Foreign Investment Codes." (1983) 1 *Hastings International and Comparative Law Review* 7.

A. Timoshenko, *Environmental Negotiator Handbook* (The Hague: Kluwer Law International, 2003).

B. Toebes, *The Right to Health as a Human Right in International Law* (Oxford: Intersentia, 1999).

A. Tolentino, "Good Governance Through Popular Participation in Sustainable Development" in K. Ginther, E. Denters & P.J.I.M. de Waart, eds., *Sustainable Development and Good Governance* (The Hague: Kluwer Law International, 1995).

K. Tomasevksi, *Responding to Human Rights Violations 1946–1999* (The Hague: Martinus Nijhoff, 2000).

S.J. Toope, "Emerging Patterns of Governance" in M. Byers, ed., *The Role of Law in International Politics: Essays in International Relations and International Law* (Oxford: Oxford University Press, 2000) 91.

J.P. Townsend, *Price, Tax and Smoking in Europe* (Copenhagen: World Health Organization, 1998).

M.J. Trebilcock, "What Makes Poor Countries Poor? The Role of Institutional Capital in Economic Development" in E. Buscaglia, W. Ratliff & R. Cooter, eds., *The Law and Economics of Development* (London: JAI Press Inc., 1997) at 15.

P. Trepte, *Regulating Procurement – Understanding the Ends and Means of Public Procurement Regulation* (Oxford: Oxford University Press, 2004).

T. Treves, "The Settlement of Disputes According to the Straddling Stocks Agreement of 1995" in A. Boyle and D. Freestone, eds., *International Law and Sustainable Development: Past Achievements and Future Challenges* (Oxford: Oxford University Press, 1999).

A. Trouwborst, *Evolution and Status of the Precautionary Principle in International Law* (The Hague: Kluwer Law International, 2002).

T.C. Trzyna, ed., *A Sustainable World: Defining and Measuring Sustainable Development* (Sacramento: California Institute of Public Affairs, 1995).

L. Udall, "Irian Jaya's Heart of Gold. Natural Resource Extraction Takes a Heavy Toll on Indonesian Island's Peoples and Habitats" (1995) 10 *World Rivers Review* 10.

M. Ul-Haq, *Reflections on Human Development* (Oxford: Oxford University Press, 1995).

United Nations Conference on Trade and Development and General Agreement on Tariffs and Trade Secretariat, *An Analysis of the Proposed Uruguay Round Agreement with Particular Emphasis on Aspects of Interest to Developing Countries* (Geneva: UNCTAD/GATT Secretariat, 1993), MTN.TNC/W/ 122.

——*Newly Emerging Environmental Policies with a Possible Trade Impact: A Preliminary Discussion – Report by the UNCTAD Secretariat* (New York: United Nations, 1995).

——*Trade and the Environment: Issues of Key Interest to the Least Developed Countries* (New York: United Nations, 1997).

United Nations Development Programme, *Capacity Development for Governance for Sustainable Human Development* (New York: UNDP, 1996).

——*Governance Policy Paper* (1997).

——*Human Development Report 2000* (Oxford: Oxford University Press, 2000).

——*Human Development Report 2002: Deepening Democracy in a Fragmented World* (Oxford: Oxford University Press, 2000).

United Nations, Division for Ocean Affairs and the Law of the Sea, *The Law of the Sea, Concept of the Common Heritage of Mankind* (1996).

United Nations Environment Programme, Report of the Executive Director, *Status of Desertification and Implementation of the United Nations Plan of Action to Combat Desertification*, UNEP/GCSS.III/3.

——*Goals and Principles of Environmental Impact Assessment* (Nairobi: UNEP, 1987).

——Final Report of the Expert Group Workshop on International Environmental Law Aiming at Sustainable Development, UNEP/IEL/WS/3/2, (1996).

——*Environmental Impact Assessment; Issues, Trends and Practice* (Geneva: UNEP, 1996).

——(UNEP) and International Institute for Sustainable Development (IISD), *Environment and Trade: A Handbook* (Winnipeg: IISD/UNEP, 2000).

——International Environmental Governance SS.VII/1, Report of the Governing Council on the Work of its Seventh Special Session/Global Ministerial Environment Forum (13–15 February 2002) UNEP/GCSS.VII/6, Annex I at 23.

United Nations High Commissioner for Human Rights, *Economic, Social and Cultural Rights: The Impact of the Agreement on Trade-Related Aspects of Intellectual Property Rights on Human Rights*, 27 June 2001, E/ CN.4/Sub.2/2001/13.

—— *Economic, Social and Cultural Rights: Liberalisation of Trade in Services and Human Rights: Report of the High Commissioner*, 25 June 2002, E/CN.4/Sub.2/2002/9.

—— and the United Nations Environmental Programme, *Meeting of Experts on Human Rights and the Environment, 14–15 January, 2002: Conclusions*, online: OHCHR, www.unhchr.ch/environment/conclusions.

—— *Report of the Special Rapporteur, Paul Hunt, submitted in accordance with Commission resolution 2002/31*, Commission on Human Rights, 59th Session, E/CN.4/2003/58, 13 February 2003.

United Nations Sub-commission on Prevention of Discrimination of Minorities, *Review of Further Developments in Fields with which the Sub-Commission has been concerned, Human Rights and the Environment*: Final Report prepared by Mrs. Fatma Zohra Ksentini, Special Rapporteur, UN Doc. E/CN. 4/Sub.2/1994/9 (1994).

United Nations Secretary-General, *Follow-up to Johannesburg and the Future Role of the CSD* 18 February 2003 E/CN.17/2003/2.

United Nations University, *Sustainable Development Governance: The Question of Reform: Key Issues and Proposals* (Tokyo: United Nations University Institute for Advanced Studies, 2002).

O. Uriarte, "La ciudadanía laboral en el MERCOSUR" *Derecho Laboral*, Montevideo 1998, Tomo XLI N° 190.

P. Uvin and I. Biagiotti, "Global Governance and the 'New' Political Conditionality" (1996) 2 *Global Governance: A Review of Multilaterism and International Organisations* 377.

G. Van Calster, "Green Procurement and the WTO – Shades of Grey" 11 (3) *RECIEL* 3.

J.L. Varela, "Regional Trends in International Law and Domestic Environmental Law: the Inter-American Hemisphere" in S.J. Rubin and D.C. Alexander, eds., *NAFTA and the Environment* (The Hague: Kluwer Law International, 1996).

D. Vignes, "Protection of the Antarctic Marine Fauna and Flora: The Canberra Convention and the Commission Set Up by It" in F. Francioni and T. Scovazzi, eds., *International Law for Antarctica* (The Hague: Kluwer Law International, 1996).

R.B. von Mehren and P. Nicholas Kourides, "International Arbitrations between States and Foreign Private Parties: The Libyan Nationalization Cases" (1981) 75 *Am. J. Int'l L.* 476.

K. von Moltke, "International Commission and Implementation of Law" in J.E. Carroll, ed., *International Environmental Diplomacy* (Cambridge: Cambridge University Press, 1988) at 90.

—— "The *Vorsorgeprinzip* in West German Policy," Appendix 3, Royal Commission on the Environment, Twelfth Report (Berlin: RCE, 1988).

—— *International Environmental Management, Trade Regimes and Sustainability* (Winnipeg: International Institute for Sustainable Development, 1996).

—— *An International Investment Regime? Implications for Sustainable Development* (Winnipeg: International Institute for Sustainable Development, 2000).

—— *The Organisation of the Impossible* (Winnipeg: International Institute for Sustainable Development, 2001).

D. Vogel, *Trading Up: Consumer And Environmental Regulations In A Global Economy* (Cambridge, Mass: Harvard University Press, 1995).

H. Walkowiaz, "AIDS in National and International Law" (Proceedings of the Ninety-Sixth Annual Meeting of the American Society of International Law, 16 March 2002) (2002) 96 *Am. Soc'y Int'l L. Proc.* 320.

P.S. Watson, J.E. Flynn & C. Conwell, *Completing the World Trading System, Proposals for a Millennium Round* (The Hague: Kluwer Law International, 1999).

A. Weale, "Ecological Modernisation and the Integration of European Environmental Policy" in J.D. Liefferink *et al.*, eds., *European Integration and Environmental Policy* (Cambridge: Cambridge University Press, 1993).

—— G. Pridham, M. Cini, D. Konstadakopulos, M. Porter & B. Flynn, *Environmental Governance in Europe – An Ever Closer Ecological Union?* (Oxford: Oxford University Press, 2000).

C. Weeramantry, "Right to Development" [1985] *Indian J.I.L.* 482.

J.H.H. Weiler, *The EU, the WTO and the NAFTA – Towards a Common Law of International Trade* (Oxford: Oxford University Press, 2000).

B. Weintraub, "Science, International Environmental Regulation, and the Precautionary Principle: Setting Standards and Defining Terms" (1992) 1 *N.Y.U. Envtl. L.J.* 173.

R.A. Westin, *Environmental Tax Initiative & International Trade Treaties* (The Hague: Kluwer Law International, 1997).

D.A. Wirth, "The Rio Declaration on Environment and Development: Two Steps forward and One Back, or Vice Versa?" (1995) 29 *Ga. L. Rev.* 599.

World Bank, *Sub-Saharan Africa: From Crisis to Sustainable Growth* (Washington: World Bank, 1989).

—— *World Bank Operational Manual on Poverty Reduction*, OD 4.15 (December 1991) (Washington: World Bank, 1991).

—— *Governance: The World Bank's Experience* (Washington: World Bank, 1994).

—— *Social Indicators of Development* (Washington: World Bank, 1995).

—— *The State in a Changing World* (Washington: World Bank, 1997).

—— *Development in Practice Series: Curbing the Epidemic; Governments and the Economics of Tobacco Control* (Washington: World Bank, 1999).

—— *A Framework for the Design and Implementation of Competition Law and Policy* (Paris: World Bank and the Organization for Economic Co-operation and Development, 1999).

—— *World Development Indicators*, CD-ROM (Washington: The International Bank for Reconstruction and Development/The World Bank, 1999).

—— *World Development Report: Knowledge for Development* (Oxford: Oxford University Press, 1999).

—— *The World Bank Inspection Panel, Resolution 93–10*, online: World Bank http://www.worldbank.org/html/ins- panel/ operatingprocedures.html.

—— *World Development Report 2000/01* (Oxford: Oxford University Press, 2001).

World Commission on Environment and Development, *Our Common Future* (Oxford: Oxford University Press, 1987).

World Health Organization, "International Health Regulations" (25 July 1969) *International Health Regulations*, 3rd ann. edn., 91983.

—— (July, 1998) 78 *Weekly Epidemiology Rec.*

—— *World Health Report 1999: Making a Difference* (Geneva: World Health Organization, 1999) 78.

—— "Revision of the International Regulations: Progress Report" (January, 1999) 74 *Weekly Epidemiology Rec.*

—— "Economics of Tobacco Control" (20 Aug. 1999) WHO Doc. A/FCTC/WG1/ 2

—— "Opening Statement by the Director-General", WHO Doc.A/FCTC/ INB1/DIV/3 (16 Oct. 2000).

—— and World Trade Organization, *WTO Agreements and Public Health: A Joint Study by the WHO and the WTO Secretariat* (WTO/WHO, 2002).

World Resources Institute, *Global Biodiversity Strategy* (Washington: WRI, 1992).

World Trade Organization Secretariat, *Trade, Development and the Environment* (The Hague: Kluwer Law International, 2000).

F. Yamin, "Biodiversity, Ethics and International Law" (1995) 71:3 *International Affairs* 529.

—— and J. Depledge, *The International Climate Change Regime: A Guide to Rules, Institutions and Procedures* (Cambridge: Cambridge University Press, 2004).

K. Ziegler, *Völkerrechtsgeschichte* (München: C.H. Beck Verlag, 1994).

D.M. Zillman, A. Lucas & G. Pring, *Human Rights in Natural Resource Development – Public Participation in the Sustainable Development of Mining and Energy Resources* (Oxford: Oxford University Press, 2002).

WEBSITES

African Human Rights Resource Centre <http://www1.umn.edu/humanrts/africa/ comision.html>

Bank Information Centre < http://www.bicusa.org>

Centre on Housing Rights and Evictions – Right to Water Programme, <http://www.cohre.org/ water>

Centre for Human Rights and Environment (CEDHA) <http://www.cedha.org>

Center for International Environmental Law <http://www.ciel.org>

Centre for International Sustainable Development Law <http://www.cisdl.org>

Center for Science and the Public Interest <http://www.cspinet.org>

Conflict Diamonds <http://www.conflictdiamonds.ca>

Cultural Survival Journal <http://www.culturalsurvival.org>

Desertification Convention <http://www.unccd.int>

Drylands Development Centre's Global Drylands Imperative <www.undp.org/dpa/frontpagearchive/2002/february/25feb02/>

EarthJustice <http://www.earthjustice.org>

EarthRights International <http://www.earthrights.org>

ECOSOC <http://www.un.org/esa>

Ethical Globalization Initiative <http://www.eginitiative.org/index.html>

ESCR-Net <http://www.escr-net.org>

European Committee on Social Rights <http://www.coe.int/T/E/Human_Rights/Esc/>

Foundation for International Environmental Law and Development <http://www.field.org>

General Direction Trade of the European Commission, DG Trade online <http://trade-info.cec.eu.int/europa/index_en.php>

Genetic Resources Action International <http://www.grain.org>

Global Policy Forum <http://www.globalpolicy.org>

Human Rights Watch <http://www.hrw.org>

International Centre for the Settlement of Investment Disputes (ICSID) <http://www.worldbank.org/icsid/>

Inter-American Commission on Human Rights <http://www.cidh.oas.org/DefaultE.htm>

International Centre for Trade and Sustainable Development (ICTSD) <http://www.ictsd.org>

International Development Law Organization <http://www.idlo.int>

International Institute for Environment and Development (IIED) <http://www.iied.org/wssd/index.html>

International Institute for Sustainable Development (IISD) <http://www. iisd.org>

International Labour Organization <http://www.ilo.org>

International Trade Center <http://www.itc.org>

Johannesburg Summit <http://www.johannesburgsummit.org>

Organization of Economic Cooperation and Development <http://www.oecd.org>

Overseas Development Institute Rural Policy and the Environment Group <http://www.odi.org.uk/RPEG/NR.html>

Partnership for Principle 10 (PP10) <www.pp10.org>

Programme of Action of the World Summit for Social Development 1995 <http://www.visionoffice.com/socdev/wssdpa-2.htm>

United Nations <http://www.un.org>

United Nations Commission on International Trade Law <http://www.uncitral.org> and ICC <http://www.iccwbo.org>

United Nations Commission on Sustainable Development <http://www.un.org/esa/sustdev/csd.htm>

UN Conference on Financing for Development <http://www.un.org/esa/ffd/ffdconf/>

United Nations Economic and Social Council <http://www.un.org/esa/coordination/ecosoc>

United Nations Environment Programme <http://www.unep.org>

UNEP – GEF Global Project on Development of 100 National Biosafety Frameworks (Global Programme Document) <ttp://www.unep.ch/biosafety/development/devdocuments/GPD.pdf.>

United Nations High Commissioner for Human Rights <www.unhchr.ch>

World Bank < http://www.worldbank.org>

World Resources Institute <http://www.wri.org>

World Trade Organization <http://www.wto.org>

OTHER MATERIALS

Communication from the European Commission on the Precautionary Principle, EC COM 1 (2000) WTO Document WT/CTE/W/147G/TBT/W/137, 27 June 2000.

Council Regulation (EC) No. 1/2003 of 16 December 2002 on the implementation of the rules on competition laid down in Articles 81 and 82 of the Treaty, <http://europa. eu.int>.

Council Regulation (EC) No. 139/2004 of 20 January 2004 on the control of concentrations between undertakings (the EC Merger Regulation), <http://europa.eu.int>.

Draft Plan of Implementation of the *World Summit on Sustainable Development*, Fourth Preparatory Commission Meeting, Bali, 7 June 2002, A/CONF.199/PC/L.5/Rev.1.

Final Act of the Conference on Oil Pollution Preparedness, Response and Cooperation, done at London, 30 November 1990, 30 ILM 733 (1991).

Final Act of the Conference for the Protection of Coasts and Waters of the North East Atlantic Against Pollution Due to HydroCarbons or Other Harmful Substances, and Accord of Cooperation, done at Lisbon, 17 October 1990, 30 ILM 1227 (1991).

Goa Guidelines on Intergenerational Equity adopted by the Advisory Committee to the United Nations University Project on "International Law, Common Patrimony and Intergenerational Equity", 15 Feb. 1988, reprinted in E. Brown Weiss, "Our Right and Obligations to Future Generations for the Environment" (1990) 84 *AJIL* 198 at 293-294.

ILA Resolution 3/2002: *New Delhi Declaration Of Principles Of International Law Relating to Sustainable Development*, in ILA, *Report of the Seventieth Conference, New Delhi* (London: ILA, 2002).

Intergovernmental Panel on Climate Change, Third Assessment Report, Working Group I, *Climate Change 2001:The Scientific Basis*, online: <http://www.ipcc.ch.>.

—— Third Assessment Report, Working Group II, *Climate Change 2001: Impacts, Adaptation and Vulnerability*, 13–16 February 2001, online: <http://www.ipcc.ch.>.

—— Third Assessment Report, Working Group III, *Climate Change 2001: Mitigation*, online: <htttp://www.ipcc.ch.>.

Report of the Expert Seminar on Human Rights and Extreme Poverty, UN Commission on Human Rights, 57th Sess., UN Doc. E/CN.4/2001/54/Add.1 (2001).

Report of the High-Level Panel on Financing for Development to the Secretary General (26 June 2001), UN Doc. A/55/1000, at 68–72.

Report of the Secretary-General on Combating Poverty, UN Commission on Sustainable Development acting as the preparatory committee for the *World Summit on Sustainable Development*, Organizational Sess., UN Doc. E/CN.17/2001/PC/5 (2001).

Report by the Secretary-General on the "Follow-up to Johannesburg and the Future Role of the CSD" 18 February 2003 E/CN.17/2003/2.

Report of the United Nations Economic and Social Commission for Asia and the Pacific (ESCAP) Ministerial Meeting in the Environment, Bangkok, *Declaration on Environmentally Sound and Sustainable Development in Asia and the Pacific* (1990)

Report of the World Summit on Sustainable Development, Johannesburg, South Africa, 26 August to 4 Sept. 2002, A/CONF.199/L.1 (New York, United Nations, 2002).

Resolution of the Conference of the Parties, Criteria for Amendment of Appendices I and II, Ninth Meeting of the Conference of the Parties, Fort Lauderdale (USA), November 7–18, 1994, Com.9.24.

Second Ibero-American Summit of Heads of State and Government, *Proposal for the Establishment of the Fund of the Indigenous Peoples of Latin America and the Caribbean, Final Version* (1992).

Second International Conference on the Protection of the North Sea: Ministerial Declaration Calling for Reduction of Pollution, 25 Nov. 1987, 27 ILM 835 (1988), Art. VII.

Statement of the UN Committee on Economic, Social and Cultural Rights to the Third Ministerial Conference of the World Trade Organisation (Seattle, 30 November to 3 December, 1999) UN. Doc. E.C.12/1999/9.

United Nations Committee on Economic, Social and Cultural Rights, *General Comment No.2: International Technical Assistance Measures*, UN ESCOR, 1990, UN Doc. E/1990/23.

—— *General Comment No. 3, The Nature of States Parties' Obligations*, UN ESCOR, 1990, UN Doc. E /1991/23.

—— *General Comment No. 4: The Right to Adequate Shelter*, E/1992/23-E/C.12/1991/4.annex III.

—— *General Comment No. 12: The Right to Adequate Food*, UN ESCOR, 1999, UN Doc. E/C.12/1999/5.

—— *General Comment No.14: The Right to the Highest Attainable Standard of Health*, UN ESCOR, 2000, UN Doc. E/C.12/2000/4.

—— *Poverty and the International Covenant on Economic, Social and Cultural Rights*, UN ESCOR, 2001, UN Doc. E/C.12/2001/10.

—— General Comment No. 15 (2002) on "The Right to Water," E/C.12/2002/11, 26 November 2002.

United Nations Human Rights Committee, *General Comment No. 6*, UN GAOR, 1982, Supp. No. 40, UN Doc. A/37/40.

World Intellectual Property Rights Organization, Intergovernmental Committee on Intellectual Property and Genetic Resources, Traditional Knowledge and Folklore, 5th sess., Doc. WIPO/GRTKF/IC/5/12 (2003).

Index